AVID
READER
PRESS

ALSO BY JOE POSNANSKI

The Life and Afterlife of Harry Houdini

The Secret of Golf

Paterno

The Machine

The Soul of Baseball

The
BASEBALL
100

JOE POSNANSKI

Avid Reader Press

NEW YORK · LONDON · TORONTO
SYDNEY · NEW DELHI

AVID READER PRESS
An Imprint of Simon & Schuster, Inc.
1230 Avenue of the Americas
New York, NY 10020

First Avid Reader Press hardcover edition September 2021

AVID READER PRESS and colophon are trademarks
of Simon & Schuster, Inc.

For information about special discounts for bulk purchases,
please contact Simon & Schuster Special Sales at 1-866-506-1949
or business@simonandschuster.com.

The Simon & Schuster Speakers Bureau can bring authors to your
live event. For more information or to book an event, contact
the Simon & Schuster Speakers Bureau at 1-866-248-3049
or visit our website at www.simonspeakers.com.

Interior design by Paul Dippolito

Manufactured in the United States of America

10   9   8   7   6

Library of Congress Cataloging-in-Publication Data has been applied for.

ISBN 978-1-9821-8058-4
ISBN 978-1-9821-8060-7 (ebook)

To Margo, Elizabeth, and Katie

Foreword
by George F. Will

Baseball fans are an argumentative tribe. Suppose (supposing is what those of us do who do not know, as Posnanski does, pretty much *everything* about baseball's history) there have been, say, two left-handed middle relievers from north central South Dakota. If so, this much is certain: Wherever two or more fans are gathered, there will be a heated dispute about who was the best of this cohort. This volume will ignite a splendid conflagration of arguments.

Do you agree with Joe Posnanski that Arky Vaughan is "the least-known great player"? If not, you also disagree with Bill James, who in his *Baseball Historical Abstract* said the two greatest 20th century shortstops were Honus Wagner and Vaughan. Posnanski says that Miguel Cabrera's 2017 Triple Crown season was the most impressive of the 17 such seasons in Major League Baseball history—better than Mickey Mantle's in 1956 (.353 average, 52 home runs, 130 RBIs). Disagree? Game on.

Those of us who for many years have relished Posnanski's baseball writings have a question or two. First, how many Joe Posnanskis are there? If the answer is "just one," our second question is: How old is he? Methuselah, the Bible tells us, lived 969 years. Posnanski must already have lived more than 200 years. How else could he have acquired such a stock of illuminating facts and entertaining stories about the rich history of this endlessly fascinating sport? He probably was there on June 19, 1846, when the 25-year-old Alexander Joy Cartwright, in a meadow by a pond in what is now the Murray Hill section of Manhattan, made one of the most important and durable decisions in human history: Cartwright decided that base ball's (it was then a two-word noun) bases should be 90 feet apart.

We all know, and not just because John F. Kennedy famously said so, that life is unfair. But, really, it is simply not fair that Posnanski has had the opportunity to gather the material in the volume. Or that he has the talent to present it in such a delightful way. His book is a deep dive into the history of an institution woven into two centuries of a nation that soon will celebrate its 250th birthday.

This is emphatically not just a compilation of what is called, by the intellectually careless, "baseball trivia." Leave aside the fact, which it is, that *nothing* about baseball is trivial. This book is, however, chock-full of fascinating facts. For example:

As a center fielder Tris Speaker made six *unassisted* double plays. Ichiro Suzuki led his league in singles 10 consecutive years and is the only person to have 200 singles in a season, which he did twice. The only player with at least 400 homers, 500 doubles, 1,500 RBIs, 1,500 runs, 300 stolen bases, and fewer than 50 caught stealing is Carlos Beltrán. Although Tony Gwynn was not a power hitter (135 career home runs), he was such a dangerous hitter he was intentionally walked 203 times, more than Ernie Banks (512 homers) or Mike Schmidt (548 homers). And for 19 consecutive seasons (1983–2001) Gwynn had more walks than strikeouts. He faced Greg Maddux 107 times and never struck out. Frank Thomas did something that neither Babe Ruth nor Lou Gehrig nor Barry Bonds did—hit .300, score 100 runs, drive in 100 runs, and walk 100 times *in seven consecutive seasons*. Among all pitchers in the live-ball era, Robin Roberts allowed the fewest walks per nine innings. (Also, from 1952 through 1955, he completed 118 of his 154 starts.) Johnny Mize was 34 and just back from war when in 1947 he hit 51 home runs while striking out only 42 times.

It is often said that baseball has had only two distinct eras, the Deadball Era, which ended in 1920, and all the seasons that have come after it. (It would not be clarifying to dignify the PED—performance-enhancing drugs—parenthesis in baseball's history as an era.) This is, however, not quite accurate.

A new era began in the early afternoon of April 15, 1947, in the borough of Brooklyn, when Jackie Roosevelt Robinson trotted out to play first base in the top of the first inning against the Boston Braves. The long exclusion of breathtaking talent from the highest level of baseball competition began to end. Willie Mays, Frank Robinson, Ernie Banks, and others were coming. Pitching records compiled by those who did not have to face Josh Gibson and Cool Papa Bell must be considered with this in mind. As must the hitting achievements of those who never faced Satchel Paige.

So, this book is, among other fine things, a rendering of justice. Among his 100 finest players, Posnanski includes, never implausibly, some of the great stars of the Negro Leagues. One pleasant aspect of this is that it gives us refreshing relief from the tyranny of modern metrics. Because newspaper coverage of the Negro Leagues was often haphazard, and because of the sometimes improvisational nature of the schedules, and because exhibition and barnstorming games were important to the players' careers, there is less statistical basis for making assessments. And that is, in a way, liberating. We must rely—how wonderfully anachronistic and quaint this is—on the judgments of baseball people *who actually saw the Negro Leagues' stars.*

If Casey Stengel thought Bullet Rogan was the best all-around player in the world, and perhaps the best pitcher who ever lived, that is good enough for Posnanski, and for me. When Honus Wagner, the greatest of all shortstops, was told that people were calling Pop Lloyd, the Negro Leagues' star, "the black Honus Wagner," he replied, "It is a privilege to have been compared with him." "Josh Gibson," said Bill Veeck, "was, at a minimum, two Yogi Berras." Roy Campanella, whose race kept him out of Major League Baseball until he was 26, but who was arguably the best MLB catcher not named Johnny Bench, said Monte Irvin "was the best all-around player I have ever seen. As great as he was in 1951 [when he was 32], he was twice that good 10 years earlier in the Negro Leagues."

Furthermore, Posnanski makes the following elegant point:

Henry Aaron was born in Mobile, Alabama, in 1934. Willie McCovey was born there four years later, six months before Billy Williams was born in the nearby town of Whistler. "If," Posnanski writes, "you ever find yourself wondering about the quality of the players in the Negro Leagues, think about this: If Aaron, Williams, and McCovey had been born 20 years earlier, all three of them would have spent their primes in the Negro Leagues, and their stories would be told as legend. People would be telling tall tales about the power of Stretch McCovey or the impossibly quick bat of Henry Aaron or the gorgeousness of Billy Williams' hitting and . . . would you believe it? I wouldn't worry about people overrating Negro Leaguers. I'd worry about people underrating them."

I assume that this small sample of Posnanski's facts and judgments has whetted your appetite for the feast that awaits you in this book. I will stop here, so that I do not further delay the fun you are about to have.

Introduction

This seems as good a time as any to tell you about my mother, Frances Posnanski, who came to the United States in 1964, less than three years before I was born. In her entire life, I suspect that my mother has not watched a complete inning of baseball. I don't mean in a row; I'm talking cumulatively. I sincerely doubt that she has actually seen three baseball outs.

Her stubborn and unyielding lack of interest in baseball undoubtedly was inherited from her father, my grandfather, Usher Perel, a gentle and learned Eastern European man who every morning—at least in my presence—would make a show of spreading out the morning paper, delicately separating the sports section from the rest of the news, and then energetically stuffing said sports section into the kitchen garbage can.

Though my mother has never watched baseball herself, she has played an enormous role in my own love of the sport. When I was nine years old, she decided to help me collect and coordinate the complete set of 1976 Topps baseball cards. She did this because while she had no use for baseball or her oldest son's growing obsession with it, she could never resist the joys of organizing. As such, she spent the summer dutifully recording the cards we collected in an accountant's ledger and arranging the cards numerically, alphabetically, by team, and by position.

"What is a Des. Hitter?" she asked me when we came across the baseball card of the Connecticut-born Joe Lahoud, a part-time slugger who had once cracked three home runs in a game for his beloved Boston Red Sox. In the photograph, Joe stood at the ready, as if waiting for his next pitch, while he squinted into the sun.

"That stands for designated hitter," I said. "Those are players who only hit, they don't play in the field."

"Well, that's stupid," she said in her thick accent, unknowingly speaking for the countless traditionalists who railed against the DH. She unwillingly created a new column in the ledger.

That was the summer that baseball took hold of my life. In the afternoons, I would play catch with my father, Steven, who had played soccer semiprofessionally in Poland but determined that being an American father meant introducing your child to baseball. And in the evenings, Mom and I would go over our baseball card collection, marveling at how many Sixto Lezcanos we had acquired—there seemed to be at least two Sixtos in each pack—and lamenting our inability to acquire even one Boog Powell no matter how many cards we bought.

"Who is this Boog Powell?" my mother would complain. "He must be some gantse macher."

"Gantse macher" is Yiddish for "big shot," but not really; like all Yiddish terms it's more sarcastic than that, more like, "Ooh, look who's such a big shot." Anyway, I remain convinced it is the only time that the term was used for Boog Powell, a wonderful and still-beloved bopper who hit 339 home runs in his career.

Boog Powell is not officially ranked in this book. I wouldn't have had to go too much larger to get to him—if this was the Baseball 350 or the Baseball 400, he certainly would have made it. Anyway, I would like to believe that his spirit is in here. What I tried to do in these pages—not to make myself some sort of gantse macher—is tell the story of baseball through its 100 greatest players. It is their stories that motivated me. This book contains almost 300,000 words, just about all of them originally written over a 100-day stretch when this series first appeared on the web pages of "The Athletic." I lived this book twenty-four hours a day during those weeks, writing, reading, learning, dreaming baseball. But, really, my entire baseball-loving life led to this book.

I suppose I should say a few words about the rankings themselves. One day, over dinner with the family, my phone rang with a Milwaukee area code call. My wife encouraged me to pick it up; the call turned out to be from Bud Selig, the Hall of Fame former commissioner of baseball. He was generally kind but, yes, he also had a bone to pick with the rankings.

You will have bones to pick, too. As you will see, in many cases I didn't so much rank the player as connect them with a number that seemed to be their match. I don't want to ruin the surprises ahead, but, just as an example, Joe DiMaggio is ranked 56th. This is much lower than he is generally ranked in such lists, but I never considered putting him anywhere else. Joe DiMaggio's legendary hitting streak was 56 games. Joe DiMaggio, in my mind, *is* 56.

Toward the end of the book, in one of the chapters, I'll put together a little key that explains a few of the numerical surprises.

That said, these are my rankings, and I stand firmly behind them, and I expect you to come hard at me with vigorous disagreements. What fun would it be otherwise? Let's be honest: It takes a lot of gall—a lot of chutz-pah, as my mother would say—to put together a list of 100 players and announce to the world, "Yes, these are the 100 greatest players of all time" (and in order, no less). It reminds me of another baseball moment I shared with my mother, this one after I had my first-ever baseball story published in the local newspaper.

"I read your story," my mother said that morning. "And it was very good. But I have one question."

"Yes."

"In here, you talk about this team scoring an unearned run."

"Right."

"Who are you," my mother asked, "to decide whether a run was earned or unearned?"

Who am I, indeed? I hope you enjoy.

A Short Glossary of Terms

Afew people have mentioned to me that I have a bad habit as a writer: I often punctuate statements with the phrase "as you probably know." Some version of that phrase was repeated, no exaggeration, dozens and dozens of times in this series—I've tried to take them all out (apologies if I missed any). My thought is: The last thing I want to do is insult the reader's intelligence by trumpeting something that they already know.

As such, I was initially reluctant to offer up this short glossary of terms, feeling that there will be a pretty good number of you who will roll your eyes and say, "Come on, I know what Deadball is" or "are you really explaining what a baseball Triple Crown is?"

But then I remember: My mother will read this book. Maybe.

So, I'm going to list off a few terms and ideas here that are prominent in the book. I will not write "as you probably know" before them, but please insert the phrase if you find yourself rolling your eyes.

Batting average/on-base percentage/slugging percentage: I use this construct a lot in the book—an example would be saying that Mickey Mantle, for his career, hit 298/.421/.557. The first number is his batting average, the second his on-base percentage, the third his slugging percentage. I believe seeing those numbers, one after another, gives you a deeper understanding of a hitter's value. And it's useful to think of .300/.400/.500 as being a standard of excellence; any numbers higher than those are very good.

Bill James: My friend Bill completely changed the way many of us have looked at baseball. He is ever-present in this book. I will mention just two of his inventions that I reference throughout. One is "Runs Created," which is a simple statistic that measures roughly, well, how many runs a player created. It is a much better method than looking at something like

RBIs or runs. The other is "Game Score," a fun system he uses to calculate just how well a starting pitcher pitched. He would probably say that I'm overstating the value of Game Score, but I love it just the same—a 100 or better Game Score is just about the perfect pitched game, and a 50 Game Score is about average.

Deadball: This is generally regarded as the period of baseball between 1901 and 1920, before the spitball was outlawed and when the baseballs were made of lesser stuff. These dead balls led to a different kind of game, one dominated by pitchers, and high average hitters who bunted a lot and stole a lot of bases. The home run was an almost insignificant part of the game. Before 1920 and Babe Ruth, no player had ever hit even 30 home runs in a season.

Hall of Fame: I talk a lot—*a lot*—about the Baseball Hall of Fame in Cooperstown, New York. Most of it is self-explanatory, but it is good to know going in that there are two ways for players to be elected to the Hall of Fame. One is for the Baseball Writers' Association of America—the BBWAA—to vote the player in. It takes 75 percent of the writers' vote for election. The other way is to be elected by special veterans' committees that the Hall of Fame puts together.

Related: I was fortunate to write—along with my friend Jonathan Hock—the movie *Generations of the Game,* which plays multiple times every day at the Hall of Fame in Cooperstown. This book would not be nearly as rich without my experience working on that movie.

Negro Leagues: These were the leagues (and there were several of them) that were created for African-American players in those years before 1947, when Jackie Robinson became the first black player in the 20th century to play Major League Baseball. There are numerous players from the Negro Leagues in this book, but looking back I truly believe there could have been more, such as an extraordinary outfielder named Turkey Stearnes. This is the trouble of stopping at 100.

OPS+ and ERA+: These are somewhat advanced statistics I often use when talking about hitting and pitching. The main thing to know is that adjusted stats like these—with the plus sign at the end—work on a 100-point scale—100 is average. Anything above 100 is above average (the higher the better) and anything below 100 is below average.

OPS stands for on-base percentage plus slugging percentage, so when you see that George Brett had a 135-OPS+, that is really good; it means he was roughly 35 percent better than league average when you take any number of things into consideration. ERA stands for Earned Run Average, and Clayton Kershaw as of this writing has a 158 ERA+, about 58 percent above average and one of the highest of all time.

Quality Start: When a pitcher throws six innings and allows three or fewer unearned runs, that's called a quality start. There are people who feel like it should take more to actually throw a quality start, but this is where we are.

Triple Crown: This is when a hitter leads the league in batting average, home runs, and runs batted in. It is a pretty rare feat. Pitchers also have a Triple Crown; it's not as famous, but this is when a pitcher leads the league in wins, ERA, and strikeouts.

Wins Above Replacement (WAR): OK, yeah, this is a big one in the book. I don't think you want a full primer on WAR, which can get pretty complicated, but I think there are two important things to know about WAR. One, it is an effort to create a one-stop shopping number, a stat that adds up everything possible to give you the full value of a player. In 2018, for example, it was calculated that Mookie Betts was worth 10.6 WAR, meaning that when you added up his hitting, his fielding, and his baserunning, he was worth about 11 wins more than a replacement player, who would be someone you might find in the minor leagues. That was one of the best seasons of the 2010 decade. There are a couple of different ways to calculate WAR—the two big baseball websites, Baseball Reference and Fangraphs, figure their WAR differently, particularly for pitchers. A ten-WAR season is very rare; a five-WAR season is generally an all-star season. A 75-WAR career is usually Hall of Fame worthy.

The second thing you should know: WAR is very controversial among baseball fans. Some love it. Some see its value but think it is overused. Some hate it thoroughly. The ranking formula I used to come up with the Baseball 100 does incorporate both Baseball Reference and Fangraphs versions of WAR.

Who missed the list: People have often asked me who just barely missed the list. Above, I did mention the Negro Leagues star Turkey Stearnes . . . but I don't want to mention anyone else. In truth, I have a list of more than 100 players who could have made this list. I think I'll save them in case the Baseball 100 ever needs a volume 2.

No. 100 **Ichiro Suzuki**

There are many words we sportswriters use way too often. We might write that something quite believable is "unbelievable" and that something that falls well into the realm of the possible is actually "impossible." But, if I had to guess, I would say that most of all we use the word "unique" too often.

I do, anyway. I have used the word "unique" in place of more precise words like "rare" or "distinctive" or "special," because "unique" has a certain power those words lack. Something wonderful, like Mike Trout's passion for baseball, sounds so much better if you call it unique. But it really isn't. Stan Musial had a similar passion for the game. So did Pete Rose, Vlad Guerrero, Bob Gibson, Dale Murphy, Willie Mays, Tom Seaver, and Raul Ibañez, along with a few hundred other people.

Don't misunderstand: Trout's devotion to baseball is something to behold. But it is not unique. Unique means the only one of its kind. Unique means unlike anything else. Everyone is technically unique, of course, but in a larger sense, as I've written before, people resemble each other and, in baseball, players almost always resemble others.

Tony Gwynn resembles Wade Boggs who resembles Rod Carew.

José Altuve resembles Dustin Pedroia who resembles Joe Morgan.

Chris Sale resembles Randy Johnson who resembles Sandy Koufax who resembles Lefty Grove.

Albert Pujols resembles Jeff Bagwell who resembles Dick Allen who resembles Jimmie Foxx.

Sure, there are many differences between these players, but the part that makes them a special part of baseball history—Gwynn's hitting genius, Sale's electric left-handed pitches, Pujols's power—reminds us of other greats. There are only so many ways to throw a baseball, hit a baseball, field a baseball, run the bases. And, even if you manage to be unique, you inevitably inspire imitators. Babe Ruth was unique, surely, for the way he swung for the fences. But soon after there was Lou Gehrig, and then Foxx and Hank Greenberg and Roger Maris and Barry Bonds.

Uniqueness is, by definition, the highest bar imaginable in baseball.

Ichiro Suzuki was unique.

There has never been one like him. And, if I had to guess, there never will be again.

No single number could ever explain a human as thrilling, as unusual, and as wonderful as Ichiro. Think of him now—that yoga-esque warm-up before each time at the plate, the way his feet shuffled in the batter's box, the geometrical beauty of the way he ran the bases, the breathtaking way he would unfold himself on his outfield throws (he seemed to be throwing *himself* as much as he was throwing the baseball). No numbers could begin to capture all that.

In fact, the numbers often do the opposite of capturing Ichiro's singular game. His weaknesses as a player—he didn't walk, he didn't hit for extra bases, he was a subpar player the last eight or so years of his big-league career—drown out the essence of Ichiro. His 107 OPS+, his sub-60 WAR, his .402 career slugging percentage, all of those things are ordinary, and this is why Ichiro often misses out on greatest-ever lists such as this one. There are any number of non–Hall of Famers like Kenny Lofton, Dwight Evans, and Andruw Jones who statistically outshine him.

But none of them are Ichiro. He was a legend before he ever played in a major-league game, before he ever came to America. Ichiro was a baseball prodigy in Japan; he was a serious young man who had the word "concentration" written in his glove before he was even a teenager. His father, Nobuyuki, raised Ichiro to be a ballplayer much in the same way that Mutt

Mantle had raised his son Mickey. But Nobuyuki, unlike Mutt, was so certain of his son's future greatness that he saved Ichiro's shoes and toys and clothes and baseball equipment for an Ichiro Suzuki museum he was sure would someday be built (and it was built in Toyoyama; tickets were $11 per person before it was closed a couple of years ago).

As a 20-year-old, Ichiro set a Japanese Pacific Coast League record by hitting .385. It was his first of seven consecutive batting titles. At age 21, he won the league triple crown. At 22, he won his third consecutive MVP award. All along, every year, he won the Japanese Gold Glove award for his extraordinary outfield defense. He was more or less the perfect player for a nation deeply in love with baseball, and it was a big shock when he decided to do something no great Japanese position player had ever done: He decided to leave Japan and see how he would match up against the best players in America's major leagues.

There were American doubts. Lots of them. Before Ichiro, no Japanese player had managed even to play 50 games in a big-league season. So Ichiro was a curiosity. More than 100 Japanese newspaper reporters, television reporters, and camera technicians chased him around during spring training in 2001 looking for clues about how things would turn out. They wrote about everything. What he ate. Where he went. They spilled thousands of words just on his batting practices. Some reporters were assigned just to count the number of times Ichiro swung the bat.

"How many times can they watch me stretch?" a beleaguered Ichiro asked.

Nobody in baseball history, not even Jackie Robinson, dealt with this sort of media scrutiny. The closest thing to Ichiro was probably another Japanese player, pitcher Hideo Nomo, who had arrived six years earlier and found himself surrounded by similar hordes of media. But it was different for a hitter, for someone who played every day. There were no safe spaces for Ichiro, no off-days. The wave crashed in again and again and again.

For a time, people wondered if Ichiro could handle all the attention, the pressure, and still adjust to the more challenging major-league style of play. For the first three weeks of spring training, Ichiro didn't pull a single ball to the right side. This was seen as a sure sign that he couldn't catch up to the fastballs. Many questioned whether a player Ichiro's size—he is now listed as 5-foot-11, 175 pounds, but in those days a reporter called him a "frail-looking 5-foot-9"—could stand up to the daily pounding of a 162-game American baseball season.

"He has looked overmatched at times," that reporter wrote during that first spring, "showing little of the line-drive, spray-hitting style that made him the best hitter in Japan."

"You have to give him time," an unnamed player said. "This is a whole different ball game."

Doubts rang loudly enough that even Mariners manager Lou Piniella stepped in to defend him . . . and in the process sounded a bit less than convinced himself.

"I can't expect him to hit .370 here," he said. "It's totally unfair. Ichiro can hit around .300 here, steal bases, and score runs."

Piniella was wrong. Ichiro could hit .370. He could do more than just steal some bases and score some runs. He started off his major-league career with two groundouts and a strikeout. And then, almost instantly, things clicked. In his second game, he singled to center and bunted for a single. Four days later, he had his first four-hit game. On May 18, he had a three-hit game and, blasting Piniella's stingy expectations, raised his batting average to .375.

When the first season was done, Ichiro had done exactly what he did in Japan. He led the league in hitting at .350. He also led the league in hits and stolen bases. He won his first Gold Glove. He became the second player in baseball history voted Rookie of the Year and MVP in the same season. And he led the Seattle Mariners to a 116-win season, tied with the 1906 Cubs for the greatest regular season in baseball history.

If you had to try to find an Ichiro comparison, you could do worse than Roberto Clemente. They are not alike—Ichiro, again, was unique—but they did play with the same whirlwind energy, the same pride for their countries. And they both had those wonderful throwing arms.

Clemente was different in that he hit with power and, while he had his own style and grace, he was a mostly conventional-looking player.

There was nothing conventional about Ichiro. He had special breathing techniques he used to stay calm in the batter's box. He moved his feet all about during the pitch and seemed to be halfway up the first-base line by the time he made contact. And he hit singles. That was his thing. Nobody has ever hit singles like him. He led the league in singles *10 years in a row.* Two players in the history of the game have had 200 singles in a season. One is Ichiro Suzuki in 2004 (when he had an almost unbelievable 225 singles). The other is Ichiro Suzuki in 2007.

See, it didn't matter what pitchers did. It didn't matter where defenders played him. Nothing mattered at all. The pitch would come, and Ichiro would chop at it, slap at it, turn on it, bunt it, ground it, bloop it, serve it, push it up the line, or line it into an open space. Then he would blaze down the line and beat the throw (if there was a throw to beat).

If Ichiro had started his career in the United States at age 20, I feel sure he would have broken Pete Rose's hit record. Rose has personally offered me 4,342 reasons why Ichiro would not have broken the record; that's the number of hits Rose had, including in the postseason. I certainly respect the power of the Hit King.

But I would say this:

1. Ichiro had 4,394 hits counting his postseason performances and years in the Japan Pacific League. And that is obviously more.

2. No, those years in Japan don't count *but* they do give us a pretty good idea of how good Ichiro would have been had he started in the United States. His statistics really did not change much when he got to the big leagues. In his seven full years in Japan, he hit .352 and averaged 177 hits per season. In his first nine years in the big leagues, he hit .333 and (because of the longer seasons) averaged 225 hits per season. I don't think it's unreasonable to believe he would have had more hits, not fewer, if he had started in the majors.

3. Ichiro is one of the very few players in baseball history whose hunger for hits came close to that of Pete Rose. For Rose, the hit record wasn't just about the mechanics of going out there day after day and rapping hits. No, it was the story of his ambition to win, to be the best. That ambition never faded. He played until he was 45. That ambition still hasn't faded; if someone would give Pete Rose a bat, he'd step in right now against anybody. Ichiro, I think, is like that too.

I talk about how Ichiro really is unique: Here's what I mean. There is no doubt that by ranking him 100, I have managed to infuriate two different camps. There are those who see Ichiro's lack of power (he had, for example, only 362 career doubles, far and away the fewest for any player with

3,000 hits), his bland .355 on-base percentage, and his good-but-not-great WAR and think he has no business being listed among the 100 greatest players ever.

Then there are those who see a guy with 3,000 hits who ran the bases about as well as anyone ever and was also one of the greatest defensive right fielders in baseball history—people who delighted in the wonder that was Ichiro Suzuki—and they ask, "How could there *possibly* be 99 players better than him?"

One day after the great Negro Leagues player, manager, and spokesman Buck O'Neil died, there was an enormous bouquet of flowers sent to the Negro Leagues Baseball Museum. Nobody knew where they had come from. Then, word got out: It was Ichiro. Understand, Ichiro had never met Buck O'Neil. He had never said a word about Buck O'Neil as far as anyone knew. But apparently, he had seen Buck around and had admired him. He felt a connection.

"Buck," Ichiro later told people at the museum, "was a man of honor."

Not long after Buck's memorial, Ichiro came to the museum. He was mesmerized by the history there, particularly the section that showed a barnstorming team of Negro Leaguers coming to Japan decades before Babe Ruth's famous tour in 1934. Ichiro was equally astonished to see a photo of a teenage Henry Aaron leaving home for the very first time, looking nervous but eager to face whatever pitches the world might throw at him.

As he walked around the museum, Ichiro didn't say much. In truth, he hardly said anything at all. But all the while, he took it in, the photos particularly. He looked into the faces of these men who played ball, who hit home runs, who pitched strikeouts, who stole bases, who made diving catches and brilliant throws even while being treated as something less than human, even while being disregarded and ignored and dismissed.

And at the end of his tour, Ichiro quietly wrote the largest check any player has ever written to the Negro Leagues Baseball Museum.

No. 99 **Mike Mussina**

S ome years ago, a baseball executive of some renown was explaining the excellence of Mike Mussina, and he said something that I will never forget. He said: "You know what? The best way I can describe Moose is—the guy's just a mensch."

That's a complicated scouting report.

"Mensch" is a fascinating word. It's a Yiddish word, and its meaning is hard to fully capture. Mensch literally translates to "human being," or "person." In the classic musical *Fiddler on the Roof,* Tevye the Milkman talks about how his son-in-law Motel has matured, and he says, "This Motel is a *person.*" He means "mensch." I don't think the translation works there.

The more common definition of mensch is "a person of integrity and honor." But this doesn't do much better at getting to the true meaning. "A person of integrity and honor" sounds like a war hero, an honest politician, a philanthropist, a person who spends life in the service of others. These people are mensches, certainly, but mensches don't have to be any of those people.

Leo Rosten, in *The Joy of Yiddish,* defines a mensch as "someone to admire and emulate, with the key being nothing less than character, rectitude, dignity, a sense of what is right, responsible, decorous."

That's better. But perhaps it's better to define mensch by using examples.

A mensch is someone who, when they borrow your car or lawn mower, returns it filled up with gas.

A mensch sends you a thoughtful handwritten note after interviewing you—even if you didn't get the job.

A mensch stands up to defend you when you're not around.

A mensch leaves a note on the windshield if they tap or dent your car.

A mensch goes back to the table to leave a few extra bucks because they feel like the tip left by the group was too small.

A mensch tells your manager or boss when you did a good job.

A mensch is the person who always brings a gift, surprises you by remembering your birthday, knows your kids' names (bonus mensch points for knowing the dog's name too), shovels the driveway of their older neighbor, offers to take a photo when seeing people struggling with their group selfie, and always remembers to pass along the promised book or recipe or recommendation.

In other words, a mensch is someone who tries to do the right thing, the kind of person many would call a "sucker."

But that doesn't bother the mensch. He or she isn't perfect; far from it. A mensch makes as many mistakes as the next person. A mensch is the person who apologizes for those mistakes, makes up for them, keeps striving to do better in situations big and small.*

Was Mike Mussina a mensch? Like I say, it's complicated.

As a pitcher, a mensch is an excellent description of Mussina. He more or less did everything right. The fact that it took him too long to get elected to the Baseball Hall of Fame is a celebration of his menschiness. He never did anything for show. He just pitched.

Look at him this way: Mussina is a stats geek who didn't play for stats, a New York Yankee who loathed attention, a pitcher who finished Top 6 in the Cy Young voting nine times but never won the thing, a starter who took five no-hitters into the eighth inning but never threw a no-hitter, a guy who won 20 games for the first time as a 39-year-old and promptly

---

* As you can see, I've spent a lot of time thinking about the word "mensch." I've spent a similar amount of time considering the French phrase *l'esprit de l'escalier,* which is literally "the wit of the staircase," but really just means thinking of the perfect retort too late.

retired rather than go for 300 victories (he finished with 270). He made it to the Hall of Fame despite a bold unwillingness to do anything extra to improve his chances of making it to the Hall of Fame. In that way, he was the ultimate baseball mensch.

Mussina was a brilliant high school pitcher in Montoursville, Pennsylvania, one town over from Williamsport, home of the Little League World Series. Milwaukee special assistant Doug Melvin was an Orioles scout then, and he saw Moose pitch and was blown away. Melvin said Mussina was an 18-year-old who pitched like he was 28. Moose had an advanced way of thinking about pitching. He saw it as a puzzle; Mussina has always been a puzzle guy, you know, crossword puzzles and such. He tried to think of the optimal way to keep hitters off-balance, to make them uncomfortable. With his pitching stuff and his keen mind, nobody in high school could touch him.

His father, Malcolm, a lawyer, told baseball teams not to draft him: Mike was going to Stanford, the mensch thing to do. Bob Melvin's scouting report was so over the top that the Orioles drafted him in the 11th round anyway, on the off-chance that they could get him to change his mind.

They did not change his mind. Moose graduated from Stanford with a degree in economics in three and a half years.

Then the Orioles drafted him again, this time in the first round. He was just about major-league ready; he made just 28 minor-league starts before getting his first big-league start in Chicago at age 22. He went 7⅔ innings and allowed four hits and one run (a Frank Thomas homer).

And he took the loss.

That more or less captures the vibe of his career: He was terrific, a bit unlucky, and he had an aversion to fame right from the start.

Mike Mussina generally takes sour pictures. If you go on the Internet and search for Mussina images—or simply go look at the photo of Mussina at the website Baseball Reference—you will see a man who seems unable to handle even the attention of a single camera. His glare is not an angry one, not a "just take the $^#% picture already" glare.

It's more like a "What's the point of life anyway?" look.

His photo persona more or less describes Mussina's general posture as a pitcher—even as he pitched in the big and historic baseball markets of Baltimore and New York, he never stopped being an introverted and small-town kid. He never seemed comfortable with all the stuff that goes with being a star big-league pitcher.

"I see him with that sourpuss," his coach Don Zimmer said, "and I say, 'How's your personality, Moose?'"

This hardly sounds like a mensch, I realize. Mussina didn't like dealing with the media for much of his career. He wasn't especially friendly with teammates. He could come across as rude and distant.

"Some days, I can't," he explained of his distaste for talking with the media. "Some days I won't because I know that I'm in the wrong frame of mind. . . . I'll be short, and it'll come out wrong."

For Moose, all of this was simply another puzzle to solve. His job was to pitch well, year after year, decade after decade. He had to figure out the best way to do his job. All those reporter questions, small talk with teammates or fans, none of that helped him pitch well. It wasn't just that he avoided the spotlight. He resented the spotlight.

See, this is the hardest part to explain: Mussina needed to feel *ordinary* in order to pitch well. He was never happy when people looked at him differently. When he went home to Montoursville and could feel like himself again, he opened up, got involved in every charity imaginable, coached the junior varsity basketball team, raised money for scholarships for kids around town, and talked to everybody, all of that mensch stuff. "Here, I'm just Mike," he would say happily.

In the big leagues, though, he couldn't be just Mike. "I think the way I've looked at it," he told *Newsday*'s Ken Davidoff, "is I'm not going to please everybody all the time. I'm better off making sure that my state of mind is OK before I worry about everybody else's state of mind. I'm the one who has to go out and do this."

In other words: Talking with people was optional. But pitching lousy was not an option.

This list of near-misses in Mike Mussina's career is long and legendary and, when taken all together, strangely touching.

- In 1992, he went 18-5—he would have won 20 games except for the eight quality starts he pitched that led to a loss or a no-decision. He finished fourth in the Cy Young voting, behind Dennis Eckersley, whose WAR that year was 2.9. Moose's was 8.2.

- In 1994, he was 16-5 and would have been a near-lock for 20 wins had the players' strike not canceled the rest of the season. He again finished fourth in the Cy Young voting.

- In 1995, he went 19-9 and would probably have won 20 had that season not been shortened because of the lockout. He finished fifth in the Cy Young voting.

- In 1996, Mussina did not pitch well; it was, in his own mind, his worst season. But he still won 19 games (and still finished fifth in the Cy Young voting) and had a clear chance at his 20th win in his last start in Toronto. He threw eight innings, allowed one run, left with a 2–1 lead. Reliever Armando Benítez blew the game in the ninth by allowing a homer to Moose's old college teammate Ed Sprague, and another 20-win season was washed away.

- In 1997, Mussina had a perfect game going with one out in the ninth inning—Cleveland only managed five balls out of the infield—when he got a 1-1 fastball just a touch up to Sandy Alomar, who lined it over Cal Ripken's head into left for a single. Mussina struck out the last two. "He threw maybe three pitches that they could hit all night," Hall of Famer Jim Palmer said. "A high changeup to David Justice. He didn't get the ball in enough to Sandy. Maybe it was two pitches they could hit. How do you do that?"

- That October, Moose was brilliant in the postseason—in two starts against Cleveland in the ALCS, he allowed one run in 15 innings. He didn't get the win in either of those games. In Game 6, Mussina allowed just one hit in eight innings, no runs; he struck out 10. Benítez gave up a homer in the 11th, and Cleveland went to the World Series.

- In 2001, now with the Yankees, Moose was probably the best pitcher in the American League. He led the league in FIP and every form of WAR, none of which existed or mattered to Cy Young voters in 2001. He lost the Cy to his teammate Roger Clemens, despite having a lower ERA, more strikeouts, fewer walks, more complete games, more shutouts, etc. But Moose didn't just lose to Clemens. He finished fifth in the voting and didn't get a single first-place vote.

- That same year, he took another perfect game into the ninth inning, this time at Boston's Fenway Park. This one would prove even more heartbreaking—he got two outs and had two strikes on the Red Sox's Carl Everett. Moose threw a high fastball to Everett, more or less where he was trying to get it. Everett fought it off and singled on a soft liner to left.

"I'm going to think about that pitch until I retire," Mussina said.

Mussina could have won 20 in 2002 but had three consecutive quality starts in September turn into losses. In 2003, he pitched brilliantly in his one World Series start against Florida and was set to start Game 7, but Josh Beckett shut out the Yankees in Game 6 to end things before Moose could take the stage.

Then, he settled into a different role as the veteran pitcher who no longer had the stuff but still tried to figure out how to get outs. It was a crossword puzzle again. He sometimes succeeded by confounding expectations; for instance, he began challenging hitters with inside fastballs after he had pitched for years on the outside half of the plate. But he took his share of beatings, too.

Then, at age 39, he got off to such a bad start that there was some talk of the Yankees removing Mussina from the rotation. But one more time, Moose found a way to solve the puzzle. He ended up leading the league in starts, walked just 31 batters in 200 innings, pitched around a whole lot of hits, kept the ball in the ballpark, and won 20 games for the first and only time in his career. He also won his seventh Gold Glove.

Then Mussina called it quits with no regrets. In his mind, he had used up all the tricks, all the sleight of hand, all the magic he had learned over his long baseball life. There was nothing left to give. A mensch knows when to say good-bye.

The day after he retired, the New York *Daily News* ran a story with a huge headline "Coopers-Frown," an opinion piece about how Mussina's career had fallen short of the Hall of Fame (and playing off Mussina's famous frowny look). Looking back, the timing on that story seems a bit cruel and more than a bit premature—what, they couldn't let him have *one day* to enjoy his career?—but, honestly, could Mussina's career have ended any other way?

Anyway, he did make it to Cooperstown. It took a while because of all those near-misses—the almost Cy Youngs, the almost 20-win seasons, the almost no-hitters. Over time, though, almosts fade, near-misses fade, and greatness endures. Mike Mussina was one of the greatest pitchers who ever lived, even if all the while he preferred everyone looking the other way.

T he thing about growing old as a baseball writer is that there are signposts all along the way. For a time, if you are lucky enough to start young, you are the same age as the ballplayers. You feel at least some of what they are feeling. You listen to the same music. You watch the same movies. Then, even as you get a bit older, maybe get married, maybe have kids, there are still ballplayers who are your age, the veteran players, the ones you can reminisce with.

Then comes a stage where you look around and realize that you are older than all the ballplayers . . . but, hey, maybe you're still younger than the manager or the coaches. Then one day a kid comes into the clubhouse and you realize that he is the *son* of a player you used to cover. Then comes a day when a team hires a manager you wrote about as a player, a manager who is still young enough to call you Mr. or Ms.

And then comes the most daunting moment, when a player you watched from the very beginning—a player you first saw as a young, scared kid full of potential and doubts—retires after a great career and is elected into the Baseball Hall of Fame.

Carlos Beltrán will someday make me feel even older than I feel now.

For most of his career, Beltrán's greatness was easily missed. His career was impacted by three special effects that I believe clouded his brilliance and made it harder to see. Well, actually, there are more than just three special effects if you count the fact that Beltrán never won an MVP award and never led the league in any major statistical category. He could have won an MVP award, particularly in 2006, and he finished second in numerous categories including runs scored, doubles, triples, once in stolen bases, and so on. Finishing second is not the same. Beltrán was also involved in the Houston Astros' sign-stealing scandal of 2017—leading the Mets to fire him before he could even begin his job as manager—and that affects the way people see him, too.

But mainly, I think there are three reasons Beltrán was underrated and underappreciated throughout his baseball career.

Special effect 1: He played his early seasons for terrible teams.

He played his first few years for Kansas City when the Royals were practically invisible. It isn't just that the team was bad, though they were bad. No, they were bad *and* they had no money *and* they never, ever made any news. They were barely in Major League Baseball. They never contended, never made any newsworthy trades, never signed any free agents. Becoming a Royals player was a witness protection program option back then.

And this was when Beltrán played some of his baseball. I happened to be a columnist in Kansas City at the time, or else, like 95 percent of baseball fans, I would have entirely missed it. I remember when Beltrán went to Houston and was absolutely incredible in the playoffs—eight homers, six steals, and 21 runs scored in 12 games—people acted like he had come from some other dimension. Who is this guy? Someone said to me during that postseason, "OK, I know you've been talking about this guy but you didn't know he was this good."

Only we did know. You couldn't miss it.

Special effect 2: He swung and missed on the biggest pitch.

In the ninth inning of the decisive game of the 2006 National League Championship Series, the Mets were down two runs, and Cardinals rookie

Adam Wainwright was trying to close things out. The Mets managed to load the bases with two outs. Beltrán came to the plate.

The first pitch was a fastball that Beltrán let go for a strike.

The second pitch was a curveball he swung at and tapped foul off his front leg.

The third was a curveball that Wainwright was trying to throw into the dirt in an effort to get Beltrán to chase. Instead, Wainwright made a mistake: He threw the pitch high. It broke right into the strike zone and Beltrán watched it go by for strike three.

That was bad timing. Hitters strike out looking all the time, but not in a moment like that. Beltrán was fooled on a pitch at exactly the wrong time, and forever after there would be at least one person in the crowd howling at him, "Swing the bat, Carlos!"

That's just how it goes sometimes.

Special effect 3: He made it look too easy.

Beltrán was a unicorn, a player so graceful that he hardly seemed to be trying. He seemed for most of his career to be cruising at about 85 percent of his potential, and the story line that constantly surrounded him was, "He should be better." I recall former baseball general manager Steve Phillips once criticizing Beltrán for various intangible and unprovable crimes (not making enough "plays," not being a leader, not coming through in the clutch) and he was hardly alone in feeling that way about Beltrán.

Looking back, though: How much better could he have been, really? For more than a decade, he was everything. He was, in some years, the best defensive center fielder in the game. He was, in some years, the best baserunner in the game. Even now, he is the greatest percentage base stealer in baseball history. He was a rare bid, a switch hitter with power—he's 28th all-time in doubles, 34th all-time in total bases, top 50 in homers and RBIs and runs created.

He also had that astonishing postseason in 2004, maybe the best postseason for any player in baseball history.

I've written about Beltrán so many times . . . I really have known him from the beginning. That beginning was 1999 at a long-vanquished ballpark complex in a place called Baseball City. Oh, Baseball City! For a time in the 1980s, the Royals played their spring training baseball at this oddball amusement park; the feeling was that it could be Disney World and Cooperstown put together. There was a short while when it thrived, I suppose, but by the time Beltrán came around, it was a ghost town. By then, all that was left of the Baseball City dream was a small part of the roller-coaster track that had not been torn down and the slightest whiff of cotton candy that still lingered for reasons no one could explain.

The Royals, too, had once been one of America's best teams but by 1999 they were equally sad. They had no owner. They had no direction. They did have a nice man named Herk Robinson running the team, though he seemed to prefer gardening to baseball. That was when a 22-year-old Carlos Beltrán showed up. He spoke little English. He was paralyzingly shy. But the talent was already awe-inspiring. "He can be as good as he wants to be," then assistant general manager Allard Baird told us. The Royals did not believe Beltrán was fully ready to play in the major leagues, but they didn't have anybody else, so they put him out there every day and told him to at least catch the fly balls hit his way.

Instead, he hit .293, scored and drove in 100 runs, and won the Rookie of the Year.

And he played with this gorgeous grace—well, let me try to tell you what it was like just watching him run from first to third. I've never seen anyone do it better. He barely seemed to be trying (that, as mentioned, was both his gift and curse), but he soared. He glided. When Beltrán was on first and someone cracked a hit to right field, it felt like Opening Night on Broadway. Beltrán would take off, and you could almost see a blur behind him like in the cartoons. His cleats seemed to land a couple of inches above the ground. The way he would make the turn at second base, wow, it was a bit like watching motorcycles that tilt and then hover over their turns. It was pure joy.

There have been faster players than Beltrán just as there were faster football receivers than Jerry Rice. Beltrán's gift, like Rice's gift, was the genius of precision. Rice routes were so exact that they say he used to step into his own spike marks. Beltrán cut the corner with such clarity and purpose, you would have sworn he had run a straight line from first to third.

So when I would hear people complain about Carlos Beltrán not living up to his potential, I would think, "Have you not seen this man go from first to third?"

Then there was his defense. One time, the Angels' Garret Anderson crushed a drive into the right-field gap, and it was a double for sure, and the Royals' pitcher that day, Brian Anderson, slapped his glove against his thigh in frustration. Beltrán, impossibly, ran the ball down, caught it without even exerting himself, then wheeled and fired to first base and doubled off Chone Figgins, who was rounding third base at the time.

"You know what blew me away," Brian Anderson would say of the catch. "There was no way he could catch that ball. No way. And then, he not only catches it, he catches it by his side. He doesn't have to dive. He doesn't have to stretch. I've never seen anything like it."

To Anderson, it was unforgettable. But, back to those Beltrán special effects, a lot of people missed it. They saw Beltrán run the ball down and thought, "Yeah, nice catch." That's how easy Beltrán made it look. He did stuff like that all the time. Once he raced back on a Mike Cameron fly ball, jumped as he got to the wall, and stole a top-of-the-wall double or a home run. To the untrained eye, it was a good play. But to people in and around the game, people who had played the outfield, people who had seen thousands of games and catches, it made their eyes pop out of their heads.

"I've been to two hog killings and a county fair," pitcher Curt Leskanic said. "And I haven't seen anything like what Beltrán did tonight."

To be fair, Beltrán did garner appreciation in the last few years of his career, when he became the grizzled veteran. He could no longer do those magic tricks he had done in his youth, but people finally appreciated his love for the sport. He played through too many injuries and kept coming back, even with his body wrecked. I don't think most people thought Carlos Beltrán would play until he was 40. But he did.

He spent the last years of his career in San Francisco, St. Louis, back in New York with the Yankees, to the Rangers, and finally back in Houston, where this time his team won that controversial World Series.

You can have a lot of fun with Beltrán's hitting numbers because so few players have been able to do so many things on a baseball diamond. Here is a list of somewhat arbitrarily chosen statistical combinations, and the players who achieved them.

- 400 homers, 500 doubles, 1,500 RBIs, 1,500 runs, 300 stolen bases: only Willie Mays, Barry Bonds, Alex Rodriguez, and Carlos Beltrán.

- 400 homers, 500 doubles, 1,500 RBIs, 1,500 runs, 300 stolen bases, and 50 triples: only Mays, Bonds, and Beltrán.

- 400 homers, 550 doubles, 1,500 RBIs, 1,500 runs, 300 stolen bases: only Bonds and Beltrán.

- 400 homers, 500 doubles, 1,500 RBIs, 1,500 runs, 300 stolen bases, fewer than 50 caught stealing: only Beltrán.

Admittedly, this sort of number shuffling is just for fun. Beltrán was not Mays, Bonds, or A-Rod—he was not Henry Aaron or Stan Musial or Ted Williams, either. He was, instead, a glorious player who was not always seen.

I must end any thoughts about Beltrán with a game from 2003, a Royals-Diamondbacks game that I think about all the time. That whole 2003 season was confusing for the Royals. They were atrocious in 2002, then even more atrocious in 2004, 2005, and 2006. But somehow in this middle year they managed to be pretty good; they were in first place for the first three or four months of the season. And in September they played Arizona, and it was a reasonably important game.

In the ninth inning, the Royals were down a run and they were facing Arizona's closer Matt Mantei, who at his peak was one of the hardest throwers in baseball. He was throwing so hard that day the Royals hitters seemed helpless. With one out, Beltrán came to the plate and in a seven-pitch at-bat he was vividly overpowered. There was no way, he realized, to get a hit. But he fouled off pitches and managed to draw a walk.

Then he stole second.

Then he stole third.

Then he scored on a sacrifice fly that was so short, the second baseman could have caught it. The second baseman let the right fielder—with his better arm—handle the catch but Beltrán still raced home and beat the throw.

It was one of the most staggering displays of sheer dominance I've ever seen on a baseball field. After the game (which the Royals, being the Royals, eventually lost), I asked Allard Baird what he thought.

"He can do anything," Baird said. That's exactly how I remember Carlos.

No. 97 **Roberto Alomar**

Sandy Alomar Sr. was a player with various valuable skills. He could play any position competently (he mostly played second base, but could shift to shortstop, third base, or the outfield if necessary). He was blazing fast (he stole more than 200 bases in his career). He could bunt when called upon. He switch-hit. All of this was enough to get him 15 years in the big leagues. One year, he even made the All-Star team.

Alomar Sr.'s weakness, if you will, was that he could not hit.

This is not meant to be mean or an exaggeration. Alomar was 5-foot-9, 140 pounds, and he hit .245/.290/.288 over that rather lengthy career. His .288 slugging percentage ties Bud Harrelson for the second-lowest of any player since the Deadball Era, which ended in 1920 when Major League Baseball banned the spitball. We'll get into that Deadball stuff later. Point is, Sandy Alomar Sr. really couldn't hit.

But teams kept playing Alomar because of his defense, his speed, and his charisma. They didn't seem to care that he really couldn't hit. Alomar got more than 500 plate appearances for the 1975 Yankees. He *led off* for the 1970 and 1971 Angels and led the league in plate appearance both years. Leading a lineup off with a player with a sub-.300 on-base percentage is a bit like leading off your stand-up comedy bit by reading the Keurig coffee machine warranty.

Look, the year Alomar made the All-Star team, he hit .251/.302/.293. That was one of his better hitting years.

And people were willing to see past all of it because the guy was so likable, so useful in other ways. As the longtime coach (and Alomar's mentor) Grover Resinger said: "Sandy is one of the three or four best second-basemen in the game—and I mean defensively, offensively, and inspirationally."

All of this is to say that there was something special about Sandy Alomar Sr.; he had a charisma that he was able to instill in his two sons, Roberto and Sandy Jr., who were both (to Sandy Sr.'s great joy) much more talented than their father.

Aren't you fascinated by baseball fathers and sons? Seven times in baseball history, a father and a son both made the All-Star team at the same position.

In the outfield, you have Felipe and Moises Alou, Ken Griffey Sr. and Jr., Gary Matthews Sr. and Jr., and Bobby and Barry Bonds.

At first base, you have Cecil and Prince Fielder.

At catcher, you have Randy and Todd Hundley.

And then, at second base, you have Sandy and Roberto Alomar.

That must be some feeling, seeing your son succeed not only at your sport but at the very same position that you played.

In all the obvious ways, Roberto Alomar was a very different player from his father. For one thing, Robbie was much bigger—three or four inches taller and he weighed 40 pounds more. This made the son a much more powerful hitter than the father. Roberto hit almost as many home runs in his first season (nine) as Sandy did in his entire career (13). In all, Robbie hit 13 or more home runs in seven different seasons. He also hit .300 for his career. His OPS was 236 points higher than his father's.

But because they were such different hitters, it's easy to miss the striking similarities: They were both second basemen, both switch hitters, both base stealers. Sandy was a great bunter; Robbie was probably the best bunter of his generation. Sandy was a defensive maestro; Robbie won 10 Gold Gloves. It's pretty clear who taught Roberto Alomar how to play the game.*

Roberto Alomar was a good player right from the start, as you might expect from a player who grew up around the game. At age 20, he played his first full season for the San Diego Padres, posting an above-average OPS+ while playing sparkling defense. He would get better with experience, but he was instantly a good Major League Baseball player.

He would become great. He finished third in the 1999 MVP voting and sixth in 1993, and in both seasons he had a strong case to be named the winner.

He really was an extraordinary offensive player. In 2001, he hit .336/.415/.541 with 34 doubles, 12 triples, 20 home runs, 113 runs, 100 RBIs, and 30 stolen bases. He had five other seasons almost as good. He led the league in runs in 1999. He hit .326 and stole 55 bases in 1993.

From a statistical standpoint, he was remarkably similar to another Hall of Famer: Barry Larkin. When putting together this Baseball 100, Alomar and Larkin were in the final group. As you can see, their numbers are shockingly alike:

Larkin: .295/.371/.444, OPS+ 116

Alomar: .300/.371/.443, OPS+ 116

Larkin stole 379 bases in 456 tries (83 percent). Alomar stole 474 bases in 588 tries (81 percent).

You will not find two players more similar than that. And they were both Gold Glove–winning middle infielders, though, as mentioned, Alomar was perhaps a bit overrated while Larkin was probably a bit underrated defensively.

---

* There is some contentiousness about Robbie Alomar's defense that must be discussed. As the 10 Gold Gloves suggest, he was widely viewed as the greatest defensive second baseman of his time. His defensive numbers do not add up that way. Robbie had a stretch from age 28 to 31 when the numbers do show him to be an outstanding infielder, but in the other years his range factor was lacking. He looked so good out there, so smooth, so effective, but it cannot be denied that all of the advanced stats show him to have been an average defensive second baseman. It's one of those times when the eyes and the stats do not meet, and you are left to decide which one you trust more.

So, how do you separate the two? You can look at WAR—Larkin's 69 WAR is slightly higher than Alomar's 66 WAR, but that's not enough to make the difference.

No, in the end, you have to make choices, and I chose Alomar because of a single word: presence. And in this, I am not talking about the quality of "presence," but simply being present. Larkin had only four seasons where he played in 150 games; Alomar had eight such seasons. Alomar had a shorter career in terms of years but he played in 200 more games. And because he managed to stay healthy and in the lineup, Alomar had a bigger impact. Alomar created more than 100 runs for the 1992 and 1993 Blue Jays, and both teams won the World Series. He created 139 runs for the 1999 Indians (who won 97 games and made the playoffs) and 138 runs for the 2001 Indians (who won 91 games and made the playoffs, too).

In all, Robbie Alomar created 100 runs seven different times, and all seven teams won at least 88 games. Five of those teams made the playoffs. Larkin created 100 runs four times. Alomar was just *there* more often.

In an imaginary scenario where both players are guaranteed to be healthy all year, I'd probably take Larkin. But imaginary scenarios are just that, and there are no guarantees. In real life, I will take Alomar because one of the most underrated talents in baseball, and in life, is just showing up.

No. 96 **Larry Walker**

L arry Walker dreamed of being a hockey goalie. Well, more specifically, he dreamed of being one hockey goalie, the estimable Billy
Smith, the ultra-successful New York Islanders goalie who was
sometimes called Hatchet Man for the way he would slash players with his
goalie stick. To the young Walker, no one seemed cooler. He grew up in a
midsized Canadian town with the wonderfully Canadian name of Maple
Ridge. It goes without saying that hockey was and is everything in
Maple Ridge.*

Hockey also was everything in the Walker family. His brother Carey
was drafted by the Montreal Canadiens. The Walker hockey games were
legend, and his father, Larry Sr., molded the hockey masks his sons wore.†

---

* Walker grew up in Maple Ridge playing hockey with a number of players who would
play professionally, most prominently National Hockey League Hall of Famer Cam
Neely. Walker remembers spending much of his time in goal just watching Neely wipe
out players like some movie cowboy clearing out a bar.

† Larry Walker has three brothers and their names are Barry, Carey, and Gary. This
seems like an important fact.

So, yes, Larry Walker would have become Billy Smith had his talent obliged. He tried his best. He even rode with a friend named Rick Herbert about 1,000 miles to try out for a professional team called the Regina Pats. Herbert made the team and played professional hockey for the next few years (racking up an impressive 192 penalty minutes one year in Portland). Walker did not make the team. He rode back 15-plus hours in the car with Herbert's father.

But he was not done trying. Walker went back to Regina the next year with Billy Smith dreams in his mind, and he got cut again. He was 17 years old and lost. He wasn't good enough for hockey. He didn't want to go to college. "I warned Larry," his father later said, "that he would have to be prepared to spend the next 50 years as a laborer."

Walker had played some baseball by then, but not much. The weather didn't suit baseball. The culture didn't suit baseball. His high school didn't even have a baseball team. But he needed to do something, so he found a team in nearby Coquitlam that played a full season, and he joined up. Walker was raw and uncertain of all the rules but he liked the feel of a wooden bat and he displayed some easy power and speed. He also had good timing: At that moment the Montreal Expos were desperate to find young Canadian baseball players to spark some interest among the fans. They offered him $1,500 to play ball, and Walker grabbed the money with the sort of joy you rarely see except when offering a trick-or-treater a full-sized candy bar.

The Expos sent Walker to Utica, where, for the first time in his life, he saw real curveballs and sliders and changeups and split-fingered fastballs. He had no idea what to do about any of those pitches so he just kept swinging and hoping. He hit .223. He was pretty sure as the year ended that he had not made contact with a single curveball or slider all season. He heard rumors that the Expos would release him. Instead, they sent him to Burlington, Iowa, and he was utterly transformed. He mashed 29 home runs in 95 games, stole 16 bases, and the Expos wondered what the heck had happened. They moved him up to the next level in West Palm Beach, and he kept on hitting.

Then he went to Double-A Jacksonville (where he was teammates with a towering young pitcher named Randy Johnson) and he continued to hit home runs and steal bases at an astonishing rate. At that point, the Expos realized that they had a future star on their hands. And that was exactly the point when Walker—in what would become a harbinger of things to come—tore up his knee playing baseball in Mexico and missed the whole 1988 season. One doctor pronounced his baseball career over. But Walker was resilient. He had to be. He would endure an astonishing assortment of injuries for the rest of his career.

Walker made it back in 1989—he went to Triple-A Indianapolis and showed off the plethora of talents he had. Again, he hit home runs, stole bases, drew walks, played great defense, and unleashed powerful throws. The man who wanted nothing but to be a goalie and slash some players who skated too close to the crease turned out to be a baseball natural.

Larry Walker loved the number three. His uniform number was 33. He took three practice swings before each pitch, set his alarm at three minutes past the hour, and famously said, "My first marriage was on Nov. 3 at 3:33, it lasted three years, ended in '93 and cost me $3 million."

Three times in his career, he hit three home runs in a game.

The first time, he took himself out of the game in the eighth inning even though he had an at-bat coming in the ninth—he didn't want four home runs.

The second time, he did stay in the game—it was still close—but grounded out when he had a chance for his fourth homer.

The third time, he hit his third homer in the 10th inning, and it proved to be the game winner.

There are three reasons, best I can tell, that so many people underrate Larry Walker.

1. His career was shortened by that constant barrage of small and large injuries I mentioned. He played 150 games in a season only once in his 17-year big-league career, and he had only 8,030 plate appearances overall. As such, his counting numbers mostly leave you wanting more. He finished his career with fewer hits than Larry Bowa and fewer homers than Andres Galarraga. And even though Larry Bowa's hit total and Andres Galarraga's home run total have nothing whatsoever to do with Walker's greatness, it's hard for people to see past that.

    Some of this wasn't his fault, by the way. He was on his way to a fabulous season in 1994 with the Montreal Expos when the players went on strike. He ended up playing in only 103 games that year but still hit .322/.394/.587. In a full season, he might have hit 60 doubles, 30 homers, driven in 120 runs, scored 110, etc.

And if he had been able to complete that season and put up those kinds of numbers, people might have had more confidence in what he did in Colorado in the subsequent years.

2. He played most of his home games in Denver's Coors Field. Because of Denver's altitude and the light air, baseballs soar there, and this was more true in Walker's time, before the team started putting baseballs in a humidor to make them less bouncy.

In 1997, Walker hit .366/.452/.720 with 46 doubles, 49 homers, 130 RBIs, and 143 runs scored. He was the league MVP. He also stole 33 bases. He also won a Gold Glove.

People disregard that year because he played half his games at Coors Field.

The next year, Walker hit .363 (won the batting title this time) with 46 doubles and 113 RBIs. He won another Gold Glove.

People disregard it because he played half his games at Coors Field.

The next year he hit .379, slugged .700 again, hit 37 homers, drove in 115 RBIs, scored 108 runs, and won another Gold Glove.

People disregard it because he played half his games at Coors Field. You see where this is going.

These are all-time seasons. But because of Coors Field, there was literally *nothing* Larry Walker could do to convince many of his greatness. From 1997 to 2002, he hit .353/.441/.648; these are Ted Williams numbers, these are Stan Musial numbers. Even when statisticians adjusted the numbers to take into account Coors Field's peculiarities and still found that Walker was extraordinary, so many people just treated those great seasons like they didn't happen.

3. Can you think of one Larry Walker moment? If you can, it's probably the time he turned his helmet around and batted right-handed against his old minor-league teammate Randy Johnson in the All-Star Game. Or the time he mistakenly gave a fan the baseball when the inning wasn't yet over. In other words, he had funny moments but never seemed to have an important one. He did play very well in his only World Series appearance, but his Cardinals were swept by Boston.

Bill James has talked often about how players who do one or two things well tend to be overrated while people who do many things well are always underrated. I'd add to that: People who do *famous* things tend to be overrated, while people who are simply good day after day but never really make headlines tend to be underrated.

Larry Walker had both underrated qualities. He mostly played in Montreal and Colorado, which are hardly on the minds of most baseball fans. He did everything well. He hit .313 for his career. He walked about as often as he struck out. He hit for power—he led the league in doubles, homers, and slugging percentage. He was a fabulous baserunner. He was a great right fielder. He had one of the best outfield arms of his time.

It is an unlikely story, the small-town Canadian kid who grew up dreaming of being a goaltender, who barely understood the rules when he first began playing baseball, becoming one of the most well-rounded players in baseball history. But that's how it turned out.

Tony Gwynn

A Haiku on Hitting

I tried not to guess
I did not anticipate
I trusted my eyes

A little less than two years before he died, I talked hitting with Tony Gwynn. The event was called "The Art of Hitting," and it remains one of the most wonderful experiences of my life. This was in 2012, just before the All-Star Game in Kansas City, and we talked hitting before a thrilled crowd at the Negro Leagues Baseball Museum. It was like talking astrophysics with Carl Sagan or poetry with Emily Dickinson or piano with Thelonious Monk.

Major-league star Matt Kemp was one of the people in the crowd that day. "If Tony Gwynn is talking hitting," he said, "I'm there."

One exchange, in particular, stays with me. Gwynn began the event by saying that when he stepped to the plate, he would look over the defense for the slightest opening. He loved hitting when there was a runner on first base because that meant the second baseman and/or shortstop had to cheat a step or two to cover for the steal or to complete the double play.

All he needed was a single step in any direction, and he would put the ball in the opening.

That made perfect sense. But then he said something that seemed contradictory. He said that he never actually tried to hit the ball to certain parts of the park.

"You didn't?" I asked.

"No," he said. "I hit the ball where it was pitched."

"Wait a minute. You just said you tried to find openings in the defense."

"That's right," he said.

"Well, isn't that trying to hit the ball to certain parts of the park?"

"No," he said patiently. "I waited for the pitch that allowed me to hit the ball where I wanted to hit it."

That's a hitting genius.

Tony Gwynn, the ballplayer, was more than a hitting genius. He was, until his mid-30s, a terrific defensive right fielder; he won five Gold Gloves. He was very fast when he first came up—he stole as many as 56 bases in a season—and even after he lost that speed he was a smart and opportunistic baserunner. And even though he was not a home run hitter, every opposing manager saw him as the most dangerous batter in the lineup. Gwynn finished his career with 203 intentional walks, just behind Frank Robinson and Willie Mays and just ahead of Ernie Banks and Mike Schmidt.

Despite his other skills, let's face it: To talk about Gwynn is to talk about hitting. Sure, you could talk with Meryl Streep about singing or Frank Sinatra about acting or Michael Jordan about golf, and it would be fine. But it would be beside the point.

Tony Gwynn hit a magnificent .338 for his career. Going back to 1961, the first year of expansion, that's far and away the highest average for any hitter with at least 3,000 plate appearances:

1. Tony Gwynn, .338

2. Roberto Clemente, .331

3. Wade Boggs, .328

4. Rod Carew, .328

5. Vladimir Guerrero, .318

Gwynn hit .309 or better every full season of his career. He hit .351 in his first full season, which was the year Prince released the album *1999*. He hit .338 in his last full season, which was the actual year 1999.

From 1983 to 2001, 19 straight seasons, Gwynn walked more than he struck out. This is one of the longest streaks in baseball history but it's made doubly impressive by the fact the Gwynn rarely walked. Most of the others who had such an amazing streak—Carl Yastrzemski, Rickey Henderson, Joe Morgan, Gwynn's contemporary Tim Raines—walked *a lot*.

Not Gwynn. Take away his otherworldly 1987 season—when he probably should have won the MVP award—and he never walked even 60 times in a season. Gwynn came to the plate to hit. He simply did not believe he could see six or seven pitches from any pitcher and not have at least *one of them* be juicy enough to hit.

So he steered clear of walks, but he almost never struck out. He whiffed just 434 times in his career. It's a different time now, sure, but just to compare: The Yankees' great young slugger Aaron Judge struck out 501 times in just his first three seasons.

In 1995, when Gwynn led the league with a .368 average, he struck out 15 times all season. The next year, he struck out 17 times. In 1999, he played in 111 games and struck out 14 times.

Gwynn struck out three times in a game once.

In 1992, he did not strike out in back-to-back games all season.

We can keep going with this. Here's a personal favorite: Gwynn faced the great Greg Maddux 107 times in his career. He never struck out. Not once. This is so mind-blowing, it's hard to even put it into words. You might think: Oh, well, Maddux wasn't really a strikeout pitcher. Except Maddux struck out more than 3,300 batters in his Hall of Fame career. He faced 11 different batters 100 or more times in his career including Hall of Famers Jeff Bagwell, Barry Larkin, Craig Biggio, and non–Hall of Famer Barry Bonds. He struck them out a combined 169 times.

But he never once struck out Tony Gwynn.*

Gwynn blended art and science as a hitter. He was a pioneer in watching replays of his own swing, so much so that his teammates called him "Cap-

---

* The legendary Nolan Ryan did strike out Gwynn nine times in 67 plate appearances— that's the most against any pitcher. Gwynn *still* hit .300 against Ryan, one of the very few who did.

tain Video." He was not the first batter to keep notebooks on every pitcher he faced, but his notebooks were spectacularly detailed. After every game, he would go through each pitch he faced (he had absurd recall) and mark them down in a color-coded system. At one point in one of our conversations, I happened to mention the old Giants pitcher Mike Krukow. Gwynn had not faced Krukow in almost 25 years and yet without hesitating he remembered specific at-bats he'd had against Krukow and offered up a detailed scouting report of how he would hit Krukow if they faced off again.

Gwynn didn't just accumulate information, though; he used it in real time. The ability to hit a baseball thrown at big-league speed is a gift of instinct. The science tells us that there's simply not enough time for a hitter to do anything against a major-league pitcher if you begin the clock the instant the ball is released. But the great hitter's clock begins long before the release; the mind considers visual cues, triggers muscle memory, scans the situation, and makes a prediction of what's about to happen.

Gwynn surveyed it all. He read the field, calculated everything he knew about the pitcher and the ballpark and the weather and the defensive alignment. And then he hit. Always.

Gwynn hit .343 at home. He hit .334 on the road.

He hit .345 against righties. He hit .325 against lefties.

He hit .346 in April, .333 in May, .344 in June, .325 in July, .348 in August, and .333 in September.

In his two World Series, he hit .371.

On the day Tony Gwynn died, I was looking through my old notebooks and stories to find something that summed up his particular brilliance for hitting. And I saw this quote: "I tried not to guess at the plate. I did not anticipate what the pitcher was going to throw me. I trusted my eyes."

And I realized there was the perfect hitting haiku in there.

I tried not to guess
I did not anticipate
I trusted my eyes

There were 45 games left in the San Diego Padres' 1994 season when the player strike happened. At that moment, Tony Gwynn was hitting .394. He had a real chance to become the first player in more than 50 years to hit .400 in a season. The season was canceled and the hope was lost.

The question has always been and always will be: Would Gwynn have hit .400 in 1994?

By my best estimation, Gwynn would have had to go something like 67-for-161 (.416 average) the rest of the way to get to .400.

Could he have done it? Could he have gone 67-for-161, a .416 average? The obvious answer is: Of course. He had done that kind of thing pretty often in his sensational career. He had a stretch like that in 1993, multiple stretches like that in 1994, a stretch like that in 1995, and so on.

But, of course, this would have been a different challenge. There would have been intense daily scrutiny. Reporters would have followed him everywhere. Pitchers would have tried even harder to work him. The pressure would have mounted. George Brett, who had been the last batter to chase .400 fourteen years earlier, talked for the rest of his life about how insane the pressure became. It was much more intense than he could have ever expected.

But Gwynn was older than Brett had been in 1980. He could handle the pressure. We'll never know for sure, but I will always believe that Gwynn would have done it, would have hit .400.

The reason I will always believe this is that, in our conversation about the art of hitting, I asked him: "Would you have hit .400 in 1994 if the season hadn't ended?"

"Yes," he said without hesitation.

"Really?"

"Of course," he said, and he looked at me funny. "Why would I think anything else?"

No. 94 **Roy Campanella**

Roy Campanella was the sixth African-American player in the major leagues. He often gets skipped over when people tell the story of integration because he arrived a year after Jackie Robinson. But when he arrived, the fate of what Branch Rickey called "Baseball's Grand Experiment" was still an open question.

Five African-American players had played in the big leagues in 1947. What few people remember—because Robinson's story is so triumphant—is that four of the five were, at that point, unsuccessful. Sure, Robinson won the Rookie of the Year Award. He led the Dodgers to the pennant. He was a star.

But Larry Doby, the first African-American player in the American League, hit just .156 in 29 games. The St. Louis Browns signed two players from the Kansas City Monarchs. One of them, Willard Brown, became the first African American to hit a home run in the American League while the other, Hank Thompson, became the first African American to hit a triple in the American League. But they both struggled mightily, were treated terribly, and they were dropped after about a month.*

---

* Brown was a huge star in the Negro Leagues and in various other countries, including

The fifth player was Dan Bankhead. So few remember him even though Bankhead was the first African-American pitcher in the majors. He labored under the strain. His son later said that Bankhead, who was from Alabama and had seen the worst of America's racism, pitched in mortal fear of hitting a batter and causing a riot. Bankhead pitched in only four games and was sent back to the minors; there would not be another black pitcher in baseball until the legendary Satchel Paige was finally given his chance with Cleveland at age 41.

As 1948 began, there was certainly no rush to add any more African-American players. Only two were called up all season. One was the aforementioned Paige, who made his first start on August 3 in front of 72,434 fans—Paige was already one of the most famous athletes in the country.

The other was Roy Campanella.

Campy was only 26 years old, but he had been playing professional baseball for more than a decade; he had started in the Negro Leagues at age 15. He was so good then that the Philadelphia Phillies tried to sign him. This was *twenty years* before the Phillies would actually play a black player. So how did that happen? Well, it was a comedy of errors—they had seen the name "Campanella," and had assumed him to be Italian. When they found out that while Roy's father was Sicilian, his mother was black, the pursuit quickly ended.

Instead, Campanella signed with the Baltimore Elite Giants of the Negro National League and caught the first break of his young career. The Giants' manager was a man named Biz Mackey, the greatest defensive catcher of his time or perhaps any time. Mackey, who is now in the Hall of Fame, spent countless hours working with Campy on the finer points of catching.

By age 17, Campy had replaced Mackey as the Giants' starting catcher. At 19, he won the MVP award in the East-West All-Star Game. By then, fans of the Negro Leagues would argue whether Campy or Josh Gibson was the best catcher in the world. Surely they were the two best.

It's hard to fully appreciate just how good Campanella was then. He was a defensive marvel with an arm that defied description . . . plus he hit

---

Cuba; he is now in the Baseball Hall of Fame even though he never returned to the major leagues. Thompson did return to play for the Giants in 1949 and he was a key player for the Giants' pennant-winning team in 1951 and the World Series champions in 1954.

with power. He led the Negro Leagues in doubles one year, in RBIs another, and he battled Gibson for the home run title in another. "Nobody discovered Campanella," the legendary Dodgers scout Clyde Sukeforth would say when people tried to credit him for finding Campy. "We looked at him and there he was."

The Dodgers were not the first team that looked at him. You know the Phillies looked first. In 1943, the Pirates invited him to a tryout and then, when white supremacist pressure grew, rescinded the offer. When we evaluate Roy Campanella's incredible career, we can do so with only one eye. We will never know just how good he was when Major League Baseball was entirely segregated.

We also will never know just how much of his greatness Campy left in the Negro Leagues. He played, literally, countless games as his Giants barnstormed from town to town. He routinely would catch two games per day, sometimes three, occasionally even four. Campy himself remembered a day when he caught both ends of three different doubleheaders. He was thought to be indestructible, and he thought himself indestructible. He was 24 when Branch Rickey asked him for a meeting, but his body was undoubtedly several years older than that.

Campy, by the way, was thoroughly unimpressed with Rickey at that first meeting. He listened to Rickey drone on forever ("He was the talkingest man I ever did see," Campanella said), and believed that he was being offered a chance to play for an all-black team that the Dodgers would sponsor. That didn't interest him in the least, and he turned down Rickey and left. It was only later, when Robinson told Campanella what was really happening, that Campy raced to send Rickey a telegram expressing his interest.

Rickey was more cautious with Campy than he was with Robinson. This may have had something to do with their very different personalities—we'll get into that in a moment—but it was mostly because Campy was a catcher. So many prejudices had built up around African-American players that it was hard to keep track, but one was that a black player could not handle the demands of being a big-league catcher.

In 1946, Campanella played in Nashua, New Hampshire. He was named the New England League MVP. More than that, though, he commanded a universal respect that was all but unknown at the time. When his Nashua manager, Walter Alston, was thrown out of a game, he named

Campy interim manager. This made Roy Campanella the first African-American to manage in organized white baseball.

In 1947, with Rickey and everyone focused on Jackie Robinson's triumph, Campanella was sent to Montreal, where he continued to amaze everyone with his extraordinary defense.

In 1948, Rickey still wanted to move slowly. Campanella was 26 and surely the best catcher in all of baseball, but the Dodgers already had a popular catcher named Bruce Edwards. Campanella started the season with Brooklyn, and in his first big-league plate appearance, he was plunked in the ribs by a reliever named Ken Trinkle. But after he had appeared in only three games, Rickey sent him down to St. Paul.

And Campanella decided to take matters into his own hands. He went to St. Paul and left absolutely no doubts; he hit .325 and slugged .715 in 35 games.

Then in early July, with the Dodgers in the midst of a losing streak and under .500, Campanella was finally called up. In his first game, he went 3-for-4 with a double, and he caught Buddy Kerr trying to steal. In his second game, he went 3-for-3 with a triple and a walk. In his third game, on the fourth of July, Campy went 3-for-5 with two home runs and four RBIs.

After that game, Dick Young of the New York *Daily News* asked why Campy "had been wasting his time in St. Paul." He, of course, knew the answer.

Campanella did slow down; hit just .258 that first year. But his defense was so spectacular he still got an MVP vote. He threw out 24 of the 36 runners who tried to steal on him, an astonishing 67 percent.

And for the next seven years, Roy Campanella was one of the greatest catchers the major leagues had ever seen. Before him, only three catchers—Gabby Hartnett, Walker Cooper, and Rudy York—had hit 30 homers in a season. Campy did it four times in six seasons. All the while he flashed that incredible arm. He led the league in caught-stealing percentage in each of his first five seasons, and his career percentage of 57 percent is still the record. There were no Gold Gloves then, but he would undoubtedly have won them all.

The sportswriters adored him. They told his fun stories day after day. They talked constantly about his leadership, about his connection to pitchers, about his ability to hit in the clutch. And they continuously voted him the league's MVP.

In 1951, he hit .325/.393/.590 with 33 homers and 108 RBIs. He was named MVP.

In 1953, he hit .312/.395/.611 with a catcher-record 41 home runs and 142 RBIs. He was named MVP.

In 1955, he hit .318/.395/.583 with 32 homers and 107 RBIs. He was named MVP.

Did he deserve all three of those MVPs? Maybe not. There's a good argument to be made that his own teammate Duke Snider had better seasons in '53 and '55. But Campanella was so widely respected and admired and loved that the writers wanted to give him *all* the awards.

In this way, he was quite different from his teammate and fellow pioneer Jackie Robinson. Though they faced the same racism, Campanella rarely mentioned it or fought back. While Robinson was a whirlwind of force and dignity and felt an impassioned duty to change the world, Campanella just loved playing ball.

"It's practically impossible," one reporter said, "to get Campy to admit that any phase of his life was especially difficult or unpleasant."

One of the most important books in my life is Roger Kahn's *Boys of Summer*. Reading that book first put the idea of becoming a sportswriter in my mind, and I've probably read it a dozen times over the years.

Well, Roger Kahn was a Robinson guy through and through; Kahn understood and related to Robinson's rage, his determination, his unwillingness to back down to any slight. Robinson had the pioneer's soul, and Kahn connected with that.

But Campanella was a complete mystery to Kahn. He would watch Campanella retrieve other catchers' face masks after foul balls, watch him chat up other batters "as though he was running for office," see him tell his funny and self-effacing stories to the other sportswriters, and he simply couldn't understand. "There's a little Uncle Tom in Roy," he quoted Jackie Robinson saying.

"It's the two faces, Carl," Kahn quoted himself telling pitcher Carl Erskine. "If you want to be a happy-go-lucky guy, fine. But if you're angry at society, which colored guys have every right to be, then let it show."

"We probably all have a lot of faces," Erskine replied.

Erskine, I think, got it right.

Jackie Robinson was a man out of time, a hero, a force of nature, a fighter. There's a reason we read about him in American history books.

And Roy Campanella was a different sort of hero. He dealt with the discrimination, the spite, the unfairness of it all by deflecting, laughing, hiding some of his feelings, and unleashing others. He was different from Robinson but, surely, no less complicated. And he too pushed the world forward.

Jackie Robinson himself came to appreciate this by the end of his life. In his autobiography, *I Never Had It Made,* Robinson talked about how people had tried to pit them against each other: "I'm happy that Roy Campanella and I survived the attempts at the old business of 'divide and conquer' that some people tried to use to make us enemies," he wrote. "It didn't work." Robinson readily admitted that he and Campy had "serious differences of opinion," but he insisted there was always mutual respect. "As time went by," he added, "my respect for Campy deepened, and I was convinced that his attitudes had changed."

Robinson recalled that at one point, many years after they both retired, they were talking in the office of Campanella's Harlem liquor store and Campy said: "It's horrible to be born in this country and go along with all the rules and laws and regulations and have to battle in court for the right to go to the movies—to wonder which store my children can go to in the South to try on a pair of shoes or where to sleep in a hotel. I am a Negro, and I am a part of this. I don't care what anyone says about me. . . . I feel it as deep as anyone and so do my children."

At his peak, Campanella was as good as any catcher in the history of baseball.

His career came to a tragic end. Campanella had always insisted that he never wanted to quit playing baseball. "They'll have to cut the uniform off me to get me out of it," he said. He made his last All-Star team in 1956 at age 34, but even by then he was physically a shell of himself. He hit just .219 and, for the first time in his career, threw out fewer than 50 percent of the would-be base stealers. Who knows how many innings he had caught by then?

He played again in 1957 and hit just .242/.316/.388. The career was winding down. But Campanella never lost hope. He planned to play again in 1958, the year the Dodgers moved to Los Angeles. He talked about how the Los Angeles Coliseum would be a great place for him to hit.

In January, Campanella was driving home in New York when his car hit a patch of ice and skidded into a telephone pole. He was just 37 years old at the time, and the accident paralyzed him. He spent the rest of his life in a wheelchair.

"You gotta be a man to play this game for a living," Campanella famously said. "But you gotta have a lot of little boy in you, too."

The year after the accident, the Dodgers played the Yankees in a special exhibition game to honor him at the Los Angeles Coliseum. More than 93,000 people attended. It remains the largest crowd in baseball history.

No. 93 Ozzie Smith

O zzie Smith was the greatest defensive player I ever saw. This is not to downplay the sheer awesomeness of Andrelton Simmons, Andruw Jones, Adrián Beltré, or Nolan Arenado, among many others defensive maestros. It's just that, to me, the Wizard invented a whole new way to play defense. He made jaw-dropping plays so often that you couldn't take your eyes off him.

He was so good that when watching a Cardinals game, you would turn the channel when they were on *offense*.

There are numbers that show his defensive radiance. In 1980, while playing for San Diego, he had 621 assists, a record that will likely never be broken. Why will it never be broken? Because many more balls were put in play in 1980; now, with the strikeout, shortstops rarely get even 500 assists. In 2019, Oakland's Marcus Semien had the most shortstop assists in baseball with 436—185 shy of Ozzie, more than one per game.

But the wonder only begins with his 1980 record season. In 1981, the strike season, Ozzie actually had a higher range factor than he did in 1980. If not for the strike, he would have broken his own record.

Then he was traded to St. Louis. And in 1982, he had an even higher range factor than he'd had in either 1980 or 1981. This was a shortstop playing at a different level. He led the league in assists eight times and finished second another four times. By Baseball Reference's defensive WAR, his fielding was worth an astonishing 44 Wins Above Replacement. Nobody is close.

Defensive WAR

1. Ozzie Smith, 44.2

2. Mark Belanger, 39.5

3. Brooks Robinson, 39.1

4. Cal Ripken, 35.7

5. Joe Tinker, 34.3

There are two Ozzie stories I want to tell here. The first comes from September 23, 1996, less than a week before he played his last big-league game. I was a 29-year-old columnist for the *Cincinnati Post,* an afternoon newspaper back in the days when such things still existed. It goes without saying that the *Post* no longer exists.

My job that day was to try to sum up Ozzie Smith's genius, and someone said to me: "Just watch him take infield practice. You'll get all you need just from that."

So, I watched. And this is what I wrote:

The baseballs roll slowly at first. The game will not begin for a couple of hours still, and all around Ozzie Smith, baseballs shoot out like fireworks. People hit them, throw them, bunt them, chase them, a hundred baseballs dance around the diamond. Ozzie Smith focuses on one ball, the one that rolls toward him.

Ozzie Smith is getting ready to perform even though there is no one in the crowd.

"Here we go," St. Louis Cardinals pitching coach Dave Duncan says.

Here we go. In baseball, great players come and go like favorite songs. They show up for a while, some hit 400 home runs or strike out 3,000 batters, and then they fade into a happy memory. Folk heroes come along less often. Ozzie Smith is one of those folk heroes. He grows better in memory.

His legend has little to do with his own numbers; it comes from numbers that were not recorded. Everybody in the National League would have hit .300 if not for Ozzie. Everybody would have broken Joe DiMaggio's 56-game hitting streak if not for Ozzie. Think of a play. There are countless to choose from. There was the time he dove one way, the ball skipped the other way, so he caught it barehanded and threw out the runner. There was the time when he flipped the ball behind his back to start a double play. There was the time he snared a line drive 15 feet to the right of second base. Then there's the time . . .

The guy stole hits from everybody, including the Beatles. Late at night, in dark bars, baseball players still sit over empty beer bottles and tell sad stories of the hits Ozzie Smith took away.

"Here we go," the Wizard says.

He fields a grounder and, without looking, throws it to first base. Then, he does it again. Again. The balls begin to come at him more often, one every 10 seconds, then once every five, and each time the baseballs spin a little faster, they skid and screech along the turf, buzzing as they approach. He catches each one softly, as if he's picking them with tweezers.

And each time, he makes perfect throws to first base without even looking up. It seems utterly impossible. He stares down, throws the ball to his left, as if he's tossing away a whiskey bottle. Each time, the ball plops softly in the first baseman's glove, which never moves. Smith rushes to his right, scoops the ball, flings it away, it lands in the first baseman's glove. He bounds to his left, plucks the ball out of the air, flings it away, it lands in the first baseman's glove.

"Are you peeking?" Duncan asks.

"For 15 years," Smith says.

The coach bounces the ball hard against the turf so that it jumps high in the air. Smith waits for it to come down and catches it on the short hop. Again. Again. It looks like he's trying to catch water from a geyser. Smith rushes in, twirls his glove in front of his chest, like a man waving away mosquitoes. Somehow, he catches the ball. He throws it without looking and in one motion, it lands in the first baseman's glove.

The ball bounces higher, higher, it seems to leap angrily off the turf, attacking Smith, and Smith continues to grab the ball with that same motion, then comes the same nonchalant throw, the same soft landing in the first baseman's glove.

"Hit it up," Smith yells at the coach. The coach hits pop-ups behind Ozzie Smith. He turns his back, runs to where he figures the ball will land, and with his back to home plate lets the ball fall into his glove like an NFL receiver. Another pop-up. Again, Smith turns his back and catches it over his head.

The coaches turn to watch him. A few players turn. Ozzie Smith, 41 years old, keeps catching the baseball over his shoulder, blind, and it is a magic trick.

And then, all at once, the symphony is over. Ozzie Smith has performed enough. He rushes around the field to pick up a few stray baseballs, and even that he does with style. He slaps his glove to the ground, and the ball ends up in the pocket.

That's when it happens. Teammate Gary Gaetti in the batting cage rips a line drive right at Ozzie, and there's no way for the Wizard to see it. His eyes are looking somewhere else. The ball comes right at his head, and there's no time to warn him, no time for him to see, no time for anything at all. Ozzie Smith reaches down to pick up a baseball. Then, at the last possible instant, without looking, he raises his arm, catches the line drive, and calmly discards the baseball with all the rest.

"Eyes everywhere," Duncan says, and he shakes his head.

Ozzie Smith was not a great hitter. He did become a pretty useful one, though, as the years went along. From 1985 to 1992, eight seasons, he had a good .361 on-base percentage. He stole 300 bases.

But he hit with no power at all—he finished his career with a lower slugging percentage than on-base percentage, a rare thing (especially rare in his case because Smith's .337 on-base percentage wasn't all that good). Of the 87 players with more than 10,000 big-league plate appearances, Ozzie Smith has by far the lowest slugging percentage.

Lowest SLG (10,000 PAs)

1. Ozzie Smith, .328

2. Rabbit Maranville, .340

3. Luis Aparicio, .343

4. Omar Vizquel, .352

5. Nellie Fox, .363

But Ozzie Smith did have a pretty famous extra-base hit that you might recall.

A couple of years ago, I worked with my friend Jon Hock on a movie we called *Generations of the Game.* It now plays multiple times every day at the Baseball Hall of Fame. It was one of the most fun things I've ever done—I mean, my job was to go around the country and interview Hall of Famers (and future Hall of Famers) about what baseball and the Hall means to them.

As part of this, I went to St. Louis to interview Ozzie Smith at his office. He was a fantastic interview, like always. He talked about how much he loved playing defense. He talked about some of his most famous plays. Of course, we also talked about the home run he hit in Game 5 of the 1985 NLCS. That came in the bottom of the ninth inning, one out, the series tied, the game tied. Smith hit it off the Dodgers' reliever Tom Niedenfuer. It is one of the most surprising home runs in baseball history.

And as Ozzie remembered it, he began to echo the famous Jack Buck call from that home run.

"*Smith corks one down the line,*" he said, and I could feel the goose bumps.

"*It could go,*" he said (Buck actually said "it may go," but it's the same thing).

"*Go crazy, folks, go crazy!*" Ozzie shouted. "*The Cardinals have won the game by the score of 3–2 on a home run by the Wizard!*"

Here we were in a generic office in St. Louis, but for a moment it was like we were at Busch Stadium all those years ago. The joy on his face, even after all these years, was so evident, so palpable—if you happen to come to Cooperstown and the Hall of Fame, look for it in the movie. Ozzie Smith played the game with irrepressible joy. He still feels it. That is his superpower.

No. 92 **Bullet Rogan**

T here's a decent chance that even if you're a devoted baseball fan—
even if you're fascinated by the Negro Leagues—you've never
heard of Bullet Rogan. I had not heard of him until I was having
breakfast one day with my friend, the legendary Negro Leagues player,
manager, and storyteller Buck O'Neil. Buck called him "Bullet Joe Rogan,"
though his name was probably not Joe. It was probably Charles Wilber
Rogan. To be fair, much of Bullet Rogan's life is a mystery.

Anyway, we were talking about Negro Leaguers who belonged in the
Hall of Fame, and Buck began to talk about Bullet Joe. He said that Rogan
threw about as hard as Satchel Paige, was perhaps the best fielding pitcher
in baseball history, was a world-class center fielder, and could handle the
bat better than anyone he'd ever seen.

Bullet Joe sounded to me more like a comic book superhero than a man.

I began to investigate. It was not easy. Rogan began his baseball career during World War I, before the official Negro Leagues began. He
played the bulk of his career in the 1920s, a time period often ignored
in the Negro Leagues books. He died in 1967, before Robert Peterson's
groundbreaking book, *Only the Ball Was White,* launched interest in Negro
Leagues baseball.

But there are clues left behind about Rogan's brilliance. For instance, the Hall of Fame manager Casey Stengel called Rogan the best all-around player in the world and one of the best—if not the best—pitcher who ever lived. Rogan's catcher and manager Frank Duncan called Rogan the best lowball hitter he ever saw. A teammate named George Carr said that Rogan was the smartest pitcher he ever saw; he never threw the same pitch to the same hitter twice.

After watching a 48-year-old Bullet Rogan crack three hits against his all-star barnstorming team, Bob Feller said: "I can't imagine how good he must have been when he was young."

What can we do with such words? What can we do when left only with legend?

As mentioned, we don't even know Rogan's name for certain. We don't know his birth date. For many years, it was assumed that he was born in 1889, but recent research suggests he was actually born in 1893. That would have made him 15 or 17 or 22 years old when he became a catcher for a semipro team called Fred Palace's Colts in his hometown of Kansas City, Kansas. Within months, he joined the army and made a name for himself as a ballplayer.

In one of his rare interviews, Rogan simply said, "I was born playing baseball."

In 1915 or so, Rogan was recruited to play for the 25th Infantry Wreckers in Hawaii, which was probably the closest thing at the time to a national African-American baseball team. This was before Rube Foster and others founded the Negro National League in 1920. The Wreckers played other army teams as well as civilian ones. Future Negro League stars like Heavy Johnson and Dobie Moore played for the Wreckers. Rogan became their best player almost immediately.

By the time he showed up to play for the Wreckers, Rogan was already well known in the army for his baseball talent. Here is part of a story that was written in the *Pacific Commercial Advertiser* in July 1915.

> The chief interest in the game was the first appearance on the local diamond of Rogan, late of the Twenty-Fourth Infantry, who arrived on the last transport. There is hardly a company commander in the Twenty-Fifth Infantry who has not made a bid for this man's assignment to their company, without success.... He played the first three

innings at third base and made a great impression. He looks like the classiest infielder the regiment has had in some time. In the fourth, he went into the (pitcher's) box and here his success was even more pronounced. He had worlds of speed and a quick delivery following a leisurely windup that is in itself puzzling to any batter. At the bat, he had three chances and in each case met the first ball pitched on the nose but each time in the direction of some fielder.

Within a year, Rogan's pitching was being celebrated repeatedly in headlines in black newspapers like the *Chicago Defender*. "Rogan Strikes Out Eighteen Men." "Rogan Wins Again." Even when he missed games, he was the big story. "Twenty-Fifth Wins Without Rogan," was another headline.

According to one story, Rogan was recommended to the owner of the All-Nations baseball team, J. L. Wilkinson (later owner of the Kansas City Monarchs), by Stengel himself. This may or may not be true; Wilkinson undoubtedly knew about Rogan already. But it's definitely true that Stengel adored and idolized Rogan. The two would barnstorm together for many years. And as manager of the Yankees, he would encourage several of his pitchers to emulate Rogan's unusual but effective no-windup pitching style.

Rogan was not a big man—he's listed at 5-foot-7, 160 pounds—but he was immensely strong. He threw as hard as any pitcher of his day even though he did not wind up. And he used an enormous bat, perhaps more than 50 ounces or heavier, that was even heavier than the bat used by Babe Ruth. Rogan was a master of hitting with that tree trunk. O'Neil said that even as Bullet Joe approached 50 years old he could still guide the ball wherever he wanted. "He taught me more about hitting than anybody," O'Neil said.

And as a pitcher, how hard did the man nicknamed Bullet throw? Again, it's hard to guess based on the snippets that have made it through the years. But Duncan, who caught Rogan and Satchel Paige, used to say that Paige was easier to catch because of his unmatchable control but that Rogan threw harder. Paige himself said that Rogan threw as hard as the legend of the day, Smokey Joe Williams.

The numbers that survive the years do tell their own story. A few years ago, a group of Negro League historians tried to piece together something like a statistical record of Negro League baseball. It is so challenging because the Negro Leagues schedule was a hodgepodge of league games, exhibition games, town games, and challenge matches against company teams. As the years have gone along, others—like the people who run the excellent Seamheads website—have made even more strides in finding some numbers.

And the numbers they have found for Bullet Rogan are astounding. In 1924, he went 18-6 as a pitcher, he hit .386 and slugged .566 as a hitter, and he led the Kansas City Monarchs to the first Negro Leagues World Series title. He was the hero of that series.

The next year, he hit .372 with power and also went 18-2 with an estimated 1.84 ERA.

In an exhibition game, he shut down a white all-star team that included Jimmie Foxx and Al Simmons. In Cuba, he pitched and hit and led his team to the national championship. In all, the historians have found (so far) that he went 135-61, placing him among the winningest pitchers in the Negro Leagues. He also hit .335 and slugged .510.

Bullet Rogan stayed around the game for years after he retired from playing. He coached, scouted, and served as an umpire in the Negro Leagues for a time. He then settled down in Kansas City, where he worked for the post office. He never talked about his baseball days, and very few people who met him understood that they were talking with one of the greatest players in baseball history.

Mariano Rivera

"They say his father was a fisherman. Maybe he was as poor as we are and would understand."

—*The Old Man and the Sea*

I was rereading Ernest Hemingway's *The Old Man and the Sea* when I came upon the Joe DiMaggio references. Hemingway adored DiMaggio. How could he not? DiMaggio spoke to all those things that Hemingway cherished: consistency, quiet elegance, and, of course, grace under pressure. DiMaggio played through pain without complaint. He delivered hits in the biggest moments. The legend built that DiMaggio never threw to the wrong base. If Joe DiMaggio had not existed, Hemingway would have had to invent him.

But he did exist. And, as such, DiMaggio was the idol of Hemingway's old man.

"I must have the confidence," the old man says to the sea, "and I must be worthy of the great DiMaggio, who does all things perfectly even with the pain of the bone spur in his heel."

Obviously, I never saw Joe DiMaggio play. But as I read Hemingway's words, I find myself thinking of a different Yankee. He too was the son of a fisherman. He too grew up too poor to understand. As a ballplayer, his career almost ended before it began. He was almost traded (twice) before he settled into his permanent role with the Yankees.

And he, like DiMaggio, was grace under pressure. He took the mound with a calmness that chilled opponents. It didn't matter the heat of the moment, the importance of the pitch, the number of men on base, the score of the game. It didn't matter if it was a breezy spring training game in Tampa, a pennant-chasing battle at Fenway Park, or the World Series clincher; he looked entirely at ease, as if the game were already over and he was sitting in a recliner and retelling the story to his own grandchildren.

Here is the strangest part of the story: The man had only one pitch. He did not throw a curveball, a slider, a changeup, a screwball, a knuckler, a fadeaway, a splitter, or a palm ball. He threw one pitch, a fastball that naturally cut to the left at the very last second. It might be right to call the pitch a "cutter," but other pitchers throw cutters. This pitch was different.

"I learned the pitch," he said, "from God."

Who could doubt that? For all his years, 18 in all, no one could hit the pitch. They knew it was coming. "Sure, you know what's coming," a fine hitter named Mike Sweeney said. "But you know what's coming in horror movies, too."

All of which is to say that if Hemingway had lived in a later time, his hero would not have been DiMaggio.

"They have other men on the team," the boy said to the old man.

"Naturally," the old man said. "But he makes the difference."

If Hemingway had lived in another time, his hero would have been Mariano Rivera.

Mariano Rivera finished more games (952), saved more games (652), and finished with the highest ERA+ (205) in baseball history.

From 1996 to 2013, he only once had an ERA above three—that was in 2007 when he was 37 years old. There was a sense then that maybe he was finally coming to an end, that hitters had finally caught up to that nameless pitch that broke a thousand bats and a million hearts.

The next year, he pitched 70⅔ innings, walked six batters (yes, six batters), saved 39 games, and had a 1.40 ERA.

In all, he pitched 141 postseason innings. He allowed just two home runs—one that mattered (Sandy Alomar homered to tie an ALDS game in 1997) and one that mostly did not (Jay Payton homered off him in a World Series game; Rivera struck out the next hitter to win the game anyway). He had an 0.70 ERA. He allowed a total of one run in his last 24 postseason appearances.

I bring up these numbers not only because they are impressive, but also because they speak to his time and place. Mariano Rivera became the first player elected unanimously by the BBWAA into the Baseball Hall of Fame, and many people were horrified by that. If you look at Rivera conventionally, he pitched fewer than 1,300 innings. His 56 career WAR is roughly the same as players who never came close to the Hall of Fame, such as Dave Stieb, Jerry Koosman, and Kevin Appier.

The fair question then: How could contemporaries like Greg Maddux and Randy Johnson, who threw four times as many innings as Rivera (and finished with more than twice as many Wins Above Replacement), not get elected unanimously while Rivera did?

I do not have a counterargument to any of this—Maddux and Johnson *should* have been elected unanimously—except to say that it isn't right to compare Rivera to them or anyone else. He was a different kind of pitcher with a different kind of role. And he impacted the game in a different way.

Rivera grew up in Puerto Caimito, Panama, and he never thought he would leave. He cleaned fish and pulled up nets as a young boy; the Yankees signed him for $3,000. Before he pitched a single big-league inning, he blew out his elbow and had Tommy John surgery. He did not actually make it to the big leagues until he was 25 years old.

He began with the Yankees as a starter and not a very good one. It is written in his permanent record: He made 10 big-league starts and went 3-3 with a 5.94 ERA. Legend has it that owner George Steinbrenner himself was ready to trade Rivera to Seattle for the light-hitting shortstop Félix Fermín. He was included in at least one other possible trade package.

But then the Yankees moved Rivera to the bullpen, and it was like the entire world went from black and white to color. He transformed. In Game 2 of the 1995 American League Division Series against Seattle, Rivera entered in the 12th inning with the score tied and a runner on first. He struck out Jay Buhner to end the threat. In his first full inning, he got three outs without letting the ball out of the infield. In his second, he struck out the side (including that much-coveted Félix Fermín). He worked around two singles in the 15th, and the Yankees won the game. It was an electrifying performance.

He had two more such appearances in that series. And even though the Yankees lost the series, they never again listened to a trade offer for Rivera. "People inquire about him all the time," general manager Bob Watson told reporters. "But that kind of arm, you don't give up."

In April the following year, Rivera was so good out of the pen, so unhittable, that Twins manager Tom Kelly said: "He needs to pitch in a higher league if there is one. Ban him from baseball. He should be illegal."

And the year after that, Rivera was made the Yankees full-time closer and you know how it went after that.

None of this would have been an option had Rivera come up in Tom Seaver's time or Warren Spahn's time or Satchel Paige's time or Walter Johnson's time. There were no closers there. Relief pitchers were utilities; they were not stars. The closer role was invented just in time for Rivera, and Rivera's one pitch was created just in time for the closer role.

And oh, that pitch. Jim Thome called it the greatest pitch in baseball history. Who can argue? Yes, we can talk all we want about Nolan Ryan's fastball, Sandy Koufax's curve, Steve Carlton's slider, Carl Hubbell's screwball, Bruce Sutter's splitter, Gaylord Perry's spitter, Pedro Martínez's changeup, and Satchel Paige's Bee ball (so named because, as Satch said, "It be where I want it to be when I want it to be there"). But all of them threw other pitches.

Rivera threw no other pitches. He came into the game, and he came at hitters with that same pitch, one pitch, again and again, fastball, sharp break to the left at the last possible instant. He learned the pitch while playing catch with his friend and countryman Ramiro Mendoza in 1997. He just tried a new grip, and the pitch came out whole, unblemished, perfect. That's why he said he learned it from God.

Counterintuitively, Rivera was not a notable strikeout pitcher. He averaged fewer than a strikeout per inning over his career and in one of his most celebrated seasons, 1998, he struck out just 36 in 61⅓ innings. In his unmatched postseason career, he struck out just seven per nine innings, which is well below many relievers of his time.

Then again, his pitch wasn't built to be missed. It was built to saw off bats. Surely, no pitch has ever broken as many bats as Mariano's cutter. It attacked lefty hitters like a swarm of bees, so much so that some switch hitters chose to hit right-handed against Rivera. But righties did not do much better; they often reached out blindly, like they were trying to hit a shadow.

Beyond that, Rivera simply had the perfect closer persona. Nothing bothered him. He failed so rarely, but when he did he simply shrugged and moved on. In 2004, he blew two saves against Boston—the Red Sox were the one team that often had his number—and the next time he pitched in Boston, fans wildly cheered him when his name was announced.

His response? "I felt honored," he said. "What was I going to do? Get upset and start throwing baseballs at people?"

No. Not Rivera. He pitched his whole life in New York, with the tabloid back pages ready to pounce on any blown save. He never looked worried. He never seemed stressed. He never offered any hope to hitters. It's impossible to know exactly where to rank Mariano Rivera on the all-time list because there was never anyone like him. I am no Hemingway, but I'll just say if I had a lead in the ninth against the Devil, I'd want Mariano Rivera on the mound.

No. 90 **Max Scherzer**

In 2015, Max Scherzer pitched three of the greatest baseball games ever pitched.

On June 14, facing Milwaukee, he threw a complete-game one-hitter and struck out 16 Brewers. The hit he allowed was a Carlos Gómez bloop single to right field in the seventh inning, just inches beyond the reach of second baseman Anthony Rendon. Scherzer had a perfect game going at the time and the hit was so flimsy and unsatisfying that even Gómez himself wasn't thrilled about it.

"I got lucky," Gómez told the *Washington Post.* "I don't enjoy it. I would enjoy it if I hit a real base hit. Because he dealt. He pitched unbelievable."

He did pitch unbelievable—up to that point, only 10 different pitchers had thrown a 100 Game Score game. Game Score, a fun invention by Bill James, is a pretty simple formula where you add points for outs and strikeouts registered and subtract points for walks, runs, and home runs. Bill designed it so that 100 is pretty much the ultimate nine-inning game.

Of the 12 previous 100 Game Scores (Nolan Ryan had three of them), seven were no-hitters. They included Sandy Koufax's, Randy Johnson's, and Matt Cain's perfect games along with Kerry Wood's 20-strikeout performance.

Scherzer threw the thirteenth nine-inning 100 Game Score in baseball history that day.

Six days later, Scherzer faced Pittsburgh. And this time, nobody even blooped a single. Scherzer had a perfect game going with two outs in the ninth inning when he faced pinch-hitter José Tábata. It was an epic at-bat. Scherzer got ahead 0-2 and kept trying to throw the high fastball by him—his high fastball had been essentially unhittable for two games—but Tábata kept fouling them off.

And then Scherzer shook off catcher Wilson Ramos until he got the sign he wanted: slider. Scherzer wanted to throw it down and away but, as he said, "it backed up on me." He left it inside and hanging. Tábata saw it clearly—the ball was probably no more than three or four inches inside—and dropped his elbow so that the ball grazed off his elbow protector.

For the second straight start, Scherzer's perfect game had ended in the most agonizing way imaginable. There were those who wanted the umpires to enforce Rule 5.05 (B), which states that the batter must make an attempt to avoid being touched by the ball. In this case, Tábata not only made no attempt to avoid the ball but seemed to make a clear effort to get hit by the ball.*

There were complaints galore about Tábata's move—Nationals outfielder Bryce Harper said that he wanted to cry. But there was one person who didn't complain at all: Max Scherzer. He got Josh Harrison to fly out to complete the no-hitter. And after celebrating a bit, he was given a number of chances to blame Tábata or the umpires for his loss of a perfect game. He ardently refused to complain at all.

"It was just a slider that backed up, and it hit him," he said in his television interview on the field. "I don't blame him for doing it. Heck, I'd probably do the same thing."

---

* There is a precedent for an umpire enforcing 5.05 (B) in such a big moment. In 1968, in the ninth inning of a game against San Francisco, Los Angeles's Don Drysdale loaded the bases. At that moment, he had a 44-inning scoreless streak, just 1⅓ innings shy of Carl Hubbell's major-league record. Drysdale threw a pitch that hit the Giants' Dick Dietz, which forced in a run and ended the streak. But home-plate umpire Harry Wendelstedt ruled that Dietz did not try to get out of the way, and the at-bat went on. Dietz ended up flying out, and Drysdale was able to stretch his streak to a then-record 58 innings.

Later, after he'd had time to think about it, he said the exact same thing.

"I left it in," he told reporters. "I have no qualms about it whatsoever. That's just baseball. He did what he needed to do, so kudos to him."

The no-hitter was not quite a 100 Game Score—it topped out at 97. But it was still one of the greatest ever games.

And the best was yet to come.

On October 3 of that year, in the second game of a doubleheader, Scherzer and the Nationals faced the New York Mets. That Mets team won their division and ended up winning the pennant, so even though it was at the end of the regular season, this was no pushover. It should be mentioned that Scherzer had thrown seven no-hit innings against the Reds in his previous start before giving up a single to Tucker Barnhart.

There would be no singles on October 3. Scherzer threw a no-hit, no-walk game. He struck out 17. It wasn't a perfect game because in the sixth inning, New York's Kevin Plawecki grounded the ball to short. Washington's Yunel Escobar fielded it cleanly but threw in the dirt and first baseman Clint Robinson could not handle it. To be fair to Escobar, it was cold and windy so there were no easy plays. But in the instant afterward, Scherzer screamed out in fury.

Later, Scherzer dressed himself down for his reaction.

"Just a play that didn't get made," he said afterward. "Yuni goes out there and competes as hard as anybody."

The Game Score for this one? One hundred and four. It was the second-highest nine-inning Game Score in baseball history behind only the aforementioned 105 Game Score by Kerry Wood when he struck out 20 and didn't walk anybody.

Remember, all those games—three of the best ever pitched—were in one season.

But here's the kicker: 2015 wasn't Scherzer's best season. It wasn't his second-best season. It might not even have been his third- or fourth-best season. It was really just another Max Scherzer season. This is just what he does.

After Scherzer's second big-league season, Arizona traded him to Detroit in a complicated three-way deal that brought Curtis Granderson to the Yankees with Ian Kennedy and Edwin Jackson going to the Diamondbacks. Why would the Diamondbacks trade Scherzer before he even got started? They simply did not believe that Scherzer, with his violent delivery and over-the-top intensity on and off the mound, would stay healthy.

Two years after the deal was made, it actually looked pretty good for Arizona. Kennedy went 21-4 with a 2.88 ERA and finished fourth in the Cy Young voting. Daniel Hudson, whom Arizona had picked up by flipping Edwin Jackson, won 16 games. Arizona went to the playoffs.

Meanwhile, Scherzer couldn't quite put it together. He had the stuff. He had the competitive fury. He even stayed relatively healthy. He also played for a really good Tigers team. But there was something missing. He pitched fine but unremarkable baseball. He didn't miss enough bats, he gave up too many hits, he couldn't quite break through. In 2011, he had a 4.43 ERA and the league hit a more than satisfactory .272 with a .455 slugging percentage against him. Such solid offensive numbers don't seem possible when you match them with the overpowering velocity and movement of Scherzer's pitching repertoire.

But nobody in baseball works harder than Scherzer to figure out how to break through. In 2012, he added a curveball. He rarely threw it that year, but it gave hitters a new pitch to consider, and combined with a couple of tweaks in his motion, Scherzer started missing bats—he led the American League in strikeouts per nine innings in 2012.

In 2013 he became a star, going 21-3 with a 2.90 ERA and a league-leading 0.970 WHIP. He won the Cy Young Award. The next year, he was almost as good, finished fifth in the Cy Young voting, and that's when he became a free agent and signed a seven-year, $210 million deal with the Nationals.

It was a controversial signing for Washington. Yes, Scherzer had been great the previous two seasons, but he was turning 30, and by then just about everyone had come to the conclusion that long-term, big-money, free-agent signings are *always* a bad idea. As Cubs president Theo Epstein said about such deals, they always have a celebratory press conference *before* the contract begins. But you never see one at the contract's end.

When sportswriter Jayson Stark polled baseball executives, the Scherzer deal was voted the most outrageous contract offered, with one executive calling it "a Bobby Bonilla joke waiting to happen." Because of the structure of the contract, the Nationals will be paying Scherzer until 2028.

"Even if he's great for four years and then declines, that's 10 more years you're still paying him $15 million. That's incredible."*

The point is, there were still many doubts about Scherzer. This turned out to be a good thing because there's nothing that Max Scherzer loves more than doubters. They fuel him, inspire him, make him uncomfortable. And he wants to be uncomfortable. He wants to feel like he needs to do something drastic to get better and better. One thing that awes his teammates and fellow pitchers is how much tinkering and adjusting he does even when he's *pitching well*.

Another awe-inspiring thing is the rage and focus he brings to every start, every inning, every batter. There are countless stories about the rage that comes over him when he's on the mound. When one young player offered him a high-five before a game, Scherzer walked right by him. "I don't do that," he later explained. "I'm in the zone."

Once he got to Washington, Scherzer added a cut fastball to his already bountiful assortment of pitches, and that completed the picture. He has been extraordinary ever since:

In 2015, he led the league in starts, complete games, shutouts, and strikeout-to-walk ratio. You already know he threw three of the greatest games in baseball history that year. He finished fifth in the Cy Young voting.

In 2016, he led the league in wins, starts, innings, strikeouts, and WHIP. He won the Cy Young Award.

In 2017, he led the league in complete games, strikeouts, WHIP, and hits-per-nine innings. He won the Cy Young Award again, despite pitching part of the season with a broken finger.

In 2018, he led the league in wins, complete games, innings, strikeouts, WHIP, hits-per-nine, and strikeout-to-walk ratio. He was second in the Cy Young voting.

In 2019, despite missing six starts, despite back pain, despite breaking his nose while trying to bunt a ball, he finished third in the Cy Young vot-

---

* The Bobby Bonilla contract is one of the most famous in baseball history. The terms seem tame now—five years, $29 million—but what made it unique was that the Mets agreed to defer payments, and he will be making $1 million per year every year until 2035. Not bad for a guy who retired in 2001.

ing and then without his best stuff or health made five postseason starts, ranging from brilliant to gritty, and led the Nationals to the franchise's first-ever World Series title.

Suddenly, that $210 million deal looks like an absolute bargain. In fact, I think we will look back at the Scherzer deal as a turning point—so many teams spent the 2019 offseason throwing around hundreds of millions of dollars just trying to get the next Max Scherzer. It's hard to compare today's players with greats from the past, especially those who are very much mid-career. Scherzer's story is nowhere near complete yet.

But it's safe to say he's already one of the 100 greatest players in baseball history.

No. 89 Mike Piazza

Mike Piazza was taken very, very late in the baseball amateur draft. And if you're into baseball trivia, you might even know he was taken by the Los Angeles Dodgers in the 62nd round of the 1988 amateur draft. That's pretty famous because Piazza was *by far* the lowest draft pick ever to make the Hall of Fame. He will remain the lowest forever because the draft doesn't even go 62 rounds anymore.

Lowest Draft Picks to Make the Hall of Fame

1. Mike Piazza, 62nd round, 1,390th overall pick (1988)

2. John Smoltz, 22nd round, 574th overall pick (1985)

3. Ryne Sandberg, 20th round, 511th overall pick (1978)

4. Jim Thome, 13th round, 333rd overall pick (1989)

5. Nolan Ryan, 12th round, 295th overall pick (1965)

You might also know Piazza was taken as a personal favor to Dodgers manager Tommy Lasorda, who happened to be best friends with a guy named Vincent Piazza, Mike's father.

What you might not know is the Dodgers did not take Piazza in the 62nd round to sign him. They had absolutely no intention of signing him. They had absolutely no intention of even making him an offer.

No, the Dodgers took Piazza in the 62nd round as a personal favor to help him find a Division I college baseball program. See, out of high school, Piazza (with the help of Lasorda) signed with the University of Miami, but he was entirely overmatched there. He got nine plate appearances and one hit. Seeing his future, he quit school.

Piazza then went to Miami-Dade Community College (again aided by Lasorda). He wasn't overmatched there—he hit .364—but he also went entirely unnoticed. Not a single Division I school showed interest. Scouts saw absolutely nothing in Piazza. He was slow. He couldn't play first base. He had no arm. He lacked power. His best tool was his hitting, and it wasn't much of a tool; most scouts did not believe he could hit at a higher level. Piazza's toolbox was empty.

But he did play hard, and he had a good attitude, and he wanted success so badly. Lasorda was smitten. He asked the Dodgers to draft Piazza just so a school might see that and be impressed and perhaps take a chance on the kid.

The Dodgers drafted him and still no school came calling. When the Dodgers scout finally called a couple of months after the draft to check in, Piazza asked for one more favor. He wanted a tryout. The Dodgers were not especially interested in giving a tryout to a 62nd round pick taken as a personal favor, but one more time, guardian angel Tommy Lasorda stepped in and helped arrange a tryout, which he personally attended with scouting director Ben Wade.

And to the Dodgers' surprise—perhaps even to Lasorda's surprise— Piazza hit the ball hard at that tryout, hard enough that the Dodgers decided they had nothing to lose. They offered Piazza $15,000 to sign. Piazza took the deal before the sentence was even finished.

Can a baseball player be made? Vince and Mike Piazza shared a dream of playing big-league ball. Vince had quit baseball when he was 16 to make a living, but he spent a lifetime loving the game—he tried at different times to become a big-league owner. Father and son built a batting cage in the backyard, and Mike hit in that cage every single day, all year round. Mike famously would dig the cage out of the snow and hit baseballs that he and his father had heated in a pan over the stove. Vince told *Sports Illustrated* the zoning board sent someone by to take a look at the batting cage, which by that point had a roof, paneling, and a heater.

"What is that?" the board representative asked.

"That," Vince replied, "is my son's ticket to the major leagues."

Can a ballplayer be made? Vince surrounded his son with all the necessary tools. Not only did Mike grow up with Lasorda as a guiding light (Lasorda is godfather to Mike's brother Tommy), but he also got to hit for Ted Williams when he was in high school. (Williams reportedly was impressed, though he was also great friends with Vince and quite possibly would have said he was impressed even if he wasn't.)

But it went beyond the opportunities. Mike more than matched his father's fervor and passion. He breathed baseball. He never let any of the constant discouragement—"you're too slow," "you're too awkward," "you're too unathletic"—affect his drive or his confidence. He was going to become a big-league player no matter what the scouts said.

And once he got his professional shot, he did not let go. The Dodgers, somewhat in desperation, made Piazza a catcher because they couldn't figure out anywhere else to play him. And Piazza picked up the position better than they expected. Piazza was hardly a natural and lacked the arm strength to become a premier defender, but he had a sense for the game, he fearlessly blocked pitches in the dirt, and he liked being at the center of it all.

More important, he blossomed as a hitter. In his third minor-league season, he hit 29 home runs and slugged .540. The next year, after being moved up to Double A and then Triple A, he hit .350 and slugged .587. Suddenly, this afterthought was one of the best hitting prospects in baseball.

And, wow, he just kept hitting. From his first day in the big leagues (when he went 3-for-3 with a double at Wrigley Field), he was the best-hitting catcher Major League Baseball had ever seen. He won Rookie of the Year after hitting .318 with 35 homers and 112 RBIs. He came back with a nearly identical year and finished sixth in the MVP voting.

And then, from 1995 to 1998, he hit .343/.411/.594 with a 1.005 OPS. He received MVP votes each year and twice finished second in the voting (first time to Ken Caminiti, the second time to Larry Walker). In 1998, he was traded twice—once to Miami and then, eight days later, to the

Mets—but he kept on hitting like no big-league catcher ever had. By WAR runs batting, here are the five greatest-hitting catchers ever:

1. Mike Piazza, 418 runs above average

2. Mickey Cochrane, 271 runs

3. Johnny Bench, 269 runs

4. Bill Dickey, 262 runs

5. Gene Tenace, 259 runs

Nobody is even close.

Many people suspected Piazza was using steroids to get stronger; you can't tell his story without at least mentioning the suspicions. They formed all around him. Piazza was, as the *New York Times* pointed out, never linked to a positive drug test or with any investigation. And on multiple occasions he firmly denied using steroids.

He did admit to using drugs such as amphetamines, Vioxx, and, briefly and most notably, androstenedione. Today andro is considered an anabolic steroid and is illegal to use without a prescription. But back then it was an over-the-counter supplement that was considered so innocuous inside the game that Mark McGwire kept it out in the open in his locker.

In any case, the steroid whispers were undoubtedly the reason it took Piazza four tries before he was finally elected to the Hall of Fame.

After retiring, Piazza moved to Miami, lived there for a time, then felt a longing for action. "There is nothing you will ever do after you retire," he told *The Athletic*, "that will give you the same buzz as playing." He decided to buy a soccer team, A.C. Reggiana in Reggio Emilia, and it turned out to be a financial disaster for him and his family as well as a heartbreaking end to a team that had played for a century. Piazza and his family still live in Italy, and Piazza manages Italy's national baseball team.

"My heart is in Italy now," he says.

No. 88 **Curt Schilling**

In 2002—the year after Randy Johnson and Curt Schilling were co-MVPs of the World Series and named co–Sportspeople of the Year by *Sports Illustrated*—someone in the Diamondbacks organization explained to me the basic difference between the two players.

The person said that with Johnson, teammates hated him on the day he pitched, loved him the other four days.

And with Schilling, teammates loved him on the day he pitched, hated him the other four days.

It's a generalization, of course, and I'm sure not everyone felt that way. But it probably does get close to the heart of the two pitchers. Johnson was a grouchy son of a gun on the days he pitched. You didn't want to be anywhere near the guy. He took the mound with a Grand Canyon–sized chip on his shoulder and intended to strike out the world, and he did not want anyone to get near him. You couldn't talk to him. You couldn't approach him. He once threw a ball (somewhat lightly) at a photographer who was too close when he was warming up. Even his wife, Lisa, wouldn't talk to him on pitch days.

"I am the intimidator," he would say about himself.

But the other days, Big Unit was pleasant and even fun to be around, assuming you could get past the natural and menacing glare and daunting 6-foot-10 frame. He played himself in the movie *Little Big League*. He played himself on *The Simpsons*. He's done a few funny commercials. He can be quite a likable guy.

Schilling was the opposite kind of story. On game days, there simply wasn't anyone you would rather have on your team. Schilling was a ferocious competitor. He loved the big moments—the bigger the better. Even in his younger days, when he was wildly inconsistent and a self-described "idiot," he thrived in the playoffs, in the World Series, when the games counted most. And when he developed into an incredible pitcher, like he was from 2001 to 2004, he maintained that love of the spotlight. Something about him would rise up when the team needed him to win. He was at his best when his team needed it.

And the other four days? Schilling was as he is now: opinionated, inflexible, thin-skinned, a loudmouth, a knucklehead, a jokester, a troll, a clubhouse politician, a nonstop yapper. "Sometimes," his Arizona teammate Luis Gonzalez said, "you need to unplug Curt to stop him from talking." Behind the scenes, teammates offered that sentiment in much more pointed ways. He drove them bonkers. He offended many of them. He was, in the words of more than one, a handful. He was, in the words of more than one, a jerk.

Some of this broke through publicly. At different times, teammates, columnists, and managers have called him "something of a con man," "a blowhard," "a phony," "self-centered," "self-aggrandizing," and "Red Light Curt" (for his relish for the television cameras).

Schilling was never that easy to figure out, though. Yes, he would pick fights, say offensive things, push the boundaries of taste and compassion. But he was also deeply generous. In his career, he won the Branch Rickey Award, the Roberto Clemente Award, the Lou Gehrig Award, *and* the Hutch Award, all of them for charity, community service, and displaying admirable character on and off the field. Schilling and Jamie Moyer are the only two players to win all four of what you might call MLB's integrity awards. He gave tirelessly of his time to support the military, to support children's charities, to support people in need. He was so devoted to the memory of Lou Gehrig that he named his son Gehrig and spent countless hours working with ALS charities.

I remember him coming out to support my friend, the late Steve Palermo, an extraordinary big-league umpire before he was paralyzed by a bullet while trying to help two women who were being mugged.

Schilling said Palermo was behind the plate for his first start. Schilling was nervous beyond words, and Palermo saw it. "Tell you what, kid," Palermo said as he walked to the mound, "you get that first pitch close I'll call it a strike." Schilling never forgot it, and Palermo would say he could always count on Schilling to help.

How do you piece it all together? How do you see the divisive cartoon character Schilling has become on Twitter and also see the guy who wrote this letter to America after 9/11:

> My first cognizant thought was, "Man, did they pick on the wrong country." Then, after watching TV, I began to realize that not only did they pick on the wrong country, but they couldn't have picked a worse target. There is no city on this planet that more represents its nation than New York does in the United States. New York is the true definition of a melting pot. Every race, religion and color are represented in New York, and on Tuesday you saw every race, every religion, every color come together as one nation of people fighting for one common goal—to save lives. I can honestly tell you that I have never been as proud to be an American as I was that day.

Would the two Curt Schillings even recognize each other at a party?

After Schilling won Game 1 of the 2001 World Series—the first World Series game in Arizona history—I wrote a column about a single empty seat in the ballpark. It was the seat Schilling left open for his father, Cliff. Schilling always left an empty seat for his father, who died of a heart attack before his son's big-league career began. To say Schilling idolized his father is to understate things; he will tell you he has never fully recovered from his father's death.

Cliff Schilling was an army man. He was tough, very tough, and the only time Curt ever saw him cry was after Roberto Clemente died. But Cliff was also profoundly decent and humble and driven; Curt would listen for his father's voice in his mind before every game. "He was my best friend," Curt said.

I wrote the column for the *Kansas City Star* on a tight deadline and went back to the hotel late and went to sleep. I woke up early the next morning. There was an email from Curt Schilling thanking me for writing it.

I've thought about that a lot since then. I didn't know Schilling then; we had never spoken one-on-one. The Internet was not all that accessible in those days; there was no such thing as Google Alerts—you had to make a real effort to find a story written by some guy in the *Kansas City Star*. I've thought a lot about Schilling, on the night after he pitched a brilliant World Series Game 1 (seven innings, three hits, eight strikeouts against the three-time defending World Series champions), going on to a computer to read about himself and then taking the time to send a note to an obscure middle-America sports columnist he had never met just to say how much it meant to him.

I can't quite figure it out. I can't quite figure him out.

The trouble with writing about Schilling is it's a no-win. Nobody wants a full story on the guy. His fans want you to talk about how great a pitcher he was or how he is being persecuted for his politics. Non-fans want you to talk about his anti-Muslim and anti-transgender social media posts or the many conspiracy theories he traffics in, a number that grows with each passing year. And neither group wants to read about the other side.

Despite all that, I do want to discuss just one controversial Schilling moment. You might remember when he joyfully retweeted a T-shirt about lynching journalists and commented, "OK, so much awesome here . . ."

It poses a question:

What responsibility does a journalist with a Baseball Hall of Fame vote have to put a check mark next to Schilling's name?

Beyond that, though, Schilling's baseball argument as an all-time great is pretty airtight. Not everybody sees it that way because Schilling won "only" 216 games and never won a Cy Young Award, and the retired pitchers who are listed as most similar on his Baseball Reference page—Kevin Brown, Bob Welch, Bret Saberhagen, Tim Hudson, Orel Hershiser—were excellent pitchers but not all-time greats.

But each of these points against Schilling is misleading. The wins thing? Nobody should care about pitcher wins these days, but even if you do, Schilling twice led the league in wins and won 20 three times. He has about the same number of wins as recent first-ballot Hall of Fame choices John Smoltz, Pedro Martínez, and Roy Halladay.

The Cy Young thing? No, he never won, but he finished second in the Cy Young voting three times, twice to legendary seasons by his teammate Randy Johnson and once to Johan Santana. He finished top four in pitcher various versions of WAR 12 times. He surely *could* have won the Cy Young Award on numerous occasions.

And as far as his similarities with those other fine-but-not-Hall-of-Fame pitchers go, they're really cosmetic. Schilling was not like any of them. He has many more strikeouts than any of them; he was a ferocious strikeout pitcher and is one of only four to have back-to-back 300-strikeout seasons. The other three are Johnson, Nolan Ryan, and Sandy Koufax. He also retired with the greatest strikeout-to-walk ratio in modern baseball history.

And an argument can be made that he's the greatest postseason pitcher in baseball history.

So, no, he wasn't Bob Welch.

Bill James invented something called the "Hall of Fame Monitor," which adds up various stats to determine the likelihood that a player will be elected to the Hall of Fame. A monitor score of 100 gives the player a good chance to be elected. At 130, the player is a near-lock for election. At 150, the player should already be in the Hall of Fame.

Schilling scored a 171 on the Hall of Fame Monitor. None of the other pitchers called "similar" even scored 100.

But again, believing Schilling is Hall of Fame–worthy does not answer the basic question: What responsibility does a journalist have to vote for someone who holds journalists in such disdain that he believes a T-shirt about lynching them is worthy of praise and a retweet? We live in a time when journalists around the world work in mortal danger of losing their lives for reporting the truth. Do you have to vote for someone who offends every fiber of your being if you believe he was a truly great baseball player?

I don't have a great answer for that. The obvious answer seems to be "no." There are people in and around the game I admire very much who have told me they would never vote for Schilling because of the things he has said, positions he has taken, prejudices he advertises, resentments he constantly stirs up. They say things like, "I don't owe him a vote. There are plenty of other great players who don't laugh about killing journalists." I don't think they're wrong. But I don't know if they're right, either.

Truth is, I can't figure out what drives Schilling. I never expect to understand. I think he was a great pitcher. As for the other four days between, well, that's another story.

Charlie Gehringer

C harlie Gehringer never celebrated himself. Ever. Sportswriters used to love him for that. And then they didn't. And then they did again. It's a baffling story.

Gehringer's story itself is not baffling at all. He could not have been more consistent, on or off the field. They called him "The Mechanical Man" because he just went out and played ball. He didn't talk. He didn't complain. He didn't boast. He didn't want fame. He just wanted to play ball and play it well; that was where his story began and ended.

"Wind him up in the spring," Lefty Gomez said of Gehringer, "turn him off in the fall, and in between, he hits .340."

Yes, the sportswriters loved him for that quiet strength: What can be more appealing than the strong-and-silent type? Hollywood has made a million movies about that Gehringer kind of hero. From 1927 to 1940, Gehringer hit .329/.411/.497, played a terrific second base, and stole some bases. Most of all, he did the same thing every year, and you never heard a peep from the guy.

When he won the MVP award in 1937 while having a year no different from all his others, he was typically silent. The *Detroit Free Press* stepped in his place with an editorial that called him "a gentleman, a devoted son and an all-around fine citizen . . . whose artistry around second base is exceeded only by his modesty on the diamond and off of it."

Sportswriters wrote that kind of stuff about Gehringer all the time. How can you not love a humble superstar?

Charlie Gehringer grew up on a farm in Fowlerville, Michigan—"a town of something like 1,200 humans in Livingston County," the *Free Press* explained—and the only thing the young Gehringer knew for sure was he didn't want to spend his life on that farm.

His father died when Charlie was just going out into the world, and his mother was adamantly opposed to his playing professional baseball. Instead, he went to the University of Michigan with the intention of becoming a coach. He played baseball, tried out for football, lettered in basketball. But it became clear that Gehringer was a raw and rare baseball talent, and he already had the Mechanical Man detachment that would become famous in later years.

"Don't get too excited about this game," Michigan baseball coach Ray Fisher said to him at practice one day.

Gehringer looked curiously at his legendary coach, as if he couldn't quite understand.

"Don't worry," he finally said with perfect equanimity. "I won't."

It was rare for Gehringer to even string four words together like "Don't worry, I won't." He did not talk. He didn't see the use of talking. Finally, against his mother's wishes, Gehringer decided he would give professional baseball a shot. He impressed Ty Cobb himself during a tryout for the Tigers in 1924 and made the club. In short order, Gehringer became a consistent All-Star, an MVP, a baseball star of the highest order. His most noticeable trait, though, remained his silence, his refusal to make a show of anything, his ghostlike ability to disappear into the background.

"He'd say hello at the start of spring training and good-bye at the end," Cobb said.

"He was a man of mechanical precision," Branch Rickey said, "and obscure so far as showmanship was concerned."

"You just forget him," teammate Doc Cramer said.

"He hadn't missed a tag or said a word in 15 years," Leo Durocher said after Gehringer missed a tag on Dizzy Dean in the World Series.

On the field, he got a little bit better every single year. As Bill James has written, "I wonder if any player in baseball history had a record of sustained improvement to equal Gehringer?"

The answer is almost certainly: no. Gehringer was always good. From 1927 through 1940, he hit .300 every year but one (in 1932 he hit .298). He scored 100 runs in all 12 healthy seasons he had. He regularly had 200 hits, 30-plus doubles, double-digit homers, and stolen bases. He regularly knocked in 100 or so runs. He regularly played 150-plus games.

But he kept finding new ways to improve. At 31, he led the league in hits and runs. At 33, he cracked 60 doubles—he's the last player to hit 60 doubles in a season. At 34, he won his first and only batting title by hitting .371 and was named MVP.

And he became a better and better defender as the years went along. "There is not a surer pair of hands in baseball . . . he is a high-class defensive ballplayer," one sportswriter wrote of the younger Gehringer, but it was as an older player that he became a great defensive second baseman. From ages 30 to 34, by Baseball Reference's fielding calculations, he was 55 runs better than average, making him the American League's best fielder at any position over that time.

On the field, he played with bland ferocity; his expression never seemed to change. He never seemed to be happy or unhappy, never seemed frustrated or to be having any fun. It was business. Off the field, he was profoundly shy. He lived with his mother and took care of her throughout his career.

Every morning, Charlie and his mother went to Mass together.

He was admired for all of it—his silent conviction, his overwhelming modesty, his "keep your head down and work hard" approach to baseball and life. One story that made all the papers involved Gehringer at a banquet. He was introduced in a typically grandiose way, and he stepped behind the lectern.

"I'm known around baseball as saying very little," Gehringer said. "I'm not going to spoil my reputation." Then he sat down.

Gehringer was elected to the Hall of Fame in a special runoff election in 1949. He had come relatively close to being elected the previous two years, but there was such a backlog of great players left over from World War II— the Hall of Fame had stopped inducting players during the war—that he simply had to wait in line. In the '49 runoff election, he was selected on

85 percent of the ballots, finishing ahead of Mel Ott, Jimmie Foxx, and 17 other players who would eventually get into the Hall of Fame.

Gehringer did not attend the ceremony. Remember how the Mechanical Man never celebrated himself? Well, this continued after his retirement. But this time, bizarrely, the sportswriters attacked his modesty. Their rage was best exemplified by the words of the legendary sportswriter Shirley Povich, who took to the pages of the *Sporting News* to attack the Mechanical Man.

"I take no great satisfaction now in having cast one of the votes that might have helped to install Charlie Gehringer in the Baseball Hall of Fame," he wrote. "I was just thinking he might have found time to detach himself for a few hours to be on the scene on a day when baseball was finding a niche for him among the immortals. That shows how easy it is to overrate a fellow."

Then he added some snark.

"It is still the highest tribute the game can offer," Povich wrote. "Of course, there's no cash award accompanying it."

This was the angle many sportswriters took: They wrote that Gehringer had skipped Cooperstown because there was no money to be made. The hypocrisy of celebrating Gehringer for his modesty for decades and then blasting him for it at the end did not seem to occur to anybody.

Anyway, as it turns out, Gehringer didn't miss the Hall of Fame so he could make money. He missed it because, at age 46, he traveled to the West Coast to get married for the first time.

From the *Sporting News:*

When Charlie Gehringer returns from his honeymoon in the West, he'll find Detroit considerably relieved that he had a legitimate excuse for missing the enshrinement ceremonies that put him in the Cooperstown Hall of Fame.... Charlie has always been shy, and as a 46-year-old bachelor, he made secret wedding plans.

And from the *Detroit Free Press:*

He wanted to get married to his Detroit girl out in California, to avoid all the fuss that this old town would have stirred up. Throughout his career, Charlie has never sought the spotlight; in fact, the spotlight has been kept out of breath chasing him.

There were a few apologies from the sportswriters after that; I don't know if Gehringer accepted them or cared about any of it. He lived a long time after his playing career. He worked for the Tigers as general manager for a short while. He had tried repeatedly to turn down the job, but they sort of pressured him into it, and he loathed every minute of it (though he did sign the young phenom Al Kaline). Gehringer later played in some old-timers' games (injuring himself once trying to stretch a hit into extra bases) and did some charitable work. He never did change, though. According to a wonderful story told by his wife, Josephine, toward the end of his life, people in Detroit would often recognize him and say, "Are you Charlie Gehringer?"

And he would say, "I'm sorry, no. My name is Schultz."

No. 86 Gary Carter

Gary Carter is one of more than a dozen baseball players who were nicknamed "Kid." This does not include more specialized versions of the nickname such as "The K Kid" (Clayton Kershaw), "The Say Hey Kid" (Willie Mays), "Kid Natural" (Ryne Sandberg), "The Big Kid" (Bryce Harper), "The Good Kid" (Lou Boudreau), "Billy the Kid" (Billy Wagner, among others) or "Da Kid" (Sean Manaea).

No, there have been more than enough players just nicknamed "Kid" to make the point: Ted Williams, Ken Griffey, Robin Yount, Charles Nichols, Billy Demars, etc. Many of the "Kids" through the years, to be blunt about it, got the nickname not out of love but because they annoyed the bejesus out of their veteran teammates. The template is Ted Williams, the most famous Kid of them all, whose teammates so loathed his youthful arrogance that they condescendingly called him "Kid" just to infuriate him, which they did.

Carter's story is a little bit different. He was not arrogant. He did not show disdain for anybody the way Williams did—quite the contrary. He truly played like a joyful kid. He ran out every drill at full speed. He played each moment with a sort of manic enthusiasm. He was just 19 at his first spring training, and he took on every part of it—the workouts, the interviews, the games, the razzing, all of it—with an exuberance that at first seemed funny but over time became less and less charming.

They began calling him "Kid," in the spirit of "Hey, Kid, slow down a little bit, pace yourself, it's a long season." The more Carter performed, though, the more irritated his teammates became and the less affection could be found in that nickname.

I've not seen it often referenced, but it's striking how similar the young Carter was to the young Steve Garvey. They were born a little more than five years apart, which meant Garvey was already playing for the Los Angeles Dodgers when Carter was going to Sunny Hills High in Orange County, California. I imagine Carter viewed Garvey as something of a role model. Garvey always loved being in the middle of everything, he loved the spotlight, loved doing the press interviews, loved being in a Major League Baseball uniform. So did Carter. He did so many interviews that after a while, teammates stopped calling him Kid and began calling him "Camera Carter" and "Lights."

And the joy! It was always there, nonstop. You would be hard-pressed to find a photograph of the young Carter when he's not smiling.

There's a particular order to Carter's career, one I think has made him spectacularly underrated. By WAR, Carter (70 Wins Above Replacement) is the second-greatest catcher in baseball history, behind only Johnny Bench. By Jay Jaffe's JAWS formula, which uses WAR to measure both a player's career value and peak value, he's again second in baseball history behind Bench. His seven-year peak is actually *higher* than Bench's— higher, in fact, than that of any catcher in baseball history.

Is he, as these statistics suggest, the second-greatest catcher in baseball history? I don't have him quite that high, but as you can see, I do have him squarely among the 100 greatest players ever.

Still, it took Carter six turbulent years to finally get elected to the Baseball Hall of Fame.

What you find so often in Hall of Fame voting is that it comes down to storytelling. Carter's contemporary catcher Carlton Fisk had a career with a clear and compelling story: A brilliant young New England athlete, tough as nails, goes to Boston, plays his heart out, hits perhaps the most famous homer in baseball history, then goes to Chicago, finds a second life on the South Side, and keeps on going and going until they tear the uniform off his back at age 45.

Another great catcher, Mike Piazza, had a career with a similarly clear and compelling story: tough Philadelphia kid, written off by everyone, drafted in the 62nd round as a personal favor to his father, turns himself into the greatest-hitting catcher in baseball history.

But Carter? How do you summarize his career? He always seemed slightly off. He was a terrific rookie, but he lost the Rookie of the Year Award to John Montefusco, whose wonderful nickname "The Count of Montefusco" has mostly outlived his pitching fame.

Carter was a superstar in Montreal when that city seemed a million miles away from everything else in baseball and when the talented Expos team kept finding ways to lose. Carter put up MVP-quality seasons for the Expos in 1978, '79, '80, '82, '83, and '84, but he did not get a single first-place MVP vote in any of those years. (Even in 1980, the year Carter finished second in the MVP voting, Philadelphia's superstar Mike Schmidt won the award unanimously.)

Carter was probably the best player in the National League in 1982, when he hit .293/.381/.510 with 32 doubles, 29 homers, and spectacular defensive numbers. He finished 12th in the MVP voting that year.

In 1984, he became just the third catcher—Roy Campanella and Bench were the first two—to lead the league in RBIs. Campanella won the MVP award when he did it, and Bench won the MVP award two of the three times he did it. Carter finished 14th the year he did it.

Sure, people knew Carter was good, but it seemed to escape notice that he was great. He played otherworldly defense, and he was a terrific power hitter. Put it all together and Carter was about as good as Yogi Berra, Bench, Fisk, Campanella, and all the other legends behind the plate.

Carter did not grow up as a catcher. He had played only a handful of games there before the Expos drafted him, and in his first two years, he played more outfield than backstop. But after five years of diligent work behind the plate, Carter made himself into a special defender. He had the physical tools: a great arm, fantastic athleticism (he was recruited to play quarterback at UCLA), soft hands, and leadership qualities. But even more, he was obsessed with doing all the little things that a catcher needs to do. In '76, in part-time play, he already was one of the best in baseball in throwing out baserunners.

The next year, 1977, he became probably the best defensive catcher in the National League. That was the last year Bench won the Gold Glove

Award; it was given to him out of respect to his extraordinary career. Carter had supplanted the legend. But, again, people just didn't see it. Carter did not win his first Gold Glove until 1980, and he won only three in his career. When you look at his defensive numbers—which include 26 defensive Wins Above Replacement, among the highest totals in baseball history—you see a catching genius. But, alas, people missed it.

In all, Carter did not get much national recognition until he went to the New York Mets in 1985. He played for the famous and wild Mets teams of the mid-1980s—Dwight Gooden, Darryl Strawberry, Keith Hernandez, Ron Darling, that lot—and in 1986, he finally got a first-place MVP vote; even though he didn't come close to winning the award, he was finally getting some of the attention he deserved.

There's some irony about that—by 1986, Carter was no longer the player he had been. A catcher's body breaks down quickly. The years of crouching and diving in front of pitches in the dirt and blocking baserunners bearing in at full speed steals a catcher's youth. In 1987, Carter hit just .235/.290/.392, and the next year was about the same. In 1989, he played only 50 games. Then he signed with the Giants, and after that with the Dodgers, and finally he returned to the Expos—you probably don't remember those years, and if you do, you probably wish you didn't. When Carter's name first appeared on the Hall of Fame ballot, some of the voters apparently could not shake this version of Carter from their heads, this creaky-bodied catcher with the stiff swing, barely flaring balls to right field. They had lost the picture of Gary Carter when he could do everything.

Carter never displayed any signs of being jaded by the game. Even after his baseball skills had frayed and worn thin, he played baseball with a smile on his face and (though he was notoriously slow) a spring in his step. It was hard to believe that even at the end, when he seemed to be overwhelmed by pain, he could be so happy. Some thought it a show, and every so often, I would hear someone say of Carter, "Oh, that guy's a phony," which he undoubtedly was not. This line of thinking reminds me of what my friend Chuck Culpepper would use whenever someone would say to him that former Florida State football coach Bobby Bowden was putting on an act as a kind and generous man.

Chuck would say, "Well, he's been doing it for 50 years; it's one heck of an act." Gary Carter was like that, too. You can't be a phony if you never break character.

Gary Carter died much too young, at age 57, after a short but fierce battle with brain cancer. At his memorial, countless people talked about his zest for life. He should have been a first-ballot Hall of Famer, unanimous even, but he did get his due in time, and the wait didn't seem to bother him much. "Though my body feels like an old man now," he told the crowd that day he was inducted in Cooperstown, "I will always be a kid at heart."

Sadaharu Oh

O ur story about Sadaharu Oh begins not with the great man himself but with a baseball player you almost certainly do not know.
His name was Hiroshi Arakawa. He was a smallish man, barely 5-
foot-4, and he had a little paunch and suspect speed and almost no natural
power. He hit just .251 for his career in the Japanese Pacific League.

Charlie Lau hit .255 in his big-league career.

Walt Hriniak hit .253 in his big-league career.

Charlie Manuel hit .198 in his big-league career.

All of them were great hitting coaches just the same.

You can probably see where this story is going.

Arakawa at some point during his career became fascinated with aikido, the Japanese martial art that roughly translates to "the path to harmony of spirit."

That is, in fact, a very rough translation. Basically: "Ai" means "to
harmonize or come together"; "Ki" means "mind, soul, spirit"; and "Do"
means "the way or path." Different people put those words together in different ways, but in general it's correct to say that aikido is a martial art, a
religion, and a philosophy about achieving harmony of the soul.

There is a wonderful story, perhaps true, about Arakawa meeting the sensei Morihei Ueshiba, who founded aikido. Arakawa was introduced as a famous baseball player, which left the Founder utterly baffled and uninterested. Ueshiba did not know baseball or any of its rules. He rather bizarrely confused baseball with the medical therapy moxibustion (which involves burning a certain kind of plant called mugwort onto the skin to boost energy) because the Japanese words are similar.

After Arakawa offered a brief explanation of what it meant to hit baseballs, Ueshiba asked, "For something like that, why don't you just cut through with a Japanese sword?"

Arakawa's life changed instantly. He realized, all at once, that preparing to hit was no different than training with a Japanese sword. They require the same discipline, the same force of will, the same level of inner peace. Arakawa was 30 years old by then, spent as a ballplayer, but he had a new path in life. He wanted to teach young people the proper way to hit baseballs.

In January 1962, a few months after his last game, he was hired to be the hitting coach for the Yomiuri Giants.

And the Giants had a talented, underachieving party guy on the team named Sadaharu Oh.

Sadaharu Oh's father, Shifuku, owned a noodle shop in Japan. I have sometimes wondered if the movie *Kung Fu Panda* was (very) loosely influenced by Sadaharu Oh's life. In the movie, the panda, Po, is the son of a noodle shop owner, and he daydreams of being a great warrior. His father does not understand at all.

Sadaharu Oh is the son of a noodle shop owner and dreamed of being a great baseball player, and his father did not understand it at all. The sensei in the movie, incidentally, is named Master Shifu, and Oh's father's name was, as mentioned, Shifuku. I am probably stretching this comparison at this point.

Shifuku was from China, and he was briefly imprisoned during World War II under suspicion of being a spy. All indications are that he was not a spy and that he was imprisoned because of the tension of the times (not unlike the way Japanese-Americans were interned in the United States during the war).

Shifuku thought of baseball as a silly and pointless pastime. He wanted his sons to do important work; he wanted Sadaharu to become an engineer. The story goes that it was Sadaharu's brother, Tetsuhiro (who also loved the game), who ultimately convinced their father to allow Sadaharu to play ball.

Oh was a natural ballplayer. Like Babe Ruth and Stan Musial, he began as a pitcher. He was a natural lefty, but he grew up swinging right-handed because he did not know that the rules allowed him to swing any other way. Even so, nothing could conceal his talent. By the time he was in high school—and high school baseball in Japan is a bit like high school football in Texas—he was a national star. He was signed by the Yomiuri Giants for roughly $60,000 (13 million yen).

And . . . he disappointed. In his rookie year, he hit just .161 and struck out one out of every three times he came to the plate. His second year, he was somewhat better, but he struck out more than 100 times—so many whiffs that fans would sometimes call him "Sanshin Oh."

"Oh" means "king." "Sanshin" means "strikeout."

"Frankly, it was easy to get him out," pitcher Hiroshi Gondo told the writer Robert Whiting. "He could not hit a fastball. You could just blow it by him." In 1961, at age 21, Oh hit just .253 with 13 home runs. He lived on the wild side. He seemed only halfway committed to baseball. His future seemed blurry at best.

That's when the Giants hired Hiroshi Arakawa. And everything changed.*

First, Arakawa told Oh to stop drinking, stop smoking, and stop partying or else there was no point in continuing their training together. Oh agreed.

Then came the baseball work. Arakawa saw Oh was mistiming his stride and lunging too soon, and this left him unbalanced when the ball arrived and helpless to adjust to its pace and movement. Oh was just guessing out there, and guessing was no way to hit baseballs.

---

* There's a point worth making here about hitting coaches and their star pupils: Their relationships tend to begin only after the hitters themselves have run out of ideas. The most famous American coach-hitter relationship is probably that between Charlie Lau and George Brett. Well, Lau approached Brett several times with some hitting advice, and Brett angrily rebuffed him. It wasn't until Brett found himself hitting .220 and in danger of being sent to the minor leagues that he began listening to Lau. In other words, Arakawa arrived at exactly the right moment for Oh.

But how could Arakawa fix this? He turned to some of the fundamentals of aikido and thought up a way to change Oh's stance entirely. He wanted Oh to stand on one leg, his back leg, as the pitcher released the ball. Arakawa called this the "flamingo stance."

Oh was not the first player to lift his front leg high as the pitcher delivered. American superstars Mel Ott and Musial did it first. It's unclear if Arakawa knew that, though. What he did know was that standing on one leg would force Oh to stay balanced, force him to be conscious of his "energy center." As the ball was delivered, Oh would then flex his right knee skyward and stride into the ball in perfect harmony. Alas: aikido.

"I had reached a point," Oh would write, "where Aikido had become absolutely necessary to what I did. Without Aikido, I would not learn to stand on one foot, I would not 'understand it.'"

Together, Arakawa and Oh practiced day after day, hour after hour. Often, Oh would use a sword instead of a bat and a sheet of paper in place of a baseball. This training transformed Oh. He had been known for his lackadaisical approach to baseball, a mortal sin in Japan. Baseball is viewed as a discipline in Japan, an art form, one that takes relentless work. Baseball training in Japan bears no resemblance to spring training in the United States. Each practice session lasts six or seven hours. There are two batting cages going at once before every game. Each game is preluded by long infield and outfield practices.

I remember former Kansas City Royals manager Trey Hillman saying he tried to cut back the grueling training sessions when he was a manager in Japan. He thought he was doing the players a favor. He found instead that players resented this. They wanted to work past exhaustion; this was an important part of the game for them. There was honor to be found in pushing themselves beyond their physical limits and dishonor in doing less than their best.

After he began working with Arakawa, Oh became the very symbol of this kind of work ethic. For more than two years, he worked with the sword. He trained his body and his mind.

And, yes, Oh began to crush baseballs. The improvement was instant. In 1962, his first year after working with Arakawa, he hit 38 home runs, which easily led the Japan Central League (no one else hit more than 25). In 1963, he hit .300 for the first time, walked 123 times, and slugged 40 home runs to lead the league again. In 1964, he hit .320/.456/.720 with a

Japanese-record 55 home runs. He did this in 140 games, by the way. He won his third home run title by 19 homers.

A few Oh stats: He won 13 consecutive home-run titles. He won 15 home-run titles in 16 years. He won two Triple Crowns. He walked at least 108 times for 16 straight seasons. His 868 career home runs is a world record. His career OPS was 1.080—and he had an OPS of 1.000 or higher every year from 1963 to 1978.

What can we make of these numbers? It's hard to say. It is certainly not easy to translate numbers in Japanese baseball to American numbers.

But there are a few points worth making:

1. We have seen many Japanese players, like Ichiro, Hideo Nomo, Hideki Matsui, and Yu Darvish, come over in the past 20 years and play at the same supreme level in the major leagues as they played in the Japanese Leagues. It's not perfect math, of course. Some Japanese stars have not played well here. Also, Oh played in a different time for Japanese baseball.

   Still, baseball is baseball. And I must admit, as someone who has spent a lot of time learning about the Negro Leagues, I'm suspicious of anyone who dismisses other leagues or baseball styles as inferior.

2. There are many, many great American players who saw Oh hit and were certain he could have been an American star. There are too many quotes from players who faced him to include here, but let me offer just a few:

   "Oh could have played anywhere at any time," Don Baylor said. "If he played in Yankee Stadium, being the left-handed pull hitter he is, I have no doubt he'd hit 40 homers a year."

   "You can kiss my ass if he wouldn't have 30 or 35 home runs a year . . . he rates with the all-time stars of the game," Frank Howard said.

   "I'm sure he would have hit in the 30s and probably in the low 40s," Frank Robinson said of the numbers of home runs Oh would have hit.

   "He sure hit me," Tom Seaver said. "He was a superb hitter. He hit consistently, and he hit with power. . . . He'd be a lifetime .300 hitter."

   "He would have hit for average and power," Don Drysdale said.

   "He'd have been a Hall of Famer," Hal McRae said.

   Pete Rose, who is not always generous when it comes to judging Japanese baseball, said Oh would have hit .300 for sure. Davey Johnson talked about how good a defensive first baseman he was. Brooks Robinson said he was just an outstanding hitter. And so on. Oh's remarkable ability was transparent to the greatest American players of the day.

3. To me, the most compelling aspect of Oh's case is his dominance. He wasn't just the best player in the league. He was *far and away* the best player in the league. He did not just win 13 consecutive home-run titles. He won eight of them by double digits. He did not just lead the league in on-base percentage every year; for a good stretch of his career, his on-base percentage was right around .500. Nine times, he slugged better than .700.

At age 37, he hit .324/.477/.706 with 50 home runs.

Could someone be that dominant in Japan and not be one of the best players in the history of the game? I simply can't see it.

According to Whiting and others, it took a long time for Oh to be embraced by Japanese fans. This seems to be, at least in part, because his father was Chinese. According to one story Oh was not allowed to play in a high school tournament because he was not full-blooded Japanese.

He was also, as a young player, overshadowed by the great third baseman Shigeo Nagashima. Together they were like the Ruth and Gehrig of Japanese baseball. But Nagashima was better loved at first, in part because he had hit one of the most famous home runs in the nation's history, a walk-off homer in front of Emperor Hirohito. Do you know what they call a walk-off homer in Japan? A sayonara home run. I love that so much.

In any case, Oh won over his country through his sheer dominance. He became the nation's ultimate sporting hero—bigger in Japan, perhaps, than any American athlete here since Michael Jordan or Muhammad Ali or Babe Ruth. Oh's unique batting style was copied. His intense discipline toward the game was celebrated. "Oh" became synonymous with Japanese baseball.

There's something fascinating and persistent about home-run records: Fans do not want to see them broken. We have seen this in America time and time again. People did not want Roger Maris to break Babe Ruth's single-season home-run record, then people did not want to see Mark McGwire break Maris's home-run record, and then people did not want to see Barry Bonds break anybody's home-run record. The same line is true in career home runs: Henry Aaron dealt with death threats as he chased Ruth's career record. And when Bonds broke Aaron's record, a huge percentage of baseball fans simply refused to accept it.

There's a similar time line in Japan with Oh. People so cherished Oh's single-season record of 55 homers—that's the reason Matsui wore No. 55 when he joined the New York Yankees—that they have lost their minds a little bit any time it was threatened. Controversy followed.

In 1985, for instance, Randy Bass had 54 home runs for the Hanshin Tigers going into his final game of the season. He was walked four straight times (four pitches each). That's suspicious enough, but in this case his opponent happened to be the Yomiuri Giants. And the Giants manager happened to be, you guessed it, Sadaharu Oh. If that seems like a pretty big scandal, well, it actually wasn't. The incident was lightly investigated and the judgment was that Oh had nothing to do with the walks (Whiting later reported that a Giants coach threatened a $1,000 fine for every strike Bass was thrown).

In 2001, Tuffy Rhodes hit 55 homers to tie Oh's record but, in eerily similar fashion, he was not given the opportunity to break it. "Nobody in the whole country wanted me to break it," Rhodes would say. Like with Bass, Rhodes was walked repeatedly by Oh's team—and again Oh insisted he had nothing with it. This time Oh's coach, Yoshiharu Wakana, went public and admitted that he made the decision to repeatedly walk Rhodes.

"It would be distasteful to see a foreign player break Oh's record," Wakana said.

The next year, Alex Cabrera also tied the record and also found it difficult to get pitches in the final games. This time Oh specifically and publicly ordered his players to pitch to Cabrera—he had grown embarrassed by it all—but his pitchers refused. Whiting writes that while Oh's passive acceptance of the way everyone protected his record is somewhat curious, there probably wasn't anything he could have done. His record was cherished by a proud nation. They would do all they could to see it was not broken.

The record would be broken. In 2013, Wladimir Balentien hit 60 homers for the Yakult Swallows, and you would think this would finally end the controversy.

But it did not. Instead, people in Japan insisted there was something wrong with the ball. And, sure enough, a thorough investigation was done, and the balls were indeed found to be juiced.

Many people in Japan still consider Sadaharu's 55 home runs to be the record. They probably always will.

Cool Papa Bell

Amillion stories begin with this basic construction: "James 'Cool Papa' Bell was so fast that . . ." He was so fast that he could turn out the light and be under the covers before the room got dark. He was so fast that he could hit a line drive up the middle and beat the ball to second base. And so on. We'll get to those. But we should begin with something true and sure: Jesse Owens refused to race him.

Jesse Owens was, as you no doubt know, the fastest man in the world in the 1930s, the fastest man the world had ever seen. One day in 1935, he set three world records. The next year, at the Olympics in Berlin, under the outstretched arm of Adolf Hitler, Owens won four Olympic gold medals. He came home to a ticker-tape parade down Fifth Avenue in New York City. He was, the papers said, an American hero.

This is the grand American legend that has passed down through the years.

But, in fact, Owens was not treated like an American hero when he returned. As an African-American athlete, he was publicly celebrated but privately scorned. On the very day of the New York ticker-tape parade, Owens was asked by management of the Waldorf-Astoria hotel to take the freight elevator down to his own reception.

While Americans across the country celebrated the way Owens embarrassed Hitler and the Nazis by triumphing over their so-called master race, President Franklin Roosevelt refused to even acknowledge Owens upon his return. Owens received no invitation to the White House. FDR did not send a letter of congratulations. This so infuriated Owens that he joined the Republican Party and spoke out on behalf of Roosevelt's opponent Alf Landon.

"Some people say Hitler snubbed me," Owens told one Baltimore crowd. "But I tell you, Hitler did not snub me. . . . I had the opportunity to meet the King of England, I had the opportunity to wave at Hitler, and I had the opportunity to meet the King of Sweden . . . but remember the President did not send me a message of congratulations because, people said, he was too busy."

Beyond such indignities, what truly haunted Owens was how few financial opportunities there were upon his return. He was, remember, a college athlete without even a scholarship. When it was discovered that he got some money for speaking on behalf of the Republican Party, he lost his amateur status. The IRS came after him, forcing Owens to declare bankruptcy just three years after his legendary performance in Berlin.

The greatest athlete in the world pumped gas to support his family.

"Everyone was going to slap me on the back, shake my hand, have me up to their suite," he said. "But no one was going to offer me a job."

And so, in desperation, he took on a whole series of exhibitions to make money. He would show up in towns across America and have 100-yard races against the fastest locals—he would give the runners enormous head starts. But this idea had only so much power—nobody was surprised that the great Jesse Owens could outrun other people—so he soon began to run against racehorses. He won most of these, too, because the races began with a starter's gun, which generally startled the horses enough to allow Owens to take a substantial lead that he held to the end.

Much has been said about how demeaning it all was, how tragic it was that the great Jesse Owens was forced to race local runners and horses . . . but Owens did not see it quite that way. He understood what it meant to be a black man in America; he would have to do what was necessary to survive. "You can't eat four gold medals," he often said.

In the early 1940s, after being hired by the Ford Motor Company in public relations, Owens began to show up at Negro Leagues baseball games, where he would challenge the hometown team's fastest players in a 100-yard sprint. Sometimes, he would give the runners a head start, sometimes Owens would jump hurdles as a handicap. Either way, he always won, even as he grew older and heavier.

And Jesse Owens refused to race Cool Papa Bell.

We will never know for certain how fast Cool Papa Bell really was. The stories and legends and myths are what have lasted. He once dropped a bunt down the third-base line and the pitcher tagged him out sliding into third . . . he scored from first on a sacrifice bunt . . . he stole 175 bases in a single season . . . he once stole two bases on one pitch . . .

"One time he hit a line drive right past my ear," Satchel Paige said. "I turned around and saw the ball hit his ass sliding into second base."

"If he bunts and it bounces twice, put it in your pocket," Double Duty Radcliffe said.

"If he hit one back to the pitcher," Jimmie Crutchfield said, "everyone yelled 'Hurry up!'"

When Buck O'Neil was asked how fast Cool Papa Bell was, he would immediately respond before the question was even finished: "Faster than that!"

The known statistics of Cool Papa Bell leave us wanting more. The tenacious and dogged baseball historians at the Seamheads website have uncovered 345 Cool Papa stolen bases in almost 1,500 games, which is certainly good but not the stuff of legend. But these numbers—like the numbers that show Josh Gibson with 238 home runs and Satchel Paige with 1,524 strikeouts—are merely a guidepost, a reminder that these players were flesh and blood and not merely the stuff of myth and legend.

But such numbers conceal as much as they reveal. The Negro Leagues were, by necessity, too chaotic to reduce to numbers. The teams played constantly, doubleheaders seemingly every day, games against factory teams and church teams and local all-star teams as well as against other teams in the Negro Leagues; this is what they had to do to survive. Cool Papa Bell played in thousands and thousands of games that can never be recorded.

What we know for sure about Bell is that he was among the best of his day. The first batch of players to come out of the Negro Leagues to the major leagues—Jackie Robinson, Larry Doby, Monte Irvin, Roy Campanella, Ernie Banks, Minnie Miñoso, Willie Mays, Henry Aaron, Don New-combe, Elston Howard, Luke Easter, and the list goes on and on—are some of the greatest players in Major League Baseball history. They offer just a glimpse of how talented the players were in the Negro Leagues.

Had integration come sooner, Bell undoubtedly would have become a major-league star himself. He hit .391 in exhibition games against white teams, and time after time he heard them say to him, "Oh, if only you were white."

You might have heard the story that Cool Papa Bell was once clocked rounding the bases in 12 seconds flat. This seems utterly impossible. Minnesota's Byron Buxton has the modern record—as timed by baseball's incredible Statcast tracking system—for the fastest inside-the-park home run. The time: 13.85 seconds. Twelve seconds seems absurd.

But here's the thing: It's probably true or at least true enough. He probably ran a 12.2 or 12.6 or something like that. We know that it's probably true because Hall of Fame owner Bill Veeck said he personally clocked Cool Papa rounding the bases (on mushy ground with his uniform flapping in the wind) in an astounding 13.1 seconds. So, certainly, in perfect conditions, you could imagine people clocking him at 12 seconds or so.

Here's another true story: In 1945, when the Kansas City Monarchs signed Jackie Robinson, they played him at shortstop even though his arm was somewhat questionable. When the Dodgers were scouting Robinson, they worried about his arm. It was arranged for Bell to hit some grounders to short and run them out to test the arm. Bell repeatedly beat the throw, which helped convince the Dodgers to play Robinson at second base instead.

Cool Papa was 42 years old at the time.

Usually, when people talk about Bell's speed, they refer to his offense. And he was a great bunter who repeatedly beat out singles. He was also a breathtaking baserunner who by all accounts scored from first on singles dozens of times through the years. No matter the numbers, he was a master of the stolen base, so much so that many years after he retired, he taught Lou Brock the art. In fact, it was Cool Papa who was there to honor Brock when he set the single-season stolen base record in 1974. Bell presented the actual base to his onetime apprentice.

"We decided to give him this base," Cool Papa proudly said to the crowd, "because even if we hadn't, he was going to take it anyway."

But it was actually on defense where Bell shined brightest. There simply wasn't a fly ball that seemed beyond his reach. When I play that "You can go back in time and see one player" game, I often choose Cool Papa Bell. I would love to see him chase down fly balls.

We began with this: Jesse Owens refused to race Cool Papa. Bell himself was convinced that this was because Owens was afraid of losing, and I have no doubt that was part of it. "If Cool Papa had known about colleges or if colleges had known about Cool Papa," Satchel Paige once said, "Jesse Owens would have looked like he was walking."

But I wonder if there was something more. Cool Papa Bell was a legend in the African-American community. So was Jesse Owens. I suspect Owens understood this, understood that there was no value in the two of them racing and bursting one of those legends. Better, instead, to leave them guessing for the rest of time.

No. 83 **Phil Niekro**

hil Niekro went to bed that Saturday night in 1985 conflicted and unsure. He really did not know what he would do the next day. He was 46 years old at the time, and he was the No. 2 pitcher for the New York Yankees, who had just been eliminated from the playoff chase. In just about every way, Sunday's game had become meaningless.

His Yankees had just lost to Toronto 5–1, and that mathematically ended New York's chances at a championship. They had entered this final three-game series trailing the Blue Jays by three games in the American League East. A sweep could have forced a one-game playoff, and New York did win the first game. But with Saturday's loss, the chase had ended, the last hope was lost, and the Sunday game, at least in the larger context of pennant races, was meaningless.

Niekro was scheduled to pitch that Sunday game.

And it mattered only because if he won, it would be his 300th victory.

Niekro had been trying for weeks to win his 300th game. He'd had four chances already, each crushing in its own way. On September 13, with more than 53,000 in the stands at Yankee Stadium, he pitched a complete game without allowing an earned run. But the Yankees lost anyway, because Gold Glove first baseman Don Mattingly uncharacteristically booted a ground ball and because catcher Ron Hassey threw a ball away. Those errors led to three runs, and the Yankees lost 3–2.

His next two times were against the Tigers, and his knuckler didn't knuckle in those. Then the Orioles beat him and the Yankees by a run, and his victory total stayed stuck at 299.

Now he was scheduled to try again . . . and he didn't really want to try again. Nothing about the timing for such a monumental achievement felt right. It was a meaningless game on the last day of the season. The game was to be played on the road—in Canada, no less—and he obviously preferred to win No. 300 in the United States.

Most of all, he knew that the Yankees were not going to bring him back. Why win his 300th game for a team that didn't even want him? Niekro expected during the offseason to sign with Atlanta, the city where he'd had his greatest successes, or Cleveland, near where he had grown up (his father was a rabid fan of Cleveland's Bob Feller) and *those* seemed the right places to win his 300th game. It also would help his negotiating position if he skipped his start and had a 300th win to offer to his new team.

So, as he went to bed, he planned to skip this start. It just made sense.

But Phil Niekro couldn't sleep. He tossed and turned all night, and when he finally gave up on sleep, he got out of bed and looked out the window and realized that, yes, he would pitch. Of course, he would pitch. He had to get win No. 300 now, before it was too late.

Phil Niekro Jr., his father, was in an intensive care unit in Wheeling, West Virginia. And he was dying.

"My father was a coal miner in Eastern Ohio," Niekro explained to me many years later. "Three shifts. That thing I remember most was him coming back from the coal mine, and I wouldn't even recognize him. I mean, he was just . . . black. All black. All I could see was his teeth.

"He would come home and the first thing he would do was come up to us on the front porch. Me and (my brother) Joe would be waiting for him. He'd have his lunch bucket with him, and he opened it up, and there was always something for us. There was a Twinkie in there or a banana. He would give me half. He'd give Joe half.

"And then, before anything else, we'd go into the backyard. We'd play catch, just me and my dad. Joe would set up on the porch and watch us. We'd play catch until it got dark. Then, when it was dark, when it was over, we'd go and have dinner. Then he would go to the stove and heat some water, pour it into the tub, and he took a bath. I remember how black that water was after he was finished.

"Then my dad would go lay down on the couch, and he'd fall asleep listening to the Cleveland Indians."

Phil Niekro felt an odd buzz as he warmed up that Sunday afternoon in Toronto. The crowd was . . . different. Niekro could not remember ever pitching in a game quite like this one, and he had pitched in more than 800 big-league games and in more than a thousand professional games if you wanted to go back to the minors. His pro career went all the way back to 1959, when he signed for 500 bucks with the Braves. They were the Milwaukee Braves then. That's how long ago it was.

The Braves sent Niekro to a Class D team in Wellsville, in southeastern New York, near the Pennsylvania border. He was a 20-year-old knuckleball pitcher. And he was terrible. He couldn't control the pitch at all. He gave up 38 runs in 35 innings. walked more than he struck out, and the manager, Harry Minor, called him in and said the team was going to release him.

"In that moment," Niekro said, "I saw myself, like my dad, working in the coal mines." Phil begged for another chance. He said he would do anything to stay, anything at all; he would mow the infield, he would be the bat boy, he would sell concessions. His earnestness impressed Minor. The Braves shipped him down a half level, to McCook in the old Nebraska State League. Niekro pitched well enough in relief to survive for another year.

More than a quarter century after that, fans poured into Exhibition Stadium as Niekro got loose in the bullpen. They were not coming for a baseball game, it seemed to Niekro. They were coming for a party. They had bought their tickets back when they thought this game might decide the season. But now that the Blue Jays had won the division, the fans had come to enjoy the afterglow.

Blue Jays manager Bobby Cox was resting his best players—the usual potent lineup heart of Lloyd Moseby, Willie Upshaw, and George Bell was replaced by Lou Thornton, a rookie named Cecil Fielder, and a former MVP at the end of his career, Jeff Burroughs. Cox sent out a pitcher named John Cerutti to make his first big-league start. It was essentially an exhibition game at Toronto's Exhibition Stadium.

Niekro felt weird about it all. This was not how he had imagined winning his 300th game. And as he looked out at the crowd coming to celebrate their title, and as he considered the halfhearted lineup that Cox and the Blue Jays were using, and as he thought about his father, the first inkling of an idea emerged from the depths of his mind, a crazy idea, one that he dared not even say out loud.

What if Phil Niekro—Knucksie, as everyone called him—won his 300th baseball game without throwing a single knuckleball?

Phil Niekro Jr., the father (Phil the pitcher was actually Phil Niekro III), was a hard-throwing semiprofessional pitcher in his younger days. Everybody in and around Lansing, Ohio—five or so miles from the West Virginia border—knew how hard Phil Niekro Jr. threw in the old Mine Workers League. His two sons, Phil and Joe, would hear legendary tales about their old man and how he played when he was young.

But then Phil Jr. hurt his arm. He wanted to keep on pitching and so he asked a teammate—a former minor-league pitcher named Nick McKay—to teach him how to throw a knuckleball. And Phil Jr. threw it beautifully right away.

"One day in the backyard," Phil Niekro, the son, said, "he threw me one. It probably hit me in the knee or something. And I had to know: What was *that*? Dad told me. He showed me how to hold it. I didn't know anything about knuckleballs, didn't know much about the big leagues or knuckleball pitchers in the big leagues.

"All I knew was that we threw it every day. That's all we'd do. He'd come back from the coal mine, and we'd go in the backyard, and we'd throw knuckleballs to each other. Sometimes my sister Phyllis caught me. Sometimes my friend John Havlicek caught me, though that was one thing John couldn't really do—catch that knuckleball. Phyllis was better at catching it.

"I got pretty good throwing it. I pitched four years of high school with it. I lost one game in high school . . . when Bill Mazeroski hit a home run off me. That was the only game I lost.

"I didn't think much about it. All I did was throw knuckleballs."

John Cerutti was a bit of a mess to start the game. Well, it was his first big-league start, and he was going up against a legend trying to win his

300th game. You could understand. Cerutti gave up a single to Don Mattingly, threw a wild pitch, and walked Don Baylor. He should have gotten out of the inning, but Dámaso García booted a ground ball. Then Cerutti plunked Willie Randolph and gave up a single to Henry Cotto and threw another wild pitch and gave up another walk before finally, mercifully, getting Bob Meacham for the third out.

The Yankees had scored three runs before Niekro even took the mound.

Niekro saw that as a sign to go through with his idea. He threw nothing but fastballs to leadoff hitter García, who flew out to center. Then, spotting his fastball and mixing in a few screwballs, Niekro struck out Rick Leach and Lou Thornton.

He made it through the first without throwing a single knuckleball.

That was probably the first inning Niekro had pitched in the big leagues without using at least one knuckleball. It was certainly the first since 1967, his first full season with Atlanta. Niekro was already 28 years old by then; it had taken him forever to work his way through the minors. And that's because nobody knew what to do with him or his knuckleball. Nobody could hit the pitch. But, also, nobody could catch it. Yes, Niekro was getting outs, but he was also inflicting significant psychic damage on All-Star catcher Joe Torre, who could not catch the knuckler and was beginning to see ghosts and question his own existence. Something had to give.

In mid-June, the Braves gambled—they traded for a sacrificial lamb, a catcher who would be willing to deal with the existential nightmare of being called a "catcher" while not being able to actually catch the ball.

They traded for Bob Uecker.

Looking back, it had to be Ueck. When the trade was made, the Braves made a big deal out of calling Uecker a "knuckleball specialist." He most decidedly was not. He'd had just a little bit of experience catching a couple of knuckleball pitchers, but that experience was mainly running to the back of the screen. As Uecker famously said, the proper way to catch a knuckleball is to wait for it to stop rolling and then pick it up.

But what Uecker had was an unquenchable willingness to look silly. "Your job is to throw the knuckleball," he told Niekro. "You throw it every pitch. It's my job to catch it."

Uecker set a big-league record with 27 passed balls—23 of them with Niekro pitching. But Uecker's sacrifice helped make Niekro's career. For the first time, Knucksie threw his knuckleball without hesitation or ambivalence. He led the league in ERA. He was off.

And he *was* great. People missed it in part because over the next 11 years he played for mostly mediocre and bad teams. Still, he twice led the league in wins, twice led the league in WAR, four times led the league in innings and complete games, etc. He made only three All-Star teams in those 11 years and he only got two first-place Cy Young votes.

It wasn't just the mediocrity of his teams. There was another big reason people did not appreciate Niekro: that knuckleball. It's such an odd pitch, such a mystery to people, that many thought of Niekro as a circus act. They thought of the knuckleball as a parlor trick. They thought of him more as a magician than a pitcher.

Niekro always (quietly) resented the implication that he was anything less than a pitcher. He was not just out there mindlessly throwing knuckleballs and hoping for the best. He studied hitters' tendencies. He threw his best pitches under pressure. Heck, how many pitchers in baseball history do you think won 300 games, struck out 3,000 batters, and then, on the side, also picked up 25 saves? In fact, there are two.

One was Walter Johnson.

The other was Phil Niekro.

Anyway, because of that knuckleball, people didn't see Niekro's greatness. And that's when this germ of an idea came into his head, this idea of pitching a whole game without throwing one knuckler.

"I wanted to show," he said, "not only myself but also everybody else— all those guys who said that the only thing that kept me in the game all those years was my knuckler—that I was *more* than a knuckleball pitcher. I wanted to show them that I deserved to be where I was."

In the second inning, Niekro walked Fielder but got Burroughs to hit into a double play, then prompted Kelly Gruber to pop out to second. Two innings down. No hits. And again, he did not throw a knuckleball.

Niekro had a no-hitter going until two outs in the fourth, when Fielder finally knocked a single on a fastball. But Niekro got out of the inning when he froze Jeff Burroughs with a fastball on the outside corner. That was especially sweet. Burroughs and Niekro had been teammates on the Braves in the late 1970s. They had faced each other so many times. To get Burroughs looking on a fastball . . . well, that meant the world to Niekro.

The Yankees made it 5–0 in the fifth, and Niekro got another 1-2-3 inning without throwing a knuckleball.

"What the hell is going on out here?" Yankees second baseman Willie Randolph said to Niekro as he approached the mound.

"Not gonna throw one," Niekro said.

Randolph looked hard at Niekro and then smiled. "Go for it," he said.

In the sixth, Niekro faced the minimum again when he got García to hit into a double play. The Toronto crowd, still high and buzzing over the Blue Jays reaching their first postseason, began to root harder for Niekro. It's unclear how many of them realized that he was not throwing the knuckleball, but they knew that seeing a pitcher win his 300th game was special.

In the seventh, Burroughs snapped out of Niekro's hypnosis, sat on a fastball, and smacked it for a double. But Niekro got out of the inning unscathed. He breezed through the eighth as well, and then came out to pitch the ninth with a now all-but-insurmountable 8–0 lead. He was going to win his 300th game. And he had still not thrown a knuckleball.

Yankees manager Billy Martin, as a practical joke, sent five pitchers to the bullpen to warm up (there was only really room for three of them). Niekro wasn't amused. But he did love it when he saw who they sent out to catch his warm-up pitches before the inning: his brother Joe.*

The two brothers embraced on the mound.

"If I lose the shutout," Phil told his brother, "I want you to come in and finish this for me."

"Shove that thinking up your . . ." Joe replied.

With that, Joe stepped behind the plate, and Phil threw his first knuckleball of the day and Joe couldn't catch it. The ball bounced high off Joe's leg.

"Just missed," Phil said.

The last inning was a dream. Niekro got Leach to bounce the ball right

---

* Joe Niekro was a superb knuckleball pitcher himself; not quite as good as Phil but he did win 221 games and in 1979 came significantly closer to winning the Cy Young Award than Phil ever did (he finished second to Bruce Sutter by just six points). Together, Phil and Joe won a combined 539 games, the most in baseball history, 10 more than the Perry brothers, Gaylord and Jim. Phil Niekro Jr., their father, unquestionably was the greatest teacher of the knuckleball in baseball history.

back to him. Out No. 1. He threw a fastball on the outside part of the plate and got Thornton to foul out to the catcher. Out No. 2.

Then Cox decided to shake things up a little bit—he sent in Tony Fernández to pinch-hit. Fernández ripped a double off a fastball, and that brought up Niekro's old pal Burroughs.

Niekro threw a fastball, and Burroughs crushed it—but pulled it just foul. Niekro smiled, at least in his mind. He still had not thrown a knuckleball, and Yankees catcher Butch Wynegar called for another fastball as per instruction.

But this time, Niekro shook him off.

Niekro threw the knuckleball, his pitch, and Burroughs swung wildly and missed. Wynegar called for another fastball. Niekro shook him off again and threw the knuckleball one last time. The last knuckleball danced as much as any Niekro had ever thrown. Burroughs swung and missed, the final out.

"In the end, I wanted the knuckler," Niekro would say, "not because I didn't think I could win without it, but because I just couldn't see myself pitching the most important game of my career without throwing one."

Niekro became the oldest man to pitch a shutout that day, passing Satchel Paige. In the years since, Jamie Moyer has passed Niekro. The list of oldest pitchers to throw a shutout is a fun one:

1. Jamie Moyer, 2010 vs. Braves, 47 years, 170 days

2. Phil Niekro, 1985 vs. Blue Jays, 46 years, 188 days

3. Charlie Hough, 1994 vs. Cardinals, 46 years, 160 days

4. Satchel Paige, 1952 vs. White Sox, 46 years, 75 days

5. Satchel Paige, 1952 vs. Tigers, 46 years, 30 days

Of course, as Niekro himself says, Paige might have been 56 when he threw those shutouts. He was surely the oldest of the bunch.

"Either way," Niekro says, "it's pretty good company."

After Niekro struck out Burroughs, everyone rushed to the mound. Joe got there first. He leaned close to his brother's ear and said, "Dad is out of intensive care. He's going to make it."

Here was how he woke up: Yankees owner George Steinbrenner had set up a radio in the intensive care unit so that Phil Niekro Jr. could hear the play-by-play of his son's game. In the seventh inning, Phil Jr. rather suddenly sat up a little bit and said, "He's pitching a good game, isn't he?"

I mean, how perfect is that?

Phil Niekro Jr. lived for three more years. He was too sick to be there when Phil and Joe became the winningest brother duo in baseball history, but he sent word that he was happy and proud to have taught his sons how to throw a knuckleball. A father, he said, just wants to give his children the tools to make it in the world.

Phil Niekro died a few months after I wrote this, and as I think about that kind man I think of the story he loved most, the story of the scout who came to the family home in Lansing and offered Phil Niekro III the chance to play baseball for a $500 signing bonus.

"I'm sorry," Phil's father said. "I work in the coal mines. We just don't have that kind of money."

No. 82 **Kid Nichols**

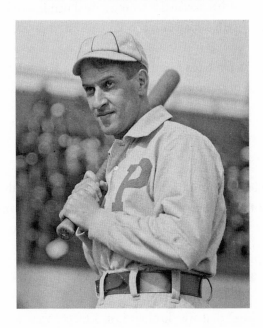

It's always fun to play the "guess the pitcher" game. So here we go: Here are the first ten seasons of two pitchers, both right-handed, born about 18 months apart. They started their careers in the same year.

One of the pitchers is infinitely more famous than the other.

Pitcher A: 267–151, 3.05 ERA, 1,125 Ks, 768 walks, 28 shutouts, 1.242 WHIP, 139 ERA+.

Pitcher B: 297–151, 2.97 ERA, 1,484 Ks, 1,001 walks, 36 shutouts, 1.234 WHIP, 146 ERA+.

Both were obviously extraordinary pitchers. But which one was better? You'd have to say it was Player B, right? I mean, more wins, lower ERA, lower ERA+, more shutouts, more strikeouts.

So, yeah, Pitcher A is Cy Young.

And Pitcher B? He was a player who is almost entirely unknown even though Cy Young himself conceded that he was the superior pitcher in their early years.

Pitcher B is a man named Kid Nichols.

Now, before we go on, nobody is saying that Kid Nichols was as good as Cy Young. This only covers their first 10 years. Cy Young was just as good for *another* 10 years and ended up with 511 wins while Nichols faded pretty quickly and finished with "only" 362 victories. I'm not saying that Nichols should have the annual pitching award named for him.

But maybe more baseball fans should know his name.

Since there's a decent chance you know nothing at all about Nichols, I'll rattle off a dozen or so tidbits that I find pretty interesting.

1. Charles Nichols was born in Wisconsin, the son of a butcher. His family moved to Kansas City when he was young and he lived there more or less the rest of his life.

2. He was called "Kid" in his first year of organized baseball because he was so slight and young-looking that he was routinely mistaken for the bat boy.

3. He began pitching for Boston in the National League in 1890, which was, as mentioned, the same year that Cy Young debuted with the Cleveland Spiders. When the 1890s began, pitchers threw from inside a "pitchers box" that was located just 50 feet away from home plate. Every year, it seemed, the men who ran baseball would change the rules of what a pitcher could and could not do.

   Nichols pitched through all of it. He won 35 games in 1892 when the pitcher was 50 feet from home plate. He won 34 games in 1893 after it had been moved back to 60 feet, 6 inches. He was 27 in 1895, the year a caught foul tip was considered a strike. He led the National League in wins every year from 1896 to 1898.

   In all, he won 30 or more games seven times, which is the major-league record and will always be the record unless the rules of the game change.

4. Nichols was not known as one of the harder throwers of his day. He was not often mentioned in the same company as Hall of Fame flame-throwers Amos Rusie or Cy Young or a forgotten pitcher named Jouett Meekin. Many believe the pitcher was moved back because of Meekin, who threw very hard *and* had an unshakable philosophy that he should begin each at-bat by throwing two fastballs close to the batter's head.

5. While Nichols did not throw especially hard, he had an unusual fastball; hitters swore that it jumped just as it got to the plate. This jump-

ball was the only pitch he threw and yet hitters couldn't figure it out. I like to think of Nichols's hopping fastball as something a little bit mystical, like Mariano Rivera's cutter.

6. In the later part of his career, Nichols befriended a young Kansas City fan named Charles Stengel, who would become known as Casey Stengel and become the most successful manager in baseball history. Ol' Casey would always say that Nichols was one of the great influences of his life.

7. Nichols, in addition to his baseball prowess, was a fantastic bowler. He won a bowling championship in Kansas City when he was 63 years old.

8. Kid Nichols wasn't the only successful bowler in the family. His wife, Jennie, for a time, held the women's record for duckpin bowling.

9. Nichols and Hall of Famer Joe Tinker opened a large theater in Kansas City together called the Tinker-Nichols Theater and they would bring vaudeville shows to town. I particularly like one mention they had in the *Moving Picture World*, which wrote that his "exploits on the diamond are well known to the fans of the older generation." Older generation. This was in 1913. Already, Nichols was being forgotten.

10. Nichols received a U.S. patent for an electronic scoreboard he invented. The scoreboard would show a baseball game in progress in almost real time, using lights to represent baserunners. He would have the display going during the World Series in Kansas City, and it was said to draw as many as four or five thousand fans.

11. Cy Young, in addition to being a rival, was a great admirer of his. "Kid Nichols forgot more baseball than 90 percent of us will ever know," he said.

12. Nichols received almost no Hall of Fame consideration in the early years. Bill James explained it this way: Nichols's greatness ended almost *precisely* when baseball exploded into the American imagination. His last 30-win season was just before the turn of the century. He was essentially done with his career before the American League existed, so he never pitched in a World Series game (although he did pitch brilliantly in the 1892 championship series when his Boston Beaneaters

breezed by Young's Cleveland Spiders). By the time that baseball was widely acknowledged as the national pastime, Nichols was home and retired.

As such, Nichols was entirely overlooked when the Hall of Fame was conceived in 1936. Nichols never even got 3 percent of the Baseball Writers' vote—this even though the famed sportswriter Grantland Rice was a huge supporter and would, now and again, make his pitch for Nichols in print or on the radio.

13. Ty Cobb, of all people, brought Nichols back into the public conversation. Cobb did not face Nichols's best—their careers barely overlapped—but in the 1940s, Cobb would rant to anyone who would listen about Nichols's greatness.

"You're a bit too young to remember," Cobb told one reporter in 1948, "but I knew a pitcher who was a real pitcher. His name was Kid Nichols. He was with the Boston Nationals early in the century."

And then, as proof, he would pull out Nichols's statistics that he carried around with him. Yeah, he walked around with Nichols's stats.

"How can they possibly keep Kid Nichols out of the Hall of Fame?" he asked in a 1948 column.*

Cobb still wielded a lot of influence in those days. The year after he wrote his column, Nichols was finally elected to the Hall of Fame by the Old-Timers Committee.

---

* Cobb also had a funny little gripe that's worth repeating here about how pitchers were becoming too brittle. "Let me tell you, those were the days," he wrote. "Pitchers didn't have sore arms, chipped bones, and all that stuff." People always love to believe that their own complaint is somehow new, but people have been grumbling about pitchers' fragility almost since the dawn of baseball.

No. 81 **Ferguson Jenkins**

Of the seventeen pitchers in baseball history who have struck out 3,000 batters in their careers, only four have also walked fewer than 1,000. Three of them—Curt Schilling, Greg Maddux, and Pedro Martínez—are of recent vintage. They pitched in a more modern game when hitters struck out unapologetically as they looked to hit more home runs.

The fourth pitcher is Fergie Jenkins.

This is just one way to show that Jenkins was a pitcher ahead of his time. He has been largely forgotten by baseball fans, in part because he was barely remembered to begin with. Jenkins had the misfortune to come of age in baseball's golden age for starting pitchers. Because of this, he was more easily identified by the things others did that he could not.

Yes, he threw hard but not nearly as hard as Nolan Ryan.

Sure, he was graceful on the mound but he was not seen as the picture of pitching splendor the way Tom Seaver or Jim Palmer was.

He could not throw Bert Blyleven's tantalizing curveball, did not intimidate hitters with a killer slider like Bob Gibson or Steve Carlton, and he certainly did not pitch in the World Series year after year after year like Catfish Hunter. In fact, his teams never won at all. Jenkins did not spit on the ball like Gaylord Perry, cut it like Don Sutton, or flutter it like Phil Niekro. He did not gyrate on the mound like Luis Tiant or lift his leg high like Juan Marichal.

What Jenkins did instead was so simple, it barely seemed like a plan: He threw the ball down and away. That was it. That was the whole thing. He pitched and lived with a singular focus that was in and of itself a superpower. If he struck out a hitter, his next pitch was down and away. Allowed a home run? Down and away. Men on base? Down and away. No-hitter going? Down and away. He never wavered and never backed down and never saw anything but that one portion of the plate. Ferguson Jenkins hit more corners than sunlight.

From 1967 to 1975—nine seasons for Chicago and Texas—he averaged 300 innings, 20 wins, and 22 complete games per year. He did this exclusively for either bad teams and teams good enough only to break hearts. Jenkins never pitched in the postseason. He is surely the greatest pitcher to entirely miss the fervor of October baseball.

Some of the players in this book are betrayed by their statistics, by which I mean that you can miss their greatness by looking specifically at their numbers. But Jenkins's statistical record tells his story faithfully. Five times he led the league in fewest walks. Five times he led the league in strikeout-to-walk ratio. Seven times he led the league in home runs allowed. He wasn't out there to fool batters. He rarely threw a curveball. He never had a changeup (though once or twice a game, just to add a little spice, he might throw a forkball).

Jenkins threw fastballs—four-seamers, two-seamers—and with each pitch, he sent a message: "This is the best I got. If you can beat me, beat me. But I like my chances."

Jenkins is the only Canadian-born pitcher in the Hall of Fame. He grew up in Chatham, Ontario, where, as he often says, he learned how to pitch by throwing rocks through the open doorways of passing railway cars. This is a common theme, one you will see again and again in the Baseball 100: So many pitchers began by throwing rocks.

The Phillies signed Jenkins when he was a teenager and traded him to the Cubs less than four years later. It was a bizarre deal. The Phillies traded 23-year-old Jenkins (and 24-year-old Adolfo Phillips) for soon-to-be-38-year-old Bob Buhl and 35-year-old Larry Jackson.

"Will Phils Youth for Age Deal Mean Champagne or Alka Seltzer?" asked the *Philadelphia Daily News*.

Answer: It meant heartburn.

"The two guys we gave up *might* help a ballclub," Phillies manager Gene Mauch told reporters. "The two guys we got *will!*"

That quote didn't hold up, either.

In the end, I'm not sure it *really* was an age-for-youth deal. Maybe. But there is good reason to believe it had more to do with race, with Jenkins and Phillips both being black. The Phillies had a disgraceful history with race; they were the last National League team to integrate, and they treated their first African-American star, Dick Allen, disgracefully. Of course, we can never know for sure, but the Jenkins trade was certainly strange: He was young and a brilliant prospect.

Whatever the reason, this turned out to be one of the worst trades in Phillies history and one of the best in Cubs history. Jenkins became an instant star for the Cubs. He finished second in the Cy Young voting in his first full year in Chicago, and he put up six Cy Young–quality seasons over the next seven years after that.

Jenkins's endurance and consistency was mind-boggling even in his time but now looks entirely made up. In a time when a pitcher can lead the league with three complete games, how do you make sense of a pitcher who, from 1967 to 1972, completed 20, 20, 23, 24, 30, and 23 games. And it wasn't like he was out there conserving his energy; he threw very hard. How did he stay healthy? How did he just keep going and going? How did his arm not fall off?

Jenkins will tell you: He didn't really have a choice. That was the real secret. He pitched in a time when all the great pitchers—Jenkins, Seaver, Carlton, Ryan, Perry, Sutton—pitched complete game after complete game. I've spoken with them about it at one point or another (with the notable exception of Carlton) and asked each to explain how they did it. Their answers are interesting but inevitably disappointing. They talk about how they play long-toss catch every day, as if that were the magic exercise. They might talk about how they did a lot of running; building up the legs was the key. They might talk about pacing themselves during games, not throwing all-out and going for the strikeouts except when absolutely necessary (this was obviously not true of

Ryan, who *always* went for the strikeout). They might talk about pitching through pain.

While all of these tricks no doubt helped, I'm not sure what you can do with any of that specifically. Pitchers today would not be able to suddenly throw 300 innings in a year if they long-tossed daily, jogged incessantly, or simply ignored the twinges in their elbows and shoulders.

The real reason so many great pitchers threw a whole bunch of innings and stayed healthy in that time was that that's what was expected of them. If they couldn't do it, they were discarded. It was survival of the fittest. Teams were willing to burn out as many pitchers as necessary to find one who could stay in there until the very end.

So, yes, while we can point to an astonishing number of pitchers like Jenkins who just kept going and going, there was a long, long list of pitchers who burned out—a short list might include Don Gullett, Dennis Leonard, Randy Jones, Ron Bryant, Steve Busby, Sam McDowell, Gary Nolan, Jon Matlack, Ken Holtzman, Tom Phoebus, John Montefusco, Bill Stoneman, Andy Messersmith, Gary Gentry, Bill Parsons, Steve Kline, and Mark Fidrych; obviously, you can go on and on. Some were stars. Some didn't last long enough even for that. They were all done by their early 30s.

That was baseball's simple calculus of the time. The ones who lost velocity or felt sharp, stabbing pain whenever they threw the fastball found a new way to get out hitters or they became scouts or insurance salesmen or something.

In other words, Jenkins threw 300 innings per year because that's what was demanded of him . . . and what he demanded of himself. Yes, there were tricks and methods. But, most of all, it was the times. Nobody should think Jenkins would throw 300 innings today.

This is the challenge of comparing players across generations: Jenkins would be a very different pitcher now. What would he look like? That's harder to say, but one thing that I'm confident in saying is that with his impeccable control and command, his great stuff, his pitching mind, his terrific athleticism (Jenkins played basketball for the Harlem Globetrotters for a couple of years), his hitting prowess (in his Cy Young year of 1971, Jenkins had 14 extra-base hits, including six homers, in his 39 games), he would be a star in any time.

After Jenkins's career ended, he endured numerous tragedies—he buried a young mother, a young wife, a young fiancée, and a young daughter.

Heartbreak followed him. "In my life," he said, "I've been a part of many funerals." He admits that living has often been a struggle.

On the mound, he always knew who he was. This never changed. In 2003, at the age of 60, he threw out the first pitch for a new Canadian baseball league. He had prepared for the moment. He hit the outside corner, low and away, just like always.

No. 80 **Carlton Fisk**

C ecil Fisk was one of those hardscrabble Depression-era men who inspire legends. Cecil was an archetype you'll recognize immediately—a New Hampshire machinist and farmer who believed in the three pillars of hard work, plain values, and American possibilities. And he was tough. They say he was chopping firewood the day before he died at age 98.

There are two Cecil Fisk stories that come to mind, both father-and-son stories. The first revolves around the final high school basketball game his son Carlton played in. Cecil called his son "Carl." Everybody else called him "Pudge," because he was a pudgy baby.

Cecil Fisk was not the sort to call anyone "Pudge."

Carl played basketball for Charlestown High, a little school in their little community. The school is gone now, a casualty of consolidation. But in those days, during those snowy New Hampshire winters, everybody in Charlestown crowded into the tiny gym where the high school team played. Everybody knew Carl Fisk.

In Carl's last game, the team faced defending state champion Hopkinton in the state semifinals. Carl was pretty badly overmatched. He was a solid 6-foot-2, making him the tallest player on the Charlestown team.

Meanwhile, Hopkinton had two considerably taller players down low, including 6-foot-9 Craig Corson, who would play as a backup for North Carolina in the 1972 Final Four.

Overmatched or not, Cecil Fisk did not raise his son to make excuses. Carl attacked the glass with frightening intensity. Carl was a leaper in those days—he had a 38-inch vertical—and he thrived on contact and force. He came at the Hopkinton big men again and again. Hopkinton built a lead. Carl brought his team back. Hopkinton built a bigger lead, a seemingly insurmountable lead. Carl brought his team back again. Carl had his team on the brink of victory when a whistle blew—a fifth and final foul on Carl Fisk. The fans stood and cheered as he came out of the game and watched from the bench in tears as his team lost by two.

For the game, Carl Fisk scored 40 points and grabbed 36 rebounds. Nobody in Charlestown had ever seen a performance quite like that.

And as Carl came off the court, he saw his father and hero, Cecil, the toughest and best man he would ever know. For the rest of his life, Carl Fisk remembered word for word what his father said to him at that moment.

"How," Cecil said, "could you miss four free throws?"

The second father-and-son story is shorter and pithier. One year, after Carlton Fisk became a big star for the Boston Red Sox, his father came to Boston to see him play. Cecil was walking through the clubhouse when a coach stopped him.

"So, Mr. Fisk," the coach said, "you're Carlton's dad, huh?"

Cecil looked the coach dead in the eye.

"No," he said. "Carlton is my son."

In Carlton Fisk's first minor-league season, the legend goes, he had a crisis of confidence so crushing that he thought about quitting the game. This happened, poetically enough, in Waterloo (Iowa). Fisk was 20 years old.

The crisis had nothing to do with his play—from his first day in professional baseball, it was clear that Fisk had greatness in him and was destined to play in the major leagues, destined to be a big-league star, perhaps even destined for Cooperstown. He hit .338 that first full professional season, slugged .600, smashed 12 homers in 62 games, and showed brilliant defensive potential as a catcher.

Red Sox scout Mace Brown told the *Boston Globe* after that season, "Carlton Fisk is one of the best young catchers I've ever seen."

No, the problem was not his play. The problem also wasn't social; he was not homesick, wasn't bothered by the bus rides or chaotic minor-league life, wasn't put off by the baseball grind. Fisk loved the grind. Fisk lived for the grind.

So what was it?

Waterloo went 53-60 in the Midwest League. And Fisk just could not handle that much losing.

You just can't overstate how much Fisk hated losing. It didn't matter to him where the losing happened—all losing was the same. Other players might not have cared about a team's record in the Midwest League, just as other players didn't care when the New Hampshire freshman basketball team lost to the University of Rhode Island. Minor-league games? Freshman basketball? What difference did it make?

For Carlton Fisk, though, each loss was pure and unbridled agony.

"After the URI loss," New Hampshire coach Bill Haubrich said in *Pudge: The Biography of Carlton Fisk,* "all the kids were showering, getting ready to watch the varsity game. Not Fisk. He stayed in the locker room, in uniform, his head in his hands. Finally, I said, 'OK, Pudge, time to get on with your life.'"

He could not get on with his life. Not after a loss. His Boston teammate Dennis Eckersley once said, "I thought it was life and death out there, I really did." Fisk thought it was even bigger than that. Every loss was the end.

Fisk played that way his entire career. He became famous for his stubborn and unrelenting determination. He suffered a devastating knee injury in 1974 on a home-plate collision with Cleveland's Leron Lee. At least one doctor doubted that he would catch again. He came back in 1975 and played better than ever. At the end of that '75 season, he hit perhaps the most famous home run in baseball history, his World Series Game 6 extra-inning blast against the Cincinnati Reds. After he hit the ball, he danced up the first base line and tried to wave the ball fair. Somehow, the ball did stay fair. "Everybody should have that moment in the universe—in whatever aspect of life they're in—that is their moment," he said.

Relentlessness was his defining trait. Fisk was, as Boston's columnist Bob Ryan once wrote, the first catcher in baseball history who would catch nine grueling innings and head straight to the weight room.

All this dedication led to him playing more games, scoring more runs and generating more total bases than any catcher before him. But he wasn't chasing numbers. The truth is that he felt compelled to do it. He had to work harder than anybody else. He had to be stronger than anybody else. He had to play longer than anybody else. He had to make all his free throws. There was no other option.

Carlton Fisk, to the end, was his father's son.

Ask Fisk to name his baseball hero, and he surprises you: It's Bill Russell. No, it's not the old Dodgers shortstop Bill Russell (admittedly, that would be even more surprising) but instead *the* Bill Russell, basketball Hall of Famer, the greatest team player in any sport, the force behind the Celtics dynasty, the Lord of the Rings.

It isn't the least bit surprising that Russell is Fisk's hero; the men share the same athletic DNA. No, what's surprising is that Russell is Fisk's *baseball* hero. Fisk actually built his own game around Russell's example.

"When he went to block a shot," Fisk says, "it wasn't just to slap it out of bounds. It was to block it and put it back in play. . . . He played angles and he played trajectories. I wanted to translate that into my job as a catcher."

Fisk loves talking about being a catcher, loves talking about that feeling of being behind the plate and considering the calculus of the moment. What does my pitcher have? How tired is he? How good is his curveball? What are this hitter's strengths? What is the hitter expecting? Who's up next? As Fisk worked through the countless variables—"I called all the pitches, there was no looking in the dugout," he says with some measure of disgust—he tried to think about it the way Russell thought about being on the court.

"He knew angles," Fisk says, "and I knew weaknesses. He knew situations, and I knew situations. . . . As Bill Russell would say, 'The reason he missed that shot is because he knew Bill was there.' That's the impact I wanted to have, the control I wanted to have. The reason this guy wasn't ready for this pitch is because he knew I was there."

Fisk was an excellent defensive catcher. He did not always get credit for that. (He won a Gold Glove in his rookie year and did not win another for the rest of his lengthy career.) Fisk played in a time when there were many brilliant defensive catchers. He played in the time of Johnny Bench, widely viewed in his day as the greatest defensive catcher ever. He played in the time of Gary Carter, who was an astonishing catcher. In his own league, he played in the time of Jim Sundberg, Bob Boone, Rick Dempsey, extraordinary fielders.

But Fisk's defensive talents were both obvious and mysterious. He had a good arm, particularly when he was young, and he was a terrific athlete. He was relentless at blocking pitches in the dirt. But more than anything, Fisk controlled games with his mind, his force of will, his relationship with pitchers. In all, he caught two Cy Young seasons, a couple of Hall of Famers, the guy who set the saves record, and he loved the role he played in their success. That was what Bill Russell did. He made everyone around him better.

Fisk was elected to the Hall of Fame in 2000, and his 37-minute speech is mentioned in Cooperstown every year because, whew, 37 minutes is a long time—it's thirty-some minutes longer than the Gettysburg Address. Fisk admitted afterward that he wasn't quite prepared for the emotion of the moment, and he had to stop and start a few times. But he also did not apologize for the length of his speech. He had a lot of people to thank. He was going to thank them no matter how long it took.*

The moment from the speech that endures came at the end, when Fisk began to talk about his father. He had made it through the part with his mother, Leona; he called her the "warmth," and said that she made the best cinnamon rolls in Sullivan County, New Hampshire. But that was the easy part. Cecil was harder.

"And the guy who contributed most to me being stubborn and me being determined," Fisk began. "My dad, Cecil."

He looked at his father in the front row.

"He always said," Fisk continued, "'Keep your eye on the ball,' and, 'Cripes, if you can't run around there for an hour or two, you shouldn't even be out there.' Well, Dad, I was out there for 30 years."

And then Fisk began to shake a little bit. Five seconds passed, 10 seconds, 12 . . .

---

* Fisk was particular that way. He also once made the Boston management redo his Hall of Fame plaque because it called him a "Vermont native." He was indeed a Vermont native, born in Bellows Falls, but that was only because Vermont had the closest hospital. Fisk saw himself entirely as a New Hampshire boy, and the new plaque made that fact clear.

"You know," he said, "sometimes good didn't seem to be good enough."

Fisk began to shake again. He nervously folded and unfolded the handkerchief that was in front of him. This time, 20 seconds of silence passed. The crowd cheered to bolster him, but the tears came just the same. Fathers and sons . . . it's a complicated business, a swirl of love and longing and friction and admiration and regret.

"I always wanted you to be proud of me, Dad," Carlton said, as he looked directly at Cecil. "And sometimes just because you could have done better doesn't mean you've done badly."

The camera turned to Cecil. He laughed loudly. He understood where this was going. Cecil had always been so hard on his son. There were no apologies; he had raised a Hall of Famer. But maybe he could have been . . . well . . . what's there to say? You can't go back.

"You know," Carlton said, his voice gaining strength, "through the years you always made sure people knew I was your son. And I'm proud of that."

Now his voice was a train pushing forward.

"But this weekend," he said, "guess what?"

And Fisk paused for just a moment, just long enough to set himself for the most important line of all.

"You're Carlton's dad this weekend," he said, and cheers erupted, and Cecil Fisk smiled deeply and nodded. He was his son's father to the end.

No. 79 **Derek Jeter**

Derek Jeter is not remembered for getting 3,000 hits. None in that club are remembered for the number itself, with the possible exception of Roberto Clemente, who reached exactly 3,000 hits before dying while trying to bring aid to Nicaragua after a massive earthquake. The number 3,000 will therefore be connected to Clemente. But he will, of course, be remembered for so much more than 3,000.

That is true of all of the 32 men who batted safely three thousand times in a career. They are all remembered for something more, something visceral, something that inflames the memory. Ripken's daily persistence. Rickey beating the tag. Mays's hat flying off. Yaz's stance. Musial breaking out of the box. Aaron's unassuming home run trot. Ichiro's chop. Cobb's sharpened spikes. Beltré's annoyance at being tapped on the head. Rose in headfirst flight . . .

Jeter, too, is remembered for more than 3,000. He is remembered for the moments. So many moments. He is, I believe, the most *seen* player in baseball history. What do I mean? Baseball used to be shrouded in mystery. How many people across America actually saw Tris Speaker play? Stan Musial? Frank Robinson? Rod Carew? Even George Brett or Dave Winfield or Lou Brock would appear rarely on television; they were mostly names in box scores (often shortened names like Mus'l and R'bnsn because the columns were too narrow for the full name). They were grainy black-and-white photographs in the local paper. They were static-speckled images on the *Baseball Game of the Week*.

Now, though, we can watch any game, see any highlight at any time and as often as we like. We can summon any play in stunning high definition . . . and high-def can look more vivid than reality. Derek Jeter came of age in a game that left nothing to the imagination. He represented that game. He was everywhere, all the time, on television, on magazine covers, hosting *Saturday Night Live*, batting in the playoffs every year, all of his superpowers and all of his rich flaws magnified and intensified and exaggerated beyond all reason.

Jeter played lead guitar in the most indomitable baseball band of this era, the 1990s and 2000s New York Yankees. He came to the plate 734 times in the postseason, more than anyone else; that is a full season of Octobers. His flip to beat Jeremy Giambi, his stuntman leap into the stands, his November home run, his jump throw from the hole, his flares to right field, everybody knows those; they are among the indelible baseball images of our time, making them among the most indelible images of any time.

But it's more than just that. We saw exactly how he looked in the on-deck circle, how he ran out to the field, how he sat on the bench. We know the models he dated. We know his quotes by heart (though most of them are hardly worth remembering—"We win as a team," "We lose as a team," "Sometimes you have to tip your cap"; Jeter spoke often but purposely revealed nothing). We can close our eyes and see Jeter doing those things he always did.

No, Derek Jeter will not be remembered for 3,000 hits. There is too much else.

And yet, it seems to me that "3,000 hits" defines Jeter. It is his life's work.

What does 3,000 hits mean, anyway? The number is only a number, not substantially different from 2,994 or 3,003. And that word, "hits," is vague. What are hits? There are singles . . . doubles . . . triples . . . home runs—and they are not all that much alike. Eddie Collins had 32 more hits than Willie Mays, but nobody would confuse one for the other. Mays totaled about 1,800 more bases even with fewer hits.

Hits are as vague a noun as, say, "cars." You have two men who own a hundred cars. One could be Jay Leno. The other could be a junkyard dealer.

Still, to reach 3,000 hits, yes, it's substantial. It matters. Three thousand hits means 200 hits a year for 15 years. It means 175 hits each season from ages 23 to 40. It means 150 hits a year for two decades.

Three thousand hits is a relentless uphill march through cold spring afternoons, stifling summer nights, endless rain delays, and twelve-game road trips. Three thousand hits is a daily battle against the hard-throwing rookie who isn't entirely sure where the ball's going, the funky reliever who hides the ball as long as he can as if reluctant to let go, the crusty veteran who has lost his stuff but gets by with a well-earned knowledge, the dominant pitcher at the height of his powers who throws lightning bolts and owns prominent real estate on both sides of the plate.

Three thousand hits means a daily fight with the odds, a mostly losing battle against darting sliders and diving fielders and math and umpires ready to punch you out on a curveball that dances an inch or two off the plate.

Three thousand hits is a life. It requires hitting when you're young and green, hitting when you're at your best and feel invincible, hitting after you can't catch up to the fastball.

To get to 3,000 hits, a batter must triumph over interminable slumps, conquer the injured list, and endure the disappointment of a few hundred perfectly struck line drives that are caught. A batter must triumph over pitches that dissolve into shadows, managers who want to know why you went hitless the last couple of days, trainers who suggest a little more rest, fly balls that die in the summer humidity, and official scorers who rule that you only reached first base because the infielder botched the play.

This goes on and on, every day, every week, every month, every summer. You can't ever win a baseball career. There is always another game, another season, another changeup that will fool you into swinging early. You can't ever claim victory because tomorrow comes and tomorrow and tomorrow and tomorrow afterward.

But for the few who reach 3,000 hits, that is something like victory. You can't luck into 3,000 hits. You can't fake it. You might fake a hot streak, a glorious season, even two or three good years. But 3,000 hits? No. The magician David Blaine once said that the hardest part of the magic bullet illusion is catching the bullet. The hardest part of getting to 3,000 hits is getting 3,000 hits. All 32 men who reached 3,000 hits are connected in this way. They all kept coming back long after their teammates stopped, long after it made much sense to keep going on.

It is a club, a real club, more than the 500-homer club or the 300-win club is. The 27 batters who smashed 500 homers aren't much of a club—they are just a bunch of different people who happened to show up at the same party. What, after all, do Reggie and Killebrew have in common? How hard would Mr. Cub have to squint into a mirror to see Manny Ramírez as his reflection? Murray and McGwire were first basemen—and that's where the comparisons start and end.

The 300-win club is no club, either. Pitching has changed. Pitchers have changed. The careers of Nolan Ryan, Warren Spahn, Walter Johnson, Randy Johnson, and Phil Niekro would not recognize each other in a bar.

But there is only one way to get to 3,000 hits—and that's to get a little bit closer every day. Pete Rose used to say that he loved getting four hits in a game because it meant he had a chance to get five. Mays and Musial attacked the game with the same sort of joy; Aaron and Yaz and Kaline with the same professional purpose. Boggs and Gwynn and Carew were tireless craftsmen. George Brett would say every game he ever played was filled with fear—fear of failure, fear of embarrassment, fear of his father's disappointment. Clemente played like that. Ripken did, too. The 3,000-hit club players are not all alike, no, but they share a singular quality. They took every at-bat seriously. There's no other way to get to 3,000 hits.

They were, for lack of a better word, always "present."

And I would argue that no player in baseball history was ever more present than Derek Jeter.

Jeter is wildly overrated. Jeter is also wildly underrated. Surely, no player in the history of the game has ever been so effusively praised for great defense with so little evidence. On the other hand, no five-time Gold Glove winner has ever been so savaged for being a defensive catastrophe.

Detractors say that if Jeter had not been a member of the overhyped Yankees, he would have been a nobody. "Imagine," they say, "what people would say about Jeter if he played his career for the Minnesota Twins."

And if that's a fair point, then it's just as fair to say that few players were treated so shabbily by the MVP voters. He could have won the award in

1998, 1999, 2006, and maybe even 2009. He won none of them. If he was so overhyped, how could he not win the award once?

The Jeter legend was one that willed his team to victory with invisible and intangible powers of grit, will, and command. This led his critics to grumble about how his best traits had to be taken on faith.

But Jeter's career is not intangible at all. He created more runs than any shortstop ever, including Honus Wagner. He scored more runs, knocked more hits, and reached base more times than any shortstop ever.

There's a reason for these clashes of opinion: Jeter was inescapable. He worked very hard to stay neutral. He spoke comforting and empty words. He carefully cultivated his image. He repelled controversy and curbed division on his teams. And yet, he inspired powerfully strong opinions, both for him and against him. When Jeter came to the plate in any ballpark in America, there were many different sorts of sounds. But there was never silence.

This gets back, I think, to the original point of being seen: Jeter was doggedly present for 20 years. I like that word: present. It can mean "the state or fact of existing." This is why kids say "present" when their name is called for attendance (or at least they did in old *Little House on the Prairie* episodes). Jeter was this kind of present for sure . . . he played in 145 or more games in 16 different seasons—that's one more season than Cal Ripken. Ten times in his career he came to the plate 700 or more times—only Rose had more 700 PA seasons. The most underappreciated contribution in sports is availability. Jeter was always available.

There's another definition of presence: "the impressive manner or appearance of a person."

And this was Jeter, too. He never changed. He, to the very end, was focused, determined, ready. If you watched him play in April 1998 or June 2009 or July 2012 or August 2000, you saw the same guy playing with the same energy.

Of the 2,747 regular-season games Jeter played, he got at least one hit in 2,114 of them. He has had multiple hits in more than 1,000 of them. He was always there, always at the top of the lineup, always recognizable at shortstop, always calmly saying the clichés that filled newspaper stories but didn't put him on the back page of the *New York Post*. Was Derek Jeter the best player of his era? No. Was he the most persistent, the most enduring, the easiest to like, the easiest to dislike, the easiest to hype, the easiest to be cynical about?

I don't even know who is second on such a list.

That's why I think Jeter, more than anyone else, is the personification of 3,000 hits. How do you get to Carnegie Hall? Practice, practice, practice. How do you get to 3,000 hits? Line drive after bloop after scorcher down the line. Eight times Derek Jeter got 200 hits in a season. No other shortstop has done that more than four. Twelve times he hit .300 or better . . . that's more often than Clemente or Brett.

He wasn't *just* getting hits. Jeter hit double-digit homers 16 times, the most ever for a shortstop. Jeter stole double-digit bases 17 times, most ever for a shortstop. Jeter scored 100 runs 13 times, most ever for a shortstop.

But the hits tell the story best: Jeter was unrelenting and undeniable. We can't remember all the hits. But we can remember that there have been more than 3,000 of them.

Jeter got his 3,000th hit on July 9, 2011, a warm and sunny day at Yankee Stadium. He came into the game two hits shy of the number. He got hit No. 2,999 in the first inning, a weak thing, a ground ball off David Price that somehow dribbled through the infield. When you're counting hits as baseball players do, you don't throw any of them back.

Jeter's chase for 3,000 had been substantially different from anyone else's because of the Yankee thing. When Adrián Beltré, for instance, got his 3,000th hit, it was a one-day thing. But not for Jeter: His countdown began way back in 2009 when he skipped a single past first base for hit No. 2,722. That moved him past Lou Gehrig and made him the Yankees' all-time hit leader.

The Yankees are the most storied team in American sports. But until Jeter came along, they did not have anyone with 3,000 career hits. It was a rare void. So for two years, people anticipated Jeter's coronation. They prepared. Jeter had his first below-average season in 2010 (though he still won a Gold Glove and made the All-Star team) and the mediocrity continued into 2011, but everyone comforted themselves knowing that 3,000 hits was coming.

And then it happened. At exactly 2 p.m., with the crowd in high pitch, Price threw a 78-mph curveball. Jeter was looking fastball, but the pitch hung over home plate the way the moon hangs over Key West. And Jeter did the last thing even his biggest fans thought possible—he crushed it. It had been two months since Jeter had homered, and he ran hard out of the box because he did not expect the ball to actually go over the fence.

But the ball did go well over the fence.

And then . . . madness. The Yankees players rushed out of the dugout. The Rays' infielders clapped slightly. A 23-year-old man named Christian Lopez, who was given his ticket by his girlfriend, fell on the ball in the left-field bleachers. The sound in the new Yankee Stadium was as World Series loud, as loud as it had been when Jeter hit his famous Mr. November home run in the 2001 World Series. Jeter rounded the bases quickly, and when he touched home plate, he ran into a bear hug from Jorge Posada. He was the 14th man to get 3,000 hits with one team. He was the second to do it with a home run. He was, of course, the first to do it as a Yankee.

But, oddly enough, it is not the home run that sticks with me from that day. It is not No. 3,000 at all. No, because the next time up, he cracked a double down the left-field line. And the time after that, he lined a single to right, his favorite kind of hit, and then he stole a base. And his fifth time up, he grounded a single up the middle, five-for-five.

And that was Jeter, relentless to the end, still knocking hits when the job was seemingly done.

Jeter wanted to go on. He wanted to play more. For most of the players in the club, 3,000 hits represents the end, the pinnacle. But the year after he got his 3,000th hit, Jeter hit the weight room harder than ever, took on a whole different training regimen, and the next year he had a renaissance season. He led the league with 216 hits. He hit .316 for the season. He finished seventh in the MVP voting. He wanted to play forever.

Nobody gets to do that, however. Injuries and age and wear and tear got him, like they get everyone, and in 2014, at age 40, he was roughly a replacement-level player on an aged and tired Yankees team. You don't get to write your own endings.

There is something they do at Yankee Stadium—when the game begins, a group of fans in the bleachers will chant the names of the Yankees players until they get their deserved acknowledgment. Some of the players have rituals to go along with this. The player might pound his chest for the fans or flex muscles or just wave happily, the way people waved on ships leaving shore.

Jeter had a ritual, too, but it was really an anti-ritual. The instant they began to chant his name (before they even got the "urr" in DEH-rick JEET-urr), Jeter would hold out his glove toward the fans. *Enough. Thank you.* He did this without looking, automatically, never losing focus on the batter. It felt perfect to me. Jeter was saluting the fans without taking his eye off the game. He was saying: "I hear you, and I love you, but I'm working right now."

That's what he was doing all these years. Working.

A Jeter teammate once said what made Jeter special was that he wasn't special, which is to say that he was always the same recognizable guy, that he played precisely the same way on a Tuesday in Texas or a Saturday in Seattle or a Wednesday at the White Sox as he did the seventh game of the World Series.

That doesn't seem possible, of course. We all have good days and bad, happy and grumpy moods, lucky and unlucky times in our lives. Life is rarely flat—it almost always feels uphill or downhill. There is no way that Derek Jeter, in America's biggest city, on America's most famous team, in a life of cheers and boos and supermodels and opposite-field singles, really stayed perfectly centered. But maybe he did. He had 3,465 hits and 200 postseason hits to show. Those numbers say what he always tried to say: He hears you. He loves you. But he's working right now.

No. 78 **Clayton Kershaw**

The movie *Moneyball* has its fans and critics, but there is an immortal moment when Brad Pitt—as Oakland A's general manager Billy Beane—sinks into his chair and says, "How can you not be romantic about baseball?" It is a question I ask myself constantly. Baseball is, yes, a game with all of the problems, flaws, controversies, annoyances, and disappointments that games played by human beings will have. For the first half of the 20th century, baseball would not let black players in. For more than 75 years, baseball's owners granted themselves an unshakable and unbreakable hold on players and their futures. Every generation, every last one, there is some form of cheating and greed and foolishness that threatens the sport.

We know all this.

But, sometimes, dammit, we baseball romantics can't help ourselves.

Think: Koufax and Kershaw.

How does that happen? How can two breathtaking and electrifying and humble and legendary lefty pitchers, both unhittable at their best, fastball and curveball, both with poetic names that start with the most devastating letter in baseball, take the same mound in the same legendary stadium 50 years apart?

The greatest baseball announcer of them all, Vin Scully, told me that on several occasions he mistakenly called Kershaw "Koufax" in his broadcast. This is how they blended together in his mind, greatness upon greatness. Vin would see one and think of the other, think of one and visualize the other, and when Kershaw and Koufax actually were together speaking a language only they could understand, Vin could not help but smile and think about how much they still resembled each other, even if almost 50 years separated them.

Koufax led the league in ERA five times. Kershaw led the league in ERA five times. Kershaw led the league in WHIP four times. Koufax led the league in WHIP four times. Koufax won three Cy Young Awards and an MVP. Kershaw won three Cy Young Awards and an MVP.

Koufax finished 165-87 in his career. Kershaw is 175-76 in his still-active career.

They are not replicas, obviously. Koufax and Kershaw pitched in very different times—and they are pitchers who reflect their own particular moment. Koufax pitched in a time when a great starting pitcher's singular task was to finish the task—he had 27 complete games in 1965 and then again in '66. Kershaw has only 25 complete games in his entire career (despite being one of the most durable pitchers of his time). Koufax pitched 335 innings in a season. Kershaw, lately, has needed two seasons to reach that many innings.

Then, these trends go the other way, too: Kershaw pitches in a time when any pitch against any batter can be hit out, and so his job is to take the mound and somehow prevent runs for as long as possible before handing over the game to late-inning specialists. Koufax's 131 ERA+ shows that he was terrific at holding teams down. His ERA+ from 1961 to 1966 was a wonderful 156.

Kershaw's *career* ERA+, however, is 158. In his six-year peak, it was an otherworldly 182.

Koufax pitched in a time of high mounds and low runs. Kershaw pitches in a time of whiffs and dingers. Koufax pitched in a time when even great pitchers rarely started in the postseason—he made seven postseason starts, and they were all in the World Series, and he was a miracle. Kershaw pitches in a time when lots of teams make the playoffs. He has made *thirty* postseason starts, and it has been a mixed bag, though in 2020 he finally put it together and won his championship.

This is all about different times. Would Koufax be Kershaw now? Probably. Would Kershaw have been Koufax back in the day? Probably. This connection between them isn't just powerful, it is indeed romantic, a connection that can get you thinking that baseball, for all its flaws, is aligned with something mystical in the universe, two Dodger lefties wearing blue and throwing overpowering fastballs and gorgeous curveballs as if time stands still.

There's a story I once heard about Kershaw; I don't know if it's true but it sounds true. It seems he was asked by a television network to do an interview about his pitching routine. Kershaw turns down more interview requests than he accepts by a factor of about 20, but he agreed to this one. The interview was set up for a pitcher's mound—I think this was during spring training and it was set up to last for 15 minutes. Remember that: 15 minutes.

Kershaw, it is pretty well known, is something of a control freak. He blocks out his time with Belichickian precision. Exactly four hours before every start he does one thing, three hours before he does another, two hours before he does something else. He has a precise moment before every start when he drinks a cup of water, when he runs, when he hits the outfield wall, when he steps into the bullpen to do exactly, pitch for pitch, the same warm-up routine.

The interview day comes, and Kershaw goes to the mound to meet his interviewer. It begins with light small talk—hey, thanks for doing this, how is your family, quite the weather we've been having lately. Interviewers will generally try a little small talk to loosen up the subject, try to make a connection, etc. I don't blame the interviewer at all. But this was Kershaw. He endured the fluffiness for about two minutes before saying something like this:

"Look, if you want to spend the time chatting about nothing, I'm happy to do that. But at fifteen minutes, I'm out of here."

When I got my interview with Kershaw, I was told it would last five minutes, and I thought of this story.

That interview, bizarrely, is one of my favorites. Because it was a challenge: What could I actually learn about Clayton Kershaw in five tight minutes?

Wonderfully, he walked in and checked out the scene—we had the cameras ready and his chair waiting—and he said just two things. First, he said, "Do I look at you or at the camera?" I said to look at me. Second, he nodded and said, "You know this is five minutes, right?"

And here's what I learned in those minutes.

1. What Kershaw admires about Koufax is his humility. That's their connection. That's their bond. When you see them together, you can feel how they are part of a club where there are no other members.

   "You come across a lot of older ballplayers that maybe want to tell you how they did it," Kershaw said, "or maybe want to impress upon you exactly how they did it, and that's the only way to do it. Sandy's not like that. He loves talking baseball. He just wants you to succeed. He's just an unusual and wonderful guy."

2. I wondered: Does he ever just look around Dodger Stadium and take in his dream life? He doesn't seem the type to spend much time thinking about himself as a boy, but he was once a boy who loved the way Will Clark hit (Kershaw wears No. 22 for Clark). He was once an unhittable high school pitcher whose greatest wish was to pitch in the big leagues. Does he think about that boy?

   It turns out that he does. Once a year.

   "I give myself that chance on the first day," he said. "I don't live in Los Angeles during the offseason. So to come back and see that third deck of seats and just get to go through that tunnel . . . it hits home for me. It's that first day that I realize it's pretty special to get to come here every day. I get to pitch on that mound. I get to run around that outfield. On that first day, I let it sink in. And that, after that, it's time to work."

3. His own humility comes from his deep faith . . . and, yes, this sense of luckiness that he feels.

   "I know that I didn't deserve this talent," he said. "So for me to get to do this every day, it really just puts things into perspective. I definitely try hard not to take it for granted."

4. Kershaw believes strongly in preparation, as you might expect for a pitcher who is so precise in every single thing he does. But I was surprised when he said that he thinks attitude is more important for a pitcher than preparation.

"Sure, you watch video," he said. "You do all these things to be at your top form, to be ready to pitch that day. But at the end of the day, my belief is that you have to just want the out more than they want the hit.

"You don't have to say it. You don't have to be arrogant about it. But, really, *nobody* is going to get a hit that day. That's the mindset you have to have. That's the mentality. You can't let up. You can't lose focus batter to batter, especially as a starting pitcher. No matter what, no matter what happens, it's all about that next pitch, and the next pitch, and the next pitch. And then you get four days to do it all over again."

5. My favorite insight into Kershaw came after I asked him at the end how much he enjoyed those special days when everything goes right. He said he enjoys them, obviously; he was clearly giddy with joy after his no-hitter against Colorado in 2014, for example. But he said that while those days are fun, he had trouble with the phrase "special days."

"If you think about it, those days when it's all going well, those aren't *supposed* to be the special days, right?" he said. "For hitters, the special days are the ones where you get a hit. That's because everybody says baseball is a game of failure . . . but that's only true for hitters. Hitters are supposed to fail. As a pitcher, you're supposed to succeed. You're not supposed to give up a hit. Hitting is the hardest thing to do in sports so, for me, I don't consider those days when things go well to be the special ones. I think that's just another day.

"The days when things don't go right, those are the special days."

There was a sixth insight: He spent quite a while with that final answer, and then I thanked him, and I looked at my watch. Clayton Kershaw had given me six minutes and 43 seconds. It was, for Kershaw, as meaningful a gift as he can give.

No. 77 **Miguel Cabrera**

Sometimes at night, when I'm looking to fall asleep, I think up base-ball lists. These could be about anything, really. They could be the best baseball players named Joe* or the best curveballers I've ever seen (Mark Eichhorn, anyone?) or my favorite ever uniforms.

One of my favorite lists contains the batters who hit the ball the hardest.

By hardest, I am not talking about those players who hit the longest home runs. That's a whole other thing. I'm talking about those batters who hit the ball so hard that corner infielders would back up a step and begin to sweat. I'm talking about batters who hit the ball so hard that you feel a different temperature in the ballpark when they step to the plate, and you catch a different look on the pitcher's face, and you anticipate seeing a a baseball hit so impossibly hard that your breath just rushes out of your body.

Though the idea of exit velocity—which is the actual mph measure-ment of the baseball coming off the bat—is new, there have always been

---

* The All-Joe team: Catcher: Joe Mauer; First base: Joey Votto. Second base: Joe Morgan. Shortstop: Joe "Arky" Vaughan. Third base: Joe Torre. Left field: Joe Medwick. Center field: Joe DiMaggio. Right field: Shoeless Joe Jackson. Starters: Iron Joe McGinnity, Smoky Joe Wood, José Fernández, Bullet Joe Rogan, José Rijo. Closer: Joe Nathan.

players who were famous for how hard they hit baseballs. Nap Lajoie was probably the first. He was followed by players like Paul Waner. Stan Musial and Ted Williams crunched baseballs. There was, Buck O'Neil always used to say, a different sound when the ball came off the bat of Josh Gibson.

I never saw them, unfortunately, nor did I see Mickey Mantle or Frank Howard, and so my falling-asleep list contains players I saw in my lifetime. I don't put them in order because this isn't that kind of list—it's just a meandering thought to set my imagination and nostalgia sparking. I think of it more like poetry.

Look at the names that come to mind alphabetically: Dick Allen. Albert Belle. Rico Carty (I loved him so—they say he refused to slide because he carried his wallet in his back pocket). Adam Dunn. Edwin Encarnación. George Foster. Joey Gallo. Josh Hamilton. Ichiro (only in batting practice; in games he guided the ball; but in batting practice he hit with ferocity). Bo Jackson. Harmon Killebrew. Greg Luzinski. Willie McCovey. Mike Napoli (this name might surprise some but not those who watched him hit at his best). Al Oliver. Dave Parker. Carlos Quentin (the leader of the Qs!). Frank Robinson. Willie Stargell. Jim Thome. Chase Utley (such a quick bat). Vladimir Guerrero. Dave Winfield. Xander Bogaerts (needed an X but he hits the ball plenty hard). Yaz. And, of course, when we get to the Zs I must name pitcher Zack Greinke, who would never forgive me for leaving him off a list such as this.

Three others deserve special recognition.

There's Tony Oliva, my father's favorite player, who hit the ball so hard that in Minnesota they still reminisce about some of his foul balls (he also was famous for swinging so hard that the bat would slip out of his hands and whirly-bird into the stands).

There's Gary Sheffield; I am proud to be on his Wikipedia page saying, "I can't imagine there has ever been a scarier hitter to face."

But, perhaps most of all, there's Miguel Cabrera.

Miggy was a hitting prodigy. At age 16, scouts lined up around his home in Venezuela to sign him; the Dodgers' scout Camilo Pascual was in the Cabrera home at midnight the first day he could sign. Instead, Cabrera signed with the Marlins for almost two million dollars, one of the largest contracts given to an international player at that point. He would have received even more interest except that people worried about where he would play defense. The Yankees, for instance, refused to get into the bidding because they worried that he was too big to be a shortstop, where he grew up playing. They were right in their own small way; he was too big to be a shortstop.

In the larger picture, however, they were very, very wrong.

Cabrera hit a walk-off home run off Tampa Bay's Al Levine in his big-league first game. He was 20, and he hit cleanup for the Marlins in the postseason, mashing three home runs in the NLCS (including a three-run homer off Kerry Wood in the first inning). He also cracked a home run off Roger Clemens in the World Series.

After that, he put up 13 consecutive seasons of such consistent awesomeness that looking at his Baseball-Reference page feels a bit like looking directly into the sun.

Life off the field was anything but consistent for Cabrera. He made a seemingly never-ending series of mistakes and bad choices. He was arrested for drunken driving. The police came to his home after a domestic dispute. He faced a lawsuit from a former mistress. He did go to an alcohol abuse center, and by all accounts he has worked hard to put his life together.

As a hitter, though? It could not have looked easier. He hit every kind of pitch. He hit to all fields. Every year, Miggy's batting average was something glorious like .324 or .339 or .328 or .316. Every year he hit 34 or 27 or 44 home runs. Every year he drove in 100 runs, every year he scored 100 runs, every year he hit 40 or 50 doubles.

I have never seen anyone hit the ball harder and find it difficult to believe that anyone ever did. There was something fundamentally different about the ball coming off Miggy's bat. His ground balls crashed through the infield. His line drives smashed into walls. Every game, it seemed, Cabrera would hit at least one ball so hard that everyone in the crowd that day went home satisfied that they had seen the master at work.

In those 13 seasons, he hit .323/.402/.566 with 502 doubles, 434 home runs, and an average of 110 RBIs per year. Few players in baseball history have had 13 seasons like those.

Since 2017, Cabrera's power has sapped as he has dealt with injuries and wear and tear. So it goes. He signed an enormous deal that pays him until he's 40, and while there probably are not that many explosions left in his bat, he should still become just the fifth player—joining Henry Aaron, Barry Bonds, David Ortíz, and Albert Pujols—to hit 500 homers and 600 doubles.

And even now, every so often, he turns on a ball and hits it so hard the eye can barely follow and the baseball becomes a blur, and it sounds like the Fourth of July.

In many ways, Miguel Cabrera did not get the full credit he deserved for his astounding Triple Crown season in 2012. I will take my fair share of the blame for that; I was one of those people who missed how special, in its own way, that season was.

It was, I believe now, the most impressive Triple Crown season in baseball history.

As you know, those words "Triple Crown" are magical in sports. They can refer to the three most significant American Thoroughbred races (the Kentucky Derby, Preakness Stakes, and Belmont Stakes) or three legendary races of motor sport (the Indy 500, 24 Hours of Le Mans, and the Monaco Grand Prix). Golf has a triple crown; so does Nordic skiing, surfing, and Brazilian football. But it's probably most famous in baseball, where the Triple Crown refers to a player leading the league in batting average, home runs, and RBIs.

The first "real" Triple Crown in baseball history came in 1901, when that hard-hitting force Nap Lajoie hit .426, cracked 14 home runs, and drove in 125 RBIs. There had been a couple of other Triple Crowns in the 19th century—a man named Paul Hines did it in 1878 and Tip O'Neill won it in 1887 in the old American Association—but that wasn't baseball as we would recognize it.

Lajoie was the first to do it in the modern era ... but even Lajoie's Triple Crown is pretty questionable. He did it in the first year of the American League. The league was still developing, there were only eight teams, the competition was pretty light. The only other Hall of Famer to finish top 10 in any of the three Triple Crown categories was one you probably never heard of, a third baseman named Jimmy Collins, who was voted in by the Old-Timers' Committee mostly for his defense.

Point is, you could argue that Lajoie's Triple Crown is not the first "real one," either.

That would make Ty Cobb's Triple Crown of 1909 (.377, 9, 107) the first real Triple Crown. But, come on, can you really say that someone had a Triple Crown season with nine home runs?

When I was a kid, it was a thing for young baseball fans to memorize all the Triple Crown winners. I would always remember the most obscure of the bunch, Heinie Zimmerman, because, I mean, his name was Heinie. He won it in 1912 with the Cubs. He hit 14 home runs.

After Zimmerman, you start to get Triple Crown seasons that look like actual Triple Crown seasons. Rogers Hornsby won it twice—in 1922 and 1925—and hit .400 both times, hit 42 and 39 homers, drove in 152 and 143 runs.

Then came a long series of all-time greats. In 1933, Hall of Famers Chuck Klein and Jimmie Foxx each won the Triple Crown in their respective leagues. Lou Gehrig won it the next year, Ducky Medwick three years after that.

In the 1940s, Ted Williams won it twice. The second time, 1947, was a strange year in the American League. Nobody other than Williams hit .330, nobody other than Williams hit 30 home runs, nobody other than Williams drove in 100 RBIs. And yet the MVP went to Joe DiMaggio, who, by the calculations of WAR, was only half the player Ted Williams was that season.

The next three Triple Crowns—Mickey Mantle in '56, Frank Robinson in '66, and Carl Yastrzemski in '67—have been celebrated more than any of the others, I would say. That's because each of them comes with a great story.*

- Mantle had been this brilliant and beloved young player with un-limited potential—think the hype of the young Ken Griffey plus the young Bryce Harper plus the young Ronald Acuña Jr.—and then he finally put it together with this unthinkable season: .353 average, 52 homers, 130 RBIs. He led the league in just about everything except on-base percentage. There's something so satisfying about seeing a prodigy put everything together.

---

* Mantle led the league in hitting *and* walked 112 times. How could he have not led the league in on-base percentage? There's only one possible answer: His brilliant .464 on-base percentage was topped by the greatest hitter of them all, a 37-year-old Ted Williams (.479 OBP).

- Robinson's Triple Crown came one year after the Cincinnati Reds traded him away for Milt Pappas and change. Robinson was known for his competitiveness. He always played a little bit angry from the day he was born. But he was particularly angry in '66. He had never hit 40 homers in a season—and never would again—but that year he mashed 49. In addition to the Triple Crown categories, he led the league in runs, on-base percentage, and slugging percentage, too.

- Yaz's Triple Crown season of 1967 is probably one of the five most famous seasons in baseball history, as he led—carried, really—the Impossible Dream Red Sox to the pennant.

This is all a long lead-up to say that after Yaz, there were no triple crowns for 45 years . . . until Cabrera did it in 2012. But everything was different by then: The Triple Crown seemed utterly out of date. I mean, look at the categories: Batting average? Who cares about batting average now that we know about the greater value of on-base percentage? Home runs? By 2012, most fans seemed pretty sick of home runs; there had been too many hit. And runs batted in? We now know that's not really an individual stat, it's team-based.

Cabrera's Triple Crown (.330, 44, 139) was so uneventful and unimportant for so many of us modern baseball fans that we actively fought against him winning the MVP award. That was the year Mike Trout emerged, and while he lost out on those old-fashioned stats, he had a higher on-base percentage, was a much better baserunner and defender, and scored 20 more runs. By WAR, Trout was worth three more wins than Cabrera.

There was enough old-fashioned thinking to give the MVP to Cabrera. But there was a fuss.

In retrospect, I'm glad he won even though I would have voted for Trout. Cabrera's Triple Crown was special in a way that should be remembered. He is the first and still the only player to win a Triple Crown since the leagues expanded in 1969. That means a lot. When Hornsby, Foxx, Williams, and Mantle won their awards, they won them in much smaller leagues against much less competition.

Take Mantle's '56 season. How many truly great hitters were in the American League that year? Yes, there was Ted Williams, but, as mentioned, he was 37 years old by then. Do you know who finished second to Mantle's 56 homers that year? Vic Wertz. He hit 32. Al Kaline was a truly great player, and he finished second to Williams in RBIs. Yogi Berra was a legendary player but was an aging catcher in the midst of his last great season. Larry Doby was a terrific player but he was coming to the end, too. Minnie Miñoso is a legitimate Hall of Fame candidate but he was not really a batting average–home run–RBI threat.

Now look at Cabrera's Triple Crown—he had to beat out Mike Trout. He had to outhit Derek Jeter, Joe Mauer, Adrián Beltré, Robinson Canó, Dustin Pedroia, and others. He had to out-homer peak Josh Hamilton, Edwin Encarnación, Prince Fielder, Paul Konerko, Chris Davis, José Bautista, Adam Dunn, Nelson Cruz—all of them capable of smashing 40 homers in a season. He had to drive in more runs than those guys and a new addition to the American League, Albert Pujols.

While Mantle won the Triple Crown against the best hitters on eight teams, Cabrera won his against the best hitters on *fifteen* teams. Mantle won his Triple Crown in a league that was still mostly segregated, in a league that might not have had a job for Miguel Cabrera himself.

Point is, you might find the Triple Crown itself to be archaic and uninteresting. But even if you do, Cabrera's was the most impressive one in baseball history.

No. 76 **Willie McCovey**

There are a few dozen players in baseball history who are all-time greats and there are a handful more who became folk heroes. The Venn diagram does not contain many who were both.

Willie McCovey was both.

He was born on January 10, 1938, in Mobile, Alabama. That was four years after Henry Aaron was born in Mobile and six months before Billy Williams was born in Whistler, a few miles away. It's one of baseball's beautiful mysteries that three Hall of Fame hitters of that magnitude were born in the same place at the same time.[*]

Aaron was, obviously, the greatest of the three. Williams had the sweetest swing.

---

[*] And if you ever find yourself wondering about the quality of the players in the Negro Leagues, think about this: If Aaron, Williams, and McCovey had been born 20 years earlier, all three of them would have spent their primes in the Negro Leagues, and their stories would be told as legend. People would tell tall tales about the power of Stretch McCovey or the impossibly quick bat of Henry Aaron or the gorgeousness of Billy Williams's hitting and . . . would you believe it? I wouldn't worry about people overrating Negro Leaguers. I'd worry about people underrating them.

And McCovey? He was the folk hero. He was the one others in the game feared.

"When he belts a home run," Dodgers manager Walter Alston said, "he does it with such authority it seems like an act of God."

"Strongest man in baseball," Willie Mays said.

"I don't think I've ever seen a player hit the ball harder than McCovey," his manager, Herman Franks, said.

"Let me just tell you," Sparky Anderson summed up, "I shake just when I walk past Willie McCovey."

What is a folk hero, after all? You might say that a folk hero is someone who blends what is real and what is not, a mingling of fiction and nonfiction. McCovey's record is there for everyone to see. And yet, he was so big, so strong, so powerful that people struggle to describe him.

The real part: McCovey hit 521 home runs in his career, led the league in homers three times, slugging three times, and RBIs twice.

The unreal part: Had his career been just slightly different—had he been given a chance earlier or played in a better-hitting time—he might have hit 900 home runs.

McCovey was so dangerous a hitter that in 1969, managers intentionally walked him 45 times, and that was the record and would stay the record for another thirty years, until Barry Bonds broke the game. The next year, they walked him 40 more times. Nobody wanted any part of Willie McCovey when he was healthy and in the batter's box.

McCovey was the seventh of ten children and, as he often said, he was the only athlete of the bunch. He dropped out of school to get a job and support the family. At 17, he went to a Giants tryout camp in Melbourne, Florida. It would turn out to be one of the most remarkable tryout camps in baseball history.

The Giants, in those days, were astonishing collectors of talent. The key was a former Negro Leagues executive named Alex Pompez. In a short time, the Giants—with Pompez playing a key role—picked up McCovey, Juan Marichal, Gaylord Perry, the three Alou brothers, Jim Ray Hart . . . I mean, that's quite a haul.

And there was someone else—another 17-year-old who happened to be at the very same tryout camp in Melbourne. He was from Puerto Rico. His name was Orlando Cepeda.

Can you imagine? Two Hall of Fame first basemen at the same tryout camp for the same team on the same day in 1955? Those sorts of convergences just don't happen. But this time it did, and it would impact two all-time great careers. For the next decade, McCovey and Cepeda would battle for at-bats, playing time, and their place in the history of the game.

Cepeda was four months older than McCovey, and he was a bit more advanced. He got to the big leagues first, in 1958. While McCovey was busy crushing baseballs in Phoenix when Cepeda got his call to the Giants. He took full advantage. Cepeda hit .312 with 25 homers and a league-leading 38 doubles. He won the Rookie of the Year Award.

McCovey made his move more than a year later, in late July 1959. Even though there were only two months left in the season, his rookie year is still something to behold. He went 4-for-4 in his first game, slugged .700 in his first month, and finished by hitting .354/.429/.656 with 27 extra-base hits. And, yes, even though he played in only 52 games, he also won Rookie of the Year.

From the start, people could see that McCovey was this unprecedented blend of size and strength and hitting genius. Lefty O'Doul called him the next Ted Williams. Giants announcer Russ Hodges marveled that he'd never seen a hitter with a better eye. ("He never swings at a bad ball!" Hodges said.)

"He might," his manager, Bill Rigney, said after McCovey's first month, "just be one of the great hitters of our time."

But what to do at first base? The Giants had an embarrassment of riches, two breathtaking hitters. Unfortunately, there is only one first base, and so the Giants tried Cepeda and McCovey at other positions. It was a no-go. Cepeda, because he threw right-handed, seemed on the surface to be more adaptable to another infield position, but after trying him at third base for four games they realized that was definitely not going to work. They tried each of them in the outfield—both right and left field—but it was not good.

And so for three seasons, Willie McCovey scrounged around for at-bats. Cepeda had gotten their first, and he was fantastic. In 1961, he led the league in homers and RBIs and finished second in the MVP voting to Frank Robinson. He was a perennial All-Star.

And McCovey? From 1959 to 1962, McCovey averaged just 88 games per season, even though he hit .283/.369/.539 over that span. He had any number of nagging and painful injuries, too, something that would haunt his entire career.

In 1963, the Giants finally committed to playing McCovey every day in left field. He promptly led the league with 44 home runs.

McCovey's entire career is a testament to the power of timing, good and bad. McCovey lost much of his early career to Cepeda (the Giants did not trade Cepeda until 1966).

And when McCovey finally was given his chance, baseball was in the midst of its lowest-scoring era since Deadball. In McCovey's prime, 1967–70, batters across baseball hit just .245 and slugged .362. One out of every seven games was a shutout. The mounds were high, the strike zone was oversized, and pitchers reigned. McCovey also played his home games in San Francisco's Candlestick Park, which was a pitcher's ballpark.

Even in this environment, McCovey was so good that managers preferred simply pitching around him.

Then there were the injuries, so many injuries: foot injuries, hip injuries, knee injuries. McCovey—like Mickey Mantle—was in constant agony, yet he played through. "He came off the field one day and he had tears in his eyes," his manager Charlie Fox said. "You don't soon forget that."

This is what makes McCovey both real and imagined: Think of what McCovey could have been! Think about him playing at Yankee Stadium in the 1990s with modern medical treatments. How many home runs could he have hit?

Then again, to talk about what could have been is to miss how great he was. Even with the winds blowing so hard against him, McCovey soared. After a down season in 1964, the year his beloved father died, McCovey returned in 1965 to hit 39 homers, second to Mays. From 1965 to 1970—when nobody was scoring runs—he slugged .578, the highest in baseball by 20 points. He led the league in homers, RBIs, slugging, and OPS in 1968, the year of the pitcher.

He had his most extraordinary season in 1969, the year he was intentionally walked 45 times. Managers gave up. In one June game against the Miracle Mets, he was intentionally walked in the first inning, intentionally walked again in the second, and then finally pitched to in the fifth (he homered). In a September game against the Dodgers that year, McCovey came up in the 10th inning with two outs and nobody on base. Dodgers manager Walter Alston walked him. "I didn't want to get beat with one swing," he said.*

In all, they walked McCovey 121 times that year. They defended him with what were, at the time, exotic defensive shifts. McCovey could handle the bat and even with his leg injuries probably could have beaten out a bunt or punched a single the other way almost anytime he wanted. But that's what the other teams wanted. "We'll happily give him four singles any time he wants them," Padres manager Preston Gómez said.

"I guess," McCovey said sadly, "I'm the least-pitched-to of any hitter in the history of baseball."

Even with all that, he hit .320/.453/.656 with 45 homers and 126 RBIs. He won the MVP award.

There was something about McCovey's hitting that didn't quite add up. He had this enormous swing that, like Joe Frazier's famous left hook, seemed to take two days to unwind. After he hit two home runs at the 1969 All-Star Game, Vice President Spiro Agnew told him, "You have the biggest shoulder swing I've ever seen."

But the sluggish look of his swing was an illusion. He hit with a surgeon's precision. From age 30 on, McCovey walked more than he struck out.

In the end, McCovey's career was wonderful. He hit 521 home runs, his 147 career OPS+ ranks among the greatest hitters, and he was elected first-ballot to the Hall of Fame. The small stretch of the San Francisco Bay that ripples behind the right-field wall at Oracle Park is now called McCovey Cove.

And he left behind images—Willie McCovey was Wes Parker nervously moving back a few inches, he was the sweat beading on Don Drysdale's forehead ("I think McCovey is the only player he was afraid of," Don Sutton said of Drysdale), he was the quickening heartbeat of Tom Seaver and the rapt attention of Bob Gibson.

---

* In the end, Alston got beat by the walk—it was followed by two more walks and an error, and McCovey scored the winning run. But that's not the point.

"Hey, Willie," the pitcher and author Jim Bouton said to McCovey as he and "a group of terrorized pitchers" watched McCovey smash terrifying home run after terrifying home run in batting practice. "Can you do that every time?"

McCovey, Bouton said, did not smile.

"Just about," he said.

No. 75 **Justin Verlander**

et's go back, if we can, to a spring day in 2001. An 18-year-old Justin Verlander and his father, Richard, sit in their home in Goochland, Virginia, and wait for the phone to ring. It is the day of the Major League Baseball amateur draft. There is some excitement buzzing around baseball as people wonder if the Twins will take college superstar pitcher Mark Prior (the Twins do not; they take hometown hero Joe Mauer instead).

Father and son feel like Justin could be a lot like Mark Prior.

They are hoping that teams will see that and take Justin high in the draft. They are hoping this will be a good day.

The funny thing is: It probably ended up being the best possible day for Justin Verlander. But it certainly did not feel like that in the moment.

Justin had been a dominant pitcher for Goochland High. He averaged exactly two strikeouts per inning—142 whiffs in 71 innings—and allowed four earned runs all season. He was skinny but tall; his 6-foot-5 frame suggested unlimited potential. He had one of those blessed arms. When he was 10 or so, Justin and his father were vacationing at the lake, and they decided to have one of those contests to see who could throw a rock the farthest.

Richard threw his about halfway across the lake and felt pretty good about it.

Justin threw his rock over the lake.

"My jaw dropped," Richard later said. It was probably that moment when they both fully understood Justin's destiny. Justin threw so hard in Little League (and with such shaky control) that multiple kids quit the league rather than face him. When he was 14, a coach named Wayne Spencer challenged Justin to throw his hardest pitch.

"Hey, Sally," Spencer yelled at Verlander while crouching behind the plate, "I've seen better arms on a chair."

Whether it was the casual sexism, the comparison to basic furniture, or the pure lameness of the joke, Verlander gritted his teeth and broke 80 mph for the first time. Not long after that, he threw 85, then 90. One scout clocked him at 93 his senior year in high school.

"I could just throw the crap out of the ball," Justin said.

Scouts knew that there was more to come. That is their job to know. They marveled at how long his arms were and how much more muscle he would put on.

"He's a lot like Jack McDowell," one scout said, comparing Verlander to another 6-foot-5 righty who would go on to become a sensation at Stanford, the fifth pick in the draft, a two-time 20-game winner and a Cy Young Award winner.

It sure sounds like Verlander was going to be a first-round pick that day in 2001, right?

Ah, but there were other things going on. For some reason, the velocity on Verlander's fastball had dropped his senior year. Why? Richard tried to explain to the scouts that this was all because of an illness, but scouts are paid to be skeptical. Dropped velocity is bad. "Is he injured?" they asked themselves. "Or worse, has he topped out?"

Then there was the question of young Justin's control. He was no longer wild enough to get kids to quit the sport, but he still had not come to any real agreements with the strike zone. "Will he harness his stuff?" the scouts asked themselves. "Will he ever develop command of his pitches?"

Baseball America predicted that Verlander would go somewhere between the eighth and 12th rounds. That was too low for the Velanders—a player barely gets any signing bonus at all when drafted that low—and so they announced that Justin had committed to play baseball at Old Dominion unless drafted in the top three rounds. This is the sort of thing players and their families do when they want to improve their stock, but it's often a bluff. And people who knew Justin Verlander felt sure that this was a bluff because the kid lived to play professional baseball; it had been his only tangible dream since throwing a rock across the lake.

Father and son sat in their home that day and waited to see just where Justin would get drafted.

The first three rounds went by . . . and Justin was not taken. This was disappointing but ultimately unsurprising; baseball teams are not easily coaxed into taking a player higher than their scouts recommend. So, the next question was: Would he go in the next couple of rounds? Would the team who drafted him make a serious offer? The fourth round went by, and no one took Justin. Then the fifth round and the sixth and the seven went by, too. It looked like *Baseball America* was right. He would go somewhere between the eighth and 12th rounds.

But the phone would not ring. Soon, the draft moved into the teens, and then it turned 20 rounds, and still Verlander's name had not been called. This led to the "what the heck" rounds, the shots in the dark, the 23rd round, the 31st round, the 39th round, the rounds where teams are buying lottery tickets—Wes McCrotty and Mark Comolli, Cesar Montes De Oca and Matthew Sibigtroth and Justin Sassanella.

In all, 1,469 players were selected in the 2001 draft.

Justin Verlander was not drafted at all.

Sports are filled with stories of great athletes inspired by the pain of being told that they weren't good enough. The most famous of these is the story of basketball superhero Michael Jordan, who as a sophomore in high school was cut from the varsity basketball team.

Well, we should tell that story because it isn't that simple: Jordan was not exactly cut. He was a sophomore, and sophomores almost always played junior varsity at Pop Herring's Laney High School in Wilmington, North Carolina. Jordan was put on the junior varsity team. But another sophomore, a now semi-famous basketball footnote named Harvest Leroy Smith, made the varsity.

Jordan never, ever forgot Leroy Smith. Never. At his Hall of Fame speech—HIS BLEEPING HALL OF FAME SPEECH—he made sure that Smith was in the crowd.

"Then there's Leroy Smith," Jordan told the crowd that day. "I got cut, he made the team—on the varsity team—and he's here tonight. He's still the same 6-foot-7 guy, he's not any bigger, probably his game is about the same. But he started the whole process with me because when he made the team and I didn't, I wanted to prove not just to Leroy Smith, not just to myself, but to the coach that picked Leroy over me. I wanted to make sure you understood—you made a mistake, dude."

Jordan got criticized for sounding a bit bitter and kind of ripping an old coach on what everyone expected to be a celebration day . . . but I've never quite gotten the criticism. It was *his* Hall of Fame day, and what he said was raw and, best I can tell, intensely honest. Jordan stripped himself down. He took basketball to a whole new place and the fuel he used was hunger and fury and the need to prove every single doubter wrong. All his life, he needed disbelievers.

It is a common story. Tom Brady, who most would call the greatest quarterback in the history of professional football, was not drafted until the sixth round, and the raw disappointment—he and his father still get tears in their eyes when they talk about it—has been a part of the fire that fueled him, even as he reached his 40s and had been celebrated as few American athletes ever have been.

There is so much power in proving everybody wrong. My friend, swimmer Melvin Stewart, sheepishly admits that after he won the gold medal in the 200-meter butterfly at the 1992 Summer Olympics in Barcelona, when he was up on the medal stand, he wanted to think good thoughts and appreciate all the people who helped him along the way. Instead, his mind instinctively ran through the list of all those people who told him he couldn't do it.

So many athletes need this negative energy to drive them forward.

When Justin Verlander went undrafted in 2001, he and his father were hurt and furious. And, yes, it drove him forward. It focused his energy. Justin almost immediately put on 15 pounds of muscle and his fastball velocity skyrocketed into the mid-90s. He showed up at Old Dominion looking entirely different from the player recruited, and the coach was awed.

"I bet some of those teams are kicking themselves now," Richard said of those clubs that had passed on Justin in the draft.

Yes, they were. Verlander immediately became one of the best amateur prospects in the country. At the end of his sophomore season, Verlander struck out 17 in a game against James Madison. His fastball was clocked at 98 mph.

"I think," one scout said after that game, "I may have just seen the first pick in the 2004 draft."

Verlander was actually the second pick in the draft, after the Padres made their lamentable and utterly forgettable choice of Matt Bush. That will go down as a great trivia question: Who was taken ahead of Justin Verlander in the 2004 draft?

On May 22, 2006, less than five years after not getting drafted by a single big-league club, Verlander—now 6-foot-5, 225 pounds, his fastball in triple digits—started against the Kansas City Royals. He retired the first 10 batters of the game. He threw a five-hit shutout, with three of the meaningless hits coming in the final two innings and his Tigers up by eight runs.

In the ninth inning, he struck out Doug Mientkiewicz looking on a pitch so absurd and unhittable that Mientkiewicz—nicknamed "Eye Chart" for obvious reasons—was still muttering about it in the clubhouse afterward. Doug was a fine player who prided himself on his ability to always put the ball in play.

"Well, I guess that's why he was the first pick in the draft," Mientkiewicz finally said as a way of comforting himself.

We told him that Verlander was actually not the first pick in the draft. His eyes bulged.

"Who was picked ahead of him?" he asked incredulously. "And you *better* say 'Albert Pujols.'"

Justin Verlander's hunger to prove people wrong has never gone away. It is part of what marks him as a pitcher, I think. His early career was strangely uneven. He could be very good; he won the Rookie of the Year and finished fifth in the Cy Young voting in his second year. But in his third year, he led the league with 17 losses and had a dismal 4.84 ERA. The young Verlander struck out fewer players than you would have expected for a guy who threw 100 mph.

But then it all clicked in—he became the game's best pitcher from 2009 to 2012. It felt like a coronation. He won a Cy Young and MVP, probably should have won a second Cy Young, and while he was terrific, it seemed pretty easy.

I don't mean that to sound like a knock. I'm just saying he threw that blazing fastball, he had a backbreaking curveball, he had an absurd changeup, and he was so flush with talent that he didn't even use his wipe-out slider much in those days. He was brilliant, but we had not yet seen his extraordinary pitching heart.

That happened after he turned 30, when he started running into some trouble with injuries and home runs and long at-bats he couldn't finish off. The doubters and skeptics returned and wondered: What's this guy made of? OK, he was terrific when he had some of the best stuff of any pitcher in baseball history and he was surrounded by All-Stars. But could he be terrific with his stuff and team fading? At age 31, he gave up the most runs in the American League. At age 32, he was hurt much of the year, and when he returned he was atrocious for two months.

Here are the stats of two dominant righties at age 32:

Pitcher A: 157-97, 3.52 ERA, 121 ERA+, won Rookie of the Year, Cy Young, and MVP, could have won two more Cy Youngs, made six All-Star teams. Had two depressing seasons in a row.

Pitcher B: 168-128, 3.34 ERA, 120 ERA+, won a Cy Young, could have won two more, made six All-Star teams. Had two depressing seasons in a row.

The first is obviously Verlander. The second is Félix Hernández.

Félix Hernández got hurt and never recovered. His career came to a sad and screeching halt.

And Verlander? Well, his injuries and decline had given him the same gift that baseball teams had given when they did not draft him in 2001. The doubters were back. And they pumped life back into him.

"People suck," he told reporter Brandon Sneed.

For the second time in his life, he used the unrestrained power of doubt (along with the love of his wife, supermodel Kate Upton) to spur him on. At age 33, he went 16-9 with a 3.04 ERA, led the league in strikeouts, and finished second in the Cy Young voting in a staggeringly close race (he actually had six more first-place votes than winner Rick Porcello).

At age 34, he was traded to Houston—adding even more doubt to his bonfire of motivation—and he went 5-0 with a 1.06 ERA to help lead the Astros to what would become their first World Series championship. Along the way, he was named the MVP of the American League Championship Series.

In 2018, he again led the league in strikeouts and finished second in the Cy Young voting.

In 2019, he won the Cy Young award, after leading the league in wins, innings, WHIP, hits per nine, and strikeout-to-walk ratio. He struck out 300 batters for the first time in his career.

Verlander's second chapter has been astonishing . . . and, as of this writing, it still isn't complete. He already has a Hall of Fame record with more than 3,000 strikeouts and 72 Wins Above Replacement. But if he can keep going, all sorts of statistical wonders are still in play.

Then again, talking about those kinds of numbers probably won't help him. I'm pretty sure he'd prefer people rip him. I'm pretty sure he's looking for the next doubt to throw into the fire.

No. 74 **Frank Thomas**

L et's start with a somewhat random stat: There have been 30 players in the modern era who created 1,000 runs while they were in their 20s.

I'm not sure how that stat hits you, but it's impressive. The stat "runs created" is calculated by adding together a player's ability to get on base with the ability to hit with power, and it does a nice job of estimating how many runs a player is responsible for. Because the game is all about runs—scoring runs, preventing runs—this is meaningful.

So let's look at it again: thirty players who created 1,000 runs in their 20s.

Of the 30 players on the list, 23 are in the Hall of Fame. These are the names you know, the greatest players ever: Ruth, Cobb, Foxx, Mantle, Mays, Hornsby, Aaron, etc.

The seven who are not in the Hall of Fame are:

- Active players Mike Trout, Albert Pujols, and Miguel Cabrera, who will surely be elected on their first ballot.

- PED-tainted players Barry Bonds and Alex Rodriguez, who, by the numbers, are two of the greatest offensive players in the game's history.

- Vada Pinson and Andruw Jones, who have interesting Hall of Fame cases that, so far, have not yet persuaded 75 percent of the voters. Pinson spent 15 years on the ballot. Jones remains on the ballot now.

So, you get it—these are 30 of the greatest young hitters in baseball history. They might be *the* 30 greatest young hitters in baseball history.

Frank Thomas stands out among them.

Only Ted Williams walked more per game than the young Thomas. Only Williams and Babe Ruth managed a higher on-base percentage. Only Ruth, Williams, Gehrig, and Foxx had a higher OPS. And you know what you can say about all of those other players? Right: None of them spent their youth playing in an integrated league.

In other words: None of them played in a league that would have allowed Frank Thomas.

Thomas was always the most obvious player on the field—it tends to be that way for 6-foot-5, 275-pound people—but while people saw the hugeness of the man, they often missed his essence. His brilliance was concealed, mysterious; his huge body was a disguise. People thought he was a slugger, one of those awesome lumbering creatures who swing mightily and hit baseballs a long way. Yes, Thomas looked like a slugger, and he moved like a slugger, and he was called a slugger, and he obviously put up some slugger numbers.

But Frank Thomas was not a slugger.

He was a hitting genius. He was a right-handed Ted Williams.

And people just didn't see that.

By the time Thomas reached the big leagues at age 22, he had grown used to his enormous body cloaking what really ticked inside. All his young life, people told Thomas that he was a football player. They didn't say he *should* be a football player. No. They told him he *was* a football player.

Thing is, he didn't want to be a football player. Baseball was his game. He was just 10 years old when his beloved younger sister Pamela died of leukemia, and he vowed to become a great baseball player in her memory.

Everybody—*everybody*—kept telling him to quit the baseball nonsense because football greatness awaited. He was so big, so strong, so athletic. Thomas was cut from his high school baseball team, but football came easy. He was not drafted by a single baseball team coming out of high school, but Auburn's Pat Dye had a football scholarship waiting for him. Didn't he want to score the touchdown that beat Alabama? Didn't he want to go to the NFL and be a great tight end like Ozzie Newsome or Kellen Winslow?

No. He didn't. He played three games as a backup tight end for Dye at Auburn, but he had a whole other plan in mind. He only went to Auburn so he could walk on the baseball team, the way Bo Jackson had before him. Thomas led the SEC in hitting his sophomore year. That allowed him to do what he had wanted to do all along: He gave up football entirely. He kept hitting. The White Sox took him with the seventh overall pick in the 1989 draft.

But even the White Sox couldn't see all of him. They saw Thomas as a pure power guy and yes, he would hit with power. But that wasn't what defined him. Thomas was a hitting savant. You know how they used to say Williams could see the seams as the baseball approached? Thomas could do that, too. You know how they say that Stan Musial's batting eye was so impeccable that umpires would refuse to call strikes against him? Thomas had that kind of eye.

At 22, while starting in Birmingham, he was already (no exaggeration) one of the most natural hitters the game had ever seen. He hit .323 and walked 112 times in 109 games.

The White Sox called him up. He hit .330/.454/.529 in 60 games.

And with that he began his onslaught on the record books and the imagination. For each of the next seven seasons, he hit .300, scored 100 runs, drove in 100 runs, and walked 100 times. You know who else in baseball history did that seven years in a row? Nobody. Not Ruth. Not Gehrig. Not Bonds. Not even Williams, though it must be said that military service got in the way for him.

None of this was by mistake: Thomas knew exactly what he was doing. He knew his stats to the fourth digit right of the decimal point. He knew baseball history. He knew his own value. Don't you think people told him to swing the bat more, to swing for the fences more, to be more of a classic slugger? Of course they did. Even Tim Raines, his best friend with the White Sox, would nudge him and push him and try to get him to be more aggressive. "Can't drive in runs when you're walking," Raines would tell him.

But Thomas, like Ted Williams, was a perfectionist. He was an artist. He couldn't swing at a pitch off the plate because . . . it was a pitch off the plate. He didn't understand how anyone could miss that. "People are always saying I can't do this, I can't do that," he told Rick Reilly at *Sports Illustrated*. "People love knocking Frank Thomas."

He refused to give in even a little bit. He had his philosophy: swing at the good pitches, spit on the bad ones, drive the ball to all fields. Everybody on the outside, all they saw was what they wanted to see. They saw the muscles. They saw the glare. Only Thomas himself understood what was on the inside. In those seven extraordinary seasons, he led the league in on-base percentage four times, in OPS four times, in walks four times, he won two MVP awards, and came close two other times. In 1997, he became the biggest man in baseball history to win a batting title.

Only three men as big as Frank Thomas—Derrek Lee and Mike Morse are the other two—have hit .300 in a full big-league season. Thomas did it *nine times*.

You can't really tell Thomas's story without talking a little bit about steroids. Thomas played in that steroid era, and he was by far the most outspoken anti-steroids hitter of his day. He called for drug testing as early as 1995. He was quoted many times hinting (or flat-out saying) that he knew other players took shortcuts and he found it revolting and against the very essence of baseball. He was the only active player willing to talk to George Mitchell for his report about PEDs in baseball.

Even in his post-playing career, he has not been shy about speaking out against those players who used (or might have used) PEDs in his time.

"I'm not happy at all," he told the *New York Post* after a couple of suspected PED users were elected to the Hall of Fame. "Some of these guys were great players. But they wouldn't have been great players without drugs. . . . I don't mind these guys doing what they want to do for their families and to make their money. But don't come calling to the Hall of Fame and say, 'I'm supposed to be in the Hall of Fame' when you know you cheated."

I've thought a lot about why Thomas was so outspoken when so few other players were. I think it's because he understood that he was destined to be in the middle of the PED story whether he liked it or not. He was enormous, muscular, and a former football player. He hit with great power and, late in his career, broke down with various injuries: He was always going to be a leading suspect in the PED hunt.

This undoubtedly drove him crazy because it's so unfair—there was (and remains) a recklessness people relied on to guess who used steroids and who did not. Thomas wasn't going to idly watch people speculate about him. He was going to control the situation just the way he controlled at-bats. He lashed out. He challenged other players. He did admit, with some embarrassment, briefly using amphetamines as a young player. But he would not let anyone group him with those who were taking PEDs. And he would not defend or shield any PED users, not even with his silence.

There's a vivid and telling scene in Reilly's *SI* piece about Thomas—it happened after ESPN baseball analyst and former utility infielder for several teams Dave Campbell suggested that the way to get Thomas out was with high inside fastballs. Campbell cited Thomas's record against Nolan Ryan; Frank was 0-for-12 with 11 strikeouts against the legend.

It's fair to say Thomas was not impressed.

"Who the @#$%^ is Dave Campbell?" Reilly quoted Thomas screaming in the clubhouse. "A %$#@! .213 hitter trying to tell me what I can't hit? A .213 hitter? Telling me I can't hit fastballs?"

The scene—which, by the way, was delightfully enhanced by his White Sox teammate Ozzie Guillen, who egged on Thomas by shouting, "That's true! You cannot hit fastballs!"—is so telling for any number of reasons. Two of them stand out.

One, he was exactly right: Campbell hit .213 in his career. That is hardly common knowledge; it means that Thomas looked it up to stoke his own rage.

Two, it showed the passion and fever behind what everybody assumed was his placid approach. Thomas was called a gentle giant more times than he cared to count. But that was part of his mask. Thomas's ambitions were vast. He came to the big leagues with the same goal as Williams; he wanted to walk down the street and have people say he was the greatest hitter who ever lived.

And for a few years there in his 20s, before the injuries took hold, he came awfully close.

No. 73 **Brooks Robinson**

Forgive me for going back in time for a moment, but Brooks Robinson demands it: I'm 10 years old and in the tiny Cleveland backyard behind the small house my parents scrounged and saved to buy. A telephone wire sags above the yard—the lowest point of the wire is just beyond our reach when we jump. There's a round hole of dirt that's not covered in grass, left over from an ill-fated attempt to dig a hole to China, and a perfect tree for climbing and a back porch that was once screened in but is now open-air thanks to the many holes in the screen. A rotted picnic table has been pushed out of the way. All around us is a chain-link fence that can be scaled in a quick three-step process.

1. Left foot to the middle of the fence.

2. Right foot to the top.

3. Right foot catapults body over.

It is one of those rare Cleveland days when the sky is entirely blue.

My father is there in the backyard. He has just gotten home from work at the factory; the oil on his pants is still fresh. He is smoking a Kent and well into his second pack by now. Dad is still an athlete—can still flash some of the quickness he displayed as a semiprofessional soccer player in Poland—but he is not a baseball player. He did not know a thing about baseball before coming to America with my mother three years before I was born. He learned about baseball on the radio, by playing softball on the company team, and by overhearing conversations.

He thought it important to know baseball for when his American sons grew older.

Now, he rolls me ground balls. Dad wears a plastic glove too small for his hand and a baseball cap that collapses on his head. He rolls me another grounder, another.

All the while, he invokes about Brooks Robinson.

"Diving for the ball isn't the hard part. Get up! Think how fast Brooks Robinson gets up."

"Get in front of the ball. Brooks Robinson always gets in front of the ball. If he misses it, he can still block the ball with his body."

"Think about how Brooks Robinson throws. Don't overthrow it. Throw it just as hard as you need to get the runner out."

"Charge the ball. Brooks Robinson charges every ball."

Every day in that backyard, with Dad and me, it is Brooks Robinson—Mr. Hoover, the Human Vacuum Cleaner, the greatest defensive third baseman who ever lived—who connects us. Every day—on sunny days like this or, more often, gray days, on a recently mowed backyard with clippings everywhere or a yard covered in dandelions or a muddy yard—I see the outline of Brooksie, imagine the spirit of Brooksie, dream of being like Brooksie. I grow up believing in superheroes: Superman, Batman, Wonder Woman, Brooks Robinson.

I cannot begin to tell you how overjoyed I was to find out Robinson learned the game from his father in much the same way I learned it from mine. My dad worked in a sweater factory in Cleveland. Brooks Robinson Sr. worked in a bakery in Little Rock, Arkansas. In our first home movie, my dad is tossing me a Whiffle ball to hit and throwing me ground balls in the grass. Brooks Sr. gave his son a sawed-off broomstick to hit with and, as one story claims, "started to hit groundballs to the older of his two boys as soon as the youngster could toddle."

Brooks Jr. was actually a natural lefty. Not many people know that. He broke his left arm and collarbone when he was very young and taught himself (with his dad's help) to throw right-handed. Can you imagine how different baseball history would have been had Robinson not broken his arm? He would have thrown left-handed . . . and, as such, he wouldn't have been able to play third base.

Robinson grew up living what you might call a romantic baseball childhood, the sort of childhood James Horner wrote music for. He played ball every day. He built up his arm throwing newspapers on his paper route (Yankees Hall of Fame catcher Bill Dickey was one of his customers). The first time he threw a football, he was named quarterback. His first date was at the local malt shop.

And when he was 13, he wrote that ubiquitous essay—the same essay, it seems, all great ballplayers and athletes write—about how he wanted to be a big-league ballplayer when he grew up. He put more effort into it than most. He found a photograph of the great ballplayer Ernie Lombardi and put it on the cover. He researched how much ballplayers were paid and included that information inside. To the question of why he believed he could become a big-league ballplayer, he wrote: "I'm slow to anger and not easily discouraged; am enthusiastic, happy, calm, and very active."

And to the question of why, he wrote: "The hours are good."

Robinson's self-scouting report was prophetic. He certainly had athletic gifts—lightning-quick reflexes to start—but it would be his determination that guided him. And his niceness. From the start, he was so impossibly nice. Everybody thought so. Niceness came naturally to him, but he also worked at it. His hero was Stan Musial, the nicest of ballplayers, and Robinson wanted to be just like him.

It meant the world to him years later when a Baltimore baseball writer named Jim Elliot said of Brooksie: "Compared to this guy, Stan Musial was hard to get along with."

Another baseball writer, Gordon Beard, when referring to how Reggie Jackson was getting a candy bar named for him, wrote: "Brooks never asked anyone to name a candy bar after him. In Baltimore, people name their children after him."

Can niceness help a ballplayer achieve greatness? Well, like the old line about having chicken soup when you're sick: It couldn't hurt. People were drawn to Robinson. They naturally rooted for him. Teammates adored him and protected him and stood up for him.

Robinson was so famous for being nice that, in 1965, a commercial for a local Baltimore bank took advantage of it.

Announcer: Tell me, Brooks, does anything ever get you mad?

Brooksie: No, not me. You can't lose your temper in this game. No, I never get mad.

Announcer: How about when you come to bat in the ninth inning with the bases loaded and strike out?

Brooksie: Well, you can't get a hit every time. No, that doesn't make me mad.

Announcer: How about when you play back for a power hitter, and he lays down a bunt you can't handle?

Brooksie: Well, that's the way the ball bounces. No, that doesn't make me mad.

Announcer: Well, how about if you buy a home and then find out you could have gotten a better rate on your mortgage with no appraisal fee and no prepayment penalties?

Brooksie: Ooh. That makes me mad!

Robinson signed with the hapless Baltimore Orioles in 1955 for $4,000. The Orioles were in just their second season in Baltimore after being the dismal St. Louis Browns. They lost 100 games the year before they signed Robinson and lost 97 the year after that. But Robinson saw the Orioles' troubles as a positive; he believed they would help him get to the big leagues faster.

In one way, he was right: Robinson played his first big-league game in September when he was 18. He went 2-for-4 with an RBI against Washington. But he did not get a hit for the rest of the season and was sent to San Antonio to polish up his game. And he didn't become a major-league regular for a few more years.

There were plenty of people who didn't see much in Robinson in those early years. Of baseball's five tools, Robinson showed only one in the minors. He couldn't hit much. He had little power. He couldn't run at all.

His arm wasn't particularly strong—there was a time when the Orioles thought he might be better suited as a second baseman. One teammate watched him play in those early days and wondered why the Orioles had signed him at all.

He did have a balletic style about him at third base, though. That was clear from the start. Was that enough? I think of the young Robinson as a bit like the young Fred Astaire, who inspired the famous screen test analysis: "Can't sing. Can't act. Balding. Can dance a little."

Robinson won his first Gold Glove for Baltimore in 1960, when he was finally given third base as his own. He won the Gold Glove in each of the next 15 seasons. Sometimes when you look back at a player using modern defensive stats, you might see a gap between the player's reputation and performance. Not with Brooksie. He was an above-average fielder in every one of the 16 seasons in which he won the Gold Glove, and he was legendary in most of them.

He was 276 fielding runs above average in those 16 seasons.

No one in baseball at any position was within 100 runs of him.

"The most amazing part," said former big-league pitcher Al Fitzmorris, who saw Robinson from across the way dozens of times, "is that he really couldn't throw. You'd see all sorts of guys like Graig Nettles and Buddy Bell and George [Brett], and they all had these rifle arms. But not Brooks. He would just lob the ball across the infield and get his guy by a step."

Robinson did it differently. He made plays with positioning and instincts and balance and timing and otherworldly reflexes. You couldn't crush the ball by him. Nobody could dive to the dirt, scramble to his feet, and throw like he could. His arm might not have been that strong, but he had the fastest release in the game. And his accuracy, particularly when starting the double play, was unrivaled. Pete Rose said he belonged in a higher league. Jim Murray wrote that when he retired, he should just take third base with him. Sparky Anderson said he could throw his glove out there, and it would start 10 double plays by itself.

"I used to stand in the outfield like a fan," his teammate Frank Robinson said, "and watch him make play after play. I used to think, 'Wow, I can't believe this.'"

Brooksie was not a great hitter most of the time. But, occasionally, he found a hitting groove. He certainly was a great hitter in 1964, when he hit .317/.368/.521 with 28 homers and led the league with 118 RBIs. He won the MVP that year. He had 300 total bases in '62, he drove in 100 runs in '66, and he hit .294 in '60.

And in the 1970 World Series, the Cincinnati Reds simply couldn't get him out. He hit .429 with two homers in the five-game series.

But it's fair to say that Robinson's limitations as a player were always a part of the story: He couldn't run, he didn't have great bat speed, he didn't walk much, and he didn't have all that much natural power. His 13-year-old self got it exactly right: Brooks Robinson was not easily discouraged. In all, he finished with more than 2,800 hits, more than 250 homers, more than 1,300 RBIs. Take away his last three seasons when his bat went dead, he was a 108 OPS+ hitter, which is plenty good for the greatest defensive third baseman in the game's history.

Look at those words again that he wrote as a child: "I'm slow to anger and not easily discouraged; am enthusiastic, happy, calm, and very active." I think that came through with the way he played—and I think that was why my dad was drawn to him. I look at Dad's life then; every day he endured the daily grind at the factory, the grouchiness of his bosses, the monotony of the grueling work, the realization there were no promotions ahead. But every day, though he was dead tired, he came home and took us to the pool, coached our Little League teams, played catch in the backyard. He did something that altered our lives just a little. Every day.

And, in a way, that was Brooks Robinson, too. Every day—it could have been a Sunday at Fenway Park, a Friday night at Yankee Stadium, a Thursday in April in frigid Minneapolis, a scorching Tuesday in July in Kansas City, or just a boring old Wednesday night in Cleveland, with the infield as hard as a rock and the sky as gray as the smoke coming from the factory chimneys. It didn't matter. He was always there, every day, on the balls of his feet, ready to charge for a bunt or dive to his left for a line drive or backhand a grounder down the line and make a throw as he fell backward.

"That's it!" my dad yelled to me as I dived into the grass in our backyard, snared the ground ball, jumped to my feet, and made the return throw. "That's it! That's Brooks Robinson!"

No. 72 **Robin Roberts**

All of us, I suppose, would have some opinions on who belongs in the "Most Underrated Pitchers Ever" team photo. Thing is, we really need to define our terms. Underrated could mean terrific pitchers who are not in the Hall of Fame but certainly could be, in which case I would put Dave Stieb in there, David Cone, Bret Saberhagen, Luis Tiant, Rick Reuschel, Billy Pierce, Johan Santana, Jerry Koosman, and any number of others.

Then again, underrated could mean really outstanding pitchers who might not be quite Hall of Fame worthy but are so much better than people remember, such as Kevin Appier, Chuck Finley, Frank Tanana, or Steve Rogers.

I think of it a little bit differently. I think Robin Roberts would be in the center of my underrated-team photograph. He is underrated in a different way. He is in the Hall of Fame, has been since 1976. It's hard to be underrated and be in the Hall of Fame.

But here's the thing: I think Roberts belongs in every discussion of greatest pitchers ever. And he's never really mentioned in those discussions. I think Roberts should be known by every baseball fan, and he really isn't. He's not even the most famous Robin Roberts going, placing a distant second behind the wonderful television broadcaster.

Robin Roberts played baseball at a time when the focus of the game was very much on the position players. Willie Mays. Mickey Mantle. Henry Aaron. Duke Snider. Frank Robinson. Al Kaline. Roberto Clemente. Pitchers, for the most part, were an afterthought. This is how baseball evolves; different eras offer a different focus for the game. Roberts's time in the 1950s was about great everyday players. But the 1960s going into the 1970s were really about pitchers: Bob Gibson, Sandy Koufax, Tom Seaver, Steve Carlton, Don Drysdale, Denny McLain, Nolan Ryan, Phil Niekro, Gaylord Perry.

In the 1980s, baseball's heroes were mostly hitters again: Tony Gwynn, Wade Boggs, George Brett, Rickey Henderson, Mike Schmidt, Dale Murphy, and the rest.

And in the 1990s, ironically, the game revolved around pitchers again. I say "ironically" because most people, when remembering the 1990s, will remember all the runs, all the home runs, all the records being shattered. But looking back, the most iconic and meaningful players of the time were pitchers: Greg Maddux, Roger Clemens, Pedro Martínez, and Randy Johnson (not to mention Tom Glavine, John Smoltz, Mike Mussina, and Curt Schilling).

Baseball has been odd that way; similar great players often clump together. Mays, Mantle, and Aaron all come at the same time. George Brett and Mike Schmidt come at the same time. Rickey Henderson and Tim Raines come at the same time.

But getting back to the point, Roberts was by far the best pitcher in the 1950s. There were some other terrific pitchers—Warren Spahn won 20 games pretty much every year of the '50s, Billy Pierce should always be included when listing underrated pitchers, and Whitey Ford rarely lost while playing for the indomitable Yankees.

But it was Roberts's decade. From 1950 to 1955, just those six seasons, he posted 46.9 WAR, which is more than the careers of *seventeen* pitchers in the Hall of Fame.

He was probably the best pitcher in the league in all six of those seasons. I once did something I called the Cy Stieb Awards where I went back to 1950 and, year by year, determined who *should* have won the Cy Young

Award (I named it for Dave Stieb, who I believe should have won three Cy Young Awards—he never won any). By my calculations, Roberts was the best pitcher in the league every year from 1950 to 1955. No other pitcher was the best six years in a row.

But now we get to reasons why people don't fully grasp Roberts's greatness—it begins with timing. Look at those years: 1950–55. Do you know what's interesting about that? Those are the six seasons just before the Baseball Writers of America gave out the first Cy Young Award in 1956. In fact, Roberts is probably responsible for the creation of the Cy Young Award in the first place. Before the Cy Young, the only award a pitcher could win was the MVP award, but that required getting more votes than all the position players. And that rarely happened. Roberts never won an MVP award, not even in 1952 when he went 28-7 with a 2.59 ERA and threw a breathtaking 30 complete games. In his last 23 starts, his Phillies went 21-2—Roberts's only two losses were shutouts. The writers instead gave it to Hank Sauer, who led the league in homers and RBIs.

Here's how Oscar Fraley of the United Press International responded to that vote:

"Anybody who knows the difference between a bunt and punt must be completely flabbergasted at the selection of Hank Sauer in the National League. Most of the voters obviously never heard of Robin Roberts ... one theory is that they were all on vacation and the ballot was filled in by the editor of the women's page."

Yes, there was always time for some light misogyny in 1950s baseball writing!

In any case, Roberts never won any big awards. He pitched in a hitter's time. He also declined rapidly after he turned 29—you might expect that from a pitcher who averaged 323 innings per season in his six big years. All of it has added up to Roberts being largely forgotten.

Roberts had one of those classic American upbringings. He grew up on an Illinois farm, went to a two-room schoolhouse (where, he always remembered, he learned to memorize "Gunga Din"). He developed his pitching arm by throwing fastballs against a barn door (protected by a mattress). He hated doing chores; there are numerous funny stories about that. His mother once told him to wash dishes or clean his room or something like that, and he declined—"ballplayers don't do chores," he said—but as consolation, he promised to one day buy her a house, just like Lou Gehrig had for his mother.*

There's something meaningful about that story, I think, something directly related to what made Roberts so good. He was a stubborn mule. He would get his mind on something—it didn't matter if it was being a ballplayer, buying his mother a house, or not doing chores—and he wouldn't get off of it. Even his father admitted to one reporter, "With Robin, we just kind of went along."

Stubbornness, as you will see, marked Roberts as a pitcher, too.

He did not play college baseball at first when he attended Michigan State. He played basketball instead and was good enough to be named the Michigan Collegiate Player of the Year by the *Detroit Free Press*. So how did baseball happen? Roberts told the story like so:

I just showed up for practice one day after the end of the basketball season. The baseball coach, John Kobs, was surprised to see me because he knew of me only from my two seasons on the basketball team.

Coach Kobs said, "What are you doing here?"

I said, "Coach, I can play your game."

He asked, "What position do you play?"

"What do you need?" I replied.

"I need pitching."

"Well," I said, "I can pitch."

It's a fun story, but I'm pretty skeptical. For one thing, there are all the other signs that Roberts grew up wanting to be a ballplayer. But even beyond that, it's hard to believe that a talent like Roberts was so nonchalant about pitching. By the time he began playing college baseball, he was already one of the best pitchers in the country.

Over the next two years, in rapid succession, he would: 1) be all but unhittable at Michigan State; 2) get an enormous $25,000 signing bonus from the Phillies; 3) blaze through the minor leagues in a month; and 4) make his first big-league start against Pittsburgh, going eight innings, allowing just five hits and two runs.

So, this whole "chance encounter" baseball story, while charming,

---

* Years later, when Philadelphia's travel secretary Babe Alexander offered Roberts $25,000 to play for the Phillies, Roberts responded by saying, "That would buy a nice house, wouldn't it?"

doesn't seem credible. It's much more likely that Roberts enjoyed basketball but always knew that his future was in a baseball uniform.

Roberts often said that he did not want to pitch; he saw himself as a third baseman. If that's true, then Michigan State did him a great favor by putting him on the mound because Roberts was a famously bad hitter.

Lowest career OPS since 1920 (min. 1,500 PAs)

1. Don Sutton, .340

2. Greg Maddux, .395

3. Phil Niekro, .395

4. Lefty Grove, .417

5. Tom Seaver, .429

6. Tom Glavine, .454

7. Robin Roberts, .464

8. Steve Carlton, .482

9. Warren Spahn, .520

10. Jackie Hernandez, .526

Poor Jackie Hernandez is the only nonpitcher on the list.

Roberts told a wonderful story about his own hitting: He said he once hit a home run off of Satchel Paige in an exhibition game. And years later, Roberts said he ran into Ol' Satch.

"Satchel," Roberts said. "You know I once homered off you."

To which Paige replied: "Roberts, I have a book with the names of all the great hitters who got a hit off me. You ain't in it."

As a pitcher, Roberts was relentless. He threw one of the hardest fastballs of his day—Ernie Banks used to say that Roberts threw even harder than Bob Gibson—but he was not a strikeout pitcher. He averaged only 4.5 strikeouts per nine innings, which even by the standards of his time was about league average.

Could Roberts have struck out more batters? Of course. But the truth is that he was too stubborn to pitch that way. He refused to go for strikeouts, and he also refused to walk anybody (he led the league in fewest walks per nine innings four times). The strikeout pitchers will throw the ball out of the zone in an effort to get hitters to chase, but that wasn't Roberts's style. He had three objectives:

1. Challenge every hitter.

2. Never beat himself.

3. Finish the game.

That was it. Everything else was for show, and Roberts was not about show.

Challenge every hitter. Among live-ball pitchers in the Hall of Fame, who do you think allowed the fewest walks per nine innings? Right:

1. Robin Roberts, 1.73

2. Greg Maddux, 1.80

3. Juan Marichal, 1.82

4. Carl Hubbell, 1.82

5. Roy Halladay, 1.94

He was not interested in fooling anybody. He threw strikes and dared hitters to hit them. Sometimes, it should be said, those hitters *did* hit them—for decades, Roberts held the record for most home runs allowed, and even now he's second on the list behind Jamie Moyer.

But the home runs he allowed—no matter how long, no matter how loud—never stopped him from challenging the next guy.

Never beat himself. Well, you know about the rarity of walks, but how about this: Roberts had just 33 wild pitches in his entire career. Thirty-three wild pitches in about 4,700 innings! How crazy is that? A. J. Burnett had 25 wild pitches in 2011 alone. Among pitchers with more than 3,000 innings pitched, only Charlie Root* had fewer wild pitches per inning than Roberts.

Roberts was also a good defensive player. He was somewhat slow to the

---

* Charlie Root is best remembered as the pitcher who gave up Babe Ruth's called-shot home run in the 1932 World Series.

plate, but in his prime he controlled the running game. And while, yes, he gave up a lot of home runs, he was actually pretty good about minimizing the damage. Only 36 percent of the home runs Roberts gave up were with runners on base. That's a pretty good percentage; it's tied for 14th among the 100 pitchers who gave up the most home runs in baseball history.*

Finish the game. Roberts's third objective was his main objective: finish what he started. He completed more than 300 games—since World War II, only Spahn completed more.

I can't write about Roberts without telling a personal story. One day, a few years ago, Roberts called me at home—this was back when we all had home phones. I had never spoken to him before. He left a message saying that he was Robin Roberts, the Hall of Fame pitcher—he introduced himself that way as if I would not recognize him otherwise—and he was in Kansas City to visit his brother. He hoped I might take him on a tour of the Negro Leagues Baseball Museum.

At first, I felt sure it was a gag. I'm kind of embarrassed for thinking that now. Robin Roberts was 77 years old when he called. He wanted to see the Negro Leagues Museum. He'd read a few of my columns, saw a bit of kindred baseball spirit, and thought I might get a kick out of talking some baseball with him. I'm embarrassed that my natural reaction was mistrust.

In the end, though, I called him back. We went to the museum together. It's one of my most cherished baseball memories. Roberts told stories for hours; he was a marvelous storyteller. Every photo in the museum,

---

* All right, since I did the work, I'll give you the results of this study: Do you know who, among the 100 pitchers, gave up the lowest percentage of multi-run homers? Answer: Hall of Famer Tom Glavine! Of Glavine's 356 home runs, 243 were solo shots. Here are the pitchers with the 10 lowest percentages for giving up homers with runners on base. You will notice a familiar name in here, Justin Verlander, who for a long time in 2019 gave up home runs at a furious rate and still ended up winning the Cy Young Award. Timing! 1. Tom Glavine, 31.7%; 2. Tom Seaver 32.6%; 3. Steve Trachsel, 32.8%; 4. Justin Verlander, 33.1%; 5. Dan Haren, 33.1%; 6. Catfish Hunter, 33.2%; 7. Cole Hamels, 33.8%; 8. Freddy Garcia, 34.0%; 9. Bartolo Colon, 34.6%; 10. Curt Schilling, 34.9%; And, while we're at it, here are the five who gave up the highest percentage of homers with runners on base. Check out No. 4: Nolan Ryan rarely gave up home runs, but when he did they were often with runners on base. 1. Murry Dickson, 50.7%; 2. Bob Friend, 49.3%; 3. Kyle Lohse, 49.1%; 4. Nolan Ryan, 47.4%; 5. John Smoltz, 46.5%.

every exhibit, every signed baseball seemed to spark a memory. What a wonderful man.

I remember one story in particular. In 1951, the Dodgers and Giants came down to the wire at the end of the season. You know how that ended—the teams were tied at the end of the season, and they had a three-game playoff that ended with Bobby Thomson hitting a home run and radio announcer Russ Hodges screaming, "The Giants win the pennant!"

What you might not know is that the Dodgers had to win their last game against the Phillies to even force that playoff. And it did not look like they would. The Phillies led the game 6–1 early and 8–5 going into the eighth inning. But the Dodgers came back to tie it.

And that's when manager Eddie Sawyer called for Roberts to pitch relief and the Dodgers' manager Charlie Dressen called in Don Newcombe to match up. Talk about a different time: Roberts and Newcombe had pitched the day before. They were on zero days rest.

The two greats matched zeroes for five innings. Finally, in the bottom of the 13th, Newcombe was spent and was replaced by a pinch-hitter. But Roberts went on.

In the 14th, Roberts faced Jackie Robinson. In all, Jackie Robinson faced Robin Roberts 176 times—more than he faced any other pitcher. They had many epic battles. Robinson won this one. He crushed a long home run, and that won the game.

And how did Roberts remember such a difficult loss? Like so: "If I don't give up that home run to Jackie, there is no Bobby Thomson home run. There is no playoff."

And he smiled. "It's a good thing I gave up that home run, isn't it?"

No. 71 **Bert Blyleven**

Let's talk a little bit about rookie cards (I warn you in advance that this will go off the rails a bit before we get back to Bert Blyleven).

It has been quite a few years since I've collected baseball cards, so I can't tell you what role rookie cards play in the baseball card world today. But I can tell you: When I was a teenager, rookie cards were everything.

My buddy Rob introduced me to the whole concept of rookie cards. When I was really young, I collected baseball cards the old-fashioned way—I put them in shoe boxes, wrapped rubber bands around them, flipped them in gambling exhibitions, put them in the spokes of my bicycle tires so that they made a clicking sound. But Rob was a real collector, and he explained to me that a player's first card, the rookie card, was special.

By special, he meant *valuable**. I had never thought of baseball cards being worth anything. But he showed me something called the "Beckett

---

* Rob didn't know that he was actually launching my sportswriting career. A few years later, I submitted a story to *Beckett Monthly*—a monthly magazine version of the *Beckett Price Guide*—and for some strange reason, the editors accepted it. I got paid three cents a word. That was my first paying gig.

Baseball Card Price Guide," which estimated the monetary value of the cards. And these cards were worth real money. A 1952 Mickey Mantle rookie card in mint condition was worth $2,700! A Tom Seaver rookie was worth $140! Heck, a Rickey Henderson rookie card from 1980 was worth $12.50 by 1983! There was money to be made!

There clearly was money in rookie cards. But how did you pick the right rookie cards? Well, it turns out Rob was sort of the Charles Schwab of rookie card investing, and he built his portfolio on two unshakable principles.

The first of those was obvious: pure speculation.

Every baseball fan around my age, it seems, has a story about some wild-goose chase baseball card investment they made. In attics across America, there are shattered retirement plans in clear notebook pages filled with Andy Van Slyke cards, José Canseco cards, Eric Davis cards, Don Mattingly cards, etc. Some of these investments sort of paid off—it isn't bad to have stock-piled rookie cards of Ken Griffey, Chipper Jones, Greg Maddux, and so on.

But mostly, those were not the ones hoarded. No, if I had to guess—based on my informal survey—I'd say the rookie cards that people went most crazy over were:

1. Gregg Jefferies. His 1988 Donruss rookie card was, I believe, the hottest item in baseball rookie card history. Why? Well, in 1987, in Double-A Jackson, he hit .367/.423/.598 with 20 homers, 26 stolen bases, 48 doubles, etc. He came up to the Mets and got three hits in six at-bats. He switch-hit. Yes, he was Mickey Mantle, everyone was sure of it. Jefferies ended up having a fine career; he led the league in doubles once, he made a couple of All-Star teams, and he is one of only a few players to get Rookie of the Year votes in two different years. But, alas, he was done at 32 and those cards are worth roughly their value in cardboard.

2. Cory Snyder. He hit with ferocious power. He had Clemente's arm. He was on the cover of *Sports Illustrated* at 24. Let's just say, it didn't quite work out.

3. Brien Taylor. First pick in the draft. No. 1 prospect in baseball. Seemed to be the future of the New York Yankees. Then he hurt his shoulder in a fight trying to defend his brother and the dream ended before it began.

4. Brad Komminsk. Slugged his way through the minors. Power and speed. Looked like the next Dale Murphy. Wasn't the next Dale Murphy.

5. Todd Van Poppel. One of the greatest high school pitchers ever. No. 1 prospect in baseball. Put agent Scott Boras on the map. Seeing those cards hurts my eyes.

6. The Phils—Hiatt, Plantier, and Bradley. Phil Hiatt ended up playing in Japan. Phil Plantier hit 34 homers one big-league season but that was about it. Phil Bradley was the best of the bunch, and he was an all-conference quarterback to boot. None of it makes their baseball cards worth anything.

Honorable mention: Rubén Sierra, Dave Magadan, Kevin Maas, Oddibe McDowell.

Moving on, the second principle in Rob's rookie card investment plan involved stat mining. What we would do was analyze a player's core stats and his age, triangulate, and bet on the players we thought might reach a Hall of Fame standard such as 300 wins, 3,000 strikeouts, 3,000 hits, or 500 home runs.

This too led us down some dark paths. For years, we collected Rich Dotson rookie cards. Why? Because Dotson had 70 wins by age 25. That's a lot of wins for that age—it still ranks 37th among players since World War II. The way we figured it, if Dotson could keep on winning—he did finish fourth in the Cy Young voting in 1983—he had a shot at 300 wins. And if he got to 300 wins, his rookie card would be worth a fortune.

Dotson, in the end, won 111 games in his career, a nice achievement. His rookie card is worth bupkis.

I should explain what I mean when saying "We collected." See, every dealer and card shop then had what they called "common cards." These were boxes and boxes and boxes filled with Sixto Lezcano and Steve Staggs and Dan McGinn and Joe Koppe and Ollie Brown cards; I think the idea was that people could go through these boxes when they wanted to fill out their sets. The commons usually went for one to three cents apiece.

We would scour these boxes for, as I say, Rich Dotson rookie cards. We briefly had some interest in Charlie Lea. That also didn't work out. We thought Garry Templeton had the potential to get 3,000 hits; he came a bit closer than the pitchers but still fell 904 hits short. I remember pulling

Terry Puhl cards out of the boxes because he too seemed to have a lot of hits for his age.

But the prize of all prizes, the card that would get us more excited than any other, well, that was easy. It was a 1971 Bert Blyleven rookie card. Even now, when I see one, I begin to feel a little bit of that thrill of going through all the Fred Kendalls and Don Minchers and Bobby Bolins and Milt Wilcoxes to finally come upon it.

What made the Blyleven card such an undervalued one? Well, Rob and I and a handful of others had analyzed the stats and we knew something in 1981 that almost nobody seemed to know:

Bert Blyleven was going to the Hall of Fame.

The notion in 1982 that Blyleven was going to the Hall of Fame was absurd. It would have gotten us laughed out of just about every baseball discussion in America. Bert Blyleven? What? Have you lost your mind? The guy had made *one* All-Star team. He was traded *three* times. He was barely above a .500 pitcher. He had never even been considered for the Cy Young.

Blyleven into the Hall of Fame? Seriously?

Seriously. Rob had done the research. He showed me the back of that 1982 card: Through age 30, Blyleven already had 2,357 strikeouts.

He was all but *guaranteed* to get 3,000 strikeouts in his career.

And that meant—Hall of Fame. Plain and simple. This was long before some of the more advanced baseball statistics came around. Blyleven scored well on those, too, but at that time we cared about two things: wins and strikeouts. Blyleven had quite a few wins already. But he had a lot of strikeouts, and he was destined for 3,000, and that meant Hall of Fame, and that meant his rookie card would be valuable. We made it our mission to fish as many Blyleven rookie cards as we could out of the common card boxes.

It actually took Blyleven a little bit longer to get his 3,000th strikeout than we expected because he missed almost all of the 1982 season with an injury, and he was not fully healthy in 1983, either. But he got No. 3,000 on August 1, 1986, for Minnesota. That day, against Oakland, he had the curveball bouncing, and he struck out a career-high 15 batters. He became just the 10th pitcher in baseball history to strike out 3,000 when he whiffed Mike Davis on a curveball down and in.

Nobody talked about the Hall of Fame for him after that game, though. Even Blyleven downplayed the achievement; he said it was nice but he was happier about moving his season record to .500 (10-10). Blyleven didn't think 3,000 strikeouts was going to be his Hall of Fame ticket. No, he still thought he would win 300 games.

And he came close. After his fantastic 1989 season at age 38—he went 17-5 with a 2.73 ERA, led the league in shutouts, and finished fourth in the Cy Young voting—he had 271 victories, just 29 shy of the magical 300.

On July 31 in 1990, Nolan Ryan won his 300th game and all the stories mentioned Blyleven because he seemed to be next. He was up to 279 victories by then. But then things went awry. Blyleven missed a start after his wife and children were in a car accident. When he got back, he immediately strained his shoulder and had to shut down for the rest of the season.

He expected to be healthy in 1991, but doctors found he had torn his rotator cuff and he missed the entire season.

That basically ended the chase. Blyleven did try to come back in 1992, but he wasn't especially effective and he won just eight games. That gave him 287, putting him tantalizingly close to 300, so he decided to come back one more time in 1993; he signed a minimum-salary contract with the Twins. "I'm not going to the minor leagues," he told reporters. "I'm not going to try with any other team. This is it. If it works out, great. If it doesn't work out, great."

It didn't work out. Blyleven got rocked all spring. The Twins released him, and Blyleven retired on April Fools' Day, which fit his reputation as a prankster.

And despite his 3,701 strikeouts—third on the list at the time of his retirement—people wrote that he probably would not get elected to the Hall of Fame because he did not win 300 games.

"He had only one 20-win season, and he never won a Cy Young Award," wrote Rochester's Bob Matthews. "I probably never would include Blyleven on my ballot for Cooperstown, but I wouldn't challenge anyone who did."

Blyleven himself fought back. "I feel like I have the numbers to be in the Hall of Fame," he told a reporter. "If you look at a Catfish Hunter or a Ferguson Jenkins or a Bob Gibson or a Bob Feller, I feel like my numbers are there."

He wasn't wrong about that:

Catfish Hunter, 224 wins, 2,012 strikeouts, 36.3 WAR

Ferguson Jenkins, 284 wins, 3,192 strikeouts, 82.2 WAR

Bob Gibson, 251 wins, 3,117 strikeouts, 81.6 WAR

Bob Feller, 266 wins, 2,571 strikeouts, 65.1 WAR

Bert Blyleven, 287 wins, 3,701 strikeouts, 96.0 WAR

Actually, as anyone who has listened to Bert on Twins broadcasts knows, Blyleven would not have referred to WAR then or now—he doesn't care much for advanced metrics. Even without them, though, he had what seemed like a strong case, and he wasn't too shy to say so.

But here's the thing: He shouldn't have had to make his case. He should have been a slam-dunk Hall of Famer. The guy struck out more than 3,700 batters, compiled an astounding 60 shutouts, put up almost 100 WAR, and, yes, would have won 300 games except for a couple of bad breaks.

So why did it take 14 years for people to finally vote him in (after an Internet campaign made him a cause)? The answer, I think, goes something like this: Some players are appreciated in their time. Some players are appreciated only years after they're done. Steve Garvey was one of the biggest stars in baseball during Blyleven's time. He did all these things that baseball fans in the 1970s and 1980s admired. He played every day. He hit .300. He got 200 hits a year. He won Gold Gloves. His team won pennants. He was called Captain America. Sportswriters adored him and wrote glowing things about him pretty much every day.

Every single day, somebody called Steve Garvey a future Hall of Famer.

Blyleven, meanwhile, did none of the things that baseball fans of his time admired. Baseball fans at the time worshipped at the altar of 20-game winners, and he only won 20 once (and it barely counts because he also lost 17 that year). He was traded five times. He never won a Cy Young. He was a goofball and a prankster and so wasn't taken seriously. His best pitch was a curveball, which isn't quite as sexy as the fastball or slider. In his best years, he played for lousy teams and so nobody cared.

Nobody ever seemed to call Blyleven a future Hall of Famer.

But as time went on and new ways of looking at baseball were discovered, their tides turned. After his career ended, people couldn't help but notice how low Garvey's on-base percentage was, how he never slugged

.500, how his defensive numbers didn't impress, how he really didn't place himself among the all-time greats (he's not in the top 100 in RBIs, homers, doubles, runs, or just about anything else). His fans keep trying to push his Hall case, and he keeps popping up on Veterans Committee Hall of Fame ballots, but the winds blow against him. He might never get elected to the Hall of Fame, something that in 1982 would have been inconceivable.

Blyleven? He got just 83 votes his first year on the Hall of Fame ballot and even fewer the next year. But soon people saw what had been hidden. He had struck out more batters than Tom Seaver or Walter Johnson. He threw more shutouts than Bob Gibson or Steve Carlton. When WAR came along, well, he had a higher WAR than Warren Spahn or Nolan Ryan. His postseason numbers (5-1, 2.47 ERA in 47⅓ innings) were very good.

It helped him that Jack Morris came on the Hall of Fame ballot at around the same time. Morris is in the Hall of Fame now, but first, he was a perfect foil for Blyleven, who won more games, struck out more batters, had a lower ERA, and even had a better postseason record. It was hard to argue that Morris was a Hall of Famer but Blyleven was not. In the end, Blyleven was voted in by the writers and Morris was voted in by the Veterans Committee.

There are still people who don't think Blyleven belongs in the Hall of Fame or that, at best, he's a borderline guy. There are still people who don't see that with his absurd curveball and rubber arm and surprisingly competitive nature, he was one of the greatest players in baseball history. But we saw it a long time ago on the back of his 1982 baseball card.

One final thought: I see the Blyleven rookie card on eBay going for as much as $145!

Then, I also see it going for as low as $2.95.

That baseball rookie card retirement plan just didn't quite work out.

No. 70 **Sandy Koufax**

I f this was a ranking of baseball names—not the lyricism of the name, necessarily, but instead a ranking of what hearing or seeing the name does to the heart and the soul of a baseball fan—then Sandy Koufax would be at the top. Think of the greatest names in baseball history, the ones that make goose bumps rise on your arms and transport you to another place and time.

The name Clemente does that. DiMaggio does that. The names Musial and Mays and Gehrig and Reggie and, of course, Babe Ruth do that.

Has there ever been a name more perfect than Mickey Mantle?

Yes. I think so. There has been one: Sandy Koufax.

"Trying to hit him," Willie Stargell said, "was like trying to drink coffee with a fork."

"A foul ball off of Koufax was a moral victory," Don Sutton said.

"The greatest pitcher I ever saw," Ernie Banks said.

"It got to the point," statistician Allan Roth said, "where when anybody got a hit off him, people would turn to each other and say, 'Gee, I wonder what he did wrong.'"

"As soon as I saw that fastball," Buzzie Bavasi said, "the hair raised up on my arms. The only other time the hair on my arms raised up was when I saw the ceiling of the Sistine Chapel."

Jim Murray: "Need a doctor? Get Jonas Salk. You want to win a golf bet? Get Sam Snead for a partner. If you want to dance, see if Fred Astaire is busy. But if you want to win a pennant or a World Series, just hand the ball to Sanford Koufax."

"This guy," Ron Santo said, "could drive you to drink."

With Koufax, myth and magnificence weave together so tightly, it is hard to separate the two—but even more to the point, it seems unkind to separate the two. He had a strange career, an odd and potent blend of luck and misfortune. He was the shooting star who is remembered forever. He was utterly boring and, at the same time, the most fascinating person ever to throw a baseball.

My prize possession when I was a teenager was a 1956 Sandy Koufax Topps baseball card. Why? It's hard to say. That card was more than a decade older than I was. I never saw Koufax pitch. I never lived in Los Angeles. I never liked the Dodgers. I'm not left-handed. I didn't even want to be a pitcher. But I would take that card out nightly and stare at it and dream.

How did Koufax do that?

Sandy Koufax grew up in Brooklyn. His parents divorced when he was three, and he quickly and permanently lost touch and contact with his father, Jack Sanford Braun. Sandy was nine when his mother married a lawyer named Irving Koufax; Sandy would forever see Irving as his father. If there was pain in all of this, as there surely was, Koufax kept it to himself like he kept all things to himself.

He showed baseball promise from his youngest days of throwing a rubber ball against the front stoop. His Jewish family, though, saw time spent playing baseball as *mishegas*—craziness. His grandmother, when she wanted to express her displeasure, would call Sandy "You baseball player." Irving wanted Sandy to become an architect and often said that baseball was a waste of time and money and hopes. "A baseball player," Sandy recalled his father saying, "you will never be."

Irving changed his mind when he went to see Sandy pitch in a sandlot game. Koufax's fastball left him breathless enough that he changed his mind entirely about baseball, and he would become Sandy's biggest fan (Irving also negotiated Sandy's first contract with the Dodgers).

Sandy liked baseball, yes, but basketball was really Koufax's game. He was, by reports, a basketball prodigy with a great jump shot and leaping skills that made him an unstoppable rebounder. He didn't want to go out for the high school baseball team and when he was talked into playing, he didn't even pitch. He played first base.*

Koufax committed to play basketball at the University of Cincinnati and played for the freshman basketball team in 1954. The University of Cincinnati was a magnet for sports legends in those days. There was Koufax playing for the basketball team. There was the No. 1 tennis player in the world, Tony Trabert, playing for the tennis team. And two years later, a certain player named Oscar Robertson joined the basketball team.

In any case, Koufax loved basketball but he could not keep his left arm hidden for long. He was coaxed into joining the Cincinnati baseball team and though he was impossibly wild, he threw so hard that scouts salivated. The Yankees were so serious about him that they sent two scouts to see him and, when Koufax balked at their low offer, they sent a third scout to talk the family into signing. The third scout was Jewish. The Koufaxes were so insulted by what they saw as the Yankees' condescension that they never forgot.

When it came down to it, the Pirates and the Braves offered the most money—the Braves offered a lot more money than anyone else. But by the time those offers came in, the Koufaxes already had agreed on a handshake deal with Brooklyn Dodgers GM Buzzie Bavasi. And though the two men would later clash, Bavasi never forgot how Sandy Koufax refused to renege when more money was offered.

The Dodgers gave Koufax a $14,000 signing bonus—this made Koufax what was then called a "bonus baby." The owners had agreed that if a team gave any amateur player more than $6,000, they could not send the player to the minor leagues. The rule was supposedly put in place to prevent the richest teams from buying all the best players, but it was probably more about discouraging big-money deals in the first place.

Whatever the reason, Koufax never pitched a day in the minor leagues. Did that hurt him? Help him? Would his career have been different—

---

* It's funny to think that on the Lafayette High School baseball team, you had Koufax at first base and a different left-handed pitcher on the mound, a guy named Fred Wilpon. Yes. That Fred Wilpon, now the former Mets owner.

better or worse—if he had been carefully developed through the minors? It's like so much of Koufax's career: We'll never really know. Koufax spent six years pitching part-time in the big leagues, trying to find control for that legendary fastball, honing what would become his devastating curveball, striking out everybody, walking everybody, and, yes, dealing with some of the arm troubles that would haunt and prematurely finish his baseball career.

Then, three rather incredible and unprecedented things happened, pretty much all at once, and all of them benefited a still raw but developing Sandy Koufax.

1. In 1962, the Dodgers moved out of Los Angeles Memorial Coliseum (which had proven to be a big hitters' park) and into Dodger Stadium, which would become one of the great pitcher parks in baseball history.

2. In 1963, in a move that almost nobody noticed, the baseball rules committee redefined the strike zone. The big talk before the 1963 baseball season will probably sound familiar: People complained that the games were too long and that umpires were not calling the strike zone properly. "The umpires have become such prima donnas," Bill Veeck wrote in a widely distributed and influential column, "that they rewrite the rules."

   In response, the rules committee changed the strike zone so that it went "from the batter's knees to the top of his shoulders." This rule unintentionally both raised the strike zone (the rule had been to the armpit) and lowered the strike zone (the rule had been the top of the knee and now it was just the knee).

   The rules committee had no idea that they had just ushered in a second Deadball era.

3. The Dodgers, more than any other team, realized that the existing rule limiting the height of the pitcher's mound to 15 inches was not being enforced. And when baseball rules are not enforced, as we have seen again and again through history, they are flaunted. The Dodgers built up the highest mounds in baseball.

Would Koufax have become a great pitcher without all these things happening at once? Certainly. He was beginning to show his great promise in 1961, before any of that happened. He led the league in strikeouts that year. He was unquestionably on his way to becoming a terrific pitcher.

But there is no question that the perfect storm of events helped turn Koufax into a superhero.

From 1963 to 1966—in cozy Dodger Stadium, with a massive strike zone to work with, pitching high off Mound Olympus—Koufax was as great as any pitcher had ever been. He won three pitching triple crowns in four years, leading the league in wins, ERA, and strikeouts in 1963, 1965, and 1966. He threw a no-hitter each year. His ERA overall for those four years was an astonishing 1.86.

At Dodger Stadium he went 50-11 with a 1.31 ERA and 21 shutouts in just those four seasons.

Unforgettable. That's what he was. He and Don Drysdale carried the Dodgers to three World Series in those four years, and Koufax was, of course, breathtaking in those games. In '63, a Dodgers sweep over the Yankees, Koufax won Game 1 at Yankee Stadium with a complete game. He won the last at home, outdueling Whitey Ford, allowing just one run on a homer to Mickey Mantle. Koufax was named Series MVP.

In the '65 World Series, he was better. That was the year he skipped Game 1 because it fell on Yom Kippur. He promptly lost Game 2, getting beaten by a brilliant pitching performance from Minnesota's Jim Kaat. The series seemed lost for the Dodgers. But in Game 5, Koufax threw a four-hit shutout, striking out 10. And three days later, in Game 7, he threw a three-hit shutout, again striking out 10.

"If I could have any pitcher in baseball history start for me in a Game 7," Sparky Anderson said, "it would be Koufax."

Koufax famously—or infamously—pitched through agonizing pain. His hand, his wrist, his index finger, his elbow, his shoulder, none of these worked quite right. The big issue was his arthritic elbow, which might not even have been a baseball injury; it was probably caused by a basketball fall he had in high school. He had special balms rubbed on his elbow. He took a pill called phenylbutazone alka to bring down the inflammation—it's not a steroid but it is no longer considered safe to use. Mostly, he simply gritted his teeth and pitched through the pain.

And after the 1966 season, at age 30, he retired because of it.

"I've had too many shots and taken too many pills," he told reporters gathered at the Beverly Wilshire hotel. "The decision was based partly on medical advice and partly on my own feeling. . . . I don't want to take a chance of completely disabling myself."

That year, 1966, was an extraordinary one for young retirements. NFL superstar Jim Brown retired in July, also at the age of 30. Two legends: gone. Many people thought they would both be back. Neither ever came back.

There was some skepticism about Koufax's reasons for retiring. Yes, everybody knew about his arm pain—KOUFAX QUITS BECAUSE OF AILING ARM was splashed across the top of the *Los Angeles Times*—and through the years there had been countless stories about his injuries, countless photos in the newspapers of Koufax dipping that elbow in giant buckets of ice water. But, many people believed that there was more behind his retirement than mere pain.

There was good reason to believe that. Before his 1966 season, Koufax and Drysdale attempted one of the boldest negotiating moves in baseball history—they negotiated together and demanded three-year deals or they would both sit out. It was a bitter fight, one they were destined to lose. And once they did lose, there was definite bitterness about it all.

Many people thought Koufax was mad at the Dodgers. They thought he was holding out for more money. They just couldn't believe that he was calling it quits. The division was so wide that Koufax refused to delay his announcement until after owner Walter O'Malley and the team returned from an exhibition tour in Japan. And when Koufax refused to delay, Bavasi refused to come to the press conference.

"He said he'd made up his mind to announce it right away," Bavasi told the press. "Then I said I could have no part of it. I wished him luck."

Yes, it was a little bit ugly. What the Dodgers didn't know—as Jane Leavy explained in her wonderful book *Sandy Koufax: A Lefty's Legacy*—was that Koufax had been planning to retire for more than a year. Fourteen months earlier, Koufax had told his friend, *San Diego Union* beat writer Phil Collier, that 1966 would be his last season. And he was so eager to retire that he didn't want to wait at all; he wanted to announce it on the plane ride back to Los Angeles after the Dodgers lost the World Series. Collier talked him out of it and broke the story two weeks later.

So was it arm pain that pushed Koufax into retirement? Yes, certainly, but it was more than that. Koufax, in his autobiography, talked plainly and openly about the true purpose of being a ballplayer. "It's a temporary life, really," he wrote, "a period between the time of our youth and the beginning of our lifetime career."

He never said so, but it seems that Koufax was ready to end his youth. Many of his closest friends theorized that, even beyond the pain, he'd simply reached the moment when it was time to move on and live a more normal life. He'd been a great pitcher. He'd won the championships. He'd struck out the world. And it was time to try something else.

In the end, Koufax became an even greater legend by leaving. We never saw his decline. We never saw his fastball after it had lost its hop or his curveball hung for hitters to pound. In the imagination, Sandy Koufax stays young forever.

In 1967, Bavasi wrote an odd and bitter piece in *Sports Illustrated* about Koufax. He said a few nice things about Koufax, particularly about his pitching, but the article was mostly a chance for Bavasi to air his grievances about the Koufax-Drysdale holdout battle; Bavasi couldn't let go. He wanted to make it clear that he had not lost to Koufax. He wanted to scold Koufax for making him look "like some sort of southern plantation owner dealing with one of his slaves."

And he just wouldn't stop at the negotiations. Bavasi attacked the very idea that Koufax had really been in all that much pain.

"Sandy did not suffer agonizing pain while he was pitching, and he never said he did, either," Bavasi wrote. "I think Roberto Clemente was on the right track when he said, 'All I know about Sandy's arthritis is that it must come after the game is over. Nobody could pitch the way Koufax does with something bothering him.' "

Bavasi believed that the media played up the injury angle to absurdity ("A real sob story," he mocked). He said that Koufax's own doctor not only told him he could still pitch but advised Koufax to pitch another year. "I don't want to pitch anymore," Bavasi quoted Koufax saying to his doctor.

Bavasi also griped about the way Koufax retired, saying that he had rushed to do it because he had already leaked it to the papers. "The finest pitcher the game had ever known wound up announcing his retirement in a hotel room with his lawyer by his side and not a Dodger to be seen," Bavasi wrote. "I felt rotten about it."

It was not a particularly generous display from the man who first shook Irving and Sandy Koufax's hands more than a decade earlier. But there's something in there that I think carries on, even if it has come to mean something different from what Bavasi meant. He wrote:

> You can learn a lot about the problems of journalism by studying the printed record of the life of Sandy Koufax. As far as I am concerned, nobody since Rudolph Valentino ever had as many myths, legends and pure balderdash written about him as Sandy.

In context, Bavasi was bashing the press for making Koufax more legendary than he was, by making Koufax sound more colorful than he was, by playing up his heroics beyond their reality, by martyring him for the pain he suffered, by turning his fastballs into thunderbolts and calling his pitching arm "the left arm of God."

But, looking back, Bavasi—whether he meant to or not—was saying something more and something lasting. Koufax was a brilliant pitcher and Koufax was a man who had the game bend to his wishes and Koufax was a legend and Koufax was a meteor that streaked across the sky before burning out and Koufax is a touchstone that baseball fans hold on to even now.

You can never separate all that. And why would you want to? Baseball wouldn't be the same without Sandy Koufax, the man, the myth, the legend, and the balderdash.

No. 69 Monte Irvin

"Sometimes," Monte Irvin said, "I think: 'Nobody saw me when I could really play.'... I've tried not to think about it. But sometimes you can't help it."

We were sitting on a bench outside a ballpark in San Diego when he said that—Monte Irvin, Buck O'Neil, and me. The day was perfect, as San Diego days tend to be, and the sky was bright and blue. The afternoon glowed. I listened as two men who spent their youth playing baseball in the Negro Leagues talked about what it meant to them.

The part that stands out was how tenderly Buck looked at his old friend as he talked about the bitterness that he could never quite leave behind.

Buck had defeated the bitterness. He had turned the pain of his life into joy. He called his book *I Was Right on Time*, and he believed it, too, believed that he played at exactly the right time, believed that the life he spent playing baseball in the Negro Leagues, managing in the Negro Leagues, celebrating the Negro Leagues, well, it was the best life he could have lived. When people asked him how hard it was to have to stay at blacks-only hotels, he talked about how the food was better there. When people asked him how sad he was that he didn't get to face Bob Feller and play with Joe DiMaggio, he talked about how he did get to face Satchel Paige and play with Josh Gibson.

When people said it must have been hard to play in the shadows, Buck shook his head no and talked about how they played in the sunlight.

"The people I feel sorry for," he often said, "were the ones who didn't see us play."

This was Buck O'Neil's great gift. He was a miracle. He let go of the bitterness.

Monte Irvin, try as he did, found it much harder to let go.

"Well," Buck said, "it's easy for me. I wasn't half the ballplayer Monte was."

To understand Monte Irvin, we must work backward. Whenever you hear someone question the extraordinary talent hidden in the Negro Leagues, give them this useful little time line.

—In 1959, Bob Gibson came to the big leagues. That was the year the Boston Red Sox became the last team in baseball to integrate. In his career, Bob Gibson won two Cy Young Awards and an MVP, and he set the modern record with a 1.12 ERA in 1968.

Two other Hall of Famers—Willie McCovey and Billy Williams—entered MLB that year, too. They too would have played in the Negro Leagues had they come along a dozen years earlier.

—In 1958, Orlando Cepeda debuted at age 20. He won the Rookie of the Year Award by hitting .312 and leading the league in doubles. He led the league in homers in '61, twice led the league in RBIs, and won an MVP award. Baby Bull was elected to the Hall of Fame.

—In 1957, John Roseboro came up to Brooklyn. He was one of the first full-time black catchers in the game and he would make four All-Star teams, win a couple of Gold Gloves. He was behind the plate catching the very best of Sandy Koufax and Don Drysdale.

—In 1956, Frank Robinson debuted. He won two MVP awards and a Triple Crown. He was one of the greatest hitters and most forceful personalities ever to play in the major leagues.

—In 1955, Roberto Clemente debuted. He won four batting titles, 12 Gold Gloves, one MVP, and finished with exactly 3,000 hits. You cannot tell the story of baseball without him. Elston Howard became the first black player for the New York Yankees this year, and he also won an MVP award in his career.

—In 1954, Henry Aaron debuted. No more needs to be said.

—In 1953, Ernie Banks debuted. He undoubtedly wished he could have played two that day.

—In 1952, a whirlwind pitcher named Joe Black entered the league. Nobody had seen anything quite like him. He was tough and thoughtful and brilliant and he won 15 games and saved 15 more (though this was before the save was a statistic) and won the Rookie of the Year Award. He almost won the MVP, too. The writer Roger Kahn called Joe Black in '52 the most ferocious pitcher he ever saw.

—In 1951, Willie Mays debuted. Again, nothing more needs to be said.

—In 1950, there were few black players signed—almost every team was reluctant to integrate. But Sam "the Jet" Jethroe finally made it. He was 33, and his legs were shot. It was said that in his prime, the Jet could outrun the word of God. As it was, Jethroe led the league in stolen bases in each of his first two seasons (along with hitting 18 home runs each year) and won the Rookie of the Year Award.

—In 1949, Minnie Miñoso debuted. He led the league in triples three times, stolen bases three times, won three Gold Gloves even though the award wasn't invented until he was in his 30s, and he finished with a career 130 OPS+. Don Newcombe also debuted that year, and he won the first Cy Young Award, along with the MVP.

—In 1948, Roy Campanella debuted. He won three MVP awards and is in the Hall of Fame.

—And in 1947, of course, Jackie Robinson and Larry Doby debuted.

Look at that list—and remember I've only chosen the all-timers—and think about how every single one of those players, every last one, would have played in the Negro Leagues had he been born just a few years earlier. This is something that is both obvious and hidden; if any of them had played their careers in the Negro Leagues, their legacies would not be 755 home runs or a whirling over-the-shoulder World Series catch or throws from right field that boggle the mind or a pitching motion so violent and wonderful that each time you think the arm will go with the ball. No, for many people, Aaron, Mays, Clemente, Gibson, all of them, would have become stories, legends, nicknames, and impossible-to-believe tales.

This is the part that I think so many miss about the greatest Negro Leagues players. People tend to talk about them as if there is some doubt about their greatness. There is no doubt. I just pointed to one or more great African-American and dark-skinned Latino players coming into the league *every single year* after Jackie Robinson crossed the line, even in those years when most major-league teams refused to sign a black player. And it's not like you have to stop there. In 1960, it's Juan Marichal. In 1961, it's Lou Brock. In 1962, it's Willie Stargell. In 1963, it's Joe Morgan.

So what happens when you count backward? It's the same story.

Now we count backward for Monte Irvin.

You might know that former baseball commissioner Bowie Kuhn was not in Atlanta on the day that Henry Aaron hit his record-breaking 715th home run in 1974. It was one of countless blunders Kuhn made in his time as commissioner. He chose instead to be in Cleveland so he could attend a dinner at the stadium club. As it turned out, he didn't even attend a baseball game; the Brewers-Tribe game was snowed out.

Kuhn's explanation, if you want to call it that, was that he'd already been in Cincinnati to see Aaron's record-tying 714th home run—I mean, how many record-shattering home runs can you expect one man to watch? And his explanation was ridiculous on its face because he wasn't there to see Aaron. The game in Cincinnati was baseball's official Opening Day. Commissioners *always* attended Opening Day.

Just a quick reminder that Bowie Kuhn was somehow elected to the Hall of Fame. He might not be the least qualified person in there—but he's definitely in the photograph.

Anyway, Kuhn sent Monte Irvin to Atlanta in his place. Irvin was working in public relations for the commissioner's office at the time. He was given an impossible task. Irvin got to the stadium late because of flight problems, and then after the home run was hit, Irvin was given the microphone so he could present Aaron with a special watch.

"In the name of the commissioner," he began, and then the boos cascaded down on him, the loudest boos you've ever heard, boos so deep and intense and heartfelt that they drowned out anything else he said. Everyone turned to Henry Aaron to see how he was reacting, and he smiled just a little bit at the boos, and that somehow made them even louder and more penetrating.

Irvin knew the boos were not for him. He had not even been sent by Kuhn himself; Kuhn was so clueless about the situation that he never planned to have any baseball presence at all in Atlanta. An old baseball writer named Joe Reichler, who worked in the commissioner's office, asked Irvin at the last minute. So Irvin knew they were really booing Kuhn. Maybe he felt some of that outrage himself.

But he also knew that Bowie Kuhn didn't receive those boos. Monte Irvin did.

And those people booing had absolutely no idea about the man at the center of it all.

In 1951, Monte Irvin was 32 years old, and he felt like half the man he used to be. He'd been playing some kind of pro ball since he was 18. He had been to war. He'd badly hurt his knee. He'd endured so many humiliations for the color of his skin. He was playing first base and left field because that was all his body had left. He had once played center field like a dream.

Still, even then, he could really hit. He was at the center of the New York Giants' hopes. "It's up to me," he said. "We can win if I can hit."

And he did hit. He hit .312/.415/.514 for the season. He led the National League in RBIs. He had double-digit doubles, triples, home runs, and stolen bases. The only other players to do that in 1951 were Jethroe and Miñoso—both of whom had played with Irvin in the Negro Leagues. Leo Durocher called Irvin the most valuable player in baseball.

He did not win the MVP award—that went to Brooklyn's Roy Campanella instead, even though that was the year the Giants beat the Dodgers in their famous three-game playoffs that ended with Russ Hodges screaming "The Giants win the pennant!" over and over again. When asked about winning the award, Campy could not stop talking about his friend Irvin.

"Monte was the best all-around player I have ever seen," Campy said. "As great as he was in 1951, he was twice that good 10 years earlier in the Negro Leagues."

How good was Irvin's age-32 season? Well, it's an imprecise thing to work backward as we are, but let's put up a few age-32 seasons:

Monte Irvin: .312/.415/.514, 24 homers, 94 runs, 121 RBIs, 147 OPS+

Henry Aaron: .279/.356/.539, 44 homers, 117 runs, 127 RBIs, 142 OPS+

Ryne Sandberg: .304/.371/.510, 26 homers, 100 runs, 87 RBIs, 145 OPS+

Kirby Puckett: .329/.374/.490, 19 homers, 104 runs, 110 RBIs, 139 OPS+

Al Kaline: .308/.411/.541, 25 homers, 94 runs, 78 RBIs, 176 OPS+

The Negro Leagues stats are incomplete. Even the stats we have are uncertain because the Negro Leagues were scattered, jumbled, league games and town games and exhibition games all swirling together. Irvin probably hit around .400 in 1940 and 1941. He spent most of 1942 playing in the Mexican League, where, best anyone can tell, he hit .397 with 20 homers in just 63 games. And he was a breathtaking baserunner, a breathtaking center fielder—he was particularly noted for his arm. "I had an arm better than anybody," he said.

Irvin used to say to Willie Mays, in a joking and serious way, "You remind me of me."

Irvin longed only to return to Mexico for baseball in 1943, but despite a bad knee and a family to support, he was drafted and was placed in a unit of black engineers who went to England, France, and Belgium.

When he returned, he was approached by Dodgers scout Clyde Sukeforth. Irvin said Sukeforth made him an offer to become the first black player in the major leagues. It made sense: In 1942, in a survey of Negro Leagues owners, Irvin was the runaway choice as the right player to break the color line in the major leagues.

"Monte Irvin should have been the first black in the major leagues," Cool Papa Bell later said. "He could hit that long ball. He had a great arm. He could field. He could run. Yes, he could do everything."

But upon returning from the war, Irvin declined the Dodgers' offer.

There has been much speculation about it. Some believed that Newark Eagles owner Effa Manley refused to let Irvin go without compensation from the Dodgers, and Branch Rickey was not about to pay for a Negro Leagues player. This is one shameful part of Rickey's otherwise noble pursuit: He refused to pay any money to the Kansas City Monarchs for the rights to Jackie Robinson.

Irvin himself said he didn't sign with the Dodgers because he simply wasn't ready to be the first. The war had been too hard on him.

"I had been a .400 hitter before the war," Irvin told author Peter Golenbock. "I had lost three prime years. I hadn't played at all. The war had changed me."

Monte Irvin was such an athletic phenom at East Orange High School in New Jersey in the late 1930s—football, basketball, baseball, track, anything you could imagine—that his teacher wrote to New York Giants owner Horace Stoneham and said: "We've got a player here you would not even believe."

Stoneham sent two scouts to watch Irvin play, though there wasn't really any point to it. Stoneham was somewhat idealistic, but he was entirely ineffective. He may have had some private thoughts about the unfairness of segregation, but he was not going to be the first owner to sign a black player.

Still, he wanted to know just how good Irvin was. Many years later, a much older Irvin played for the Giants, and he asked Stoneham: "What did they say about me?"

"They told me," Stoneham reported with real sadness in voice, "that you were the next Joe DiMaggio."

Back on that park bench in San Diego more than a half century later, Buck O'Neil stayed silent and listened as his friend talked about the pain.

"Why did they think we could not play?" Irvin asked. "That's always been my question when I think back to the Negro Leagues. The ball was the same size. The bats weighed the same. The fields were no smaller. Why did they think we could not play?"

No. 68 Gaylord Perry

Gaylord Perry cheated. He did not hide that fact—well, check that, he did actually hide it, but then he didn't, and then he did again; that was his game. But anyway, he did not run from it. He titled his autobiography *Me and the Spitter: An Autobiographical Confession*. In it, he talks at length about cheating and begins with the day he said changed his life, the day he decided to live his life as a baseball outlaw.

That day was May 31, 1964. It was the second game of a pretty meaningless doubleheader against the abysmal Mets. But it wasn't meaningless at all for Perry. His career was in the balance that day. He had to make a choice.

And he made his choice.

Jim and Gaylord Perry (Jim was about three years older than his brother) grew up on the family farm in Williamston, a small town in the northeastern part of North Carolina. Sports meant everything to the Perrys, particularly Jim and Gaylord's father, Evan, who had been a fabulous athlete as a young man. Evan had not been given the chance to chase his athletic dreams because there were fields to be plowed and a big family to support.

Evan was not going to let the same fate fall on his two boys. They played ball in the cow pasture every day. And they played with purpose. Them Perry boys were going to play big-league ball.

"All them Perry boys want to do is play baseball," a neighbor once said. "And their dad is even worse."

Among the many charming stories Gaylord Perry tells about his childhood is one about how, just before his first day of high school, his father took him to the store to get him everything he would need to make it in school and in life. The Perrys didn't have much money, so the shopping trip was a big deal. Evan took his son to the general store. They walked past the school clothes. They walked past the school bags. They never even considered looking at any books. They walked directly to the sporting goods section, where Evan picked out a new baseball glove for his son.

Then he took Gaylord past the work boots and past the everyday shoes and picked out a pair of new football cleats.

And then they paid and left. That was it. That was high school shopping. Evan Perry raised both of his sons on the belief that if they worked hard enough, they could be ballplayers. And there wasn't anything bigger than that.

Jim was first. He was the biggest thing in Williamston—an all-state center, a brilliant pitcher, he would have been the team's star quarterback, too, except he gave up football so he could focus on his pitching. He was an advanced pitcher, too; Gaylord insisted that his brother walked just one batter his entire sophomore season.

Then came Gaylord.* He was the kid brother, but he was about as gifted as Jim. As a basketball star, he averaged 30 points and 20 rebounds a game. As a pitcher, he threw even harder than Jim. They played on the same high school team for one year, and that year Jim and Gaylord combined for eight shutouts in the state tournament and led Williamston High to the state title.

---

* The connection between Gaylord and Jim Perry would stay strong—eerily strong. On September 21, 1975, Gaylord Perry beat the White Sox by throwing a complete game and allowing two runs. That made his career record 215-174. And that exact moment, Jim Perry's career record was—impossible as this is to believe—215-174. Freakish, right? Unfortunately, it didn't last. Jim's career had ended a couple of weeks earlier, so that's where his numbers stopped. Gaylord pitched for another eight seasons, winning 99 more games (and losing 91) to finish at 314-265.

Jim went to Campbell University out of high school and then signed with Cleveland. Gaylord didn't stop for college. He signed with the Giants right out of high school for one of the biggest deals ever given a high school pitcher. The papers reported the deal being close to $100,000, but Gaylord always said it was more like $75,000.

He gave half of his signing bonus to his parents. Gaylord always remembered giving his father the money, and Evan Perry being so overwhelmed that he teared up and blew his nose and, in Gaylord's words, "it sounded like a boat whistle on the Roanoke River."

OK, let's get back to that pivotal day when Perry decided to become an outlaw, May 31, 1964. It was six years after he signed with the Giants, and things were not going too well. Jim had become a star with Cleveland; he led the league in wins and shutouts in 1960 and made the All-Star team in 1961. The Twins then traded for him, and Jim Perry would help lead Minnesota to the 1965 pennant.

Gaylord? Nobody could figure him out. He had good enough stuff. He was competitive. People liked him. He dominated at times in the minor leagues. But something just wasn't quite clicking for him in the majors.

"Gaylord Perry remains an enigma to the San Francisco Giants as he gets what could be his last chance with the National League Club," the Associated Press wrote about him during 1964 spring training. The team was losing patience. In his first two seasons, he'd managed just 11 starts and a few more games in relief, and he was already 25 years old. Time was running short. As the 1964 season began, he was put in the bullpen, where he was good some days, not good on others. The Giants finally gave him a start in early May, and he gave up seven runs in seven innings.

"He just wasn't sharp," his manager, Alvin Dark, said.

It was unclear at that moment if the Giants would ever give him another chance to start a game. And then, destiny called.

Perry pitched well in a relief appearance, and then came the pivotal day. It was at Shea Stadium and more than 57,000 people were in the stands to see it, even though the Mets were in last place at the time. Perry was at the very bottom of the list of pitchers Alvin Dark wanted to use, particularly after the Giants took a 6–1 lead in the second game. But the Mets somehow came back to tie the score. It went into extra innings. And it kept going.

And finally, in the 13th inning, the fateful call went to Perry.

He almost blew the game right away. He gave up back-to-back singles to Amado Samuel and Roy McMillan, which should have set up the Mets nicely. But Giants outfielder Jesús Alou made a fantastic throw to get Samuel at third base.

Then in the 15th, Perry gave up a leadoff single and a sacrifice bunt, and things looked bleak. Radio announcer Russ Hodges said, "Gaylord looks like the grim undertaker there on the mound." And that's when exhausted Giants catcher Tommy Haller walked out to the mound and said the words that would change everything: "Gaylord," Haller said, "it's time to try it out."

They both knew exactly what Haller meant.

It was time for Perry to throw the spitball.

He'd thrown it a couple of times in games before, more as a lark than anything else. Haller had seen how devastating a pitch it was, how it dropped like a boulder being pushed over the edge of a cliff in a Road Runner–Coyote cartoon, how batters could not make solid contact with it, how sweet those double-play ground balls looked coming off the bat.

On the downside, the spitball was illegal and had been for almost 50 years.

"Was I ready to be an outlaw?" Perry asked.

"You know all that stuff about desperate times and desperate measures," Perry answered.

And so he began. He got his first spitball double play when Galen Cisco bounced a ball right back to him. That ended the inning and the threat. The game went on and on and on and Perry kept on drenching the baseball and kept on getting double plays until the Giants finally scored in the 23rd inning. In all, he pitched 10 scoreless innings, striking out nine, forcing three double plays. He'd seen the future. And the future was wet.

The rest of that season, he had a 2.57 ERA and the league hit .229 against him. In 1966, he won 20 games for the first of five times. He became the first pitcher to win Cy Young Awards in each league. He set an American League record by winning 15 games in a row. He won more than 300 games. He passed Walter Johnson's all-time strikeout record (though Nolan Ryan and Steve Carlton got there weeks earlier). Etc. Etc.

All the while, Gaylord Perry threw spitballs.

Or maybe he didn't.

That was for umpires to figure out.

Perry would be elected to the Hall of Fame in his third year of eligibility.

In 1971, Perry started Game 1 of the National League Championship Series against Pittsburgh. He ended up throwing a complete game and winning—probably but not definitely by loading up on a whole bunch of spitballs. There were a few stories that postseason about Perry and the spitball, with one of his unidentified teammates saying that he didn't throw it much by then.

"Only when he's in trouble," the teammate said.

Anyway, after the game, a reporter thought it would be cute to ask Gaylord's five-year-old daughter, Allison, if her father threw a spitball. Allison did not even blink.

"It's a hard slider," she said.

Later, Allison went up to a writer and said, "I know where he hides the stuff."

"Where?" the writer asked.

"In his garage," she said.

The best I can tell, sports fans hate some cheaters and love others, and I think it comes down to style. Barry Bonds, whatever else you want to say about him, did not charm. Roger Clemens, whatever else you want to say about him, did not charm.

Perry charmed. He made everybody laugh. He did it all with a wink and a nudge and a slap on the back. He touched his hat, his shoulder, back to his hat, his chest, as if he was going for the Vaseline, going for the spit, going for the tobacco juice, and there was no way to know if he was or wasn't. Umpires constantly checked on him, but Perry had turned the story around. In his story, the umpires were the bad guys, they were the federal agents trying to catch Junior Johnson moonshining.

Perry was a rogue. Bonds was a villain.

Perry is Han Solo. Clemens is Darth Vader.

Yes, of course, it's a different kind of cheating—but, more, it's a matter of style.

My favorite Perry pitch was not actually the spitball, it was something he called the "puffball." He would so load up on the resin bag (Perry apparently would sometimes put flour in the bag instead of resin) that when he threw the pitch, a big cloud of resin would explode so you could not even see the ball. It looked like a spaceship coming out of light speed. It was ridiculous and funny, but also quite effective. The puffball was outlawed in 1981 because of Perry.

Did Perry ever *fully* admit to cheating? Yes. Also, no. At some point, he came to appreciate that people didn't really want to know, that his story was so much better as a mystery and a legend. He did what he had to do to survive, to win games, to get another team to sign him. He was that lovable bandit who kept himself one step ahead of the law. Perry threw greaseballs and puffballs and doctored balls, sure, but he also didn't throw them, he just pretended to throw them, and that worked, too.

He also did a whole lot of baseball things well. He developed impeccable control. Players couldn't steal a base off him. He fielded his position. He found new ways to get batters out the second, third, fourth, and fifth time through the lineup—he completed more than 300 games in his career. He got sure outs, he coaxed double plays, he disrupted timing, and he fooled umpires and hitters for two decades.

In his autobiography, Perry admitted throwing spitballs. But then he said—the book came out in 1974—that he had stopped throwing them. And then he said that, well, maybe he didn't stop.

And he ended it all by saying that maybe he never threw the spitter at all.

"Do I still wet them?" he asked the reader. "I sure know how. But that doesn't mean I do it—or even that I ever did it. Maybe I'm just kidding. Maybe I got the Mets out in 1964 on sheer talent."

No. 67 **Hank Greenberg**

The trouble with retelling history is that it's hard to fully capture the times and the stakes and the danger. This is true of wars and discoveries and the rise and fall of empires. It's true in the biggest moments of sports history, too. Jackie Robinson's story, for instance, has become familiar to the point of predictable, as if it was fated that a Black man would break baseball's color barrier, overcome the threats and intense pressures, and prove what we knew was true all along about equality. The more the story is told, paradoxically, the more familiar it becomes, and the harder it is to fully consider what baseball and America would have been like in the very real possibility that Robinson had failed.

Between 1900 and 1924, with anti-Semitism spiking all around the world, more than two million Jewish immigrants poured into America in the hopes of finding a better life. This led to an ugly American backlash. Immigration was slashed. The Ku Klux Klan reemerged after many dormant years and focused some of their terrorism on Jews. Henry Ford published numerous anti-Semitic screeds. Father Charles Coughlin blamed Jewish people for purposely causing the Depression on his weekly radio show, which was listened to by millions of people. Charles Lindbergh— who after flying across the Atlantic had become the most famous and beloved man in America—spoke out against what he called subversive Jewish influence.

Around this time, in a national poll, more than half of America agreed with the statement that "Jews are different and should be restricted."

It was against this backdrop that Hank Greenberg began to play Major League Baseball.

Henry Greenberg was an awkward young man. He looked off-balance when he ran. He had a robotic stiffness. John McGraw saw Greenberg play around this time and immediately and unconditionally deemed him too big and clumsy for big-league ball. It was a terrible blow to Greenberg for a couple of reasons. One, Greenberg had wanted, more than anything, to play for his hometown Giants—his father, David, a casual Giants fan, had personally asked McGraw to give his son a tryout—and two, McGraw had made quite a show in the papers about wanting to sign a Jewish ballplayer.

"I would give $100,000 for a Jewish player who had even the prospect of being a real star," he told the *New York World*.

If McGraw had no interest in signing Greenberg (or, indeed, even letting him shag fly balls at the Polo Grounds as Greenberg once requested), what chance did he have out there in the rest of the world?

What McGraw couldn't see—or wouldn't see—was that Greenberg was going to become a big-league ballplayer no matter what limitations he might have been burdened with. He hit until his hands bled. He played pepper for as much as eight hours a day to develop his nimbleness and hand-eye coordination. He exercised obsessively. He squeezed a rubber ball at all times to strengthen his forearms. He jumped rope to strengthen his flat feet. He did track and field explosion exercises to help him get a faster break out of the batter's box.

He did all this with a seriousness that astounded and baffled those around him. "Hank never played the games," his high school basketball coach Irwin Dickstein said. "He worked them."

Greenberg's family did not understand why their ultra-serious son was dedicating so much of his time and energy to something as foolish as baseball. His mother and father had emigrated separately from Romania, and they raised Henry (mostly known as "Hymie" as a child) in an Orthodox house where Yiddish was the language. His father, David, had worked his way up from a textile worker to the owner of the factory, and, unlike many of the fathers in this book, he liked baseball. He liked the Giants. But he also did not see baseball as a viable career path for a Jewish boy in America. Hank fully expected that he would end up going into his father's business.

But Greenberg still worked at baseball with the earnestness and determination that would mark his career.

By 1933 there had been Jewish baseball players in the majors, but there had never been a Jewish baseball star. In truth, there had never been a Jewish-American sports superstar at all, other than some Jewish boxers such as Benny Leonard and Battling Levinsky, who had become world champions. The early days of basketball were dominated by Jewish and African-American players, but the sport was mostly unknown then. Baseball was everything in those days.

The only time anyone seemed to talk about Jews and baseball when Greenberg made it to the big leagues was when referring to the gangster Arnold Rothstein's role in fixing the 1919 World Series.

Greenberg was a sought-after prospect. McGraw didn't see it, but the Yankees did. Paul Krichell, the Yankees' scout, went after him hard even though the Yankees already had a pretty decent first baseman named Lou Gehrig. At a game together, Greenberg recalled Krichell leaning over to him as Gehrig stepped to the plate: "He's all washed up," Krichell said. "In a few years, you'll be the Yankees' first baseman."

But Hank Greenberg was nobody's fool.

"That Lou Gehrig looks like he has a lot of years left," Greenberg responded, and he signed with the Detroit Tigers instead. At 21, while playing in Beaumont, Texas, along with an old neighbor and high school buddy Izzy Goldstein, he hit 39 home runs; the next year he was playing for Detroit and hit .301 with moderate power.

Greenberg made his first big mark the next year when he led the league with 63 doubles and helped the Tigers become pennant contenders. He was thrust into the national spotlight; in later years, Greenberg would often say that he would have preferred to stay quiet and unknown, keep his Jewishness to himself, but that wasn't an option for someone as proud and serious and brilliant as Greenberg.

Soon, his religion became front-page news.

The Tigers and Yankees were in the middle of a ferocious pennant race as the Jewish high holidays began in 1934. There was a swarming sense of desperation in Detroit. It had been a quarter century since the Tigers had won a pennant, and more than 20 since they even challenged for one. An opportunity like this felt impossibly rare, and the team was being led by a Jewish player, and now Greenberg talked about how he had promised his parents that he would sit out Rosh Hashanah, the Jewish New Year.

The outcry was enormous. The Tigers needed him! When Rosh Hashanah came around, the Tigers' lead was just four games, and the Yankees were already ubiquitous. Teammates and Tigers management implored Greenberg to play. Panicked fans sent in a flood of pleading letters. Rabbis were consulted. One rabbi was quoted in the *Detroit Free Press* suggesting that while Rosh Hashanah was a holy day, it was not clear that Greenberg needed to miss the game.

Suddenly, lots of Detroit baseball fans became Talmudic scholars desperately interested in debating the intricacies of Jewish customs.

Greenberg played on Rosh Hashanah. He did more than play. With the Tigers trailing by a run in the 7th inning, Greenberg stepped in against Boston's Gordon Rhodes and hit a game-tying home run. Then, in the ninth, with the score tied 1–1, Greenberg stepped in again and smashed a massive walk-off home run that one Detroit writer compared to a drive by the legendary golfer Bobby Jones. Greenberg was mobbed as he ran around the bases. Detroit fans happily shouted "Happy New Year!"

The moment was celebrated with some of the sappiest prose imaginable. A man named Bud Shaver wrote this for the *Detroit Times:* "The traditional tenacity of the world's oldest and most beleaguered people today had played its part in a pennant race.... They were propelled by a force of desperation and pride of a young Jew who turned his back on the ancient ways of his race and creed to help his teammates."

Nine days later came Yom Kippur, the Jewish day of atonement. And this time no rabbis needed to be asked. There are no outs for Yom Kippur. A Jewish person is supposed to spend the day fasting and reflecting and no circumstances can alter that.

And this time, Hank Greenberg sat out.

Sure, it didn't hurt that the circumstances were much different. The Tigers had built a 7½ game lead on the Yankees with 11 games to play, so they were almost assured of the pennant. Still, there was just as much written about Greenberg's absence on Yom Kippur as there was about his Rosh Hashanah heroics. The most famous of these was Edgar Guest's poem in the *Detroit Free Press*, "Speaking of Greenberg." It ended like so:

Came Yom Kippur—holy fast day worldwide over to the Jew
And Hank Greenberg to his teaching and the old tradition true
Spent the day among his people and he didn't come to play
Said Murphy to Mulrooney, "We shall lose the game today.
We shall miss him on the infield and shall miss him at the bat
But he's true to his religion—and I honor him for that."

People have argued ever since about Guest's intention—was he celebrating Greenberg's refusal to play, or sort of poking fun at it? Either way, I think we can all agree it's a lousy poem.

But that poem was reprinted in papers all over the country. It cemented Greenberg's fame, and it gave America something new to consider. In Henry Ford's city, in a time when many people were speaking out against what they called the seditious influence of Jewish bankers worldwide and Jewish decision makers in the FDR administration, Hank Greenberg became America's first Jewish sports star.

Greenberg was never entirely comfortable with his place as a Jewish hero, but there wasn't much he could do about it. The name-calling followed. The threats hounded him. He dealt with all of it quietly. And he always hit. In 1935, he led the league in homers (36) and RBIs (168) and won the MVP award.

After an injury-lost season, he came back in 1937 and 1938 and finished painfully close to two cherished records. In '37, he drove in 183 RBIs, one shy of Lou Gehrig's American League record. He never quite lived that one down; he was only three RBIs behind with two games to play, but he finished the season 1-for-7 with two RBIs and just missed.*

In 1938, Greenberg had a chance to break Babe Ruth's record of 60

---

* If you look at Greenberg's Baseball-Reference page, you will see he drove in 184 RBIs in 1937. Here's what happened: In 2012, a baseball historian named Herm Krabbenhoft discovered that when they counted his stats, they missed an RBI Greenberg had in the second game of a June 20 doubleheader. So you would think that Greenberg actually tied the record without knowing it; but as it turns out Krabbenhoft also found a missing RBI for Gehrig in 1931. So now, officially, Gehrig has the American League record with 185 RBIs, and Greenberg is second with 184.

homers. He had 58 home runs with five games to play. (Roger Maris had 59 homers with five games to play when he broke the record in 1961.) "I figured I'd get three more easily," he later wrote.

But Greenberg tensed up. He didn't hit a single homer in those final five games. There has long been a debate about whether his Jewishness—with the news of Nazi Germany growing bleaker by the day—played any role in his drought down the stretch. Breaking Babe Ruth's home run records took a toll on all the challengers through the years. Stress caused Maris to lose some of his hair down the stretch in 1961. Henry Aaron endured boxes and boxes of hate mail and racist threats as he chased Ruth's career homer record.

Greenberg, meanwhile, was trying to break Ruth's record just a month before Kristallnacht—the Night of Broken Glass—when Jewish businesses and synagogues were attacked in Germany and Austria and tens of thousands were sent to concentration camps. This is the moment many historians mark as the beginning of the Holocaust.

Greenberg publicly insisted—and would for the rest of his life—that he felt like most players supported his chase and he did not succumb to the pressure of the moment. But some friends and teammates insisted that he was overwhelmed by it all. Charlie Gehringer said that Greenberg wasn't sleeping at night. Another unnamed teammate said, "He walks up and down the dugout during batting practice telling everybody that he isn't worrying about it, isn't thinking about it. But he's thinking about it all the time."

Either way, he fell two homers short of the record. He would insist that he felt worse about missing Gehrig's record because he saw himself more as an RBI man than a home run hitter.

In 1939, Greenberg missed a few games with nagging injuries and so he *only* hit .312/.420/.622 with 111 runs and 113 RBIs. A down year. In 1940, he led the league in doubles, homers, RBIs, slugging, and OPS and won his second MVP award. He was 29 years old and at the height of his powers. He would miss parts or all of the next five seasons for World War II.

Greenberg was the first big baseball star to be drafted by the military; he was drafted several months *before* Pearl Harbor. At the time, baseball fans watched closely to see how players responded to the war. If they were less than gung ho about going to war, the fans and media hit hard. A news photographer showed up for Greenberg's military physical. "I should punch you in the nose," Greenberg said. He'd already received hate mail based on rumors that he had asked for a deferment (Greenberg always insisted that he did not).

At the physical, the doctor discovered that Greenberg had flat feet. This only made matters worse: One newspaper editor reportedly circled Greenberg's feet and scribbled "$25,000"—Greenberg's salary at the time—suggesting that Greenberg had bribed the doctor.

"I was the perfect patsy," Greenberg would write bitterly of that time. "Here the country was getting ready for a world war, and I was trying to duck the draft—it was right down the press' alley. They hounded me."

He entered the draft voluntarily and was ordered to report on May 7, 1941—one week before Joe DiMaggio's hitting streak began and seven months before Pearl Harbor. He thought he was making a one-year commitment. After Pearl Harbor, though, he reenlisted. He would miss the next four and a half years for World War II.

Greenberg was not the same player after the war. His body was beaten up. He had seen things that changed him. But in 1946, at age 35, he still managed to lead the league in homers and RBIs one more time. In all, he played seven seasons where he got 600 or more plate appearances. He led the league in doubles in two of them, homers in four of them, and RBIs in four of them. He won two MVP awards, finished third two other times, and received MVP consideration in all six.

The ending of his career, though, was unfortunate. On Greenberg's 36th birthday, a story appeared in the *Sporting News* claiming that Greenberg wanted to finish his career with his hometown Yankees. There was a photograph included of Greenberg holding up a Yankees uniform—an entirely unfair shot. The photo was taken in 1943, before Greenberg played in an exhibition game to raise money for the war effort, and the Yankees uniform was the only one available for the photo. Greenberg insisted that the story was entirely made up and he had no desire whatsoever to leave Detroit or play in New York.

None of these details mattered to Tigers owner Walter Briggs Jr. He was outraged. He didn't like Greenberg anyway; they had fought bitterly over salaries through the years. According to Greenberg, Briggs told his general manager: "We don't deserve that kind of treatment from a player to whom we've been overly generous. This is too much. Get rid of him!"

The Tigers got rid of him. It was reported that the Tigers sold Greenberg to the Pittsburgh Pirates, but technically, they waived him with the knowledge that no American League team would pick him up (if they tried, the Tigers sould simply pull him back from waivers). That meant that he would be available to the lowly Pirates of the National League; all it would cost them was the $10,000 waiver fee. Greenberg heard about it on the radio. Shortly afterward he got this cold telegram from Tigers GM Billy Evans:

THIS IS TO INFORM YOU THAT YOUR CONTRACT HAS BEEN ASSIGNED TO THE PITTSBURGH CLUB OF THE NATIONAL LEAGUE. TRUST YOU WILL FIND YOUR NEW CONNECTION A MOST PROFITABLE ONE.

Greenberg was stunned and hurt and very angry. "It just took the heart out of me," he would say. He promptly retired.

The Pirates were frantic. The acquiring of Greenberg was the first bit of good news for the franchise in two decades. Ticket sales had jumped. Pirates owner John Galbreath went to see Greenberg and pleaded with him to play one more season. What followed was one of the most extraordinary negotiations in baseball history.

Greenberg said that he liked the dimensions at Briggs Stadium. Galbreath said he would bring in the fences at Forbes Field to match them.

Greenberg said he was tired of riding trains and buses. Galbreath said he would fly Greenberg to road games.

Greenberg said he was too old and set in his ways to have a roommate. Galbreath said he would set it up for Greenberg to have his own suite on the road.

Greenberg asked for $100,000. Galbreath gave it to him, along with the opportunity to buy stock in the team (that Galbreath would buy back after the season). Greenberg's wife was given a racehorse. He was promised his unconditional release after one season. The Pirates were that desperate for their own star.

And you know what? It mostly worked out for both sides. Greenberg's body was shot and he could no longer hit like he had. Still, he led the league with 104 walks, posted a .408 on-base percentage, and cracked 25 home runs. That really wasn't too bad.

And he worked hard with a 24-year-old slugger named Ralph Kiner, who mashed 51 home runs that season.

And Pittsburgh's attendance almost doubled, even though the Pirates were no better than they had been the year before.

So, that was something. After the season, at age 37, Hank Greenberg retired.

Greenberg would continue a life in baseball, eventually becoming the general manager of the Cleveland Indians. His personality did not fit the job. He fired manager and Cleveland hero Lou Boudreau because of philosophical differences; feuded with Larry Doby, the first African American to play in the American League; and lost brilliant young shortstop Luis Aparicio over a few hundred dollars. Cleveland went from being one of the best franchises in baseball to one of the worst, and Greenberg played a significant role in that.

Greenberg also fell short of the Hall of Fame the first seven times he appeared on the ballot. It isn't entirely clear why he had to wait so long other than the fact that the writers, at that time, didn't seem eager to vote *anyone* into the Hall of Fame. In 1949, for instance, there were *fifty* players on the ballot who would eventually be elected into the Hall of Fame, including Greenberg. The writers as a group didn't vote for *any* of them. The same was true in 1950.

Finally, in 1951, the voters began the slow process of electing players—they voted in Mel Ott and Jimmie Foxx. In '52 they picked Harry Heilmann and Paul Waner. Slowly, slowly, the Hall of Fame door began to open a little bit, and finally in 1956, it was Greenberg's turn.

No, it never should have taken that long. He remains one of only five players to finish a career with a .300 batting average, .400 on-base percentage, and .600 slugging percentage (Ruth, Foxx, Williams, and Gehrig are the others). There was some talk about how he was not a great all-around player, but that's probably been overstated. He was slow, but he made himself into an adequate first baseman, a tolerable outfielder, and an average baserunner.

He was also a pioneer. Baseball, because of its place in American life, has had a few players who inspired others to expand their minds and open their worlds: Jackie Robinson; Roberto Clemente; Ichiro Suzuki. And so on. Hank Greenberg sometimes lamented that he had to carry this extra burden as a Jewish player, but he carried it powerfully.

One story, perhaps apocryphal, is that Jo-Jo White once inspected Greenberg carefully, looking for horns. What is unquestionably true was that Greenberg and White became roommates and friends. "You're just like everyone else," White once said to Greenberg, somewhat in wonder.

No. 66 **Robin Yount**

You probably have not heard of a ballplayer named Larry Yount. He was a promising pitcher from Woodland Hills, California. He had a presence about him. The Houston Astros took him in the fifth round in 1968, and he was advanced enough that the Astros tried him out in Triple A in his first professional year. At 19, he dominated in Hampton, Virginia, and the next year he was pretty good in Columbus, Georgia.

The Astros had their eye on him. He had grown to be 6-foot-2, he gained 30 or 40 pounds after turning pro, his fastball had become an imposing pitch. Houston thought about keeping him with the big-league team after spring training in 1971 but sent him down to Triple A instead, where he struggled a bit. Still, he showed enough stuff to get his first call to the big leagues.

On September 15, 1971, with the Astros trailing, 4–1, in the ninth, Houston manager Harry "the Hat" Walker signaled for Yount to come in and replace pitcher Skip Guinn.

Only a few of the 6,513 fans who had come to the Astrodome to see the game remained, but there's always a little bit of extra buzz when a new prospect makes a big-league debut. Larry Yount was pumped up. His future had arrived. He barely even noticed in the bullpen when his elbow began to twinge a little as he threw. Nerves probably. As he took the mound, he tried to take it all in. The crowd. The size of it all. The history. It was the beginning! Where would it end? All-Star Games? The World Series? The Hall of Fame?

It was all possible as he approached the mound that night.

The first batter he would face was All-Star Felix Millan, who hit .300 the year before. After that, he would face one of the league's leading hitters, Ralph Garr. Fast. Hit line drives. And if he could get through those two he would then face the great Henry Aaron. What a night. What a moment. This was a time for dreaming.

But as Yount threw his first warm-up pitch he realized that the twinge in his elbow was something more. It hurt a lot. A knife. He threw his second warm-up pitch and it hurt even more. A horrible realization came over Larry Yount: He couldn't pitch. He tried a third pitch but grimaced before he even released the ball, and the pain was so overwhelming that he almost fell to the ground. He had no choice but to call out his catcher and the team trainer to the mound.

"I can't go," he said as he fought back the feelings that roared inside him.

"Are you sure?" they asked him, and they asked him again and again, and all Yount could do was nod. He walked off the mound.

He came out of the game without throwing a single pitch. He believed—the way Burt Lancaster believed in *Field of Dreams*—that there would be other days. But there were no other days. Larry Yount tried to make it back to the big leagues. But he never did. He became a real estate developer instead.

His official big-league career line: 1 game, 0.0 innings, 0 hits, 0 walks, 0 strikeouts, 0 batters faced. He is the only pitcher in baseball history to be in the record books without throwing a single big-league pitch or getting a single big-league out.

Twenty-one months later, Larry Yount's younger brother, Robin, was taken by Milwaukee with the third overall pick of the 1973 amateur draft. Robin played just 64 games in low Class A, hit OK, fielded OK, and was called up to the big leagues, where he stayed for the next 20 years.

Robin Yount's agent? His brother Larry.

Before we get into the wonders of Robin Yount, let's talk for a moment about that 1973 draft. The top four picks in that draft are pretty fascinating.

The Texas Rangers had the first pick and they took a local high school pitching phenom named David Clyde. He had been so good as a high school pitcher that the Rangers decided to try something entirely new—they put Clyde right into a Texas uniform and had him start his first major-league game against Minnesota only three weeks after he finished high school.

Well, the Rangers in that time were in desperate need of attention; people in Dallas barely knew they existed. The game was a circus—literally, there were parading animals, belly dancers, fireworks, a band—and more than 35,000 people showed up, the first-ever Rangers sellout. Some say that game played a pivotal role in keeping baseball in the Dallas–Fort Worth area.

"Maybe," American League president Joe Cronin said afterward, "this is God's way of bringing major-league baseball to Dallas–Fort Worth."

But if the game did play a role in keeping baseball in Dallas, it did no favors to David Clyde. He actually pitched pretty well, but after that he was burdened with unfair expectations, a lifestyle he was not ready for, and, soon after, debilitating injuries. His career flamed out.

With the second pick, the Phillies took John Stearns, who was known less for baseball and more for being a famously contentious and ferocious football star at Colorado. When he was a sophomore defensive back and punter with the Buffaloes, he told *Sports Illustrated*, "I can't enjoy football without going savage. Going psycho. I would like to be remembered around the conference as a bad dude."

He was called "Bad Dude" after that.

Stearns was drafted by the NFL's Buffalo Bills in the 17th round but chose baseball instead. He was traded to the Mets in the Tug McGraw deal of 1974 and had a fine big-league career, making four All-Star teams and setting a National League record for catchers with 25 stolen bases in 1978.

Third, the Brewers chose Robin Yount, a high school shortstop. And with the fourth pick, the Padres chose Dave Winfield, an all-world college pitcher and outfielder and athlete at the University of Minnesota. I don't have any idea how Winfield dropped to fourth in that draft, considering his extraordinary athletic talent. He was also drafted by the Atlanta Hawks in the NBA draft and by the Minnesota Vikings in the NFL draft. Fun fact: In the NFL draft, just like in MLB, Winfield was taken just a few picks after Stearns.

Yount and Winfield became the only pair of future Hall of Famers ever taken back-to-back in the first round of the MLB draft.

Yount was one of the youngest players in baseball history to play every day. Even now, he has records to show it.

Most plate appearances through age 20: 1,661

Through age 21: 2,324

Through age 22: 2,869

Through age 23: 3,495

Yount, however, was not a great young player. He had tremendous talent . . . "He's the most complete young ballplayer I've ever seen," a scout told *Sports Illustrated*'s Pat Jordan when Yount was just 18.

But there was something missing. Through four seasons he had an 86 OPS+, an atrocious defensive record, and a powerful sense that baseball was unfulfilling. It was this last part—this growing realization by everyone that Yount didn't even like baseball very much—that made baseball people wonder if he would ever live up to his potential.

As the 1978 season began, at age 22, Yount began looking hard for a way out of the game. He was miserable. He felt underpaid and unappreciated. He didn't like playing for a noncontender. He didn't feel at home at all in Milwaukee and missed California. He suffered the first real injury of his career.

And it didn't help that the Brewers played a little hardball with him. There is a moment in every young baseball player's career when they fully come to the realization that Major League Baseball is less a game and more a business than they had hoped. Brewers general manager Harry Dalton told the media that while the team had several untouchable players, Yount was not one of them because they weren't sure about his commitment. They didn't *want* to trade him, Dalton said sneakily. But they were not *opposed* to trading him.

That was when Yount announced that he was thinking of walking away from baseball and becoming a professional golfer. When he was young, he said, he loved playing golf and was quite good at it. He had not chosen baseball; baseball had chosen him. His heart was on the golf course.

It was a big story with many reporters taking Yount at his word. Looking back now, it all seems ridiculous; there is virtually no chance that Yount could have made it as a pro golfer. It wasn't impossible, but it was next to impossible. Yount was a two-handicap golfer, which is better than almost everyone reading this. And he was obviously a fantastic athlete, so you cannot entirely write off the possibility that with dedication and practice he would have improved dramatically. But it needs to be said: There are more than 75,000 golfers playing today who carry a two handicap. Yount was nowhere close to being ready to go on the PGA tour.

Still, it was a big story across baseball. And looking back, it was less about golf and more of a cry for help.

"He doesn't want to play baseball anymore," a person close to the situation told the *Milwaukee Journal* in 1978. "He doesn't like it anymore."

Things changed rapidly, though. The Brewers gave him what, at the time, was a fat contract: five years, $2.35 million (that's not $2.35 million per year; that's the entirety of the contract or $587,500 per year—it was a different time). Yount got married. And, maybe for the first time, he got serious about baseball. Before the 1979 season, he showed up early for spring training and explained that he was now trying to become the best player in the league. He had needed to get the golf dream out of his system.

And in 1980, he had his first huge year, hitting .293 with a league-leading 49 doubles, 10 triples, 23 homers, and 121 runs scored. He made his first All-Star team and received his first MVP consideration.

In 1982, he became the best player in baseball. He hit .331/.379/.578, led the league in hits, doubles, and total bases, led the Brewers to their first and still only World Series, won the shortstop Gold Glove, and won the MVP award. It was, all things considered, the best season of the 1980s.

1. Robin Yount, 1982: 10.5/9.8 WAR (Baseball-Reference/FanGraphs)

2. Cal Ripken, 1984: 10.0/9.8 WAR

3. Rickey Henderson, 1985: 9.9/9.7 WAR

4. George Brett, 1980: 9.4/9.1WAR

5. Wade Boggs, 1985: 9.1/8.8 WAR

And Yount stayed pretty much at that level for a few years. He led the league in triples in 1983 and scored 105 runs in '84. In 1985, to protect his health, the Brewers moved him from shortstop to the outfield, and he put up consistently good seasons. From 1986 to '89, Yount hit over .300 every season and was a base-stealing and triples-hitting machine.

In 1989, he hit .318/.384/.511 with 21 homers, 19 stolen bases, scored and drove in 100-plus runs, and was awarded his second MVP. True, this wasn't as good as his first MVP season—in retrospect, I'd probably have given the award to Rickey Henderson or Wade Boggs—but it was still a fantastic season.

And by this point, his career numbers really started adding up—this is a benefit of starting so young. He reached 3,000 hits, and even now is 20th all-time in hits (3,142), 21st in doubles (583), and 16th in games played (2,856). He's top 50 in most other categories, too, like runs scored, extra-base hits, games played, and times on base.

There is one odd thing about Yount's long and brilliant career: He made only three All-Star teams. How did that happen? He made it in 1980 and started at shortstop in '82 and '83. Once he moved to the outfield, though, he never again played in another Midsummer Classic. Three All-Star Game appearances are astonishingly low for an all-time great player who won two MVPs.

Here are the All-Star Game appearances for players with multiple MVP awards:

24: Stan Musial and Willie Mays

20: Mickey Mantle

19: Ted Williams and Cal Ripken

18: Yogi Berra

14: Frank Robinson, Ernie Banks, Johnny Bench, Barry Bonds, and Alex Rodriguez

13: Joe DiMaggio

12: Mike Schmidt

11: Miguel Cabrera

10: Joe Morgan and Albert Pujols

9: Carl Hubbell and Jimmie Foxx

8: Roy Campanella and Mike Trout

7: Lou Gehrig, Hal Newhouser, Roger Maris, and Dale Murphy

5: Hank Greenberg and Frank Thomas

3: Robin Yount and Juan González

Yount didn't mind; he never really wanted attention. Even when he was elected to the Baseball Hall of Fame in his first year of eligibility (1999), he was still mostly anonymous because he was elected the same year as supernovas Nolan Ryan and Yount's close friend George Brett.

During that week, someone asked Yount how it felt to be the third wheel with those two legends.

"It's good to be Ringo," he said.

No. 65 **Ernie Banks**

T here's something, dare I say it, sacred about the perfect combination of a great player and a legendary quote. Think of Muhammad Ali and "I am the greatest." Think of Lou Gehrig and "Today, I consider myself the luckiest man on the face of the earth." Think of Joe Namath and "We're going to win the game, I guarantee it." Think of Satchel Paige saying "Don't look back. Something might be gaining on you."

These are a few words that somehow capture the essence of a player, of a moment, of that little bit of magic that makes someone unforgettable. It doesn't always have to be a sweeping quote. It could be John Kruk saying, "I ain't no athlete, I'm a ballplayer." You see those few words and you know exactly who Kruk was and what he was about.

Or think about Allen Iverson saying, "We're talkin' about practice?"

Or think about Joe Montana, in the middle of the Super Bowl, just before leading his 49ers on their game-winning drive, looking at the stands and telling a teammate, "Look. Isn't that John Candy?"

Or think about the wonderful golfer Roberto De Vicenzo, just seconds after he signed the wrong scorecard and cost himself a chance at winning the Masters: "What a stupid I am!"

There are so many of these. Rasheed Wallace's "Ball don't lie." Joe Louis's "He can run but he can't hide." Garry Templeton's "If I ain't startin', I ain't departin'." John McEnroe's "You cannot be serious!" Reggie Jackson saying, "I didn't come to New York to be a star, I brought my star with me"; Kevin Garnett saying, "Anything is possible!" Marshawn Lynch saying, "I'm just here so I don't get fined."

But the greatest combination of them all, the player and words that fit together the most perfectly, most poetically, most beautifully, well, that's not a contest.

"It's a beautiful day for a ball game. Let's play two."

That's Ernie Banks.

Think of the gorgeousness of those last words: "Let's play two." I've never bought into the "a picture is worth a thousand words" cliché—it depends on the words. *Let's play two!* In just three words, you understand Banks in a way that no photograph, no painting, no snapshot could ever quite capture. *Let's play two!* Three words express Banks's endless joy for baseball. Three words that make the heart sing.

I went in search of when exactly Banks first started saying those words. I couldn't pinpoint it exactly, but I did find out that Banks didn't become famous for saying "Let's play two" until near the end of his career—1969 to be exact—when his Cubs and the New York Mets fought for the pennant.

Banks was already 38 years old then, and he was on his last legs. He drove in 100 runs that season, which created the illusion that he was still a dangerous hitter. But he really wasn't by that point. He hit just .253 with a 92 OPS+. He was at the end. Banks would play barely 100 more games after that season before retiring.

Still, that was a seminal year. The Cubs were in the pennant race that year for the first time in a generation, the first time in Banks's career, and because of that writers discovered Banks all over again. The first reference I can find to Banks saying, "Let's play two" comes in a story by a legendary Canadian baseball writer named Clancy Loranger. If you live in Vancouver you might still recognize the name because the street that leads up to Nat Bailey Stadium is called Clancy Loranger Way.

On June 10, 1969, Loranger wrote this about Banks:

"He just loves to play the game, and one of his favorite expressions is, 'Hey, hey, let's play two today.' "

This reference—"one of his favorite expressions"—suggests that Banks had been saying "let's play two" for a long time.

A few weeks later, the most famous baseball writer in America at the time—the New York *Daily News'* Dick Young—wrote about the quote, but again in a way that suggested it was already well known. He wrote that the Mets "want to be able to pull the switch on Ernie Banks' famous exuberant phrase, 'It's such a beautiful day, let's play two.'"

It is strange that "Let's play two" was already a "famous exuberant phrase," but none of the writers seemed to mention it before.

Another story that appeared around the same time quoted him this way: "Isn't this wonderful? It's a crime to take money for playing baseball. We all ought to be in San Quentin. . . . Let's play two games today. It's too nice a day for just one game."

Later in that season, *Sports Illustrated's* Mark Kram documented Banks's exuberance—"There are no clouds in Ernie's life," he wrote—in a way that sealed Banks's place as baseball's happiest warrior:

> Banks is particularly animated during batting practice, that soft time in baseball . . . he sings, jabs at some down-home philosophy and jabbers in a weird patois that dwarfs the ordinary apostles of boosterism. If he is in St. Louis, he will say: "St. Louis! Home of the mighty Cardinals and the great Stan. St. Louis! Great city. Meet me in St. Louie . . ." If he is in New York, he will say: "New York, the Big Apple, the Melting Pot of the World. Home of Oh! Calcutta! and those pesky Mets."
>
> In Chicago, he overflows.
>
> "Henry Aaron," he says dramatically, looking over at Aaron. "Henry Aaron! The most dangerous hitter who ever lived. Hall of Fame, here he comes. Henry, let's play two today."
>
> Aaron, shaking his head, looks at him curiously.

Banks learned to *play* baseball from his father, Eddie, who played pro baseball for a team called the Dallas Black Giants. But he learned to *love* baseball from Buck O'Neil.

Buck used to tell my favorite "Let's play two" story. That one happened in 1962.

You should know: Banks's career was at a crossroads in 1962. That was the year he moved from shortstop to first base. Banks didn't like first base—"Presents many problems," he said of the position, "not the least of them is what to do with my feet. Sometimes I seem to have too many and sometimes not enough"—but the Cubs asked him to make the switch to protect his worn-down body.

Before the switch, Banks was a shortstop—and a transformational one. There had never been a shortstop like him in the history of the game. He was superb defensively, but that wasn't what separated him. His base-running, while enthusiastic, certainly did not separate him. He hit .300 or so every year, but there were other shortstops who did that. He was an utterly unbreakable force (he played in 717 straight games), but even that was not unprecedented.

No. It was the power that made Banks remarkable. From the day he first picked up a bat, Banks hit with power. His father used to tell of all the windows he broke as a child. In 1955, he became the first shortstop ever to hit 40 home runs. How big a deal was it? Only one other shortstop in baseball history—Vern Stephens—had ever even hit 25 home runs.

In 1957, Banks became the second shortstop to hit 40 home runs.

In 1958, Banks became the third shortstop to hit 40 home runs (47 to be exact, which stayed the record for 43 years until Alex Rodriguez broke it).

In 1959, Banks became the fourth shortstop to hit 40 home runs.

In 1960, Banks became the *fifth* shortstop to hit 40 home runs.

There had never been a slugging shortstop before him. Those words pushed together—slugging shortstop—were a baseball oxymoron until Banks came along. Shortstops were supposed to be little guys who bunted a lot and turned a bunch of double plays. But Ernie Banks—he was feared. Banks twice led the league in intentional walks—unimaginable for a shortstop! He led the league in homers twice, led the league in RBIs twice, and he won two MVP awards for two terrible Cubs teams. They didn't give MVPs to players on bad teams often in those days, but that's how jaw-droppingly good he was.

From a purely analytical standpoint, Banks compiled more than 50 WAR in just seven seasons. That's more than five shortstops in the Hall of Fame had in their entire careers.

This leads to a larger point about the Hall of Fame: To me, Banks had done all he needed to do as a shortstop to be elected to the Hall. But would he have been elected had he retired rather than move to first base? No. He would not have. For one thing, he wouldn't have played enough years to be eligible.

But, even if you look past that—he would have had a .290 batting average, a couple of MVP awards, 298 career home runs, a Gold Glove, a few All-Star Game starts. He was also the first black player on the Chicago Cubs. Everybody knew he was utterly unique.

But he would have only had 1,355 hits. There's no way that the writers would have considered voting for him, even if he was a seminal player.

Of course, Banks didn't retire then. He moved to first base and became a different kind of player. His body was pretty well wrecked. His first base defense was adequate—less so as the years went on. His batting average and on-base percentage dropped precipitously; he hit just .258 with a .306 on-base percentage in his last 1,312 games.

But by playing those 1,312 games, he was able to compile the big career numbers that win Hall of Fame votes. He became the 11th player to hit 500 home runs. He finished with more than 1,600 RBIs, which was 13th on the all-time list at his retirement. He lasted long enough for the fans and writers to discover his inspiring optimism even though he never played in the World Series. He was Mr. Cub!

And Ernie Banks was elected first-ballot with 84 percent of the vote.*

In the end, Banks is in the Hall of Fame and that's what matters. All I'm saying is that Ernie Banks was one of the greatest players in baseball history for seven years, and that's the guy I think of when I see his plaque.

Buck O'Neil was Banks's first professional manager with the Kansas City Monarchs. Reportedly, it was Cool Papa Bell who first spotted Banks's great talent and recommended him to the Monarchs. When Banks showed up in Kansas City, his baseball talent was obvious . . . but believe it or not,

---

* If that vote total seems a bit low for an all-time legend like Banks, well, it actually wasn't low for his time. The writers were a persnickety bunch in those days. They refused to vote in Eddie Mathews. Yogi Berra and Whitey Ford were not elected on the first ballot. Banks's 84 percent of the vote was a higher percentage than Warren Spahn got, and some considered Spahn to be the greatest pitcher in baseball history.

he was very shy to the point of silence in those days. He would sit quietly in the back of the team bus, never say a word, never let anyone know what he was thinking or feeling.

"I was learning," Banks told me when I asked him about this. "I already loved baseball. But Buck showed me how to express that love."

Buck and others facilitated Banks's signing with the Cubs. (He actually didn't want to go at first.) Banks never played a game in the minor leagues. He went right from the Monarchs (where he had hit .347) to becoming the first black player for the Cubs (where in 10 games he hit .314 with two homers). The next year, 1954, he was the Cubs' starting shortstop and he finished second in the Rookie of the Year balloting to Wally Moon.

The year after that, as you know, he became the first shortstop to hit 40 homers in a season.

By then, he would express his joy for everyone to see and hear—it was something his teammates saw for years before it became nationally known. That joy was in everything Banks did, the way he would show up to the ballpark early, the way he would bounce around giddily during batting practice, the way he would talk about each game like a kid talking about an upcoming birthday party.

"Maybe it's sacrilege but I believe Banks was a con artist," John Roseboro once said. "No one smiles all the time, naturally, unless they're putting you on. Every day of our lives isn't a good one."

But every day *was* a good one for Ernie Banks. His mother had wanted him to be a minister. His father wanted him to be a baseball player. He became both. The ballpark was his pulpit, the crowds his congregation, the batter's box his sanctuary.

Banks, like all pioneers, dealt with pressures and fury. He was called all the names. He received his share of threats. He was denied meals in restaurants and denied entry into hotels. He dealt with it his way—not with Jackie Robinson's fierceness or Satchel Paige's larger-than-life personality or Roberto Clemente's determination, but simply by being Ernie Banks.

It's a beautiful day. Let's play two.

Which brings us around, at last, to August 18, 1962. The Cubs played a doubleheader in Houston; the home team was called the Colt .45s then, and they played their games at Colt Stadium, where the heat was unbearable and the mosquitoes so large and feisty that outfielders used to wear towels under the hats to protect their necks. "Like sheiks," Buck O'Neil used to say.

"Those mosquitoes were so big," Buck said, "we used to say that everybody should move in groups because otherwise, a mosquito might carry one of us back to the nest."

The day in question was scorching hot—92 degrees according to the official box score, but Buck swore it was at least 110. Banks came to the ballpark smiling, like always, and he went through his routine. He took the dugout steps two at a time. He looked up into the sky, felt the heat attack him in waves, and, in Buck's memory, said his part: "It's a beautiful day for a ballgame. Let's play two!"

Banks struck out three times in the first game.

He fainted before the second game and so couldn't start.

He recovered just enough to pinch-hit in the ninth inning with the score tied 5–5. Don McMahon struck him out.

"Beautiful day, Ernie?" Buck asked him in the clubhouse after the doubleheader and he had this mischievous smile on his face. Banks was crumpled by his locker, and he was so depleted that he could barely look up. But then he too smiled.

"They're all beautiful days, Buck," he said. "Just that some days are more beautiful than others."

No. 64 **Johnny Mize**

Johnny Mize was not elected into the Hall of Fame by the Baseball Writers' Association of America. In truth, he never came close to being elected. The highest percentage he got was 43.6 percent in 1972. This was during what you might call the dark period of Hall of Fame voting. The writers, seemingly, didn't want anybody in the Hall of Fame.

They refused, even, to vote in Yogi Berra on first ballot. I mean, seriously, Yogi Berra?

From 1957 to 1971, the BBWAA voted just nine players into the Hall of Fame. And they didn't want to vote in that many. They were fine with voting in Bob Feller, Ted Williams, Stan Musial, and Roy Campanella—all of them made it in with some ease. Jackie Robinson was elected on the first ballot, but made it by only five votes.

The other four players elected—Ducky Medwick, Red Ruffing, Luke Appling, and Lou Boudreau—were voted in only because the Hall of Fame kept insisting that the writers do *something*. None of them were elected the old-fashioned way of garnering 75 percent of the vote; the Hall of Fame asked the BBWAA to hold runoff elections just to get them to vote *somebody* in. That's how bad it got.

Now, there are those who like this stingier approach, who believe that Hall of Fame standards should be extraordinarily high. And that's fine, in theory. But in reality, the BBWAA did damage to the Hall of Fame during this stretch for two reasons:

1. Their reluctance to vote players in infuriated the Hall of Fame, which needs a steady flow of new players to keep the place vibrant and alive. So the Hall empowered their Veterans Committees, which in those same years, 1957–71, elected thirty-six people to the Hall, including some of the most questionable choices in the Hall today. The year that tells the story is 1971. The writers didn't vote in anybody even though all-time great players like Yogi Berra, Johnny Mize, and Duke Snider were on the ballot.

   And that same year, the Veterans Committee voted in a whole bunch of not-great players, most of whom you probably wouldn't know: Rube Marquard, Chick Hafey, Dave Bancroft, Harry Hooper, Jake Beckley, Joe Kelley. The Veterans Committee also voted in former Yankees executive George Weiss, who refused for as long as he could to sign a black player.

   The BBWAA thought it was protecting the Hall of Fame much the way that people who created Prohibition thought they were protecting American values. And all either really did was open up the back door.

2. In their fog of stubbornness, the writers badly missed on a true legend in Johnny Mize. It is, in my opinion, one of the two biggest misses in BBWAA history (the other is coming up shortly on this list) and a thorough embarrassment.

How good a hitter was Mize? He was Lou Gehrig good. He was Stan Musial good. He was Mel Ott good, Frank Robinson good, Joe DiMaggio good, Albert Pujols good. There is one player in baseball history, just one, who hit more than 50 homers and struck out less than 50 times in a single season. That was Johnny Mize in 1947.

And he did that as a 34-year-old who had come back from the war.

They called Mize "Big Cat." He liked to say that he got the nickname in the minor leagues from a teammate who admired the way he picked balls in the dirt as a first baseman—like a big cat. Others insisted he got the name because of the plodding way he moved around. Either way, Big Cat grew up in Demorest, a tiny temperance town in the northeast corner of Georgia.

One trivial but fun fact is that Mize had family relations to the two giants of baseball of the time—Ty Cobb and Babe Ruth. He was apparently a distant cousin of Cobb's and his first cousin, Clara Mae Merritt, married Ruth.

Mize was not, at first, a baseball player. Tennis was his game. We hear a lot about baseball players who starred on the football field or basketball court; you rarely hear about ballplayers playing tennis. But Mize was a remarkable young tennis player with extraordinary hand-eye coordination. He would talk proudly about how long he could keep a rally going while hitting a tennis ball against the barn using a broomstick. He had no doubt that it was this training that led to his greatness as a hitter.

After growing several inches and gaining 50 pounds in his early teen years, he was recruited to play baseball. At 15, just after entering high school, he played for the local college team, Piedmont College. At 17, Frank Rickey—brother of Branch, and a Cardinals scout—saw Mize play just once and signed him.

Mize could hit like few ever have, so how did the writers miss so badly on him? Part of the reason was that Mize's timing was always just off. He signed with a dominant Cardinals team, and this delayed his entry into the big leagues by at least three years. Mize was a fantastic hitter in the minor leagues right from the start, undoubtedly big-league ready, but he played first base. The Cardinals' best player at the time was their first baseman, Ripper Collins, who led the league in slugging in 1935. Collins was such a fixture at first base that the Cardinals agreed to sell Johnny Mize to the Cincinnati Reds.

Had Mize gone to the Reds, that might have launched his career earlier. But again, Mize had bad timing. He badly pulled a groin muscle just before the sale. When he went to Reds training camp, he could barely swing the bat. The Reds returned him to the Cardinals as damaged goods before the 1935 season.

In retrospect, that wasn't the best move the Reds have ever made.

Mize got healthy and finally made it up to the Cardinals in 1936 as a 23-year-old. He hit .329 and slugged .577 as a rookie. That convinced the Cardinals to trade Collins and insert Big Cat as their everyday first baseman.

Over the next six seasons, Mize hit a combined .332/.414/.590. At different times, he led the league in doubles, triples (despite his famed slowness), home runs (twice), batting average, total bases (three times), slugging percentage (four times), and RBIs (twice). He twice finished second in the MVP balloting, once to Reds pitcher Bucky Walters and the other time to Reds first baseman Frank McCormick.

If the Cardinals and not the Reds had won the pennants in those two years, Mize surely would have won both of those MVP awards.

He was a craftsman at the plate in the truest sense of the word. He became famous for using different types of bats for different situations. He preferred a light bat against hard throwers and a heavy bat against those who changed speeds. He liked a lighter bat late in games, particularly on hot days, and he used a heavier one on colder days, especially in the early innings.

It got to the point where Mize had so many bats—he began the 1940 season with 43 of them—that the clubhouse people complained they couldn't travel with them all. Mize replied: "How do you expect me to work without my tools?"*

In December 1941—four days after the bombing at Pearl Harbor— Giants manager and legend Mel Ott engineered a trade to get Mize. Ott saw a bit of himself in Mize. In '42, Mize led the league in RBIs for the Giants. And then he went to the navy for the next three and a half years.

That's another bit of timing that made people miss his greatness. When talking about great players who lost prime years to World War II, Johnny Mize is often forgotten. He probably would have approached 500 home runs and various other legendary numbers if not for the war.

Mize was still breathtakingly good when he returned. In 1947, he had his extraordinary 51-homer, 42-strikeout season. He also led the league in runs and RBIs. The voters gave the MVP to Boston's Bob Elliott, who did not have nearly as good an offensive year but did have a higher batting average.

---

* There are so many great stories about Mize and his knowledge of baseball bats. In 1950, Mize suggested to Phil Rizzuto that he should use a heavier bat. Mize reached into his own bat collection and pulled one out and handed it to Scooter, who had been a .265 or so hitter since the end of the war. Rizzuto, rather suddenly, hit .324 and won the MVP Award. When asked what made the difference, Rizzuto said: "I began using Johnny Mize's bats."

In 1948, Mize again led the league in homers—by one. That one homer mattered a lot because it prevented Stan Musial from winning the Triple Crown in his greatest season. Mize finished second to Musial in RBIs, slugging, OPS, total bases, and WAR.

And then a crazy thing happened—the Yankees bought Mize for $40,000. It was crazy because nobody even knew the Yankees wanted him, not even Yankees manager Casey Stengel, who said, "It's news to me. I don't even know what I'm going to do with him."

Stengel eventually figured out exactly what to do with him: Mize became the Yankees' ultimate bench bat. In the 1949 World Series against Brooklyn, Stengel pinch-hit Mize in the ninth inning of Game 3 with the score tied 1–1. Mize singled to right, scoring two, and the Yankees went on to win the game and the Series.

Mize thrived as a part-time player. He mashed 25 home runs in part-time duty for the 1950 Yankees. In 1952, in another World Series against Brooklyn, he hit .400 with three homers in five games. In 1953, at age 40, Mize played in his last All-Star Game.

There were two pretty famous couplets written about Mize while he was with the Yankees—the poems are famous because "Mize" is so easy to rhyme, I think. The first appeared in a *Boston Traveler* headline—it was written by an anonymous copy editor:

To Criticize Mize is Unwise
His Bat Supplies His Best Replies

The second was written by a famous sportswriter of the time, Dan Parker. He wrote it before the 1953 World Series.

Your arm is gone, your legs likewise
But not your eyes, Mize, not your eyes

There's a story from that Series that I love. In Game 3, the Dodgers' Carl Erskine struck out what was then a Series-record 14 hitters. Mize couldn't believe it. All game long, he screamed at his teammates, "Why are you swinging at that miserable, bush curve?"

But with one out in the ninth, Mize was sent in as a pinch-hitter. And . . . Erskine struck him out on a miserable, bush curve.

"A sweet out," Erskine said.

Mize, ironically, became more famous as a part-time player with the dominant Yankees than he was as a dominant player with a fading Cardinals team. As a respected older player, he won five World Series rings with New York.

But then, it seems, baseball writers began to think of Mize as *only* that respected older player. They forgot about the time when he was as good a hitter as anybody. Mize was finally elected to the Hall of Fame in 1981 by the Veterans Committee. Mize did feel some bitterness about being overlooked by the writers, but he generally took such things in stride. When he finally reached the podium in Cooperstown, he told the crowd: "I had a speech ready. But somewhere along in 28 years, it got lost."

No. 63 **Steve Carlton**

T he greatest trade in Philadelphia Phillies history happened because two pitchers wanted more money. In Philadelphia, a good pitcher named Rick Wise felt he deserved a huge raise. And why not? He was immensely popular in Philadelphia. He had come off an excellent and highlight-filled 1971 season. He went 17-14 with a 2.88 ERA. He made the All-Star team. He was fifth in the league in shutouts. Also, he threw one of the most famous no-hitters in baseball history against the Big Red Machine, famous not only for its dominance (his walk of Dave Concepción was the only baserunner of the day) but also because Wise hit two home runs in the game. No pitcher had ever done that—thrown a no-hitter and hit two home runs in a game. Nobody has done it since.

Wise was 25 years old. He'd made $25,000 in 1971. He felt like he deserved $50,000.

The Phillies were outraged by Wise's salary demands. Double his salary? They offered $40,000 and not a penny more and told him to take it or leave it. He didn't take it.

At the same time, in St. Louis, Steve Carlton wanted his salary raised to $65,000. He was coming off his first 20-win season and believed he should be compensated for that.

Cardinals owner Gussie Busch did not agree. Busch was sick of Carlton's demands; the two had a bitter salary fight after Carlton's fantastic 1969 season, when he went 17-11 with a 2.17 ERA, struck out 210 in 236 innings, and set a major-league record by striking out 19 in a nine-inning game. The two went to war over money at the end of that year, and Carlton came away with a $50,000 deal. Gussie Busch developed a grudge that would never go away.

Busch could barely believe that Carlton wanted even more money. Wasn't $50,000 enough for any ballplayer? He unwillingly went to $60,000, and when Carlton turned that down, the owner had had enough. He had heard about the Wise fight in Philadelphia (and heard Wise wanted a more palatable $50,000), and he ordered his general manager, Bing Devine, to offer a straight-up deal: Steve Carlton for Rick Wise.

Devine, reportedly, kept delaying the call in the hope that Busch would just forget about it. Busch would not forget; he asked Devine about it every single day. He wanted Carlton gone. *And* he wanted Carlton to be sent to Philadelphia, baseball's wasteland, a team and town so dysfunctional that Carlton's teammate Curt Flood went all the way to the Supreme Court to avoid being traded there.

Finally, Devine ran out of time. He made the offer, and the Phillies jumped all over it.

The point is: The Cardinals are the ones who initiated the best trade in Phillies history and probably the worst in St. Louis history.

But that's not how it looked to Phillies fans at the start. Wise was beloved, and he loved Philadelphia. People were furious after Wise's wife, Susan, angrily quoted GM John Quinn saying, "We'd never trade Rick Wise; this is the fellow we're going to build around."

The consensus among the newspapers was that Wise would thrive in St. Louis, where he would finally get a chance to play with a good team. The *Daily News** wrote, in a matter-of-fact way, that he was a sure 20-game winner with a good-hitting team like St. Louis.

And Carlton? Nobody quite knew what to make of him. He seemed unsteady, inconsistent, odd. How would he perform in Philadelphia, where losing had become a state of being? "He will be hard-pressed to

---

* Boston later traded Wise to Cleveland for Dennis Eckersley, which gives Wise the rare distinction of being traded for two Hall of Famers in his career.

win 20 in his pretty new powder-blue uniform," the *Philadelphia Inquirer* decided.

Attitudes about Carlton changed rapidly, however. You might know that Tim McCarver—who would become a legendary broadcaster—became Carlton's personal catcher. But what you might not know is that he was also Wise's personal catcher. So when the Wise-Carlton trade was made, reporters flocked to McCarver to see what he thought.

McCarver at first said they were equal in talent. "They're so comparable," he said, "that you have to start looking to the finer points like how they field their position. When you have to start looking to things like their personalities, things like that, you know they're awfully close."

He then broke it down, pitch by pitch, and actually gave the edge to Wise for his fastball *and* his slider. Think about that: Steve Carlton had one of the greatest left-handed fastballs in baseball history, and he would develop *the* greatest slider in baseball history, righty or lefty. But even McCarver didn't know that yet.

My Opinion: Best Sliders in Baseball History

1. Steve Carlton

2. Bob Gibson

3. Randy Johnson

4. Clayton Kershaw

5. Dave Stieb

McCarver would learn fast. See, in 1972, Carlton stopped throwing his slider for reasons that seem more mysterious as the years go along. He had picked up that slider in Japan after the 1968 season while trying to figure out a way to get out the legendary Japanese slugger Sadaharu Oh. The first two times they faced each other, Oh homered. Carlton, figuring he had to do something different, tried the slider he had been playing around with. Oh buckled. "I knew I had something," Carlton told *Sports Illustrated.*

Carlton used that slider to great effect in 1969, when he became one of the best pitchers in baseball. But he junked it at some point in 1970. Why? Some thought it was because the Cardinals felt like it put too much strain on his arm. Some thought it was because he lost confidence in it.

My favorite version of the story is that he gave up the slider on June 29, 1970, after giving up two home runs on sliders to a 39-year-old Ernie Banks. "That son of a gun can still hit," Carlton said after that game, and it warms the heart to think of Mr. Cub himself sending Carlton into a canyon of self-doubt.

Unfortunately, that story isn't true. Both homers were hit off fastballs—the first one right down the middle, the second one up and away. The source for this is Carlton himself, who was still talking to the media in those days.

So why did he really give it up? Nobody really knows.

But as soon as Carlton got to Philadelphia, he began to throw it again. And barely a month later, reporters went back to McCarver to ask about Carlton. Suddenly, McCarver sang a very different tune.

"Pound for pound, I think Steve probably throws harder than anybody else in the league," he gushed. "And he was zipping that slider. When he has that working well, nobody is going to touch him."

McCarver was right: Nobody touched Carlton in 1972. It was one of the greatest seasons a pitcher has ever had. He actually got off to a mediocre start—in early May, with Carlton and team struggling, new general manager Paul Owens announced that every player on that doomed team was available for a trade. "If they want to talk about Carlton, I'll listen," he said.

Then Carlton went on a pitching stretch for the ages. On June 7 against Houston, he struck out 11 in seven innings and allowed just one run. In his next outing against Atlanta, he pitched a complete game, struck out nine, and allowed one run. And in his next start, he threw 10 scoreless innings (though the Phillies lost in 11).

And he was off. For the next four months, while playing for the worst team in the league, Carlton went 22-4 with a 1.54 ERA, 208 strikeouts, 61 walks, and just 10 home runs allowed in 251 innings. He twice threw back-to-back shutouts. He completed 23 games. He had 19 starts during the stretch with a Game Score higher than 70, which is amazing. In this century, no pitcher has had 19 starts with a Game Score higher than 70 in a full season. Carlton did it in four months.

In the end, he won 27 games while Philadelphia won only 59. That's a famous stat, so it's interesting that Carlton probably would not have won many more games for a better team. Looking game by game, Carlton did not have many tough losses that year, and he actually got a couple of cheap wins. Sure, he might have won 30 for a great team. He also might have won just 25.

The better statistic is WAR. His WAR—12.1 (Baseball-Reference), 11.1 (FanGraphs)—is the highest for any pitcher since World War II.

How good a pitcher do you have to be for someone to just say "Lefty," and people know it's you?

Time to jump into a rabbit hole! When you think of Carlton, what's the first thing that comes to mind? His 1972 season? Maybe. His four Cy Youngs? Maybe. His eccentric interview after he was elected to the Hall of Fame? Maybe.

But there's a good chance you will think about his silence.

Steve Carlton famously did not talk to reporters.

Actually, at first he did talk to reporters with some enthusiasm, but then he stopped. When? How? It's a lot more complicated than I first thought. There's a general story, one that I believed, that Carlton stopped talking to reporters in 1973, the year he led the league in losses. The story went that he felt like the media had kicked him around for long enough. It's a story that makes sense.

But, alas, it isn't true.

Carlton was a loner all his life. He grew up on a chicken farm in Miami, and he felt happiest when he was out hunting and fishing alone. He didn't like school. He didn't particularly like people. He didn't even like baseball all that much; basketball was his favorite sport. But he knew that he had a lethal left arm—literally. He discovered the power of his pitching arm by throwing rocks at living things. He knocked doves off telephone wires. He once threw an ax with such precision that it cut off the head of a quail. He even claimed he had killed a rabbit with a perfectly thrown stone. "That doesn't seem possible," he said, "but I hit it smack in the head."

So when the coach refused to start him on the basketball team his senior year, Carlton quit the sport entirely and focused on becoming a professional pitcher. He threw hard enough to get a tryout with the St. Louis Cardinals, and he signed with the club for $5,000.

From the start, reporters found him interesting because he was so different from other ballplayers. When he was 14, he began to read books about metaphysics and that became his lifelong passion. "It was the only subject that interested me," he told one reporter. "It's a personal thing. I'm looking for what the answers are going to be at the end of life if you live a certain type of life."

Carlton had this complicated philosophy about pitching and training and life that involved a blend of Eastern religions, weird exercises (like thrusting his arm into huge buckets of rice), mental focus, physical exhaustion, and absolute commitment. As Bill James once wrote, "I would try to explain it to you but I don't understand it." Many reporters probably thought he was a bit of a crackpot, but great athletes are not "crackpots." They are "colorful" or "eccentric."

The story that he stopped talking to reporters in 1973 is compelling because it fits his time line. He did grow annoyed by the increased interview requests after his amazing 1972 season. Then, 1973 was a lousy year all the way around. He came to spring training with a severe chest cold—something close to pneumonia—and he pitched lousy most of the year. Reporters hit him pretty hard. It's easy to imagine him stopping interviews right then.

But he didn't stop. Carlton talked to the press all year in '73.

Well, what about 1974? There's another version of the story that goes like this: Carlton stopped talking to the press after *Philadelphia Daily News* baseball writer Bill Conlin shredded him in print.

That story is half true: Conlin did indeed shred him. It happened during spring training; Carlton was so bad that his manager, Danny Ozark, threatened to pull him as the Opening Day starter. "There is a 60 percent chance he won't start opening day," Ozark harrumphed after a particularly bad Carlton outing. Reporters raced over to Carlton to ask if he was worried. "No reason to be," he said. "I never get anybody out in the spring."*

One day after Ozark's outburst, Conlin began a two-day newspaper series called, yes, this is really what it was called: "The Disaster of Steve Carlton." In it, he wrote at length about Carlton's massive decline after his incredible '72 season and predicted, with some confidence, that Carlton would never again be that pitcher.

"Norman Mailer never matched 'The Naked and the Dead,' " Conlin wrote. "What's Jonas Salk done lately. Johnny Vander Meer pitched back-to-back no-hitters and vanished. Maybe we should accept the probability that Carlton peaked during that one season of grandeur and remember it is difficult to recapture the way we were."

---

* Carlton did start that Opening Day, by the way.

Who would blame Carlton for refusing to talk to the media after that? But, in fact, Carlton kept talking to the media throughout the 1974 season. Carlton was quoted just days after the hit job. He was hit with a Billy Williams line drive in his start against the Cubs. "All I had time to see was 'Chub Feeney,' and 'Sewn in Haiti,'" Carlton said.

In 1975, Carlton signed a three-year deal with the Phillies, and for the first couple of months of the season, he was the opposite of silent. You couldn't shut the guy up. He talked about how much he loved Philadelphia. He talked about how he was looking to have his best year ever. He talked about his perceived feud with catcher Bob Boone. And so on and so on.

But in June, we caught the first glimpse of the Carlton silent treatment. It happened on June 16, 1975. That day, Carlton pitched six innings against the Cubs at Wrigley Field, gave up three runs, and hurt his left elbow. Reporters gathered around to ask about the injury. Here's how the *Daily News* reported it:

> Carlton will usually grunt after a tough outing. When he finally emerged from the trainer's room, Carlton cowled to his locker.
>
> Did it start bothering him in the sixth when Andre Thornton and Manny Trillo were pounding back-to-back homers?
>
> No answer. The question was repeated. Carlton spun away from his locker and sent a towel toward a receptacle. He strode to the shower.

It seemed like a one-time deal, a bad day, and Carlton talked again to the press in his next outing. But two weeks later, after a dreadful performance in Cincinnati, Ozark tore into Carlton in the papers. I mean, he *really* tore into Carlton; it's shocking by today's standards to see a manager just bludgeon his superstar:

"He was so inconsistent from one hitter to the next. That's the thing that concerns me more than anything. No consistency. And his breaking ball was terrible. He just had no idea what he was doing. . . . I think it's more a lack of concentration than anything else. . . . If he can't get his mind on what he's trying to do, I don't know how we can help him. If he keeps this up, he won't be worth anything on the market. The other clubs see it too."

Once again, Carlton stopped talking to the press. In late July, *Philadel-*

phia Daily News columnist Stan Hochman made the first public mention of it: "Mr. Carlton was unavailable after the performance," he wrote. "He was off doing his Greta Garbo bit. Some nights, Mr. Carlton does his 'Invisible Man' bit. He does not enjoy meeting the media, on the grounds that his theories of pitching will be misunderstood since they are on a higher plane."

But even through this, Carlton did not fully shut out the press. Carlton talked to reporters sporadically for the rest of the season, and in 1976, he was once again quite talkative. After he won his 20th game in '76, he was so happy that this series of words appeared in the *Philadelphia Inquirer:* "'This is the happiest day of my life,' Carlton bubbled." Yes, the papers reported him bubbling.

He talked in 1977, too. By now, he was definitely withdrawn, often defiant, but as one reporter wrote that year: "Eventually he will return to his dressing cubicle where he will politely, although at times somewhat painfully, unravel his performance in detail before the notepads, cameras and tape recorders."

The rabbit hole does seem to end in 1978. That year, the Phillies won the National League East, but at the same time the team had a cold war with the local press. Numerous players—particularly Bake McBride and Garry Maddox—stopped talking to the press for a time. Carlton was one of those players.

But unlike McBride and Maddox, Carlton's rage never thawed. I think there's a simple reason for it: Carlton found that he *liked* not talking to the press. What was the downside for him? He was free to concentrate on his pitching. He didn't have to endure an endless repeating of the same question. OK, true, he wouldn't be able to get his message out—but he didn't really have a message he wanted to get out anyway. Maybe those reporters would knock him in the papers but, in Carlton's mind, they were doing that anyway.

By 1979, it became known across the sports world that Carlton was the guy who didn't talk to the press. He was mocked repeatedly for it.

And? From 1980 to 1983, he won two Cy Young Awards, could have won a third, won his 300th game, and passed Walter Johnson to become the all-time strikeout king. (Nolan Ryan would take that title later.) He later said not talking to the press cleared his mind and allowed him to become the pitcher he was meant to be.

In later years, it became pretty clear that Carlton was smart to not talk to the media, because there were all kinds of bats flying around in his attic. In 1994, after he was elected to the Hall of Fame, he did a series of interviews, including a long interview in his home in Durango, Colorado, with Pat Jordan. The result was an astonishing portrait of racism, homophobia, fear, nonsense, and anti-Semitism. A few lines probably will suffice:

He believes that the last eight U.S. presidents have been guilty of treason . . . that the AIDS virus was created at a secret Maryland biological warfare laboratory "to get rid of gays and blacks, and now they have a strain of the virus that can live 10 days in the air or on a plate of food, because you know who most of the waiters are," and finally, that most of the mass murderers in this country who open fire indiscriminately in fast-food restaurants "are hypnotized to kill those people and then themselves immediately afterwards," as in the movie *The Manchurian Candidate*. He blinks once, twice, and says, "Who hypnotizes them? They do!"

Carlton quickly released a statement saying the entire article was untrue and suggested that Jordan "became so disoriented (in the thin air of his hometown of Durango) that he lost his grasp on truth and decency."

Pat Jordan, as only he can, grumped back: "Steve is the most fearful man I've ever met."

No. 62 **Smokey Joe Williams**

In April 1952, the *Pittsburgh Courier* put together a panel of 31 experts—"thirty-one of the top baseball men in the country," is how they were described—and had them pick what the paper called "The All-Time... All-America Baseball Team." The famous team has sometimes been called "The All-Negro Leagues Team," but it was not exactly that. It was, instead, a collection of the greatest black players from 1910 to 1952.

Now, because it was 1952, there is not much space between "greatest black players" and "greatest Negro Leagues players." At this point, only five of the sixteen major-league teams were integrated. Still, the committee did choose Jackie Robinson, who only played one year in the Negro Leagues. He is the only player on the starting team who made it because of his play in the major leagues.

The team is fascinating on many levels, including, as you will see, the vote for our featured star, Smokey Joe Williams. But before we get to him, let's look at the all-time lineup. If you are a fan of the Negro Leagues you will probably recognize all the names . . . except one.

1B: Buck Leonard

2B: Jackie Robinson

SS: Pop Lloyd

3B: Oliver Marcelle

LF: Monte Irvin

CF: Oscar Charleston

RF: Cristóbal Torriente

C: Josh Gibson

Seven of these eight players are in the Hall of Fame . . . and one is not. The missing player is the one I suspect you do not recognize—Oliver Marcelle.

But it's no fluke that Marcelle is on this team. He was usually placed on such teams. When Pop Lloyd put together his greatest all-time team, Marcelle was on it. When Smokey Joe Williams put together his greatest all-time team, his third baseman was Oliver Marcelle. Of all the forgotten great players in Negro Leagues history, it seems pretty clear that Marcelle is the most forgotten.

He was a Creole from Louisiana, and they called him "the Ghost." Buck O'Neil used to say that nickname came from his tendency to disappear after games. On the field, the Ghost was a defensive wizard at third base and a line-drive hitter. Off the field, he was a volcano of rage. His talent was impossible to miss; after one exhibition game against major leaguers, people began calling him "the Black Frankie Frisch" after the Gas House Gang Cardinals great.

His fury was also impossible to miss. He supposedly took a bat to the head of Oscar Charleston (O'Neil always doubted the story, believing that if Marcelle had, Charleston would have killed him). He had part of his nose bitten off in another fight. He was arrested for being on the scene when a man was murdered (he was released after it was determined he didn't fire the gun). He was traded by the Lincoln Giants twice in the same year, 1925, because the team kept going back and forth on whether or not his extraordinary talent made him worth the trouble.

"He has been a stormy petrel throughout his entire career in New York," the *New York Age* reported after one of the trades. "Possessed of an unusually quick temper, he got the enmity of many fans because of his willingness to argue and even fight with umpires."

So why is Marcelle not in the Hall of Fame while all the other players on the list are, along with two Negro Leagues third basemen he convincingly beat in the poll, Judy Johnson and Ray Dandridge? It could be his temper. It could be his questionable off-the-field exploits. But I think it's something else, something to do with storytelling.

As we have talked about—and will continue to talk about—the statistics from the Negro Leagues are, by definition, incomplete. It isn't just because the record-keeping was less diligent. The Leagues themselves were not set up for keeping statistics. The seasons were a jumble of league games, town games, exhibition games, doubleheaders after doubleheaders (sometimes on the same day). Some of the games were played in the nation's best stadiums in the biggest cities and some of the games were played on rock-hard fields surrounded by rickety benches in small towns. We can—and some people do—uncover numbers that can bring some clarity.

But mostly, what we are left with are the stories. The legends. The memories. Marcelle, maybe because he played in the early days of the Negro Leagues, maybe because he was difficult to know, maybe because of his tendency to disappear, maybe because of his anger issues, maybe because his steady style of play didn't inspire folk tales, did not inspire enough stories. Was he the best third baseman in the Negro Leagues?

The people in 1952 who saw him and everyone else play sure thought so.

All of which leads us to Smokey Joe Williams.

In addition to picking a lineup, the *Pittsburgh Courier* experts also chose a pitching staff. And when talking about Negro Leagues pitching, everything starts with Satchel Paige, the most famous and the most celebrated pitcher in the history of the Negro Leagues. Paige got 19 votes, more than any position player with the exceptions of Josh Gibson and Oscar Charleston.

Smokey Joe Williams got 20 votes.

Now, yes, it's true, you can make too much of this. We're talking about a one-vote difference—and it's not like Paige and Williams were competing for one spot: The voters got to choose four pitchers for the staff. The voters only made it clear with their votes that those two were miles ahead of every other pitcher (Bullet Rogan finished third in the voting with nine votes).

But, yes, it is actually pretty incredible. As mentioned, Paige was the all-time Negro Leagues legend. His exploits were so incredible that sportswriters in the white press would routinely write about him while he was in the Negro Leagues—that simply didn't happen for almost anybody else. He was bigger than life, the pitcher that black and white players alike idolized and adored.

Add in that Paige was at the height of his fame in 1952. He was 45 years old (at least), but he was pitching brilliantly for the St. Louis Browns (he made the All-Star team and got an MVP vote). He was just about the most famous baseball player in America.

Smokey Joe Williams, meanwhile, had died the year before virtually unknown. He pitched some of his best ball before the Negro Leagues even existed.

Still, he got more votes than Satchel Paige.

How good must he have been?

They called him "Smokey Joe" (sometimes spelled "Smoky") and they also called him "Cyclone Joe." Williams did not seem to have a preference between the two nicknames. Both got the point across and the point was this: He threw hard.

How hard? Again, we have to rely on the legend.

One Negro Leaguer said that he threw so hard that he needed two catchers per game because the first catcher's hand would be too swollen to go on after the fifth inning.

Williams grew up in a town called Seguin, Texas, not far from San Antonio. There isn't too much known about his childhood except that he became a pitcher "probably as soon as I discovered I had an arm." He loved the way a baseball felt in his hand, loved it so much that he would carry one around in his pocket wherever he went. At night, he would put the baseball under his pillow and rest his head on it.

He was a late bloomer . . . or anyway, it seems that way. We don't know because, like with Paige, we don't actually know when Williams was born. At different times, people thought he was born in 1879, 1885, and 1886. The settled year seems to be 1885, which means he was 25 years old when he signed to play with the Chicago Black Giants in 1910. This was a full decade before the Negro Leagues officially came into existence.

In his first game, he supposedly threw the ball so hard that Hall of

Famer pitcher and eventually founder of the Negro Leagues Rube Foster said, "Slow down a little there."

To which Williams replied: "If I really throw hard, they won't see the ball at all."

He pitched for the next 25 years. Williams was 6-foot-4, weighed about 210, and he bounced all around the United States as well as Cuba and Mexico. He was not as charismatic as Paige—who was—but he was a sensation everywhere he went.

"When I wasn't pitching, I had to play the outfield," Williams said. "In those days, there was no two-platoon system. You had to pitch to everyone, lefties as well as righties. And you had to finish every game you started unless there was an emergency. We had no pinch-hitters. Couldn't afford them."

We do know Williams threw thunderbolts, and not just from his nickname or the legends. He threw so hard that he was matched up regularly in exhibitions with two of the greatest major-league pitchers of the day, Walter Johnson and Pete Alexander. Observers said that Williams threw at least as hard as the two big-leaguers (some said he threw harder). One legend, possibly true, is that it was white Hall of Famer Ross Youngs who saw Williams's fastball and coined the nickname "Smokey Joe."

"If you have ever witnessed the speed of a pebble in a storm," Negro Leagues owner Frank Leland said, "you have not even then seen the equal of [Williams's] speed."

He didn't just throw hard—he had impeccable control. That combination made him nearly unhittable. Bozeman Bulger, one of the pioneers of sportswriting and a man who ghostwrote Giants manager John McGraw's newspaper columns, said that Williams was as good a pitcher as Christy Mathewson—that was telling because Bulger and Mathewson were close friends.

Ty Cobb said that Williams would have been a "sure 30-game winner in the major leagues."

"You have a little respect when you face guys like that," Frankie Frisch said of Williams.

Waite Hoyt, many years later when he was a broadcaster, saw Bob Gibson pitch and said that he had seen a pitcher like Gibson before, and his name was Smokey Joe Williams.

The statistical record, slight as it unfortunately is, backs up the legend.

Williams was 45 years old when he struck out 27 Kansas City Monarchs in 12 innings in one of the first professional games under lights (though, to be fair, nobody could see too well under those portable lights; Monarchs pitcher Chet Brewer struck out 19 the same day).

Eighteen years earlier, while pitching for the New York Lincoln Giants, Williams threw a no-hitter to outduel a great Negro Leagues pitcher named Cannonball Dick Redding.

Most of all, Williams dominated white teams in exhibition games. In his life, he beat Walter Johnson, Pete Alexander, Chief Bender, Rube Marquard, and Waite Hoyt, just to name the Hall of Famers. James Riley's research pointed to Williams going 20-3 against white exhibition teams, including one game against the New York Giants when he struck out 19 (that was actually one of his three losses).

There's joy and sadness in studying the Negro Leagues—joy in discovering such wonderful players as Smokey Joe, and sadness that he was denied the chance to play in the major leagues and denied his place in baseball history. We can do something about the second part at least. The *Pittsburgh Courier* team is a snapshot, a chance to understand just how great some of the players were.

Many years later, by the way, Buck O'Neil asked his friend Satchel Paige how it felt to finish second to Smokey Joe in the poll.

"They got that right," Paige said.

No. 61 **Arky Vaughan**

Through the years, I've tried several times to answer a seemingly simple question: Who is the least-known great player in baseball history? I've tried various polls, surveyed many baseball fans I know, etc. I've had a theory about it, one that obviously relates directly to Arky Vaughan, whom there is a reasonable chance you don't know.

For this essay, I tried another method. I created a survey with 60 players, some of them all-time greats, some of them obscure Hall of Famers (who were not, in my view, all-time greats), some of them good players who are not in the Hall, some of them regular old baseball players you might have come across in a baseball card pack. And I asked people to estimate what percentage of baseball fans would know the name and the player.

It's hardly scientific, but it is interesting. Using the results, I rated the players on a scale of 0 to 4, with 0 meaning that basically nobody has heard of the player, and 4 meaning that everybody has.

The most famous players in the poll—and I suspect some of the most famous baseball players ever—are:

1. Babe Ruth, 3.98

2. Jackie Robinson, 3.96

3. Willie Mays, 3.91

4. (tie) Henry Aaron, 3.89; Lou Gehrig, 3.89

I didn't include many famous players on the survey—no Ty Cobb, Joe DiMaggio, Mickey Mantle, or Pete Rose. But you know that they would be up here in this stratosphere. Others in the poll who were just about universally known included Mike Trout, Albert Pujols, Roberto Clemente, Sandy Koufax, and David Ortiz.

Then there was the next level—players *most* people know, but not everybody. Here are some of those players and their scores:

- Carl Yastrzemski, 3.08

- Satchel Paige, 3.05

- Darryl Strawberry, 2.84

- Willie McCovey, 2.61

- Warren Spahn, 2.53

- Phil Niekro, 2.48

- Dale Murphy, 2.44

- Ferguson Jenkins, 2.11

- Al Kaline, 2.05

I was surprised Kaline was that low and surprised again that Strawberry was that high, but fame is a moving target.

The least famous players in the poll were:

1. Roger Connor (0.11), a 19th-century first baseman who held the home run record in 1921 when it was broken by a guy named Babe Ruth. He's in the Hall of Fame.

2. Ross Youngs (0.11), an all-out hustling ballplayer of the 1910s and 1920s who hit .322 for his career and died at age 30 from a kidney ailment. He is in the Hall of Fame.

3. Billy Consolo (0.12), a light-hitting and well-liked shortstop who is probably best known for his lifelong friendship with Sparky Anderson. He's not in the Hall of Fame.

4. Norman Stearnes (0.13). I didn't play fair here. Norman Stearnes is better known as Turkey Stearnes, a Negro Leagues superstar and one of the greatest hitters in baseball history. He's in the Hall of Fame.

5. Bob Elliott (0.13), a star player in the 1940s and early 1950s. He was the first third baseman to win an MVP award (in 1947), and he was so admired that his teammates called him "Mr. Team." He's not in the Hall of Fame but was still terrific.

Numerous other Hall of Famers scored very low in name recognition. See how many of them you know: Rick Ferrell, Earle Combs, Mickey Welch, Earl Averill, Billy Herman, Addie Joss, George Kelly, Travis Jackson.

And all Negro Leaguers, with the exception of Satchel Paige, scored low, even Oscar Charleston (0.70), who some believe was the greatest player in baseball history.

All of this brings us to the center of it all: Arky Vaughan. Vaughan scored a 0.78, meaning he is barely known.

I am convinced that, pound for pound, Arky Vaughan is the least-known great Major League Baseball player.

I say "pound for pound" because there's no reason for him to be so little known. He didn't play in the Negro Leagues and didn't play before 1900. He played in a golden era of baseball—in the time of Ruth and Gehrig and Williams and Jimmie Foxx and DiMaggio—and he was certainly not overlooked in his own time. He made the All-Star team every year, he won a batting title, led the league in multiple categories throughout his career, and he came close to winning an MVP multiple times even while playing for mediocre Pirates teams.

He even played in a World Series for Jackie Robinson's Brooklyn Dodgers.

Still, nobody knows him. How did history skip right past him? A few years ago, I was watching a Kansas City Royals baseball game, and a trivia question came up: *What shortstop since 1900 had the highest batting average for a full season?*

The choices were:

1. Honus Wagner

2. Arky Vaughan

3. Nomar Garciaparra

4. Luke Appling*

The announcers, Ryan Lefebvre (who is a longtime friend) and Rex Hudler, talked and talked about how they had never heard of Arky Vaughan and how surely *nobody* had ever heard of Arky Vaughan. They just kept going on and on about it, as if "Arky Vaughan" were some made-up name from some made-up time.

Vaughan is one of the greatest players ever. He's also a fascinating story; there could be a movie about his life. I'm not at all sure why fame has eluded him.

Joseph Floyd "Arky" Vaughan was born, obviously, in Arkansas, which is how he got the famous nickname that stayed with him all his life. But, in fact, Arky Vaughan didn't live in Arkansas. His family moved to California when he was just seven months old.

This was because his father, Robert, found a job working for Standard Oil in Fullerton, California. There are two archetypal father types in this book. There's the father who is dead set against baseball, sees it as a waste of time, etc. And then there's the father who relentlessly pushes his son to become a ballplayer. Robert Vaughan was neither. He took the Standard Oil job so his children would have a good school to attend. He doted on his three boys and encouraged them to enjoy life and chase their own passions.

Arky was an athletic phenom; it didn't matter the sport. He was a football sensation and received several football scholarships. Baseball was his love.[†]

The scouting of Vaughan is a joyous story. The Yankees had heard great things about him and sent one of their top scouts, Vinegar Bill Essick (who had convinced the Yankees to sign DiMaggio), out to sign the kid. It seemed like a simple transaction.

---

* The answer was Luke Appling, in case you're curious. He hit .388 in 1936.

[†] Vaughan played peewee football with a kid named Richard Nixon. Many years later, after Nixon became president, he put together his own list of the greatest baseball players ever. Nixon listed his old teammate as the greatest shortstop in baseball from 1925 to 1945.

But at the same time, Pittsburgh scout (and owner of the Wichita, Kansas, minor-league team) Art Griggs happened to be vacationing in Los Angeles. He received a tip about a kid in Fullerton with the potential to become a big-league star. But here's the twist: The player was not Arky Vaughan. No, instead it was Vaughan's teammate Willard Hershberger, a fantastic-hitting catcher whom you may have heard of for tragic reasons.

Vinegar Bill had no idea he had competition for Vaughan, so he took his time getting to Fullerton, stopping along the way to scout other players. Griggs, meanwhile, went straight to see Hershberger . . . and once Griggs saw Vaughan play he knew that he just had to have him. Griggs signed Vaughan on the spot, leaving poor Vinegar Bill in a lurch when he finally got to town. The Yankees tried to make it right, offering the Pirates $40,000 for Vaughan's services.

The Pirates turned it down. They might or might not have known what they had with Vaughan, but they figured if the Yankees wanted him that badly, they might as well see what they had.*

Vaughan played for Griggs's team in Wichita for one season in 1931. He hit .338 with 16 triples and 21 homers. He was the Pirates' starting shortstop the next season.

And Vaughan just kept on hitting in the big leagues. Vaughan's rookie year, he hit .318 and surely would have won the Rookie of the Year award, had it existed. In his second year, he hit .314 and led the league in triples. In his third year, he hit .333/.431/.511, leading the league in walks and on-base percentage.

His shortstop defense, however, was a major issue. Vaughan had a strong arm and good range, but he made errors. Lots of them. He committed 46 errors in his first year and 46 more his second. The Pirates were

---

* Vinegar Bill Essick ended up signing Hershberger as a sort of consolation prize. Hershberger was a talented but deeply troubled young man. His father, Claude, had killed himself when Willard was 18. Willard Hershberger was in the Yankees' minor leagues for eight seasons before getting traded to Cincinnati, where he hit .316 in part-time duty for three seasons. In the middle of the 1940 season, after repeatedly reaching out for help, he killed himself. He is the only player in major-league history to die by suicide during the season.

so desperate to get his defense straightened out that they brought in their greatest player, all-time legend Honus Wagner, to coach him up. What an extraordinary confluence of talent: Here were two of the greatest shortstops in Major League Baseball history coming together.

Wagner coaching Vaughan is one of my favorite baseball connections because while Wagner is one of the greatest players of all time—and a supremely nice man—teaching wasn't exactly his thing. I always love hearing stories of all-time greats like Ted Williams or Bob Gibson trying to teach others to do what came so naturally to them. According to the fine book *Honus Wagner: A Biography*, Wagner worked an hour or two every day with Vaughan. After a few days, someone asked Arky how it was going.

"I'm not sure," Vaughan said. "When I asked Mr. Wagner what to do, he said, 'You just run in fast, grab the ball and throw it to first base ahead of the runner.' But he didn't tell me how."

Vaughan did develop into a pretty good defensive shortstop; perhaps some of those Wagner lessons stuck with him. He was, however, error-prone his entire career.

As a hitter, though, he was all but unmatched. His pinnacle season was 1935, when he hit an extraordinary .385/.491/.607, leading the league in all three slash numbers. Vaughan was hitting .400 on September 10 but then slumped and hit just .229 down the stretch. Even so, he became the first shortstop to slug .600 in a full season. He was certainly the best player in the National League, but he didn't win the MVP award because the Pirates were not a factor in the pennant race. The Chicago Cubs won the pennant, and the award went to Chicago catcher Gabby Hartnett.

Vaughan hit .300 every year from 1932 to 1941. He led the league in walks three times. He was breathtakingly fast—his Hall of Fame teammate Paul Waner would say he never saw a player run from first to home like Vaughan. He led the league in triples three times, runs scored three times, and stolen bases once.

Through age 29, Vaughan was hitting .324/.415/.472 and had more than 1,700 hits, which is more than Pete Rose, Stan Musial, or Derek Jeter had at that point in their careers.

Then his story took some odd turns.

After the 1941 season, the Pirates rather unexpectedly shipped Vaughan to Brooklyn for four nonentities that included a 37-year-old pitcher nicknamed "Hot Potato" and a 34-year-old backup catcher named Babe Phelps, whom people called "Blimp."*

What happened? Well, it turns out the deal was spurred by the Pirates' new manager, Frankie Frisch, who will return to our story later. Frisch was a great player, but he, perhaps more than any player in baseball history, suffered from what George Brett has called "Dirt Disorder." This disorder can be described like so: The farther a person gets from the dirt, the easier the game looks.

Frisch would spend his entire life telling stories about how much better baseball was in his day. They were entertaining stories—the press ate them up—but they annoyed the bejeebers out of the younger players who seemed pretty sure they were as good as all those guys in Frisch's time.

Vaughan was famously quiet and modest, but he was proud, too, and it's fair to say he was not impressed by Frisch's nostalgia. And the feeling was mutual. Frisch wanted players like himself: aggressive and loud and largely uninterested in taking a walk. He shipped Vaughan off to Brooklyn to play for Leo Durocher.

For Vaughan, this made things even worse—the Frisch-Vaughan relationship was practically Bogie-Bacall compared to the way Durocher and Vaughan butted heads. Durocher was everything Vaughan despised; he was obnoxious and cold, he played mind games, and he wanted all the credit. Durocher was famous for his "nice guys finish last" quote (though he didn't exactly say it the way people have come to understand it). Vaughan was the ultimate nice guy. Those two had no chance together.

The breaking point, according to Hall of Famer Billy Herman, came when Durocher suspended pitcher Bobo Newsom and then ripped him in the newspaper, saying Newsom had thrown a spitball during the game despite being told not to throw the illegal pitch.

Well, it wasn't true. And when Vaughan read the story, he was outraged. He barged into Durocher's office with the newspaper in his hand. Here's how Herman remembered what came next:

---

* It's never great when you already have a strong baseball nickname like "Babe" and people still insist on calling you "Blimp"—though, to be fair, Blimp Phelps had once been a very good player. He hit .310 and made three All-Star teams in his career. Blimp played one year in Pittsburgh and retired.

"Leo," he said, "did you tell this to the writers?" "Yeah," Durocher said, "I told them that." Arky didn't say another word. He went back to his locker and took off his uniform—pant, blouse, socks, cap—made a bundle of it and went back to the office. "Take this uniform," he said, "and shove it right up your ass." And he threw it in Durocher's face. "If you would lie about Bobo," he said, "then you would lie about me and everybody else. I'm not playing for you."

Vaughan then returned to the clubhouse, sat down, and refused to enter the game. Some of the other players wanted to join him, but in the end, only Vaughan held out. Around the seventh inning, the Dodgers' Branch Rickey came down and convinced Vaughan to put his uniform back on. Still, Vaughan would not enter the game.

He did eventually start playing again. In 1943, he hit .305 and led the league in runs and stolen bases. But playing for Durocher had made the game miserable for him, and his father had always told him to follow his heart. The next year, even though Rickey himself came out to the West Coast to try to talk him into returning, Vaughan simply stayed home in California and took care of the family ranch while World War II raged on. He had retired. He wasn't going to play for Durocher ever again.*

Vaughan did return to baseball and the Dodgers in 1947, shortly after Durocher was suspended for associating with gamblers. You will note the year and remember that was the season of Jackie Robinson breaking the color line. Vaughan played his own small role in that, too.

"[Arky] was one of the fellows who went out of his way to be nice to me when I was a rookie," Robinson would say. "Believe me, I needed it."

Vaughan hit .325 in part-time duty, and he hit a double and drew a walk in three plate appearances in his first and only World Series. The next year, though, Durocher was back, and he promptly made a public statement about how one player's charm simply eluded him. Everyone knew exactly who he was talking about. Vaughan hit just .244 and hated every minute of playing for Durocher, and that was the end of that. He left the major leagues for good at age 36.

---

* While his war with Durocher is well documented, Arky's son Bob said he once asked his father to name the best manager he ever played for. "Durocher," Arky admitted quietly.

Vaughan did play a little bit for the minor-league San Francisco Seals when he got back to California, and he played well enough that big-league teams tried to lure him back. He never returned.

Four years later, Vaughan and a friend were fishing on a lake with an ill-fated name—Lost Lake—when a storm swept in and the boat capsized. The water was ice cold, and an eyewitness said Vaughan swam back to help his friend. About 10 yards from shore, both men submerged and never returned to the surface. Arky Vaughan was 40 years old.

In the immediate aftermath of the tragedy, just about everyone in baseball spoke glowingly about Vaughan, from Jackie Robinson to Enos Slaughter, Branch Rickey, National League president Warren Giles, and coach Cookie Lavagetto, who said, "I never knew a finer fellow or a better team man."

And, almost immediately after that, baseball fans and writers left him behind. In the 1953 Hall of Fame voting, with his death still lingering, he got literally one vote. One. Through the years, despite being the greatest shortstop of his day, Vaughan never got even one-third of the writers' vote. The legendary sports columnist Red Smith once called him "baseball's most superbly forgotten man."

Why was he forgotten? I guess you could try to explain by saying he played for mostly mediocre teams, he had a reputation as a poor defensive shortstop, and his short career blunted his magnificent hitting talents. But none of that really explains it. My guess is his personality naturally led to his being forgotten. He was so quiet and modest. He was not colorful in the ways that entertain sportswriters. He was simply a great ballplayer with strong values.

Then Frankie Frisch reentered the picture. See, Frisch was by far the loudest and most persuasive voice of the Hall of Fame Veterans Committee in those years—the group was often called "Frisch's Committee." And Frisch's committee voted in just about all of his old cronies with the Giants and Cardinals. Many of those unknown Hall of Famers including some I listed at the beginning of this—George Kelly, Travis Jackson, Ross Youngs, Freddie Lindstrom, Dave Bancroft, Jim Bottomley, Chick Hafey, and others—were Frisch's teammates with the Giants or Cardinals. He was, for a few years there, the key master guarding the door of the Hall of Fame.

And, as we know, Frisch didn't like Vaughan. And so it wasn't until years after Frisch died that Vaughan got his Hall of Fame due.

His induction into the Hall of Fame finally happened in 1985, and it mostly happened because an influential sportswriter named Milt Richman took up his cause. Richman was on the Veterans Committee by then, and he talked up Vaughan's case. But he did more than that. That year, about a month before the election, he wrote a long and widely distributed story praising Vaughan's brilliance.

"As exceptional a ballplayer as he was," Richman wrote, "Vaughan was every bit as noble a human being. This isn't something I found out about him in a book. It's what I discovered for myself from knowing him. I think I can sum him up best by saying he was another Brooks Robinson."

Richman was able to stir up some strong emotions for Vaughan; by the time of the vote, numerous other writers had chimed in. It led to Vaughan's election.

Fittingly I suppose, few noticed. Lou Brock and Hoyt Wilhelm were elected that year, too, and most of the headlines were for them. There were also headlines for another Veterans Committee choice, Enos Slaughter, who had been complaining about being passed over every year for more than a decade. "I never could understand it," Slaughter grumbled. "It's been a bitter pill for me to swallow all those years, but fans across the country have never given up. . . . I didn't like being passed over all these years, and I don't pull any punches about it. But it's better late than never."

Meanwhile, Vaughan entered the Hall almost unnoticed. He probably wouldn't have minded. The Hall of Fame did put out a special commemorative envelope for Vaughan, as it does for all Hall of Famers.

They misspelled his name.

No. 60 Pete Rose

There are so many things to say about Pete Rose—his playing, his gambling, his hustle, his competitiveness, his mistakes, his triumphs, his family, his stubbornness, his hits, his misses, his suspension, his records, his crimes, his passions . . . where do you begin? He is sitting in a sports memorabilia store in Las Vegas, and he is selling his autograph, and barkers are outside in the mall trying to draw people in by shouting, "Come see the Hit King!" He is older and heavier but still very much Pete Rose, unmistakable, undaunted, and he kicks out the metal folding chair that stands next to him and he says, "Sit down!" as both an invitation and a challenge.

Where do you begin with Pete Rose?

One question that comes to mind is this: Could any of us have been Pete Rose? That is not to ask if any of us could have lived the erratic and blinding life Rose has lived or gotten 4,256 hits but instead to ask: Could any of us, if we had just wanted it badly enough—if we had just wanted it as badly as Pete Rose himself—could any of us have played Major League Baseball?

Did the rest of us not make it to the big leagues simply because we did not want it enough?

Or did Pete Rose want it too much?

If you are or ever were one of those kids who desperately dream of becoming a big-league ballplayer—and I certainly was—you know that each day on the journey is one of discovery, both for good and ill. Your mind opens up to the game when you see baseball players with breathtaking gifts. You see Tony Gwynn hit, you see Mike Trout slug, you see Rickey Henderson steal, you see Roberto Clemente throw, and you wonder: Is any of that inside of me?

And you go out into the world to find out. You throw baseballs against walls and step in against pitchers who seem to be throwing from 10 feet away and you brace yourself as you stand under a high fly ball. Maybe you have some success. Maybe you make a local All-Star team. But, for most of us, this is only where discovery begins. Then comes the hard stuff. You get hit by a pitch for the first time, and it leaves a bruise, and maybe you never dig in so confidently. You face your first decent curveball and wonder how you could ever hit that. You let a ground ball go through your legs and feel the embarrassment. Maybe, with the game on the line, you hope that the ball doesn't get hit your way.

The big-league dream grows a little bit fainter with each small defeat.

How long can you deny the reality that you're probably not good enough? I was 12 or 13 and cursed with self-awareness. Most of us are. I looked around and realized I wasn't the best player on my South Euclid Tris Speaker Little League team. If I wasn't the best player on my own team I certainly wasn't the best player in South Euclid. And South Euclid is just one small suburb in Cleveland. And Cleveland is just one city in Ohio. And Ohio is just one state in the Rust Belt. And the Rust Belt is just one region of a big country.

The math gradually overwhelmed my dreams.

What is childhood but a gradual realization?

Now, look at Pete Rose. He was small. He was awkward. But he was not cursed with self-awareness—that's the one thing we know for sure about Rose. The only truth of his childhood, the only thing he completely believed in, was that he was going to be a Major League Baseball player. There was no other option. He was Harry Rose's son.

Harry Rose—everybody in town called him "Big Pete"—was a legendary athlete on the West Side of Cincinnati. Nobody had ever seen a tougher character. He played semipro football well into his 40s, often with broken bones. He determined on the day his son Lil' Pete was born that he was going to be a ballplayer.

Harry's brother-in-law, Buddy Bloebaum, a former minor leaguer, suggested that they teach Lil' Pete how to switch-hit right away. And so Pete Rose has been switch-hitting literally for as long as he can remember. When he was 8 years old and began Little League, his father approached the coach and demanded that Lil' Pete be allowed to switch-hit.

In return, Harry promised that his son would never miss a game, never miss a practice, never take a vacation, and that he would play his heart out every single moment. The deal was struck. And for Pete Rose, the deal was for keeps. It has lasted a lifetime.

Pete Rose played catcher for a while because no other position seemed to suit him; but it turned out he was too small and frail to hold up there. Then he became a second baseman because his arm wasn't strong enough to play short. The doubts about his baseball future were there, swirling all around him, but Lil' Pete never saw them. Never felt them. There's something about the way he's wired that prevents him from feeling doubt (or shame), fear (or regret), a crossing of the wires that led naturally to him becoming the all-time hit leader *and* the most famous athlete in American history to be permanently suspended from his sport. Rose knew that nothing could ever stop him, and nothing ever did.

He didn't even play high school baseball as a senior—he'd repeated the ninth grade and so was ineligible. He instead spent that year playing sandlot baseball with auto mechanics and factory workers and construction workers on rock-strewn fields around town. He wasn't really a prospect. But he did have one thing going for him.

Remember Buddy Bloebaum?

Right, Pete's uncle; he was a part-time scout for the Cincinnati Reds. He lived a big life, too. He played minor-league ball. He was a pool hustler. And he was unafraid to go after what he wanted. Bloebaum burst into the offices of Reds general manager Gabe Paul and farm director Phil Seghi and made Rose's case. He said that while Rose seemed small, he would grow. He said that nobody in the world played harder than Rose.

He also made the compelling argument that the Reds needed to give the local kid a chance. The team had missed on another West Side kid named Don Zimmer, who had become an established big leaguer at the time. "You can't miss again," Bloebaum insisted. And, really, what would it cost them to take a chance? Bloebaum said he could get Rose to sign for a measly $5,000. Paul gave Bloebaum the money. The Reds shipped Rose to a Class D team in Geneva, New York.

And Pete Rose began the journey that he always knew was his destiny.

Here's something that people don't often say about the young Pete Rose, but it's true: The guy was breathtakingly fast. It's hard to picture the speed if you only caught Rose at the end, when he was in his mid-40s, thick, and entirely focused on blooping singles over infielders' heads, but the young Rose was blazing fast. In his first full season in pro ball—Tampa, 1961— Rose hit an astounding 30 triples. He stole 30 bases. He was so fast that his first nickname was actually "Scooter."

That year, a scout clocked him running to first in 3.7 seconds, this supposedly against a strong headwind ("I can do 3.5 easy," he told the local reporter). To give you an idea what that means, Billy Hamilton and Byron Buxton—widely regarded as the fastest players in baseball today—are clocked at 3.7 seconds to first base.

"He's only a tick slower than Vada Pinson," one Reds official gushed, "and Pinson is the fastest player in baseball."

But it wasn't Rose's speed that captured the imagination. No, it was his attitude. He was utterly mad. He never stopped. The guy ran to first base on walks. He ran from the on-deck circle into the batter's box. He sprinted on and off the field between innings. He kept going on the bases until somebody dared stop him. There were no rundowns for Pete Rose because he just kept going. He would see outfielders with the ball in their gloves and *still* take off for the extra base.

His Tampa manager Johnny Vander Meer, a once-wonderful pitcher who had thrown back-to-back no-hitters for the Reds, was the first of many managers to fall under Rose's spell.

"Hitting and speed are not his greatest assets," Vander Meer said. "I've seen a lot of players who had all the tools to be great, but they weren't aggressive. Rose is aggressive every minute of every day. He's aggressive when he's batting, running or playing the infield."

Vander Meer then offered two folksy quotes about Rose that should be included:

1. "He's got more stomach than a parachute-jumper."

2. "He runs like a scalded dog."

At his first major-league spring training camp in 1962, Rose was so manic on the field that during one game against the Yankees, Whitey Ford leaned over to Mickey Mantle and said sarcastically, "Look at Charlie Hustle over there." Ford meant the nickname derisively, and everybody at first kept using it to poke fun at Rose. But he loved it. He was no longer Scooter.

He was Charlie Hustle.

Most of the Reds (and many of the writers and fans) loathed Rose when he competed for a big-league job in '63. Part of it was the hustle, the arrogance, the hot dog element that was always a part of his nature. But most of all, people just didn't want him to beat out Don Blasingame, the Reds' likable second baseman. Blasingame was 30, and he had paid his big-league dues, and he could really handle the bat. He was also one of the best bunters of his time. Nobody wanted this arrogant kid to take Blasingame's job.

So players tore into Rose, mocked him, alienated him, did all they could to make him miserable.

Rose played right through all that because of course he did. He found a mentor and kindred spirit in none other than the great Frank Robinson. To Rose, Robinson was the ballplayer's ballplayer, the ultimate example of how you play the game. He was tough. He was fierce. He was a brilliant hitter and he broke up double plays with wild abandon. He would do what he had to do to win.

Robinson, meanwhile, saw an underdog in Rose. They spent many dinners together talking baseball and life. Robinson, probably more than anyone else in the big leagues, taught Rose how to play the game.*

Rose took Blasingame's job early in 1963. Over the next 24 years, he would play more games, come to the plate more times, and knock more hits than anybody in the long history of Major League Baseball. He got on base more than anybody. He hit more singles than anybody. Only Tris Speaker hit more doubles. You can lose yourself in Pete Rose's numbers.

---

* Near the end of his life, Robinson went public and announced that Rose doesn't belong in the Hall of Fame. I know that it broke Robinson's heart to say it. But, again, he had talked to Rose endlessly about playing the game right.

He became the biggest name in baseball through the sheer power of his ambition. Was Rose ever the best player in the game? Probably not, no. You could argue that he was never the best player on his own team, though that's not fair since Rose spent the prime of his career as teammates with all-time legends Joe Morgan, Johnny Bench, and Mike Schmidt. But it is true that Rose's game had gaps. He didn't hit with much power. He played defense with enthusiasm but not always with effectiveness. His .375 lifetime on-base percentage is good but not legendary.

Still, Rose made himself the center of the baseball universe. To watch Pete Rose play ball—the mad dashes to first on walks, the dangerous head-first slides, the way he stretched singles into the doubles, his insistence on backing up every single play no matter what—was to enter that magical world of baseball nostalgia.

Yes, you know how Pete Rose played?

He played the way old ballplayers *imagine* they had played.

And he loved the game; Lord, did he love it. Do you know what Rose used to do at night after the ball game ended? He would drive home, park his car in the driveway, and then stay in the driver's seat for hours scanning the radio dial so he could listen to West Coast games. How much did he love it? In the 11th inning of that famous 1975 World Series Game 6 at Fenway Park, with the Reds trying to win the whole thing, with the Red Sox trying to stave off elimination, with so much tension in the air, he turned to Carlton Fisk and said, "Wow, this is some kind of game, isn't it? We'll be telling our grandkids about the game."

Then, at first base, he turned to Carl Yastrzemski and said, "This is the greatest game I ever played in!" And Yaz, who took the game seriously enough to never get caught up in moments, was so taken by Rose's enthusiasm that he nodded.

Rose would talk about baseball for hours with anybody willing to match his enthusiasm. He was exceedingly kind to young players, buying them dinners, offering them constant advice. He was the sort of leader that other players followed. He played baseball with a crackling energy that inspired countless kids to become ballplayers themselves.

But, there is another side to it all. With Rose, there is always the other side. How can you hear the story of him sitting in his car and listening to West Coast games without wondering if he was betting on them? How can you talk about his limitless thirst without talking about his troubling off-field life? It's all part of the same person. And many of the same sports-writers who celebrated him as a god when he played baseball the right way savaged him as a charlatan when he was suspended for gambling, jailed for tax evasion, revealed to be a poor excuse for a husband and father, and credibly accused of statutory rape.

Baseball is not life.

But it is for Pete Rose.

Pete Rose still signs autographs in Las Vegas. This month, five hours a day, noon to 5 p.m., you can catch him at the Art of Music store at the MGM Grand Casino or—if he's not there—at the Art of Music store at the Mirage. He will not sign autographs every day. He will take a couple of weekends off.

He signs everything. He'd prefer to sign the merchandise that the store is selling, but for a price he will sign personal items, whatever they might be. He has signed the Dowd Report, which led to him getting permanently suspended from baseball, the police mug shot after his arrest for tax evasion, and the Hall of Fame ballots that excluded him because he's ineligible. He has, rather famously, written, "I'm sorry I bet on baseball" on baseballs and then signed those.

"What do I care?" he told me once. The way he figures it, if people pay, he will sign. On eBay, you can get a baseball signed with his hit total (4,256), one signed with "Charlie Hustle," one signed with "HOF??", one signed with "I wish I were in the HOF," one signed with "I wish I landed on the moon." The items he will sign are limited only by the imagination of the person asking.

I've sat with him while he signed autographs. Much of it is downtime—he is in the store every day so there's no real urgency; he will be back tomorrow if you miss him today. Still, fans do come, a few every hour, and sometimes they ask him about the time he knocked over Ray Fosse in the All-Star Game ("You know, I was the one who got hurt!" he says) or about his National League record 44-game hitting streak ("I should have caught DiMaggio," he says), or about his simmering feud with Johnny Bench ("He wouldn't be in the Hall of Fame if it wasn't for me," he says), or about the Hall of Fame ("I don't even think about it," he says, but without conviction). He will tell wonderful baseball stories if the mood strikes him. He will talk about how he was wronged by any number of people if the mood strikes him—that mood strikes more often.

Has anyone ever loved baseball as much as Pete Rose? I don't think so. Has anyone ever lost so much in baseball by following his worst impulses? I don't think so.

And yet . . . I don't sense that Rose has changed, not in the way that people seem to want or expect or even hope for. He's been Pete Rose all his life. He has been that same Cincinnati kid who never doubted his future greatness, Charlie Hustle dashing to first base on a walk, the guy who (of course) was there to catch the ball that Bob Boone bobbled in the World Series, the unquenchable force who got to 3,000 hits and decided that wasn't enough, wasn't close to enough, and so he just kept hitting even after his hometown Reds didn't want him anymore, even after the Phillies released him, even after he seemed finished in Montreal, even after he became the Reds manager and the only manager in baseball who would put his name in the lineup.

Pete Rose has had the same kind of compulsive pull throughout his life—for baseball, for the ponies, for sports betting, for sex, for cars, for action.

Change? He can't change. And he wouldn't even if he could. It's all part of the same story.

There are so many misconceptions about Pete Rose's permanent suspension and Hall of Fame eligibility. Here is the basic time line:

February 1989: Rose went to have a private meeting with baseball commissioner Peter Ueberroth. The *New York Times* reported that the meeting was about Rose's gambling.

March 1989: Ueberroth, having been advised that *Sports Illustrated* was about to publish an exposé of Rose's longtime gambling on baseball, announced that MLB had started an investigation into "serious allegations."

April 1, 1989: A. Bartlett Giamatti became commissioner of baseball. Giamatti revered baseball. His books about the sport were called *A Great and Glorious Game* and *Take Time for Paradise*. The last thing in the world he wanted was to start his tenure having a nasty fight with one of baseball's greatest figures. But Rose would give him no choice.

June through late August 1989: There were numerous back-and-forth fights between Giamatti and Rose, with Giamatti insisting on having a hearing and Rose suing baseball to prevent it.

August 24, 1989: Rose was permanently banned from baseball.

Here's the part of the story that was missed at the time: Giamatti wanted to make a quiet deal. He did not want to permanently suspend Rose. He wanted to discreetly handle Rose's gambling and move on to more important ways to improve the game. He had a plan, one that now seems quite sensible.

See, there are actually two parts to Baseball's Rule 21, the "Thou shalt not gamble" rule:

The first part states that any player who bets on a baseball game they are *not* involved in will be declared ineligible for one year.

The second part states that any player who bets any sum on a game they *are* involved in will be declared permanently ineligible.

You see the difference, right? If Rose bet on the Astros-Pirates game, yes, it's against the rules but it's not a mortal sin—that comes with a one-year suspension. It is only betting on *your own team* that leads to the permanent ban, which makes a lot of sense if you think about it. The rule is intended to prevent players from throwing games or purposely not playing their best.

Giamatti knew from the information he was given that Rose had bet on his own team while managing the Reds. But he gave every indication that he was willing to charge Rose with the lesser offense. All Rose would have to do was admit he gambled on baseball and promise to make amends and he would have been suspended for a year and then given a chance to return to baseball. That seemed a reasonable punishment to Giamatti.

But, alas, a Rose is a Rose is a Rose is a Rose. He refused. He defiantly refused. He would not admit betting on a single game. He would not change his life one bit.

And he did what he knew how to do: He fought. He sued Giamatti and MLB. He tore at Giamatti's integrity repeatedly. He refused to even meet with Giamatti, and he continuously called the whole thing a witch hunt.

Rose seemed sure he would win. And he did win a couple of battles. He found a Cincinnati judge who issued a temporary restraining order against Giamatti. Another Cincinnati judge attacked Giamatti for "prejudging Rose." But Rose's lawyers knew—in a way that Rose probably never did—

that these were nothing but stall tactics, that sooner or later he would have to cut a deal. And the trouble was: The nastier Rose fought, the worse the deal became.

On August 24, 1989, the deal was done . . . and it was the worst possible deal Rose could have cut for himself. It was reported as a settlement, but it was nothing of the kind.

Baseball suspended Rose forever and got him to sign an agreement stating so:

"Peter Edward Rose acknowledges that the commissioner has a factual basis to impose the penalty provided herein, and hereby accepts the penalty imposed . . . and agrees not to challenge that penalty in court or otherwise. He also agrees that he will not institute any legal proceedings of any nature against the commissioner or any of his representatives."

So what did Rose get? Nothing. Yes, the Rose team insisted that they *did* get something. They got MLB to stop their investigation of Rose (which presumably would have led to some pretty bad stuff). They were able to free Rose from admitting that he bet on baseball. And they got a promise that MLB would not publicly accuse Rose of betting on the Reds.

But, in the end, none of that held up. Yes, MLB stopped the investigation, but so what? They had already given him the baseball death penalty. Rose didn't have to admit he bet on baseball, this is true, but there was no chance he was going to be let back in the game with that admission. And finally, while Giamatti hemmed and hawed when reporters asked if Rose bet on his own team, the lifetime ban spoke for itself.

The Rose team deluded themselves into believing that Giamatti's initial plan of having Rose serve just a one-year suspension was still on the table.

"This is a very sad day," Rose said. "I've been in baseball three decades and to think I am going to be out for a very short period of time hurts. . . . I've never looked forward to a birthday like I'm looking forward to my new daughter's birthday. Because two days after that is when I can apply for reinstatement."

It was true that he could apply for reinstatement. And Giamatti promised to keep an open mind. But he made it clear that no player with a lifetime ban had ever been reinstated.

"It isn't up to me," he said. "It is up to Mr. Rose to reconfigure his life in ways I would assume he would prefer. I am not here to prescribe them, to dictate them or to diagnose."

And then . . . Giamatti died eight days later. He was replaced by his dear friend Fay Vincent, who remains one of the most passionate hard-liners against Rose.

Pete Rose has never come close to being reinstated and it's pretty clear he never will be.

But what about the Hall of Fame? That is actually a slightly different story. After Rose was suspended, Giamatti was asked specifically about the Hall. He said Rose's place in history would be left up to the Hall of Fame voters. "When Pete Rose is eligible," he said, "[BBWAA secretary] Mr. Jack Lang will count the ballots, and you will decide whether he belongs in the Hall of Fame."

His predecessor as commissioner, Peter Ueberroth, agreed: "I believe Pete Rose will be elected to the Hall of Fame." Shortly after that, Hall of Fame associate director Bill Guilfoile confirmed that Rose would be on the ballot, and the baseball writers would decide, based on the totality of his baseball life, if Pete Rose belonged in the Hall.

But Fay Vincent, among others, couldn't see the logic of that. How could someone permanently banned from baseball be given baseball's greatest honor? In 1990, against the wishes of the BBWAA, a movement began to remove Rose from the ballot. And it was a fait accompli. The Hall of Fame board had a vote and decided that nobody who has been permanently banned from the game would appear on the Hall of Fame ballot.

Edward Stack, the Hall of Fame director, absurdly made it sound like Rose was not the motivating force behind this decision.

"We're cleaning up our rules of election," he said. "This is probably something that should have been done years ago. . . . I don't remember [Rose's] name being specifically mentioned. Pete Rose was not the subject of our discussion."

People will argue whether Rose's name should appear on the ballot, but I don't actually think it matters. I don't think Rose ever would have gotten 75 percent of the vote. And I don't think he will ever get in the Hall of Fame. Yes, there are those who favor putting him in after he dies, which seems particularly cruel, but most of them misunderstand his ban. It's not a lifetime ban. It's a *permanent* ban. I could be wrong, but I just don't see how enough momentum builds for removing the ban after he dies.

It's a sad story. It is Rose's own fault—not only for breaking one of baseball's most cherished rules but for refusing to come clean and accept his punishment right at the start. I feel quite sure that even after all he did, if he had said to Giamatti that he was wrong and he wanted to change his life, he would be in Cooperstown and in baseball today.

But, then, he would not be Pete Rose.

No. 59 **Reggie Jackson**

On September 5, 1970—in the midst of his most nightmarish baseball season—Reggie Jackson stepped to the plate as a pinch-hitter. It was a gorgeous afternoon, a Saturday day game in Oakland, and it was Fan Appreciation Day on top of that. But it hardly felt like an event. Fewer than 10,000 fans showed up to be appreciated. And Reggie was deeply unhappy.

He had established himself as a superstar in 1969. He had 37 home runs at the All-Star break, which was ahead of Roger Maris's (and Babe Ruth's) record pace. In 58 games from April 24 to July 2, he hit .324/.444/.852 with 31 home runs. It was unheard-of stuff. And despite a season-ending slump—he hit just two home runs in his last 30 games—he still managed to hit 47 home runs and lead the league in runs, slugging, and OPS. He finished fifth in the MVP voting but, even with the late-season collapse, he was probably the best player in the league.

Nothing had gone right since that season ended—this was largely because Jackson had the misfortune of playing for one of the game's most notorious and exhausting quacks, Athletics owner Charlie O. Finley. The two men clashed like titans. First, they fought over money. Jackson demanded $60,000 after his brilliant season. Finley was insulted and countered with $35,000. Jackson was insulted and threatened to quit baseball. Finley, according to Dayn Perry's fascinating book, *Reggie Jackson,* was so desperate to get Jackson to sign that he would call repeatedly in the middle of the night in the hopes that Jackson would "in the fugue of near-sleep accept his latest lowball offer."

So, yeah, Finley was that kind of nut.

Jackson did not cave in; he held out almost all of spring training. Finally, Finley offered $45,000 and a stipend to pay for an apartment in Oakland. Jackson didn't want to take the deal, but he had pushed the negotiations as far as he could. Then he exacted his own revenge. Finley did not specify what *kind* of apartment so Jackson rented the most luxurious apartment he could find in the city, one right next to Finley's own apartment.

It was like a *Tom and Jerry* episode.

Then Jackson went into the worst slump of his life. Finley, seeing his chance to take the upper hand, demanded that his manager, John Mc-Namara, bench Jackson. He also tried desperately to send Jackson to the minor leagues, but Jackson refused to go.

Jackson tried to fight back in the press with various charges and insults. But his heart wasn't really in it. Being on the bench broke his spirit. At one point, he grew so anguished that he called Finley and begged for a truce. He said that he would lay off Finley in newspaper stories if Finley would just put him back in the lineup. Finley was briefly satisfied, but even after being returned to the lineup, Jackson struggled. Finley had him benched again.

On September 5, Jackson was on the bench for the sixth day in a row. He was contemplating quitting. He sat for the first eight innings and then in the bottom of the eighth, with the A's up a run and the bases loaded, Jackson was sent in to pinch-hit for pitcher Paul Lindblad. Kansas City brought in lefty Tom Burgmeier to face him.

On the first pitch, Burgmeier threw an inside fastball that caught too much of the plate and Jackson unleashed with all the frustration and anger that had been bubbling inside. He caught all of it, and when Reginald Martinez Jackson caught all of a baseball, it was something to behold. He sent the ball soaring deep into the center-field bleachers, a grand slam, one of the longest home runs Reggie ever hit, and he hit so many long ones.

Jackson stood at the plate and watched the ball rise, as he sometimes did, and then he lumbered slowly around the bases. The few fans still at the game cheered madly. When Jackson got to home plate, he threw off his batting helmet and then he looked up to the owner's box. He could not believe what he saw—there was Finley smiling and applauding like he'd had something to do with that.

And that, finally, was too much.

Jackson lifted his middle finger toward Finley. Then he unmistakably shouted out the two easiest words in the English language to lip-read, the two words that one newspaper called "the classic defiant unprintable" and another called "one of your more obscene expressions."*

Finley stopped cheering at that point. He tried to make light of it after the game—"I thought it was pretty clever," he told reporters—but privately he was outraged.

Jackson, after the game, told reporters that he would never apologize, and he would absolutely not be back in Oakland in 1971. He hinted that he would challenge the reserve clause if necessary to get out of town. When it was pointed out that Curt Flood had taken his challenge all the way to the Supreme Court only to fail, he said: "You've heard it said that the wrong man challenged the reserve clause. He was older, he had his best years behind him. My best years are ahead of me."

In the end, Jackson did apologize—Finley had threatened to fine him $5,000 if he didn't—and he didn't challenge the reserve clause. He played in Oakland for Finley for four more years. The A's would win three World Series titles while Jackson made four All-Star teams, won an MVP award, and became baseball's biggest star.

Such was the life of Reggie Jackson.

Jackson did not grow up poor, but he did grow up haunted. He was six when his mother, Clara, left with three of his siblings and never returned. He was in high school when his father, Martinez, did six months in jail for bootlegging. Reggie was one of the few black students at his various schools in Wyncote, a neighborhood in southeast Philadelphia. He would say that he heard racial slurs throughout his childhood.

Martinez was the biggest influence on Reggie's life. He was a veteran

---

* My favorite lead of the day came from Ron Bergman in the *Oakland Tribune*, who wrote: "What did Reggie Jackson say?" As if he was either too delicate or simply couldn't make it out.

(he'd flown during World War II), a ballplayer (he'd played on the fringes of the Negro Leagues), an obsessive gambler, a ladies' man (which was why Clara took half the kids and left), and a tailor. He was often distant, but he loved watching his son excel at sports. When Reggie was a senior in high school, he was captain of the football team, the basketball team, the baseball team, *and,* as the son of a tailor, he took all the measurements for the senior letterman sweaters.

Reggie Jackson was an athletic marvel. There were always baseball scouts sniffing around, but his best sport was football. He was heavily recruited by schools around the country to be a halfback. Perry wrote in his book that both Georgia and Alabama recruited him to become their first black football player, but I'm skeptical about that. This was 1964, the year Lyndon Johnson signed the Civil Rights Act and a full seven years before either team would integrate. Alabama had not yet enrolled a black *student,* much less a black athlete. There might have been some communication, but my best bet is that neither school was ready for Jackson.

Not that it would have mattered: Jackson had no interest whatsoever in going anywhere near the South. His father had driven the bus of the Newark Eagles Negro Leagues team for a while and he told terrifying stories about his time below the Mason-Dixon Line. Reggie had plenty of other options: Penn State; Oklahoma; Syracuse. He remembered that Notre Dame and Michigan showed some interest, too.

Jackson eventually chose Arizona State because he liked the idea of going far from home and he admired the Sun Devils' famously tough head coach, Frank Kush. As an added bonus, Arizona State had a fantastic baseball program run by Bobby Winkles. When he asked Kush if he could play baseball as well as football, Kush grunted yes, if he maintained a B average. Jackson played on the freshman football team—freshmen were still ineligible to play varsity football—and was effective as a runner and a receiver. But he already seemed to know that baseball was his future.

He bonded immediately with Winkles and would come to see him as a second father. Winkles repeatedly told Jackson he had a chance to be a great ballplayer. And the summer after that freshman year, he arranged for Jackson to play on a team run by legendary Baltimore Orioles scout Walter Youse.

It is interesting that Winkles did not mention to Youse that Jackson was black. Youse had been working with brilliant young ballplayers for many years, but he never had a black player on his team before. Jackson remembered Youse seeming a bit reluctant at first. But then he watched Jackson hit home runs that boggled the mind. He watched Jackson throw like no one he had seen other than perhaps Pittsburgh's Roberto Clemente. And then he clocked Jackson running to first.

"Hey kid," he yelled at Jackson after the run. "How about doing that again. This watch must be broken."

Reggie ran again and the clock said the same thing: 3.8 seconds. He then timed Jackson running 3.4 seconds to first on a drag bunt. "Reggie is about as fast as Mickey Mantle when Mantle was 19," he told reporters. "I've never seen a boy Reggie's size move the way he does."

At that point, he was so taken with Jackson, he called Baltimore Orioles farm director Harry Dalton. They watched Jackson together, with their mouths agape. "He's the kind of prospect you see once every 20 years," Youse said. And they were both deeply frustrated because they knew they could not get him. Baseball had, that very year, started an amateur draft (Jackson's Arizona State classmate Rick Monday had been the first pick) and that meant that Jackson could not be signed like in previous years. He would go to the team with the top pick in the draft, and that team was the New York Mets.

They never doubted even for a moment that Jackson would be the first pick.

Jackson went back to Arizona State, quit football with Kush's blessings, and filled the void left behind by Monday. He set school records for home runs and RBIs. Scouts drooled. The newspaper stories all predicted exactly what Youse and Dalton had foreseen: The New York Mets would take Jackson with the first overall pick.

Only, the Mets didn't take Jackson. They took a high school catcher named Steve Chilcott instead. Jackson was selected second by the Athletics.

It still might be the most controversial pick in the history of the draft, in part because Jackson has repeatedly claimed that the Mets didn't take him because he was dating a white woman. Jackson's version is that a day or two before the draft, Winkles told him, "The Mets think you're gonna maybe cause a problem, socially."

Winkles, however, has denied saying that and has insisted that he had no way of knowing before the draft what the Mets or any other team was going to do.

The Mets, for their part, said they took Chilcott because the team was desperate for catching and because the legendary Casey Stengel, who had retired as a manager but was still doing some scouting for the team, saw Chilcott play and fell desperately in love. "He's going to be better than [Yogi] Berra," Stengel reportedly said.

Chilcott, of course, did not end up being better than Yogi Berra or Dale Berra or Geronimo Berroa. He was cursed with countless injuries and batting slumps for seven difficult minor-league seasons. He never made it to the big leagues.

In his book *Becoming Mr. October,* Jackson lamented extensively about the fact that the Mets didn't take him first. He wondered how much different his life would have been had he played in New York right from the start.

The brilliant defensive catcher Jim Sundberg told me that Jackson was the smartest hitter he ever saw. Yes, it is true that Jackson happened to be standing right next to Sundberg when he said this (Reggie merely nodded in agreement). But he meant it.

You didn't hear people call Jackson a "smart hitter" when he played. Guys who strike out a lot just don't get called "smart" very often, and nobody struck out more than Jackson. This is still true, which is simply remarkable. Hitters are striking out more than they ever have in baseball history, and yet Jackson's record remains.

Most career strikeouts:

1. Reggie Jackson, 2,597

2. Jim Thome, 2,548

3. Adam Dunn, 2,379

4. Sammy Sosa, 2,306

5. Alex Rodriguez, 2,287

But Sundberg explained—rightly so, I think—that Jackson's strikeouts were not a sign of weakness but were instead part of his brilliant calculations. Jackson wasn't interested in playing baseball the way other people wanted him to play. When he first began playing for the A's, Finley brought in the great Joe DiMaggio to teach him how to shorten his swing and make more contact.

"They're all trying to hit home runs," DiMaggio grumped. "Jackson swings for the fences at every ball."

DiMaggio was famous for not striking out—until his difficult final season, he had more career home runs than strikeouts. And Jackson was deeply respectful of the Yankee Clipper, saying, "You can just sit around with him on the bench and let him talk and you can gain knowledge."

But, Reggie Jackson wasn't shortening his swing for DiMaggio or anybody else.

He had a clear vision of the kind of ballplayer he was going to be, and that vision didn't involve pulling back just so he could hit a few more ground balls. He was going to hit home runs, lots and lots of home runs, and in order to do that, he developed a plan, one he called "calculated anticipation."

When Reggie stepped to the plate, he looked for a certain pitch in a certain place.

And he swung hard.

If he got the pitch, he destroyed. If he didn't get the pitch, he flailed.

Most great hitters—like George Brett, for instance—will tell you this is no way to make a living as a hitter. And Brett is mostly right; guessing isn't much of a plan against the best pitchers in the world . . . that is, unless you guess right a whole lot.

And as Sundberg said, "Nobody anticipated pitches better than Reggie Jackson."

He was uncanny about getting the pitch he wanted. He relentlessly studied tendencies. He adjusted from pitch to pitch. He goaded pitchers into throwing the pitch he wanted, sometimes pretending to be fooled by that pitch in an earlier situation. He would choke up on the bat to convince pitchers that he was looking fastball and then wait on the curve. He would move up in the box, suggesting that he was looking for the curve, and then wait for the fastball.

Sundberg says that Jackson, more than anybody he ever saw, bent pitchers to his will.

Jackson's will led to home runs. He called them dingers and taters and they are what he lived for. "Home runs," he famously said, "are where the money is."

Yes, Jackson made his career exactly what he wanted it to be—a larger-than-life demonstration of his extraordinary power. He was a periodically good outfielder with a strong arm. He was a fast baserunner when he was young. But it was the home run that mattered, and he hit 563 of them—he retired in sixth place on the all-time list behind only Henry Aaron, Babe Ruth, his hero Willie Mays, his role model Frank Robinson, and Harmon Killebrew.

And he did that during a particularly dead time for homers and often in pitchers' parks—in another time and place he might have hit 600 or 650 or even 700 homers.

But with Reggie, it was more than just the number of home runs. Each bomb was its own work of art. How many unforgettable homers did he hit? He blasted one off the transformer on the roof at Tiger Stadium during the 1971 All-Star Game—that has been estimated at 539 feet, though at least one observer claimed it would have been well over 600 had it not been stopped.

The third home run he hit in Game 6 of the 1977 World Series—the one off a Charlie Hough knuckleball*—probably went 475 feet.

He hit a 500-foot home run in Anaheim and a home run in Kansas City that left old Municipal Stadium and bounced off Brooklyn Avenue—people in Kansas City still talk about that one. But then people in Kansas City also still talk about the homer he hit off Larry Gura in 1976, one that bounced off the back of the right-field bullpen.

In Minneapolis, he hit a home run off Jim Perry in '69 that was so absurd, the *Minneapolis Star Tribune* ran a photo with an arrow pointing to the beer sign at the top of the center-field scoreboard. There's where the ball hit.

In 1972, Nolan Ryan threw him a hanging curve in Oakland, and Jackson hit what Ryan would call the longest ball ever hit off him.

Jackson launched one of the longest home runs ever hit at old Arlington Stadium, one of the longest home runs ever hit at old Cleveland Municipal Stadium, one of the longest home runs ever hit at Fenway Park, one of the longest home runs ever hit at Memorial Stadium. This was the essence of Reggie; he wanted to send fans home with something that they would never forget. Joe DiMaggio wanted him to shorten his swing? Ri-

---

* "He threw the pitch," Jackson said of the moment, "and I said, 'Oh boy!'"

diculous. He would have quit baseball first. He didn't play ball for scraps. He played ball to have a candy bar named for him.*

I don't know that anybody in baseball history has ever wanted to be a superstar more than Reggie Jackson.

"Fans don't boo nobodies," he said when they booed him.

"I didn't come to New York to be a star," he said after signing with the Yankees. "I brought my star with me."

"The only reason I don't like playing in the World Series," he told reporters, "is I can't watch myself play."

"I am the best in baseball," he wrote in his first book. "That may sound conceited, but I want to be honest about how I feel."

He was always honest about how he felt . . . or, perhaps more to the point, he never hid how he felt. Through the Finley Wars, through the Billy Martin Battles, through the George Steinbrenner Skirmishes, through the glorious times and the terrible slumps, he needed everyone around him to know exactly how he felt.

I think about two Jackson moments from the 1978 World Series. The first comes from Game 2. It was the top of the ninth, the Los Angeles Dodgers led the Yankees by a run, and there were two men on base. The Dodgers brought out a hard-throwing rookie named Bob Welch. And Reggie stepped up to the plate.

He was already Mr. October by then.

If you are old enough, you will remember how the scene played out on television—it was not unlike the final scene of *The Natural*. The brilliant young pitcher. The great slugger. The camera closed in tight on Welch's face, then on Reggie in the box. The count went full. The runners took off, which Reggie would say jolted his attention. Jackson swung his usual swing—he surely was not trying to poke a game-tying single. No, he swung full, like he was trying to deposit the ball somewhere in the hills. He missed. He slammed his bat so hard that it broke in his hands. Dodger Stadium became a wall of sound.

Now, the memory jumps ahead six days to Game 6. The Yankees led 5–2 in the seventh inning, and Welch was brought in to keep things where

---

* That candy bar—the Reggie bar—came out in 1978, and the best line about it came from Jackson's teammate Catfish Hunter: "When you unwrap a Reggie bar, it tells you how good it is."

they were. With a man on, Jackson stepped back to the plate. I have always loved the way Jackson remembered the moment in *Becoming Mr. October:*

"He threw hard every time he came in. But the first time I saw him he was fresh as a daisy. The last time, you know, the coffee had been on the stove a little bit. And I had smelled the aroma enough to be able to understand the taste."

He really was a poet. Reggie Jackson went up to the plate to hit a home run against Bob Welch. Then, he hit the home run. The coffee tasted fine.

No. 58 **Jeff Bagwell**

In Kansas City, at what is now Kauffman Stadium, there's a statue of Frank White just beyond right field. People who are not from Kansas City might not understand that. White hit just .255 in his career. He stole some few bases. Yes, non-Royals fans might know about his defense—he won eight Gold Gloves as the Royals' second baseman—but they probably don't appreciate his otherworldly fielding the way Kansas Citians do.

In Kansas City, it's simply accepted fact: Nobody ever played second base like White.

White was like a dancer and a bullfighter on the hard and scorching hot Astroturf at Royals Stadium. Ground balls seemed to pick up speed with every bounce. He jumped on high choppers that attacked like angry bees. Nobody was better at going back on bloops and inconveniently placed pop-ups. His first baseman John Mayberry used to yell "Frank!" instead of "I got it."

But even with all this, it might still puzzle out-of-towners why White's number was retired by the team and why there is a statue of him at the ballpark. Well, it's this: White grew up in Kansas City. He learned to play ball on Kansas City streets in the shadow of old Municipal Stadium. When he was a hopeful young player, he spent his summer working construction on what would become Kauffman Stadium.

When he became an All-Star, a Gold Glover, a World Series hero, he came to represent all the dreams of Kansas City kids hoping to be Royals themselves.

There are a few players around baseball who were like that, players who mean more to their communities than anyone on the outside can know. There's Pete Rose in Cincinnati, for example. Tony Gwynn did not grow up in San Diego (he grew up a couple of hours away in Long Beach) but he went to play college ball at San Diego State and came to represent all that is that wonderful city. Rickey Henderson grew up in Oakland, Ryan Zimmerman played college ball close to Washington, Cal Ripken's father was a Baltimore Orioles coach. There are others.

But it seems to me that no player in baseball history—not even Rose or White—had the stars aligned to become a hometown hero the way Jeff Bagwell did in Boston.

Look: He was born in Boston. His father Robert had grown up in Watertown, Massachusetts—sixteen minutes away from Fenway Park—and he played college baseball at Northeastern. His mother, Jan, grew up in a large Irish family in Newton, Massachusetts—also sixteen minutes away from Fenway—and she played in Boston park softball leagues for years after high school. Both of them spent the best parts of their early lives at Fenway Park. Jeff Bagwell is as New England as the Kennedys.

Oh wait, we didn't even mention the grandmother. What does every cliché New England kid need? A grandmother who lives and dies with the Boston Red Sox—and Jeff Bagwell had one of those, too: Alice, his mother's mother, who religiously listened to games on the radio and scoured over the box scores in the *Boston Globe*.

Yes, when Jeff was a child the family did move a couple of hours away to Killingworth, Connecticut, but even that is still in the Red Sox sphere of New England. When Jeff was just a year old, his parents taught him to throw a baseball. The Red Sox dream was launched. Sure, he was small as a kid, but he refused to give up because his baseball hero was a normal-sized guy who hit like he was a giant.

Jeff Bagwell grew up idolizing Yaz. How could it have been any other way?

Seriously, this is a Boston Red Sox movie, right? And it only gets better because Bagwell was considered a nonprospect in high school. As *Middletown Press* reporter Jim Bransfield said in the Society for American Baseball Research's comprehensive book, *Jeff Bagwell in Connecticut*: "I remember one scout telling me that he had a plus bat but couldn't run, didn't have much of a glove, had an ordinary arm and didn't have a position."

Without a pro offer, Bagwell went to the University of Hartford, which was the only Division I team to offer him a scholarship. There, he met more New England characters. His first coach, Bill Denehy, had grown up in Middletown, Connecticut, and pitched for the New York Mets for a while. He played the hard-nosed coach who humbled the cocky young Bagwell. At one point, Denehy moved Bagwell from short to third, and Jeff complained about it.

Denehy looked him straight in the eye and said: "You're too $*%&#*# slow to play shortstop."

Denehy was fired shortly afterward for a reason that has nothing to do with our story here but is too good to skip. It seemed that the Hartford and UConn players had a massive fight on the field during a game, and Denehy's post-fight commentary to one reporter was to say he hoped that when UConn assistant coach Mitch Pietras came to town, somebody would bomb his car.

Dan Gooley—a fourth-generation Irish American born in New Haven, Connecticut—became the new Hartford coach. He had such a huge impact that Bagwell named him in his Hall of Fame speech.

Put it all together: Here's a New England kid raised by New England parents, coached by New England coaches, he's an obsessive Red Sox fan who idolizes Yaz, and he has Grandma Alice cutting out Sawx box scores back in Newton. How can this story end any other way but with this kid stealing the hearts of Boston fans? I mean, just cast Matt Damon and Ben Affleck right now.

And then it looked like it would happen. The Red Sox took him in the fourth round of the 1989 draft, and he went to Winter Haven and hit well, then he went to New Britain and hit even better. Then Bagwell went to Boston, where he played for 20 years for the Red Sox and hit a million doubles off the Green Monster and put his name in the all-time Boston book alongside Ted and Yaz and Bird and Russell and Brady and Bourque and . . .

OK, none of that happened.

The Red Sox instead traded him for a 37-year-old reliever named Larry Andersen.

Seriously. It has to be one of the biggest bummers in baseball history.

There's no way to explain that trade now, no way to give enough context. Sometimes, managers and general managers of teams with bad bullpens lose their minds. The Red Sox are not the first nor last team to have this happen.

In 1993, for instance, the Royals had bullpen woes and rather suddenly determined they could not live without a guy named Stan Belinda for the stretch run. Belinda was their only hope. So the Royals traded one of the best pitching prospects in baseball, Jon Lieber, who went on to win 131 games and finish fourth in the 2001 Cy Young balloting.

Belinda, as you might have guessed, did not prove to be a difference maker in Kansas City.

The Red Sox in 1990 were even more desperate to win—it's hard to replicate now that they've won a bunch of championships, but from 1919 to 2003, the Red Sox were in a constant state of panic. Their desperation was particularly acute in 1990. The memories of the heartbreaking 1986 World Series loss were still vivid. In 1988, the Red Sox got swept by Oakland in the ALCS. The fear that the Red Sox would never, ever win a World Series again was at its peak.

And the 1990 Red Sox were a good team with severe bullpen problems. It had everybody in Boston shouting at shadows and lampposts. Something had to be done. But what? Well, Larry Andersen was pitching well in relief for Houston. Yes, he was 37. Yes, he had bounced around the game—been traded, purchased, released, and signed as a free agent. But he found a nice groove in Houston in 1989 and 1990.

And when you are as frantic as the Red Sox were, frankly, you'll do some crazy things.

So the Red Sox traded Bagwell for Andersen.

"Larry is a veteran major-league reliever who should bolster our bullpen for the stretch run," Red Sox general manager Lou Gorman said. "Although the price was high, we are happy to have acquired a pitcher with postseason experience."

The price was high? Yeah, the price was high—the Red Sox traded a brilliantly talented 22-year-old kid who was born and raised to be a Red Sox superstar for a month's worth of Larry Andersen. Sure, the Red Sox tried to explain it away. They said they already had a third baseman they liked in Scott Cooper (and another named Tim Naehring) and a first baseman they liked more in Mo Vaughn, and so Bagwell was the odd man out.

"I admire Jeff Bagwell, and I hope he goes on to have an outstanding career," Gorman told reporters. "But right now my job is to help the Red Sox win a championship."

Yeah, Lou didn't do that. Andersen pitched a few innings, the Red Sox lost the ALCS to Oakland in four straight again, and Andersen bolted for better weather in San Diego.

When Jeff Bagwell called his grandmother Alice to tell her about the deal, she cried.

I've had an ongoing argument—well, not so much an argument as a joyful discussion—with my friend, television producer Michael Schur, about whether Jeff Bagwell or Gary Sheffield was more intimidating at the plate.

Mike, for good reason, sides with Sheffield. I totally get it. Sheffield at the plate was like a man being held back from a fight. He waggled that bat back and forth, and his whole body was like a rattlesnake coiled to strike, and you could almost hear him shouting "Let me at 'em, let me at 'em!" before every pitch was released.

Bagwell was exactly the opposite. He would get into that weird batting stance—legs spread as wide apart as they could go—and he looked like he was sitting uncomfortably on a stool. He had his bat pointed straight up to the sky, and he was entirely motionless. That was the eerie part to me, the part that makes me think that Bagwell might have been even more intimidating than Sheffield. He would just stand there, a statue, an ice sculpture, a Hollywood cowboy just before the draw, and then he would unleash the shortest right cross of a swing you ever saw.

If I may, I'd like to compare the two giants to a couple of Rocky opponents.

Sheffield was Clubber Lang, shouting and attacking and pitying all fools.

Bagwell was Ivan Drago, standing there with that blank look on his face and then saying, in the worst Russian accent west of John Malkovich in *Rounders:* "You vil lose."

They're both frightening. But I lean slightly toward Bagwell—or, maybe I should say slightly *away* from Bagwell.

That intimidation factor makes it easy to overlook just how well-rounded Bagwell was as a player. He was one of the best baserunners of his generation—he actually had multiple 30-30 seasons—and he was a terrific defensive first baseman. He walked 100 times in a season seven times, and from age 24 to age 32, he walked more often than he struck out.

If not for his last two seasons, when he was mostly done, he was a .300/.400/.500 career hitter.

Ted Williams called Bagwell the closest thing he saw in the modern game to Frank Robinson, which is just about the highest praise imaginable.

Bagwell's best season was the strike season, 1994, but his season was not shortened by the strike. One day before the season prematurely ended, Bagwell was hit by a pitch from Andy Benes and broke his left hand. That was a common theme for Bagwell because of the way he crowded the plate. He broke that hand three straight seasons on hit-by-pitches.

The 1994 season had been astonishing. He hit .368/.451/.750 with 39 homers, 116 RBIs, and 104 runs in just 110 games—and he did it while playing half his games in the hitter's death trap that was the Houston Astrodome. Bagwell hit an extraordinary .373 in the Astrodome that season, far and away the highest average any Astros player had ever managed in that place:

Highest Astrodome Batting Averages (minimum 150 at-bats)

1. Jeff Bagwell, 1994: .373

2. José Cruz, 1978: .353

3. Jeff Bagwell, 1998: .347

4. Dave Magadan, 1995: .344

5. Craig Biggio, 1991: .343

It's always tempting to wonder just what Bagwell's 1994 numbers might have looked like had he played a full season. But in Bagwell's case, because of the injury, the timing of the strike helped him. He won the MVP award unanimously, and almost certainly would not have won it had the season played to its conclusion.

Bagwell was never again quite as good as he'd been in 1994, but he came close repeatedly. In 1999, he had 42 homers, 30 stolen bases, and led the league in runs and walks. The next year, he scored 152 runs, which is the most scored by any player since Lou Gehrig in 1936.

In 1997, he had 40 homers, 40 doubles, 30 stolen bases, and 100 walks.

The list of players who have done that is one—Jeff Bagwell and Jeff Bagwell alone.

Bagwell did not make it into the Hall of Fame right away. It actually took him seven ballots to get elected. The reason was that some people suspected him of using PEDs. He was never connected to steroids in a public way—no positive drug tests, he was not mentioned in the Mitchell Report or by José Canseco, nobody in the know ever publicly charged him, and he publicly denied using. But there were whispers just the same, and Bagwell did offer a fascinating and perhaps telling quote in 2001 about using steroids:

"In my case, the temptation is always there. One thing I know is I can go home after my career is over and say, 'I did it myself.' . . . Now let me tell you, if I'm on the bubble, the amount of money that's in the game, I probably would already have a needle in my butt. There's too much money out there. If it does make you better, why wouldn't you at least give it a shot to hang on? All you have to do is have one big year. Next thing you know you're around for five or six more."

And then this, on his judgment of players who do use PEDs:

"Sometimes I don't blame them. Yeah, it might be kind of risky but they still have a family to feed. That's the big question. You have to go with yourself and determine what's more important to you."

Bagwell was finally elected in 2017. He went in, of course, as a member of the Houston Astros because that's the only major-league team he ever played for. He would say he had no regrets.

No. 57 **Rod Carew**

R od Carew and Nolan Ryan were great friends. They actually lived
right next door to each other in 1979. It was a pretty fascinating
time for them because, as Jaime Aron—coauthor with Carew
on the book *One Tough Out*—says, that was the year Carew became the
highest-paid player in baseball. The very next year, Ryan took that title
away by becoming the first player to get paid $1 million in a season.

You want to talk about trying to keep up with your neighbors.

But it made sense. Ryan was the game's most unhittable pitcher. And
Carew, as *Time* magazine splashed on its cover, was "Baseball's best hitter."

"He has no weakness as a hitter," Catfish Hunter told *Time*. "Pitch him
inside, outside, high, low, fast stuff, breaking balls, anything you throw he
can handle."

OK, we want to get back to Carew and Ryan, but first, there's a wonderful Carew-Catfish story to be told. In their careers, Carew and Catfish
faced each other 111 times, and Carew owned the guy. In all, he hit .347
with seven home runs, a 1.015 OPS. But there was one game in particular
that stood out—August 24, 1977. Hunter was on the Yankees by then,
and Carew had cracked two hits against Hunter in their first game of the
season.

"How many you think you're going to get off our guy tonight?" Yankees catcher Thurman Munson asked Carew around the batting cage before the game.

"Eh, maybe a couple," Carew said.

"Yeah, no way," Munson said.

Carew smiled. "Not only that," he said. "I'm gonna tell you what the pitch is and where I'm gonna hit it before he lets go."

Munson responded with some of his favorite words.

When Carew came up in the first inning, Munson picked up some dirt and put it on Carew's shoes and muttered, "He's gonna drill you." Carew laughed.

"He's not going to drill me," Carew said. And then Carew looked out to the mound in his famously piercing way and as Hunter went into his windup, Carew said, "Fastball away, line drive to left field." In came the fastball away. Carew's bat flashed. The ball shot out to left field for a single.

With that, Munson stepped in front of the plate and started screaming more of his choice words.

Umpire Ron Luciano, who was working second base that day, smiled and bowed toward Carew.

Carew's genius as a hitter, he often said, came down to three things. First, there was his confidence. He exuded it. He radiated with it. He often began days by asking a new teammate, "You know what's my favorite song?" The teammate would look at him in a puzzled way. And he'd say, "It's the national anthem because every time I hear that song, I'm gonna get two or three hits."

"I wanted every pitcher to know," Carew wrote in his book *Hit to Win,* "that I was the best there was."

You can't fake that kind of confidence. Well, that's not right: You *can* fake it, but big leaguers see through false bravado, mock it. Nobody doubted Carew's certainty was very real.

Carew's second secret to hitting wasn't something he could teach: He had magical hands. The greatest hitters had gifts. Henry Aaron had those incredible wrists. Ted Williams had superhuman eyesight. And Carew had those hands, quicker than the eye. He would use them to adjust, in real time, to whatever pitch was thrown. Nobody else could hit like that.

Speaking of Williams, Carew often thought about the Splendid Splinter. They hit so differently. Williams believed that the blueprint for hitting involved waiting for the right pitch. You might have seen Williams's famous strike zone chart—Warren Buffett has one in his office—where Williams assigns every single part of the zone with a batting average. The balls in the middle of the zone led to a .400 average, Williams believed, while the balls down and away lead you down the path to hitting .230. So the key was to swing at balls in the middle of the zone and not swing at balls down and away.

Carew didn't think like that at all. To him, every pitch in the zone (and some pitches out of the zone) were opportunities. You just had to hit the pitch where it was meant to be hit.

"Ted didn't think you could have any success on pitches outside," Carew says. "But I was hitting .350 or .400 on those pitches because I knew I could get my hands out there and just hit the ball to the opposite field."

Carew's third secret to hitting had something to do with the many different batting stances he used. If you are old enough to remember Carew in his prime, you know that announcers never stopped gushing about how he had a different batting stance for every occasion. He had designer batting stances for great pitchers. He had specialty batting stances for different counts. Carew was the man of a thousand stances.

Why did he have so many different batting stances?

This is where his friendship with Nolan Ryan comes in.

Carew was a mostly conventional hitter before 1973. He was a terrific hitter—he won two batting titles, won the Rookie of the Year award, started in five All-Star Games—but he had not yet started changing batting stances every time out. He maintained the same classic, upright stance every time, and he let his hands do the hitting. Nobody could throw a fastball by him.

Then came Ryan. And his fastball was fundamentally different from all the rest. Carew couldn't touch him. By September 23, 1973, Carew had faced Ryan 25 times and managed just five hits. More than that, he struck out 10 times. This was utterly unacceptable: Carew saw pitchers as a puzzle, and like all puzzles, each could be solved.

He faced four pitchers in his career more than 100 times, and he hit .300 off each of them. He faced 18 pitchers 60 times or more. He hit .331 total against them. You might fool him for a while but Carew knew that sooner or later, he would solve every pitcher.

But Carew could not solve Ryan. There seemed no solution for a 100-plus mph fastball that seemed to jump a foot just as it approached the plate. He kept thinking about it and thinking about it until finally, he came to the basic two-pronged problem of trying to solve Nolan Ryan.

1. Carew could not hit Ryan's high fastball.

2. Carew could not lay off Ryan's high fastball.

These were tough things to admit to himself. Carew, to this day, prides himself on how he hit fastballs. Ask him what he would hit in today's game against the ubiquitous 95 and 100 mph fastballs, and he will smile broadly, channel Ty Cobb, and tell you: "Only about .285. But I am 74 years old."

So it crushed him to admit that Ryan's high fastball was too fast and rose too quickly. Scientists will tell you there's no such thing as a rising fastball because gravity doesn't work that way, but scientists don't have to hit Nolan Ryan. The science doesn't change the fact that Ryan's rising fastball jumped over more bats than any pitch in baseball history.

What could Carew do? He thought about how to get his hands higher so that he could get on top of that Ryan fastball but came to realize that he couldn't do it. So, paradoxically, Carew decided to do the opposite. He decided to go into a special crouch just for Nolan Ryan.

"I lowered myself all the way down like I'm sitting in a chair," Carew says. "And I'm not striding or anything. I'm just standing there and using my hands. That forced me to stay down."

This was the point: The crouch wasn't to help him hit Ryan's best pitch. It was a reminder to *lay off* Ryan's best pitch. Carew struck out his first time up on a high fastball and dropped even lower into his stance. His next time up, he singled to left. Then he pulled a single to right. Then he cracked a single to center.

"Stand up like a man!" Ryan screamed at Carew, and Carew smiled. His next at-bat, he ripped a double to the left-field gap. That gave him four hits off Nolan Ryan in one game . . . I can't say for sure, but he might be the only player to ever get four hits off Ryan in a single game.

And that was when Carew realized just how valuable it was to switch batting stances. By crouching against Ryan, he was baiting Ryan to stop throwing that high fastball. It didn't always work but it often worked. Of the 34 batters who faced Ryan 70 or more times—a list that includes Pete

Rose, Tim Raines, Andre Dawson, Robin Yount, Reggie Jackson, and Mike Schmidt in addition to a bunch of near–Hall of Famers—Carew was the only one to hit .300.

He used this strategy with other pitchers. He would crowd the plate to make them think he was looking for an outside pitch. He would crouch low to make them think he was expecting something down and away. He would step up in the box like he was looking for something off-speed and step back in the box like he was looking for a fastball.

"Can you dictate from the setup position what kind of pitch you want thrown?" Carew asks in his book on hitting. "Absolutely. Any hitter can set up a pitcher. Why not? They do it to us all the time."

And here was the best part: Carew never *really* changed his full batting stance . . . it was an illusion. Again, this was the genius of Carew. Yes, he changed the way the stance looked, but the basics were the same. He always had his back foot in the same place. He never really moved around in the box. He always locked his eyes on the pitcher in the same way. He brought the same hitting approach each time.

He just made it look different enough to make pitchers crazy.

The story of how Rod Carew made it to the big leagues is incredible no matter how many times you hear it. He was born on a segregated train in Panama—his mother, Olga Teoma, was in one of the back cars when she went into labor. There was a nurse on the train named Margaret Ann who came back to the car to calm down Carew's mother while a doctor named Rodney Cline delivered the baby.

If Carew had been a girl, he would have been named Margaret Ann.

Instead, she named him Rodney Cline Carew after the doctor.

But Margaret Ann does not leave the story. She became very close to the family—she was Rod Carew's godmother. And she knew that Carew's father, Eric, was abusive. "There wasn't a time in my life," Rod wrote later, "I wasn't licked or punched or whipped, often for no reason whatsoever."

Carew's mother desperately wanted to get Rod away from his father. When Carew was 14, Margaret Ann asked if he would like to come live with her in New York. Olga jumped at the chance. "I had the feeling," Carew said, "a whole new world was opening up for me."

It didn't open right away. He did not play high school baseball. He never made the team. It might have been racially motivated or maybe it was a language barrier. Whatever the reason, Carew did play for a sandlot team called the Bronx Cavaliers and hit the ball so hard that a few scouts came to see him. He signed with the Twins for $5,000.

He is sure none of it would have happened except for the nurse who almost gave him his name.

Carew came pretty darned close to hitting .400 during his amazing 1977 season. That wasn't the only year that he fluttered around .400.

In 1974, he was hitting .400 on June 27 and was still a legitimate threat for .400 through the middle of July.

In 1975, he was hitting an astonishing .421 on June 9, and was still within striking distance as late as July 26, when he was hitting .386. He didn't exactly slump the rest of the way (he hit .311) but in order to maintain a .400 average, you have to keep hitting .400. That's why it's so hard.

In 1978, he was hitting .400 in late May.

In 1979, he was hitting .414 after two weeks but fell off quickly from there.

Point is, Rod Carew got off to *a lot* of hot starts.

But 1977 was special. That was the year that he made his best run at .400. He had—as usual—gotten off well and was hitting .411 as July began that year. He dropped about 20 points of batting average in July (by hitting a mere .304) and seemed pretty much out of the chase for .400.

On September 13, Carew was hitting .376, which is an incredible batting average. Do you know how many players since World War II have played 150 games and hit .376 in a season?

Two.

1. Rod Carew

2. Stan Musial, 1948, when he hit .376 on the nose.*

In any case, he was going to have a historic season no matter what. But Carew always said that he never stopped wanting hits. And in his last two

---

* The key to this stat is the playing time. When Tony Gwynn hit .394, much of that 1994 season was lost to the strike. When George Brett hit .390, he was hurt and played in 117 games. Larry Walker played in 127 games when he hit .379 in 1999. Ted Williams played 132 games when he hit .388 in 1957.

weeks in 1977, he went crazy. He started 13 games. He got two or more hits in 11 of them. In all, he hit .500 down the stretch, bunting and slashing and lining hits day after day.

The surge wasn't quite enough—he got his average up to .388 but could not quite get it any higher. He led the league in runs, hits, triples, on-base percentage, OPS, and intentional walks and won the MVP award even though his Twins were not really in contention.

He finished eight hits shy of .400. And that's what he remembered.

Here's one last thing to think about 1977: Carew was one of the best in baseball history in reaching on error. Nobody can say if that's a skill or if that's more luck, but that year Carew had seven hits taken away because they were called errors. Add those seven hits and . . . oh so close to .400.*

---

* In 1980, George Brett finished five hits shy of .400. That year, he reached on an error five times. So that is the closest anyone has come to hitting .400 since Ted Williams.

No. 56 Joe DiMaggio

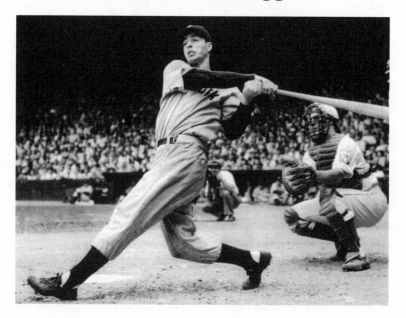

J oe DiMaggio was in the midst of a little slump when he took the field
on May 15, 1941. He was confused by it; he had started the year so
hot and he felt like he was still hitting the ball pretty hard, but all luck
had abandoned him. He was cracking line drives right at shortstops. He
was smashing would-be doubles that were just within the reach of outfielders. His batting average dropped below .300. He wondered when the
black cloud would pass over.

On May 13, he faced Cleveland's Bob Feller, and he went hitless. This
time luck had nothing to do with it. After the game, he muttered: "I don't
think anybody's ever going to throw a ball faster than Feller does. And his
curve? It ain't human."

So when the game on May 15 began, DiMaggio was in a foul mood.
He wasn't hitting. The Yankees were losing. New York manager Joe Mc-
Carthy made everybody come to Yankee Stadium early for extra batting
and fielding practice. The Yankees lost 13–1 to the White Sox to fall below
.500. The lede in the New York *Daily News* that day read: "The Yankees
held secret practice at the Stadium yesterday morning, and they should've
made the ball game that followed a secret too."

DiMaggio managed a single off a pitcher named Eddie Smith. It was, the *Daily News* pointed out—a bit too enthusiastically—his first hit in three days.

The most wonderful things so often begin in the plainest ways.

The next day, DiMaggio broke out. He got two massive hits, one of them a 430-foot home run off White Sox pitcher Thornton Lee—"one of the longest ever seen at the Stadium," the *Daily News* crowed—and the other a 400-foot triple.

It would be a while before anyone noticed that the streak had begun.

Joe DiMaggio was already baseball's biggest star when the streak began. He'd won the previous two batting titles. He'd won the 1939 MVP convincingly over Jimmie Foxx and Feller. He was a lifetime .343 hitter, celebrated for his center-field defense, and his Yankees had won the World Series in four of his first five years.

But . . . he wasn't yet DIMAGGIO, all capital letters. You have to remember, DiMaggio came of age in a time of legends. Babe Ruth had only just retired when DiMaggio began. Lou Gehrig was DiMaggio's teammate until he could no longer go on. Foxx and Hank Greenberg were at their peak, Mel Ott was still cracking hits and homers with the crazy batting style, and Feller, as DiMaggio himself admitted, threw a baseball as hard as anyone ever had.

Then in Boston, a thin kid named Ted Williams suddenly appeared and hit rockets.

What was DiMaggio's claim to be among the immortals? He was a terrific ballplayer, yes, but he didn't yet have anything he could call his own. His lyrical four-syllable name would become famous—"Where have you gone, Joe DiMaggio," Simon & Garfunkel sang—but in those tense years before World War II, DiMaggio sounded foreign, and foreignness was feared. Stereotypes filled so many of the stories written about him—the boy eating his mama's spaghetti, the slick black hair, the constant mentions of olive oil. "Although he learned Italian first," *Life* magazine assured fans, "Joe, now twenty-four, speaks English without an accent and is otherwise well adapted to U.S. mores."

And then there was this: DiMaggio wanted to be paid fairly. This was considered unseemly in his day. He held out for more money after his sensational 1937 season, when he led the league in homers and total bases. "DiMaggio is an ungrateful young man and is very unfair to his teammates to say the least," Yankees owner Jacob Ruppert told reporters. "I've offered $25,000, and he won't get a button over that amount. Why, how many men his age earn that much? As far as I'm concerned, that's all he's worth to the ballclub and if he doesn't sign, we'll win the pennant without him."

DiMaggio was outraged, but in those days there really wasn't anything to be done. The press was against him. The fans were against him. He sheepishly signed for $25,000, at which point the victorious Ruppert ungraciously said: "I hope the young man has learned his lesson."

When DiMaggio returned, the fans booed him. He never forgot that. Ever.

So, yes, Joe DiMaggio in 1941 was a star. But he lacked . . . something.

He cracked a single on May 17 and went 3-for-3 the next day against the St. Louis Browns. He doubled off Denny Galehouse on a Monday, scraped a single off St. Louis's Elden Auker in the bottom of the eighth on a Tuesday, and got two hits off Detroit pitchers on a Wednesday (in that game, the bigger story was his perfect throw that nailed Charlie Gehringer trying to go first to third on a single).

It is striking, looking back, to see how easily the streak could have died before it ever got going. He singled in his last at-bat against Detroit's Archie McKain. He got just one single in five tries against Boston in a 9–9 tie. He blooped a single off Lefty Grove when the Red Sox crushed the Yankees 10–3. At this point, the streak was 11 games but it did not yet feel like a streak.

He got four hits and hit his second tape-measure homer of the streak in Washington on May 27. Two days later, reporters made the first mention: "In the fourth, Joe DiMaggio led off with a single to left, stretching his hitting streak to fourteen straight games."

He was barely stretching this thing along. In the nine games between May 28 and June 5, DiMaggio got just one hit in eight of them. The whole thing didn't *feel* like anything yet. In one of those nine games—a 13–0 loss to Boston—DiMaggio made three errors. Nobody cared about a fledgling streak. On June 1, the *Daily News* called out DiMaggio for "getting his slumps." On June 3, DiMaggio's lone hit was a homer, but the Yankees lost again and found themselves mired in third place behind Cleveland and Chicago and just a game up on Boston and Philadelphia to stay out of the second division.

June 4 was a rainy and dour day in New York; it was the day Lou Gehrig's funeral services were held. The Yankees were in Detroit—well, many of them were. Bill Dickey left Detroit for the funeral (DiMaggio's first wife was there as well). But DiMaggio stayed in Detroit to play and the next day he went 1-for-5, a triple off Hal Newhouser. The Yankees lost again. But the streak was at 21 games.

On June 8, DiMaggio managed two hits in each game of a double-header in St. Louis. The streak moved to 24 games.

The *Daily News*' Jimmy Powers was still unimpressed. In his famed "Powerhouse" column, he wrote that, yes, DiMaggio had a hitting streak going, but that his "batting average has really been fattened at the expense of pushover pitchers, fellows on the lowly A's, Browns and Senators." Powers then ran a chart showing that DiMaggio was hitting .231 against Cleveland and .222 against the White Sox—the Yankees' top contenders—while he hit a combined .448 against lowly Philadelphia, St. Louis, and Washington.

"Y'otto use the big club on th' big bat on the big teams," he advised DiMaggio in an accompanying comic.

When DiMaggio reached 26 straight games—two-for-four against Chicago with a game-winning homer in the 10th—the story began to take shape. Who had the longest hitting streak anyway? It was a pretty obscure trivia question at the time. Hitting streaks had been tracked but were not considered big news. It turned out the modern record belonged to George Sisler, who hit in 41 straight games. Reporters rushed to find Sisler, who was running a sporting goods store in St. Louis.

"If my hitting streak is going to get broken," Sisler said, "I'd like to see Joe DiMaggio do it."

The reporter asked Sisler if he'd gotten any breaks during the streak. "Lucky hits?" Sisler said, and he thought about it for a second. "I don't recall any offhand."

DiMaggio homered the next day and doubled the day after that to tie the team record at 29 games. And then—he got a lucky hit. On June 17, DiMaggio failed to get a hit his first two times up and, his third time, hit a ground ball to short. The ball hit a divot in the infield and bounced up and over the glove (and head) of White Sox shortstop Luke Appling.

"That," DiMaggio would say, "was the luckiest hit of my streak."

But as Sisler had said: There are no lucky hits for great hitters. The streak moved to 30, a Yankees record.

An infield single extended the streak to 31—that was the same day that Joe Louis knocked out Billy Conn in a fight the whole country was talking about. Funny thing, DiMaggio's streak was already something special, but in total he wasn't hitting any better than normal. He'd hit .347 for three weeks; that was basically his lifetime average at the time. But hitting streaks require timing, and he had that. Then he cracked three hits against the White Sox, four hits against the Tigers on Ladies' Day at Yankee Stadium, and two more hits including a homer against the Tigers a couple of days after that.

As DiMaggio kept hitting, reporters began to realize they were covering something pretty new. Every day, people would ask each other "Did DiMag get a hit today?" Reporters sought out Ted Williams and asked him if he wanted to have a hitting streak like DiMaggio's. His answer is almost as legendary as the streak itself.

"I sure have," he said. "I'd like to break every hitting record in the book. When I walk down the street I'd like for them to say, 'There goes Ted Williams, the best hitter in baseball.'"

It turned out that Ty Cobb, who had a 40-game hitting streak in his career and could be ruthlessly dismissive of younger players, was rooting hard for Joltin' Joe. "DiMaggio is wonderful," he said. "Would he hit the dead ball? He'd hit anything. He would be a great star at any time in the history of the game."

And then, because he was Cobb, he added: "I think DiMaggio could be even greater than he is. I don't think he conditions himself properly during the winter months."

Then he said that Bob Feller was not as fast as Walter Johnson.

Well, this was what you got when you interviewed Ty Cobb.

Looking back, DiMaggio himself was stunningly relaxed. He laughed as reporters nervously surrounded him as if they didn't want to jinx him.

"Talking," he said cheerfully, "is not going to stop it."

"Are you worried?" they asked him.

"Why should I worry?" he asked. "The only time to worry is when you're not hitting."

He made it 37 straight games. No. 38 came on a double in his last plate appearance against Auker. Two hits in each of his next two games, and Joe DiMaggio was at 40 games, one away from tying Sisler's modern record.

And at this point, yes, the DiMaggio streak had become the biggest sports story in the country. It's funny, nobody had really cared about hitting streaks before—not when Sisler or Cobb did it. Nobody could even put into words why a hitting streak even mattered—does it help your team win more if you spread hits out just so over a number of days? Probably not, no, but there's something so satisfying about a hitting streak, something that speaks to the heart.

Every day, you wake up, and you hope that something good will happen.

During a hitting streak, it does.

And then there was this: The streak perfectly captured the rhythms and sensibilities of Joe DiMaggio. There he was, every day, same look, same gracefulness, same sense of purpose. "There is always some kid who may be seeing me for the first or last time," DiMaggio would say 10 years later. "I owe him my best." This was his legacy, his play for immortality: As the sportswriters sang, he came to play every day, and he never threw to the wrong base, and he never made a mistake on the base paths, and he never threw away an at-bat.

And if the sportswriters exaggerated—and they perhaps exaggerated more for DiMaggio than anyone—it was forgivable because he was Joltin' Joe.

He tied Sisler in the first game of a doubleheader at Washington by rapping a double in the sixth inning. In the second game, his single off reliever Red Anderson in the seventh inning got the *Daily News* to break out their war headline type: DIMAG SETS HIT RECORD.*

"How do you feel, Joe?" reporters asked.

"How would you feel?" he asked back. "Great! Terrific! Silly! Terrific! Anything you want."

At some point—pretty late in the process, to be honest—reporters figured out that Sisler's record was not the actual all-time record. "Wee Willie" Keeler, famed for saying that his job was to "hit 'em where they ain't," had hit in 44 straight games over two seasons, from 1896 to 1897. It was a pretty suspect record, to be honest, as it was spread over two seasons and baseball in the 1890s was a very different game from what it would become.

---

* The full headline was: DIMAG SETS HIT RECORD; YANKS WIN 2; FLOCK SPLITS. Headlines used to be so much fun.

But with Sisler out of the way everybody needed something new to talk about, so Keeler's record became the new target. DiMaggio broke Keeler's record on July 2 with a home run off Boston's Dick Newsome (he had been robbed of hits twice by great fielding plays).

You couldn't really say that breaking Keeler's record captured the public's imagination. There were just 8,682 in the crowd that day.

After then, with no more worlds to conquer, DiMaggio just kept on hitting because he was DiMaggio. The Yankees played a doubleheader on Lou Gehrig memorial day—with 55,000-plus in the stands—and DiMaggio ripped four hits in the first game, two more in the second. That moved the streak to 48.

He got to 50 with another four-hit game, this one against the St. Louis Browns.

Two hits against St. Louis made it 51. In a four-game series against the White Sox, he spread out seven hits to move his streak to 55.

Then the Yankees went to Cleveland, and DiMaggio reached that number that sits forever next to his name: 56. You can see him cutting through that baseball poster with 56 written on it. You will think of him if you are buying groceries and 56 turns out to be the price. DiMaggio and 56 are utterly inseparable.

In 56 games, Joe DiMaggio hit .408/.463/.717, but this is hardly the point. As many have pointed out, for the *entire* 1941 season, Ted Williams hit .406/.553/.735.

No, the point is that he just kept the thing going. The streak finally ended on July 17 in Cleveland in front of the largest crowd to watch a night game up to that point—67,468. DiMaggio hit three infield grounders that day. The first was a smash down the third-base line; Cleveland third baseman Ken Keltner made a backhand stab and fired across the infield to beat DiMaggio by a step and a half.

DiMaggio's next ground ball was hit just as hard, but closer to Keltner, who threw him out easily. And his third grounder was a tailor-made double play to shortstop Lou Boudreau. Shortly after the game, DiMaggio was photographed making zeroes with his thumbs and index fingers—his first oh-fer in more than two months.

"It couldn't last forever," DiMaggio said, but he was wrong about that. It has lasted forever.

No. 55 **Bob Feller**

The museum is gone now ... well, not gone exactly. The lovely brick building is still up, surrounded by trees and grass and greenery. Time still stands still around it. But the building is the Van Meter City Hall now, which means that people come by to get building code permits and set up house inspections and the like. If you want to build a shed in Van Meter, Iowa, you stop in and ask if you need a permit. (If it's smaller than 160 square feet, you do not.)

But Bob Feller's face is still etched into the side of the building.

That is because this was once the Bob Feller Museum. It was never exactly thriving—it's tough to thrive as a museum about an old ballplayer in a small town a half-hour west of Des Moines—but it was a joyful treat for baseball fans who wanted to step into another time. Sometimes Feller himself was there to give a quick tour and sign a few autographs and tell a few stories.

He was at the museum one of the times I came, and I remember how he pointed to a baseball signed by Babe Ruth. He'd bought that baseball as a boy; it cost him $5. And how did an Iowa farm boy raise $5? Well, sure, he trapped 50 gophers. In those days, in Van Meter, they'd give you a dime for every gopher you brought in.

With the $5 in his pocket, he went to a ball game in Des Moines with his beloved father, Bill, and he saw the Babe Ruth baseball, and he bought it and kept it for the rest of his life.

The museum was filled with stories like that—romantic, a bit corny, sweet, unabashedly American.

I loved that little museum, not so much for what was in it but for how it told Feller's story. It was exactly how *he* wanted his story told. Feller was a particularly complicated man. He was a patriot—he volunteered immediately after the bombing of Pearl Harbor—and a man who fought all his life for things he believed in. He also was president/CEO and chairman of the "In my day, ballplayers were ballplayers" conglomerate. He never tired of telling people how much better baseball once was and how much worse it had become.

He probably signed more autographs than any player in baseball history (the joke was that it was harder to find a baseball that *did not* have a Feller autograph on it than one that did). He also was the first prominent player to regularly charge money for autographs.

On the one hand, he set up the most successful barnstorming tours with Negro League players, and he was the very first to lobby for Satchel Paige's entry in the Hall of Fame. He would talk at length about the great talent of black players when it wasn't popular. "Bob," his friend Buck O'Neil said, "mostly had his heart in the right place."

On the other hand, the great Negro League pitcher Chet Brewer said Feller didn't pay Paige or any of the Negro League players their fair share, and he had a long-standing feud with Jackie Robinson. Also, through the years, he made numerous racial statements that were, at best, insensitive.

He was often modest and self-effacing and utterly charming. Nobody loved baseball more. But he could also be a magnificent grump who promoted himself to an absurd degree.

"Let me ask you," he growled at me once, "if I don't promote myself, who will?"

You cannot sum up Bob Feller's story easily. There was too much there.

But the museum—ah, everything was simple in that museum. In that sweet little place, Bob Feller got to tell his story without the complications and squabbles and business dealings gone wrong and the profound grief that came later in his life. In the museum, Feller could spin his fairy tale.

And Bob Feller's fairy tale was mostly true.

———

Once upon a time, a boy named Bobby Feller was born in a nine-room farmhouse in a village called Van Meter. He was born in a time before television, before radio, when the movies were silent and half the cars in the United States were Model Ts. There were 500 or so people in Van Meter then; they lived a life without complicated choices. You got your hair cut by Fred Fritz at the barbershop in the town square. Bread was seven cents a loaf at Jack England's grocery store. If you needed nails or lumber or tools, you went to O. V. White's hardware store.

Once a day, you could hear the train whistle of the Denver Rocket as it rolled by on the Rock Island railroad tracks on the outskirts of town.

Bobby could not remember exactly when the idea of becoming a ballplayer first emerged in his mind; it just seemed to always be there, like consciousness. When he was 7 or so, he wrote a school essay about being a tree. But unlike the other trees, he wasn't cut into lumber.

"They made me into a home plate for the baseball diamond," he wrote. "And that's the end."

By then, he had begun to throw a rubber ball against the side of the house. His father, Bill, would watch him sometimes and could not help but notice that there was an unusual grace and power about the way his oldest son threw a ball. One can never be sure of such things, naturally; a loving father might see in his child gifts that are not quite there. But an idea began to emerge in Bill Feller's mind.

"I think I know what I want that youngster to become," he told Bobby's mother, Lena, who was a schoolteacher in town. "I want him to play baseball. I don't want him to be a farmer. Baseball is a good life."

Two years later, Bill Feller came home with a stack of packages. Inside, there was a Rogers Hornsby glove, a Ray Schalk catcher's mitt, a full baseball uniform complete with striped stockings, a pair of spikes, a green bat, and, mostly, a half dozen of what Bob himself would call "good baseballs, not the nickel rocket kind."

With all that equipment, Bobby started his own team. He played third and second base in those days, and he dreamed of hitting like Hornsby. Soon everybody in town knew about Bill and Bob Feller, the father-and-son duo who dreamed about a big-league life.

"You'll never grow baseballs on your farm," Bobby's fourth-grade teacher, Miss Wycoff, told him. "They're not good to eat, you know. But if the game makes you happy, and you don't fall down in your studies, go right ahead."

The game did make him happy—blissfully happy. Every day, Bobby and Bill Feller would play catch after working the farm. Where do you think the whole idea of the movie *The Natural* came from?

"You've got a gift, Roy," Roy Hobbs's father told his son in the movie. "But it's not enough. You gotta develop yourself. Rely too much on your own gift, and you'll fail."

"If you lose your health and your money, you can regain those," Bill Feller told his son in real life. "But if you lose your integrity, it is gone forever."

All the while, Bob threw baseballs harder and harder. He still had this idea in mind that he was going to be the next Hornsby. But Bill was a plainspoken and realistic farmer, and he saw no reason to chase after false hopes. This was how Bob Feller would recall the pivotal conversation he had with his father:

"Bob," Bill said, "what do you think about pitching?"

"I like it," Bob said.

"Now don't get me wrong, son," Bill continued. "I think you're a great batter and a mighty fine fielder. But, you know, I think you might pitch better than do any of those things."

"Maybe you're right, Dad," Bob said. "I guess I do strike out more fellows than I hit home runs."

"In the big leagues, a pitcher is mighty important," Bill reminded him, "even if he comes out of his hole just once every four days. Now, you tend to your pitching."

Bobby did tend to his pitching. And Bill would go around town and embarrass Bobby by telling everybody, "Listen, now, you fellows hang on to earth long enough and we'll get you the best seats for a World Series."

Then, when Bobby was 14, Bill Feller decided that his son needed a place to improve his pitching. That's when he decided to build a ballpark on his farm in Iowa.

Where do you think the whole idea of the movie *Field of Dreams* came from?

"We'll lay it out up there on the hill right above the Racoon River," Bill told his son as they walked along the farm. "We'll clear the pasture, roll the field, put in seats, sell cold drinks and sandwiches. . . . Folks will come all the way from Des Moines just to see you pitch."

"People will come, Ray," Terrence Mann said in the movie. "People will most definitely come."

Bill and Bobby did build that ballpark—they called it Oakview Park— and people did come from as far as Des Moines to see him pitch. The Fellers once counted more than a thousand people in the stands.

Bobby Feller was a phenomenon by then. As a junior in high school, he was throwing no-hitters and striking out everybody. Cleveland's famed scout Cy Slapnicka came to Iowa and met with father and son and signed the kid for a buck and a baseball autographed by the Cleveland players.

As wistful and sweet as this might seem, it must be said here that Slapnicka wasn't allowed to sign a 16-year-old kid for any amount of money, even a buck. Major-league teams were forbidden from signing a kid off the sandlots or out of high school. That was supposed to be the exclusive right of minor-league teams. They signed the players, developed the player and then, if the player was good enough, sold the player to a big-league club. This was a way minor-league teams could remain solvent. The Des Moines Demons already had their eye on Feller and were not pleased in the least to see Cleveland swoop in and take away their big-money ticket. Owner E. Lee Keyser would bring his official complaint directly to Commissioner Kenesaw Mountain Landis himself. That turned into a nasty fight.

But Slapnicka didn't care. He had seen Feller throw, and he figured signing Feller directly was worth whatever penalties might come later. Slapnicka got Bob a job selling peanuts around League Park in Cleveland and waited for the moment when his phenom was ready to pitch against big leaguers.

He didn't have to wait long. Feller's unofficial debut happened on July 6, 1936. He was 17 years old, and he was brought in to pitch three innings in an exhibition game against the legendary Gas House Gang St. Louis Cardinals. He came in to relieve an old-timer named George Uhle, who some believe invented the slider and was definitely the one to coin the name.

Uhle to Feller. The papers said that Cleveland was showing its "yesterday and tomorrow."

The first batter Bobby faced was a rookie catcher named Bruce Ogrodowski, who saw one pitch, just one, and was so frightened by it that he turned toward Cleveland manager Steve O'Neill and shouted, "Just get me out of here in one piece!" Ogrodowski bunted to avoid further embarrassment.

Loud-mouth Leo Durocher barked at Feller that he had nothing . . . and he struck out twice. Feller also struck out Pepper Martin and Ripper Collins, two of the best players in the game.

The Cardinals couldn't stop gushing after the game.

"One of the fastest balls I have ever looked at," Joe Medwick gushed.

"He's fast all right . . . and let me tell you something: He knows how to pitch," Martin said.

"Best prospect since Dizzy Dean," Cardinals manager Frankie Frisch said, and Dean himself agreed.

"He can't miss," Dean said. He even took Feller aside to talk to him and give him some advice.

The most effusive praise was from home plate umpire Red Ormsby, who had been calling games for more than a decade. "I don't care if he's only 17," Ormsby said. "He showed me more speed than I have ever seen uncorked by an American League slabster. And I don't except Walter Johnson either."

The newspaper headlines naturally followed. "Faster than Johnson" . . . "Ol' Diz Sees Younger Self" . . . "This 'Feller' Must Be Good."

Feller pitched a few games in relief before making his first big-league start on August 23, 1936. He didn't disappoint; he pitched nine innings and struck out 15. Nobody had ever had a debut like that. Opposing batters talked about how they had never seen anyone throw so hard. Bobby was still in high school!

The newspaper coverage is best exemplified by this sentence, which appeared among the accolades:

"This lad, who learned to throw by pegging at a makeshift backstop in his father's cow pasture, this boy wonder not long out of short pants, this high school boy has a future brighter than the sun."

Brighter than the sun. On September 13, with Bill Feller proudly watching from the stands, Bobby struck out 17 Philadelphia Athletics to set an American League record.

Here's a trivia question to try on your friends: Name the two players who struck out their age in a major-league game:

The first is Feller, a 17-year-old striking out 17.

The other was Kerry Wood, who at age 20 struck out 20.

Feller wasn't just fast. He was wild. Really wild. On the day he struck out 17, he also walked nine and hit a batter. Doesn't that remind you of yet another movie, one called *Bull Durham*?

"It feels 'out there,'" Ebby Calvin Laloosh said after winning his first professional game in *Bull Durham*. "A major rush. I mean it doesn't feel 'out there' but it feels 'out there.'"

"What are you going to do," Bob Feller asked a reporter, "if you pitch the ball and they can't hit it?"

After the game, someone asked Bill Feller how it felt to watch his 17-year-old son set the American League record for strikeouts.

"Familiar," he said. "We've been dreaming about it for years."

That's more or less where the beautiful fairy tale of Bobby Feller ends. You felt this part so strongly when you went to the Bob Feller Museum and made your way around Van Meter. Everything about Feller's childhood, his debut, it all seemed so cinematic, so innocent, so pleasant. Sure, it's partly an illusion. But it's a nice illusion.

After that season ended, Kenesaw Mountain Landis threatened to make Feller a free agent because of the unethical way Cleveland signed him and tried to hide him as a peanut vendor. But Feller and his dad wanted to stay in Cleveland, and so they asked Landis to let them stay.

In 1939, at age 20, Feller emerged as the best pitcher in baseball, and he was the best pitcher in baseball in 1940, and he was probably the best pitcher in baseball in 1941, too. He was still wild but overpowering. He led the league in strikeouts four years in a row, leading the league in walks three of those four years.

Feller had 107 wins and 1,233 strikeouts through his age-22 season, and both of those are modern records that will likely never be broken.

There seemed little doubt that he would break all the modern records by the time he was done.

But then came reality. The war. Feller enlisted in the navy on the day Pearl Harbor was bombed. He served and lost almost four full prime seasons.

He was still a great pitcher when he got back—in 1946, he started 42 games, completed 36 of them, threw 10 shutouts, and set the modern record with 348 strikeouts. He was still just 27 years old. There was a hope that Feller would just keep on going as if the lost years were to be forgotten.

But time doesn't work like that. Feller would have more good seasons—he led the league in strikeouts two more times and he won 22 games in 1951—but he would never again be great. His career numbers, as striking as they are—266-162, 3.25 ERA, 2,581 strikeouts, three no-hitters, 12 one-hitters—come with an air of sadness. He should have been even better.

Feller, in some ways, never got over that. For many years, he carried with him a typewritten sheet of paper titled "What if there had been no war." On it were Feller's imaginary statistics as figured by a devoted baseball fan and autograph collector from Seattle named Ralph Winnie.

In all, Winnie figured Feller would have finished with 373 wins, more than 3,700 strikeouts, five no-hitters, and 19 one-hitters. That seems reasonable enough, though anyone who has seen a time-travel movie knows that it's risky to mess with history. Maybe Feller would have been even better than that. Maybe he would have hurt his arm. In any case, I vividly remember the first time he showed me the sheet—I was still a kid—and the way he said, "Pretty impressive, huh?"

There was quite a bit of pain in Feller's later life. His first wife, Virginia, grew addicted to barbiturates and amphetamines and their private lives were difficult for 25 years before they finally divorced in 1971. He endured various financial difficulties, which was one of the reasons why he spent so much of his later life on the road signing autographs and making appearances. He found himself in the middle of numerous controversies, mostly of his own making.

He was rightly celebrated, however, as an all-time great. Feller did have much kindness in him. Toward the end, he often seemed beaten up by life and could come across as crusty and grumpy, but to see him showing a kid the correct grip for throwing a fastball and a curveball—something I was lucky enough to see numerous times—was to see the fairy tale come back to life. In those moments, he looked so deeply happy.

No. 54 **Chipper Jones**

Chipper Jones grew up idolizing Mickey Mantle, which is a bit weird if you think about it. The timing doesn't really work. Jones is five years younger than I am, and Mantle retired a year before I was born. But as you probably guessed, Jones didn't need to see Mantle play in order to understand.

His father, Larry Sr., saw Mantle play. And Larry decided to raise his son to be the next Mickey Mantle.

Fathers and sons. They are at the heart of so many baseball stories.

Step 1: Come up with the name

If you want to raise a legendary ballplayer, obviously, you must begin with a good ballplayer name. Mutt Mantle knew long before his son was born that he would be called "Mickey," after the great catcher of the day, Mickey Cochrane. Mutt was probably unaware that Mickey Cochrane was not actually Mickey Cochrane; his name was Gordon Stanley Cochrane. He got the nickname "Mickey" for the least appealing reasons—people around the neighborhood in Bridgewater, Massachusetts, kept calling him Mickey to slight his perceived Irish heritage, which makes even less sense when you discover Cochrane was Scottish.

Nobody who knew Cochrane well ever called him Mickey. He hated that name.

But Mutt Mantle didn't know or care about any of that. His favorite ballplayer was called "Mickey," and so his son would be called "Mickey."

When you paired Mickey with the last name Mantle, well, sparks flew. Mickey Mantle! It sounds like baseball.

Compared to a baseball superhero name like Mickey Mantle, well, Larry Jones had a problem. He gave his son his own name, Larry Wayne Jones Jr., and let's be honest: You would have a hard time coming up with a less inspiring or unique baseball name than "Larry Jones." There had already been four professional players named Larry Jones, and not one of them had made it to the big leagues. The father worried a lot about it.

But, sometimes, yes, destiny provides an answer. Less than a week after Larry Jr. was born, Great-aunt Dolly came by to get her first look. And the first thing she said was: "Why he's a chip off the old block!"

Chip became Chipper. And Chipper Jones, wow, that had a whole different ring to it. Larry Sr. would tell his son again and again that, yes, people might have a hard time remembering a player named Larry Jones.

But, he said, they would never forget Chipper Jones.

Step 2: Teach 'em to switch-hit

It has become a cliché because so many of the greats—Mickey Mantle, Chipper Jones, Pete Rose, Marla Hooch—were taught by their dads to switch-hit at a young age. It was Mutt Mantle who came up with the idea.

You might not know this, but Mutt Mantle didn't just want Mickey to switch-hit. He also wanted Mickey to switch-throw, to be fully ambidextrous. That idea didn't last too long; by the time Mickey was 8 years old, he was so sick of throwing the ball left-handed that he begged his father to let him stop. Father and son struck a deal. Mutt would stop making Mickey throw left-handed if he would promise to never hit right-handed against a righty pitcher.

Every single day, after working those long and merciless hours in zinc mines, Mutt Mantle would return home and work with Mickey on his switch-hitting. Mutt would pitch right-handed. Mutt's father, Charles, would pitch left-handed. Those sessions were not intended to be fun. Mickey was training to become a hitter unlike any in baseball history.

Yes, it was a novel idea. Before Mantle, there had never been a big-league switch-hitter with power from both sides of the plate. The closest thing was probably Roger Connor in the 1880s, back when 16 home runs might lead the league. But that doesn't really count. The great switch-hitter of Mutt and Mickey's time was Frankie Frisch, who slapped and bunted and slashed his way around the diamond. Ripper Collins was a switch-hitter who led the league in home runs one year. But he didn't even try to hit homers left-handed—87 of his 94 career homers were from the right side.

How different was Mickey? At his retirement, there had been 10 seasons when a switch-hitter smashed 30 home runs. All 10 belonged to Mickey Mantle.

Larry Sr.'s vision for Chipper was the same as Mutt's vision for Mickey—basically, he wanted his son to switch-hit with power just like the Mick. The dream came from an experience: Larry Sr. had been in Baltimore's Memorial Stadium on one of the 24 days that Mickey Mantle homered there. That home run sailed right over Larry's head in the right-field bleachers, and seeing that ball so close, well, it connected Larry Sr. to Mickey somehow. He developed a dream to become Mickey Mantle himself. He was a good high school player, played some ball in college, even got a tentative offer from the Cubs to try out.

But by then, Larry Sr. knew that he would not become Mickey Mantle. He instead became a teacher and a high school baseball coach. He bought a Mickey Mantle signature bat that he kept in his den as an inspiration and a reminder.

Then Chipper was born, and Larry's dream took off again. He determined his son would switch-hit like Mickey Mantle.

And, to his delight, Chipper wanted it as much as his father did. He loved the challenge from the very beginning. He even tried to train himself by brushing his teeth left-handed, throwing baseballs left-handed, even signing his name left-handed.

And on Saturdays, after the NBC Game of the Week, Larry Sr. and Chipper would go to the backyard and replay the games they had just watched. Chipper would hit from the same side of the plate as the imaginary hitter he was impersonating. Years later, in his book *Ballplayer,* Chipper could still remember the exact batting stances he used when he was pretending to be players with the Dodgers, his favorite team.

He would lead off as Davey Lopes, a righty. As Steve Garvey, he would hold his hands in tight and low. As Dusty Baker, he'd hold the bat high and point it toward the sky. But he especially loved hitting as one of the lefties—as Kenny Landreaux or Franklin Stubbs or Mike Scioscia. And, most of all, Chipper loved batting like Reggie Smith, a switch-hitting force from both sides of the plate.

The better Chipper became as a switch-hitter, the more Larry Sr. dreamed.

"Nobody switch-hit like Mantle in the day," Larry Sr. told a reporter. "I thought that was a neat thing. I wanted that for Chipper."

Step 3: Show 'em some tough love

In 1948, Mickey Mantle was playing for a semipro team called the Baxter Springs Whiz Kids. He hit three massive home runs against a Columbus, Oklahoma, team. Afterward, Mutt was asked what he thought about his son's incredible performance.

"He coulda done better," Mutt replied.

When Chipper was 7 years old, his father pitched tennis balls to him. In those days, Chipper had a nasty habit of bailing out toward the shortstop when he swung right-handed. That is known as "stepping in the bucket," and it's not a particularly good way to hit. Larry Sr. repeatedly instructed his son, "Step at me! Step at me!"

But Chipper just couldn't do it. He kept bailing out until, finally, Larry Sr. told his son, "Look, I'm not going to hit you. I would never hit you."

Chipper nodded and stepped into the box to try again. His father promptly threw the next tennis ball right at his face, knocking out a baby tooth. Chipper began wailing, and his mother came over and screamed at her husband, "What the hell is wrong with you?"

Larry Sr. was a bit sheepish about it—mostly he worried Chipper would never want to step in the box again. But, of course, Chipper was in the box the next day.

And he stopped stepping in the bucket.

———

Chipper Jones was, best I can tell, one of three players to be taken No. 1 over a more hyped talent by a hometown team. Jones grew up in Jacksonville, Florida, just five or so hours south of Atlanta, and he was taken ahead of super-prospect Todd Van Poppel (who actually didn't go until the 14th pick because he and his still-developing agent, Scott Boras, were asking for record money). That worked out pretty darned well.

In 2001, the Minnesota Twins took St. Paul catcher Joe Mauer over Mark Prior. That too worked out pretty darned well.

And in 2004, the San Diego Padres took local Matt Bush over Justin Verlander.

Well, two out of three ain't bad.

Mutt Mantle idolized Mickey Cochrane. Mickey Mantle idolized his father. Larry Wayne Jones Sr. idolized Mickey Mantle. Chipper Jones idolized his father. This is a baseball chain, Mutt to Mick to Larry to Chipper, the baseball circle of life.

The young Chipper was an athletic marvel, not unlike Mickey. He was very fast, and he was much bigger than Mantle, and he had natural power from both sides of the plate. Mickey and Chipper both began their professional careers as shortstops, and both were moved off the position because of erratic fielding (Chipper committed 56 errors his first full season in the minors).

Both were considered phenoms before they ever took a big-league swing.

Both had early injuries that set them back. Mantle hurt his knee during the 1951 World Series while trying to avoid Joe DiMaggio on a fly ball hit between them. Chipper tried to avoid a tag during a spring training game against the Yankees and blew out his ACL. He missed the whole 1994 season.

In retrospect, it wasn't a bad season to miss. That was the strike season. And then, in 1995, you might recall that baseball owners tried that silly replacement player thing for a while and Opening Day wasn't until late April. Chipper was in the lineup for Atlanta's Opening Day, and he got two hits and scored three runs, and even though the crowd was restless and bitter about the strike (only 24,091 showed up), the only thing that really mattered to Chipper was that his dad was in the crowd to see it.

It was all pretty magical after that. Chipper hit 23 homers and finished second in the National League Rookie of the Year balloting to the electrifying Japanese pitcher Hideo Nomo. Then Chipper was all but impossible to get out in the playoffs, and the Atlanta Braves won their first (and still only) World Series.

The next year, he hit .309/.393/.530 with 30 homers, 114 runs, and 110 RBIs and finished fourth in the MVP balloting. He got MVP votes each of the next seven seasons.

Chipper's peak was from 1998 to 2002, and the thing that was so incredible about those years is how alike they look. He won the MVP in 1999 when he hit .319/.441/.633 with 45 home runs, 110 RBIs, and 116 runs.

But that year wasn't very different from 2001, when he hit .330/.427/.605 with 38 home runs, 102 RBIs, and 113 runs.

In those five seasons, he didn't hit lower than .311 or higher than .330. He drove in 100 RBIs every season and scored 100 runs all but one. His on-base percentage was always .400, his slugging percentage always well into the .500s (or .600s), and he averaged 15 stolen bases per year. He was the same awesome player year after year.

The second half of his career was more mercurial. Batting average is not the best stat, as we all know, but his yearly batting averages illustrate the up-and-down nature of Jones's later career. In 2004, he hit a career-low .248, and his career seemed to be winding down. But from 2006 to 2008, he hit .324, .337, and an astounding .364, when for part of the summer he seemed like a threat to hit .400.

And then he faded. He missed a lot of time in those later years, and he played in a lot of pain. That too was a lot like his hero, Mickey Mantle.

There's another thing that connects them: Chipper Jones and Mickey Mantle both had incredible plate discipline. Both finished their careers with more walks than strikeouts. Mickey walked more than Chipper, but Chipper struck out less than Mickey, so it was more or less a wash.

All those walks—more than 1,500 of them, sixteenth all-time—probably cost Chipper some of those landmark numbers that people like to talk about. He got to 468 homers but not quite 500. He got to 2,726 hits but not quite 3,000. He finished right about 35th in most categories, including total bases (33rd), doubles (32nd), homers (35th), and RBIs (35th).

Some of those counting numbers could have been higher if Chipper had been less disciplined at the plate. But he wouldn't have been as good a player.

Larry Wayne Jones Sr. was the only hitting coach his son would ever have or would ever need. The men talked after every game, went over every at-bat, worked through every slump.

My favorite Chipper Jones stat is the one I think best describes their relationship: He is the only switch-hitter in baseball history with a .300 batting average from both sides of the plate.

Mantle hit .330 hitting from his natural right side but .281 as a lefty.

Frankie Frisch hit .326 as a lefty but .292 as a righty.

Bernie Williams, Víctor Martínez, José Vidro, and Dave Hollins were .300 hitters from the right side.

Roberto Alomar, Pete Rose, Bip Roberts, Lance Berkman, Jerry Mumphrey, and Johnny Ray were .300 hitters from the left side.

But only Chipper Jones, with his .303 batting average as a lefty and his .304 batting average as a righty, did it from both sides. It showed what a perfectionist he was, what a perfectionist Larry Sr. was, what their relationship and commitment achieved. "You can always do better," Larry Sr. used to tell his son, which was a more sensitive but no less effective way of saying, "He coulda done better," the way Mutt Mantle did after his son hit those three home runs.

Fathers and sons. Actually, in my favorite Chipper father-son story, well, Chipper is the dad. Chipper Jones rather famously named his son "Shea," in part after Shea Stadium. See, Chipper Jones was a killer at Shea Stadium.

"Is that my stadium?" Shea used to ask his father when they went to New York.

"Yep, that's it," Chipper said to him.

Every time Chipper was in New York, somebody in the city would ask how his son Shea was doing, and they would ask, "Wow, you really named your son after Shea Stadium because you hit so well there?" And Chipper would smile.

He did hit well there. Chipper Jones hit .313/.417/.558 at Shea Stadium, which closed in 2008. Those are incredible numbers when you're hitting on the road, in New York, facing all those fans.

But here's the best part. Do you know what Chipper hit everywhere else through 2008? He hit .310/.408/.548. Almost exactly the same numbers.

When he was healthy and young, every stadium was Shea Stadium to Chipper Jones.

No. 53 **Buck Leonard**

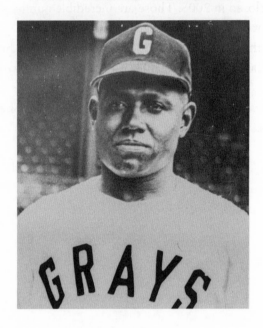

My favorite ever baseball saying, I think, is this one: "Trying to throw a fastball past him is like trying to sneak the sunrise past a rooster." There's something so beautiful about how those words connect, something rhythmic and poetic and wonderful.

Best I can tell, those words have been said about three hitters:

Curt Simmons said them about Henry Aaron.

Bob Feller said them about Ted Williams.

And everybody in and around the Negro Leagues said them about Buck Leonard.

I'm not sure who was first. I don't know that it matters. What does matter is that people talked repeatedly about Buck Leonard being the rooster. How can you judge the greatness of Negro Leagues players without a thorough collection of numbers? This, as you have no doubt noticed, is one of the recurring themes of the Baseball 100. Legend plays a role—it has to play a role. Cool Papa Bell was so fast that he hit a line drive to center and was hit by the ball as he slid into second. Josh Gibson hit a ball so high and far in Pittsburgh that it did not come down until the next day, when his team was in Philadelphia. Satchel Paige had a catcher who kept a raw steak under his glove to cushion the blow, and by the fifth inning, it had turned into hamburger. Sam "the Jet" Jethroe was faster than the word of God.

And trying to throw a fastball by Buck Leonard was like trying to sneak the sunrise past a rooster.

Walter "Buck" Leonard always seemed taller than his 5-foot-10 frame. There was a graceful way he carried himself—upright, upstanding, proud. He came to pro baseball later in life. He was raised in a churchgoing family in Rocky Mount, North Carolina, and his father died when he was 12. He then shined shoes to support the family. He stopped going to school at 14 because there was no black high school in town* and went to work in the local hosiery mills. Soon after, he started working full-time for the railroad. He put brake cylinders on train cars.

Baseball was, in those days, a bright light in a gray life. Leonard had a knack for it, and he played on some semipro teams around North Carolina. He was always the best hitter in town but he wondered: What future was there for him in baseball? The major leagues were obviously a nonstarter, and it was hard to know how to even begin catching on with a Negro Leagues team. He preferred a steady paying job and he played baseball in his spare time.

It probably would have stayed that way, but then the Depression hit, and Leonard lost his job at the railroad. The Depression, of course, was hard on many millions of Americans, but it was particularly hard on African Americans. There were no jobs and little hope. When Leonard was offered $15 a week to play ball for the Portsmouth Black Revels team, he knew that was the best offer he was going to get. Buck Leonard was already 25 years old.

Then, finally, he caught a break: One of the greatest ever pitchers, Smokey Joe Williams, saw him play and was impressed. In 1934, Williams was tending bar in New York when he came across the legendary owner of the Homestead Grays, Cumberland Posey. He told Posey about Buck Leonard and recommended that the Grays sign him.

Posey was quite the character. He is the only person enshrined in both the baseball and basketball halls of fame. He's in the Basketball Hall of Fame as a player—he played at Duquesne under the assumed name of Charles Cumbert and led the team in scoring three straight years. Then

---

* Years later, Buck Leonard went back and graduated from high school.

he created his own team, the "Loendi Big Five," which was the Harlem Globetrotters of the time; they won four consecutive Colored Basketball World Championships.

In baseball, Posey was a fine player for the Grays but he made his mark as an owner and talent evaluator. Nobody worked harder to acquire great players—he was quite ruthless about it, often raiding other teams' talent. Incredibly, 11 of the 18 Negro Leagues players in the Baseball Hall of Fame played for Posey at one time or another. "He was," sportswriter Wendell Smith wrote, "the smartest man in Negro Leagues baseball."

In 1937, Posey paired Leonard with his great slugger Josh Gibson, and almost immediately people began calling them the Black Lou Gehrig and the Black Babe Ruth. The Gibson-Ruth connection always seemed a little bit forced to me. On the surface, yes, you have two of the all-time great power hitters, maybe *the* two greatest power hitters, but they were very different men. They were almost direct opposites in personality, demeanor, style of play, position, even which side of the plate they hit from.

But Gehrig and Leonard? Now, that was a match. They shared similar styles (Leonard readily admitted that he tried to copy Gehrig's batting motion when he became a pro). Gehrig was a little bigger and might have hit with more power. Leonard was a little more athletic and was a better defender.* But their similarities ran even deeper. They were each steady and humble men. They played without flash, without ego, with a quiet resolve that everyone around them admired. Lou Gehrig was the most beloved player in the major leagues. Buck Leonard was the most beloved player in the Negro Leagues.

Both Gehrig and Leonard loved turning on fastballs. They each pulled line drives that would tear the glove right off your hand. "You could put a fastball in a shotgun," fellow Negro Leaguer Dave Barnhill said of Leonard, "and you couldn't shoot it by him."

The stats that exist back this up. According to the best numbers avail-

---

* Leonard's fielding exploits are almost as legendary as his ability to crush fastballs. Dodgers scout Elwood Parsons—who, according to author Larry Lester, was a police court bailiff and a chemistry instructor when Branch Rickey made him the first Black scout—once saw someone smash a line drive down the first-base line so hard that Leonard simply did not have time to move his glove. So, Leonard just caught the ball barehanded and tossed it around the infield like nothing had happened.

able at the Seamheads website, Leonard hit .343/.446/.578 over his career, which is strikingly similar to Gehrig's .340/.447/.632—though, again, comparing the stats of players in such different worlds probably does not do either man justice. They were playing the same game but in very different circumstances.

"It was tough playing in the Negro Leagues," Leonard said. "A lot of riding. A lot of playing. Some seasons we would play 210 ballgames. You're riding every day, playing in different towns. No air-conditioning. Meals were bad. When I first started playing, we were getting 60 cents a day on which to eat, and we stayed in rooming houses."

Leonard never came especially close to playing in the major leagues, but he did have one brief moment of hope. In 1943, with the war going on, Washington Senators owner Clark Griffith asked Leonard if he would want to play in the major leagues. Leonard said yes, and Griffith said he was going to try to make it happen. It never happened and it's unclear how seriously Griffith even tried. The Senators and Griffith did not actually sign their first black player until 1954, seven years after Jackie Robinson.

Leonard would always say that in his younger days, he never really thought about the major leagues. "It does no good," he said, "to mourn for what you can't have."

But after Robinson crossed the line, Leonard—like so many of the greatest Negro Leagues players—began to think about what might have been.

"I don't think anybody really felt sorry for himself until after Jackie Robinson integrated the Brooklyn Dodgers," he said with some sadness in his voice. "Then everybody started thinking: 'Maybe we should have been there all along.' It was a shocking thought. Some of us weren't prepared for it."

When Leonard was 44, Bill Veeck approached him about playing for the St. Louis Browns. Leonard knew that he was too old to do it. That scout, Elwood Parsons, spoke with Leonard around that time about the success that Robinson, Roy Campanella, and Don Newcombe were having with the Dodgers.

"I'll never forget Buck's eyes filling with tears," Parsons said. "And he said, 'But it's too late for me.'"

Buck Leonard went back to Rocky Mount and worked for the school district. He helped out with the minor-league team there. He was 65 years old in 1972 when he went into the Hall of Fame with his old teammate and friend Josh Gibson. Also elected that year: Sandy Koufax and Yogi Berra. Leonard said: "I will do everything in my power to honor and uphold the dignity of baseball." He didn't need to say that. He lived his whole life that way.

And when reporters asked him how he felt about not playing in the majors, he shrugged and said it wasn't meant to be.

"I only wish," Leonard said, "I could have played in the big leagues when I was young enough to show what I could do."

No. 52 **Adrián Beltré**

The Los Angeles Dodgers signed Adrián Beltré for $23,000 when he was just 15 years old. That was not only a great bargain, it also was illegal and unethical. Teams were not allowed to sign players until they turned 16.

It's daunting how often you dig into baseball history and find people and teams skirting the rules.

In many ways, the Dodgers simply did what Cleveland had done when they signed an underaged Bob Feller: They figured that even if they got caught and punished, it would be worth it. And, in both cases, it was. Beltré, like Feller, was born to be a ballplayer. But in Beltré's case, he was *literally* born to be a ballplayer. Months before he was born, his father, Bienvenido Beltré, went to his friend Felipe Alou (who was a minor-league manager in the Expos organization at the time) and explained that his wife was pregnant and would soon give birth to a great ballplayer.

"I am going to train him," Beltré's father said, and he asked for help. Alou thought that his friend was, perhaps, a little too enthusiastic to raise a ballplayer. But he agreed to help.

"I have a soft spot for him," Alou would say of Adrián, "because I used to hold him."

The younger Beltré was just a scrawny kid when the Dodgers first saw him at their training center. He weighed no more than 130 pounds. But they saw the otherworldly bat speed. They saw the amazing throwing arm. They saw the future. And they figured: Why wait for the Christmas rush? Let's just wrap him up now.

As baseball decisions go, this was an undeniably smart move. Beltré was incredibly advanced. At 17, he mashed 26 homers and played lights-out defense in Class A ball. At 18, he battled briefly for the minor-league triple crown and left Baseball America so breathless that when talking about his skill set they had to admit: "He hasn't shown any weaknesses in two years of minor-league ball."

Beltré was in the big leagues at the age of 19.

But the Dodgers couldn't say he was 19 because that would have encouraged people to do the quick math and realize that they signed him before he was eligible. So, problem solved, they just said he was 20 years old. And they might have gotten away with it except that when Beltré's agent, Scott Boras, gushed on and on about how amazing it was to reach the big leagues at 20, Beltré responded, "No, I'm only 19."

Boras looked into it and found, yeah, he really *was* only 19. He did the calculations and realized what the Dodgers had done.

This led to—well, a lot of craziness. According to an amazing story uncovered by writer Jorge Arangure Jr., Boras went to the Dodgers and demanded they pay Beltré a fair compensation to make up for signing him too early. That was all he wanted; he had no interest in making any of this public. But the Dodgers balked, insisted they did nothing wrong, and that's what led Boras to take the facts to commissioner Bud Selig.

In the end, Selig found that the Dodgers signed Beltré at 15 *and* they falsified his birth certificate—comically whiting out April 7, 1979, and replacing it with April 7, 1978—*and* they simply ignored the birth date on his passport.

Selig awarded Beltré $50,000, shut down the Dodgers' Dominican academy for a year, and banned them from signing any Dominican-born amateur players for that same year.

But Selig let the Dodgers keep Beltré rather than make him a free agent. In the end, alas, the Dodgers were right. Cheating was worth the risk.

In early 2001, Beltré needed an emergency appendectomy in the Dominican Republic. He'd already established himself as one of the terrific young
players in the game—in 2000, he'd hit .290/.360/.475 with 20 homers—
and after the surgery, the papers reported that he was fine.

He wasn't fine. The surgery was botched. Beltré stayed in the hospital
for a month; he lost 24 pounds and even after he was released he was still
not able to eat solid food or work out. By that time, he admitted that things
had not gone well but still felt like he would be ready by the time he got to
spring training.

"I was a little scared," he admitted. "Things weren't looking too good. I
tried to stay positive but it was tough. They said it was simple surgery, but
it got pretty ugly. But now I know I will be OK."

Only, again, he was not OK. He came to spring training wearing a co-
lostomy bag. The Dodgers still did not sound worried; they made it clear
in the papers that Beltré would be rolling along in just a few weeks. "If he
was older, it would be a little more of a concern," one Dodgers official said.
"But he is young and such a good athlete."

Then a second wound opened up, causing significant bleeding. He
needed a second surgery and lost another 10 pounds. He still wasn't eating solid food at the end of spring training. He started the season on the
injured list and stayed there for the first six weeks of the season.

And when he finally returned, he was different from the vibrant young
player he had been. It wasn't clear at all that he would ever be that player
again. From 2001 to 2003, he hit just .254/.300/.421—a 92 OPS+. His
defense took a step backward. Questions swirled all around him. Had
the multiple surgeries taken too much out of him? Was he not dedicated
enough? Had he lost his mojo? In 2003, the Dodgers brass made various
public statements suggesting that they had grown tired of waiting for Beltré to develop into a star.

The 2004 spring training began with a hot rumor that the Dodgers
were going to deal him to the Yankees to replace Aaron Boone, who had
blown out his ACL playing basketball. But the deal fell through the cracks
and the Dodgers decided to just stick with Beltré for another year and
hope for the best.

The Dodgers, partly in an effort to get Beltré going, hired a new hitting coach, a former All-Star and Gold Glove–winning third baseman named Tim Wallach. It's a common story; teams often will bring in a new coach who seems like a perfect match to help a struggling player. It so rarely works but teams keep on trying—it's like speed dating, I guess.

In this case, Wallach proved to be exactly the right person at the right time. He worked with Beltré on a few physical things—closing his stance and repeatedly asking him to hit the ball the other way. Every day during batting practice, he would match up Beltré and teammate Shawn Green in a special-rules home run derby where only opposite-field and straight-away homers counted.

This helped, but Wallach's big influence was in helping Beltré rebuild his confidence. He saw a young player—Beltré was still just 25—who had lost faith in his own talents. He saw a young player who didn't trust himself, which is why he so often went flailing after outside sliders. "He didn't know who he was as a player," Wallach would say. The two men talked every day until, more and more, Beltré found himself just *knowing* what to do.

"It is a whole different feeling at the plate," he told reporters. This was in May 2004. Beltré had gotten off to an extraordinary start—he was hitting .389 and slugging .704 after the first month of the season. He was leading the league in batting average, homers, RBIs, and pretty much everything else except walks (Beltré never developed an appetite for walks). He was hitting the ball so hard that it actually sounded different coming off the bat, and various writers began to compare that to the sound of the ball hitting Barry Bonds's bat.

Nobody thought that kind of hitting would last—but it did. When the season ended, Beltré hit .334, slugged .629, and led the league in home runs even while playing in cavernous Dodger Stadium. Plus he was a sorcerer on defense, making every play and flashing one of the greatest arms ever for a third baseman.

How good a season was that? When talking about the greatest third base seasons ever, I'd say these are the top five candidates:

- Cleveland's Al Rosen in 1953 led the league in homers (43), RBIs (145), runs (115), and lost the batting title and Triple Crown by one point to Detroit's Mickey Vernon. Rosen was a good-but-probably-not-great defender.

- Kansas City's George Brett in 1980. That was the year he almost hit .400. He finished the year with an absurd .390/.454/.664 line and was a better third baseman than he got credit for, but he did only play in 117 games that year.

- Philadelphia's Mike Schmidt in 1980 led the league in homers (48), RBIs (121), and total bases (342); he scored 100 runs, won the Gold Glove, and won the MVP award.

- Alex Rodriguez in 2007 hit an incredible 54 homers, drove in 156 RBIs, led the league with a 1.067 OPS, and stole 24 bases in 28 attempts. His defense was about average.

- Beltré in 2004.

The difference between Beltré and those others, though, was that nobody saw him coming. The other four were established stars. All-Stars, MVP candidates. Beltré was known throughout baseball only as an underachiever. And then he had this extraordinary season at exactly the most cynical time, when baseball fans were skeptical that any player who suddenly had a great season could be doing it clean. Many simply wrote off the whole thing.

Beltré lost the 2004 MVP to Barry Bonds, who had perhaps the strangest season in baseball history. Bonds hit .362/.609/.812 with a record 232 walks including an impossible-to-believe 120 of them intentional. Bonds broke the game. There is an argument to be made that when you include defense, Beltré's season was just as good.

At the end of the season, Beltré signed a five-year, $64 million deal with the Mariners (who outbid the Dodgers; it was a different time). His career went dark again—he disappeared just as suddenly and mysteriously as he had emerged. His home run total dropped from 48 to 19. His batting average fell by 80 points. Every other day, it seemed, someone else was talking about what a huge disappointment Adrián Beltré was.

In retrospect, he wasn't as bad as people thought. He was roughly a league-average hitter in his time in Seattle (.266/.317/.442), this even though he played most of those games with a bad thumb. Safeco Field in Seattle wasn't a good ballpark for him. And all the while, he remained a breathtaking defensive third baseman.

But nobody was too interested in the details. Beltré was 30 years old, he had been in the big leagues for 12 years, and at that moment he had a couple of Gold Gloves, had a lifetime 105 OPS+, and one legendary season that the vast majority of people chalked up as a fluke.

Nobody would have *ever* expected that guy to be on this list.

But Adrián Beltré—one of the most joyous players in baseball history—was only getting started.

Before the 2010 season, the Red Sox signed Beltré to a one-year, $10 million deal. For Boston, it was a simple calculation—the money was right, the commitment was light, and they had an opening at third base. The Red Sox figured that no matter what Beltré hit (he had a lifetime .179 batting average at Fenway Park, so expectations were not high), he would be good enough defensively to make the deal worthwhile.

"I'll tell you this," his old manager John McLaren told the *Boston Globe.* "You're gonna see some things defensively that are gonna make you say to yourself, 'Did I really just see that?' He's one of the best I've ever seen."

For Beltré, signing a one-year deal was a chance to show that he really was a star. "Thank God I'm in a good financial situation," he told reporters, "so I could consider taking a little risk."

He hit .338 the first month of the season but did not homer, so people wondered if his power was gone. It was not. By year's end, he hit .321, led the league in doubles, hit 28 homers, drove in 102 RBIs, and played his usual sensational defense. He was one of the best players in the league.

The Rangers offered him a six-year, $96 million deal to take him away from Boston. And what can you say of his time in Texas? It was beautiful. It was glorious. Over the next seven seasons, he hit .308/.360/.517, won three more Gold Gloves, played in the World Series, and spread joy throughout America.

And then came a big surprise: People started adding up all the numbers through all the years; wow, it was like compound interest. Three thousand hits? How did that happen? He hit 477 home runs—only Mike Schmidt and Eddie Mathews among third basemen had more. He hit more doubles (636) than any third baseman except George Brett.

He finished with more hits (3,166) and RBIs (1,707) than any third baseman, period.

And all the while, he played third base like a dream. Beltré is 10th all-time in defensive WAR—that's at any position—and among third basemen, it's Brooks Robinson, Adrián Beltré, and then everybody else.

But, mostly, there was the joy. All that joy. Where did it come from? Until he got to Texas, people knew of him only as an enigma, a great defender, a hitter who didn't walk, a guy who had one incredible season in the mid-2000s.

Then he put on that Rangers uniform and it was like donning a superhero cape. Everything about him just lit up. He was fun. He was hilarious. He was quirky and weird and silly and so happy every day. You would go to games just to see what he might do. You can only guess that he had this exuberance inside him all along, but it was only the last few years that he felt confident enough to let it out for everyone to see.

Let's count down my five favorite Beltré moments:

No. 5: That time Minnesota pitcher Tyler Duffey hit Beltré in the rear end with a pitch. Beltré dramatically rubbed his butt for quite a long time as he walked up the first-base line and then started laughing as he reached first base.

No. 4: That time against the Astros when he sort of tried to stretch a single into a double—baserunning was never his strong suit—and got caught in a rundown. He did stay in the rundown for a surprisingly long time but just as he was about to be tagged out by José Altuve, he suddenly and cheerfully took off running toward the pitcher's mound.

No. 3: That time in September 2016 when Beltré lined a double to center field. It was a bit of a goofy play from the start as Brewers center fielder Hernán Pérez tried to field the ball between his legs. But the best part happened at second base. Beltré slid in headfirst and had his hand on the bag. Brewers shortstop Orlando Arcia kept a tag on for a long time hoping Beltré might take his hand off by mistake. Beltré responded by putting his left hand on the bag and lifting his right. Arcia then tagged that hand, so Beltré put his right hand back on the bag and lifted his left, back and forth like someone playing a shell game. So much fun.

No. 2: That time in 2017 with the on-deck circle. The Rangers and Marlins played a pretty meaningless game that went off the rails—the Marlins ended up winning that game 22–10. Beltré had three hits in the game—moving his career total to 2,996—when in the eighth inning, he was warming up too far away from the on-deck circle in the eyes of umpiring crew chief and 34-year-veteran Gerry Davis.

At first, Beltré seemed to think Davis was kidding—who cares where an on-deck hitter is warming up in an 18–6 game in the eighth? When he realized that Davis was not kidding, Davis demanded he move closer to the on-deck circle. Instead, Beltré dragged the on-deck circle closer to him. Davis threw him out and then threw out Rangers manager Jeff Banister, which only made the whole thing funnier.

No. 1: That time—no, it isn't one time, it's a thousand different times—teammates tried to touch the top of Beltré's head. It was often his teammate, friend, and straight man Elvis Andrus, but others would jump in. Beltré just hated when people went for his head, and the act, like Beltré himself, just never stopped being entirely hilarious and awesome and sublime.

No. 51 **Al Kaline**

I f you just looked at the back of his baseball card—especially one of those old Topps cards that had only the most basic of statistics—you would wonder what was so special about Al Kaline. See, Kaline never hit 30 home runs in a season. He didn't crack 400 homers or hit .300 for his career. He never won an MVP award.

And yet, he became Mr. Tiger and one of the greatest players in baseball history.

When I was a kid, I truly believed that the only thing that mattered in life was talent. I constantly thought about talent, worried about talent, concentrated on talent. When the idea first hit about becoming a sportswriter, I couldn't sleep at night for fear that I lacked the talent to do it. My philosophy of life then was that people are born to greatness.

But it isn't true. Sure, Al Kaline had talent. He was a baseball prodigy. He never played one game in the minor leagues. At age 20, he might have been the best player in the league.

But look again at that baseball card. It wasn't talent that made him Mr. Tiger.

———

This will sound familiar: Nicholas Kaline wanted his son to be a ballplayer. At some point, I need to count the baseball stories that begin with the dreams of the father. Nicholas Kaline was a broom maker in Baltimore, and he believed that if things had been different—if he'd been given a chance—he might have become a great ballplayer. He wasn't going to make the same mistakes with his son. Nicholas taught son Al to throw a curveball at 8 years old. He planned to raise himself another Bobby Feller.

Here's the funny part: Feller wanted to be a hitter. And Kaline wanted to be a pitcher. Feller became a pitcher after making the unmistakable calculation that it was his best route to the big leagues. Kaline became a hitter because his high school coach said he already had enough pitchers. He put Kaline in center field instead.

The kid hit right away. Kaline seemed to have a natural understanding of baseball that eluded other kids. Anderson remembered having a conversation with the whole team about "going with the pitch," which is to say adjusting their hitting based on the location of the ball. All of the players nodded as if they understood, but they didn't really. How do you go with the pitch, anyway?

Kaline, in his first at-bat, rifled an outside pitch the other way for a single.

Kaline was a bonus baby, which is to say he signed for so much money ($15,000) that, by rule, the Detroit Tigers had to keep him on the big-league roster. Kaline played in 30 games as an 18-year-old. He wasn't great, but he wasn't overmatched, either—he did hit a homer off Cleveland starter Dave Hoskins.

In those days, Kaline's defining skill was his speed. They called him "the Baltimore Greyhound." And, apologies in advance, just seeing that nickname, "the Baltimore Greyhound," is going to send us on a tangent: Don't you miss those days when ballplayers got nicknames that fit that particular pattern:

"The" + "Where they came from" + "Fun noun, usually with the same first letter."

Mickey Mantle was "the Commerce Comet."

Cap Anson was "the Marshalltown Infant."

Amos Rusie was "the Hoosier Thunderbolt."

Bob Feller was "the Heater from Van Meter."

Frankie Frisch was "the Fordham Flash."

Spec Shea was "the Naugatuck Nugget."

So, no, they didn't all work. But I love that particular nickname construction. We do have one player now who has a nickname like that: Some people will call Mike Trout "the Millville Meteor." That's perfect for a timeless player like Trout. But I'd actually like to see it used more often, and I have a few suggestions:

Mookie Betts is "the Nashville Nighthawk."

Cody Bellinger is "the Scottsdale Smasher."

Anthony Rendon is "the Houston Hammer."

Justin Verlander is "the Goochland Gun."

Kirby Yates is "the Hawaiian Punch."

Or, you know, we could forget the whole thing.

Back to Al Kaline. He became a regular at age 19 and finished third in the Rookie of the Year balloting. He did not have a particularly good year offensively—he hit .276 with no real power or walks—but he made his mark as a defensive wonder in right field. He moved like a greyhound, as you know, and his arm, whoa, it was magical. He led the league in assists, but that arm could not be summed up by mere numbers.

In one game, he threw out a runner trying for an extra base in three straight innings.

In another, he dived for a ball, couldn't come up with it, and then, while sitting on the grass, he picked up the ball and threw out Dale Mitchell trying to take second.

There was just something about this kid. His talent was unmissable. It wasn't an easy year for him because the players hazed him and taunted him. "I had a guy grab my uniform, saying he didn't want me around," Kaline would say later. But he was still good enough that one writer put Kaline on his MVP ballot.

Then, at age 20, Kaline became a superstar—it was, at the time, probably the greatest season a 20-year-old ever had. And even now, it's surely in the Top 5.

Best seasons ever for 20-year-olds:

1. Mike Trout, 2012: Hit .326/.399/.564 with 30 homers, a league-leading 49 stolen bases, and a league-leading 129 runs.

2. Alex Rodriguez, 1996: Led the league in hitting (.358) doubles (54), runs scored (141), and total bases (379).

3. Al Kaline, 1955: Led the league in batting average (.340) and hits (200), scored and drove in 100 runs, mashed 27 homers, and undoubtedly would have won a Gold Glove if the award had been invented.

4. Mel Ott, 1929: Didn't lead the league in much because Rogers Hornsby was around but he did hit .328 with 42 homers, 151 RBIs, and 138 runs scored.

5. Ty Cobb, 1907: Hit .350 to win the first of 11 or 12 batting titles (more on that in the Cobb chapter). He also led the league in hits and RBIs.

Baseball had a new star. People could not stop gushing.

"He's made some catches I still don't believe," Yankees manager Casey Stengel said.

"He's just one of those naturals," his teammate Ned Garvin said.

"The kid can't miss," Joe DiMaggio said.

"He's the greatest right-handed hitter in the league," Ted Williams said.

The last of those compliments was particularly meaningful to Kaline, who idolized Williams. They had spoken once when he was 18, and Williams had passed along eight words that Kaline believed was the holy gospel of hitting:

Wait for your pitch and then hit it.

Every time Kaline would get in trouble, get in a slump, feel off rhythm, he would repeat that mantra to himself: Wait for your pitch and then hit it. He always told young hitters that the way to mess yourself up as a hitter was to complicate things.

Kaline finished second in the 1955 MVP voting to Yogi Berra, who, bluntly, did not have as good a season. Kaline finished third the next year to Mickey Mantle and Berra. Mantle won the Triple Crown in 1956 so this isn't to knock that vote, it's just to point out that you couldn't really win an MVP in the 1950s and early 1960s if you weren't a Yankee—from 1950 to 1963, the Yankees won 10 of the 14 American League MVP awards. Kaline finished second in the MVP voting in 1963 to another Yankee, Elston Howard.

But, though he would go on to do so much, you could argue that things peaked for Kaline at 20. He never led the league in hitting again. He only once scored 100 runs in a season, only twice more drove in 100 runs. His body broke down repeatedly. And he began to sour on the game.

The souring part began after he got into a brutal salary dispute in 1956. He had finished second and third in the previous two MVP races but was still making just $15,000 a year. Mickey Mantle, it was well known, was making $60,000 a year. To Kaline, it just seemed fair for him to get a substantial raise.

So when the Tigers sent him a contract offering only a $3,000 raise, he sent it back unsigned.

This might seem reasonable now, but in 1956, in a blue-collar city like Detroit, it was seen as outrageous. Sending back a contract? Who did he think he was, anyway? Tigers president Spike Briggs was apoplectic. The next day, he was speaking at a dinner and he made it abundantly clear just how wronged he felt on behalf of the Detroit Tigers and their many hard-working fans.

"Al thinks he's as good as Mickey Mantle and wants more money than Mantle," Briggs said. "I don't agree with him, and he isn't going to get it. . . . I sent Kaline a contract over the holidays with a $3,000 bonus for last year. I got the contract back unsigned. I didn't get thanks for the bonus or even a holiday greeting."

Wow! Not even a holiday greeting! Kaline could not even believe how unfair Briggs had been. "I definitely didn't ask for Mantle's pay," Kaline angrily told a reporter, and he explained that all he wanted was a fair raise that matched his play. But it was too late. The Tigers knew exactly what buttons to push. Kaline settled for the Tigers' stingy raise, and to make matters worse, he was booed heartily when he returned to Tiger Stadium.

Yes, it's true, Detroit fans booed Mr. Tiger.

Kaline burned with rage. His composure and professionalism later would often be compared to that of Stan Musial, Baseball's Perfect Knight. But that sort of happy warrior stuff came naturally to Musial. Not so for Kaline. He was a perfectionist and his temper was always on a slow boil.

He smashed bats. "I just never thought I should make an out," he said.

He rebelled against the constant pressure the press put on him. "They wanted me to be Ty Cobb," he said. "But who can be Ty Cobb?"

"There was a time when Al Kaline was not a very pleasant person to be around," the legendary Detroit sportswriter Joe Falls said.

Mostly, he resented that people thought everything came easy to him. Nothing comes easy. Kaline played with a painful left-foot injury that bothered him his entire career. He played the game so hard that he suffered constant injuries—he broke his collarbone diving for a ball (he made the catch), he was knocked unconscious after running into a wall, he broke his hand slamming his bat after a strikeout.

This is what I mean by the limitations of talent. The young Kaline, the player Garvin called a natural, did not become great because of that talent he had. No, Al Kaline became great because he kept going through it all—through the frustrations, the slumps, the unfair criticisms, the agonizing salary disputes, the terrible injuries—and all the while he kept growing as a player and a man, kept finding his better self. Despite the injuries, he played more than 2,800 games, which is more than Derek Jeter. Even after he lost his Baltimore Greyhound speed, he remained a smart and superb baserunner and he kept playing right field like a dream; after they started giving out Gold Gloves, he won 10 of them.

"There have been a lot of great defensive players," his contemporary Brooks Robinson once said. "The fella who could do everything is Al Kaline."

And even though he played through the 1960s, the worst-hitting environment since Deadball, Kaline hit double-digit home runs for 19 consecutive seasons and climbed his way to 3,000 hits and more than 1,600 runs scored and almost 1,600 RBIs.

He was also at his best in his biggest moment, the 1968 World Series. He hit .379 and slugged .650 and got the game-winning hit in Game 5.

Through it all, Kaline came to represent something larger than baseball. He came to represent fortitude and kindness and dignity. Remember how Falls said he could be unpleasant to reporters as a young player? Well, after his 2,000th hit, Kaline didn't want to talk to reporters. He was not a stats guy, and he cared only about the team, and he just didn't see it as a big deal.

But after shrugging off reporters, Kaline had second thoughts. He realized—perhaps for the first time—that whether he saw it as a story was not the point. Those reporters still had to write it. He walked up to Joe Falls and said quietly: "I should have understood what they wanted. Will you apologize to them for me?" And Falls said that after that, Kaline never declined to talk.

He took the same approach on the field. In 1960, as a 25-year-old, Kaline was thrown out of a game for arguing with an umpire. On the way back to the locker room, he realized that he had been wrong. After the game he found the umpire to say he was wrong and that he was sorry. From that point on, umpires talked often about the class and graciousness of Al Kaline.

It was the same with the fans. He had a hard time forgiving Tigers fans after those early boos, after they attacked him for trying to get himself a fair salary. But he soon came to appreciate that they looked to him as the luckiest of souls. And, whether he felt lucky or not, whether he felt in pain or not, he owed them that dream.

"Fans don't want much," he once said. "All you have to do is smile and say 'hi!' and shake their hands. They're happy."

Fifteen years after his initial bitter salary battle, Kaline again made the papers for a contract dispute. This time, though, he was a legend. He was Mr. Tiger. He was as much a part of Detroit as Motown. And this time, the Tigers offered Kaline the team's first-ever $100,000 deal. He wouldn't take it.

"I don't deserve such a salary," he said. "I didn't have a good enough season last year."

We should talk, for a moment, about Kaline's last game because he made a decision that day that he would always regret. The Tigers were lousy that year; they lost 90 games, and on a cold Wednesday, October 2, 1974, they played the AL East champion Baltimore Orioles in a meaningless game. There are many similarities between Kaline's last game and the last game of his hero, Ted Williams, the game John Updike immortalized in his famous *New Yorker* story "Hub Fans Bid Kid Adieu."

"I, and 10,453 others, had shown up primarily because this was the Red Sox last home game of the season," Updike wrote, "and therefore the last time in all eternity that the regular left fielder, known to the headlines as Ted, Kid, Spliter, Thumper, TW, and, most cloyingly, misTer Wonderful, would play in Boston."

On this day 14 years later, even fewer people—just 4,671—would show up to see Mr. Tiger play in Detroit. Williams had homered in his final plate appearance, a glorious end. There was a small hope that Kaline would connect one more time, giving him a nice even 400 homers for his career. If he could do it, Kaline would become the first American Leaguer ever to have 3,000 hits and 400 home runs.

These sorts of round numbers fuel the most precious of baseball dreams. Even Ted Williams didn't have 3,000 hits and 400 home runs.

But hope for Kaline to homer was a mere illusion. His left shoulder hurt so bad he could barely swing the bat. He would not have played at all except it was his final game, he had to play, and so he was put in as the team's designated hitter and in the first inning he struck out looking against the Orioles' Mike Cuellar. Simply swinging the bat hurt too much.

In the third inning, though, he did swing and he got pretty good wood on a pitch from Cuellar. He watched dispiritedly as the line drive sank and landed in the glove of a charging Al Bumbry.

Then came the fifth inning, and the small but spirited crowd prepared themselves for Kaline's next at-bat. But Kaline did not come out of the dugout. Instead, a pinch-hitter—a 25-year-old utility player named Ben Oglivie (who years later would lead the league in home runs)—stepped to the on-deck circle. The crowd began to boo. They booed louder as Oglivie stepped toward the plate as he intended to hit. They booed even louder when he grounded out to second against Wayne Garland.

Things grew so contentious that in the sixth inning some fans began gathering around the Tigers' dugout just to scream at manager Ralph Houk.

But it wasn't Houk's decision to pull Kaline. No, Kaline himself had decided that he'd had enough. His shoulder hurt too badly. He'd suffered enough for this sport. "I'm glad it's over, I really am," he told reporters at the end of the game. "I don't think I'll miss it. On the Fourth of July, I'd love to be at a lake instead of at the ballpark for two games."

And, it should be said, Kaline didn't miss it. He really had given all he had to give. He went home to spend the year with his son, who was a senior in high school and would soon be off to college. He spent many days at the lake. He stayed around the game as an announcer and team consultant until he died in 2020 at age 85.

"I can honestly tell you," Mr. Tiger told me once, "I gave my best."

Sure he did. How many baseball Misters are there? You have Mr. October (Reggie), Mr. November (Jeter), Mr. Baseball (Uecker), and Mr. Met (Mr. Met). There's Mr. Mister if you want truly terrible 1980s pop-rock.

But the most beloved of all the Misters are those who became synonymous with their team and their city. There's Mr. Cub, Ernie Banks. There's Mr. Padre, Tony Gwynn.

And there's Mr. Tiger, Al Kaline.

But Kaline did leave baseball with one regret.

He regretted taking himself out of that last game.

Why? Was it that he didn't give himself another shot at that elusive 400th homer? Nah. "I've never been a stats guy," he said. "Anyway, eras in baseball are all different. The game changes so much. I knew how many great hitters had hit 400 or 500 home runs, and to me, it wasn't like I was in their class."

Was it that the way he pulled himself out of his last game simply didn't symbolize how he played the game? Nah. He'd given all he had. He didn't need a show at the end to know what he was about.

No, the reason he regretted it was the most Al Kaline of reasons: He regretted taking himself out of the game because that meant he put Ben Oglivie in a position to get booed. And Ben just didn't deserve that.

No. 50 **Nolan Ryan**

Nolan Ryan was the greatest pitcher who ever lived. Nolan Ryan was the most frustrating pitcher who ever lived. Nobody struck out more batters. Nobody walked more batters. Nobody was harder to hit. Nobody so willingly let baserunners steal. Nobody threw more no-hitters. Nobody threw more wild pitches. He was unbeatable. Nobody in modern baseball lost more.

It is as if Ryan is not actually a pitcher but something else entirely—an alien, a cartoon character, a folk hero, a saxophone. Trying to find a place for Ryan on a list like this is a bit like trying to figure out where the Beatles belong on your list of favorite pastas.

Nolan Ryan was a sophomore in high school when he threw a softball from one end zone to the other on the Alvin High School football field. Ryan was unimpressed with himself. He'd done stuff like that before. But it profoundly impressed Alvin High baseball coach Jim Watson, who immediately asked Ryan to pitch on the varsity team.

From the start, no one could touch Nolan Ryan's fastball.

From the start, everybody was scared to death of Nolan Ryan's fastball.

"He didn't know *where* the ball was going," Watson said in the book

Nolan Ryan: The Making of a Pitcher. "And neither did the batter, which worked to his advantage."

In many ways, that's Ryan's story in a single quote.

Ryan would often say that he developed his arm strength by throwing *Houston Post* newspapers into people's driveways with his father, Lynn. It's a romantic story, but quite likely true—Nolan and his father had a 1,500-customer paper route.*

Ryan threw more than just newspapers, however. The young Nolan was always throwing stuff—rocks, sticks, tennis balls, marbles. He didn't care; he threw and threw all his childhood. He just liked throwing, and this was convenient because Nolan's older brother Robert was a catcher in search of a pitcher. "I guess he's the one who made me a pitcher," Nolan later said.

Picking up the story—Ryan threw so hard in high school that multiple scouts came after him, and at the same time he was so wild that multiple scouts went running for the hills. The one who stayed with Ryan was named Red Murff, and he had once been a strong-armed Texas pitcher himself. Murff got only 26 games in the big leagues with Milwaukee, but in that short time he did strike out Frank Robinson, Ernie Banks, Jackie Robinson, Willie Mays, *and* Roberto Clemente. In 50 innings, that's pretty impressive work.

Murff was a Mets scout, and he often said that fate brought him to Clear Creek, Texas, where he saw Ryan pitch for the very first time. He was so excited by Ryan's potential that as soon as he got home, he wrote a note to himself to mark the occasion:

> This skinny high school junior HAS THE BEST ARM I'VE EVER SEEN IN MY LIFE. This kid Ryan throws much harder than Jim Maloney of the Cincinnati Reds or Turk Farrell of the Houston Colt .45s (I saw them pitch Thursday night, 4-23-63).

Other scouts saw the arm, but none were as moved as Murff was. "He seemed to see something in me no one else did," Ryan would say. The Mets took Ryan in the 12th round of the very first amateur draft.

To understand the quirks of the draft, look at the Mets' picks that year:

---

* Another all-time great, third baseman Brooks Robinson, also developed his arm by throwing newspapers into people's driveways.

First round (second overall pick): Les Rohr. Won two big-league games.

Second round: Randolph Kohn. Never made it.

Third round: Joe Moock. Great name. Played in 13 big-league games.

Fourth round: Ken Boswell. Had an 11-year career, 5.5 WAR.

Fifth round: Doug Britelle. Never made it.

Sixth round: Harold Roberson. Never made it.

Seventh round: Michael McClure. Never made it.

Eighth round: Roger Harrington. Never made it.

Ninth round: Louis Williams. Never made it.

10th round: Roger Stevens. Never made it.

11th round: Jim McAndrew. Won 37 big-league games.

12th round: Nolan Ryan.

The Mets managed to sign Ryan for almost nothing—Murff took Ryan bird hunting and they agreed to terms. The Mets then sent him to Marion, Virginia, where, as an 18-year old, Ryan threw 78 innings, struck out 115, walked 56, hit eight batters, and generally confused everyone.

"Now that I've been in baseball," Ryan said, "I like it better than I thought I would."

Even though he immediately put up Nolan Ryan–type numbers, he wasn't yet Nolan Ryan. That first year, he threw side-armed rather than using the long, slow, over-the-top windup that would inspire a generation. He had a side-to-side, sweeping curveball rather than the top-to-bottom curve that would wipe out hitters for two decades. He was so skinny that despite spending all offseason—on the Mets' command—drinking a meal-replacement drink called Sego, he couldn't add a pound to his 6-foot-2, 168-pound frame.

But Ryan's style was taking shape. He began to throw overhand as a 19-year-old, and he pitched 202 innings in Class-A Greensville and Double-A

Williamsport. He struck out 307, walked 139, threw 22 wild pitches, and went 17-4 with a 2.36 ERA.*

Late in that first full minor-league season, Ryan pitched a game that foreshadowed his career. He was pitching for Williamsport against Pawtucket, and he was incredible. He struck out 21 batters. Nobody could touch him. And yet Williamsport lost the game 2–1. How do you lose a game when you strike out 21 and nobody can touch you?

He did it the Ryan way. He gave up the tying run when Dave Nelson (who would go on to a 10-year big-league career) singled and promptly stole second, stole third, and stole home. Ryan gave up the winning run in the 10th inning when a player named Don Gadbury reached on an error, moved to third on a wild pitch, and stole home.

Nobody was ever slower to the plate than Nolan Ryan.

Ten days after that game, Ryan made his big-league debut. "I'm scared to death," he told reporters. He was pretty good in his debut—he faced Atlanta, lasted two innings, struck out the first batter he faced (pitcher Pat Jarvis), and also struck out Hall of Famer Eddie Mathews. But he did get a fastball up on Joe Torre, who cracked it over the left-field wall.

"I knew it was a little high when I threw it," Ryan said after the game. "It kept on getting higher after Torre hit it."

Seven days later, he made his first big-league start, and that one was a disaster. Ryan lasted just one inning, gave up four runs, four hits, and two walks and threw a wild pitch.

But there is something else to know about Nolan Ryan's first inning as a big-league starter.

He did strike out the side.

Nolan Ryan was drafted into the Army Reserves in 1967. He returned in June and immediately struck out 18 batters in seven innings for Jacksonville. "As great as Nolan Ryan is pitching," Dick Young wrote in the

---

* He also gave up more walks than hits, something he would do again in the big leagues in 1977 when pitching for the California Angels. That year with the Angels was something else—he walked 204 batters in 299 innings, but the league only hit .193 against him and he allowed only 198 hits. He remains the only pitcher in baseball history to throw 250 innings and allow more walks than hits.

Daily News, "I just know that the day the Mets bring him up, he'll get a sore arm."

That's exactly what happened. Ryan's arm just popped. He went to see doctors, who couldn't figure out what was wrong. They suggested exploratory surgery. Ryan said no, or more specifically, "Hell no." After further observation, the doctors discovered that his forearm tendon was torn and it needed surgery. Ryan said no, or more specifically, "Hell no." He said he'd fix the arm himself.

People began to realize there was something different about this guy. He did fix the arm himself. By 1968, he was throwing harder than ever for the New York Mets.

Everything the guy did was like that, like something out of a Marvel movie.

The record in the non-Nolan world for strikeouts is 4,875, held by Hall of Famer Randy Johnson.

Ryan struck out 5,714.

The record in the non-Nolan world for walks is 1,833, held by Hall of Famer Steve Carlton . . . just ahead of the 1,809 walks by another Hall of Famer, Phil Niekro.

Ryan walked 2,795.

The record for most no-hitters in the non-Nolan world is four, held by Hall of Famer Sandy Koufax.

Ryan pitched seven no-hitters.

The record in the non-Nolan world for stolen bases allowed is 547, held by Hall of Famer Greg Maddux.

Ryan allowed 757 stolen bases.

The pitcher over the past 100 years with the most errors in the non-Nolan world is Hall of Famer Don Drysdale, with 59.

Ryan committed 91 errors.

The record for fewest hits per nine innings in the non-Nolan world is 6.8 and is currently shared by Koufax and future Hall of Famer Clayton Kershaw.

Ryan allowed 6.6 hits per nine innings.

The modern record in the non-Nolan world for wild pitches is 226 and belongs to Niekro, who threw a knuckleball that would do whatever it wanted to do.

Ryan threw 277 wild pitches.

The modern record for losses in the non-Nolan world is 279 and belongs to Hall of Famer Walter Johnson.

Ryan lost 292 games.

The record for most complete games allowing two hits or fewer in the non-Nolan world is 25, also held by Walter Johnson.

Ryan threw 37 two-hitters or better.

You understand the point, right? He's incomparable. Anything a pitcher can do, he did better. Anything a pitcher can do, he did worse. There's nobody else in his category. This didn't happen by accident. Other pitchers were going for their thing. Nolan Ryan was going for *his* thing.

What was that thing? Former batting champion Ralph Garr told a story about Ryan that I think comes closest to explaining. In May 1979, Ryan's Angels played Garr's White Sox in a Sunday afternoon game. Garr led off, stepped to the plate, struck out on three pitches that were nothing more than blurs, and when he got back to the dugout he shouted out in his distinctive high-pitched voice that could be heard for miles around: "Boys, we got *no* shot today."

He was right. Ryan threw a two-hit shutout and struck out 11.

This is what Ryan was going for every time he pitched. He pitched just to win games. He pitched to dominate. He pitched to intimidate. He pitched to make the best hitters on earth simply give up hope. He pitched every game with the intention of leaving behind something indelible.

Randy Johnson and Tom Seaver combined for an amazing 67 three-hitters (or better) in their awesome careers. Ryan alone had 69 of them.

Sandy Koufax and Pedro Martínez combined for an amazing 215 games with 10 strikeouts. Ryan alone had 215 such games.

Every time out, Ryan aimed for history. He refused to compromise, to moderate, to make any concessions at all. Yes, he could have sped up his windup so that base stealers didn't run on him at will. Wouldn't do it. He could have spared a couple of miles per hour off the fastball to refine his control. Wouldn't do it. He could have stopped aiming for corners when he was behind in the count, could have been more efficient by not always going for the strikeout, could have taken a few wild pitches off the career total by easing up just a little bit.

Would. Not. Do. It.

Ryan wasn't into trade-offs. He wasn't negotiating. He had what I feel sure is the hardest fastball ever thrown and, by God, he was going to throw it. He had a curveball that dropped like a hawk going after its prey, and, by God, he was going to throw it. He intended to strike out 27 batters every game. He intended to throw a no-hitter every game. And each batter who made contact, each batter who managed a hit, didn't change the fundamental truth of Nolan Ryan's ambitions.

It only made him slightly moderate his goals to striking out 26 batters and throwing a one-hitter.

I don't think you can overstate just how many batters Nolan Ryan walked. As you can see above, he walked almost 1,000 more batters than any other pitcher in baseball history. You can add the entire careers of Hall of Famers Pete Alexander, Robin Roberts, and Mike Mussina and still not get to Ryan's total.

How many walks? Ryan allowed fewer hits per inning pitched than anyone ever. But if you look at WHIP—that's walks plus hits per inning—he drops out of the top 10, out of the top 50, out of the top 100, out of the top 250. He's 291st.

Walks were just part of the deal. The slow windup was just part of the deal. The pitches in the dirt, the errors, even losing all those games, all of it was just part of being Nolan Ryan, the most unhittable pitcher who ever lived. He wanted to fly. And he did fly. Could he have curbed his pitching style and been more effective? Maybe. He never considered it.

All in all, Nolan Ryan chose to be Nolan Ryan.

And what fun would it have been otherwise?

No. 49 **Warren Spahn**

First we'll use Spahn
then we'll use Sain
Then an off day
followed by rain
Back will come Spahn
followed by Sain
And followed we hope
by two days of rain.
　　　—Gerald V. Hern poem
　　　　on the 1948 Braves

Warren Spahn was, as they used to say in his time, one smart cookie. He wanted to be a first baseman. His father, Ed, didn't want that. Ed raised Warren to pitch on the sound principle that teams will always need left-handed pitching (while also figuring that, as a lefty, his son had limited options in the field). Ed Spahn was pretty relentless about it; he made his son pitch so many baseballs at so many targets that after a while Warren dreaded coming home.

Throughout, though, Warren saw himself as a hitter. Hitting was what he loved, not pitching, and in some ways that never really changed. You might know that Spahn hit 35 home runs in his big-league career, behind only Wes Ferrell and Bob Lemon among pitchers. He always felt more comfortable, more at home, when talking to hitters. Those were his people.

So he fought his father throughout his childhood. Yes, he'd pitch at those targets because he was a good son, but he insisted that he would never become a pitcher. OK, he'd develop a fastball and a curveball, but he would never become a pitcher. Fine, he'd throw until his arm hurt but he'd *never* become a pitcher.

Then he got to high school and Warren saw the team's all-state first baseman. "That guy," he said to himself, "is a lot better than I am."

That's when Warren Spahn became a pitcher.

Warren Edward Spahn was named after one of the worst presidents in American history: Warren G. Harding. The name was pure timing. Harding took office barely a month before Spahn was born; he had run on a campaign of "return to normalcy" and had won in a landslide, taking more than 60 percent of the vote. Ed Spahn sold wallpaper in Buffalo, a little less every year, and nothing appealed to him more than the idea of returning to normalcy. He so believed in Harding's magical ability to take America back to the past that he chose to name his son after the president first, himself second.

Through the years, many players were named after presidents but most of them were minor players. Here are some of my favorites:

Pete Alexander: Grover Cleveland Alexander, one of the greatest pitchers ever, was named for Grover Cleveland, the only president to serve two nonconsecutive terms. Few used the name "Grover" when referring to him—they called Alexander "Pete" or "Ol' Pete," and he's usually referred to as Pete Alexander now. Grover Cleveland Alexander also has a distinction that will never be matched: He is and will always be the only player ever named for a president who then had a president play him in a movie. Ronald Reagan played Alexander in the lamentable but so-bad-it's-good movie *The Winning Team*.

Tommy Bridges: He won 194 games in his big-league career and appeared in six All-Star Games. His full name was Thomas Jefferson Davis

Bridges—he was named after the third president and the president of the Confederacy. There have been more than a half-dozen players named for Thomas Jefferson.

Sweetbread Bailey: He wasn't a great pitcher—or even a good one—but he did pitch briefly for the Cubs and Dodgers after serving in the army during World War I. His nickname is wonderful. But his full name might be even better: Abraham Lincoln Bailey.

Lil' Stoner: Here might be my favorite—Lil' Stoner won 50 games for the Tigers between 1922 and 1929. His full name was Ulysses Simpson Grant Stoner—which is wonderful, even if Ulysses S. Grant's middle name wasn't really Simpson (that was his mother's maiden name, but Grant's name was Hiram Ulysses Grant). But that's not the best part. Lil' Stoner had a brother named Benjamin Franklin Stoner, another named Theodore Roosevelt Stoner, and another named Washington Irving Stoner.

Max Venable: He played 12 years as a utility outfielder for the Giants, Expos, Reds, and Angels. His full name is William McKinley Venable. He named his son William as well but made the middle name "Dion" instead of McKinley. Will Venable was a significantly better player than his father; he played nine years in the big leagues, hit as many as 22 homers, and stole as many as 29 bases in a season.

Ted Lilly: He was named after Teddy Roosevelt—his full name is Theodore Roosevelt Lilly—but still went by Ted instead of Teddy. He won 130 games for six teams between 1999 and 2013.

Woody Williams: There have been two players called Woody Williams in the big leagues. This is the hitter: He played for the Cincinnati Reds during World War II and in 1944 he led the league in plate appearances and at-bats. He is notable for having hit just one home run in 1,369 plate appearances and for being named Woodrow Wilson Williams.

Cal McLish: He won 92 games in his big-league career and in the late 1950s with Cleveland emerged as one of the league's better pitchers. He received MVP consideration in 1958 and 1959. But it is his name that made him a legend—the full name was Calvin Coolidge Julius Caesar Tuskahoma McLish.

Ted Wieand: You've never heard of him. He only pitched six games in his very short big-league career but he gets a special mention because he was named for a Roosevelt—but not Teddy. His full name: Franklin

Delano Roosevelt Wieand. He was born in Walnutport, Pennsylvania, one month after the inauguration of FDR.

And, as you know, Warren Spahn was named for Warren G. Harding.

Spahn used to tell a story about his first big-league disappointment. In 1942, he came up to the big leagues to play for the Boston Braves. He was, at the time, unfinished as a pitcher but he could throw hard so he got the call. His manager was Casey Stengel,* and he pitched a couple of games as a 20-year-old.

He was shipped out on his 21st birthday, however. Spahn said he was brought in as a relief pitcher against the Dodgers on April 20, 1942. At the mound, Stengel ordered him to intimidate Brooklyn shortstop Pee Wee Reese. "This hitter has been beaned and got his skull broke," Spahn quoted Stengel saying. "I want you to throw your first two pitches at his head."

That, to say the least, was not Spahn's style. In his long, long, long career—he would become the first pitcher since that other presidential namesake, Pete Alexander, to throw 5,000 innings—Spahn hit only 42 batters. He was the nicest of men and the purest of competitors, and everything in his soul told him not to throw at Reese. But he was also 20 and he had been given a direct order, so he sort of, kind of threw two balls near Reese's shoulder before walking him.

Here's what Spahn said happened next. Stengel rushed out to the mound and took away the ball and said this:

"You're out of the game. And when you get to the dugout, keep walking 'til you reach the clubhouse. There's gonna be a bus ticket there back to Hartford. You'll never win in the major leagues. You got no guts."

Now, the story is not literally true. Spahn *did* face Reese first when he came into that game in 1942, but he didn't walk him. He got Reese to pop out to the catcher. And he didn't get pulled from the game, either; Spahn pitched on for another four innings. He actually faced Reese a second time and got him to hit into a 6-4-3 double play.

But his big-league season did end with a walk. Spahn walked a catcher

---

* Stengel was also Spahn's manager with the Mets in 1965, which led to one of Spahn's many famous quotes: "I pitched for Casey Stengel before and after he was a genius."

named Cliff Dapper,* who played just eight games in the big leagues. That walk loaded the bases, and you could definitely imagine the fury of Stengel. He pulled Spahn and did send Spahn to Hartford the very next day.

Details aside, the story is wonderful because whenever Spahn told it, he would linger for a second on the part where Stengel said he had no guts. And then he would continue with this line: "So, anyway, after I won the Bronze Star at the Battle of the Bulge . . ."

Spahn did indeed earn the Bronze Star and a Purple Heart at the Battle of the Bulge. If you are a fan of *It's a Wonderful Life,* you might remember that as the narrator recounted what each character did during World War II, "Marty helped capture the Remagen bridge." The bridge over the Rhine at Remagen was actually called the Ludendorff Bridge, but Spahn, like the fictional Marty, really was there. He was wounded on that bridge.

After the war, Spahn had new feelings about baseball. He had resented his father for making him throw all those pitches as a boy. But now he was grateful. "After what I went through overseas," he said, "I never thought of anything I had to do in baseball as hard work."

Spahn won 20 games for the first time in 1947. And then he won 20 in 1949, 1950, 1951, 1953, 1954, 1956, 1957, 1958, 1959, 1960, 1961, and 1963. I could have just said he won 20 games 13 times, but that wouldn't give you the full scope of the achievement. Sure, the game has changed entirely since Spahn's time, but it's still worth mentioning that since 2013, there have been just a dozen 20-game winners *combined.*

Spahn succeeded with an unmatched combination of guile and street smarts and command and joy and a second-level understanding of how to get hitters out. He is most known for throwing a pitch everybody called a screwball but he never stopped adding pitches and tricks and windup adjustments. He knew hitters and knew that what they liked least was unpredictability.

---

* One rabbit hole leads into another: Cliff Dapper is famous in his own right. Though he played in only eight big-league games, he has the highest batting average for any player in baseball history with more than 15 plate appearances. He hit .471 in 17 at-bats. He also owned an avocado and lemon farm with Duke Snider. But most famously, Dapper was the only player ever traded for an announcer. In 1948, Dapper was dealt by the Dodgers to the minor-league Atlanta Crackers for the broadcaster Ernie Harwell, who would call Dodger games until another legend named Vin Scully took over.

"Hitting is timing," Spahn said, "and pitching is upsetting timing."

Which takes us back to Spahn's screwball. He began working on it sometime in 1954. He still threw very hard then, but part of his genius was that he always thought ahead. He could already see that day in the not-too-distant future when his fastball and curveball would lose their effectiveness. He began throwing the screwball a lot in 1958. "Most pitchers wait until they lose their stuff to change their style, wait until they've had a couple of bad years," catcher Del Crandall said in awe. "Spahnie anticipated it and had it ready when the fast one began to lose steam."

"In this business," Spahn said, "you have to anticipate your needs."

You might notice that I referred to the pitch as one everybody called a screwball. This is because there's a timeless question: Was Spahn's pitch *really* a screwball? It remains a mystery. A true screwball is sort of a curve with a reverse motion—it is devastating on the arm. When throwing a textbook screwball, you have to snap your wrist away from your body, exactly the opposite of what you do on a curveball. "When I threw the screwball," the master of the pitch, Carl Hubbell, explained, "I came right over the top and turned my arm clear over and let the ball come out of the back of my hand."

Is that how Spahn threw it? Well, to be honest, we don't know. In 1962, Spahn was the subject of a story in the *Ottawa Citizen* weekend magazine where he allowed a photographer to take a photo of the grip he used. In it, he held the ball between his two middle fingers but also seemed to be touching one of the seams with his index finger and pinkie—Spahn called it a full-hand grip. Let's just say it looks extremely awkward. And he said he did turn the ball over the way Hubbell had.

But there's reason to believe that that might have been a Spahn prank—he was famous for those—because a little later, he was interviewed about the screwball and he said that he didn't have a special grip at all. In fact, he said, it just happened naturally. Spahn said that he threw what he thought was an overhand curveball to St. Louis's Terry Moore. "He struck out," Spahn recalled, "and later he said to me, 'Hey, where did you get that screwball?' He swore it broke away from him. That indicated that I had a natural ability to throw a screwball, so I began to fool around with it."

Long after he retired, he explained the screwball to the great baseball writer Roger Angell and a whole different picture emerged:

"Look, it's easy," Spahnie said. "You do this." His left thumb and forefinger were making a circle, with the other three fingers pointing up, exactly as if he was flashing the "OK" sign to someone nearby. The ball was tucked comfortably up against the circle, without being held by it, and the other fingers stayed up and apart, keeping only a loose grip on the pill. Thrown that way, he said, the ball departed naturally off the inside, or little finger side, off the middle finger, and would then sink and break to the left as it crossed the plate. "There's nothing to it," he said optimistically. "Just let her go," he said.

That is a wonderful and vivid description of a pitch. But the pitch is most definitely not a screwball. That is a circle change, the pitch that made Tom Glavine famous, not to mention Pedro Martínez, Zack Greinke, Cole Hamels, and many others. Did Warren Spahn really throw an entirely different pitch from what he's so famous for throwing? It's a good bet: Years later, reliever John Franco threw his circle change with such velocity and spin that he too insisted it was a screwball. Baseball history does repeat.

Spahn won 363 games in his career, more than any pitcher since Deadball. Greg Maddux came up eight wins shy, Roger Clemens nine wins short. He also threw more shutouts than any pitcher in the last 100 years. Spahn was elected into the Hall of Fame in 1973.

Still, Spahn might be best known as the first part of that famous Spahn and Sain poem. That timeless rhyme—*Spahn and Sain / And two days of rain*—comes from 1948, when the Boston Braves won their first pennant in almost 40 years. The Braves' lineup was a creaky one, filled with all sorts of 30-something hitters like Bob Elliott and Jeff Heath and Eddie Stanky and Tommy Holmes. The pitching staff was loaded down with a bunch of middling pitchers left over from the war, like Bill Voiselle, Vern Bickford, and Red Barrett.

But they had Warren Spahn.

And they had Johnny Sain.

On September 6, the Braves had built a two-and-a-half-game lead, and manager Billy Southworth decided he was taking no more chances. He was going to ride Spahn and Sain to the bitter end. This began with a doubleheader against the Dodgers. He started Spahn in the first game and let him go 14 innings until his team finally scored its second run.

He started Sain in the second game, and he pitched a shutout.

Because of two open dates and two consecutive rainouts (there's your two days of rain), the Braves didn't play again until September 11. It was another doubleheader. Southworth started Sain in the first game (nine innings, one run) and Spahn in the second (nine innings, two runs, one earned).

After another doubleheader, he brought back Sain on two days' rest (nine innings, three runs) and then Spahn on three days' rest (nine innings, two runs). Then Sain again was back on two days' rest (nine innings, two runs) and Spahn pitched on two days' rest (nine innings, one run).

Sain was granted three whole days of rest before he threw his next complete game (nine innings, three runs).

That was when the wear and tear finally began to get to Spahn. He pitched on three days' rest and got knocked out of the box in the third inning. His next time out—on full rest—he was rocked by the Dodgers, giving up seven runs in five innings, including homers by Eddie Miksis and his old nemesis Pee Wee Reese.

Sain pitched the next day (nine innings, three runs, two earned) and Spahn pitched poorly three days after that (seven innings, eight runs, six earned). Sain pitched the second day of that doubleheader, again on two days' rest. By then, the pennant was wrapped up.

In all, Spahn and Sain started 15 of the Braves' last 22 games and carried the Braves to the World Series. In that Series against Cleveland, Spahn and Sain started four of the six games. They each won a start, each lost a start, and Cleveland took the series in six.

Sain would never have another year like that one. He won 24 games, led the league in innings pitched, and finished second in the MVP to Stan Musial in his greatest season. Sain would win just 70 games after that.

Spahn, meanwhile? In fact, 1948 was one of his worst seasons. He would pitch another 17 years and win 319 more games.

"I don't think Spahn will ever get into the Hall of Fame," Musial once said, "because he'll never stop pitching."

No. 48 Ken Griffey Jr.

Every era, it seems to me, has a ballplayer who most perfectly captures the essence of cool. True: Cool is a moving target; what's cool in one generation is decidedly uncool in another. Even the words change—cool, hip, groovy, daBomb.com, fire, outta sight, GOAT, baller, the bee's knees—and they change so fast that the surest way to reveal yourself as old and out of touch is to use a word for cool that long ago lost its currency.

New ballplayers—like new musicians, new writers, new actors, new comedians—always come along who, in the wonderful words of Tulane English professor and student of cool Joel Dinerstein, "embody the unspoken, unconscious needs that have not yet reached consciousness in young people."

Every era needs that cool. In the time of Humphrey Bogart, the ballplayer was Joe DiMaggio: silent, solitary, ready for whatever might come along. Mickey Mantle's power and speed matched with his wild nights out—he was cool the way Sinatra's Rat Pack was cool. Roberto Clemente was cool like Billie Holiday; watching him play inspired feelings that felt unfamiliar and glorious. Reggie Jackson was 1970s cool like the Fonz. Bo Jackson was 1980s cool like Arnold Schwarzenegger's Terminator.

And then came Griffey.

What was it about Ken Griffey Jr.? Well, it wasn't one thing. It was that gorgeous left-handed swing. It was the limitlessness of his talent. It was the way he wore his hat—baseball cap backward in a way that drove traditionalists mad—and the way his smile just beamed. Maybe most of all, it was the joy that just seemed to glow off of him. The instant he showed up at Oakland-Alameda County Stadium for his very first big-league game, the instant he hit a double off Dave Stewart in his first time up, he became his generation's favorite player.

With that, he made baseball feel current and alive in a way that it didn't the day before. That's the thing the coolest of the cool do. The coolest players make the game burst into color, like that moment in *The Wizard of Oz* when Dorothy lands in Oz.

When Ken Griffey Jr. turned 30—November 21, 1999*—he had a shot at being the greatest player ever.

Baseball is unusual in that in the minds of so many, the greatest player ever stays locked in place. In football, as the years progressed, the greatest player ever skipped around, Jim Brown to Joe Montana to Lawrence Taylor to Jerry Rice to Tom Brady. Basketball, too—Bill Russell, Wilt Chamberlain, Kareem Abdul-Jabbar, Magic Johnson, Larry Bird, Michael Jordan, LeBron James.

Baseball, though: Babe Ruth towered over the game in a way that is just different.

For the minority of people willing to consider someone other than Ruth, there is an opportunity, a chance for someone to come along and join Ruth at the top of baseball's mountain. As he turned 30, Griffey had a chance to be that guy. At that moment, he was hitting .299/.380/.569. He had hit 398 home runs, which was more than anyone ever at his age. He had won 10 straight Gold Gloves, something only Willie Mays had

---

* You probably know this legendary bit of baseball trivia, but if you don't, I wish I could be there to enjoy it with you: Ken Griffey Jr. and Stan Musial—two of the greatest and most beloved left-handed-throwing and -hitting outfielders in the history of the game— were both born on November 21 in Donora, Pennsylvania. Now, you tell me baseball isn't mystical.

done as a center fielder. He averaged 52 homers per year the previous four seasons, which suggested the best was yet to come. He already had more than 70 WAR.

The last part, no matter how you feel about WAR, was awe-inspiring. At that point, only six players in baseball history had compiled 70 WAR by their 30th birthdays, and they were the titans: Ruth, Mantle, Rogers Hornsby, Mel Ott, Hank Aaron, Jimmie Foxx.

Junior still seemed so young, so new, so certain to be great for many years to come. Put together his achievements, his charisma, his boundless joy . . . well, there are still those who will tell you that Ken Griffey Jr. is the greatest player of them all.

Trouble is, time can be cruel. Nobody wanted Ken Griffey Jr. to ever get old.

And, sadly, he got old when he was still young.

Griffey was traded to Cincinnati by request just 10 or so weeks after he turned 30. He was plenty good in his first year with the Reds—he hit 40 homers and slugged .556—but something wasn't the same. He hit .271, his lowest full-season average since he was a rookie. For the first time since that rookie season, he did not win a Gold Glove.

And the joy? Something happened to the joy.

Maybe it came from his breaking down. Maybe it was because he was in constant pain. Maybe it came from getting older; maybe he had just been beaten down by all the demands and requests and media questions and everything that comes with being the icon of your sport. But something changed.

After age 31, Ken Griffey Jr. was rarely a great player. He averaged fewer than 100 games per season in his last 10 years. Injuries robbed him of his speed and elasticity, and he became a subpar outfielder. His batting average plummeted to .260 in those final years, and though he did knock 192 home runs to push his career total past 600, it wasn't the magical number that it had been before (Barry Bonds and Sammy Sosa beat him to it).

Late in Griffey's career, it was reported that his Reds manager wanted to use him as a pinch-hitter but could not because Griffey was napping in the clubhouse. There was never any real clarity about the story, but less than a month later, Griffey retired in the middle of a four-game series.

Time can be so cruel. A whole generation of kids saw only *that* version of Ken Griffey Jr., just as a whole generation of kids sees only *this* version of Albert Pujols. The older Griffey was just trying to keep things together.

But the young Junior: He was this blinding light of wonder.

So many amazing and absurd things happened in 1994 that it's all but impossible to remember them all. That was the season of the baseball strike, and so it is a season of what might have been. Tony Gwynn might have hit .400. The Montreal Expos might have won the pennant (and what would *that* have meant for the future of Montreal baseball?). Matt Williams might have broken Roger Maris's single-season home run record.

And Ken Griffey Jr.—well, a couple of crazy things happened to Griffey.

First, yes, he too might have broken Maris's record if the season had gone on. He was on pace. He had 40 homers through 111 games. Maris, in his year, had 41 at the same time.

But you know what? He probably would not have broken Maris's record had the season gone on. Why not? Because 1994 was the year that the roof came down in Seattle.

Well, it wasn't the roof, exactly—it was the insulation tiles attached to the roof. On July 19, four 26-pound tiles at the Kingdome came crashing down on the choice seats just behind home plate. This, thankfully, happened a few hours before the game so nobody was sitting in those seats. But some players were warming up on the field. They saw it. And it was pretty scary.

Seattle officials immediately and rightly shut the place down and canceled all Mariners home games until further notice. Within a day, they realized they would not be able to play another game at the Kingdome until all 40,000 tiles were removed.

So the Mariners went on the road and stayed on the road. They asked about playing in a nearby baseball stadium in Tacoma or Vancouver, but MLB said no, all games had to be played in major-league parks. And for the next 20 games, the Mariners were vagabonds playing "home" games at Boston,* Anaheim, Kansas City, and Arlington, Texas.

---

* Trivia fun: The Mariners have played in a dome their entire history but have had one home rainout in their 40-plus-year history—can you name it? Answer: It was on Thursday, July 21, when they were scheduled to play a home game but instead got rained out at Fenway Park.

Could Griffey have broken Maris's record while playing every single game on the road? I doubt it. For one thing, he loved hitting in the King-dome. For his career, Griffey hit .310/.396/.605 in the Kingdome, and over the next five seasons, he would hit 123 homers in 344 Kingdome games, which is pretty darned close to 1961 Maris territory.

For another, players generally hit more home runs at home. Griffey, for his career, was typical in that way: He hit a homer every 14 at-bats at home and every 17 at-bats on the road. Add in the pressure and the exhaustion of going from city to city without a place to call home. I just can't see Griffey doing it.

Of course, I wish we could have seen him try. It seems impossible but Griffey was at the height of his powers. There didn't seem to be anything beyond his reach.

For much of the 1990s, there was an ongoing argument. Who was bet-ter: Barry Bonds or Ken Griffey Jr.? Here were two left-handed-hitting, left-handed-throwing outfielders who were sons of iconic 1970s baseball players.

Barry, for his part, played like a mirror image of his father. They were power and speed. They both played great defense. They were fury. When 30 homers and 30 stolen bases were a mark of staggering brilliance, no-body did it more often than Bobby and Barry Bonds.

Junior, meanwhile, looked like his father but their games were quite different. Ken Sr. could fly; he was one of the fastest players in all of base-ball in his day. He never stole more than 34 bases in a season, but that was only because the Reds rarely gave him the green light. (Joe Morgan always said he got distracted when there was a stealing teammate.) Senior was an electrifying baserunner who always believed he could have stolen 100 bases in a season if given a chance. Ken Jr. was fast as a young player but not that fast.

Ken Sr. was a corner outfielder with a less-than-average arm. Ken Jr. was a center fielder with a powerful arm.

Their swings were different, too—Senior's swing was a blunt instru-ment, a slash more than a swing, a thing designed for line drives and grounders into the hole. He was basically a .300 hitter (he finished at .296). Junior's swing, of course, was majestic, gorgeous, the Grand Can-yon of swings, the Machu Picchu of swings, the "Here Comes the Sun" of swings. It tilted upward, and when bat met ball, you could feel the breath rush out of your body.

So, yes, Junior and Barry. The argument raged on. Looking back through a statistical lens, Barry was probably the better player because he got on base more, made fewer outs, and made more things happen on the bases.

Their stats in the 1990s:

Bonds: .302/.434/.602 with 299 doubles, 42 triples, 361 homers, 343 stolen bases, 8 Gold Gloves, 3 MVPs, 80.2 WAR.

Griffey: .302/.384/.581 with 297 doubles, 30 triples, 382 homers, 151 stolen bases, 10 Gold Gloves, 1 MVP, 67.5 WAR.

But people don't have to see baseball with their heads; that's part of the beauty. For many fans, the choice was Griffey because he did play center field, the game's great stage, and he did hit a few more home runs, and his game had a grace and an energy and a delightfulness that they couldn't find in Bonds's game. That doesn't mean one side was right or one side was wrong. It's baseball. There's room for all the opinions.

After 1999, though, they went separate ways. Bonds made his choices to bulk up and he became an absurdity. Time made Griffey's choices, and he declined and ached. When it came to their legacies, to their places in Cooperstown, Griffey was elected just three votes shy of unanimity. Bonds has not been elected, and there seems no clear path for him ever to get elected.

Baseball, as you already know, really is a game of the heart.

For a time, I lived in Cincinnati, and there was a supermarket in my neighborhood, and in that supermarket's parking lot there was an X carved into the concrete. That X was supposedly where one of Ken Griffey Jr.'s high school home run balls was found. Sometimes I would stand at that X and look around. You couldn't even see a baseball field from there. It did not seem possible. But that was the whole point of Ken Griffey Jr. He did not seem possible.

No. 47 **Wade Boggs**

W ade Boggs makes more sense if you think of him as a misunderstood artist. Many artists are underappreciated in their time. It is said that Vincent Van Gogh sold only one or two paintings during his life. Emily Dickinson could not find a publisher for her poems. Edgar Allan Poe was penniless, *The Great Gatsby* got mixed reviews, and Georges Bizet's opera *Carmen* was universally panned.

Boggs was a bit like that. He wasn't exactly underrated. That's not the right word. He made All-Star teams. He was famous. He made the Hall of Fame.

But misunderstood? Yes. But you get the sense that very few people ever really got him.

Let's start with a fact you might not believe: When Boggs was in third grade, everybody called him Babe Ruth. That's right. Boggs, who spent just about his whole major-league career avoiding home runs as if they were poison, began as Babe Ruth. He hit the ball so much farther than anyone else that when his team played pickup ball in the neighborhood, it was only allowed four players in the field while the other team got six.

He was such a bomber that when he was 12, he was intentionally walked 12 straight times in Little League.

How natural a hitter was Boggs? His father, Win, used to say that when Boggs was 19 months old (the family was living in Puerto Rico at the time; Win was a career air force man), he simply picked up a bat, naturally held it just right, and laced the first pitch he saw for a double.

Boggs was a big kid—he was young when he hit his adult height of 6-foot-2 and even in high school he weighed more than 175 pounds—and it seemed certain that he would simply slug his way into professional baseball. But something weird happened his senior year. He went hitless in nine consecutive games. At first, he thought himself profoundly unlucky—he felt like he was hitting line drive after line drive right at different fielders—but after a while, he wondered what the heck was going on.

That's when Win gave his son the book that changed more hitters' lives than any other.

He handed Wade *The Science of Hitting* by Ted Williams.

"There are certain good pitches to hit," Boggs told a reporter a few games after reading the book, as if he had come across the secret of life. "And I started looking for those."

He went 26-for-35 the rest of the way and finished his senior year hitting .485.

If Ted Williams was baseball's Socrates, philosophizing about waiting for good pitches to hit, Boggs was Plato, his most ardent disciple. Boggs would sacrifice everything—home runs, cheers, acclaim, and even his rightful place in baseball history—to live by that most basic principle.

Boggs expected to be a first-round pick out of high school in 1976. How could he not be a first-round pick? You couldn't get him out. He hit the ball so hard. There was a pitcher in the Tampa area, a guy named Sam Spence, who was the talk of local scouts. Cleveland ended up drafting him in the second round. And . . . Sam Spence? Boggs *crushed* that guy. If Spence was a second-round pick, Boggs had to be a first-round pick, a high first-round pick, maybe even the first overall pick. He told everybody that unless he was a first-round pick, he was going to play college baseball at South Carolina or somewhere like that.

Boggs was taken in the seventh round by Boston.

He was furious. He didn't get it at all. It would take him years to get it. Boggs had a very clear picture of himself: He was a hit machine, an on-base machine, no pitcher on earth could get him out. How in the world could baseball scouts miss him?

And the truth is: They didn't miss him, not exactly. They just saw someone different. They didn't care about his batting average. They certainly didn't care about his on-base percentage. They saw an awkwardly tall kid who couldn't run, didn't throw all that well, didn't really fit into any defensive position, and, for some reason, was not interested in hitting home runs.

Boggs got married six months after finishing high school. Then he went to Class A Winston-Salem and hit .332 and struck out 22 times all year. His on-base percentage was over .400. He thought that was pretty darned good.

Nobody else thought it was good at all.

"You'll never make it to Boston hitting like *that*," a Red Sox roving instructor told him.

What Boggs saw as his art—he never swung at a bad pitch and consistently hit the good pitches through holes and into open spaces—the Red Sox saw as a one-way ticket to nowhere. The guy was 6-foot-2 and he hit 13 extra-base hits all year, only two of them homers. That wasn't going to work. He was too slow to play the outfield and not nimble enough to play in the middle infield, and by the rules of the day, you couldn't have a corner infielder hit two measly home runs.

They tried to work with him. *Pull the ball! Stop chopping at it!* He would humor the coaches in practice. But in the games, he'd just go back doing it his way. In Double-A Bristol, he hit .311 with a .400 on-base percentage again, but he hit just one home run all year.

So, the Sox sent him *back* to Bristol, and he hit .325 with a .420 on-base percentage. This time around, he didn't hit a single home run.

The kid was a mule. He just refused to play the game the way coaches told him. The Red Sox did send him to Triple-A Pawtucket in 1980, and he hit .306 with twice as many walks as strikeouts. He was one of only two players in the league to hit .300—and he just barely lost the batting title. I mean *barely*. It's a good story, actually. Boggs was leading Toledo's Dave Engle by less than a point going into the ninth inning of the last game of the season. Engle was on deck when a teammate hit into a double play, which seemed to give Boggs the batting title. But in the bottom of the ninth, with Toledo up 6–0, Pawtucket's Ray Boyer drew a walk, bringing Boggs to the plate.

Boyer jogged to second in the hopes of getting thrown out and ending the game so that Boggs could win the title. But the catcher wouldn't throw. Then he went to third and again the catcher wouldn't throw. On the next pitch, Boyer took off for home and scored on a wild pitch.

Boggs then grounded out and lost the batting title to Engle by 0.6 points.

Engle was called up to the big leagues the next year and finished fifth in the Rookie of the Year balloting. Boggs? He was sent back to Pawtucket. The Red Sox were uninterested in batting titles. They were uninterested in a guy who walked a lot and almost never struck out. They were uninterested in a player whose third-base defense was shaky enough that the manager mostly used him as a designated hitter. But mostly, they were uninterested in a player who hit just one home run all season long.

"My swing is built for Fenway!" Boggs insisted to reporters.

Nobody believed him. In Pawtucket the next year, he hit .335, walked more than twice as often as he struck out (like always), and even added a little power to his game by hitting 41 doubles and a career-high five home runs. The Red Sox continued to be uninterested. "All I do is hit .300," he griped to one reporter, "yet I've never read or heard once that I'm a prospect."

Boggs grew so frustrated, he wrote a letter to Red Sox vice president Edward Kenney asking, "Am I a prospect?" Kenney replied that he was, but Boggs didn't believe him so he had his brother-in-law—a sportswriter in Tampa—ask Red Sox manager Don Zimmer the same question.

Zimmer's response did not fill Boggs with optimism. Zimmer's response was: "Who?"

"I guess they only want home run hitters," Boggs said. "But do they watch batting practice? I can hit them as far as anyone. My extra-base hits are picking up as I get older and stronger. I hit the ball off the center-field fence a lot."

Finally, in 1982, Boggs made the club by default. The Red Sox didn't know what else to do. They couldn't just keep sending him back to the minors—Boggs had to be the only prospect in baseball history to compete for *five* consecutive minor-league batting titles—but nobody seemed interested in trading for him. Boggs played in just 13 games in the first two and a half months of the season. He hit .250 with zero home runs and one RBI in those 13 games.

But on June 22 against Detroit, in the bottom of the 11th inning with the scored tied 4–4, a 24-year-old Boggs did something nobody expected. He hit a walk-off home run. The Red Sox were so thrilled, they put him in the next game. And the next. And the next.

And for the next three months, Boggs hit about .400.

It was staggering stuff. He used the Green Monster in left field as his own personal canvas. He banged doubles off it with regularity—some of them line drives, some of them long pop-ups that just caressed the monster on their way down. In all, he hit .349, the highest batting average for a first-year player in more than 50 years.

Then he began the most incredible run of batting-average seasons since his teacher Ted Williams. In his first full season, Boggs hit .361 and won the batting title. He also walked 92 times, scored 100 runs, played above-average defense at third, and was probably the second-best player in the American League behind Cal Ripken Jr.

Did people see his talents then? No. He finished 12th in the American League in MVP balloting. He wasn't chosen for the All-Star Game. And in Boston, well, the headline on a Bob Ryan story in the *Boston Globe* more or less sums up the feelings: "For All His Totals, Wade Boggs Has Yet to Prove Himself in the Clutch."

Ryan was pretty direct in his column.

"There is no evidence to suggest he is a man you want to send up there in the late innings with men in scoring position," Ryan wrote. "In fact, some people are suggesting he is naught but a glorified Matty Alou. The immortal Matty was the greatest spacer-out of base hits of all time."

Whether or not Ryan was fair to Alou—who hit .333 from 1967 to 1969 when more or less *nobody* hit for average—he was entirely wrong about Boggs. What he missed is that Boggs didn't just hit for impossibly high averages. He also walked.

And the year Ryan criticized his ability to hit in the clutch? He hit .368 with runners in scoring position. He hit .373 in high-leverage situations. He hit .615 with the bases loaded. To be fair to Ryan, those stats were not accessible in 1982. Still, Ryan and others simply *believed* that Boggs couldn't hit in the clutch because it fit the image they had created.

In 1984, Boggs hit .325 with a .407 on-base percentage. Eh. Nobody noticed.

In 1985, Boggs put up one of the great seasons of the 1980s, leading the league with a .368 batting average, 250 hits, and a .450 on-base percentage while playing excellent defense. He finished fourth in MVP balloting. That was his peak when it came to the MVP. He never finished in the top five in MVP voting again.

Isn't that incredible? It's one thing that Boggs never won an MVP award—other great players like Al Kaline, Eddie Murray, Tony Gwynn, David Ortiz, and Derek Jeter never did, either. But all of them came closer than Boggs did. He never once received a first-place MVP vote from anybody.

In 1986, Boggs led the league with a .357 batting average and a .461 on-base percentage for the pennant-winning Red Sox. He also led the league in WAR that season (not that anyone knew that then). He was worth two or three more wins than teammate Jim Rice, but Rice got four first-place MVP votes. Boggs, as you know, got zero.

In 1987, Boggs led the league with a .363 batting average and a .461 on-base percentage. That was a juiced-ball year, so he even added some home runs to the mix, 24 of them, more than he had hit the previous three years combined. He led the league in OPS and WAR and intentional walks. He finished a distant ninth in the MVP balloting.

In 1988, Boggs led the league with a .366 batting average and a .476 on-base percentage (the highest in almost 25 years) and was also first in doubles, runs, and intentional walks. For the third straight year, he led the American League in WAR. I don't need to tell you he finished sixth in the MVP voting, again finishing well behind a Boston teammate, Mike Greenwell.

In 1989, Boggs didn't win a batting title or lead the league in WAR (he finished second to Rickey Henderson). He hit a mere .330, and, yes, sure, he led the league in on-base percentage, runs, and doubles, but everybody decided he'd had a down year. He finished 21st in the voting behind, among others, another teammate, this time Nick Esasky.

Nobody in baseball history has been that good for that long and been so widely overlooked.

Boggs was a kook. He ate chicken before every game—Jim Rice dubbed him "Chicken Man."

He was militant about time and numbers. Boggs left home for the ballpark at precisely 3 p.m. He sat down at his locker at precisely 3:30. He walked into the dugout at precisely 4. He warmed up his arm at 4:10 and went to take his ground balls at 4:17.

He had a thing about the number 17. He always took 117 ground balls during infield.

He took batting practice at 5:17 p.m. whenever possible. He always ran his pregame sprints at 7:17. His sprint time was so well known that Blue Jays manager Bobby Cox once had the scoreboard operator in Toronto make the clock jump from 7:16 to 7:18 just to mess with Boggs.

But it wasn't just 17. He liked 18, too—18 is a special number in the Jewish faith because it's the numerical equivalent of the word *chai,* meaning life. Boggs isn't Jewish, but before every at-bat, he would sketch out the Hebrew word *chai* in the dirt.

Those kinds of fanatical superstitions probably had something to do with people seeing Boggs more as a flake and less as a genius.

Then came Margo Adams.

If you're too young to remember that whole fiasco, well, that's probably for the best. In 1989, it came out that Boggs had been involved in a four-year affair with a Costa Mesa, California, mortgage broker named Margo Adams. I know: A ballplayer having an affair might not strike you as earth-shattering news.

But Margo Adams *was* earth-shattering news because after the affair ended, she sued him for $12 million (the suit was later thrown out of court). She did a two-part interview with *Penthouse* magazine revealing all sorts of embarrassing intimate details and worse—if anything could be worse—Boggs's supposed secret opinions about some of his teammates.

In response, Boggs did an emotional interview with Barbara Walters on *20/20* in which he apologized at length—making him one of the first athletes ever to apologize to the nation through the media for some indiscretion—and painted Adams as a vengeful person who kept the relationship going with blackmail-like threats.

The whole thing was inescapable. Every day, it seemed like something new was happening with the Boggs-Adams story.

Boggs always insisted that it didn't affect him as a ballplayer, but things changed for him after it. His last three years in Boston combined, he didn't even hit .300. And then he was gone.

———

In 1992, Boggs was involved in another bizarre controversy, not as famous as the Adams thing but, in some ways, even more impactful on his late career. In a September game against Detroit, with Roger Clemens pitching for the Red Sox, Tony Phillips led off the fifth inning by hitting a weak ground ball toward third. Boggs may or may not have mishandled the play. The official scorer, Charles Scoggins, decided he did and ruled it an error.

It didn't seem especially important at the time. But then Clemens got wild. He walked Lou Whitaker and, after a strikeout, walked Cecil Fielder. He then allowed a sac fly and a double to score two runs. Because of Boggs's error, those were recorded as unearned runs.

But Boggs did not believe he had committed an error.

After the game, Boggs sent some Boston public relations person up to see Scoggins, who admitted he didn't see the play closely. Scoggins agreed to change it from an error to a hit.

This took the error off Boggs's register. But, more noticeably it put two new earned runs on Roger Clemens's stats. And this was a bigger deal because Clemens, at the time, was fighting for the ERA title.

Boggs's complaint made Clemens's ERA jump from 2.24 to 2.31.

Clemens would have undoubtedly freaked out under any circumstances; he had pretty well-known temper issues. But this was a particularly tense moment. He was going for his fourth Cy Young Award, which would have tied him with Steve Carlton for the most ever. He just couldn't fathom a teammate fighting to cost him that. And for what? So he wouldn't have an error on his record? Who cared about that?

Clemens unloaded on Boggs, calling him a selfish player who only cared about batting average. Clemens talked about what a terrible teammate he was (Clemens said he'd always worked hard to support Boggs's quest for batting titles and was shocked when Boggs didn't try to help him win the Cy Young Award). And then, just as a little "take that with you" jab, he dived back into the Adams stuff, which was finally beginning to fade from the public eye.

Boggs responded angrily, saying, "What, are we giving out errors now just because he's Roger Clemens?" That did not help.

Shortly after that, Boggs's back began to hurt. Doctors told him the pain was stress related. He was miserable. Boggs finished the season with a near-sacrilegious .259 batting average. He blamed Clemens. He no longer felt wanted in Boston.

And he left. But he did not just leave for some random team; no, he signed with the Red Sox' much-despised rival, the New York Yankees.

Boggs was never quite the same player after leaving Fenway Park, where he hit .369/.464/.527 for his career. But with the Yankees he did become a .300 hitter again with his usual .400 on-base percentage. He must have looked sleeker in pinstripes because he won two Gold Gloves after years of having his defense maligned. He really wasn't a great fielder by then but he was still good and he had been passed over several times when he was probably the best defensive third baseman in the league.

And he was a member of the 1996 Yankees, who won the World Series. There is an iconic image of Boggs sitting on a police horse after the game. That image took the heart out of a generation of Red Sox fans who had tried so hard to love him.

There's a funny little legend that continuously pops up about great singles hitters like Ichiro Suzuki or Gwynn or Rod Carew or Pete Rose or, yes, Boggs. The legend is that while none of them hit many home runs, they *could* have if only they had wanted to. Each of them could, on command, hit home runs in batting practice, and this suggested that they each were holding back their power in dedication to the hitting art form.

I actually don't believe that Ichiro or Gwynn or Carew could have been great home run hitters.

But I kind of do believe it with Boggs.

I believe that because, even years later, Boggs would show up at celebrity games and old-timers' games, particularly in Cooperstown, New York, and he would hit home runs to thrill the crowd. Put a bat in Boggs's hands and he really could do anything.

What he wanted to do was live up to the ideal he set for himself after reading Ted Williams's book. Home runs didn't figure into the equation he devised: Get hits. Get on base. Don't make outs. Galileo preached that the earth revolves around the sun. Boggs preached that a player should never swing at the wrong pitch. Neither's view was much appreciated in his time.

No, Boggs was not overlooked. He was famous. He got to 3,000 hits, and he made 12 All-Star teams, and he received more than 90 percent of the vote his first year on the Hall of Fame ballot. Still, there are many who believe he was a very good player but not a great one, a terrific hitter for average but not in the class with the all-timers.

But he was one of the greatest hitters in the history of baseball. Boggs knew it even if others missed it. "Rod Carew told me once that for those who know you, no explanation is necessary," Boggs said. "And for those who don't, none is possible."

No. 46 **Eddie Mathews**

I n 1969, with baseball in trouble, with 3,000 fewer baseball fans in attendance per game than at the beginning of the decade, Commissioner Bowie Kuhn did what baseball commissioners tend to do when faced with such crises: He ordered up a celebration of baseball's past.

Baseball: always looking backward to look forward.

Here's what Kuhn did: He announced that since 1969 was baseball's centennial,* it was the perfect time for fans and sportswriters to choose baseball's all-time team.

The idea was fun, probably the most fun thing that stick-in-the-mud Kuhn ever did as commissioner, but because he was a bumbler, the process was entirely baffling. First, he asked individual teams' fans to pick their own centennial team. That worked fine for Yankees fans and Red Sox fans and other fans of teams that had been around for a long time. But

---

* What exactly made 1969 baseball's centennial? Well, in 1869, the Cincinnati Red Stockings became the sport's first openly professional team. The Red Stockings were surely not the first professional team, as players had been paid under the table for years, but, hey, myth is a part of the game. And you do not need a great excuse to have a party.

what were fans of the four expansion teams in Kansas City, Seattle, San Diego, and Montreal supposed to do?

What were Oakland fans supposed to do? They had just gotten their team. What about Houston fans? They'd only been around for a few years.

The Mets had only been around since 1962 and they had been terrible, so Kuhn asked their fans to pick all-time Brooklyn Dodgers and New York Giants teams.

The Angels had only been around since 1961 and Kuhn told those fans to pick an all-time Angels team.

Giants fans were asked to pick two teams—a San Francisco Giants centennial team and a New York Giants centennial team (Willie Mays made both).

You can almost see baseball fans running around like the panic scene in *Airplane!* while Kuhn was in the middle saying: "OK, now, does everybody know who they're supposed to be voting for?"

Once the votes were somehow counted and tabulated, the results were handed to a select group of baseball writers led by Dick Young. *They* were supposed to somehow turn that mess into baseball's Centennial Team.

The funny thing is that despite all the mayhem, the team came out and it actually worked. There was a big celebration in Washington that featured the new president, Richard Nixon, one of the biggest baseball fans to ever hold office. People had fun arguing about the team. Kids learned more about baseball history. It really did turn out well.

And here's that team:

1B: Lou Gehrig

2B: Rogers Hornsby

SS: Honus Wagner

3B: Pie Traynor

LF: Ty Cobb

CF: Joe DiMaggio

RF: Babe Ruth

C: Mickey Cochrane

RHP: Walter Johnson

LHP: Lefty Grove

Looking back, that list holds up reasonably well. Yes, by 1969, it should have been abundantly clear that Mays was the greatest center fielder, but how can you argue with DiMaggio?*

Cochrane over Yogi Berra and Roy Campanella was questionable but you could make the argument.

Many fans complained that Sandy Koufax was snubbed in favor of Lefty Grove, but in my opinion Grove was the right choice.

But there is one choice that stands out as being utterly absurd.

How in the heck was Pie Traynor selected over Eddie Mathews?

On January 16, 1974, Mathews got word that he had not been elected to the Baseball Hall of Fame. It was his first year of eligibility, and he got just 32 percent of the vote.

"I didn't make it," he told his wife.

"You didn't make what?" she asked in return.

Mathews hit 512 home runs in his career, a record for third basemen at the time. He played in 12 All-Star Games, twice led the league in homers, scored 100 runs eight times, and slugged .500 for his career. No other third baseman had ever accomplished so much. Cobb said he had seen only three or four perfect swings in his lifetime, and one of them belonged to Mathews.

He had worked hard on that swing. Mathews spent hours and hours in his backyard trying to swing just like Ted Williams. He later told *Sports Illustrated*—Mathews and *SI* were powerfully connected because Mathews was on the first cover—that he had spent his whole childhood studying to be a ballplayer.

Like with so many of the great ones, Mathews's father was a pivotal figure, but it was his mother who truly turned him into the classic pull hitter. His mother used to pitch to him while his father played the field. After

---

* In addition to being named the all-time center fielder, DiMaggio was also called the "greatest living ballplayer." He loved that title so much, he insisted on being introduced that way at every function for the rest of his life.

almost hitting his mother with a line drive, a new rule was added—if he didn't hit the ball to right field, there were extra chores to be done.

Mathews had the looks of a matinee idol, too. "With those beautiful muscles," *Sports* magazine gushed in its 1957 story "Baseballs' Ten Handsomest Men," "he can make a girl believe anything."

Mathews also had been a World Series hero, hitting the walk-off bomb in a pivotal Game 4 of the 1957 World Series.

With all that, how could Mathews have received only 32 percent of the vote? It's hard to figure. He did hit .271 for his career, which is not all that impressive. But that was largely due to his late-career decline; he hit .300 three times and was basically a solid .280 hitter for the bulk of his career. He was not a celebrated defensive third baseman because he committed a lot of errors, especially early in his career. But he was certainly adequate as defender and, in retrospect, he was quite good in several years.*

So—32 percent of the vote? What gives? Mathews told himself not to worry about it. "I've had several calls from the media today wanting me to say something, but I am not interested in stirring up any controversy about the Hall of Fame," he said. "If I make it someday, naturally, I'll be appreciative. Meanwhile, I'll survive."

A year later, Mathews got word that he again had not been elected to the Baseball Hall of Fame. He'd gotten 40 percent of the vote this time. He avoided all reporters; there didn't seem to be anything to say that wouldn't insult people that he didn't want to insult—like Ralph Kiner.

See, Kiner was elected that year. What in the world did Kiner do that was better than Mathews? Kiner was a home run hitter who drew walks. That was his whole game. Mathews hit 150 more homers and walked 400 more times in his career. Plus, Kiner's defense was famously brutal no matter where they put him, his career was painfully short, his teams were never a factor. By WAR, which would not be invented for many years, Mathews was twice the ballplayer Kiner was.

Mathews knew that he was a much better player than Ralph Kiner. But

---

* There is a funny story about how in 1952, the year Mathews came up, Boston Braves manager Tommy Holmes had an idea to make him into an outfielder. And supposedly one day, Holmes was hitting fungoes to the outfielders and he hit one into foul ground. Mathews chased after it and smashed right into baseball commissioner Ford Frick. That was the end of the outfield experiment.

what good would come from even suggesting that? Mathews stayed quiet and hoped for better things in a year.

On January 22, 1976—one year later—Mathews got word that again he had not been elected to the Baseball Hall of Fame. His vote had climbed a little but only a little—it was now 49 percent. More than half the voters still did not think he was a Hall of Famer.

Two pitchers were elected that year—Bob Lemon and Robin Roberts. Mathews had never faced Lemon, but he had hit .323 and slugged .613 in more than 200 plate appearances against Roberts. "He sure looked like a Hall of Famer to me," Roberts said after his own long-overdue election. "I hope they vote him in next year."

On January 19, 1977, Mathews got word that he had not been elected to the Baseball Hall of Fame, and that one hurt most of all. That was the year Ernie Banks appeared on the ballot.

Banks hit .274/.330/.500 with 512 home runs in his career.

Mathews hit .271/.376/.509 with 512 home runs in his career.

They seemed perfect matches.* They were infielders, both born in 1931, both fantastic sluggers at exactly the same time. Yes, Banks was a shortstop, but he moved to first mid-career; Mathews played 1,000 more games at third than Banks did at short.

Banks was elected on the first ballot with about 84 percent of the vote.

Mathews was passed over again.

This time, Mathews did speak out. "Ernie called me this morning," he said. "He was excited, super happy. He told me I should have made it. . . . He deserved it. I'm proud of him."

But he could not help but ask: How in the world did Banks get elected in his first year of eligibility while he was still standing on the outside? Why did the voters keep overlooking him? Why couldn't he get the respect that his career so obviously earned him?

"I'm disappointed," he said. "But I'm not going to jump off a bridge. I've had disappointments before."

So can we get to the bottom of this mystery? Why did it take so long for Mathews to get elected? For that matter, what happened in that centennial vote in 1969? Mathews was a much greater player than Pie Traynor, but

---

* In fact, Mathews seems to have been clearly superior. His advantages in WAR (96.6 to 67.5), OPS+ (143 to 122), and runs created (1,723 to 1,511) are massive.

that's not even the worst part. No, the worst part is that Mathews was *not even a finalist* for the greatest-ever third baseman. No, the finalists were Traynor, Brooks Robinson, and, bizarrely, Jackie Robinson, who started just 249 games at third base in his entire career.

What happened?

"You have to wonder," the *Los Angeles Times'* legendary Jim Murray wrote, "whose toes Eddie Mathews stepped on."

Sometimes, the answer is a bit too obvious.

Mathews had stepped on the sportswriters' toes.

To be as fair as possible, Mathews was not always an easy man to like. He clashed often with sportswriters and photographers and players and, well, basically anyone who wasn't a teammate. In his career, he had epic fights with Frank Robinson and Don Drysdale ("Eddie almost demolished him," Henry Aaron remembered) and almost came to blows with Jackie Robinson. He never hid his contempt for opponents. The other team, he would say, is the enemy.

He was particularly difficult as a young man. One typical story of the young Mathews was of a time he was driving recklessly and a police officer tried to pull him over. Mathews turned off his lights and slipped into a side street; the officer caught him and charged him. When the newspaper photographer showed up, Mathews threatened to break his arm.

It wasn't that Mathews was mean. He was generally a very nice guy. But he ran hot. Teammates swore by him—"He was our spiritual leader," Aaron would say—while opposing players and fans liked to dislike him. "Popularity," Dick Young said when someone asked him why Banks was elected while Mathews was not, "does count in baseball, in voting, in life."

And that really was Mathews's story. In 1969, for instance, everybody loved Traynor. He was one of those fine ballplayers who kept getting better and better in memory. He hit .320, which sounds much better than it actually was because everybody hit for average in his day. That's not an exaggeration. In 1930, when he hit a career-high .366, the whole league hit .303. He finished *ninth* in the league in batting with that .366 average.

Meanwhile, he gained a reputation as a defensive maestro that grew each year. Perhaps he was. The defensive statistics do not support the reputation.

In fact, none of the advanced statistics support Traynor's reputation. By WAR, he is 36.2 career Wins Above Replacement, placing him 627th all-time alongside wonderful but not legendary players like Cecil Cooper, Alex Gordon, Don Buford, and Wally Joyner.

But by 1969, Traynor had become one of the game's most beloved characters. He was quoted constantly in the *Sporting News*. He was a sports broadcaster. And, most joyfully, he was the announcer for Studio Wrestling in Pittsburgh, which had some of the greatest legends in pro wrestling history like Bruno Sammartino and Killer Kowalski and George "the Animal" Steele, who would eat turnbuckles. Traynor was a lovable guy.

I mean, the guy was named Pie.

Mathews was not lovable like that. He also was not lovable like Banks. He was not lovable like Brooks Robinson.

The writers finally did vote him into the Hall in 1978. He called it the greatest day of his life, but then used the occasion to unload on the modern ballplayer. "The one thing I'm proudest of," he said, "is that every day I played, I gave the best I had. I don't think the players today do that. And I don't think they're as happy as we were.

"I feel sorry for them. Every day you read about how they don't like the way the uniform fits or their locker is too close to the shower. For the money they make, I don't think the production or attitude is there."

Someone asked him if he would manage in the big leagues again—he had managed the Braves in the early 1970s.

"No," he said. "Basically, it's because of the attitude of the players. They're making good money, but they can't run to first base. You ask them why, and they say, 'I can't get my head together.' You ask them to take extra batting practice, and they say they have to take the wife to the grocery store. It's not the same."

He said that he felt bad for a couple of the other old-timers—Duke Snider and Enos Slaughter and Pee Wee Reese—who were still waiting to be elected. He knew that pain.

"I'm just a beat-up old third baseman," he told the Cooperstown crowd on the day of his induction. "I'm just a small part of a wonderful game."

Mathews and Aaron were teammates for 13 seasons. When Aaron broke Ruth's career home run record, Mathews was his manager. The two are bonded in so many ways. And it's funny, people expected for years that one of them might break Ruth's record.

But they almost always thought it would be Mathews.

Career Home Runs at Progressive Ages (*denotes an MLB record)

Age 20: Mathews 25; Aaron 13

Age 21: Mathews 72; Aaron 40

Age 22: Mathews 112; Aaron 66

Age 23: Mathews 153*; Aaron 110

Age 24: Mathews 190*; Aaron 140

Age 25: Mathews 222*; Aaron 179

Age 26: Mathews 253; Aaron 219

Age 27: Mathews 299; Aaron 253

Age 28: Mathews 338; Aaron 298

Age 29: Mathews 370; Aaron 342

Age 30: Mathews 399; Aaron 366

Age 31: Mathews 422; Aaron 398

Age 32: Mathews 445; Aaron 442

Age 33: Aaron 481; Mathews 477

Age 34: Aaron 510; Mathews 493

Age 35: Aaron 554; Mathews 509

Age 36: Aaron 592; Mathews 512 (final total)

Age 37: Aaron 639

Age 38: Aaron 673

Age 39: Aaron 713*

Age 40: Aaron 733*

Age 41: Aaron 745*

Age 42: Aaron 755* (final total)

I love that chart so much because of what it represents. Mathews was the hare, Aaron the tortoise. Mathews smashed homers until he burned out. Aaron kept on hitting home runs because he was unlike anyone else. Both of them played the bulk of their careers in a brutal home run park in Milwaukee—Mathews hit 36 more homers on the road over his career; Aaron hit 26 more road home runs while playing in Milwaukee.

And they fed off each other. Mathews inspired fire in Aaron and Aaron inspired peace in Mathews. Eventually it led them both to the Hall of Fame. Believe it or not, they own the all-time career home run record by teammates. That doesn't seem possible—I mean, how could it not be Ruth and Gehrig?

But Ruth's and Gehrig's careers overlapped less than you probably think. Gehrig didn't play his first full season until 1925, when Ruth was 30. They still hit 859 homers as teammates, which is incredible.

But Aaron and Mathews hit 863 home runs as teammates. That record won't get broken.

Here's one final note that's interesting: While Aaron broke Ruth's all-time home run record, Mathews got him on another record. Mathews is, and always will be, the Milwaukee Braves' all-time home run leader. He hit 452 home runs for Milwaukee. Aaron is second on the list with 398.

No. 45 **Bob Gibson**

"Are you from *Sports Illustrated*?" Bob Gibson asked, and I nodded because in those days I was from *Sports Illustrated*. He glared at me for a moment—that famous glare, the one that used to melt hitters. He seemed ready to say something, but he stopped before he started, as if there was no point to bring up something from so long ago.

That is when the man walked up to him. He was an older man, quite a few years older than Gibson, and he wore thick glasses. White hair stuck out of the crumpled Cardinals hat on his head.

"Mr. Gibson," this man said. "Oh, do I remember the way you pitched. I remember all those batters you hit. They were so scared of you."

Gibson smiled hard. How many times had he heard this? Too many times. Again and again through the years, people came up to him to say exactly this: You were so scary. You were so intimidating. You were so angry. You owned the plate. You stared them down until they wished they were somewhere else. You glowered. You scowled. You had them shaking in their cleats. You weren't like those wimpy pitchers today. You hit them. You showed them.

They meant well, Gibson knew that, and this time like most other times he simply thanked the man in a voice that was higher pitched and warmer than expected. That gentle voice always came as a surprise. He signed a baseball and handed it back to the man. Together we watched the man walk off so happily.

Then Gibson looked at me with a bewildering expression on his face.

"Is that all I did?" he asked. "Hit batters? Is that really all they remember?"

This will be an attempt to tell a different kind of Bob Gibson story. I can't tell you that it will satisfy. The canonical story of Gibson as an intimidator, as a headhunter, as an indomitable force, yes, it's irresistible. And it is largely true. There are so many stories within that story, so many witness accounts of Gibson's badassery. For instance, you might know that a hitter named Pete LaCock—son of the game-show host Peter Marshall—hit a grand slam off Gibson in 1975. It happened to be in the last inning of Gibson's last appearance in the big leagues.

Years later, they faced each other in an old-timers' game. Gibson plunked LaCock with the first pitch. "I've been waiting *years* to do that!" he shouted out.

That wasn't even the only time Gibson threw at someone in an old-timers' game. Gibson once brushed back his dear friend Reggie Jackson. Why? Because Jackson had the gall to homer off Gibson . . . in the *previous* old-timers' game.

I mean, seriously, who else has two classic stories about throwing at hitters in an old-timers' game?

There have been other intimidating pitchers, others—Don Drysdale, Early Wynn, Big Unit, Sal Maglie—who would move you off the plate, make you dance, knock you down if you got too feisty. It was Wynn who famously said that he would knock down his own grandmother if she dug in on him, and when told that made him seem a little bit less than well-adjusted, he shrugged. "Well," he said, "my grandmother can hit."

Still, Gibson stands alone in this category. He is the archetype, the terrifying pitcher standing tall and dangerous on the mound. If—as NFL Films reminds us—the name "Lombardi" evokes images of duels in the snow, the name "Gibson" evokes images of a batter lying flat in a cloud of dust and the merciless man on the mound, simmering, daring, never ceding ground, never forgetting.

There is a near-limitless collection of famous quotes about Gibson's terrifying presence:

Dick Allen: "Gibson was so mean, he'd knock you down and then meet you at home plate to see if you wanted to make something of it."

Joe Torre: "Bob wasn't unfriendly when he was playing. I'd say it was more like hateful."

Don Sutton: "He hated everyone. He even hated Santa Claus."

Norm Cash: "If he's pitching, I'm coming up sick."

Red Schoendienst: "He couldn't pitch today because they wouldn't let him. The way he'd throw inside, he'd be kicked out of the game in the first inning."

Tim McCarver: "I remember one time going out to the mound to talk with Bob Gibson. He told me to get back behind the plate where I belonged and that the only thing I knew about pitching was that I couldn't hit it."

Dusty Baker: "The only people I ever felt intimidated by in my whole life were Bob Gibson and my daddy."

Perhaps the most telling words about Bob Gibson's persona came from Henry Aaron in his poetic advice to Dusty Baker:

Don't dig in against Bob Gibson.
He'll knock you down.
He'd knock down his own grandmother.
Don't stare at him, don't smile at him, don't talk to him.
He doesn't like it.
If you happen to hit a home run, don't run too slow.
And don't run too fast.
If you want to celebrate, get in the tunnel first.
And if he hits you, don't charge the mound.
Because he's a Golden Gloves boxer.

This was Bob Gibson's corner of baseball, and even now it grows larger every year.

But Bob Gibson never believed that stuff told his real story.

"That's a whole lot of !@#$%^," is how Gibson explained it. "I wasn't trying to intimidate anybody—are you kidding me? I was just trying to survive, man."

The writer Roger Kahn told a story that might start getting us a bit closer to the real Gibson—not the legend, not the bully, but the real man, flesh and blood, pain and triumph. It's still a story of toughness. But this one has a twist.

In January 1971, Kahn picked up the phone at his home and, to his surprise, heard the voice of Bob Gibson on the other line. "Do you think I'm worth a column?" Gibson asked. They had a mutual friend who believed sportswriters were focusing too much on Gibson's fierce reputation and not enough on the deep and intelligent and proud man behind that reputation. Gibson thought about it and then called up Kahn, who was writing for *Esquire* and who was just finishing up what would become his classic book *The Boys of Summer*.

Kahn agreed that, yes, Gibson was worth a column. They agreed to talk over dinner after Gibson pitched on Opening Day.

That Opening Day game turned out to be a classic. Gibson locked up at Wrigley Field with another great pitcher, Ferguson Jenkins. For nine innings they each allowed just one run.

Then came the 10th. In those days, extra innings didn't mean a starter's day was over. Jenkins pitched a scoreless 10th inning. Gibson gave up a walk-off home run to Billy Williams.

"You gonna talk to Gibson *now*?" Stan Musial asked Kahn after the game.

"We've had the date since January," Kahn said sheepishly.

"Better you than me," Musial said, and he walked away laughing.

Kahn cursed his bad luck. Then he stalled. He stayed in the press box for a long time, talking to other writers and then some baseball people. After a good while, he finally caught a taxi to the hotel and told the driver to take a scenic route. When he got to the hotel, he braced himself for an angry Bob Gibson. Instead, he found four messages, the first three wondering where the heck he was and the fourth telling him to meet Gibson at a nearby restaurant.

When he got to the restaurant, Gibson was sitting alone and waiting.

"Where you been?" Gibson asked.

"I didn't think you'd want to talk right away after losing a game like that."

And Gibson's entire face changed. He was not angry, not exactly. Instead, he was deeply annoyed. There was that cartoon reputation. Did this reporter—the one people told him was serious and different—really think Gibson would have him fly out to Chicago for an interview only to postpone because he lost a ball game?

"Hey," Gibson said, "did you come out here to work or play around?"

Nobody knew for sure why they called Bob's brother "Josh." That wasn't his name. His given name was Leroy Gibson. Still, everyone called him Josh. You might suspect that they named him after the great Negro Leagues player Josh Gibson, but Bob never thought so. "The kids in the ghetto," he once wrote, "never paid much attention to professional sports."

Josh was 15 years older and the closest thing Bob ever had to a father. Bob was the youngest of seven, and his real father died three months before he was born. His mother, Victoria, worked at a laundromat and cleaned houses.

The first home Bob Gibson can remember was a four-room shack without heat on the north side of Omaha. His most vivid memory of the place was that he was once bitten by a rat there.

In time, the family moved to a segregated government housing project called Logan Fontenelle. It was, as Gibson often wrote, the ghetto, but he came to think of it as "heaven in Nebraska." True, it was segregated and it was rough—there were daily fights—and overt racism was palpable and a daily part of life. But the units were heated and there was a ballfield in one corner, and a kid was judged by how fast he could sprint around one of the two homemade tracks that looped around the place.

Most of all, he had Josh, who was a singular figure, an almost unknown American hero. Josh had been a supreme athlete as a kid, but at 18 he went to war, and when he returned, he was different. Angrier. He earned a degree in education, then a master's degree in history. Still, he could not get hired as a teacher or a coach.

Instead, he took a job at a local meatpacking plant and coached at the YMCA. He had an astonishing impact on some of the greatest athletes of his time.

For instance, Josh taught Bob Boozer how to rebound. Boozer went to Kansas State, where he was one of the most dominant players in the history of college basketball, a two-time All-American. He played in the NBA for 11 seasons, averaging almost 15 points a game.

Josh worked with Gale Sayers on his ball carrying. Sayers went on to become one of the greatest players in NFL history.

Josh was Johnny Rodgers's first baseball coach. Rodgers won the 1972 Heisman Trophy and had perhaps the most famous punt return in the history of college football.

Josh told Marlin Briscoe that no matter what anyone said, he was a quarterback. And although it was short-lived, Briscoe became the first black man to be a professional starting quarterback when he got into a game for the Denver Broncos against the Cincinnati Bengals in 1968.

And in 1947, when Bob was 11 years old, Josh made his brother the most important project of all. Why 1947? Well, it's pretty obvious: That was the year Jackie Robinson joined the Brooklyn Dodgers. That opened up all new possibilities for African Americans, and Josh expected his youngest brother to become a major-league baseball player.

It wasn't a prophecy. It was an order. Josh turned all of the anger and regret that bubbled inside him on his brother. Every single day, he threw the hard fastballs at Bob to make him lose any fear of hitting. Every single day, he smashed hard ground balls at Bob in the expectation that he would become a great infielder like Jackie. Pitching then seemed out of the question. "He figured it would be a long time before black pitchers would make much of a dent in the big leagues," Bob wrote in his autobiography.

Bob resented Josh and every now and again would race home to their mother and tell her to make Josh stop. She would tell Josh just that.

But the next day, they were at it again.

Once, Josh hit a ground ball at Bob that skipped off a rock, bounced up high, and smashed Bob's face, just above his left eye. It left a permanent scar. Bob Gibson said that scar served as a constant reminder of what he was supposed to do.

Josh wanted his brother to have a backup plan, so he also pounded against Bob on the basketball court, moving him around, making him fight for space.

After a couple of years—and the arrival of the first great African-American pitcher in the major leagues, Don Newcombe—Josh built a pitching mound at a nearby school. He would take Bob out there and make him throw fastball after curveball after fastball until his arm felt disconnected from his body.

For years, Bob did not understand why his brother was so much harder on him than he was on the other kids in the neighborhood. "I resented it," Bob said. But Josh knew how tough the road was going to be for his brother. He knew what the odds were. And he was leaving nothing to chance.

Gibson signed with the St. Louis Cardinals in 1957, and his first stop was Columbus, Georgia. His memories of the eight games he started in the South in the 1950s would always remain pungent and bitter and too personal to talk about. That was how baseball began for him. He made it to the big leagues in 1959 when he was 23, then got beat around for a year and a half. He became a full-time starter in 1961 and led the league in walks. He was no instant sensation. He did not win 20 games until 1965, when he was 29 years old.

"People don't know what it was like to be a young black pitcher in those days," he said, not defensively but as a point of fact. The way Gibson saw it, people wanted him to fail. Hitters wanted him to fail. Racists wanted him to fail. Opposing fans wanted him to fail. He had to beat them all. Every game was for survival, every hit a dagger aimed at his heart, every loss a disaster from which he might not recover.

"In a world filled with hate, prejudice and protest," he wrote in his 1968 book, *From Ghetto to Glory,* "I find that I too am filled with hate, prejudice and protest. I hate phonies. I am prejudiced against all those who have contempt for me because my face is black and all those who accept me only because of my ability to throw a baseball. I am not proud of that ability. It is not something I earned or acquired or bought. It is a gift."

That is what people missed about Gibson. The very thing they loved about him—his pitching gift—did not explain him. When people used to say he scared people, he'd scoff, "You think Roberto Clemente gets *scared?*"

When people used to talk about how hard he threw, he'd scoff, "Hank Aaron could hit God's fastball."

When people would talk about the nastiness of his slider, he'd scoff, "You don't think Eddie Mathews or Billy Williams knows how to hit a slider?"

No, they refused to see how *hard* he worked at his craft, how inventive he had to be to win, how much it all took out of him. They treated him like he was a bully. Bullies can't win major-league games. Didn't they see that he never threw the same pitch in the same location to the same batter? Didn't they see that he fielded his position better than anyone else?

(He won nine straight Gold Gloves.) Couldn't they see how good a hitter he was, how much he helped his own cause? He had 73 extra-base hits in his career, one of the highest percentages for any pitcher ever. He had 18 sacrifice flies for his career, which is a record.

In the 26 games he homered, he threw six shutouts, and the Cardinals went 23-3.

Two of those games were in the World Series.

"I wasn't mean," Gibson said. "I don't buy into any of it. You hear people talk about this glare that I had. You know, I've been wearing glasses for almost 60 years. I wasn't glaring. . . . I just couldn't see the catcher's signals. I was just trying to see. That's all. But people turn everything into something else."

I've told that story to so many people around baseball—the glasses story. And they nod and laugh. "Yeah," they say, "that's what he told me, too. It was his glasses."

And then they lean in close and say, "It wasn't the glasses."

One more Bob Gibson story: Remember at the time when he reacted strangely after asking if I worked for *Sports Illustrated*? Turns out he *was* thinking about something—thinking about how he had not talked to a *Sports Illustrated* reporter in many decades.

Gibson said he stopped talking to *Sports Illustrated* after the magazine ran a story about him that he thought was filled with condescension and disdain. When he was writing his autobiography, he tried to find that story, but *Sports Illustrated* couldn't locate it, which upset him all over again. The past was filled with a lot of hard memories. "I'm sorry," I said, and he waved me off.

"It's not your fault," he said. "That's why I'm talking to you."

"I'll find that story for you," I said.

"It doesn't matter," he replied.

I looked for that story for a long time. I went through the archives and searched every single story that even mentioned Bob Gibson. Finally, I came across one that seemed closest to what Gibson was describing—it was in the March 1960 edition, and it was called "The Private World of the Negro Ballplayer." This didn't feel like an exact match, though, because it barely mentioned Gibson and did not quote him, but it did have paragraphs like this:

Slang is a rich field. The words mullion, hog-cutter, drinker and pimp apparently came from the Negro leagues. Drinker and pimp barely survive today. A pimp is a flashy dresser, and a drinker—so Jimmy Banks, a Negro Memphis Red Sox first baseman, told me—is "a fielder who can pick it clean. He catches everything smooth. He can 'drink' it." Ernie Banks also told me about some other words, but I have been unable to find them used in the majors. A choo-choo papa was a sharp ballplayer. An acrobat was an awkward fielder. A monty was an ugly ballplayer, and a foxy girl was a good-looking girl. Unfortunately, my research came to an abrupt end when I foolishly asked Banks if he had a nickname. "I'm a ballplayer, man," he said as he walked away. "I'm not gonna nickname myself. Man, you have to calm down!"

This seemed a bit like the condescension Gibson described, but it wasn't clear why he personally felt wounded by it. There were a couple of anonymous quotes—maybe one of those was his? There were a couple of broad references—maybe one of those hit him hard?

I didn't know the answer for years. And then, while writing this, I found the real story.

It turns out it wasn't the story itself that upset Gibson. It was a photograph in the story—there's an image on the second page that shows Gibson talking with George Crowe in an empty clubhouse.

The caption read: "In a dressing room empty of whites, pitcher Bob Gibson consults Crowe."

The caption made it sound like either there was a special dressing room for black players or all the white players leave when black players talk. That made Gibson angry.

But what made him even angrier was that Gibson believed the photographer doctored the photograph. He insisted that when the picture was taken, there were white players all around them.

"I don't know photo techniques and lab stuff," Gibson said to Kahn in that *Esquire* story, "but when the guy took it, we were sitting with some whites. And when they printed it, all the whites were gone. We were two segregated cats."

That was what set him off so much that he didn't talk to *SI* for 50 years.

He thought the magazine, like so many through the years, had purposely made him an outsider.

Bob Gibson never asked for a favor. He wanted only to be judged the way others were judged. Did anyone say Tom Seaver won games because he was mean? No. Did anyone say Sandy Koufax won games because he was intimidating? No.

Bob Gibson struck out 3,000 batters and he pitched his way into the Hall of Fame because he had worked all his life to become a great pitcher. "I was just doing my job," he said.

In 1968, the year he was at the height of his powers, he made 34 starts and finished 28 of those games. "I couldn't come out," he said. "We needed me to pitch."

He had a modern-record 1.12 ERA. "Well, we never scored any damn runs," he said.

He threw 13 shutouts. "I felt like if I didn't throw a shutout, we'd lose," he said.

"It was hard," he said. "People make it sound like it was easy, like all I had to do was stare at a hitter or throw inside and they'd wilt. It wasn't like that. It wasn't easy. There wasn't anything easy about it."

When Bob Gibson died in 2020, the *New York Times* headline was "Bob Gibson, Feared Flamethrower for the Cardinals, Dies at 84." And I thought about that old man in St. Louis, the one who kept saying to Gibson, "Boy were they afraid of you."

"Nobody was afraid of me," Gibson said that day, but that wasn't exactly right. He was a brilliant pitcher for all the reasons listed here . . . but they *were* afraid of him. There's a famous story about Gibson when he was in college at Creighton and threw a high fastball inside to a hitter named Jesse Bradshaw. The hitter twisted violently out of the way and, in the process, swallowed his chewing tobacco. He soon became Rev. Jesse Bradshaw.

He helped a lot of hitters get religion.

What Bob Gibson meant to say was that he was afraid of nobody.

No. 44 **Cal Ripken Jr.**

Cal Ripken was a smart ballplayer. You probably knew that, but here's proof: When he was 10 years old, he was a batboy for a semipro baseball team managed by a canny old baseball man named Fred Baldwin. At some point during the season, Baldwin became convinced that a rival team was stealing their signs. To counter, instead of changing signs and making a whole big mess of things, Baldwin just had Ripken give out the signs.

He figured that nobody would be watching the batboy.

Ripken did it easily. He knew all the signs by heart. He was born knowing all the signs.

Ripken's intelligence about sports isn't just limited to baseball, by the way. Ripken was also an all-state soccer player in high school. He amazed his teammates with his instincts. He was always around the ball. That team won 18 games in a row and would have won the state title except Cal left late in the season because baseball training was beginning and, as promising a soccer player as he was, nothing on earth was more important to Cal Ripken than baseball.

Ripken signed with the Baltimore Orioles when he was 20. He signed with an old Orioles scout named Poke Whalen. He signed at the end of a summer game. Ol' Poke didn't even have a pen on him; they had to borrow one from a spectator in the crowd.

Here's how baseball smart Cal Ripken was: In one minor-league game, he was on second base when a nasty windstorm came through and knocked out the lights for a few seconds. When the lights came back on, Ripken was standing on third.

"The guy's value to the team cannot be measured," the *Pensacola News Journal*'s Al Padgett wrote in his column "The Wise Ol' Al."

And maybe you realized this, maybe you didn't: This is not Cal Ripken Jr. we are talking about. No, this is the original, the first; this is Cal Ripken who became a coach and a mentor and, briefly, a manager. He was Cal Ripken the ballplayer first. He was a catcher and a good one until he hurt his shoulder after being hit with consecutive foul tips. Once, in an intrasquad game, the opposing skipper knew about Ripken's shoulder injury and had the first eight players on base try to steal.

Cal Ripken threw out all eight.

"I couldn't throw hard," he told a reporter. "But I got rid of the ball quick."

Cal Ripken wanted to be a great ballplayer. He understood the game on a level that few ever have. He loved the game in a way that few ever have. But, alas, Cal Ripken could not hit, not even enough to get picked up as a handy backup catcher somewhere. Still, he played on for as long as he could—played on even after the club had told him he was not a prospect.

Cal Ripken was playing ball in Topeka, Kansas, on August 24, 1960—this was months after the Appleton, Wisconsin, paper ran a story saying that Orioles no longer saw him as a big-league possibility. He was playing for the Fox Cities Foxes of Appleton that year, and on that August night, his Foxes beat the Topeka Reds 10–7 in 10 innings. Ripken went 1-for-4 in the game, and the hit was a run-scoring single.

After the game, he went back to the hotel and found out that night that his first son was born. His wife, Vi, had decided to name the boy Calvin Edwin Ripken Jr.

Ripken didn't know at that moment that his name had just changed. He would no longer be Cal Ripken. No, he would become Cal Ripken Sr. He never thought that was right, never thought his name should have that "Senior" thing at the end.

After all, as he so often said, "I was here first!"

———

Another Calvin, the wonderful writer Calvin Trillin, has a theory about families—he believes that each family passes down a singular message. This can be something touching like "We worked hard so you can get ahead," or something formidable like "It's your job to carry on the family name," or something supportive like "No matter what happens we will always be there for you," or something cold and harsh, such as "You're on your own."

In Trillin's own family, the message was his father's "You might as well be a mensch (good person)," which Trillin loved, particularly because of the way it was worded. This wasn't an order ("You must be a mensch") or even a suggestion ("You probably should be a mensch"). It was, instead, a studied observation about life, as if his father had studied the other paths and had concluded, yeah, in the end, you might as well be a mensch.

In the Ripken household, it seems to me, the message was the same but not in Yiddish.

The Ripken motto: Hit the cutoff man.

This, too, wasn't exactly an order or a suggestion. It was a way of life. Cal and Vi Ripken did not push baseball on their oldest son. Who knew better than the Ripkens that baseball was a hard life? Cal Sr. was gone all the time, off playing or managing, spending summers in places like Rochester or Appleton or Leesburg or Elmira. There wasn't much money in it. There wasn't much steadiness in it. No, they didn't insist on young Cal playing ball, far from it.

But young Cal insisted. He came out of the crib ready to play. "All he ever wanted to be," his mother said, "was a ballplayer."

And once Cal Jr. made it clear that he wanted to be a ballplayer, well, yeah, Cal Sr. stepped in and made sure that he would become a *real* ballplayer, someone who would play the game right, someone who would, yes, hit the cutoff man. That was the Oriole Way!

What was the Oriole Way? It was a baseball philosophy—back up your teammate, don't compound your mistakes, communicate, perfect practice makes perfect, take pride in fundamentals, don't make two throws when one will do, hit the cutoff man—but it was more than that. It was a way of life. From 1966 to 1980—15 seasons that perfectly overlap Ripken's childhood, teenage years, and entry into pro baseball—the Orioles won six pennants, two World Series, and they won 97 or more games eight times. They only had a losing record once.

"The great thing," Baltimore native Richard Ben Cramer wrote in *Sports Illustrated*, "was not what they won but how they did it. This wasn't the richest club. As a business, it wasn't even good. . . . But these were ball fans. They would hoot an outfielder out of the park if he threw some rainbow over the cutoff man's head. The Orioles were all about defense. Sometimes they made brilliant plays. But they always made the routine plays. That was the Oriole Way."

No one believed more deeply in the Oriole Way than Cal Sr. In the minor leagues, he taught it to every young Orioles player so that by the time they got to Baltimore, by the time they got to play for Manager Earl Weaver, they understood.

Cal Jr. was born inside The Oriole Way in the same way that the man who changed everything was born inside the Matrix. When he was 12, his father started taking him to every ball game in Asheville, where he would take part in infield and batting practice. During the games, Cal Jr. would sit behind home plate intently and study the game. Was the hitter anticipating that curveball? Why was the third baseman playing there? What is the pitcher thinking with the count 2-2? How did he know that he could take that extra base? Sometimes, he would go up to Asheville players like Al Bumbry or Doug DeCinces and ask a long stream of questions about their approach, their strategies, what they were thinking about out there.

And after games, he would go into his dad's office and pick his brain for hours about every single decision made—this was their time, father and son, bonding over the thing they each loved more than anything else: baseball.

Cal Ripken Jr. wasn't a phenom. As a freshman, he stood just 5-foot-7, weighed less than 130 pounds. He grew fast, very fast, too fast, and by the time he was a senior, many scouts thought he was too big (and awkward) to be an everyday player. They scouted him, instead, as a pitcher. He was not a flamethrower—he probably threw in the mid-to-high 80s—but he had impeccable control and a smooth style that reminded some of Jim Palmer, which made sense since Cal Jr. basically grew up on the legend of Palmer.

Later, Ripken would say that if any other team had selected him, he would have become a pitcher.

But the only team that mattered did select him—the Orioles took him in the second round of the 1978 draft. Cal Jr. was thrilled and he was terrified. He was thrilled for the obvious reason—playing for the Orioles was the only fully formed dream he'd ever had. And he was terrified because he knew people would think he had only been drafted because of his dad.

Sure enough, in his first year at Bluefield, he heard some of those nepotism charges. He looked entirely overmatched. At shortstop, he committed 33 errors in 62 games. At the plate, he went 270 plate appearances without a single home run. He slugged .301.

The Orioles quickly moved him to third base. He had grown to 6-4 and he weighed 200-plus pounds. He was simply too big to play short. Anyway, the Orioles had another prospect, a former college star named Bobby Bonner, who looked like the shortstop of the future.

Ripken liked third base a lot. He felt a bit less pressure there. He could think more about his hitting—and he began to hit with some power. In 1980 in Charlotte, he hit .276 with 25 home runs. The next year, in Rochester, he hit .288 with 23 home runs. The Orioles were impressed enough to call him up at the end of the season.

On Opening Day in 1982, he was at third base for the Baltimore Orioles and he went 3-for-5 with a homer. He'd arrived! Then he hit .089 for the next 17 games. He had not arrived! Then he hit .313 and slugged .528 over the next 51 games. He'd arrived again!

On July 1, Orioles manager Earl Weaver tried something crazy that would change Ripken's life—and baseball—forever.

Before Cal Ripken Jr., there had never been a shortstop the size of Cal Ripken. Now there are a couple of 6-foot-4, 200-pound shortstops—Carlos Correa and Corey Seager—plus a whole bunch, like Didi Gregorius and Troy Tulowitzki and Trevor Story and Jordy Mercer, who are basically that height and weight.

Before Ripken? Zero. Nada. It just didn't make sense—how would someone that big get down for all those ground balls? How could someone that big have enough range to make all the plays? How could someone that big stand up to the daily pounding of being a shortstop?

It was canon; shortstops were small, and they were fast, and they were light on their feet. Everybody knew that. A shortstop was Scooter and Pee

Wee and Little Louie. A shortstop was Rabbit and the Gnat and the Flea and Rooster. Bucky was a shortstop. Maxie was a shortstop.

"Killer" was not a shortstop. "Boomer" was not a shortstop.

Ripken was supposed to be a killer, a boomer; you just didn't put guys like him at short. Heck, Ripken himself didn't want to be a shortstop.

But that Earl Weaver . . . he just loved to try stuff. The Orioles were in fourth place, and they weren't scoring runs, and they'd been blown out in their previous two games and Weaver was in his last season as a manager. He had to do *something* bold and nutty and slightly infuriating; that was just in his nature.

On July 1, for a game against Cleveland, he put Ripken at shortstop and put Floyd Rayford at third. "The way we've played the last two nights," Weaver said, "we have nothing to lose."

It wasn't intended to be permanent. It wasn't even an experiment. It was just a one-game thing that Weaver hoped might jump-start the club; he flatly told reporters that he had no intention of keeping it this way. The reporters rushed over to Ripken to ask how he felt about it, and he was . . . not exactly happy. He was a rookie and he was only beginning to feel comfortable in the big leagues. "Last year, I hit around .230 at short," he lamented. "I hope it won't affect me at the bat."

His shortstop debut was hardly sterling. He went 0-for-4 with three strikeouts and in the eighth inning, Weaver moved him back to third base.

That seemed to be the end of that.

But there was Ripken back at shortstop the next day. He hit a home run. But Rayford looked terrible at third base—he made two errors—and again everyone expected this nonsense to end.

But no—Ripken was back at shortstop the next day (2-for-5, one home run), and the next day (0-for-4) and the next day (0-for-4 again) and the next.

"It takes guts to make that move, Earl," an unnamed dugout visitor told the *Baltimore Sun* when that day's lineup was posted. "[Owner] Edward Bennett Williams, [GM] Hank Peters, most of the organization and probably the fans would rather see the kid left alone at third, where he is more comfortable and where he is doing so well. Either it's guts, or it is a move of a guy who knows he is retiring at the end of the season."

Weaver dug in. "I liked the way he's handled himself," he said. "It's way too early to compare them, but the way he moves around reminds me of Marty Marion."

I love how at first Weaver said it was way too early to compare Ripken to anyone and then immediately compared Ripken to seven-time All-Star and MVP winner Marion.

As time went on, people began to realize that Weaver was serious about this—he probably had been from the start but didn't want to tell anybody. Ripken as shortstop went on a hitting tear—for the next two weeks, he hit .393 and slugged .672.

The reports about Ripken's defense at shortstop in those early days were generally filled with bland and unfulfilling words like "surprisingly solid" and "capable" and "adequate." Even Ripken himself would say, "I think I'm a better third baseman." This, I think, is how it goes for pioneers. People have a hard time seeing past their own expectations and preconceptions. Everybody thought he'd be too big, too lumbering to be a good shortstop, so when he made plays, they would think, "Huh, surprisingly good!"

But they couldn't see: Ripken wasn't a "surprisingly good" shortstop.

He was a miraculous one.

Yes, that's the word—*miraculous*—because, in the end, the scouts and doubters and skeptics were not exactly wrong about Ripken. He *was* too big to play shortstop the way others had played it. He *was* too slow to react to ground balls the way wizards like Ozzie Smith did.

So, instead, Ripken invented a whole new way to play shortstop using his particular talents.

One, he had an almost supernatural sense of where the ball would be going. That came from a lifetime of watching his father's teams play ball, all those years of studying hitting and pitching and positioning, all those talks with Cal Sr. about how to set up an infield, all the communication he had with pitchers and fielders.

You don't need great range when you can anticipate where the ball will be hit.

Two: He had a sensational arm. It was one of baseball's great natural wonders. People never really appreciated that arm because he didn't throw the ball full speed every time the way his contemporary Shawon Dunston did. Often it looked like he was putting no effort at all into his throws. But when you combine the quickness of his release (something he picked up from Brooks Robinson), the accuracy of his throws, the arm strength of a onetime pitching prospect, and the perfect balance that comes from countless hours of perfect practice, you end up with something mind-boggling. Ripken's arm was mind-boggling.

Because of that arm, Ripken could play 10 feet deeper than other shortstops and still make all the plays.

"One time about 1988 or 1989," Bill James wrote, "Baseball America did a survey of players with the best tools. They listed the Royals shortstop, Kurt Stillwell, as having the 'Best Infield Arm' in the American League. I'm a Royals fan; I thought, 'Wow, I never realized his arm was that good.' The Orioles came to town shortly after that, and I went to all three games and focused on the shortstops' throws. It was preposterous to suggest that Stillwell threw as well as Ripken. Stillwell had a good arm. But Ripken played 5–10 feet deeper than Stillwell and zipped the ball effortlessly to first base; every throw was hitting the first baseman shoulder high."

Three: He was a disciple of the Oriole Way. There has never been a more fundamentally sound player than Cal Ripken Jr. He was raised that way. He was equally good going to his left or his right, equally good coming in or going back, he was as good as any shortstop has ever been making backhand plays, and he turned the double play precisely. In 1990, he set a big-league record by making just three errors all season—that year, he went 95 straight games without an error. Four times in his career, he made fewer than 10 errors in a full season.

Even now, many people do not appreciate just how great a defensive shortstop Cal Ripken was. He rarely dived. He rarely made barehanded plays. He covered ground without people noticing.

In 1983, Ripken's second full season (and his MVP season), he had a league-leading 534 assists. The next year, he had an astounding 583 assists. How astounding? It's the American League record for any position. In all, Ripken led the league in assists seven times and finished top-five another four times.

Sure, it helped that he played every single day. But the guy had a magnet in his glove.

And after Ripken, big players across America realized they could play shortstop, too.

You can't tell the story of Cal Ripken Jr. without mentioning the streak. He played in 2,632 consecutive games over more than 16 seasons. There was a nationwide celebration when he broke Lou Gehrig's consecutive-game record in 1995. Baseball needed the good vibes; this was one year after the strike season and baseball fans were still angry. Ripken became a symbol for all that's good about baseball, which probably isn't too far from the truth.

But I prefer a different Ripken streak, one I find even more remarkable. He once played in 8,243 consecutive innings—that's 904 consecutive games at shortstop, every inning, every day, every night, every season, always. He played 11 innings on the second day of the streak; he played 14 innings on an April day in 1983, 16 innings on a May day in 1984, 15 innings on a June day in 1985, 13 innings on a July day in 1986, and 12 innings on an August day in 1987.

He played and played and played. People begged him to stop, take a ninth inning off once in a while. They criticized him for burning himself out. They ripped him whenever he went into a batting slump or power slump—it would be different, the critics insisted, if only he would take a rest now and then.

He was actually called greedy by some just for playing every inning of every game.

He played on. It was not part of some grand philosophy. Ripken played every inning because this was all he ever wanted to do, all he ever wanted to be.

Fittingly, it was his father, Cal Sr., who stopped that streak in 1987. Cal Sr. had finally become the Orioles' manager—just in time to witness the downfall of the Oriole Way. He had hoped to become a manager in 1983 after his friend and mentor Weaver stepped away. But the team wanted experience, and they gave the job to another longtime friend, former Giants manager and Yankees coach Joe Altobelli instead. Altobelli was the manager when the Orioles won the 1983 World Series.

Then things began to disintegrate. Altobelli was fired. Weaver came back but couldn't spark any of the old magic. Only then, after the Orioles had their first last-place finish ever, was Cal Ripken Sr. given a chance to manage.

By then, the Orioles didn't have any pitching. They lost 95 games in 1987, they started 0-6 in 1988, and Ripken was fired. He stayed on to coach because that's what he was about.

Anyway, in September 1987, in a Monday game at Toronto's Exhibition Stadium, his Orioles were getting thrashed. The Blue Jays built a 17–3 lead. And Cal Ripken Sr. decided enough was enough for his son— he had two hits in the game, but he'd been slumping for months. He was so obviously exhausted—mentally, physically, emotionally, everything. Dad pulled his son in the top of the eighth. Ron Washington came in to play shortstop. "It was my decision, not his," Cal Sr. said. "I wanted to get that monkey off his back."

"It's a blank feeling," Cal Jr. said. "I'm not sitting here feeling sorry for myself or regretting what went on tonight. I might need a little time to reflect. . . . I thought today would be like yesterday and like every day for the last five years."

It was simple, really. Cal Ripken Jr. had wanted to play every inning for the rest of his life.

No. 43 **Yogi Berra**

April 18, 1950: Opening Day, Fenway Park, Yogi Berra came up in the second inning. The Red Sox already were up 3–0. Joe DiMaggio had led off the inning with a triple, and Berra hoped to knock him in, put the Yankees on the board, and get his season off to a good start. It was his first at-bat of 1950. Boston's Mel Parnell struck him out.

"Bad balls? Sure, why not? I got to hit at something. They don't throw me any good ones."

—Yogi Berra, April 19, 1947

The last time I saw Yogi Berra, he was looking at a gray New Jersey sky and hoping—praying, even—that the Yankees game would not be rained out. He was 86 years old by then, and the thought of a summer night without a ball game saddened him.

He loved the game to his last day on earth. He particularly loved watching Derek Jeter play ball. Yogi would sit in his house and stare at the television silently, but when Jeter came to the plate Yogi could feel his heart thumping, his stomach fluttering; he felt like a kid again watching Jeter play. He wanted Jeter to succeed so badly; he loved the kid. Jeter was special. He was respectful. He was like one of the old-time players. He gave his all every play, every day.

And it would wreck Yogi when Jeter struck out. Why did the kid strike out so much? Jeter struck out almost 2,000 times in his career—he routinely struck out 100 times a year. It drove Yogi bonkers. They would talk sometimes, and Yogi would tell him to stop with the strikeouts.

Jeter would look at Yogi and smile and say he would try. But Yogi wasn't joking.

"Stop swinging at all those bad pitches," Berra would say.

May 14, 1950: Yankee Stadium, fourth inning. Yogi Berra came to the plate with the bases loaded and New York leading Philadelphia 3–1. The Athletics brought in Bobby Shantz to face Berra. Shantz struck him out.

"[Manager Casey] Stengel won't let me. Only pitchers. Pitchers ain't nothin'."

—Yogi Berra, January 30, 1953, on if he
played golf during the season

So, as you can tell, we are trying to do two things at once here, which goes hard against Yogi's famous advice: "You can't think and hit at the same time." Did Berra actually say that? Maybe. Maybe not. He remembered in 1960 possibly saying something like it to Bucky Harris, but he wasn't too sure. At some point, it grew pointless trying to differentiate between things he actually said and things people credited him with saying.

"I didn't really say everything I said," he explained to fans during the media caravan in 1986, after he became a bench coach for the Houston Astros. They laughed. But he wasn't joking.

The Yogi quotes—or Berra-isms, as they were called as far back as 1948—are unquestionably fun. How many millions of speeches around the world started with a Yogi line? But Yogi Berra was always more than those quotes, some of them real, some of them make-believe. So, one of the things we're doing here is drilling deeper and finding *real* Yogi Berra quotes, things he most definitely said. Maybe if we do that we can get a little closer to the man, the catcher, the three-time MVP, the greatest winner in baseball history, and hopefully we can also find the soldier and the husband and the family man.

The second thing we're doing: In between each section, we are pulling out a few at-bats from Yogi's remarkable 1950 season. They are not good at-bats. But there's a reason for it, a reason you will probably figure out before we get to the big finish.

June 3, 1950: Yankee Stadium. First game of a doubleheader. With the score tied 1–1 in the seventh, Berra came to the plate against Chicago White Sox pitcher Bob Cain, who was pitching a gem. Cain struck him out.

"Drinking makes people ugly. I'm ugly enough to start with."

—Yogi Berra, December 27, 1953

There are, I believe, three kinds of Berra-isms.

The first kind are simple malapropisms. Sportswriters loved those, particularly when Berra was young and the butt of so many jokes. "He learned me his experience," Berra supposedly said of Yankees legendary catcher Bill Dickey teaching him the finer points of catching.

The second kind of Berra-ism tends to build around a comical misunderstanding—sort of the *Three's Company* of quotes. An example of this was that time his wife, Carmen, said she went to see the movie *Dr. Zhivago* and he supposedly said, "What's the matter with you now?" or the time a waitress at a pizza joint asked if he wanted his pizza cut into four or six pieces, and he supposedly said four because he couldn't possibly eat six pieces.

The third kind, the most famous kind, are simple and slightly goofy statements he might have made that, upon review, have a touch of wisdom. For instance, when Mets outfielder Ron Swoboda came up with the idea of trying out Frank Robinson's batting stance, Yogi is credited with the classic: "If you can't imitate him, don't copy him." We know what he meant! There are books and books of these sorts of Berra-isms:

"We may be lost but we're making good time."

"It's so crowded nobody goes there anymore."

"When you come to the fork in the road, take it."

"Ninety percent of baseball is half mental."

"Half the lies they tell about me aren't true."

Berra was so renowned for these sorts of pearls that everywhere he went, people naturally listened for them. They would stand silently around him, hoping he might drop a classic line. He didn't like that sort of pressure. Berra was a shy person by nature. But sometimes, he delivered. A man and a woman once approached him at the Yogi Berra Museum in Little Falls, New Jersey, and didn't even hide their intentions. They asked him to just invent a classic Berra-ism on the spot.

Berra shook his head and said: "If I could just make 'em up on the spot, I'd be famous."

They laughed uproariously, and Berra shrugged. He accepted his place in American culture. But, no, he didn't love it, didn't love the way people parsed his every word, didn't love that some of the quotes made him come across as a simpleton, didn't love being turned into a cartoon character *again*.*

Yes, he released books of quotes. He even titled one of them *It Ain't Over 'Til It's Over*. Hey, you give people what they want. But he really wasn't that guy.

He was a proud, sensitive, tough, and undaunted American hero.

Oh, and he also didn't say, "It ain't over 'til it's over." But we'll get back to that.

June 27, 1950: Yankee Stadium. Second inning, scoreless game, nobody on base and Berra faced Bob Kuzava, a big left-handed pitcher who would become his teammate the very next year. Kuzava struck him out.

> "I'm not much of a talker. At home, my wife does all the talking. And at Yankee Stadium, when I'm talking contracts with [Yankees general manager] George Weiss, he does all the talking."
> —Yogi Berra, January 21, 1955

When you look through the newspapers, week after week, it's stunning to find that most of the time Berra was quoted, it involved money. It was another time, and Berra had to fight for his salary every year. Every January (sometimes late December—"always after Christmas," Berra said), there was the inevitable outbreak of stories about Berra wanting more money, the Yankees refusing to give it to him, and various speculations on how far the dispute would go.

Berra hit .322 and was third in the league in RBIs in 1950—he had to fight for more money. He won the MVP in 1951—he had to fight for

---

* The "Yogi Bear" people always insisted they came up with that name on their own; Yogi sued Hanna-Barbera but then withdrew the suit, deeming it too much trouble.

more money. He won the MVP in 1954 and 1955—he had to fight for more money.

In all, Berra finished top four in the American League MVP voting every single season from 1950 to 1956, seven consecutive years, and the Yankees won six pennants and five World Series over that time. But come January, Berra had to remind the Yankees again who he was and why he deserved a raise. Weiss was famously cheap, even for that time, when all general managers were cheap.

Weiss was cheap, but he was not dumb. He knew that the best way to keep the Yankees hungry was to pay as little as possible. That didn't just put more cash in the pocket of the owner; it also made the players desperate for postseason bonus money. He was not unaware that whenever a new player came to the Yankees, the veterans would pull him aside and say: "Shut up, do your job, and you'll get a World Series share."

Yogi was deadly serious when it came to money talk. He was proud of his playing. He was proud of what he brought to the Yankees. He had a family to support and worked numerous offseason jobs (in 1952, for instance, he was a salesman for American Shops in Newark). He held out or threatened to hold out just about every year.

"If I do my job," he told reporters in 1950, "they'll have to pay me."

"I'm going to have my best year," he told reporters in 1951, "and Weiss will pay through the nose."

"I think I'm entitled to more money, don't you?" he asked the New York *Daily News'* Dick Young in 1954, after he won his second MVP award.

In 1955, after his third MVP season, he had this famous exchange with Weiss:

"You know, not all the papers agree you're entitled to the MVP," Weiss said.

"I only read the papers that say I am the MVP," Berra replied. "I don't read them other papers."

July 7, 1950: Yankee Stadium. This was the day that Berra was named starting catcher in the All-Star Game for the first time in his career. Berra came up in the first inning against Dick Littlefield, a Red Sox rookie. Littlefield struck him out. Berra came up again to face Littlefield in the third. Littlefield struck him out again, this time on a pitch a foot over Berra's head. "Case," he said to manager Casey Stengel, "that was the lousiest pitch I ever got strike out on."

"I had to correct his grammar," Stengel said. So I told him, "No, you mean that was the HIGHEST pitch you ever got strike out on."

"Those guys who make fun of me in the papers, how much do they make?"

—Yogi Berra, February 9, 1951

In the early years, people mocked Berra for his looks. They mocked him for his awkwardness. They mocked him for his grammar. They mocked him for reading comic books. They mocked him for his size, for the funny way he talked, for the way he would swing at any pitch, for the way his mind worked. They mocked him even knowing how much it hurt.

They mocked him because every punch line was just a bit funnier with Yogi Berra's name in it.

But Yogi Berra was so much more. Lawrence Peter Berra was there at Utah Beach on D-Day. He was Seaman 1st Class Berra then, and he was in a 36-foot rocket boat, and the image that stayed with him, the one that endured for 70 years, was how hauntingly beautiful the sky looked as an impossible number of planes soared overhead. Yes, he should have been scared, but he was too young to know that for sure, and he stared up at the sky and could not get it out of his head that it looked like a fireworks show, Fourth of July in the park. He was momentarily mesmerized until his lieutenant shouted: "Put your head down if you want to keep it!"

He put his head down and kept it down. For the next 12 days, he worked in a rocket boat that shot at anything that flew under the clouds, including one of their own Allied planes. He fished men out of the water. He watched men drown. He himself could have drowned when the boat capsized; he and the rest of the crew held on until they were rescued and taken back to the transport.

Not long after that, a German bomb dropped perilously close to the transport. It was as close to death as Yogi Berra cared to be. "I wouldn't have cared if it hit," Berra later said. "I was too tired to be scared."

So, Berra had seen things by the time he got to the Yankees. He felt it deeply when they called him an ape, when they talked about how ugly he was, when they called him stupid. Sometimes, he wanted to fight. But what good would that do? Instead, he pounded line drives all over the field, threw out anyone who dared try to steal on him, exposed hitters' weaknesses like few catchers ever had. And he won! Nobody won like Yogi.

———

August 1, 1950: Briggs Stadium. Berra faced Detroit's Dizzy Trout in the second inning. Trout struck him out.

August 6, 1950: Cleveland Municipal Stadium. Top of the seventh, Yankees up 9–0, Berra faced Cleveland's tiny righty reliever Marino Pieretti—they called Pieretti "Chick." Pieretti struck out Berra on a pitch in the dirt.

August 13, 1950: Yankee Stadium. Fourth inning, Yankees trailing 2–1, Johnny Mize led off against Philadelphia's Lou Brissie. Mize never struck out, but he did that day—struck out looking, in fact. Berra followed. Brissie struck him out looking, too.

Jimmy Piersall: "If you give the pitchers a sign to throw at me, I can bash your head in with this bat and plead temporary insanity."

Berra: "We don't throw at no .200 hitters."
—Spring training exchange, March 1957

There's a statistic about Berra that blows the mind: From 1957 through 1981—25 seasons of baseball—New York teams won 13 pennants. You can do the math:

The Yankees won 11 of those pennants in 1957, '58, '60, '61, '62, '63, '64, '76, '77, '78, and '81.

The Mets won two pennants, in 1969 and 1973.

Yogi Berra was a player, coach, or manager on every single one of those teams.

How does that happen? From his first season as a player in 1947, all the way to his last season as Yankees manager in 1985, New York teams won 15 World Series titles, and Berra got championship rings in 13 of those—the only two he missed were when the New York Giants won in '54 and the Brooklyn Dodgers beat his Yankees in '55.

Again—how does that happen? What sort of sorcery did Berra have that always put him on the winning team? The Yankees have won 40 pennants. Berra was involved in more than *half* of them. Or, to put it another way, look at the non-Yankees teams with the most pennants:

Dodgers: 24

Giants: 23

Cardinals: 23

Yogi Berra: 21

Athletics: 15

Red Sox: 14

How did this small man from the Hill in St. Louis play his part for so many winning teams? Certainly, he was a terrific hitter with an uncanny ability to hit the ball hard. Certainly, he was a terrific catcher who had a knack for handling pitchers—Stengel called Berra an extension of himself. Certainly, he was the ultimate teammate: smart, alert, always aware, always present.

Still, that doesn't quite explain all those wins, all those pennants, all those World Series, even after he stopped catching, even after he stopped playing every day, even when he was just a coach or manager.

"Eh," Berra explained, "I was lucky."

September 6, 1950: Fenway Park. Top of the fifth, Yankees down 4–1, Berra faced Mel Parnell, the pitcher who struck him out to start the season. Parnell struck him out again.

September 16, 1950: Briggs Stadium. More than 56,000 people in the stands, two runners on in the top of the seventh, the ultimate Yogi Berra moment. Dizzy Trout pitching for the Tigers. Trout struck him out.

> "I never thought we were really out of it. You're not out of it until it's mathematical."
>
> —Yogi Berra, September 21, 1973

Read that quote again because *that* is what he really said. He didn't say, "It ain't over 'til it's over." For years now, my pet project has been getting to the bottom of the most famous Berra-ism of them all, to figure out where it came from. It has been baffling and frustrating. People have long believed he said it during the Mets' amazing 1973 pennant run.

I've pored over newspaper clippings for hours and hours. And it's very clear that Berra did not say it then for two reasons:

1. There's no record of him saying it.

2. The next year, in 1974, with the Mets floundering and falling out of the race, Berra definitely did say, "You're never out of it until you're out

of it." And if Berra really had said, "It ain't over 'til it's over," someone would have made a comparison between the quotes. Nobody did.

So what did he really say? I would be embarrassed to tell you how much time I've spent trying to find out. For a long time, I thought the 1974 "You're never out of it until you're out of it" quote was the origin, and people later Yogied it up.

But now I believe it is the above quote that launched things. It was late in that 1973 "Ya Gotta Believe" season. The Mets had just swept the Pirates four straight to move their record to 77-77. And even though that record seems unimpressive, it actually gave New York a half-game lead in the division.

That's when Berra said, "You're not out of it until it's mathematical."

Which, if you think about it, is a better quote than "It ain't over 'til it's over." It makes much more sense—you always have a chance until you're mathematically eliminated. And there's a certain kind of poetry to it. I like the "until it's mathematical" phrasing.

But to become an enduring Berra-ism, it needed to be less logical, a little more nonsensical, a little more fun. Take "You're not out of it until it's mathematical," add his later "You're never out of it until you're out of it" quote, mix in a couple of contractions, and, voilà, you have your Berra-ism: "It ain't over 'til it's over."

And sure enough, in 1975, sportswriters began to pepper their stories with lines like, "As Yogi Berra said, 'It ain't over 'til it's over.'" It became a symbol of the man, one of the most quoted phrases in the English language and the title for Yogi's autobiography.

I still prefer "You're not out of it until it's mathematical."

September 20, 1950: Comiskey Park. First inning, two outs, Berra faced the White Sox' Ray Scarborough, a veteran pitcher whose one claim to fame was that Ted Williams said he couldn't hit him (it wasn't true). Scarborough struck him out.

OK, that's it. So why did I go through 12 different strikeouts for Yogi Berra in 1950?

Because those were the only 12 strikeouts he had all season.

There has never been another baseball season quite like it. Yes, if you're a baseball aficionado you might scream, "Wait! What about Joe Sewell! He had a season where he struck out just four times!" And so he did. But Sewell's whole purpose as a batter was to not strike out. He hit one home run that year. (Later in his career, he hit 11 homers while striking out three times, which is remarkable, but again, not a power-hitting season.)

So it goes with all the Nellie Foxes and Dale Mitchells and Don Muellers who refused to strike out. They bunted and slashed and made contact. They didn't strike out because that was the essence of their whole game.

But that wasn't Berra's game. He was a power hitter. He hit 28 home runs that season, and that ratio—28 homers, 12 strikeouts—makes him one of only six players in baseball history to hit twice as many homers as strikeouts. Joe DiMaggio in his magical 1941 season hit 30 homers and struck out 13 times. Tommy Holmes, in that war-torn 1945 season, hit 28 homers and struck out nine times.

But Yogi was *different*. For one thing, he was a catcher. Think about the wear and tear. Berra in 1950 hit 28 home runs, drove in 124 runs, scored 116 runs, played 148 games as a catcher . . . and struck out just 12 times. It's beyond belief.

Even more—he swung at everything. Pitchers threw it high, low, inside, outside, in the dirt, over his head, toward a beer vendor, into the dugout, and Yogi was swinging.

Which takes us back to the beginning, takes us back to Yogi Berra, nearing the end of his life, looking out the window, seeing the gray skies, hoping that the game would not be rained out. He wanted to see Jeter play another day. He wanted to see that Jeter had taken his advice.

"Derek," he said, "you can't go around swinging at all those bad pitches."

"But Yogi," Jeter said, and he had that mischievous smile on his face, "you did."

Berra didn't miss a beat. "I hit 'em, kid," he said. "I hit 'em."

No. 42 **Jackie Robinson**

M ichael Jordan was a great basketball star—the greatest ever?—
and at age 31, he signed to play minor-league baseball. Jordan
had baseball talent. He was fast and a fantastic competitor,
maybe the toughest competitor in the history of American sports. He hit
.202 in the minor leagues and lasted a year.

Tim Tebow was a great football star—maybe the greatest college quarterback ever—and at age 28, he signed to play minor-league baseball. He
tried for years. Tebow had baseball talent. He was strong and fast and a
fantastic athlete. But he hit .223 for his minor-league career and finally
understood he would never break through.

Jackie Robinson was a great football star—one of the greatest football
players in America—and also a great basketball star and also a great track
star. At age 26, he signed to play minor-league baseball. He had talent. He
was an extraordinary athlete. He was a fantastic competitor.

He became one of the greatest baseball players who ever lived.

There are differences, of course, differences in age, differences in athleticism, differences in the times when they played.

The biggest difference, I believe, was that Jackie Robinson knew that
he could not fail.

———

We tell and retell the story of Jackie Robinson because it is the most important sports story in American history. We talk about the profound unfairness and hatred behind segregation. We talk at length about the pain and fury Robinson endured, the threats, the taunts, the constant pressure. We talk about Jackie's indomitable will, how he was, in the words of Buck O'Neil, "different from the rest of us." We talk about the shrewd courage of Dodgers executive Branch Rickey. There are movies about all this, songs about this, plays and poems and many books about this, countless stories.

All this is as it should be.

But I do think we miss just how *unlikely* Jackie Robinson's story really is.

You might have heard that baseball was Robinson's fourth-best sport in college. That is true, as far as it goes, but it doesn't quite get us all the way to the point.

Jackie was a little brother first. Mack Robinson was four and a half years older than Jackie, and he was one of the great track athletes in American history. In Berlin, under the outstretched arms of Nazi Germany (and in an old pair of spikes he'd been using all year), Mack broke the Olympic record in the 200-meter. Unfortunately for his place in American history, Jesse Owens stayed a step ahead and broke the record first. Still, Mack won a silver medal and later NCAA championships and if the times had been different, he would have been an American superstar.

Instead, he became a street cleaner (later fired by the city of Pasadena, California, in a purge of black workers) and worked various jobs throughout his life. Jackie Robinson was forged not only by his brother's athletic brilliance but also by the way he was treated afterward.

Jackie, too, made his first splash as a track star; he set the junior college record for the long jump. According to one story, perhaps apocryphal, he broke that record on his last jump of the event—he was in second place, and he came to his brother Mack (who was running in an exhibition) and said, "Can I borrow your shoes?"

"No," Mack said, but then he relented and took off his shoes and gave them to his brother, who promptly broke the record.

Next, Jackie was a football star. He was Gale Sayers before Gale Sayers—fast, graceful, untouchable, and most of all, instinctive. "But I don't know what I'm going to do," he protested when the *Los Angeles Times* sent out a photographer to try to capture his moves. In 1939, his UCLA coach Babe Horrell saved what he called "razzle-dazzle stuff" just for Jackie. And Robinson responded by averaging 12.2 yards per carry. That was a record.

He was also a terrific safety with an incredible ability to anticipate plays. That year, UCLA trailed Stanford by a touchdown late in the game. Stanford had the ball, and Robinson reportedly looked over at his panicked coach and shouted out, "What are you worrying about?" On the next play, Robinson intercepted a pass and returned it deep into Stanford territory. UCLA scored and the game ended in a tie.

But even here, like with his brother Mack, Robinson was second best. He was part of what would undoubtedly become the most influential backfield in the history of college football. The quarterback that year was Kenny Washington, an incredible talent who threw passes, ran with power and speed, and was the force behind the defense. A few years later, Washington became the first African American to sign an NFL contract after the league became fully segregated in 1946.

There's a baseball angle with Kenny Washington, too. We'll get back to it.

After Washington graduated, Robinson became the Bruins' star. Hall of Fame coach Clark Shaughnessy, who innovated the T formation and was coaching at Stanford, said of Robinson in 1940: "When the field is spread out, he is the most dangerous man that I have ever seen in football."

But that UCLA team was flat-out awful; the Bruins ended up 1-9 and only once scored more than 14 points in a game. That game was against Washington State; the Bruins won 34–26, and Robinson was otherworldly. He scored three touchdowns—two of them winding, beautiful runs of 60 and 75 yards—and he also threw for a touchdown.

But that was a rare bright spot in a gloomy season, and Robinson shouldered some of the blame. A couple of reporters suggested he gave up on the team once he realized things were going badly. But mostly, it was written that Robinson was an extraordinary talent and opponents created game plans specifically designed to stop him. "Generally," the *Los Angeles Times* reported, "he has been pretty effectually bottled up this year—partly because he has been a marked man in every contest, partly because few opponents have dared kick to him or pass into his territory, partly because Washington has not been around to keep Robinson and his teammates 'in the groove.'"

After the season ended, Robinson was selected to play on the college All-Star team that faced the Chicago Bears. He scored a touchdown.

Next, Robinson was a basketball star. The Cal basketball coach, Nibs Price, once called him "the best basketball player in the United States." Jackie twice led the Pacific Coast Conference Southern Division in scoring and sportswriters called him the "Ebony Luisetti" after Stanford's Hank Luisetti, who a few years earlier had revolutionized basketball with a scoring form that would become known as the "jump shot."

Robinson was generally overlooked as a basketball player. Even after he led the conference in scoring, he was left off the all-conference team. But there were those who could look beyond color and see Robinson for the star that he was. In January 1940, when University of Southern California star Ralph Vaughn was featured on the cover of *Life* magazine with the simple caption "Best Basketballer," *Oakland Tribune* columnist Art Cohn was unimpressed:

"Now that all the picture mags have glorified Ralph Vaughn of USC as 'America's No. 1 basketball player' it is interesting to note that he wasn't even the best player in Los Angeles. Because Jackie Robinson of UCLA, playing on the Coast's weakest team with NO support even remotely comparable to that which Vaughn received from a championship team, has just won the Conference individual scoring title."

There simply wasn't anything he couldn't do athletically. Track? Tennis? Golf? Swimming? He could do it all.

Then there was baseball. He was a big baseball star in junior college, and he got off to a fantastic start in his one and only season at UCLA. He debuted against Los Angeles City College on March 10, 1940, and went 4-for-4 and stole three bases, including a steal of home.

That day has become romanticized in the years since. Some have said he stole four bases. Cohn wrote that he hit a home run. It's not entirely clear if any of this is true, and UCLA actually lost the game. What we do know is that things unquestionably went downhill for Jackie Robinson after that.

In his next baseball appearance, against Cal, Robinson came in as a pitcher late in the game, with UCLA leading 16–13 and the sky getting darker. He stalled repeatedly to try to get the umpire to call the game for darkness. "I can't see the plate," Robinson moaned repeatedly and, to prove his point, threw consecutive wild pitches. The umpire eventually did call the game, but Robinson was branded a complainer.

You could see Robinson's raw baseball talent shine now and again during that season. He stole home for UCLA's only run in a loss to Santa Clara, he homered in a win over Cal, he beat out three bunts against the San Diego Marines. But mostly, he didn't care all that much.

"I guess I didn't put as much effort into baseball as I did into the other sports," Robinson would say later. "Like most Negro athletes, I just assumed that baseball was a sport without a professional future. I played it solely for the fun of it."

He cared so little about baseball that during the season he broke away to join the track team. He had given up on the long jump when he found out that the Helsinki Olympics were canceled for the war, but the UCLA track coach asked him to come back, so he did and without practicing he smashed the conference long-jump record.

How bad was Robinson's baseball season at UCLA? According to Arnold Rampersad's authoritative *Jackie Robinson: A Biography*, Robinson hit .097 for the season. He led the team with 10 errors. The numbers are difficult to add up—like in the Negro Leagues, it's difficult to tell what games counted and what games were exhibitions—but it is certain that Robinson was a huge disappointment as a baseball player.

This is where Washington reenters the picture—because it turns out Washington was a *great* college baseball player. Washington hit .454 and .350 in two varsity seasons, played brilliant shortstop, and bashed a 450- or 500-foot opposite-field home run at Stanford that left people so breathless they were still writing about it in the papers weeks later.

Washington concentrated more on football after that, but the point is that he was a bigger baseball prospect than Robinson. Leo Durocher loved his game so much that he reportedly asked Washington to go play for a time in Puerto Rico and try to make it into the major leagues as a Puerto Rican player. USC coach Rod Dedeaux said Washington had a better arm, more power, and was a better defender than Robinson.

In 1940, Dave Farrell—a writer for the communist newspaper the *Daily Worker*—wrote an open letter to Larry MacPhail, then the president of the Brooklyn Dodgers, in which he pleaded for baseball to "break the foolish tradition which has kept the Negro out of Organized Baseball. It's an insane bar, sinister today."

He suggested that the Dodgers sign a black player. And while he did mention Robinson, his bigger suggestion was Kenny Washington.

"You have been looking for a heavy-hitting outfielder," Farrell wrote. "I don't know how much you've put out to get one. Let me tell you about Kenny. He hit the longest ball I've ever seen. Kenny batted .400. . . . And he has the kind of arm that throws forward passes 60 yards."

The Dodgers did not pay attention to the call (Washington did get a tryout with the Giants in 1950, but he was well past his prime by then). But the point remains that in 1940, Robinson was a football player first, a basketball player second, a track star third, and a baseball player last and least.

Then, in 1942, he entered the U.S. Army and didn't pick up a bat or ball for nearly four years—they wouldn't let him play baseball at Fort Riley because of the color of his skin.

Now, with all that in mind, try to look at the situation with fresh eyes. It's 1945 and here's Jackie Robinson. He's 26. He's known as a football player and track star. He'd played one season of college baseball and hit .097. He has a bum ankle. He is hyperaware of his surroundings, of the basic unfairness of the world around him, and has no illusions about things changing. Oh, and also, there's an unspoken agreement in baseball that no one will sign a black player.

You tell me: How likely was the Jackie Robinson story then?

When Robinson was honorably discharged from the army after winning his court-martial case—years before Rosa Parks, he was arrested for refusing to go to the back of the bus—he immediately signed up to play football for the Los Angeles Bulldogs in 1944. In his season debut, in front of 9,000 people in San Francisco, he passed for two touchdowns and broke off several thrilling runs. At Los Angeles's Wrigley Field a few days later, he gained 101 yards on eight carries before going down when his ankle gave way.

He also signed up with a traveling basketball team.

Then things happened, and they happened so fast that the mind blurs. First, he signed with the Kansas City Monarchs in late March in what seemed to many a publicity stunt ("The versatile Jackie Robinson, of football fame, is due at camp this week" the *Pittsburgh Courier* reported). Everybody knew what a great athlete Robinson was, but nobody knew if he could play baseball.

And yet, less than two weeks later, Robinson was given a tryout by the Boston Red Sox.

That was a big deal, even though the tryout itself was a sham meant only to satisfy a Boston city councilman named Izzy Muchnick. He had gone public with a letter from Red Sox executive Eddie Collins, who bizarrely insisted that Black players did not want to play in the major leagues. After Muchnick responded saying that this was nonsense, Collins said that the Red Sox would happily give a tryout if Muchnick could find any such players.

So Muchnick, along with *Pittsburgh Courier* writer Wendell Smith, brought three players to a tryout: the blazing-fast Sam "the Jet" Jethroe, a talented young infielder named Marvin Williams, and Jackie Robinson. Everyone knew going in that nothing tangible would come from the tryout—heck, the Red Sox would become the *last* team to sign a black player, not the first—but every step, even tiny ones, were worth taking.

And Jackie was incredible that day. "You never saw anyone hit the way Robinson hit that day," Muchnick would say. "Bang, bang, bang—he rattled it!"

Robinson was so good that Boston manager Joe Cronin did go public in saying Robinson had impressed him. That was as far as that went, but it was at least something.

The tryout was soon forgotten, and Robinson began traveling with the Monarchs . . . and he loathed every minute of it. He hated the buses. He hated the doubleheaders and the night games. He also didn't like the way the Monarchs' operation worked; he asked for a contract when he arrived at camp and was told that their back-and-forth letters constituted the contract. All of it felt small-time to him.

He only stayed because, in his own words, "I needed the money."

"The teams were poorly financed, and their management and promotion left much to be desired," Robinson wrote in his autobiography. "Travel schedules were unbelievably hectic. . . . This fatiguing travel wouldn't have been so bad if we could have had decent meals. Finding satisfactory or even passable eating places was almost a daily problem. There was no hotel in many of the places we played. . . . Some of the crummy eating joints would not serve us at all. You could never sit down to a relaxed hot meal. You were lucky if they magnanimously permitted you to carry out some greasy hamburgers in a paper bag with a container of coffee."

For the rest of his life, Robinson would talk about how miserable he felt in the Negro Leagues, but it must be said that he was playing during the war, when so many of the best players were gone. Also, this was before Jackie had married Rachel; he was desperately lonely. On top of that, playing in a segregated league, while difficult for all the players, was particularly galling for Robinson, whose sense of justice was perhaps his most powerful tool.

"We were conditioned," Buck O'Neil would say, "to simply accept what was happening no matter how unfair it was. . . . But Jackie wasn't conditioned like that. He saw when something was unfair and he thought, 'We have to change that now.'"

Robinson did begin to play terrific baseball for the Monarchs. In the papers, he was still being pitched as the "All-American football player" and "UCLA's all-around athlete." But in June, his manager Frank Duncan called him "just about the best infielder in Negro baseball and [he] should improve with more games under his belt."

In July, he was hitting around .350 and showing great daring on the bases. A columnist named Bill Burk wrote of him, "If he were white, the park would be filled two hours before game time with major-league scouts, managers and owners all trying to sign him up to a contract."

Then in late August, the Monarchs played the Chicago American Giants in Davenport, Iowa. The Giants won the game 8–7. But there was something more important happening. "Many of the fans," one sportswriter wrote, "were disappointed by the absence of Jackie Robinson, much-publicized shortstop for the Monarchs."

Robinson was in Brooklyn signing a deal with Branch Rickey and the Brooklyn Dodgers.

What would the social media world say now about the Dodgers signing an almost 27-year-old former college football, basketball, and track star who'd had a few good months playing for a barnstorming baseball team in a league depleted by the war?

Would the reaction and expectation really be *that* different from Jordan or Tebow?

Well, sure it would be different because all anybody cared about then was the race question. Many—white and black—were doubtful that Robinson could make it big in the big leagues. Numerous Negro Leaguers talked about how many better players there were in the league; his old teammate Newt Allen believed Robinson's arm was too weak for shortstop. Negro Leagues pitchers talked about how he was befuddled by breaking balls.

Meanwhile, various major leaguers expressed doubt, most famously Bob Feller, who pitched against Robinson in an exhibition tour and said he could be beaten by inside fastballs. Then, of course, there were all those who believed—or chose to believe—that no African-American player could handle the everyday intensity of big-league baseball.

But Jackie Robinson was a man of faith. I do not just mean faith in God, though he was indeed a religious man. He also had extraordinary faith in himself and his destiny. He believed deeply that he was the one meant to cross baseball's color line. He believed deeply that God would not have led him down this path only to fail.

That faith filled him with something more powerful than confidence.

He knew that he would succeed because to do anything less would be unthinkable.

When he arrived at Sanford, Florida, for spring training, a mob of racists threatened him and Rachel. But he had faith. When he fell into such a frightful hitting slump during spring training that even generally supportive sportswriters began to openly question him, he had faith. When there were rumors and whispers that teammates would not play with him, that opponents would refuse to take the field against him, that the league would not back him up, that even Rickey was waffling, he had faith.

Then, powered by that faith, he became the Jackie Robinson in the American history books.

There's another thing about Robinson that is easy to miss in those books: Man, he was good. He has become such a cultural icon, such an important figure, that it's easy to miss the ballplayer.

In 1947, his first year with the Dodgers, Robinson hit .297, walked 74 times, scored 125 runs, led the league in stolen bases, and hit 12 home runs. That made him Major League Rookie of the Year (they did not give one in each league then). He was almost instantly the best bunter in the game; he led the league in sacrifice hits, too.

In his second year, he had the same year except he added a few more doubles and triples.

In his third year, he won the MVP award. Robinson's 1949 season was incredible—.342/.432/.528, stole 37 bases (most in the league in almost 20 years), scored 122 runs, drove in 124 runs, played fantastic defense at second base. He posted a spectacular 9.6 Wins Above Replacement. It was one of three times he led the National League in WAR.

He hit. He walked. He hit for power (five seasons with a .500 or better slugging). He ran the bases with abandon and spirit. He played fantastic defense. He was not regarded as a defensive star when he played, but his defensive numbers are consistently brilliant no matter what position he played—second, third, first, all of them.

Much has been made of those defensive numbers, by the way. Some have wondered why they're *so* good when his reputation was more muted. I have my own theory about that: I think Jackie Robinson was an amazing defensive player because he was entirely focused all the time. Here was one of the greatest American athletes ever, in both mind and spirit, and he was driven by an ideal. Think of that apex of athleticism and purpose; he had to be in the moment every moment.

In the end, he was going to succeed because he had to succeed. Human beings really are capable of such extraordinary things.

No. 41 **Tom Seaver**

T ake a moment for yourself, if you will, and think about the great players—the truly great ones, the all-time players—who you got to see play live. On July 5, 1985, when I was 18 years old, I saw Tom Seaver pitch in that mausoleum of a ballpark, Cleveland Municipal Stadium. If the records are correct, there were 6,024 other people there, too. In memory there were maybe a few dozen. The place felt deader than normal. The Tribe was the worst team in the American League.

Cleveland started a guy named Jerry Reed, same name as the singer who performed "She Got the Goldmine (I Got the Shaft)." That detail doesn't matter at all for this piece, but it seemed significant enough at the time; basically it was all we could talk about. Jerry Reed made 12 big-league starts in his career. This was his third.

Seaver, meanwhile, was making the 603rd start of his career. He was almost 41, and he was pitching for his third team, the Chicago White Sox. He was no longer the perfect pitching machine. In his youth, at his best, Seaver blended a blistering fastball with a heart-stopping curveball with a vicious slider with a toughness that came from his time in the Marines with a flawless motion that looked like it was pulled out of a "How to Pitch" pop-up book.

And that mind! Everybody talked from the start about Seaver's pitching mind. He seemed to know, instinctively, exactly what pitch to throw at exactly what time. "Blind people," Reggie Jackson once said, "come to the park just to listen to him pitch."

By 1985, yes, Seaver was worn down, tired, his fastball had slowed, but he still knew things about pitching, things they don't teach in books or discuss during mound conferences. He knew things about pitch location and changing speeds and being unpredictable and picking up a hitter's weaknesses. That year, even without his best stuff, he was still among the better pitchers in the American League.

And that day, he baffled and befuddled Cleveland's lineup. He gave up two hits in the first five innings and just kept on going. He had a shutout going into the ninth—the score was 8–0—and only a few of us stragglers remained in the stadium. Only then did Seaver lose his rhythm and, probably, his interest. He gave up a couple of singles and a three-run homer to Tony Bernazard. Seaver looked pretty mad at himself when he was taken out, but it still ended up being his 296th career victory.

After the game, Cleveland's manager, Pat Corrales, offered a quote that makes more sense to me the older I get.

"Seaver's the same guy I watched in 1967," Corrales said, "except that he doesn't throw as hard."

In 1974, at the height of his greatness—he had already won two Cy Young awards and led the Mets to two pennants and a World Series title—Seaver released one of the oddest and most enjoyable baseball books every written. It is hard to categorize. It is not a biography. It is not a tell-all. It was not even written by Seaver, for the most part.

The book is called *How I Would Pitch to Babe Ruth*.

It is not what you might expect. The book is actually a collection of some of the greatest baseball articles ever written—none of them by or about Tom Seaver. Included in the book are John Updike's "Hub Fans Bid Kid Adieu," about Ted Williams's last at-bat; Jack Olsen's marvelous story about how Al Kaline suffered for his craft; Jerry Izenberg on Stan Musial; Ring Lardner on Ty Cobb; a couple of Roger Kahn stories about the Boys of Summer Dodgers.

Every piece in the book was accompanied by a prologue Seaver wrote. For the Josh Gibson story, for instance, he wrote about his own feelings about segregation (opposed). For the Stan Musial story, he wrote about how he always wanted to bat one time using Musial's famous peekaboo stance (he never had the guts to try it). But for many of the others, he did, as the title suggests, offer how he might have pitched the all-time greats if given the chance.

Here for your enjoyment are a few of those—how Seaver would pitch to some of the best hitters of all time:

Henry Aaron: This wasn't imagination; Seaver and Aaron matched up 93 times (Seaver held him to a .220 average, but Aaron hit five home runs). Each matchup was special, because Aaron had been Seaver's hero. The first time Seaver faced Aaron, it was 1967, and Seaver had to turn away from the plate and look out to the outfield just to compose himself. He wrote that it felt so familiar because he had dreamed it so many times. Seaver then turned back around, blanked his mind, and threw an inside fastball; Aaron grounded into a 5-4-3 double play.

Five innings later, he faced Aaron again, threw the same inside fastball, and watched Aaron deposit it over the left-field wall.

How Seaver would pitch Aaron: Unpredictably, never throwing the same pitch twice.

Ernie Banks: Seaver and Banks faced each other 31 times, so there were no secrets between them. Seaver generally owned Banks, holding him to a .138 average. But, Seaver admitted, this was largely because he didn't face Banks at his peak.

Seaver remembered one pitch in particular. It was a day game at Wrigley Field in June 1968, and Banks was mired in a slump, having gone 0-for-18 in his previous four games. In the bottom of the sixth, Seaver had Mr. Cub down 0-2 and threw a curveball about six inches off the ground. Banks golfed it off the left-field catwalk for a home run. "Yes, sir!" Banks said to himself as he rounded the bases, "a home run in Wrigley Field!" Seaver couldn't help but smile.

How Seaver would pitch Banks: Start with hard stuff up and inside and try to put him away with sweeping pitches just off the plate . . . but beware that you keep those pitches far away.

Johnny Bench: They faced each other 96 times, with Seaver holding Bench to a .179 average. (In the middle of Seaver's career, Bench was his catcher with the Reds.)

But that low average doesn't really describe the battle between them;

Bench hit two home runs off Seaver. While Seaver feared nobody on the mound, he came closest to fearing Bench. In Game 1 of the 1973 National League Championship Series, Bench came up in the ninth inning. Seaver had struck out 13 and was throwing his fastball by everybody—but not Bench.

Seaver threw a fastball—"It just didn't seem to have anything on it," he would say quietly afterward—and Bench crushed it to left for a walk-off homer.

Four days later, in Game 5 of the series, Bench came up in the first inning with runners on second and third and two outs. Seaver never hesitated. He intentionally walked him.

How Seaver would pitch Bench: Carefully.

Mighty Casey: They never faced each other. Seaver expected that Casey would be a tough man to face in a clutch situation.

How Seaver would pitch Casey: He wasn't sure of the pattern—probably fastballs up and in, sliders away—but one thing he definitely knew: Seaver would not have thrown three fastballs down the middle of the plate like the pitcher did in the poem.

Roberto Clemente: They faced each other 65 times, and Seaver generally got the best of it—he held Clemente to a .242 average with 21 strikeouts.

How Seaver would pitch Clemente: Fastballs and sliders on the extreme outside corner of the plate. If you could hit that tiny spot—"Imagine a box in that corner just big enough to hold one baseball," Seaver said—Clemente would tip his cap and head back to the dugout. But miss it by the tiniest of degrees and there would be hell to pay.

Ty Cobb: The book was written in 1974, and in it Seaver called Cobb's hit record of 4,189 unbreakable. A little more than a decade later, Pete Rose broke it.

How Seaver would pitch Cobb: "I'd keep the ball low, trying to make him hit on the ground rather than a line drive to the outfield. . . . And if Cobb bunted and I had to cover first, I'd be very careful."

Rogers Hornsby: Seaver, unfortunately, does not go into how he would pitch Hornsby, which is a shame because I'm dying to know. But he did talk about Hornsby's obsessive views about hitting. Hornsby believed that a hitter should never drink a beer, should never read a book, and should never see a movie because of the effect it can have on the eyes.

Seaver was dubious about the book and movie part. "Reading and seeing movies helps you train and stimulate your mind while also helping you relax," he wrote.

And as for abstinence from beer? Seaver said, "Well, it's fine to take care of your body, but nobody likes a fanatic."

Mickey Mantle: Seaver faced Mantle one time . . . sort of. It was at the 1968 All-Star Game. Seaver was 23 years old and throwing just about as hard as anyone in baseball history. Mantle was 36, his body was closer to 60, and he was at the end. Mantle got a long standing ovation before the Seaver at-bat began just for showing up.

Seaver threw four fastballs down the middle, and Mantle struck out.

How Seaver would pitch Mantle: He would throw fastballs, but certainly not the down-the-middle fastballs he used in the All-Star Game. "At his peak," Seaver said of the four fastballs he threw, "Mantle probably would have hit one of them through the dome."

Willie Mays: Seaver faced Mays 26 times and allowed just five hits, none of them a home run. But Seaver readily acknowledged that he never faced the *real* Willie Mays. By the time Seaver came along, Mays's bat had slowed. After that, Mays was Seaver's teammate with the Mets.

Seaver tells a funny story: At the All-Star Game in 1970, Mays complained, "Hey, when you gonna throw me a changeup? You throw me that fastball away, that slider away, I can't hit that stuff anymore. I'm an old man! Throw me a changeup, man."

Seaver promised he would.

And the next time he faced Mays, did he throw Mays a changeup? Absolutely not. He threw nothing but hard sliders that ran away like the Road Runner, and Seaver struck Mays out three times. Seaver didn't believe that Willie Mays would ever grow old.

How Seaver would pitch Mays: Hard stuff away, away, away, as far away as possible.

Frank Robinson: Seaver faced Robinson 15 times—seven of those in the 1969 World Series—and allowed just two singles. But he never forgot a lesson he learned from one of those singles. It was the World Series. Seaver had a 2-2 count and threw what he thought was the perfect fastball just on/off the outside corner. Robby fouled it off.

So he came back with the same pitch, another perfect fastball on/off the outside corner. Robby fouled it off.

That was it: The setup was complete. Seaver had the great man looking outside, and so he reared back and threw the best inside fastball he knew how to throw—and Robinson turned on it and hit it so hard the Seaver would say he never forgot the *sound*, much less the harrowing speed.

How Seaver would pitch Robinson: Away, away, away—and never, ever try to get cute.

Babe Ruth: Here's the title of the book. With Ruth, Seaver let his imagination go and actually played out a couple of at-bats.

How Seaver would pitch Ruth: Seaver would start Ruth off with a sinking fastball, low and on the outside corner of the plate. He imagines getting a strike call as Ruth lets the pitch go by.

With the count 0-1, Seaver would relax and tell himself he was in control of the at-bat now. He would try the same pitch again, low and away, but envisioned Ruth letting it go by for a ball. No more playing around. Seaver would come in with a slider that would begin on the inside of the plate and break hard and in. It's hard to tell how many sliders Ruth saw in his career, but he certainly never saw one like this. He would swing and miss. Strike two.

Now Seaver would have Ruth's attention. The Bambino would dig in. He would probably expect another exploding slider; that pitch would undoubtedly fill his mind. Seaver instead would throw that fastball again, down and away, perfect spot—and Ruth would strike out with a big swing.

In the sixth inning, though, they would meet again. Seaver would still feel strong. He would decide to challenge Ruth with a high fastball—let's see if this guy can handle the high heat. Ruth would turn on it, send it high into the right-field stands, and Seaver would watch Ruth run, pigeon-toed, around the bases.

Ted Williams: For a thinking pitcher, Williams is the ultimate puzzle. Nobody thought more about hitting than Williams. Nobody thought more about pitching than Seaver. This would be a true battle of wits.

How Seaver would pitch Williams: He had no idea. His first idea was to try to get Williams to chase breaking balls out of the zone. Unfortunately, Seaver had no confidence whatsoever that this would work. People tried throughout the 1940s and '50s to get Williams to chase breaking balls, and the guy never did—he led the league in walks eight times and walked more than 2,000 times overall. The "get him to chase" plan did not seem too promising.

So what was left? "I guess I'd settle for the low outside corner," Seaver wrote sheepishly. And after that? Hope.

Almost exactly a month after I saw Seaver pitch in Cleveland, he went to Yankee Stadium with a chance to win his 300th game. There did seem something cinematic about it—Tom Terrific returning to New York for one final bit of glory. His greatest years were with the Mets, that 1969 season when he carried the Miracle Mets to the title, his 1971 season when he went 20-10 with a 1.76 ERA and a career high 289 strikeouts, his 1975 season when he led the league in wins and strikeouts and won his third Cy Young. He was larger than life in New York, and there are people who to this day have still not recovered from the day in 1977 that the Mets dealt him to Cincinnati.

Now he was back in the city for his biggest moment, and there was a flood of stories about Seaver leading up to the game. Reporters followed him everywhere. One of the biggest crowds of the year poured into Yankee Stadium.

"Pressure?" Seaver asked a reporter. "Sometimes media doesn't understand pressure. I've always believed that it brings out the best in exceptional athletes."

Yes, pressure focused him, always. When we went to interview Tom Seaver for the Hall of Fame movie a couple of years ago, he was having a pretty good day. In the last years of his life, he suffered from dementia and it grew progressively worse, but at this point he still had good days and he talked so beautifully about the game and what it meant to him. There is so much I take away from his words that day, but mostly I think about something he said to his brother and idol, Charles, who died years ago.

Charles would ask Tom: "What's it like when there's 50,000 people and you're standing on that little plot of ground 60 feet, 6 inches away from home plate?"

Seaver: "I said, 'Charles, you learn how to control your emotions and make them positive.' I learned that in the Marine Corps. You are always going to have emotions. You can't say it's not there. You have to use those emotions for positive energy."

How did you do that?

"For me, it was very simple," Seaver said. "I loved what I was doing. I was like an artist, a physical and mental artist. I would take those emotions, whatever they were, and focus them on what I had to do out there. I loved all of it. I loved 60 feet, 6 inches. I loved the history of the game. Sandy Koufax. Christy Mathewson. Walter Johnson. I loved them.

"I understood the Walter Johnsons. Understood—that's not the right word. I *knew* them. In my heart and brain, I knew them. They were artists, and I was an artist, and I loved being a part of that history."

Beautiful. This takes us back to Yankee Stadium, August 4, 1985. Seaver was in the bullpen before the game, warming up as the crowd poured in, and White Sox pitching coach Dave Duncan came by to watch. After a few pitches, Duncan's face went a bit white, and he stopped Seaver.

"Tom," he growled, "you don't have squat tonight."

Seaver smiled and nodded. He would go out that day with squat, with nothing but his mind and his heart and all the things he picked up through the years. He would pitch a complete game, allowing six measly singles and just one run while striking out seven. Another brilliant game in a brilliant career. He did it with absolutely nothing on his pitches.

Here's the best part: Do you know what Tom Seaver said after Duncan told him that his pitches had nothing on them?

He said: "Dave, you know that. And I know that."

He paused and pointed toward the Yankees dugout.

"But they," he continued, "they don't know that. And by the time they realize it, I'll figure something out."

No. 40 **Roberto Clemente**

"I grew up in Wisconsin, rooting for the Milwaukee Braves, loving Aaron and Covington and Bruton and Spahnie and Mathews and Adcock, but nonetheless Clemente was my favorite player. . . . I thought he was the coolest thing I had ever seen—the way he looked in a uniform, the way he walked to the plate, the way he rolled his neck, his looping underhand throws to second and his rifle shots to third and home. We all have someone in childhood, and not necessarily an athlete, that we connect to in some magical way, and for me it was Clemente."

—David Maraniss, author of *Clemente: The Passion and Grace of Baseball's Last Hero*

Let us begin with Pancho Coimbre. He was an outfielder in the 1930s and 1940s. According to legend and the best statistics available, Coimbre did not strike out a single time in the Liga de Béisbol Profesional de Puerto Rico from 1939 to 1942. Not once. It is something people in Puerto Rico still talk about.

Coimbre was by all accounts a genius of a hitter, Tony Gwynn before

Tony Gwynn. He sprayed hits to all fields, he was a blur on the bases, and he had an outfield arm to fear. He was, however, too dark-skinned to play in the major leagues. He played in the Negro Leagues instead, and he was a star, twice starting in the East-West All-Star Game while playing for the New York Cubans.

"Coimbre," Satchel Paige once said, "could not be pitched to. No one gave me more trouble."

Now let us move next to Perucho Cepeda. He was known as "the Bull" (which is why his son Orlando drew the nickname "Baby Bull") and he could do everything on a baseball diamond. He crushed line drives into gaps. He ran with abandon. He was a shortstop and, by reputation, an amazing one. He played with unbridled fury. At different times, he was called Puerto Rico's Ty Cobb and Puerto Rico's Babe Ruth—one writer called him Puerto Rico's Babe Cobb, as if being compared to only one of the great American baseball legends was not quite enough.

Cepeda, like Coimbre, was too dark-skinned to play in the major leagues. But unlike Coimbre, he refused to play in the Negro Leagues even though he was recruited many times.

"As a black man," Orlando Cepeda would write of his father, "he had neither the inclination to endure segregation nor the temperament to buck racism in the United States."

This was undoubtedly true: Perucho's temper was something to behold. When he was 44 years old, he was still playing and lashed a single. When someone in the crowd mocked the way he ran—like an "old man"—Cepeda jumped into the stands and pummeled the man. The fight was intense enough that the police arrested Cepeda and took him to the police station, where the guard on duty shook his head and said, "Perucho. Please." And then they sent him home.

Let us begin with all the black players from Puerto Rico—some whose names have traveled through the years, and some whose names have not— who would have been good enough to play in the big leagues if things had been different. And not just Puerto Rico. Black players from the Dominican Republic, too. Cuba. Venezuela. All of Latin America.

Roberto Clemente carried their spirit with him.

It was their power inside him, their yearning inside him, their rage inside him. It was their force that not only made him a great hitter and a great fielder and a great baserunner and a great man but also made him cool in the almost indescribable way that drew in David Maraniss, among so many others.

"Nobody," Clemente once said, "does anything better than me in baseball."

When Roberto Clemente came of age as a ballplayer in 1954, the Milwaukee Braves offered him the most money. Later that same year, the Braves offered another promising young player, Sandy Koufax, the most money.

Could you even imagine a future Milwaukee Braves team with Koufax and Warren Spahn in the same rotation, Clemente and Henry Aaron in the same outfield?

It wasn't meant to be. In both cases, but for slightly different reasons, the players chose to take significantly less money and join the Brooklyn Dodgers. Koufax chose the Dodgers because Brooklyn was his home and because he and his father shook on the deal before the Braves' higher offer came in. Clemente chose the Dodgers because he thought he would feel more at home with New York's large Puerto Rican community.

As it would turn out, neither player would spend much—or any—time in Brooklyn. In Koufax's case, the team would move to Los Angeles just as he began to figure out how to be a big-league pitcher.

And Clemente? Well, here's the crazy part: Brooklyn signed Clemente, but it's clear, looking back, that the team almost certainly knew he would never be a Dodger. That deal is one of the strangest in baseball history. They signed Clemente for $15,000: $5,000 as salary, $10,000 as a signing bonus. In those days, when a player signed for that much money, he became what was called a "Bonus Baby." That meant the team had two choices:

1. Keep Clemente on the big-league roster for two full seasons.

2. Place the player on the waiver wire after one season.

Obviously, teams almost never chose the second option—you wouldn't sign a player for that much money only to let other teams take him away after a year. But that's exactly what the Dodgers did. They sent Clemente to Montreal. It turns out, as Dodgers executive Buzzie Bavasi later conceded, that the Dodgers had signed Clemente only to keep him away from the rival Giants.

"We didn't want the Giants to have Willie Mays and Clemente in the same outfield and be the big attraction in New York," Bavasi said.*

Once the Dodgers sent Clemente to Montreal, they knew he was gone. They had to know; there had been a bidding war in Puerto Rico for him. But they still tried to hide him. Clemente got just 155 at-bats with Montreal and hit just .257. The Dodgers felt stuck between what Maraniss called "two seemingly contradictory notions." On the one hand, they wanted to develop Clemente's great talents. On the other hand, they knew that the more they developed those talents, the more likely it would be that another team would take him away.

So, with all of these contrasting and conflicting incentives flying around, the Dodgers simply shut down. They didn't play him. They didn't develop him. They left Clemente isolated and miserable and distrustful and haunted, feelings he never quite overcame throughout his career.

It was a waste of time because you can't hide a jewel like Clemente. There's a wonderful story about Clemente and Clyde Sukeforth, the Dodgers scout who had brought Jackie Robinson to Brooklyn to meet Branch Rickey. When Rickey went to Pittsburgh to run things, he took Sukeforth with him. And in 1954, Sukeforth went to Montreal to watch Clemente play with the Royals.

As usual, Clemente was on the bench, but Sukeforth watched outfield practice and saw that arm. He watched batting practice and saw that bat speed. As the game began, he got up to leave, but first he went over

---

* Bavasi also told SABR's Stew Thornley in an email that there was a race question to consider. In 1954, the Dodgers had five black players on the team (six if you count Joe Black, who pitched only seven innings). Bavasi said he asked Jackie Robinson himself if it would hurt the team's makeup to add Clemente and jettison a popular white player, George "Shotgun" Shuba. According to Bavasi, Robinson was adamant about keeping things as they were, saying that choosing Clemente over Shuba would mean "setting our program back five years." If this happened, it is indeed disturbing, but I'm deeply skeptical about it. Bavasi is, best I can tell, the only source for this, and he was 90-plus years old when he said that. He also said he briefly struck a deal with Branch Rickey not to take Clemente because of their friendship, which doesn't sound right, either.

to Royals manager Max Macon, smiled, winked, and said, "Take care of our boy."

Even if the Dodgers had been able to hide Clemente in Montreal, there was nothing they could do when he went back home to Puerto Rico to play winter ball for Santurce. He played in the same outfield as Willie Mays, and the two of them wrecked the league. Every day, it seemed, they did something magical offensively or defensively. Both players hit homers in the All-Star Game.

"The Dodgers never should have let him play winter ball," White Sox general manager Frank Lane said. "That's where he attracted all the attention. I doubt if a club would have taken him based on his .257 batting average in Montreal. I know if I had him, I would have paid him $2,500 or $3,000 not to play this winter."

Lane was being a bit silly here—the clubs knew full well about Clemente's brilliance. But it is true that the sportswriters did not. When Rickey's Pirates took Clemente with the first pick in the offseason draft, there was a reported "gasp of surprise" from the writers. The United Press correspondent called Clemente "a surprise selection. He batted .257 last year."

It's hard to believe sportswriters could have been so far behind.

But they were: Everybody in baseball knew what the Pirates had gotten. And Rickey just glowed. He had not only signed a great prospect for less than half of what it cost his old club, but he'd also settled an old score with the Dodgers. He had taken away the greatest outfielder they ever signed.

Roberto Clemente's game was big in every way. He swung hard, and he swung at everything. He ran the bases with a touch of madness, like a man at the brink who has decided there is nothing left to lose—no player after World War II hit more triples. He threw to kill—no right fielder since Deadball gunned down as many runners, and only one right fielder since Deadball (his replacement, Dave Parker) threw more balls away.

His game was not quite elegant the way, say, Joe DiMaggio's game or Aaron's game was elegant; there was a quiet grace to the way they played. There was nothing quiet about Clemente. In full flight, he was a jarring presence, a blur of angles—elbows, knees, shoulders, all of them running off in different directions, an asterisk in motion. In the language of Hollywood, he was not conventionally beautiful. He merely redefined what beauty means.

Clemente was bold and beautiful and principled and combative and sensitive and prideful and deeply, gloriously weird. This part gets missed. Clemente's hypochondria was legend: According to C. R. Ways's 1972 story, Clemente complained through the years of (1) tension headaches, (2) a nervous stomach, (3) a tendon rubbing against the bone of his left heel, (4) malaria, (5) bone chips in his elbow, (6) a curved spine, (7) one leg being heavier than the other, (8) hematoma of the thigh (from a lawn-mowing accident), (9) slipped discs, (10) a paratyphoid infection he contracted from hogs on his farm, (11) food poisoning, and (12) insomnia.

Particularly insomnia.

"When I wake up in the morning," Clemente said during the 1971 World Series, "I pray I am still asleep."

"If I could sleep," he said another time, "I could hit .400."

Clemente thought, not without reason, that sportswriters tilted things to make him look bad. "They talk to me," he said. "But maybe they don't like me so they write about me the way they want to write."

But in many ways, Clemente wouldn't have been Clemente without being misunderstood. "Anger for Roberto Clemente," *Pittsburgh Press* columnist Roy McHugh wrote, "is the fuel that makes the wheels turn in his never-ending pursuit of excellence. When the supply runs low, Clemente manufactures some more."

In 1956, Clemente had his first good year. He hit .311 and showed off his great arm and great defensive instincts. But that year was filled with conflict. He was fined by his manager, Bobby Bragan, for missing a sign. He was admonished repeatedly for not running out fly balls. He ran through a third-base coach's sign and even though he ended scoring the winning run, the headlines focused on his rashness. Then, later, he missed a steal sign and was fined for that (though the fine was later rescinded).

It went on and on like that; every week it seemed Clemente found himself in the middle of some new fight. This, alas, was the price of being a pioneer. People kept calling him Bob instead of Roberto. They mocked his English. They mocked his complaints. They treated him—and, as he continuously pointed out, all the other Latin American players—differently from the other big stars in the game. "You are all the same," he shouted at *Pittsburgh Press* sportswriter Phil Musick the first time they spoke. "You don't know a damn thing about me."

They *should* have known him because I don't think any player in baseball was as nakedly honest as Clemente. He hid nothing. He spoke out his thoughts, his gripes, his dreams, his hopes, his rages, and his ambitions. He left himself exposed by leading with his heart every single day.

"If I am going good," he once said, "I don't need batting practice, but sometimes I take it so the other players can see me hit."

"Baseball," he once said, "has given me the opportunity to know people, to hurt people once in a while, but mostly to love people."

"When I put on my uniform," he once said, "I am the proudest man on earth."

You, of course, want to hear the weirdest of all Clemente stories. So here goes: On August 8, 1969, the Pirates were playing in San Diego against the Padres. Home-plate umpire Lee Weyer rang up Clemente on a questionable strike-three call. Clemente went off and got himself tossed out of the game for the third time in his career.

He stewed for a long time in the clubhouse, then got dressed in his usual jacket and tie and went back to the hotel with the team. As he was walking through the lobby, he saw his teammate Willie Stargell holding a bag of delicious-smelling fried chicken.

"Where did you get that?" Clemente asked.

"There's a place just down the road," Stargell said.

Clemente immediately left the hotel, walked to the restaurant, and got himself a bag of fried chicken. He still was thinking about the third strike as he walked back to the hotel, when suddenly a car pulled up beside him. There were four men in the car. One of them was brandishing a gun. "Get in," the driver said.

So Clemente got in. The man with the gun pointed it at him, and they drove silently for a few minutes before pulling off on a side road that overlooked Mission Valley. All of them got out of the car.

"OK," one of the men said to Clemente, "take off your clothes."

He took off his clothes while one of the men held the gun close to Clemente's face; at one point, Clemente said the man put the barrel of the gun in Clemente's mouth. While he was undressing to his shorts, one of the men noticed the ring he was wearing and told him to take it off. It was the diamond ring Clemente had received for playing in the All-Star Game. He took it off and handed it over.

"Take it," Clemente said. "Take the money. But please don't kill me. Please don't kill anybody over money."

Now the men were looking at him curiously. Did he seem familiar? They rifled through his wallet and saw his MLB Players Association card. They asked him what it meant; he said he was a ballplayer for the San Diego Padres. He did not expect the men to be particularly knowledgeable baseball fans; he figured his best shot was to say he was a local player.

And, like that, their entire posture changed. They gave him back his clothes and told him to get dressed, making sure he put his tie and jacket back on. Then they drove him back toward the hotel, gave him his wallet and ring, and let him go.

Just as Clemente began to walk away, he heard tires squeal and saw the car make a U-turn. He was still overwhelmed by what had just happened, and he worried that they had changed their minds about letting him go. Clemente looked for a rock that he might throw at the car. But then the car pulled over and the window rolled down.

One of the men handed Clemente his bag of chicken.

This story perfectly divided Clemente's world. Many people thought the story was made up—it had to be made up, it was just so crazy, so silly, so ridiculous. One of his teammates said it couldn't be true because no mugger would ever give back the money. Various writers poked fun, saying this was just Clemente being a fabulist.

Others, though, saw the story as a perfect reflection of the power that was Roberto Clemente.

Clemente died on the last day of 1972, just three months after getting his 3,000th hit, a double to left field off the Mets' Jon Matlack. He died in a plane crash; he was on his way to Nicaragua to bring supplies and support after a devastating earthquake. He was 38 years old. He was coming off another .300 season in a career filled with them.

In some ways, his death overshadowed his life. Clemente was a hero.

He also was one incredible and singular ballplayer.

"Public figures who die young always have a special glow, from Marilyn Monroe to JFK," Maraniss said. "There is no afterlife, which in sports, in particular, can be dreary and disappointing. The fact that Clemente not only died young but died in such a heroic way certainly adds to his story and the way he is perceived, and . . . I would not have written a book about him if not for that. But I loved him long before, and it was for the way he played."

Yes. The way he played. Think of the most exciting plays in baseball. The triple. The right fielder trying to throw out the runner going to third. The play at the plate as the runner tries to advance. The batter going after and connecting with a pitch way too high or way too low. The diving catch. Clemente epitomized these plays throughout his career. He played the game his way. He wouldn't walk. He did not swing for the fences. He did not give up on a ball or a throw or a pitch. He made fans feel deep emotions.

"When I heard he died," Musick wrote, "I wished that sometime I told him I thought he was a hell of a guy. Because he was, and now it's too late to tell him there were things he did on a ball field that made me wish I was Shakespeare."

Clemente's style, his energy, his zeal on the field, it remains so infectious and irresistible and timeless . . . especially that last one. Clemente is timeless. You see other players in old film footage, and their power, their grace, their grandeur gets lost. Even the greatest—Ruth, Walter Johnson, Jimmie Foxx, DiMaggio, Paige—they all look a little out of date in film, a little out of time.

But not Clemente. To see him swing the bat 50 years ago is to see him swing the bat now, to see him unleash a throw from right field, to see him run the bases; it is as current and alive as anything in the moment. Clemente is an ageless summer song that takes us back and takes us forward at exactly the same time.

No. 39 **Nap Lajoie**

So much of life is style. Napoleon "Larry" Lajoie was, in so many ways, every bit the hard-bitten character that his great nemesis Ty Cobb was. As a rookie with Philadelphia, Lajoie would repeatedly come to the ballpark inebriated. Once, after a particularly rowdy night, he got into a fight with a heckler on the way to the park and was arrested. Another time, he showed up so drunk that his manager, George Stallings, put him in the game just to humiliate him. Lajoie promptly made a two-run error, screamed at fans, got pulled from the game, and was suspended for four days.

Lajoie was suspended a lot, actually. He got suspended for throwing a wad of chewing tobacco into the face of an umpire (and then chasing down the umpire after the game, threatening him all the way). He was suspended another time for viciously arguing balls and strikes and calling the umpire "crooked." He once grew so mad that an umpire would not replace a baseball that had gone black from dirt and spit and grime, he simply picked up the ball and threw it over the grandstand the way a petulant child might. The game was ruled a forfeit.

Lajoie broke his thumb while battering a future Hall of Fame teammate, Elmer Flick, who said Lajoie had been bullying him for more than a year. Lajoie got into a lot of fights.

And you know how Cobb was infamous for spiking players? Well, nobody spiked more players than Larry Lajoie, as he was generally called. He once spiked three fielders in the same inning, a record that is unlikely to be broken.

And yet, through it all, unlike the fierce and solitary Cobb, everybody adored Lajoie. People adored him so much that they tried to get him one more batting title, a story we'll tell in just a moment. They adored him so much that they followed him into a new league, something called the American League, after he left Philadelphia in a nasty contract dispute. They adored him so much in Cleveland that they literally named the team after him, the Cleveland Naps, and kept that name until he was too old to keep hitting.

See, beyond the rough-and-tumble, Lajoie was just so friendly and fun-loving, he was irresistible. "He was a pleasure to play against, too, always laughing and joking," Pittsburgh's Tommy Leach said. "Even when the son of a gun was blocking you off the base, he was smiling and kidding with you. You just had to like the guy."

So much in life is a matter of style.

Lajoie was, you might say, the sixth person elected into the Baseball Hall of Fame. You have that famous first class—Cobb, Babe Ruth, Honus Wagner, Christy Mathewson, Walter Johnson—and Lajoie finished sixth in the voting. The next year, three more players were elected, and he received the highest vote total of the three, more than Tris Speaker or Cy Young. He was revered, not only for his achievements—lifetime .338 average, 3,000 hits, the first person in the 20th century to win the Triple Crown, four batting titles, an unmatched reputation as a defender—but also for the graceful way he played the game.

"He plays so naturally and so easily," Connie Mack said of him, "it looks like a lack of effort."

Or as Ogden Nash put it in his poem "Lineup for Yesterday":

L is for Lajoie
Whom Clevelanders love
Napoleon himself
With glue in his glove

Batting average races used to matter. During Deadball in particular—but even well into the 1940s and '50s—there would be almost as much newspaper coverage around the country of batting races as pennant races. There would be weekly update stories, sometimes even daily updates, about Rogers Hornsby taking the batting lead from Zack Wheat or Harry Heilmann's efforts to hold off Tris Speaker. Batting races were like reality TV shows long before television; fans knew the characters involved and rooted for their favorites and against the others.

In 1910, there was a particularly exciting twist to the batting race. Hugh Chalmers, a flamboyant promoter who had made his name selling cash registers, had just founded his own automobile company, Chalmers Detroit. And he was particularly proud of the company's new car, the Chalmers Model 30 Roadster, a 30-horsepower behemoth that he called the envy of the world (with a $2,000 sticker price, more than $50,000 today). These were the early days of automobiles, when nothing seemed more exotic than a beautiful car.

So it was a big deal when Chalmers announced that the company would give a Model 30 to the batting champion of baseball.*

Cobb was the heavy favorite to take the batting crown and the car. He'd won the 1909 title by 30 points over Eddie Collins, and he had the highest batting average in baseball in 1907, too. He was still just 23 years old and at the height of his game; he had blazing speed and a ferocious will, and nobody seemed likely to even challenge him. "I hope to be lucky enough to own a new Chalmers next fall," Cobb said before the season began.

And Lajoie? To be honest, he was one of the least likely contenders. Yes, he had won four batting titles in his career, but those had been years earlier—by 1910, Lajoie was 35 years old and had slowed considerably. In 1908, he didn't even hit .300.

But it was Lajoie who got off to the incredible start. In late May, the papers reported that he was hitting .433 (or so—the newspaper numbers,

---

* You will see it written sometimes that Chalmers planned to give a car to batting champions in both leagues, but that was not the plan. It was always going to be one car. In 1910, Sherry Magee won the National League batting title. He did not get a car. He was pretty bitter about it.

as you will see, were notoriously inaccurate). He was way ahead of Cobb and everybody else. On June 16, he was still hitting over .400 while Cobb was hitting .388 (or so). This was exciting—a two-man race between the grand old legend of baseball and the hard-charging upstart who would dare take his place. It was a nationwide phenomenon, not least because people were betting like crazy on their favorite to win.*

And there were twists! Turns! At some point in August, Cobb started seeing something blurry cross his vision through his right eye. He took some time off. "Ty Cobb Going Blind" was the headline that appeared in papers across America. "Specialist Says He Is in Danger of Losing Sight."

Then, just as suddenly, the blurriness faded and Cobb was back in the lineup, ripping singles and doubles and triples like always.

On September 1, the *Lowell Sun* reported that Cobb took a substantial lead.

"Recently," the paper reported, "Cobb overtook [Lajoie]. The chances are that Cobb will beat Lajoie out for the batting honors."

But was that right? On September 2, the *Lethbridge Herald* broke the news that the batting leader was not Cobb, and it was not Lajoie, either. It was, instead, Fred Snodgrass.

"Fred Snodgrass of the Giants is probably the most talked about player in the country today," the *Herald* wrote under the headline SNODGRASS LEADING THE WAY FOR THE PRIZE AUTOMOBILE. "Snodgrass' present average is about .405[†] while Cobb's is around .380."

On September 4, the *Washington Post* had Cobb hitting .362 and Lajoie hitting .359, and leading the league was . . . Philadelphia's Amos Strunk at .438 (though he was just 14-for-32).

On September 5, *Sporting Life* had Lajoie leading Cobb .372 to .365.

In other words, nobody really knew what was going on. It now seems strange that even though batting races were just about the biggest thing in American sports, nobody actually *kept track* of the numbers. It shouldn't have been that hard; I mean, you take hits, you take at-bats, you do some long division, voilà, done. But the official numbers were kept secret by

---

* According to Jon Wertheim's story "The Amazing Race," one Cobb fan reportedly died of a heart attack while arguing with a Lajoie fan.

[†] Snodgrass was really hitting about .345.

the leagues. Ban Johnson, the president of the American League, wanted to be able to announce the batting champion on his own time and in his own way.

America was enraptured by a horse race in the dark.

Cobb's eye issues popped up again—and just when the Tigers were playing Lajoie's Naps. What an unlucky break. The Cleveland papers were dubious and ripped Cobb repeatedly, but Cobb seemed unbothered by it all. While Cleveland and Detroit played, Cobb sat in the stands wearing frosted eyeglasses.

When Cobb came back, he got at least one hit in each of his final 14 games. He hit .532 in those 14 games and seemed to have put the batting title away. After cracking a single and a double in Chicago against the White Sox on October 7, Cobb decided to call it a season. He said that his eyes were bothering him again.[*]

The batting race came down to the last day, even though the papers had more or less declared it over. "Ty Cobb Cinched Auto" was the newspaper headline in the *Ottawa Citizen*. Different papers had different numbers, but most[†] agreed that Cobb had a sizable lead. Even Lajoie's hometown Cleveland papers called his chances "mightily slim."

Lajoie thought the whole thing was ridiculous. He complained about how inaccurate the tabulations were. Even more, he complained about official scoring.

"They ought to have traveling scorers just like umpires," he said. "The official figures kept now are jokes. Just for instance, the last time I was in Boston I hit a ball to deep short. The shortstop, Wagner, went for it and fell down. He was charged with an error. The same thing occurred in New York, and I got a hit.

---

[*] Strangely, Cobb's eyes were good enough that he immediately left to play for an all-star team that was put together to help the Philadelphia Athletics prepare for their World Series against the Chicago Cubs. This was a real thing in those days. The leagues were in such competition that players from other American League teams—in this case, Cobb, Speaker, Walter Johnson, and other stars—really did get together to help the pennant winner prepare to play the National League team.

[†] Not everybody thought Cobb was winning. The *Philadelphia Inquirer*'s George L. Moreland did a detailed study and had Lajoie up by two points.

"I'm not kicking, understand, over the loss of that one hit. But it just goes to show how unfair the methods of scoring are under the present system."

Looking back now, with the help of countless baseball fans who have intensely researched the race, we know that Cobb was leading going into that last day by seven points.

He had 194 hits in 507 at-bats for a .383 average.

Lajoie had 219 hits in 583 at-bats for a .376 average.

So the race really was all but over. Cobb was off playing with an all-star team. True, Lajoie did have a doubleheader against the hapless St. Louis Browns, but he would need a miraculous two games to make up seven points of batting average.

Well, miraculous or corrupt—nobody could have predicted the madness that would follow.

Rowdy Jack O'Connor—also known as Peach Pie O'Connor—was a longtime catcher in the wild early days of baseball. He was Branch Rickey's teammate for a while, and what Rickey remembered most about him was that he had this trick where he would spit tobacco juice into a hitter's eye while the pitcher was winding up. This, apparently, was quite effective.

Rowdy Jack once threatened the umpire Hank O'Day with such ferocity—he promised not only to attack O'Day personally but also to bring a mob of Cleveland fans with him—that O'Day refused to take the field in Cleveland until his safety was guaranteed.

That year, in 1910, Rowdy Jack became manager for the St. Louis Browns. "While he has retained the belligerence," the *Pittsburgh Press* assured baseball fans, "he has passed up the rowdyism."

Maybe. But his team was a fiasco. They came into the final doubleheader 22 games behind the next-worst team in the American League.

Nobody knows for sure what motivated O'Connor to do what he did on that day, October 9, 1910. Many assumed he did it because he loathed Cobb, which is never a bad guess. Others thought he did it out of admiration for Lajoie, which is also not a bad guess.

Others suggested O'Connor did it because, like so many others, he had big money on the batting race, which is probably the best guess of all.

Whatever his reasons, O'Connor decided that he was going to get Larry Lajoie a batting title and a new Chalmers automobile. He did not even try to hide his intentions. In the first game of the doubleheader against Lajoie and the Naps, Rowdy Jack inserted himself as the catcher. He was 44 years old and had not played in a game in more than three years.

Then, he put a 22-year-old rookie named Red Corriden at third base and gave him specific instructions to play Lajoie deep because otherwise "he'll take your head off."

And so he set up one of the greatest scams in the history of baseball.

The first time Lajoie came up, he lifted a fly ball to center field. He hit it pretty well—Lajoie would later say he crushed it, which was almost certainly an exaggeration—but most newspaper accounts thought it was definitely playable for rookie centerfielder Hub Northen. Northen did not get to the ball; it went over his head for a triple.

"It was a clean and hard hit, but there were many in the stands who were of the opinion that a more experienced outfielder would have captured the ball" was the nuanced opinion of the *Washington Post*.

That was hit No. 1—and it lifted Lajoie's average to .377.

That hit was the least controversial Lajoie at-bat of the day.

Next time up, Lajoie noticed that Corriden was playing deep. And by "deep," I do not mean that he was playing at the back of the infield dirt. No, this guy was playing in left field. Lajoie couldn't run by then and loathed bunting—he was famous for hitting the ball hard—but he wasn't a fool. He bunted the ball down the third-base line. It wasn't a great bunt, but it didn't have to be. By the time Corriden raced in for the ball, Lajoie was on first and he was 2-for-2.

That made Lajoie's average .378—five points back.

Third time up, Corriden was back in left field again. Lajoie laid down another bunt, Rowdy Jack didn't even go for it, and Corriden raced in too late.

Lajoie's average was .379.

Fourth time up. Same thing. Corriden in left field. Rowdy Jack all but incapacitated. Another bunt. Another hit. The first game was over, and Lajoie's average was .380, just three points behind Cobb.

People in the crowd and the press box probably wondered how long these teams could keep this charade going. The answer came with Lajoie's first at-bat in the second game. He came up, Corriden was still planted in left field, Lajoie bunted for a single, and his average was .381.

Then there was a complication. Lajoie's second time up, everything was set up just like before. But this time, Lajoie's bunt was too hard and not down the line enough—it rolled to shortstop and future Hall of Famer Bobby Wallace. And Wallace, incredibly, bobbled the ball, and then realized there was no time to make a throw. This didn't actually hurt Lajoie's batting average because a run scored on the play and the official scorer ruled it a sacrifice.

But that official scorer, E. V. Parrish—a sportswriter for the *St. Louis Republic*—did not give Lajoie a hit on the play. He ruled an error on Wallace.

If that seems reasonable enough, well, it wasn't for the St. Louis Browns. Within minutes, Browns coach and scout Harry Howell raced up to the press box to ask how the play was scored.

"A sacrifice hit and an error," Parrish said.

"Can't you stretch it a point and make it a hit?" Howell asked.

"I can. But I won't."

Howell argued for a couple of moments, then left. A few minutes later, a Browns batboy came up to the press box and asked to speak to Parrish privately. When Parrish refused, the boy handed him a note written in pencil.

It read: "Mr. Parrish—If you can see where Mr. Lajoie gets a B.H. [base hit] instead of a sacrifice I will give you an order for a $40 suit of clothes—sure. Answer by boy. In behalf of—I ask it of you."

The note was sent by Howell. And I'm sorry, I don't care how much Rowdy Jack and the Browns hated Cobb or how much they loved Lajoie, you can't tell me that they would go to this sort of effort without some real money on the line.

Lajoie came up three more times, Corriden played left field for all three, and Lajoie bunted for singles each time. We now know that raised his batting average to .384 and gave him the batting title. But nobody knew that then. Nobody knew anything then; it was all confusion and darkness. Lajoie still thought he needed that extra hit.

How badly did he want it? After the game, Parrish got a call at home. He picked up and recounted this conversation:

"You don't know who this is."

"I do not," Parrish replied.

"This is Mr. Lajoie."

"Who?"

"Mr. Lajoie. I understand that you are having some trouble regarding my hits in today's games."

"No. No trouble."

"Don't you think I should have had nine hits in nine times at bat?"

"If I had thought so, I would have scored it as such."

Lajoie then asked Parrish to meet him at the hotel, where they could discuss the matter face-to-face. Parrish refused. The conversation ended abruptly there.

"Never before in the history of baseball," the *Washington Post* wrote, "has the integrity of the game been questioned as it was by the 8,000 fans this afternoon."

"In 'Fixed' Game, Browns Loaf and Let Larry Win," the *St. Louis Star-Times* wrote, along with a photo of Lajoie under the caption "HE WON (?) THE AUTOMOBILE—HA HA!"

"Some things that happened looked funny," umpire Billy Evans said.

"Race tracks were closed for less than this," H. W. Lanigan wrote.

There wasn't much for Lajoie and O'Connor to do in the immediate aftermath except feign shock that anyone would question their efforts. "He fooled us," O'Connor insisted, and Lajoie confirmed his strategic brilliance.

"The talk about my not earning those eight hits in St. Louis, though, makes me tired," Lajoie wearily told writers. "The first time up I smashed one to the outfield that went over Northen's head, yet some say he misjudged it. Then I hit one that Wallace was lucky to knock down. If that wasn't a hit, there never was one. Then we get down to those six bunts I beat out. Suppose Corriden did play fairly well back. If he had played in for a bunt and I had swung hard on the ball, I suppose the youngster would have been roasted to a turn because he did not play deep."

Yeah. Well, for one thing, it was actually seven bunt hits, not six, and the one Wallace was "lucky to knock down" was barely moving, and it was well known that Lajoie couldn't run, so there was no reason to play in on a bunt and . . . well, his explanation, like most explanations of the kind, was just kind of pathetic.

Ban Johnson found himself in a bad spot. On the one hand, he had to investigate this mess. On the other, he did not exactly want to uncover anything that would make Larry look bad—Lajoie *was* the American League; he practically founded the whole thing by leaving the National League and coming over in the first place.

So, he did what sports commissioners have done ever since: He investigated his own way. He brought in O'Connor and Corriden and Howell for questioning. Days later, O'Connor and Howell were fired and banished from the American League. (Rowdy Jack did reappear in the Federal League.) Corriden was forgiven because he was just a rookie following orders.

And Lajoie was left alone entirely.

But there was still a batting race to decide and a car to give out. The papers had more or less settled on Lajoie winning the car mathematically—.387 to .383 was the general consensus—but they all knew it was illegitimate. Some suggested that Johnson just forget all about the numbers and simply award Cobb the batting crown.

Johnson had a better idea: If the numbers didn't work, he would simply change the numbers. On October 16, the same day that Rowdy Jack and Howell were made to disappear, Johnson announced the final numbers.

And the winner was—Ty Cobb! What a lucky break!

Cobb, Johnson announced, had 196 hits in 509 at-bats for a .384944 batting average.

Meanwhile, Lajoie had 227 hits in 591 at-bats for a .384084 batting average.

Cobb had won by 0.000860 points!

"I am simply delighted, delighted, delighted," Cobb told reporters.

"The Cobb-Lajoie affair is a closed matter," Johnson said.

And while everybody smelled a rat, well, in those days, long before Baseball-Reference and FanGraphs, nobody fully understood what had just happened. For one thing, even if the numbers were legit, Ban Johnson's long division was terrible.

Cobb's average should have been .385068.

And Lajoie's should have been .384095.

But basic math aside, the numbers were not kosher. Johnson, in cahoots with his statistician Bob McRoy, had gone through the schedule and magically "discovered" that Cobb had not been credited for the two hits he got in the second game of a September 24 doubleheader. It was a statistical oversight, they said, and with those two hits, Cobb's average jumped up to .385.

But as Pete Palmer and Leonard Gettelson would discover some 60 years later, those hits in fact *had* been entered into the record already. Johnson double-counted them to give Cobb the batting title. It was a sham meant to nullify a sham. It was baseball's most notorious statistical makeup call.

Looking back, you can understand Johnson's predicament. He didn't want to investigate Lajoie, who was probably in on the fix. He didn't want to try to figure out what role gamblers might have played in this mess. But he also didn't want to give Lajoie the batting title. Adding two hits to Cobb's record seemed the cleanest and easiest way out.

The trouble is that by changing the numbers, he changed baseball. Many, many years later, when Pete Rose was chasing Ty Cobb's hit record, he was chasing the once sacred number of 4,191. But, in fact, Cobb's hit total was two less than that, 4,189. Palmer tried to get Commissioner Bowie Kuhn to change the record *before* Pete Rose broke that record, but as usual, Kuhn erred on the wrong side of history and refused to do anything about it. Pete Rose "officially" broke the hit record on September 11, 1985, when he lined his 4,192nd hit off Eric Show at Riverfront Stadium.

Rose *actually* broke the hit record three days earlier at Wrigley Field, with a first-inning line drive to left against Reggie Patterson in a game that ended in a 5–5 tie because of darkness.

Well, it just goes to show that baseball numbers are so much more ephemeral than we would like to believe. A hit called an error . . . an error called a hit . . . a bunt that rolls just foul . . . a fly ball that clashes against a bright sun . . . it's all what we make of it. Cobb got the batting title. Now, we know, Lajoie had the higher average.

Chalmers gave them both a car.

No. 38 **Carl Yastrzemski**

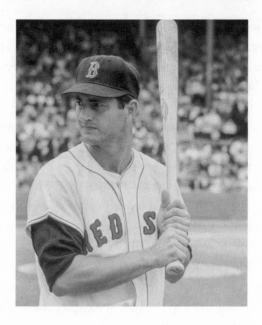

I n the Hall of Fame voting of 2020, one person decided not to vote Derek Jeter into the Hall of Fame. That person, one of 397 voters, remains anonymous, and I expect he or she will continue to stay silent because there's a mob of angry people who are ready to pounce on social media if they ever find out who the heck didn't vote for Jeter.

Does that nonvote really matter? No. Jeter's plaque will look just like all the other plaques in the Hall of Fame. There is no gold star affixed or special privilege for being elected unanimously. Frankly, it might even be a little embarrassing to be elected unanimously when you are surrounded by immortals like Henry Aaron and Willie Mays and Johnny Bench, who were not.

So why does anybody care about Jeter's meaningless one nonvote?

Part of baseball is getting bothered about stuff that doesn't really matter.

One of those things happened in 1967. It doesn't matter at all. And yet, 50-plus years later, it is still pretty enraging. It involves today's hero, Carl Yastrzemski.

Karol Yastrzemski (later changed to Carl, but we will refer to him as Karol to avoid confusion between father and son) was a potato farmer by day and a baseball dreamer the rest of the time. Karol had been a talented ballplayer as a young man—the Dodgers and Cardinals made tentative offers—but there was a depression going on, and it was not the right time to take chances. Karol worked in the fields and told himself there would be time for baseball later. Then he hurt his shoulder, and his baseball dream ended there.

"He never told me," his son Carl would write, "but I always sensed that he determined that the hard times, the chance that slipped away, the difficult farm life, none of that would happen to me."

When Carl was 18 months old, Karol gave him a plastic baseball bat, and according to family legend, the boy and the bat were inseparable after that. Father and son played countless imaginary games between the Yankees and the Red Sox—Carl's two favorite teams—and Karol would always pitch. Carl would bat right-handed or left-handed depending on which batter he was pretending to be.

And when father and son weren't playing ball—mainly during winter—Carl would be in the garage swinging a lead bat at a baseball hanging from a string over and over again until his shoulders hurt so much that he couldn't even lift the bat. There, he would throw the ball against the wall to develop his arm strength. There, he would do push-ups, pull-ups, speed drills; he jumped rope; he created weight-training devices with pulleys and wires and whatever else he could find around the garage.

If that story sounds familiar . . . it should. It's the story of Larry and Chipper Jones. It's the story of Mutt and Mickey Mantle. It's the story of Bill and Bob Feller. It's the story of Ed and Warren Spahn. Each father-son baseball story has a different pitch, a different tone; some are sweet, some are difficult, some are destructive. Like all of them, Karol and Carl had a dream.

The dream was to sign the biggest contract ever given to an amateur player.

Where did an ultra-specific dream like that come from? Answer: Paul Pettit. You will ask: *Who in the heck is Paul Pettit?* It's a good question. He's all but unknown now, but his story is one of the craziest in baseball history. Pettit was a left-handed pitching phenom in California. In high school, they called him the Wizard of Whiff, and he threw six no-hitters, three of them in a row at one point. He struck out so many hitters in his amateur career that nobody seemed able to keep count—one paper said he struck out 945 in fewer than 450 innings—and he definitely had one 12-inning game in which he struck out 27.

"He's the Bob Feller type," Branch Rickey swooned.

OK, so Pettit was a big prospect. But that wasn't why the young Yaz cared. No, now we have to introduce another obscure name: Frederick Stephani. Who? Stephani was a German-born screenwriter and director who had a brief moment of fame in the mid-1930s when he wrote and directed a 13-part serial based on the comic strip *Flash Gordon*, starring Olympic swimming champion Buster Crabbe. It was terrible; even for the time, its special effects were laughable.

But Stephani stayed in the entertainment business. He wrote and directed such film classics as *Two Grooms for a Bride*. He also directed four episodes of the television series *My Friend Flicka*.

And Stephani had his own dream: He wanted to tell the Great American Sports Story. Unfortunately, he didn't have much money or backing, so the stories of actual baseball legends like Stan Musial or Ted Williams or Joe DiMaggio were out of his price range. Then he had a revelation: What if, instead of telling the story of an established baseball legend, he simply found a *future* legend before anyone else? Simple!

In 1949, he found his future legend: Paul Pettit, the Wizard of Whiff. He signed Pettit to an $85,000 personal services contract even though Pettit had, in his own words, "never even appeared in a high school play." Stephani also included a free honeymoon to Hawaii, should he choose to marry his high school sweetheart, Shirley. (He did!)

Three months later, the Pittsburgh Pirates wanted to sign Pettit to, you know, actually play baseball. To do that, they had to first negotiate with Stephani. The Pirates bought out his $85,000 contract and then, on top, gave Pettit and his family another $15,000. This made Pettit the first amateur player ever to sign for $100,000.

Pettit's baseball career didn't pan out. Three weeks into his pro career, he hurt his elbow. Adjusting to the elbow injury, he hurt his shoulder. With the shoulder injury, he lost his windup and delivery and fastball. But he did make it into 12 big league games for the Pirates. He gave up 28 runs in 30 innings and went back to California, where he became a teacher and a coach. His story does end happily: He coached and taught for 30 years, was married to Shirley for 65 years, and, even now, still gets occasional fan letters.

The impact Paul Pettit's signing made on the Yastrzemski family was seismic. Once Carl saw a kid not much older than him signing to play baseball for $100,000, he knew his destiny.

"I had this feeling," he would later write, "this drive, that I would become the highest-paid bonus player ever."

Young Yaz was an extraordinary athlete. He was, like his future Red Sox teammate Carlton Fisk, a great high school basketball player. You will sometimes see it written that Yastrzemski set the Long Island high school scoring record, breaking the mark of another fair athlete named Jim Brown. I'm not sure he did break that record—Brown averaged 38 points a game, and in newspaper accounts, Yaz's scoring did not seem quite that high. But the larger point remains. He was an amazing high school basketball player.

First and foremost, though, he was a baseball phenom. Every team in baseball wanted him. New York brought him to Yankee Stadium for a tryout, and the second he put on the pinstriped uniform, it felt right. He took about 10 swings in batting practice and knocked four of the balls into the right-field seats. That was all the Yankees needed to see; he was promptly sent up to the office of farm director Lee MacPhail.

"Carl," MacPhail said, "would you like to play for the Yankees?"

"I sure would."

"We think you can make it," MacPhail said, and then he turned to Karol and said, "We'll give him $40,000 to sign."

The Yastrzemskis did not have a lot of money. As Carl would later say in his autobiography, $40,000—about $350,000 in today's money—was more cash than he or his father could fathom. It was the largest bonus the Yankees had ever offered a high school player.

But . . . Paul Pettit.

"It's not enough," Karol said.

Lee MacPhail almost fell out of his chair. He asked Karol to think about it and a few days later sent a scout whom the family knew, Ray Garland, to up the offer to $45,000. The elder Yaz took the offer sheet, pulled out a pencil, and crossed out the number. He wrote a new figure in its place and slid it back over.

He had written $100,000, the same amount Pettit had signed for.

"The Yankees never offered that kind of money to anybody," Garland yelped.

"That's what it will take," Yaz Sr. said.

That was the end of the Yankees' pursuit. Carl wasn't too happy about it—he wanted to play for the Yankees—but the Yastrzemskis had made a deal with themselves after seeing Pettit's signing bonus: It was $100,000 or bust. Carl decided to delay signing with a team and instead went to play baseball and basketball at Notre Dame, which was another dream of his father and the family's priest and confidant, Father Joe Ratkowski.

But Yastrzemski never would play varsity sports at Notre Dame. He was too much in demand, and after a year the offers started getting larger. The Phillies tried first. They offered $60,000, which Karol brushed off as if it was nothing. Then Phillies owner Bob Carpenter personally got involved and raised the offer to $80,000, explaining that, after tax considerations, that was actually as much real money as if they offered $100,000.

"What do you think, Mr. Yastrzemski?" Carpenter said.

"I think," Karol said, "we want $100,000 and the rest of his tuition."

Well, the Phillies agreed. That's how good Carl was. They offered $102,000 and tuition and were ready to make the announcement to the newspaper when Karol made one final request: He wanted Philadelphia to pay an extra $10,000 if Carl, for any reason, decided to quit college. The way Karol figured it, the Phillies were planning on paying that money for school anyway. So if Carl had to drop out because baseball was too overwhelming, shouldn't the Phillies *give him* the money instead?

"Why would we pay $10,000 to Carl for dropping out of college?" Carpenter asked.

That was the end of the Phillies.

The Cincinnati Reds came next, and they were not fooling around: They walked in the door with a $100,000 offer (to be paid in five $20,000 payments) plus tuition plus a $10,000 check for Carl if for some reason he decided to quit school.

Karol took the offer sheet, smiled, crossed out the big number, and wrote a new one: $150,000.

It was outrageous. Why had the price gone up so high? The Reds scrambled and came up with $125,000. But it wasn't enough.

Detroit tried, too. They pushed their offer past $125,000. But they too fell short of $150,000—and neither Yastrzemski was too excited about Carl playing in Detroit. And the Tigers were out.

Finally, it was the Red Sox's turn. And right away, Carl could tell that his father was softening. The Red Sox were Ted Williams's team! The Yastrzemskis stayed at a hotel around the corner from Fenway Park, and right away they felt like this was the place. When Boston offered $100,000 and tuition, Karol asked for $125,000, but his son knew this time they would sign.

And they did, for $115,000—the largest bonus ever given to an amateur player. They had outdone Paul Pettit.

Not everyone was impressed, however.

"The Boston Red Sox paid freshman shortstop Carl Yastrzemski of Notre Dame a $100,000 bonus to sign," wrote Wilton Garrison in the *Charlotte Observer*. "Odds are 100-to-1 he will never make the majors. And they still wonder what's wrong with baseball!"

One more little story about Yaz and money: Years later, the legendary former speaker of the house Tip O'Neill revealed that Yastrzemski had once shown some interest in politics. O'Neill said he would heartily endorse Yaz, who then asked how much, say, the lieutenant governor of Massachusetts makes. O'Neill told him it was $12,500 per year.

"And that," O'Neill said, "was the end of his political ambitions."

The newspapers, for some reason, called him Paul Yastrzemski when he first joined the Carolina League. But they soon got to know Carl. He hit .377 with power and speed for Raleigh. He had every intention of making the Red Sox the very next year, and he brought his dad with him to spring training to help him get ready.

Yastrzemski played well that spring, but he would have to wait another year to get to the big leagues. The reason? Ted Williams was playing one more season. "Don't ever let anybody monkey with your swing," Williams famously told Yaz that spring, then the great man returned to his place in left field one more time. He hit .316 with 29 homers, one of them in his last plate appearance.

All the while, Yastrzemski was learning how to play left field in Minneapolis. He had been a second baseman and a shortstop before. But he took to left field easily. Yaz hit .339 and prepared himself to step into the shadow of the Green Monster and Ted Williams.

There's something poetic about Williams and DiMaggio—the two great slugging heroes of the 1940s—being replaced immediately by extraordinary players.

DiMaggio played center field for the last time in 1951, and Mantle played center field in 1952.

Williams played left field for the last time in 1960, and Yastrzemski played left field in 1961.

Mantle and Yaz would become icons themselves, of course. In his own way, Yastrzemski became as much of a Boston icon as Williams, even if he did it in a different way. Williams was a turbulent artist, a mercurial genius at the plate who hit .400 and warred with sportswriters and pulled balls through defensive shifts designed just for him and once spat at fans.

Yastrzemski? "He's a dull, boring potato farmer," his teammate Bill Lee said, "who just happened to be a great ballplayer."

Paradoxically, it was Yaz's lack of flash that made him so captivating. He lived baseball. He was first to the park. He left the park reluctantly. He did not show it (or much of anything), but he was every bit the perfectionist Williams was at the plate. "If he went 0-for-4, he couldn't live with it," his teammate Joe Lahoud said. "He could live with himself if he went 1-for-3. He was happy if he went 2-for-4. That's the way the man suffered."

Yaz kept going and going for as long as his body would let him. He endured. He, not Williams, was the first Red Sox player to get 3,000 hits. He still has the team record in hits (3,419), extra-base hits (1,157), doubles (646), runs (1,816), and RBIs (1,844). Yaz was not particularly fast but even so, since the end of the Deadball Era, the only Red Sox player to steal more bases than Yaz is Jacoby Ellsbury.

Yaz's 3,308 games are not only the most for any Red Sox player but also the most for any American Leaguer and more than any National League player with the exception of Pete Rose.

Yastrzemski played in 18 All-Star Games and won seven Gold Gloves and three batting titles, and he did it all modestly, quietly, the way heroes do.

And because he was around for so long—a Boston institution, the sportswriters often called him—it's easy to miss just how good he was at his best. Yaz had three of the greatest seasons of the past 60 years, even if two of those seasons were concealed by circumstances.

In 1968, he hit .301 with 23 homers, 74 RBIs, and 90 runs. That looks like a perfectly fine year, not very different from a thousand others. But it was, in fact, a breathtaking one because that was the Year of the Pitcher.

His .301 average led the league, he walked 119 times, he played unmatched outfield defense, and he posted a 10.5 WAR, the second-highest total of the decade behind his own 1967 season.

Few have ever fully appreciated how good he was that season. He finished ninth in the MVP.

In 1970, the story was similar. He hit .329 with 40 homers and 102 RBIs, which looked good but not otherworldly. But that .329 average was a virtual tie with batting champion Alex Johnson, and Yaz's 40 homers were behind only Frank Howard and Harmon Killebrew; his 102 RBIs ranked him seventh. That got him fourth in the MVP voting, which isn't bad. But throw in that he led the league in runs, on-base percentage, slugging percentage, and total bases. His 9.5 WAR was the best in baseball and the second-best total of the decade.

His other legendary season—1967—well, nobody missed that one. It might be the most extraordinary year in baseball history.

Get ready for the infuriating part of the story.

The Boston Red Sox were terrible in 1966, terrible in 1965, terrible in 1964. There was no reason to believe they would be anything other than terrible in 1967, too.

They weren't terrible, but for the first half of the season they weren't especially good, either. They hovered around .500 and after losing to Baltimore 10–0 in the second game of a doubleheader on July 13, they were in fifth place.

Then Carl Yastrzemski got hot—not a normal sort of hot streak but something almost unprecedented. Over the next 10 games, he hit .371 with five home runs. The Red Sox won all 10 games and were, like that, a half game out of first place.

Boston plodded around for a month or so and fell back into fourth place. Then came Yaz again. Over the seven games, he hit .360 with three homers, nine RBIs, and nine runs scored. The Red Sox won all seven games and were tied for the American League lead.

This was how 1967 went. Yaz almost single-handedly carried the Boston Red Sox toward their impossible dream. There is only so much one player can do in baseball. In 1920, when Babe Ruth out-homered every other team in the American League, the Yankees finished third. In 1924, when Rogers Hornsby hit .424 and led the league in everything, the Cardinals finished 65-89. In 1991, when Cal Ripken had his greatest season and one of the greatest shortstop seasons ever, the Orioles finished 67-95.

But in 1967, Yaz made the Red Sox win. And he did it by being superhuman at exactly the right times.

On Sunday, September 17, the Red Sox lost their third game in a row. They fell back into a third-place tie with Minnesota, a game behind Detroit and Chicago. This set up one of the wildest finishes in baseball history, a four-team scramble for a pennant.

And who made the difference? You know it: Yaz. From September 18 to October 1, Boston played 12 games. In those games, Yastrzemski hit .523 with five homers, 14 runs, and 16 RBIs.

And the Impossible Dream Red Sox won the pennant.

Overall, in the 29 pivotal games of 1967, Yastrzemski hit .433 with 13 homers, 32 runs, and 36 RBIs and the Red Sox won 25 of them. He kept it going in the postseason—he hit .400 with three homers in the World Series—and Boston was able to push a superior Cardinals team to a seventh game before falling to the indomitable spirit of Bob Gibson.

Yaz's 1967 season was incredible in every way. He won the Triple Crown. His 12.5 WAR is the highest for any position player not named Ruth. And most of all, he played his best precisely when the Red Sox needed it most; this was the stuff of sorcery. Yastrzemski wasn't just the MVP of 1967. If you were picking an all-time MVP, you'd probably pick Yaz in '67.

And yet, of the 20 votes cast for the MVP that season, Yaz got only 19.

Which means, of course, that one person did not vote for Carl Yastrzemski.

It doesn't matter. Of course it doesn't matter. It's just like the Jeter nonvote—when you see the list of MVPs, there's no special treatment for those elected unanimously. But still it lingers, it irritates; how could someone *not* vote Yaz as MVP in 1967? What happened?

I'm not sure you want to know.

That man voted instead for César Tovar, a utility man for Minnesota who hit .267/.325/.365.

OK, the rage you're feeling now, people felt it then, too.

"Ridiculous and irresponsible!" grumped the *Boston Traveler*'s Bill Liston. "A first-place ballot for Harmon Killebrew could have been justified.

If the voter wanted to render under Cesar the things which were his, he should have given him a banjo as befitting a .267 hitter."*

"The vote for Tovar was parochial and pathetic," wrote Joe Trimble of the New York *Daily News*.

"One member of the Twins, who received MVP support himself, commented on Tovar's first-place vote," wrote the *Chicago Tribune's* Richard Dozer. "He told me, 'I couldn't believe it.'"

"If Cesar Tovar is deserving of one Most Valuable Player vote over Carl Yastrzemski," wrote Bud Tucker of the *San Gabriel Valley Tribune*, "my name is Isador Plotnik, and I drive a cab in Brooklyn."

The *Sporting News* actually wanted the voter punished: "We believe that the BBWAA, within its ranks, should take some action to penalize the writer for his unwise vote by banning him from ever serving again on a selection committee. The vote for Tovar was a black eye for the BBWAA."

Things got so heated that the *St. Paul Pioneer's* Arno Goethel—one of the two Minnesota-area voters to get an MVP vote—went public to say it was *not* him. "My vote," he said, "went Yaz first, Killebrew second and Tovar sixth."

That meant the offending vote belonged to the other Minnesota writer, Max Nichols of the *Minneapolis Star*. But here's the thing: To Nichols's credit, he didn't hide. Detroit's Joe Falls called Nichols to see if he would go on the record about his vote. And Nichols did. Not only that, but he didn't back down or say it was an honest mistake.

"From what I saw, Tovar was the most valuable player in the league," he said. "He played six positions for the Twins, and I saw him win games for them at all six positions. . . . We didn't have the best of player relations on our club, but Tovar never got mixed up in any of the clubhouse politics. He kept plugging away no matter where they put him.

"I go by what I see, not by what I read in the papers or what somebody tells me. . . . I don't know why it had to be unanimous. If that's democracy—that I had to vote the same way everyone else voted—then we're living in two different democracies."

Falls had called to lambaste Nichols, but he found himself gaining respect for the guy because he stood his ground. Sure, Falls thought the pick

---

* Light hitters were called "banjo hitters" in those days. Sometimes you will still hear the expression, but not nearly enough.

was outrageous. "But at the same time," he wrote, "I respect his right to vote for whoever he chooses."

And can't we all learn a lesson from that? Can't we all just accept that different opinions are not bad, that baseball would be a pretty boring game if we all just agreed on everything about it, that the world works better when it has people who think differently than the rest?

Yes. Well, OK, but there is one problem.

See, Max Nichols quit the Twins beat at the end of August 1967. He went to work on the city desk and didn't see a single baseball game after that. So, um, yeah, he voted for César Tovar as MVP in a year in which he didn't see Yastrzemski play in September, didn't see Yastrzemski play during one of the greatest stretch runs in baseball history.

"I guess I didn't see Yaz in his best games against the Twins," he conceded.

Could you even imagine what Nichols's Twitter feed would look like now?

No. 37 **Pedro Martínez**

P edro Martínez still remembers—he will always remember—just standing there, on a dirt path, under an open window at Campo Las Palmas. He could hear Los Angeles Dodgers scouts and coaches clearly talking about him. Martínez was 16 years old then, and he had just finished his Dodgers tryout, and he felt great about it. He always felt great about his pitching. At that exact moment, Martínez was entirely certain that he was destined to become one of the greatest pitchers in all of baseball. No other possibility had ever occurred to him.

Only, through the open window, he heard otherwise.

"He is not going to develop," one of the voices said.

"Was he anything special?" asked another.

"To be honest, there's nothing I like so much."

Martínez stared at the window, and he felt an emotion that he had never experienced before. "I started to feel the ground beneath me giving way," he wrote in his autobiography. It was not just rejection. It was not just sadness. It was an earth-shaking shock, like walking outside one day and seeing fish floating all around you. He simply could not make sense of what they were saying; his entire reality, his understanding of the world, his entire sense of self was being rocked.

At that age, he knew only three things for sure.

1. He knew the Dodgers were going to sign him.

2. He knew that he was going to America.

3. He knew that he was going to become one of the greatest pitchers in all of baseball.

It wasn't a question of faith. It wasn't about dreams. No, it was knowledge, like two-plus-two-equals-four knowledge, like the knowledge that the sun comes up each day. And yet the more the men on the other side of the window spoke—he's too small, he's too thin, he doesn't project, he's not like his brother—the more confused Martínez felt. How are you supposed to feel when everything you know turns out to be a lie?

And with the lie came questions: What if the Dodgers didn't sign him? What if he was not destined to be one of the great pitchers in all of baseball? What would he be then?

"It felt," he wrote, "like a machete took another hack at the branch I was standing on. I could hear the frightening, splintering sound as the branch began to give way under my scrawny legs and sent me tumbling down into a black void so deep I couldn't fathom where I'd land."

Then came salvation in the form of a new voice. Eleodoro Arias had once been a pitcher for the Dominican national team. He later became the winning manager of the team. He was a voice of power in his country, particularly when he talked about pitching. He understood pitching in ways that simply eluded others.

Everyone quieted to hear what Arias had to say.

"*Tiene el corazón de un león,*" he said.

He's got the heart of a lion.

And that is how the legend of Pedro Martínez began.

There is a marvelous evolution of pitchers who came from the Dominican Republic. We might call it: the Road to Pedro. The road begins—if such roads can be said to have a beginning—with a glorious pitcher named Bombo Ramos. Ramos was an electrifying and charismatic right-handed pitcher in the 1940s; he was basically the country's Satchel Paige, to the point where he, like Satch, would actually name his pitches. His best pitch he called "La Diabla," which translates to "She Devil."

Ramos died tragically at age 25 in the "Tragedy of Rio Verde" plane crash in 1948, which killed 32 players on the Santiago team.

Juan Marichal saw Ramos pitch. Marichal was just 10 years old but his life changed; he knew from that moment on that he was destined to become a great pitcher himself. He enthusiastically copied Ramos's side-armed pitching motion and threw hard enough that he was signed by the Giants. When he got to the minor leagues, a manager named Andy Gilbert saw him pitch and worried that his motion was too violent. There was no way he could stay healthy throwing the ball that way.

"Do you want to learn how to throw overhand?" Gilbert asked. Marichal nodded. They worked together and, curiously, Marichal found that when throwing overhand, he felt most comfortable if he kicked his front leg high to the sky. That became his trademark. And he pitched his way to the Hall of Fame.

Joaquín Andújar idolized Marichal and wanted to become a pitcher in the major leagues, too. He could not do that high kick the way Marichal could, so instead, he came at hitters with attitude and fury and a million different pitching angles—over the top, three-quarters, side-arm. Andújar was a whirlwind, a tornado. He got to the major leagues just as Marichal was departing, and he made four All-Star teams and led the league in wins one year. He was fantastic in the 1982 World Series. He struck out more than 1,000 hitters, and after many of those whiffs, he would point at the hitter and fire, as if his index finger and thumb were a Derringer. Yes, Andújar was, as he often said, "One Tough Dominican."

Shortly after Andújar came Mario Soto. He was about the same size as Marichal and Andújar, but he too had his own unique style. He developed a bewildering swing-and-miss circle changeup that left hitters baffled. Soto twice led the National League in strikeouts per nine innings—in fact, his 9.6 strikeouts per nine innings in 1982 was, at the time, the most for any National League pitcher not named Sandy Koufax or J. R. Richard.

Then there was José Rijo. The Yankees signed him at 15. He was too young to see Marichal pitch at his best (though he would marry Marichal's daughter, Rosie) but he resembled the great man in many ways. He was a complete pitcher—fastball, slider, splitter, changeup—and from 1988 to 1994 (after a sluggish start to his career) he was about as good as anybody in the game. He went 87-53 with a 2.63 ERA over those seven years, and in 1990, he led the Cincinnati Reds to the World Series and then went 2-0 with a 0.59 ERA against Oakland. He was named World Series MVP.

Finally: Ramón Martínez. He was different from the rest in that he was much taller (6-foot-4) and he was a pure power pitcher. He grew up idolizing Soto, the strikeout king, and Ramón was a strikeout pitcher himself. In his first full season, 1990, he went 20-6 with a 2.92 ERA and led the league in complete games. He also struck out 223, including 18 in one shutout against Atlanta. He finished second in the Cy Young voting to Doug Drabek, coming as close as any Dominican pitcher ever had to winning the award (his hero, Soto, had also finished second one year).

"He throws fastballs," Dodgers manager Tommy Lasorda said when asked what he liked about Martínez. "No tricks. No funny stuff. He throws fastballs like the great ones did."

Finally, the road leads to the greatest of them all, one of the greatest who ever lived: Ramón's little brother Pedro. Their father, Paolino Martínez, might have been part of that road, too, had circumstances been different. Paolino was a superb pitcher; he reputedly had a nasty sinker. He was invited to join his friends Matty and Felipe Alou at a Giants tryout. They went and signed. He did not go. It is probably because he could not afford the cleats and was too embarrassed to go without them.

All of the pitchers had so much in common. They all grew up poor, grew up playing baseball with some variation on tree branches as bats and rolled-up socks as balls. Pedro found that the best baseballs of all were the heads of his sister's dolls. He grew up like Marichal and Soto and Rijo had, poor, hungry, exhausted from work, listening to the rain crash against their zinc roofs. Curtains separated the rooms in the Martínezes' dirt-floor house in Manoguayabo.

But while Marichal and Andújar and Soto had to imagine what a baseball life might look like, Pedro knew. The extraordinary part was the confidence. Pedro will say that all through his childhood, he never shut up. And much of the time he talked about what life would be like when he was a great pitcher. He was so sure. The way he saw it, he was all of the great Dominicans rolled together—he had Marichal's majesty and Andújar's rage and Soto's changeup and Rijo's resourcefulness. . . .

And he had his brother, Ramón, to guide him.

How could he miss?

Pedro Martínez raced through the minor leagues—but not fast enough for his own taste. He almost quit when he didn't make the club out of spring training in 1993, he was so angry. But his brother settled him down, and the Dodgers brought him up after three days when Todd Worrell blew out his arm.*

Martínez pitched in relief in 1993, and he was pretty spectacular. He struck out 119 batters in 107 innings and allowed the league to hit just .201 and slug just .283 against him. Dodgers executive Fred Claire was so awed by young Martínez's arm and presence that he told everyone to stop even asking him about the trade rumors.

"I won't trade Pedro Martínez," he told a reporter from the *Ocala Star-Banner*. "I don't care who they offer."

Claire then traded Martínez to Montreal for Delino DeShields.

What the heck happened? What makes teams trade away once-in-a-lifetime stars like Martínez? For the Dodgers, it came down to a couple of things. One, they really wanted a second baseman. They had made an offer during the season to their regular second baseman, Jody Reed, but they couldn't reach an agreement (it didn't go well for Reed, either, who became a free agent and signed for a huge pay cut with Milwaukee).

"If he had said 'yes' to our offer," Claire said of Reed, "we would not have traded for a second baseman."

To be as fair as possible, DeShields had been pretty good for Montreal in 1993—he hit .295 with 72 walks, he stole 43 bases, he was an above-average defender. No, he would never be that good with the Dodgers, but Claire didn't know that at the time of the trade.

But the bigger problem was this: They totally whiffed on Martínez. They had seen the arm. They had seen the confidence. They had seen the

---

* There's a story about this; Martínez had been so good in spring training in 1993, he couldn't believe it when the Dodgers sent him down. It was not unlike hearing those scouts bash him when he was standing under that window in the Dominican Republic. He was standing by the bus and he was close to tears when suddenly Dodgers star pitcher Orel Hershiser came off the bus. He handed Martínez a baseball and went back on. On the ball, it said: "You're a true big leaguer. I'll see you soon. Orel."

feistiness—which, yes, sometimes seemed over-the-top. They knew what Martínez was about . . . and they somehow could not see that he was about to become one of the greatest starting pitchers in baseball history. How did they miss it?

Well, it seems, they simply let a bunch of old scouting methods impact their thinking. Scouts thought he was too small—not even six feet tall! Scouts thought he was too slight—he would probably end up in the bullpen! Scouts thought he was too volatile a personality—he might implode! Scouts thought his delivery was too violent—an injury hazard!

There are always reasons to doubt. It's always safer to doubt.

But then you trade Martínez for DeShields, and it wrecks your franchise for a generation. That's not an exaggeration. From 1994 to 2003, the Dodgers were often good but never good enough. They twice made the playoffs but didn't win a single playoff game. They brought in an international field of talented young pitchers—Hideo Nomo (Japan), Chan Ho Park (South Korea), Ismael Valdéz (Mexico), Pedro Astacio (Dominican Republic), Darren Dreifort (Kansas), and, of course, Ramón—but never found their ace.

Martínez became the greatest pitcher in the game.

What made Martínez *so* great? It is one of baseball's most challenging and wonderful puzzles. There are obvious pieces there. He had a good fastball, a great changeup and brilliant control, he was a ferocious competitor, etc.

But how do those pieces add up to make PEDRO MARTÍNEZ, all capital letters, as he was from 1997 to 2003? He was not of this world. In a time when hitters dominated the game, when home runs sailed, Martínez went 118-36 with a 2.20 ERA (with an unprecedented 213 ERA+) and 1,761 strikeouts against 315 walks. Hitters hit .198 against him with a .297 slugging percentage.

How good was he? Well, look at him through the FanGraphs prism—FanGraphs evaluates pitchers based on how many strikeouts, how many walks, and how many home runs they allow. By those measures, Martínez's 1999 has an argument as the greatest season ever. He struck out 313, walked 37, and allowed only nine homers all year. By FanGraphs' WAR, it's the second-greatest season of the last century behind only Steve Carlton's famous 1972 season.

Now look at him through the Baseball-Reference prism—

Baseball-Reference evaluates pitchers based on how many runs they allow, the ballpark where they play, and how good the defense is behind them. By those measures, Martínez's 2000 season has an argument as the greatest ever. That year, he had a 1.74 ERA (when the league-wide ERA was 4.92), struck out 284 in 217 innings, and walked 32, even *fewer* than he had in 1999. His ERA+ of 291 that year is the highest in modern baseball history by a long shot.

Highest ERA+ in Baseball History

1. Pedro Martínez, 2000, 291

2. Dutch Leonard, 1914, 279

3. Greg Maddux, 1994, 271

4. Greg Maddux, 1995, 260

5. Walter Johnson, 1913, 259

In the last 100 years, only four pitchers—each of whom threw many more innings—had a higher Baseball-Reference WAR than Martínez's 11.7.

So, how does a puzzle like that come together? What separated him? What took him to his own planet?

Think, if you will, of the famous story of the rice and the chessboard. There are countless versions of the legend, but the simple one is of a man who saved the king's life and, in return, wanted to marry his daughter. The king said no but offered anything else in his kingdom. The man pulled out a chessboard and said, "Then all I want is this. Give me one grain of rice for the first square on the board, then double it for every square after that."

It seemed so little to ask. The king said yes without hesitation . . . but you know how this ends. There are 64 squares on a chessboard. By the 21st square, simply by doubling, we are over a million grains of rice.

By the 30th, we have crossed a billion.

At the 39th square, the number is larger than a trillion.

By square 64, the number is 9,223,372,036,854,780,000—which is not *quite* as many stars there are estimated to be in the galaxy, but close enough. It is more rice than there is in the known universe.

And so Martínez's skills are the grains of rice that keep doubling. You start with a mid-to-high-90s fastball; that's already the core of an excellent pitcher. Now double it because of Martínez's absurd command. Now double it again because he had that time-stopping changeup. Now double it again because he could mix in a cut fastball that worked like a slider and make hitters chase doom into the dirt. Now double it again because he was an intense competitor who insisted that the inside of the plate belonged to him. Now double it again because he came at hitters with all sorts of different arm angles, leaving them to wonder where the ball would come from next.

Now double it again because nobody in baseball history—nobody at all—was more confident, more sure, more certain about his greatness than Martínez.

Now double it again because . . .

It is true that Martínez was mostly done at 33. He did not quite get to 3,000 innings for his career. The fact he won 219 games (against 100 losses) probably cost him a few Hall of Fame votes—he didn't appear on 49 ballots—even though anyone counting wins entirely missed the point of Pedro Martínez. It is true, Martínez did not have the huge numerical careers of his great contemporaries Randy Johnson, Roger Clemens, or Greg Maddux.

But at his best, he was better than they were, I think. I've said it before; if the devil ever gives me one pitcher to play for my soul, I'm taking Martínez circa 1999 and 2000. He wasn't just the greatest pitcher I ever saw. He was the one pitcher who you knew would damn well move the devil off the plate.

No. 36 **Christy Mathewson**

The Pennsylvania town called Factoryville doesn't have a factory in it . . . and never really did. There had once been a cotton mill across the Tunkhannock Creek, but the place closed almost immediately after Factoryville was founded. And after that, Factoryville—like Iceland—lived on as a direct counter to its name, a quiet and peaceful valley of trees and lakes and creeks, all but untouched by the Industrial Revolution, an idyllic *A River Runs Through It* sort of place.

Factoryville was where Christy Mathewson grew up.

You intuitively know everything you need to know about Mathewson because you intuitively know what the Great American Ballplayer represents. In Mathewson's time—not coincidentally—there was an enormously famous literary character named Frank Merriwell. In the early part of the 20th century, an author named Gilbert Patten wrote more than 300 books about Merriwell, an impossibly corny but outstanding athlete at Yale who also solved mysteries and never drank and never smoked and stood for justice.

His very name tells his story: He was called Frank for his candidness, Merry for his joy for living, and Well for his robust health and athleticism. He was the kind of character who always scored the winning touchdown, always knocked the game-winning hit, always handled everything with quiet modesty and dignity, always did the right thing.

Everyone knew that Frank Merriwell was really Christy Mathewson.

Matty was too good to be true. He grew up working on a farm surrounded by an apple orchard. He learned to pitch by throwing stones at the birds and squirrels that flew and scurried about. He was the best student at school, the best athlete on the fields, the dutiful son who did his chores without complaint, the free spirit who spent his free time fishing the creeks of Factoryville, and on Sundays, he sat upright in the front pew at church, and he took in the preacher's words with rapt attention.

Christy's mother, Minerva, thought for sure that Christy would become a preacher.

There is a broken window story that is telling—there often is with young ballplayers. Christy loved showing off his arm and one day he did so by demonstrating for some older kids that he could throw a ball clear over his house. He did this quite easily and the ball crashed through a neighbor's window.

Mathewson immediately admitted what he had done to the neighbors and his parents. He saved and saved until he had raised the money necessary to replace the window.

Mathewson grew tall and handsome. He became a college football hero and the president of the junior class at Bucknell. He played center in a brand-new sport called basketball.

But even after he went into the rough-and-tumble world of baseball, he never stopped being that deeply honest kid who admitted breaking the window. He promised his mother that he would never pitch on Sunday. And he never did. While his teammates might have chased women and liquor, Matty could be found at the local library or art museum. He was a voracious reader—the Bible, of course, every day, but he also read books on horticulture and philosophy and history. He loved the novels of Victor Hugo. (He read Les Misérables three times.)

"He was the only man I ever met who in spirit and inspiration was greater than his game," the famous sportswriter Grantland Rice said.

There is a story, perhaps apocryphal (but perhaps not), that goes like this: Once, while playing for the Giants, he slid into home on a close play. The slider stirred up such a huge dirt cloud that the umpire could not see what happened. He looked and squinted but was stumped.

"How was it, Matty?" the umpire said after a couple of seconds.

"He got me," Mathewson replied, and the umpire called him out.

"Why would you admit that?" the catcher asked later, and Mathewson replied, "I had to. I'm a church elder."

There is a broken window story worth telling about John McGraw—there often is with young ballplayers. If you know McGraw, you know the story is very different from Matty's story. McGraw's childhood was entirely different. He was called Johnny McGraw then (his father was John) and he grew up in the harsh-sounding town of Truxton, New York. Johnny was the oldest of eight children.

His father had reluctantly fought in the Civil War and never fully recovered from it. He went to work for the railroad to make ends meet, but they rarely did.

Johnny loved baseball and only baseball; the game was the one bit of sunshine in an otherwise dismal childhood of poverty and pain. Johnny scraped together every penny he could to buy a real baseball, and he was so proud of that ball he would carry it around in his pocket like it was a gold watch. He didn't want to soil that baseball, so he mostly threw stones instead. While he worked for the railroad with his father, Johnny would gather stones, put them in a pile, and practice his throwing when he could find a few spare moments.

John hated baseball; he beat Johnny regularly for wasting his time playing ball. There are a couple of different views of John McGraw, the father, that have passed down through the years. Some references say he was an alcoholic. Others, though, say he was profoundly sober. All say he was beaten down by life. He fought in a war he did not believe in. His first wife died in childbirth. He could not support his family no matter how hard he worked. Seeing his son waste his time playing ball set off a fury inside him that John McGraw could barely contain.

And then came the most devastating tragedy of all: In 1884, Johnny's mother and four of his siblings died in the town's diphtheria epidemic.

That leads to the broken window story. Johnny McGraw would not stop playing ball, and he broke many windows in his life. But the window he broke after his mother died sent John McGraw into a black rage unlike any of the others. John beat his son with such ferocity and purpose that Johnny's siblings thought he might die. When Johnny finally escaped, he

raced upstairs, packed the few things he had, left the house, and never returned.

Johnny McGraw was 12 years old.

McGraw did not grow tall or handsome like Matty. He did not become
a big man on campus or the personification of the All-American boy. No,
he became the opposite, another American sports archetype, a cigar-
smoking, pony-playing, hard-drinking whirlwind. McGraw became the
fiercest ballplayer who ever stepped on the field. He'd do anything at all to
win. As a hitter, he'd bunt, slice, chop, bloop, draw walks, get hit by pitches,
anything at all to get on base (his .466 career on-base percentage is third
behind only Ted Williams and Babe Ruth).

Later, as a manager, he'd pit his players against each other, threaten
them, fine them, intimidate them. According to Rogers Hornsby, no wall-
flower himself, McGraw used to walk up and down the dugout bench and
growl, "Wipe those damn smiles off your faces."

Would he cheat? Are you kidding? He practically *invented* baseball
cheating (along with baseball classics like the hit-and-run). You know that
phrase "Baltimore chop"? That's a ball that is chopped down in front of the
plate and bounces so high that by the time the fielder gets to it the batter is
at first base. McGraw invented it. In Baltimore, he paid the groundskeeper
to not water the dirt in front of the plate so that it grew as hard as cement
and the ball would bounce higher off of it.

He would do *anything* to win. You know how Ty Cobb sharpened his
spikes? McGraw invented that, though his most famous and effective
cheating method was covertly grabbing the belts of opponents trying to
tag up from third base so they couldn't go anywhere.

"In playing and managing, the game is only fun for me when I'm out
in front and winning," he famously said. "I don't give a hill of beans for the
rest of the game."

And no one—I mean, *no one*—could be as cruel as McGraw. He rode
players like no one else. He tore apart umpires like no one else. As one reporter wrote, "He has the vilest tongue on any ballplayer. He adopts every
low and contemptible method that his erratic brain can conceive to win a
play by a dirty trick."

Or as someone, perhaps an umpire, perhaps Giants coach Arlie
Latham, once said: "McGraw eats gunpowder every morning for breakfast
and washes it down with warm blood."

And here is where the whole thing gets strange and wonderful: John McGraw and Christy Mathewson were the best of friends. They were like a father and a son, like an older and younger brother. They helped each other become legends.

Under McGraw's watchful eye, Mathewson won 253 games with 77 shutouts—three of them in the 1905 World Series alone. He was elected to the Hall of Fame with the first class, alongside Babe Ruth and Cobb and Wagner and Walter Johnson.

With Mathewson as his star, McGraw won five pennants and a World Series title; McGraw won more after Mathewson retired, but he never won another after his dear friend died tragically at the age of 45.

They had nothing in common, the preacher and the cheat. They grew up in different worlds. They saw the world in completely different ways.

And yet they loved each other deeply and unequivocally; their friendship might be the most famous in all of baseball history.

People, you see, are complicated.

Mathewson told a fun story about how he developed the incredible screwball pitch—the "fadeaway," he called it—that marked his career. It happened the day he arrived to play for the New York Giants. He was already something of a phenomenon—in fact, it was an old pitcher called Phenomenal Smith* who had discovered him a couple of years earlier.

When Matty got to the Polo Grounds, the Giants manager—a future Hall of Fame shortstop named George Davis—insisted on personally seeing what the kid had to offer. He stepped into the batter's box, and Mathewson threw him some fastballs. Davis nodded. They had some nice heat on them.

Then Mathewson threw some curveballs. It's fair to say that Davis was less impressed; he whacked those all over the park. "Put that in cold storage," he yelled at Mathewson. "That ain't good in this company. A man with paralysis in both arms could get himself set in time to hit that one."

Mathewson was shaken. That curveball had been plenty good to get people out all his life. When Davis asked him if he threw anything else, Matty shrugged and said that he'd been working on this freak pitch but it wasn't anything he had thrown in games.

---

* Smith was called "Phenomenal" because when he was 16 or so years old, he played in a town game and struck out 16 batters and didn't allow a single ball into the outfield.

"Let's see it," Davis said. And with that, Mathewson unleashed the screwball. He held it like a curve and twisted his wrist counterclockwise so the ball would break the opposite way of a curveball.

Davis swung and missed.

"I will never forget how Davis' eyes bulged," Matty would write years later. Davis asked a bunch of left-handed-hitting Giants to face the fade-away, and none of them could hit it. That would begin the legend.

Sure, it's easy to see all the reasons why Mathewson and McGraw should have been at each other's throats. But there were connecting points, two in particular. One, they were both intensely competitive. With McGraw, this was readily apparent, but Mathewson—as much of a gentleman as he was—could be every bit as ferocious when it came to winning and losing.

When Matty was at Bucknell, for instance, his baseball team struggled. He barely managed a winning record. It's fair to say that he did not lose gracefully.

"No pitcher," he griped, "can win games when his men don't field well behind him or when they refuse to bat in any runs."

In 1902, after his first good season with the Giants, Mathewson went 14-17 despite leading the league in shutouts. That was the year the Giants hired McGraw, but before that, after losing 4–3 to Boston in July that year, Mathews went off in much the same way he had in college.

"I can't win with them behind me," he told reporters.

Even McGraw was not beyond Mathewson's fury over losing. In 1914, Matty wrote a story for something called *Everybody's* magazine. The story was titled "Why We Lost Three World's Championships" and it was about the Giants' failure in three World Series. In it, he tore apart his teammates ("With very few exceptions the men are not of championship caliber"), ripped everybody for caring only about what the press said about them ("The Giants are the greatest 'newspaper ball club' I know. Most of the men read everything that is printed about them") and, yes, he ripped his dear friend McGraw for building a team of "puppets" that would do anything and everything he said and, as such, fold in the biggest moments.

"Now the Giants that have won the last three National League championships do not stand on their own feet," Mathewson wrote. "They are McGraw. His dominant personality is everything. . . . Unlike McGraw [Philadelphia manager] Connie Mack had not been forced to build a team of puppets worked from the bench by a strike. The Athletics could stand on their own feet. Mack has long encouraged them to do that."

So, yes, Mathewson could hold his own with McGraw in that sore loser department.

The second connection, though, was bigger—they both loved thinking about baseball. They both loved talking about baseball, arguing about baseball, working up strategies about baseball (Mathewson, near the end of his life, invented a tabletop baseball game similar to Strat-o-Matic), teaching baseball, and, perhaps most of all, writing about baseball.

McGraw did not fashion himself a Shakespeare, but he was close friends with Bozeman Bulger, a popular sportswriter of the day, and together they wrote hundreds of newspaper articles and an autobiography.

Mathewson, meanwhile, well, he was a terrific writer—so good that his classic *Pitching in a Pinch* is still in print. The book was utterly beloved by the great American poet Marianne Moore. And it is a wonderful book. In it, Mathewson spins baseball tales, offers pitching advice, talks about jinxes, breaks down the pitcher-hitter battle, offers inside stories about great players like Honus Wagner (couldn't hit the spitball!), and tells a timeless story that we'll retell in full in a moment, for soon-to-be-obvious reasons.

In the summer of 1925, Mathewson grew tired and weak. A cough haunted his final days. He had not been healthy since serving overseas during World War I, where he had been exposed to mustard gas. He had managed to fight through for a while but the last years of his life were filled with pain. And then it ended, suddenly. On October 7, 1925, the same day that his onetime rival Walter Johnson beat the Pirates in Game 1 of the World Series, Mathewson died. He was 45 years old.

McGraw was stunned. He knew that his friend was in poor health but he did not think it was critical. He was not ready. "I knew Matty as a great pitcher, one of the greatest of all," he told reporters that day. "And I know him as a loyal friend. He stood out as an athlete. He stood out as a man." And then baseball's toughest warrior, the man who ate gunpowder and drank blood, broke down in tears and could not speak anymore.

There's a Mathewson story that connects closely to recent events in baseball, specifically the Houston Astros cheating scandal, where they used cameras to steal catcher's signs and then banged on garbage cans to let hitters now what was coming. This feels like a modern story, but as Mathewson wrote in *Pitching in a Pinch,* it's actually about as old as the game itself.

Mathewson writes that, at first, people warned him to never, ever throw high fastballs to one of the greatest hitters of the 19th century, Ed Delahanty. Matty tried to follow the advice, and he fed Delahanty breaking balls and off-speed pitches, which Big Ed smacked all over the ballpark.

Finally, Mathewson grew so sick of getting knocked around that he ignored the advice and tried throwing high fastballs. And you know what? Delahanty couldn't hit them. From that point on, Matty threw nothing but fastballs up, and he never had much trouble with Big Ed after that.

Because Mathewson was such an inquisitive pitcher, he wondered just how Big Ed got his reputation as a man who crushed high fastballs.

And it led to this story:

In 1899, nobody hit like the Philadelphia Phillies. They led the league in batting average, on-base percentage, runs, hits, doubles, and total bases. Their pitching wasn't good enough to make them a pennant winner, but that lineup—which starred future Hall of Famers Nap Lajoie, Elmer Flick, and Delahanty—terrorized pitchers across the National League.

You couldn't throw a high fastball by any of 'em.

Why not? It turns out there was a much less famous player, a long-time backup catcher named Morgan Murphy, who was at the heart of the matter. Murphy never played. But what he *did* do was sit in the manager's suite, a high room that overlooked the field from behind center field,* and with a pair of $75 binoculars, would zoom in on the catcher's signal. Yes, Murphy would steal the signs.

Stealing catcher signs was a common practice. A player and manager named Mike McGeary—who had the pleasure of managing the Philadelphia Whites, Providence Grays, and Cleveland Blues in his colorful career—apparently used an umbrella to let hitters know which pitch was coming. If the umbrella was up, that meant the pitch would be up.

Murphy had even more evocative ways of alerting the hitters about the upcoming pitch—these were much more elegant than, say, banging a gar-

---

* Though he was known for doing this at home, it's likely Murphy did it on the road as well when he could. In Brooklyn, he once rented a room across the street from the ballpark.

bage can. According to a story by Matt Albertson, Murphy would some-times adjust an awning in centerfield to get the word out. He sometimes waved a newspaper. My favorite: He would take a simple strip of fabric and hold it vertically for a fastball, horizontally for a curve.

But in 1899, he tried something different, something more nefarious. After stealing a sign, he would press a button. The button would set off a buzzer strapped to the leg of Phillies player and third-base coach Pearce "Petey" Chiles. After being buzzed, Chiles would—"verbally," according to newspaper reports—let the hitter know what pitch was coming.*

As long as the Philadelphia hitters knew what was coming, they feasted on high fastballs. Delahanty hit .410. Lajoie hit .378. Flick hit .342. That's how the reputation began. After a while, pitchers realized there was no point in trying to get high fastballs by them.

But then the Phillies got caught. Cincinnati's third baseman Tommy Corcoran noticed that Chiles's leg would twitch before pitches. He walked over to where Chiles was standing, pawed at the dirt with his cleat, and found a transmitter in the ground.

This created a stir. Baseball was a rough-and-tumble game in 1899 and the fans undoubtedly expected some cheating. But this was something dif-ferent. As the *Philadelphia Inquirer* put it: "The introduction of electricity as an adjunct to the presentation of the noble national sport opened up possibilities."

As you might imagine, the Phillies owner promptly admitted the whole thing, apologized to the rest of the league, and dedicated himself to promoting fair play in baseball.

Joking!

No, in fact, the team owner, Colonel John Rogers, denied everything in the most absurd and transparent way imaginable. He said that the thing Corcoran found in the ground was not a transmitter at all; instead, the box was actually a lighting switchboard that an amusement company had installed for when they needed lights for their stage show.

And the buzzer thing? Haha, no, see that was just a practical joke the team had pulled on Chiles; they had told him they were going to shock

---

* I'm not sure how he did this verbally—I am guessing they had code words—but the newspaper account made it sound like Chiles would scream out, "HEY, FASTBALL UP-STAIRS!"

him; see, it was just a big misunderstanding—and the Phillies would certainly never do anything like that.

It goes without saying that nobody bought the Colonel's explanation. The transmitter was removed, Petey Chiles moved to coach first base, and the Phillies' batting averages dropped 35 points over the next two years (though part of that was the exit of Lajoie in 1901).

"After the buzzer had been discovered and the delivery of pitchers could not be accurately forecast," Mathewson wrote, "this ability to hit high fast ones vanished."

You imagine that Mathewson, who read the Bible every day, might have seen the Astros saga and quoted Ecclesiastes 1:9.

What has been is what will be, and what has been done is what will be done; there is nothing new under the sun.

No. 35 George Brett

Through the years, I've probably written more words about George Howard Brett than any other Hall of Famer, probably any other ballplayer including Buck O'Neil, whom I wrote a book about. I've written about Brett almost hitting .400 in 1980 a half-dozen times at least. I've written repeatedly about the ways throughout his career that he rose to the occasion. I've written about the pine-tar incident so many times. I've written about his relationship with his father, about his hatred of the Yankees, and about his one baseball regret: that he didn't come back to spring training in 1994 and just try to make the club like a long-shot rookie.

I have written about George so often that at some point—quite a while ago, now that I think of it—when I would show up to interview him, he would shout in exasperation, "What do you want *now*?" Because it wasn't just the big stories. There were countless little ones, too, George talking about his brother Ken or George sharing golf tips or George predicting a better season for the Royals or George explaining hitting or George celebrating old friends or George watching me hit.

That last one was fun. I went to Royals fantasy camp one year. It was a gift from my wife, and it remains one of my favorite memories. I could tell you a hundred embarrassing stories from that week—though more likely,

I would tell you about the hit I got off Bret Saberhagen, who, in the glow of memory, was throwing 90 that day—but George was at the center of the big story.

He was coaching a different team across the field that day. Our team (Frank White was our manager) was playing Big John Mayberry's team. I came up, and Big John rode me pretty hard: "C'mon, Big Joe! Let's see it, Big Joe! Whaddya got, Big Joe!?"

And then, the most unusual thing happened: I connected. You know that feeling when you hit a baseball so well that you don't even feel the vibration in your hands? I had not experienced that feeling since I was 13 years old. But it happened that day, and it was miraculous, and the ball soared. I have no idea where it landed because I was huffing and puffing my way toward first base at the time, but when I did look up, I saw that the ball had rolled to the wall.

It should have been a triple . . . or, more to the point, I should have been the sort of person who turned it into a triple. But I was not that man, doubt I have ever been that man, and I happily jogged in for my stand-up double. From the opposing bench I heard Big John's voice again, this time with a bit of surprised respect: "Big Joe!"

I don't tell you this only to make sure that my hitting accomplishment is forever memorialized in a book, though that might be part of my motivation. In addition: News of a roly-poly sportswriter cracking a double to the wall travels quickly at fantasy camps. The next time I came up, there was a surprise visitor looking through the chain-link fence: George Brett. He had left his own field in the middle of his game just to come see me in a different way—not as a sportswriter constantly badgering him for time, not as an interviewer seeking ever-more-personal details of his relationship with his dad, and not as the columnist in the morning paper who, quite often, had no idea what he was talking about.

No, he came to see me as a *prospect.*

"Hey, I heard there is some kind of hitter over here," he said as he arrived. "Gotta check him out."

With that, I was nervous beyond words. Because in that moment, he was not George Brett, the center of a story. No, this time, he was *GEORGE BRETT*, capital letters, who cracked 3,154 hits in his career, who bashed three home runs off Catfish Hunter in a playoff game, who leaped to his feet to fight Graig Nettles, who carried the Kansas City Royals to the 1985

World Series, who came within five hits of hitting .400, who twice in big moments saw searing high fastballs from Goose Gossage and deposited them into the right-field seats.

This was the George Brett who filled my imagination as a boy. He was neither my favorite player nor did he play on my favorite team. But he was bigger than favorites, bigger than teams. In the 1970s, in the early '80s, there were those things that shaped my childhood—the fall of Skylab, Evel Knievel, Atari football, *The Love Boat* theme song, Farrah Fawcett posters, Conjunction Junction, Roger Staubach, "Up your nose with a rubber hose," Kentucky Fried Chicken, Muhammad Ali, gas lines, Fonzie, the Harlem Globetrotters. Brett was one of those. And there he was, standing there, watching me, and I was 13 again.

"Let's see it!" he shouted out.

The last pitch was a curveball six inches off the plate. That's how I saw it then, that's how I remember it, and that's how I'll tell it to my grandchildren if I ever have any. It was a curveball a foot off the plate, and even though I had two strikes on me, I pride myself on plate discipline, and I was not about to swing at a pitch two feet off the plate. I mean, who am I? Vlad Guerrero? No, I'm not swinging at a pitch three feet off the plate, no matter what the situation, even if George Brett is watching.

A curveball. Five feet off the plate. Give me a break.

"Strike three," the umpire said. And then George Brett, who had come from over two fields away just to see me hit, dropped his head and shouted out: "Really? That's why I came over here?"

And then, before jogging back to his field, he added one more thought: "Harder than it looks, ain't it?"

Fear drove George Brett. His father, Jack, made sure of that. There's a piercing scene in the movie *I, Tonya* in which Tonya Harding is trying to understand why her mother, LaVona, had been so cruel. "Did you ever love me?" Tonya asks.

"You think [skating champion] Sonja Henie's mother loved her?" LaVona asks back. "Poor $&!@# you. I didn't stay home making Apple Brown Betty. No, I made you a champion! Knowing you'd hate me for it! That's the sacrifice a mother makes."

That was the sacrifice Jack Brett made. "I wanted him to replace Mickey Mantle," Jack once said of George, and if Mantle's father, Mutt, was ruthless, Jack Brett was even more than ruthless. No, George didn't hate his father—people often got that part wrong—but by God, he feared his father. And it was fear, terror, that forged Brett in life and in baseball.

"I was scared every single day," he said.

There's a famous story about the 1980 season, when Brett almost hit .400—five hits short, as mentioned. When the season ended, George called his father like he always did and heard his father shout: "Do you mean to tell me you couldn't have gotten five more !@#$*%^ hits?"

The trouble is that the story sounds funny. You can imagine Jack Brett joking as he said it, the crusty old man finally conceding in his own way that the son he'd been pounding and humiliating for a couple of decades had finally done good. It's especially funny when comic strip punctuation marks replace the most important word.

But Jack Brett wasn't joking. He didn't actually say "!@#$*%^." No, what he said was, "You couldn't have gotten five more fucking hits?" with full emphasis on the expletive. Jack meant to tell his son that while other people might celebrate a .390 season and all that came with it, they both knew, deep down, in ways that no one else could, that George was, in the final summation, a failure. Five bleeping hits? Come on. Did he really try his best that game in Cleveland? Did he really run out the ground ball in Baltimore? Did he really have to swing at that breaking ball in Boston?

They both knew the bleeping answer. He was soft. He was lazy. He was wasting the talent that God gave him. Even as he dared to hit .400, it was the same sad song.

This had been their duet ever since George was a kid. Yes, Jack had punched George. Yes, Jack had kicked George. ("That," George remembers him saying after the kick, "is for embarrassing the family." George had struck out twice in a Little League game.) Yes, Jack had threatened George repeatedly. But while that stuff stung, that wasn't where the real pain came from.

See, it was George's older brother, Ken, who was supposed to take the family name to the stars. Ken was everything George was not—a straight-A student, captain of every team, high school quarterback, modest hero, recruited to West Point. He was the fourth pick in the 1966 draft, and he was such a good pitcher *and* hitter that the Red Sox were not even sure which way to go with him. They decided to try him as a pitcher, and he became the youngest to ever appear in a World Series game.

"Ken," said future 20-game winner Scott McGregor, who grew up with the Bretts, "was my idol."

Then came the Ken Brett injuries and many trades and all those things you never foresee with phenoms. He had a fine big-league career. But it wasn't the dream.

And George? He was a knucklehead. He didn't care about school. He was cocky. He wanted to goof around. He loved the beach, just hanging around the water near their home in El Segundo, California, even though he knew that every time he came home smelling of the ocean and dripping sand, his father would explode: "You're wasting your life!"

The explosions were better than the silences. Sometimes, on those car rides home from Little League games, Jack Brett was so angry, so disgusted, so humiliated that he would put a death grip on the steering wheel and stare out the windshield and not say a single word.

George had talent. Jack knew that. George had a strong arm. He could run. The bat showed promise. But he was a screwup, and Jack couldn't tolerate that. Even when the Kansas City Royals took him early in the second round—one pick ahead of a college third baseman who would end up sharing the 1970s and '80s with him: Ohio University's Mike Schmidt— Jack doubted that George would make it.

And while Brett didn't wow anybody in the minors—he didn't hit .300 in any of his four seasons, didn't show great power, made a lot of errors at third base—he moved up the ladder fast. The Royals were a young franchise then in desperate need of young stars. They called up Brett in early May 1974, a few days before he turned 21.

In his second start, he went 3-for-4 against the Yankees. The next day he homered in Texas. This was going to be easy!

No. It wasn't going to be easy. Brett went into a severe slump, hitless day after hitless day. By the end of the first month, he was hitting .216. His father reminded him nightly and with venom that he was blowing it, blowing the only chance he would ever get. George believed his father. He was such a wreck that when Royals manager Jack McKeon scanned the bench in search of a pinch-hitter, George tried to avoid eye contact just like a kid in grade school who doesn't want to get called on by the teacher.

Then hitting coach Charlie Lau sat next to him on the team plane. Lau was a 41-year-old former catcher; he seemed so much older to George. Lau had been a .255 hitter in the major leagues, but he was an avid student of hitting, and by the end of his career, he had picked up a few ideas that he thought could help young hitters. He became a batting coach for wacky Charlie Finley in Oakland, and in 1970 he helped the A's offense emerge, led by his star pupil Joe Rudi (who hit .309).

"Charley Lau and I go back to 1953 in the Army," A's manager John McNamara said. "We've been good friends ever since, but even I didn't know he was as smart as he is."

Lau was crotchety and had a quick temper (he tried to start a fight with announcer Harry Caray once) and later would struggle with alcohol abuse. But he cared about young hitters. On the plane that day, he said to Brett: "I've been watching you, George. You can be a good hitter. But it's going to take an awful lot of work. If you give me your heart and soul, I'll make you a great hitter."

George didn't know quite what to say to that. He wasn't used to encouraging words. He also wasn't used to taking advice. His first instinct was to rebuff Lau, but he was hitting .216. "Do I listen to Charley if I was hitting .300? Hell no!" he would say.

So he went to the cage to work with Lau and within five minutes—five stinking minutes!—Brett was suddenly roping line drives all over the park.

"Hey!" George shouted out in glee. "I got it!"

"You haven't got anything, mullet head!" Lau grumped, and George shut up and listened. Together, over weeks and months and years, they built the eternal swing.

With that swing, George would win three batting titles in three different decades. With that swing, George would crack 665 doubles, more than any American League player not named Ty Cobb or Tris Speaker. With that swing, George would almost hit .400 (five bleeping hits) and dominate two World Series and become a baseball icon. He would be elected to the Hall of Fame with 98 percent of the vote.

But even with that swing, Brett never stopped being afraid.

"Every game," he said, "I thought I would embarrass myself. Every day. I thought, 'What if the ball goes through my legs?' 'What if I strike out and fall down?' I would look up into the stands and see all those people and think about how much it meant to them. What if I let them down? What if we lose because of me? Every day I thought about those things."

He would do things to try to overcome that fear. For instance, he would watch old game film of himself hitting rockets, not to dissect the swing but to try to capture the feeling. He would give himself pep talks when he stepped into the batter's box: "You are the best hitter in the league! This pitcher doesn't want any part of you! You are the best hitter in all of baseball!"

He would challenge himself before every game.

"Today," he would say out loud with no one else around, "you are going to be the best player on the field."

Also, he would rage. He would get into fights with opponents and teammates alike. He crashed into second base harder than anybody to break up double plays. He would tear the clubhouse phone off the wall, particularly after getting into another argument with his father. You might remember a time he came flying out of the dugout, Hulk style, and tore after umpire Tim McClelland after being called out for using too much pine tar on his bat. It's one of the most played highlights in baseball history.

"I broke a guy's leg once in a collision," Brett would say. "I'm not proud of that. There were times it was too intense for me. There were times when my hunger to win went overboard."

This isn't to say that Brett hated it. Quite the opposite. He absolutely loved it. He had as much fun as anybody. He was the king of Kansas City, the Joe Namath of Kansas City. He played hard on the field, and he played hard off the field. He was teammates with all these terrific and forceful players—Hal McRae, Amos Otis, Frank White, Willie Wilson, Fred Patek, Al Cowens, Dan Quisenberry—and they fought each other and loved each other like family, and they won a bunch of division titles, and they played the reviled Yankees for the pennant over and over again, then won a World Series, and it was an absolute blast. Brett really was like a kid out there.

Many years after he retired, I would still see him on the field during spring training moving with the joy of a deer that had just learned how to run.

But, yet, no matter how great he became, before every game, that familiar fear would return. He would hear his father's voice in his head, and he would worry again about embarrassing himself, and he would try to shout it down by telling himself, "You're the best baseball player on the field." But sometimes, yes, Jack's voice overpowered his own.

Jack Brett died in 1992. He was diagnosed with cancer a few weeks before his death, but when family members wanted to tell George, he stopped them. "He's in the middle of a slump," Jack said. "He's having a hard enough time. Wait until he turns it around."

By then, George was already a legend; he would get his 3,000th hit that season. Jack knew by then that his son would be enshrined in Cooperstown. There was nothing left to prove. Still, to the end, Jack wanted his son to push for greatness. The last time they talked was after a May 22 game when the Rangers beat the Royals, 10–7. By that point, there were no secrets between father and son.

"How did you do?" Jack asked.

"I went 0-for-4," George said, and he expected his father to jump down his throat like always. But this time, Jack would pause for a long time before finally asking, "Well, did you at least hit the ball hard?"

That's when George fully understood that the end was near.

"I did, Dad," George said. "I hit it hard."

George lied. He did not hit the ball hard. He struck out three times, and the fourth was a soft grounder to first. But sons and fathers are not easy. Jack Brett died the next day.

There is one more George Brett story that comes to mind. On October 11, 1985, he had one of the greatest playoff performances in baseball history. His Royals were trailing Toronto two games to none in the best-of-seven AL Championship Series.

"Climb on my back," Brett told his teammates before the game began.

In the first inning, he homered off Doyle Alexander to give Kansas City a 1–0 lead (it was one run rather than two because Willie Wilson got caught stealing just before the homer).

In the third inning, he made probably the greatest defensive play of his life—"You won't see a better play than that," his manager, Dick Howser, gushed—when he fielded a Lloyd Moseby smash and made a jump throw home to get Damaso Garcia as he was trying to score the tying run.

In the fourth inning, Brett led off with a crushing double that hit the very top of the wall. Then he moved to third on a fly ball and scored on Frank White's sacrifice fly. That made it 2–0.

Then the Blue Jays erupted for five runs, seemingly putting the game—and potentially the series—out of reach.

But no. In the sixth, Brett hit his second home run, this time with Wilson on base, to tie the score at 5.

And in the bottom of the eighth, Brett singled on a ground ball to right. He went to second on a sacrifice bunt. He went to third on a groundout to short—a risky play, but Brett was always an aggressive and superb base-runner. He scored the winning run on a bloop single by Steve Balboni.

It was a 4-for-4 game, with two home runs, four runs scored, three RBIs, and a defensive play for the ages, and Brett did it at exactly the moment the Royals needed it.

"I came back into the dugout in the seventh inning, and I looked at George," his teammate Bud Black said that night. "He was wide-eyed. He wasn't blinking. There was a gleam in his eyes. He was so attuned to the game, it was spooky. You didn't want to say anything to him."

But here's the thing: If you ask Brett about that game, his greatest game and one of the greatest games in Royals history, this is what he will tell you:

"That double, it should have been a triple. I didn't run hard enough out of the box."

George is Jack Brett's son to the end.

No. 34 Cy Young

Ford Frick, the commissioner of baseball, had an idea: He wanted to create an award especially for pitchers. The way he saw things, pitchers were just not getting their due credit. Two pitchers, in particular, came to mind. One was Bob Feller, who had led the American League in wins six different times, but never won the MVP award. The writers gave those six awards to Joe DiMaggio (three times), Ted Williams, Hank Greenberg, and Yogi Berra.

Didn't Bobby Feller deserve one of those awards? Frick thought so.

He felt even more strongly about a pitcher in his favored league, the National League. Every year from 1950 to 1955, Frick believed that Robin Roberts had a powerful case as the league's most valuable player. During that stretch, he led the league in wins four times and in innings pitched five times, but the writers kept overlooking it. One year, they gave the award to his teammate Jim Konstanty, who pitched 150 fewer innings. Another year, they gave it to Hank Sauer for a perfectly fine but hardly awe-inspiring season—that was the season Roberts went 28-7, for crying out loud.

Frick couldn't shake this idea: Pitchers deserved their own award.

When he announced the idea of a pitchers-only award, however, many people rebelled against it. The writers misunderstood Frick's point and began referring to it as a "most valuable pitcher award," which suggested that Frick wanted to prevent pitchers from being considered for actual MVP. That bothered Frick immensely. He tried again to explain.

"Say for example that we would come up with a pitcher who won 30 games in a season," Frick said. "He probably would deserve to be the most valuable player along with winning the pitching award. I certainly didn't intend to take anything away from pitchers. I am a friend of the pitchers. That's why I thought it was a good idea to set up this award."

Ironically, one of those people who felt most snubbed was Feller, who had helped inspire the idea in the first place. Feller thought that Frick's pitching award amounted to nothing more than a consolation prize and that if Frick was serious about honoring pitchers, what he should have done was announce that the league should just give out one hitter award (rather than one to each league) and one pitcher award every year. He actually put a lot of thought into his idea; he even came up with a new voting group that would include:

One fan from each team

One reporter who covered each team

One player from each team

The manager of each team

Meanwhile, others thought the whole thing was ridiculous because pitchers were already getting their fair share of MVP awards. For all the griping by pitchers, United Press's Oscar Fraley wrote, they were not getting overlooked. He wrote that nine different pitchers had won an MVP, the most for any position. He went on to say that if baseball really wanted to honor underappreciated players, it should give out an award for the most valuable third baseman. Only two had won MVPs at that point.

So the pitcher award thing was considerably more controversial and contentious than you would think now. But in 1955, something happened that pressed Frick to follow his instincts and just introduce the award.

That was the year that Cy Young died.

He was Denton True Young—Dent to his friends—until he was 23 years old. Until that year, Young was a farmer in his hometown of Gilmore, Ohio.

He liked baseball and was quite good at it; he pitched now and again for a semipro team nearby for a dollar an appearance. But he never saw baseball as a profession until that year, 1890, when he began to think about settling down and getting married.

That's when the ball club in Canton, 45 miles or so away, offered him the princely sum of $60 a month to pitch.

Here's how the *Cleveland Plain Dealer* described his arrival as a ballplayer:

> Several days ago, a big farm boy arrived in Canton on a load of hay and after selling his produce he took in a ball game. It struck him that pitching a ball was a rather easy way of earning a livelihood and he applied for a job to the Canton officials.

No, it didn't go exactly like that—he didn't just show up to sell produce—but it is true that Young was a small-town boy without sophistication or worldliness. What he did have was a fastball that shocked the senses. It would be fun to know just how hard Young threw when he showed up in Canton that spring. It must have been something, because the Canton newspaper actually worried for the safety of team's catcher, Henry Yalk (this was before catchers were allowed to wear padded mitts).

"It is conceded by all who have seen him pitch," the *Canton Repository* wrote, "that he throws the swiftest ball ever seen in this city. Yalk, it is thought, will be able to fill the bill all right after he gets a little practice. At least, he says, he is not afraid to try it."*

Young was an instant star in Canton, striking out 13 in an exhibition game. The paper *immediately*—first day—began referring to him as Cyclone Young. I doubt that any player was given a legendary nickname so quickly (except maybe Shoeless Joe Jackson). Cyclone Young in short order became Cy Young, and just days after Cy Young threw an 18-strikeout no-hitter against McKeesport, the Cleveland Spiders of the National League bought his rights for $300.

Young became a star just as quickly in Cleveland as he had in Canton. In his first start, he allowed just three hits, an 8–1 win over Cap Anson's

---

* Years later, Honus Wagner would say, "Walter Johnson was fast but no faster than [Amos] Rusie. And Rusie was no faster than Johnson. But Young was faster than both of 'em."

Chicago team. The performance was so impressive that Anson, the biggest man in baseball at the time, tried to purchase Young.

"He's too green to do your club much good," he reportedly told Gus Schmelz, the Spiders' manager. "But I believe if I taught him what I know, I might make a pitcher out of him in a couple of years. He's not worth it now, but I'm willing to give you $1,000 for him."

To which Schmelz responded: "Cap, you can keep your thousand, and we'll keep the rube."

The newspapers were awestruck, too.

"Mr. Young is a tall, very well put together and athletic young man of sundry summers," the *Cleveland Leader and Herald* wrote. "He pitches the ball, not hardly that either, rather he sends lessons in geometry up to the batter with a request for solution. Mr. Young seems to know almost as much about curves as an engineer on a railroad in West Virginia."

That last part suggests that Young already threw a curveball in addition to his vaunted fastball. There is some dispute about this. Christy Mathewson wrote that Young was a pure fastball pitcher in the first half of his career and didn't develop his curveball until the second half. Young himself suggested the same, saying that a pitcher should learn control first before worrying about curveballs.

But curves or not, surely there has never been a more adaptable pitcher than Cy Young:

In 1892, he won 36 games with a National League–leading 1.93 ERA.

The next year, the league moved pitchers back from 50 feet to 60 feet, 6 inches and a rubber slab replaced the pitcher's box.

In 1893, he won 33 games and led the league in Fielding Independent Pitching (which works only with strikeouts, walks, and home runs allowed).

The next year, foul bunts were classified as strikes.

From 1894 to 1900, he went 181-112 with a 138 ERA+ and he led the league at various times in wins, strikeouts, shutouts, complete games, WHIP, and FIP. He and Kid Nichols were the two best pitchers in the game over that stretch of time.

In 1901, the upstart American League declared itself a major-league challenger to the National League.

Young jumped to the AL and led the league in wins in 1901 and 1902. He won the pitcher triple crown in 1901 with 33 wins, a 1.62 ERA, and 158 strikeouts.

In 1903, foul balls were classified as strikes in the American League.

Young again led the league in wins in 1903 along with complete games, shutouts, and innings pitched.

In 1904, the mound was lowered.

Young had a career-high 10 shutouts in 1904 and led the league with a 0.937 WHIP. He threw the first perfect game in American League history.

In 1908, pitchers were no longer allowed to muddy up a new baseball.

That year, Young won 20 games for the 16th and final time in his career. His ERA was 1.26. He also threw a no-hitter that year.

Think about how much the game changed over those years. He was a guy who pitched his first game against Anson when the rules for pitching were all different, and he pitched his last game against a young upstart named Zack Wheat, who would become teammates of Jimmie Foxx, who would be teammates with Al Benton, who would be teammates with Minnie Miñoso, who would be teammates with Harold Baines, who would be teammates with Bartolo Colón . . .

. . . who would be teammates with Jacob deGrom, who won the last two National League Cy Young Awards.

How did he do it? How was Young one of the best pitchers in baseball in 1892 and also one of the best pitchers in 1908, when the game was entirely different?

There are undoubtedly numerous reasons, but I can't help but wonder if it came down to this: Young was a timeless pitcher. That is to say, he didn't rely on gimmicks or intimidation. Yes, he had a few tricks. He always claimed to have four different pitching deliveries—one where he turned his back entirely on the hitter—in order to throw off timing. He threw every kind of pitch, including the spitter, when necessary.

But, mostly, he threw fastballs and he threw them at the corners. Young's control and command were supernatural. He led the league in fewest walks per nine innings an astounding 14 times.

"I aimed to make the batter hit the ball," Young used to say, "and I threw as few pitches as possible."

Mathewson often gets credit for being baseball's first great thinking pitcher, but Mathewson himself insisted that Young got there first. "Old Cy Young," Mathewson said, "has the absolutely perfect pitching motion."

Young's pitching transcended the times, transcended the rules, transcended the hitter's ability to adjust. He threw his pitches directly and repeatedly into hitters' most vulnerable spot—it really went back to what the *Cleveland Leader and Herald* wrote at the very start: "he sends lessons in geometry up to the batter with a request for solution." He kept asking those geometry questions until he was in his mid-40s.

"There was no hitter that ever gave me trouble," he said and then with a little smile he added, "at least not the second time around."

Young has the record with 511 wins and that record will never be broken. He also has the record for most losses (315), starts (815), and innings (7,356), and he faced almost 30,000 batters, and none of those records will ever be broken, either. He faced four thousand more batters than any pitcher in baseball history—that's roughly four seasons' worth in today's game.

Most batters faced:

1. Cy Young, 29,565

2. Pud Galvin, 25,415

3. Walter Johnson, 23,405

4. Phil Niekro, 22,677

5. Nolan Ryan, 22,575

Still, it's the win total that everyone remembers.

"Someday," Red Smith wrote in 1955, "a batter will improve on Babe Ruth's 60 home runs in a season. Maybe a Joe DiMaggio yet unborn will hit safely in 57 consecutive games. Perhaps a new Rube Marquard or Tim Keefe will pitch 20 victories without defeat. But Cy Young's 511 victories—nobody's ever going to threaten that because it is impossible and always was."

How much should really be made of that win record? That's debatable. It has long been considered baseball's most unbreakable record—even in the 1910s, people called it unbreakable—but is it really a *legitimate* record? Half of his numbers were collected in the 1890s, when baseball was very much in its development stage, and half of them came in what we now consider "modern baseball."

If you simply took away the years before the pitcher moved back to 60 feet, 6 inches, Young's win total is 439 wins—that would still be a record but not far ahead of Walter Johnson's 417 and not quite so unreachable.

If you count only the years since the American League came into existence, Young has 225 wins.

That is to say that while Young's 511 victories have become one of baseball's magic numbers, it is also unrepeatable. That mountain doesn't exist anymore.*

But here is my favorite part about Young's 511 victories.

He always *insisted* that he had really won 512.

And when I say insisted, I mean it—he wouldn't stop talking about it. In virtually every interview he gave in the last years of his life, he griped about an official scorer cheating him out of a win in 1898. He would go and on about it, citing various sources, breaking down all the details of how the win was lost and so on.

It got to the point where some reporters would simply credit him with 512 victories because he was so sensitive about it.

That seems odd, doesn't it? What, in the end, is the difference between 511 and 512 wins? How could that matter? And yet it did; it mattered a great deal to Cy Young, a modest man who nonetheless wanted credit for all the victories in his extraordinary life.

When Young died on November 4, 1955, there was a great outpouring of love and support from the baseball world.

"He was truly one of the real workhorses of old-time baseball," Ty Cobb said.

"One of the true pioneers of the game," Tris Speaker said.

"He had the three requisites of all great pitchers," Elmer Flick said. "Speed, control, endurance."

"His great record will likely stand forever," American League president Will Harridge said.

"He was the greatest pitcher of all time," Ed Walsh said.

He was so beloved that Connie Mack's daughter refused to even tell her father about Young's death. Mack was 92 years old and she said that

---

* In 1963, Sandy Koufax told a reporter that he thought the record could be broken. He was 27 then and he had 93 victories—not that far behind Young's 131 at the same age. It was pointed out to Koufax that Young averaged 28 victories a year for his next nine seasons. "It's not inconceivable," Koufax said. But it was, even for Koufax, who only lasted three more seasons.

news like that could send him into a depression from which he would never recover. Cy Young was that great. He was that beloved.

And when he died, Frick understood exactly how he would finally break through all the noise and make his pitcher's award a reality.

He would simply call it the Cy Young Memorial Award. Nobody could argue with that.

No. 33 **Jimmie Foxx**

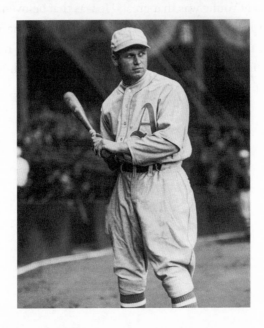

He really hated it when people misspelled his name "Jimmy."

Who can explain the sensitivities of human beings? Jimmie Foxx was, by all accounts, a sweet and good-natured man. He was famous for his ever-present smile. This was true even later in his career when he battled alcoholism and money problems. As we shall see, *A League of Their Own* didn't get him quite right.

But, even so, he really didn't like that name "Jimmy."

Baseball was his father's dream. Dell Foxx was a tenant farmer in Sudlersville, Maryland, across the Chesapeake Bay from Baltimore. Dell was also the power-hitting outfielder for the local town team. He might have become a terrific big-league ballplayer—all of his friends and family thought so—but unlike many others, he never seemed to feel any regret about missing out on the big leagues. He did not curse missed opportunities. He was, by accounts, a happy man—happy to be a moderately successful farmer, happy to be a fine ballplayer, happy to harness-race on the weekends at the local track.

And, most of all, Dell was happy to play ball with his son, Jimmie.

He began throwing balls to Jimmie from their earliest days together. There was, Jimmie always insisted, no pressure attached to these games of catch, no expectations, no deferred dreams to live up to. It was pure joy. Father and son would play catch every day after farming, and there was nothing in the world that made both of them happier.

"I recall one Sunday afternoon," Mildred Barracliff, Jimmie's cousin, told author Mark R. Millikin for his Foxx biography, "when Jim showed us his new baseball glove. I think he must have been about eight years old then. His father, at that time, threw hard balls to him, and Jim never missed. My father said, 'By gum, Dell, you're throwing the ball too hard. If he missed one, it will kill him.' Dell answered, 'He won't miss it. He'll catch it. He's going to be a big-league catcher.'"

Jimmie Foxx was an extraordinary athlete. He was breathtakingly fast (he was a superstar sprinter and high jumper in high school), impossibly strong (they called him "The Beast"), a soccer star, a basketball star, a volleyball star, and he had such a strong arm that many thought he'd be better off as a pitcher. Queen Anne's County's athletic director John Bruehl called him the greatest natural athlete he ever saw, which would be praise coming from anybody. But Bruehl had once scrimmaged against Jim Thorpe, who was named the greatest athlete of the first half of the 20th century.

Bruehl was not the only person to make the Thorpe comparison. When Foxx was 18 years old, a famous sportswriter of the time named Stoney McLinn—who served as ghostwriter for many of the great athletes of the time, including Ty Cobb—wrote that Foxx "has that athletic sense that made an all-around star of the quality of Jim Thorpe."

The Hall of Famer Home Run Baker—who probably played against Dell Foxx because they were from the same area—signed a 16-year-old Foxx to play for a new team, the Class D Easton Farmers, in 1924. There's a great story Baker told about the first time he saw Jimmie Foxx. Baker was lost in the Maryland backwoods when he came upon a young Foxx pushing a plow on the family farm.

"Where's the closest town?" Baker supposedly asked.

"That way," Foxx said and with one hand he picked up the plow and pointed in the direction.

It's too good to be true, but Foxx was supernaturally strong. In any case,

Baker gave Jimmie a tryout. "What position do you play?" Baker asked. "All of them," Foxx said. "Except shortstop. I don't like shortstop."*

Baker signed Foxx, and the kid was so good that within a few weeks, the Philadelphia Athletics bought out his contract. Foxx was just 17 years old when he pinch-hit for a rookie pitcher named Lefty Grove. Foxx cracked a single. He got nine at-bats that first season. He managed six hits.

There's a wonderful connection between Jimmie Foxx and another teenage sensation of the time: Mel Ott. Foxx signed with the Athletics when he was 17 and was raised by Connie Mack. Ott signed with the Giants one year later at age 17 and was raised by Mack's great rival John McGraw.

Foxx's first great year was in 1929, when he hit .354/.463/.625 with 33 homers, 123 runs, and 118 RBIs.

Ott's first great year was in 1929, when he hit .328/.449/.635 with 42 homers, 138 runs, and 151 RBIs.

The two would become two of the biggest stars of the 1930s.

Foxx became famous first because his Athletics were the elite team in baseball. People called him Double X. And in that first great season in 1929, the A's won the American League pennant by 18 games. They then beat the Chicago Cubs in the World Series in five games. Foxx hit .350 with two homers in the series.

The next year was a virtual repeat. Foxx hit 37 homers, scored 127 runs, and drove in 156, and the A's won the American League by eight games. They beat the Cardinals in the World Series. Foxx hit .333 with two doubles, a triple, and a home run in the series.

The next year, 1931, was not quite as good. Foxx failed to hit .300 for the first time in his career, though he still managed 30 homers and 120 RBIs. The A's won the pennant but lost the World Series to the Cardinals in seven.

And that's when the winning ended. The A's finished second in 1932 despite Foxx's best season—he hit .364/.469/.749 with 58 homers, 169 RBIs, and 151 runs scored—and the team dropped to third the following year despite another extraordinary season from Foxx. By 1934, the A's

---

* Foxx did end up playing two innings at shortstop in 1933. In his big-league career, Foxx played every position on the field except second base.

were in free fall. Mack had terrible money problems and had to sell off his best players. It would be 40 years until the A's won another pennant.

Let's go back to that 1932 season for a moment. That was the year Foxx challenged Babe Ruth's home run record of 60—already considered untouchable even though it was just five years old. Foxx had an absurd stretch in late May, hitting 14 homers in 26 games, and he had 29 home runs by the end of June.

He kept going. On July 10 that year, he hit three home runs in Cleveland to move his total up to 33. He hit another two in Detroit a week later to push to 38. He hit homers on three consecutive days in mid-August to get his season total up to 47. He got Nos. 50 and 51 on September 3.

Then he went into a bit of a homer slump, managing just two homers over the next two weeks. That seemed to end the drama, but Foxx did give it one final gallant effort, hitting five home runs in his last five games to finish the season with 58 home runs, which remarkably is still the American League record for right-handed batters.

The American League record for most home runs by a right-hander:

1. Jimmie Foxx (1932) and Hank Greenberg (1938), 58 homers

3. Alex Rodriguez (2002), 57 homers

4. Rodriguez (2007) and José Bautista (2010), 54 homers

6. Mark McGwire (1996), Alex Rodriguez (2001), and Aaron Judge (2017), 52 homers

Foxx won the MVP award in 1932 and won it again in 1933. That year he won the Triple Crown, hitting .356/.449/.703 with 48 homers and 163 RBIs.

He won a third MVP award in 1938 with the Red Sox, when he almost won the Triple Crown again. He led the league in average (.349) and RBIs (175), but his 50 home runs placed him second to Greenberg, who had matched his right-handed record with 58 home runs.

In 1939, Foxx teamed up with a 20-year-old rookie named Ted Williams to make one of the great teammate combinations ever. Foxx hit .360 with 35 home runs. Williams hit .327 with 31 home runs and 145 RBIs. They played together for two more seasons—the Kid idolized Foxx and they were friends for the rest of their lives. "He was a real peach of a guy," Williams told SABR's Bill Jenkinson in 1986 as he fought back tears.

In 1942, at age 34, Foxx was benched and then waived by the Red Sox. He ended up being sold to the Chicago Cubs. "People have been saying I was through for seven years," Foxx said after getting sold. "I feel like I still could go out there and do a good job."

He could not. He hit just .205 with three homers for the Cubs and he announced his retirement.

He did come back for the Cubs and Phillies in 1944 and '45, but those were sad encounters; he was finished as a hitter. His greatest moment in those two seasons came on the mound; he appeared in nine games as a pitcher for the Phillies in '45, and on August 19 he pitched 6⅔ innings, striking out five and picking up his only win. He also had a three-game stretch from September 6 to 16 where he pitched 6⅓ innings of relief without allowing a single hit. Newspaper stories referred to him as ancient.

He was 37 years old when he retired.

In his career, Foxx hit 534 home runs—when he retired for good in 1945, it was second on the all-time list behind only Ruth. He was elected to the Baseball Hall of Fame in 1951. He was thoroughly beloved, not only for his power but also for the bighearted way he played.

Jimmie Foxx, like Stan Musial, was never thrown out of a game.

So now let's talk about Jimmie Foxx . . . and Jimmy Dugan. The latter, Dugan, is a fictional character, but real in the minds of so many. Tom Hanks made him real. Dugan was the manager of the Rockford Peaches in the movie *A League of Their Own*. In his backstory was a career of towering home runs and blackout drunkenness.

Dugan was based on Jimmie Foxx. They were both legendary right-handed power hitters. They both hit 58 home runs in a season in the 1930s (Foxx in 1932, Dugan in 1936). They both retired young. They both had drinking issues. They both managed in the All-American Girls Professional Baseball League.

But they were not the same. Dugan's drinking drove him out of the game; he rather famously hurt his knee after jumping out of a hotel room because of a fire he had set.

Foxx's story is much sadder and much darker. He did indeed grow to like the big-city life after he got to Philadelphia. He liked being seen around town. He liked wearing expensive clothes. Ted Williams always thought the young Foxx was just trying to emulate Ruth. In the early days, Foxx's drinking was light and social and, in the eyes of teammates, under control.

Then, in 1934, while playing in an exhibition game in Winnipeg, Foxx was beaned by a left-handed pitcher named Barney Brown. The fastball hit Foxx in the forehead and knocked him unconscious. He was hospitalized for four days. The doctor insisted that although he had a mild concussion, the effects were minimal—he should be back to his normal self in just days.

In reality, he was never the same. Foxx suffered from vicious sinus headaches and blurry vision for the rest of his life. He played through it all, never complaining. But his friends said that his drinking increased dramatically after that. Williams said he once saw Foxx down a dozen little bottles of scotch on a team flight. He drank, Williams said, to numb the pain.

Still, there are no surviving stories of Foxx as a blackout drunk. He did not show up to the ballpark drunk. He did not start fights or lose his good nature. While some have said that drinking contributed to the early demise of Foxx the ballplayer—he retired the first time at 34—it was more likely the long-term effects of the beaning along with the many injuries he suffered through the years.

Dugan's and Foxx's times in the AAGPBL were also very different. Dugan was brought to the league by Walter Harvey, the candy bar magnate who was based on Chicago Cubs owner Philip Wrigley, the chewing gum magnate and cofounder of the real AAGPBL.

Wrigley had nothing at all to do with bringing Foxx into the league. In fact, Wrigley had separated from the league many years before Foxx managed the Fort Wayne Daisies. While Dugan managed during World War II—an important plot point in the movie—Foxx did not manage until 1952, long after the war was over.

Dugan took the job for the money. Foxx didn't need the money at the time; he had a job as an executive with Mid-States Freight Lines. He took the job because he thought it sounded fun to get back into baseball (he had just been elected to the Baseball Hall of Fame).

Dugan had to endure the annoyances of the exasperating batboy, Stillwell Angel, the son of one of the players, Evelyn. In real life, Foxx's stepdaughter, Nanci, was the team batgirl and loved every minute of it.

Dugan resented the women at first and didn't see them as ballplayers. Foxx respected the players from the very start and was universally liked by them.

"He never lost his temper; he was never violent," one of the Daisies' players, Wilma Briggs, told Millikin for the book. "He was a kind man, a gentleman to me and all my teammates."

Teammate Dottie Schroeder added: "Jimmie Foxx was very generous. I liked him immensely."

"He was a father figure to me that season," Pat Scott said.

"It was pretty terrible what that movie did to him," Katie Horstman said.

Wilma Briggs—whose father was such a big Foxx fan that he named her brother James Emory Foxx Briggs—did recall Foxx drinking from a little bottle that he would carry with him. But others insisted that Foxx never drank when managing the team. Either way, Foxx managed them with quiet respect. He would only offer advice or tips if asked.

"You know how to play ball," he reportedly told one of the players. "There's not much I can add."

Foxx managed the Daisies for only one year. He said it was a fun time, but the bouncing buses were hard on him, and he dealt with numerous health issues that year. He moved with his family back to Philadelphia and became a paint salesman.

The years after he managed in the AAGPBL were hard on Foxx. He bounced from job to job. He managed the University of Miami baseball team for a short while in the late 1950s, but he was let go after his team had a losing record in 1957 (some say he was fired because he lacked a college degree). He had lost his money in a couple of bad investments and because he generously gave away so much of it.

People offered him various jobs to cash in on his name, but he rarely took them, perhaps out of pride. In 1961, he declared bankruptcy. In 1963, he had a serious illness that doctors originally thought was a heart attack but turned out to be something more mysterious.

"They told me to cut down on work," Foxx said. "That wasn't very hard. I'm pretty lazy."

The ending was unrelentingly sad. In May 1966, his wife died, and the last year of his life was a fog of depression and loneliness. He felt forgotten. Foxx seemed to lose the great smile that had been his trademark. He died in July 1967 of asphyxiation; there was a piece of meat lodged in his throat. He was not yet 60 years old.

The papers did write about the great career of Double X. But even in that, there was sadness. Almost all of the stories spelled his name "Jimmy."

No. 32 **Mel Ott**

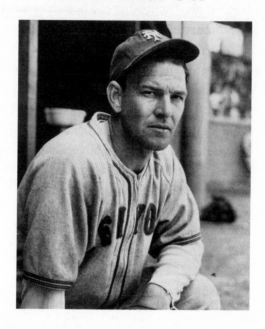

Mel Ott was a nice guy. No, sorry, that's not exactly what I meant to say: Mel Ott was *the* nice guy. You know Leo Durocher's famous quote, "Nice guys finish last?" What he actually said was this:

"Take a look at that No. 4 there. A nicer guy never drew breath than that man there. . . . Take a look at them. All nice guys. They'll finish last. Nice guys. Finish last."

So Durocher wasn't saying "Nice guys finish last"—at least originally— as one broad statement about how all nice guys finish last. No, he was talking specifically about the New York Giants baseball club being filled with nice guys, particularly that No. 4, and how despite their niceness (or, perhaps more directly, because of their niceness), they would finish last.

And No. 4? Right: That was Mel Ott.

Nice guy? Unquestionably. Sportswriter Arnold Hano called him "baseball's legendary nice guy." Arthur Daley wrote that he had "charisma long before that overworked word emerged from the dictionary for every-day use." The South's sportswriting Shakespeare, Fred Russell, called him a "clean, fine, wonderful man."

He was this kind of guy: One time, the famed New York bar owner Toots Shor was at a table schmoozing with Sir Alexander Fleming, the

Nobel Prize winner who discovered penicillin. And just then, Ott walked through the door.

"Excuse me," Shor said as he rushed off. "Somebody important just walked in."

Ott grew up in a small Louisiana town called Gretna, just on the other side of the Mississippi River from New Orleans. Ott did not look like a great athlete at first blush. He was small, and though he was a physical marvel, he appeared a bit soft around the edges. But, really, his athletic genius was invisible to the eye anyway. He had the ability to adapt. The great college basketball coach Jack Hartman was asked often how his Kansas State teams managed to play with, and often whip, those teams that had "superior talent," and he said with some real impatience in his voice: "Talent is just being where you're supposed to be and doing what you're supposed to do."

That was Mel Ott. He was where he was supposed to be. He did what he was supposed to do. He picked up baseball from two uncles who played on a local semipro team. He gravitated toward catcher because that's where the smartest player was supposed to play.

And despite his lack of height or bulk, he taught himself how to launch baseballs inconceivable distances. How did he do this? Well, it began with the high front-leg kick that he would make famous. By all accounts, he taught himself that kick right at the beginning. He would practice by standing around on one leg so he could perfect the balance required.*

I also think Ott might have been the very first disciple of launch angle, which is all the rage with hitters these days. Most would probably say that Babe Ruth was the first to aim at hitting the ball in the air since he all but invented the home run as a weapon, but it wasn't scientific for Ruth—nothing was scientific for Ruth. It was scientific for Ott. By the time he was 14, he was already so well known around his hometown for hitting long home runs that crowds at games would pass around the hat and give him coins in appreciation, admiration, and awe.

At this point, Ott was probably about 5-foot-5 and weighed maybe 130 pounds.

What followed was a spectacular series of happy events. First, a 16-

---

* Though the leg kick would become more pronounced later when he worked with the great hitter and pitcher Lefty O'Doul.

year-old Ott was recruited to play for a lumberyard team in nearby Patterson, Louisiana.

But this wasn't just any lumberyard team. It was the nation's largest lumberyard, and it belonged to a millionaire named Harry Palmerston Williams. He was a story all to himself—in later years, Williams would become one of the pioneers of aviation. But even at that point, he was a millionaire and a man of many connections.

Williams saw Ott hit and was entirely blown away.

And it just so happened that one of his connections—one of his best friends, in fact—was a guy named John McGraw, the manager of the New York Giants. The next time he was in New York, Williams gushed about Ott so enthusiastically that McGraw immediately sent a short and direct telegram to the Ott family in Louisiana.

Report to McGraw, Polo Grounds, New York—John J. McGraw.

Ott ignored the telegram, either because he believed it was a joke or he was scared that it was not. He was still in high school at the time, a small-town farm kid who had never been out of Louisiana and certainly had no concept of what New York might be like. When Williams heard that Ott had not gone to see McGraw, he personally went to Patterson, bought Ott a ticket, and put him on a train to New York. He also sent along a note— Williams might as well have attached it to Ott's shirt with a safety pin.

> The bearer, M. Ott, is the young catcher whom you asked me
> to send you in September. We have just finished our season and
> this youngster has shown up remarkably well. He is, as I told you,
> inexperienced and green, but seems to be a natural hitter and
> receiver. You, of course, will know what you want done with him,
> and I would appreciate hearing from you at a later date what you
> think of him.
>
>   Yours sincerely,
>   H. P. Williams

Ott would say he was shaking from nerves during his tryout, but if so, nobody noticed it. Frankie Frisch, who watched the whole thing, said that Ott immediately began crushing hard line drives and that the longer the tryout went, the longer those line drives sailed.

"This lad," McGraw said that very day, "is going to be one of the greatest left-hand hitters the National League has seen."

McGraw was going to make absolutely sure that his prophecy came true—he wasn't taking any chances about it. He refused to send Ott to the minor leagues; McGraw wasn't about to let some minor-league manager screw this kid up. He also prohibited anyone on the team from offering advice; McGraw didn't want any of those knuckleheads messing up the most perfect natural hitter he'd ever seen.

Instead, he kept Ott close. In 1926 and '27, Ott played sparingly for the Giants (but well—in 117 games before he turned 19, he hit .309). All the while, McGraw worked on him. McGraw believed Ott's future was as an outfielder, not a catcher, so they worked on his defense. McGraw and Lefty O'Doul sharpened his high leg-kick swing without changing it. Day after day, McGraw grilled the kid with thoughts, ideas, strategies.

At age 19, Ott began playing every day and he hit .322. But by age 20, Ott was ready to be one of the game's biggest stars. He hit .328/.449/.635 with 42 homers, 151 RBIs, 138 runs, he led the league in walks, and he was already an excellent right fielder with a great arm.

Ott would be that player, more or less, for the next 16 years, through the Depression, through the New Deal, through World War II. He led the league in homers six times, in walks six times, in on-base percentage four times, in OPS+ five times. He was metronome consistent. In 1932, he hit .318 with 38 homers, and in 1934, he hit .326 with 35 homers, and in 1936, he hit .328 with 33 homers, and in 1938, he hit .311 with 36 homers.

When you put up numbers with that sort of consistency, they do begin to pile up. In 1945, Ott became the first National League player to hit 500 home runs. And here's a crazy trivia question: When Ott hit his 500th homer, who was second in the National League for home runs and how many did he hit?

Answer: Chuck Klein with 300 homers.

Yes. Three hundred. Rogers Hornsby was just below that with 298.

This gives you an idea of how fundamentally different Ott was. He retired with the National League record for homers (511), runs (1,859), and walks (1,708). McGraw had gotten his first-day scouting report exactly right.

One of the great questions in baseball: Who was the greatest player to never win an MVP award? There are arguments to be made for Wade

Boggs, for Eddie Murray, for Mike Piazza, for Manny Ramírez, for Al Kaline, for Derek Jeter, for Kirby Puckett, for Bob Feller.

I believe that Boggs is the greatest player to never come close to winning an MVP.

But for the bigger question—greatest player to never win an MVP—the right answer is surely Mel Ott. He led National League position players in WAR five times and finished in the top three another three times. His best MVP finish was in 1942, when he led the league in runs, homers, walks, and OPS—he finished third in the MVP voting that year behind St. Louis Cardinals pitcher Mort Cooper and outfielder Enos Slaughter.

He actually lost the MVP to a pitcher three different times—Cooper, Dizzy Dean, and his teammate Carl Hubbell.

It's one of the stranger quirks of baseball that so many of those great players who never won an MVP were thoroughly beloved by the fans and the press. You wouldn't think it would work like that. It's true there are a handful of players like Albert Belle and Ramírez and maybe Murray or Duke Snider or Eddie Mathews, whose failure to win an MVP might be attributed to the fact that some writers didn't like them.

But Mel Ott? The ultimate nice guy? The press adored him, just as the press adored Kaline, Ortiz, Jeter, Puckett, and Feller. It just goes to show that while it's easy to talk about voter bias—and I'm sure it exists—such things are never quite as simple or straightforward as people want to make it.

The Polo Grounds, where Ott and the Giants played home games, was an odd place. The New York Gothams began playing ball in a Harlem meadow below Coogan's Bluff in the late 1880s and over time the Gothams-turned-Giants played in various incarnations of the Polo Grounds built on the same spot.

The Polo Grounds evolved into a horseshoe-shaped ballpark, with absurdly short fences down the lines in left field (279 feet) and right field (257 feet). But the walls jutted out so quickly that the right- and center-field gaps were more than 400 feet away. To straightaway center, it was always more than 450 feet and, by the time the Giants left New York, it was 475 feet.

The extreme dimensions led to some extraordinary moments. At one extreme, Bobby Thomson's Shot Heard 'Round the World that won the

Giants the pennant in 1951 was a fly ball lofted to the right spot down the left-field line. It might not have been a home run in any other park.

Meanwhile, three years laters, Vic Wertz hit a 440-foot smash to straightaway center field; Willie Mays turned and ran and made the most famous catch in baseball history. It probably would have been a home run in *every* other park.

In his career, Mel Ott played 1,367 games at the Polo Grounds, far and away the most of any player. Nobody else played even 1,000 games there. And in his career, he hit 323 of his 511 home runs at home. Is that a lot? Um . . . yes. It is the highest home run percentage for any player with 500-plus home runs:

1. Mel Ott, 323 of 511 homers at home, 63.2%

2. Frank Thomas, 312 of 521, 59.9%

3. Ernie Banks, 290 of 512, 56.6%

4. Jimmie Foxx, 299 of 534, 56.0%

5. Jim Thome, 339 of 612, 55.4%*

So, yes, Ott certainly took advantage of the Polo Grounds, as any good hitter should. He pulled the ball to take advantage of that short fence down the line, and the older he got, the more he focused on hitting home runs at home. After 1941, he hit 100 of his 123 homers at the Polo Grounds, an astonishing 81 percent.

In 1943, he hit 18 home runs.

He hit all 18 at the Polo Grounds.

But what's most interesting about this is that while Mel Ott hit so many home runs at the Polo Grounds, he was actually a fantastic hitter on the road. He just did it differently.

Ott hit 14 points higher on the road (.311 to .297).

Ott hit 63 percent of his doubles and 71 percent of his triples on the road.

---

* In case you are wondering—this surprised me—the lowest percentage of home runs hit at home belongs to David Ortiz, at 44.5 percent. I suppose that shouldn't be that much of a surprise; Fenway Park is a tough place for lefties to hit homers. Ted Williams (47.6 percent) is among the lowest percentages as well. One other fascinating tidbit: Babe Ruth hit more home runs on the road than at home.

Ott, perhaps more than any other player, simply adjusted and became a different hitter on the road than at home. On the road, he was a line-drive hitter who took fewer walks and put more balls in play. At home, he was more patient and pulled the ball toward the fences.

Which Ott was the better player? It's actually not that easy to tell. Here are the numbers:

Ott at home: .297/.422/.558 with 181 doubles, 21 triples, 323 homers, 953 runs, 950 RBIs, 955 walks.

Ott on the road: .311/.408/.510 with 306 doubles, 51 triples, 188 homers, 904 runs, 920 RBIs, 766 walks.

With the help of statistician Tom Tango, we can tell you that by advanced statistical measures, Ott was better at home. The difference in homers and walks is simply too great to make up with a higher average and more doubles and triples.

But there's another way to measure it, a simpler way: Tango calls this stat "Runs Participated In." For this, you add up runs scored plus RBIs, subtract home runs, and divide it by plate appearance.

Mel Ott at home: 1,580 runs, .282 RPI

Mel Ott on the road: 1,636 runs, .285 RPI

By this method, Ott was almost exactly as good at home as he was on the road, even though he batted in entirely different ways. That's a good way to think about the genius of Mel Ott.

No. 31 **Greg Maddux**

On May 17, 1988, Greg Maddux threw 10 shutout innings at Wrigley Field against the St. Louis Cardinals. This sounds pretty typical for Maddux—the guy threw a lot of shutout innings wherever he happened to be pitching—but at that point in his life and career, pitching that well was still a new sensation for him.

Maddux had only just turned 22, and he was coming off what can only be described as a disastrous season. In 1987, Maddux finished with the worst ERA (5.61) and highest WHIP (1.638) in the National League. He had a few nice moments—a four-hit shutout in Montreal, for example—but all in all, it was so bad that the Cubs sent him back to Des Moines for a few days in the middle of the season just to get his head on straight.

He was even worse when he got back from Des Moines. In the last month and a half of the season, batters hit .347 against Maddux, he walked 19 batters in 27⅓ innings, and the Cubs lost all seven games he appeared in.

Then he got off to such a bad start at spring training in 1988 that he couldn't even sleep at night. In Maddux's mind—and this is important to know when looking at his career—the words *pitching* and *confidence* were practically synonyms. He never felt like he was throwing baseballs out there. He was throwing confidence. Each pitch in his mind was measured not so much by movement and location as by conviction.

He worked through things in spring training, and by Opening Day he did feel more positive and self-assured. He threw a three-hit shutout to kick things off in Atlanta.

"I'm just more confident out there," he told the press after that one.

Then he went to St. Louis and pitched well again. He felt even better about himself. During the offseason, he'd gone down to pitch in Venezuela and he had worked with pitching coach Dick Pole on a more devastating curveball. He had started to believe in the pitch.

"Last year, if I threw 100 pitches, I'd throw five curveballs," he said after the St. Louis game. "This year, if I throw 100 pitches, I'm throwing between 20 and 30 curveballs. I just have so much more confidence in that pitch."

Confidence again. He kept going—he got a complete-game victory against the Expos.

"I feel like I can be more aggressive," he said. "I'm more confident with all of my pitches."

He and the Cubs beat the Giants 3–2.

"I have a lot of confidence now," he said. "But I'm not overconfident."

And on May 11, he pitched the best game of his life—a 10-inning, three-hit shutout against the Padres. He so blinded the Padres with his barrage of pitches and audacity that San Diego manager Larry Bowa went off on his players: "Hopefully," he said of his own team, "one day they'll come out there and start hitting. They're professional athletes and they're paid to hit."

Finally, we get to the game that changed everything, May 17 against the Cardinals. Here's what happened: He pitched 10 scoreless innings, just like he had against the Padres. But in this case, the Cardinals pitchers—led by John Tudor—matched him and the game was scoreless going into the 11th.

Maddux was spent. He'd already thrown about 150 pitches, but nobody cared about pitch counts in those days, least of all Maddux. He wanted to stay in. After getting Ozzie Smith to line out and Willie McGee to hit a harmless bouncer to first, though, he allowed a ground-ball single to Tom Brunansky, a line-drive single to Bob Horner, and an infield single to Tony Peña. That loaded the bases for Luis Alicea.

The men battled back and forth until the count was full. And that's when Maddux threw a fastball that sank just so and prompted Alicea to ground the ball to second baseman Ryne Sandberg. "I couldn't ask for a more routine ball," Sandberg would say.

But it turned out the ball was not routine at all. On the way toward Sandberg, the ball hit something. What? Nobody could tell. There were no rocks out there. Sandberg thought the ball might have hit the lip where the grass and the infield dirt meet, but reporters didn't think so. Alicea thought the ball hit a hole of some kind. Maddux thought it hit a ghost.

Whatever it hit, the ball jumped impossibly high, grasshopper style, over an outstretched Sandberg. That was a single. Two runs scored. And Maddux lost the game.

"It was like someone letting the air out of your balloon," Maddux would say.

Now, you will ask, what is the lesson to take from that? I mean, it wasn't Maddux's fault; he'd gotten the groundout. It wasn't Sandberg's fault that the ball took an absurd and unpredictable hop. Lesson? Is there even a lesson? Maybe it's that baseball isn't always fair? Sometimes it's better to be lucky than good? Sometimes, even when you get everything just right, things don't work out? Maybe the lesson is that you shouldn't leave a pitcher in after throwing 160 pitches?

No. There was a lesson—one only Greg Maddux could understand.

And it was this: He should have thrown his changeup that inning.

What? How did he get that? See, Maddux knew in his heart as he stood on the mound that the changeup was the pitch. But he heard conflicting voices in his head. What if he hung the changeup? How would he feel then? What is it that pitching coaches always say? "If you are going to get beat, get beat with your best pitch." His best pitch was the fastball. Maddux heard all of that stuff and he didn't throw the changeup when he knew that was the pitch to throw.

Maddux left that game disgusted with himself. He'd had a brief crisis of confidence. That wicked bounce that cost him the game, yeah, that was the universe telling him that was the punishment for not following your instincts.

And he would never, ever make that mistake again.

Greg Maddux is my favorite pitcher of all time. It wasn't a voluntary choice. I don't have any special love for any of the teams Maddux played for. I don't have any personal connections to Maddux. I wouldn't even say that I am partial to pitchers of Maddux's particular style; I've always preferred power pitchers over the cerebral ones like Maddux.

But Maddux utterly enthralled me. I used to circle his start dates on my calendar; I never did that for another pitcher, not even Pedro Martínez in his prime, not even Dwight Gooden in 1985, not even Max Scherzer when he was throwing near no-hitters and perfect games every other start. I loved those guys and so many others, but Maddux was something else for reasons that, even now, I'm not entirely sure I can put into words.

Maybe it's this: I love baseball, and I love sleight-of-hand magic, and Maddux was the closest thing I've seen to a bridge between the two.

Many stories about Maddux through the years have made a big deal of how average (or below average) his stuff was, particularly his fastball. Analysts continually said his fastball topped out at 84 or 85 mph, for instance. This is no doubt exaggerated. Even in his last year in the big leagues, his slider would get into the upper 80s. At his peak, he threw in the low 90s with regularity.

But while the stories may have overstated things for effect, it is certainly true that Maddux did not work with those one or two dominant pitches that have marked the greatest pitchers ever. Take a look at the 10 or so greatest pitchers since 1950—we'll list them in order of WAR:

1. Roger Clemens: High-90s fastball, almost unhittable split-fingered fastball

2. Tom Seaver: Rising high-90s fastball that leaped over bats

3. Maddux

4. Randy Johnson: High-90s fastball and one of the greatest sliders in baseball history

5. Phil Niekro: A knuckleball that danced

6. Bert Blyleven: One of the greatest curveballs in baseball history

7. Gaylord Perry: His daughter called it a hard slider

8. Pedro Martínez: High-90s fastball and a changeup that would break your heart

9. Steve Carlton: High-90s fastball and one of the greatest sliders in baseball history

10. Nolan Ryan: 100-mph fastball, optical illusion curveball

If you want to add Sandy Koufax, you think high-90s fastball and backbreaking curve. If you want to add Bob Gibson, you think high-90s fastball and a slider that buckled the knees. You don't want to oversimplify things—these pitchers were not great simply because of one or two sensational pitches. But they had the pitches.

And Maddux? He never had a pitch that you would rank among the greatest of all time—if you were ranking the top 20 or top 50 fastballs or sliders or curveballs or changeups, you probably wouldn't put Maddux on any of those lists.

Then again, he wasn't trying to make any of those lists. He didn't measure his fastball with velocity or his circle-change by deception or his curveball with the sharpness of the break. No, everything Maddux threw was defined by two words: *late movement*.

"The last 10 feet," he says. "That's what worked for me. It was not so much the whole 60 feet, 6 inches. It was what the ball did in the last 10 feet that mattered. And if your ball's doing something in that last 10 feet, that can be just as impressive as how fast it goes over 60 feet."

One of the greatest sporting events I've ever covered was Maddux's absurd eight scoreless innings against the New York Yankees in Game 2 of the 1996 World Series. The Yankees ended up winning that series—they touched up Maddux for three runs in Game 6 to win it all—but there was something extraordinary about that earlier game. Maddux was a maestro—82 pitches, 62 strikes, two strikeouts, no walks, a ground-ball symphony.

1st inning: Two groundouts and one lineout to left

2nd inning: Three groundouts

3rd inning: Two groundouts and a caught stealing

4th inning: Two groundouts and one infield lineout

5th inning: Three groundouts

6th inning: Two groundouts, one a double play

7th inning: One groundout, two strikeouts

8th inning: Three groundouts

What I remember most was the Yankees' clubhouse after the game. They were not awed by what had just happened like players might be after getting shut down by Martínez or Roy Halladay or Clayton Kershaw. No, quite the opposite: They were *mad*. Player after player talked about how they should have *crushed* Maddux. The pitches were right there! The chances were everywhere! Yes, Maddux is good but really they just beat themselves.

"The pitches were nothing special," Bernie Williams insisted.

"You feel so comfortable against him," Joe Girardi said.

"It looks so easy," Paul O'Neill said.

"The ball was there for us," Williams said. "The ball was there for us!"

Understand, it wasn't disrespect—they all respected Maddux. It was more like they had the reaction people have when they see a particularly awe-inspiring magic trick. You will see people wandering out of a David Copperfield show in Las Vegas, and they are a little bit dazed, a little bit confused, a little bit angry at themselves that they couldn't quite figure out how that car appeared or how he knew the exact numbers that people in the audience would choose.

"The Gibsons, the Koufaxes, and Drysdales did it with power and intimidation," a befuddled Yankees manager Joe Torre said. "He does it with (pause, think, pause) a lot of finesse."

How did he do it? The question was always in the air. From 1992 to 1998, seven seasons, Maddux went 127-53 with a 2.15 ERA, he won four consecutive Cy Young Awards, he led the league in ERA four times, in WHIP four times, in Fielding Independent Pitching four times, in fewest homers per nine four times, in fewest walks per nine three times, in strikeout-to-walk ratio three times . . . it's like he ascended the mountaintop and became a pitching flash of light as he connected with the universe. And nobody quite understood how.

OK, let's get to the legends. I mean, obviously, this is a big reason I loved the guy, a big reason you loved the guy—his career overflows with these legendary stories that are particularly and singularly his. You tell a legendary story about Ryan and it will involve speed and force. You tell a leg-endary story about Gibson and it will involve violence or the threat of it. You tell a legendary story about Koufax and it will involve a game, surely a World Series game, when he was utterly invincible.

But Maddux legends? They're a whole other thing.

There is a legend that once Maddux was sitting in the dugout watching the game closely. And then, suddenly, he turned to a teammate sitting next to him and said, "Watch out." The next pitch was lined foul directly at the teammate's head, and he ducked out of the way just in time.

There is a legend that in 2006, his Dodgers teammate Brad Penny, who was coming off a game where he got badly roughed up by the Mets, asked Maddux if he would call the pitches for him from the dugout the next time out. Maddux did. The game was against the Cubs. Penny threw seven shutout innings, striking out six and walking nobody.

There is a legend that, while watching José Hernández batting, Maddux noticed a slight shift in the batting stance. "We might have to call an ambu-lance for their first base coach," he told a teammate. The next pitch, blam, a line drive, smashed into the chest of Dodgers first base coach John Shelby.

There is a legend that once, when asked to intentionally walk a batter, Maddux told manager Bobby Cox, "Why would I do that?" He then ex-plained that he would throw three pitches, and on the third one, he would get the batter to hit a pop foul to third.

Do I even need to tell you what happened?

There's a legend that once when he was with the Cubs, Maddux just started screaming at Atlanta's David Justice for no apparent reason. After Justice struck out, he was enraged. He never forgot it. Later, when they were teammates, Justice asked Maddux why he did that. "Why do you think?" Maddux said. "To get in your head. And it worked."

There's a legend—my favorite legend, not least because it's definitely true—that after he won his 17th Gold Glove, breaking Jim Kaat's record, he got a congratulatory message from Kaat. But, Kaat pointed out that he still held the record as the oldest modern pitcher to ever steal a base. Kaat was 41 in 1980 when he swiped a base against the Pirates.

In July that year, when playing for the Padres against the Braves, Mad-dux knocked a single off Charlie Morton and then, yep, stole second base. He was 42 years old.

I guess what I'm saying is that Maddux should be *everybody's* favorite pitcher ever.

Do I even need to tell you what a thrill it is to sit down with Greg Maddux and talk pitching? I did this not too long ago.

"My favorite part of pitching," Maddux said, "well, there are lots of favorite parts, really. The best part of pitching was that you got to hit and, if you got a hit, well, that was the best part. But for the most part, for pitching, I think my favorite part was being able to sit in the video room and figure out how to steal a strike."

Stealing strikes. It was the first time I'd ever heard that term. I'm not sure if Maddux invented it or if he simply took it to a different level from anyone before him. But it perfectly suited Maddux's personality. You remember the glasses. You remember that people called him the Professor. In addition, Maddux lives in Las Vegas, and he thinks like a gambler. His father, Dave—after a career in the air force—became a poker dealer and Greg himself is reputedly someone you wouldn't want to see at your poker table.

So, yes, stealing strikes sounds exactly like a Maddux thing.

"It comes down to understanding the game," he said. "Understanding the situations of the game. There are several times every game where the hitter will just give you a strike. And as a pitcher, strikes are incredibly valuable."

So what does it mean to steal a strike? Maddux gives an example: Let's say he faces a batter early in the game and gets him out on the first pitch. He files all that information away. The next time that batter comes up, Maddux knows that the hitter will take the first pitch. So, fastball, over the plate, something any pitcher can do, and that's a stolen strike.

That would make the count 0-1 and do you know what batters hit against Maddux in their careers when behind 0-1? Right: .215/.242/.302.

Another example: Let's say Maddux starts a hitter off with a ball. He didn't do that much, particularly in his prime. For instance, in 1995, he started off hitters with strikes more than 63 percent of the time. But on those times when he fell behind in the count 1-0, he often knew that the hitter would be looking middle-in. "I know," he would say, "that he's not going to swing at a breaking ball for the first strike. So, I throw a breaking ball for a strike on the outside half, he's not swinging, I've evened up the count.

"To me, that was what I got the biggest kick out of—being prepared to maybe steal four or five pitches a game. I always felt like you can't win the game on seven or eight pitches, but you sure can lose it. So I was always looking to eliminate as many of those pitches as I could."

This is second-level stuff, right? I mean, here was a guy who thought about the entire number of pitches he threw in a game and he worked backward to eliminate the small handful of pitches that might beat him . . . mind-blowing. The magician Teller told *Esquire*'s Chris Jones one of my favorite ever bits of wisdom: "Sometimes magic is just spending more time on something than anyone else might reasonably expect." Maddux's magic, at least part of it, came from thinking about pitching at depths others simply never approached.

"What's interesting," Maddux said, "is that it seems like the better the hitter, the easier it is to get them to take a strike. It's the guys that kind of go up there and kind of just see the ball and react, it's a little tougher to steal a strike off those guys."

He smiled: "You get them out in a different way."

If we are going to talk about stealing pitches, we do need to talk about the Maddux strike zone. If you go back and look at Greg Maddux clips on YouTube—and by all means, you should do that right now because it's really fun—you will see a whole lot of called strikes that are not, by today's baseball definition, actually strikes. Many of these pitches are not even all that close to being strikes—they are two, three, four inches off the plate, sometimes more.

Even in his time, Maddux—along with his Hall of Fame teammate Tom Glavine—was pretty famous for getting pitches off the plate. After that famous Yankees World Series game, for instance, Joe Torre said, "He gets a lot of calls," though he quickly added, "and he deserves to get them."

Did he "deserve" to get them? What does that even mean? Why would Maddux deserve to get strike calls that other pitchers do not get?

Many years ago, when I was a teenager, I went to see a show featuring a hypnotist. The hypnotist called a dozen or so people up on the stage, including a friend of mine, and then proceeded to hypnotize them and have them do various absurd but harmless things—act like a chicken, sing a song out loud, etc. My friend, who was normally shy and reserved, did these things as enthusiastically as everyone else. It was quite funny.

When he came down, I asked him how it felt to be hypnotized. And he said that he wasn't. He said that he felt relaxed and at ease and strangely confident, but that he didn't feel *compelled* to do any of the things the hypnotist asked. No, he wanted to do them because he thought it was fun and silly and, anyway, he wanted to be part of a great show.

I can't help but think that Maddux's pitching had that sort of hypnotic effect on umpires. He could do anything he wanted with a baseball. He could make the ball jump and dive and sidestep, and he threw it exactly where he intended just about every time. It was mesmerizing. Who doesn't want to be part of that? Think about it: It's a big moment, bases loaded maybe, game on the line maybe, and he throws a pitch exactly where he wants it, one that buckles the hitter, one that sends the crowd into a frenzy, a pitch that may or may not be one inch off the plate. And he's *Greg Maddux*.

Who wants to be the party pooper to wreck the show and call it a ball?

No. 30 Johnny Bench

Ted Bench had one of those extraordinary arms that left people around him breathless. He was a catcher, naturally, and every time he would make the throw to second, even if it was just at the end of the warm-up pitches, people around him would *ooh* and *ahh* and whistle. Many people thought with an arm like that, Bench should have become a pitcher.

But they didn't understand. Ted Bench was a catcher. Not a pitcher. It wasn't a choice. That's just what he was.

Ted often ran into people who just didn't understand how it was. Take his high school baseball coach. Ted somehow got sideways with the guy, never really knew why, and at some point in Ted's senior year, the coach decided to put him on the bench for a few games. It was probably some sort of lesson-building thing, but Ted didn't particularly think that was the way to coach a team, and he sure didn't think that there were any lessons to be found when sitting.

At some point during the stretch, the coach told Ted to get into the game.

"Naw," Ted said. "I don't wanna go in. If you don't start me, I can't go in."

And he quit the team. Then he quit school altogether and went into the army. That's just how it was.

Bench did play catcher in the army. He still had that glorious arm, the one that made other ballplayers swoon, and he could hit some, too, and some of the other soldiers told him that after the war ended he ought to play pro ball. He thought he might do that but the war went on too long. By the time he got out, he was 26 years old and married and had a sore elbow.

So Ted did the adult thing. He got a job driving a propane truck in Binger, Oklahoma. He played a little sandlot ball around Binger (he would tell stories about facing Satchel Paige), and his sons would swear he hit the longest home run in baseball history when he crushed one into a far-off cornfield. But more than that, he worked and he tried to instill his own baseball dream into his three boys. The oldest, Teddy, was more artistic; he idolized Elvis. Baseball just wasn't his thing.

The second-oldest, William, did like baseball, and he had some talent—he was a catcher, too—but he didn't have that impossibly rare combination of talent and ambition.

Then came Johnny Lee. And he had everything.

By the time he was two, Johnny Bench was already showing off a powerful throwing arm that made one think of his old man's. Johnny was born with supernatural hand-eye coordination; he could catch anything his dad threw at him.

Johnny loved baseball. Loved it! When he was three, another small-town Oklahoma kid named Mickey Mantle made his debut for the New York Yankees, and the Bench family had their road map. Together, they would go to Helms Grocery and get a gallon of Neapolitan ice cream and rush home to catch Mantle and the Yankees on the Game of the Week. It was some of the happiest times of young Johnny's life.

"Ralph Terry?" Ted used to grumble while watching the Yankees pitcher throw. "Hell, I could hit that guy." And Johnny believed it.*

---

* Terry wasn't the only pitcher that Ted Bench believed he could hit. Ted watched Bob Gibson throwing on television and he said the same thing: "Hell, I could hit him." In 1968, Johnny Bench faced Gibson for the first time. The first time up, he struck out looking. The next two times up, he struck out swinging. "Dad," he said to Ted the next time they spoke, "you couldn't hit him."

The greatest athletes, you often find, don't have the doubts that burden the rest of us. They feel destined. Johnny Bench seemed to know for sure, long before he could have known, that he was going to be a big-league star and, even more, a hero for kids across America. He wrote his first "I'm going to be a major-league baseball player" essay when he was in the second grade. He wrote an updated version of it for a class just about every year after that.

How sure was he? Here's my favorite Johnny Bench story, one of my favorite baseball stories. When he was in the seventh or eighth grade, Bench got a C in penmanship. This hit him hard on two different levels. On one level, Johnny didn't get C's in anything. He was a perfectionist in every way, and so the grade itself was unacceptable.

But the subject made it much worse. A C in penmanship qualified as a full-blown emergency. How would Johnny sign all the autographs for all those kids looking for a hero if he couldn't write his name legibly, much less artfully?

So here's what he did: He went down to Ford McKinney's Texaco station, and he practiced signing his name again and again until the loops in the *h* and two *n*'s in Johnny were exactly the same height and width and had the same natural flow. Once he got that down—and it definitely took quite a while—he worked on adding flourishes to the *J* and the *B* so that people would know they were getting an autograph that mattered.

He practiced and practiced, trying out different techniques, giving the letters different looks, until he felt like he had the autograph just right. And when he did get it just right, he began signing it over and over and offering the autograph to people.

"Keep this," he would say. "I'm going to be famous."

He liked doing this so much that he went down to the gas station where he worked and signed autographs and he did it again the next weekend and again the next. By the end, Ford McKinney had so many Johnny Bench autographs that he simply stuffed them in a shoe box for safekeeping. Many decades later, he told Bench he still had that shoe box somewhere or other.

But here's the best part of all: You know the story is true by simply looking at Johnny Bench's autograph. It's flawless. It's spectacular. It's a work of art. You see ballplayer autographs, and some of them are illegible and some of them are majestic and some of them seem halfhearted. All of them tell a story, and when you see Johnny Bench's sublime signature, perfectly balanced, the same every time, and you see his story, you see all the hopes of a 12-year-old boy in Oklahoma signing autographs at the local gas station because he knew that someday he would be the greatest catcher in the world.

Johnny Bench was in a hurry. You don't practice your autograph at 12 if you're not in a rush. The Cincinnati Reds drafted him in the second round of the first amateur draft, 1965, and they offered a measly $6,000 to sign. He signed anyway because, as I said, he was in a hurry, and in that state, you don't worry too much about the details.

"John," the Reds scout Tony Robello told him, "if you make it, you will have more money than you could ever want."

Bench knew that this was a bunch of salesmanship, the sort of thing teams say to rubes when trying to save cash. Bench was no rube. But he also knew that Robello was right, that soon enough he would be a big-league star, and he'd have all the money he wanted, and the prettiest girls would be fighting over him, and there was no point in haggling over a few thousand bucks when the future was so bright.

So he signed fast, and at 18 he went to play for the Peninsula Grays, a Class A team in Newport News, Virginia. It is all but impossible to fully capture the impact he had in Newport News. Sure, you can look at the numbers—he hit a robust .294 with 22 homers in 98 games and you can imagine that he played defense like no one had ever seen—but even that doesn't describe how much the people in Newport News loved him.

Put it this way: There was a sign in left field at the ballpark there that read HIT A HOMER HERE, WIN A FREE SUIT. Bench hit 10 balls over that sign, two in one game. Yes. He won 10 free suits.

"Forget Babe Ruth," he told people. "Remember Johnny Bench."

That might look arrogant in print, but the way he said it—with a smile and a wink that made you understand he was kidding and he was serious at exactly the same time—made people fall in love. It was like this: When he hit four home runs in two games, everybody—including the sports editor of the local paper, Charles Karmosky—panicked. They weren't ready for him to leave yet.

"What are you trying to do, move up?" Karmosky asked him after that fourth homer.

"I like it here," Bench assured him, and Karmosky wrote a whole column assuring people that Bench was content in Newport News.

He couldn't stay. After a few weeks, the Reds did call him up to Triple-A Buffalo, and the Peninsula team was so proud (and heartbroken) they scheduled "Good Luck Johnny Bench Day." Unfortunately, it rained, but even so, they retired his number, No. 19. That's right. Bench's 98 games on the Peninsula were so spectacular that they retired his jersey number before he left town.

His manager, Pinky May, who had played with the Philadelphia Phillies during the war, called him "the best 18-year-old prospect I've ever seen."

The Reds called him up to Cincinnati the next year and on his first day, he made a pronouncement to everyone on the team: He was to become the Reds' starting catcher. His name was Bench, but like his father, he had no intention of sitting on one. And if there were a few veterans who seethed about that, well, that was their problem.

No one, not even the harshest cynics, could deny his brilliance. Ballplayers like him just didn't exist before. Even though he happened to play his first full season in 1968, the Year of the Pitcher, he still hit .275 with 40 doubles and 15 homers as a 20-year-old. It was good enough to win the Rookie of the Year. But it was his catching that left everyone slack-jawed. Randy Hundley had popularized one handed-catching, but Bench, as I wrote in *The Machine,* made one-handed catching an art form:

> He had huge hands—he could hold seven balls in one of them—and he would scoop pitches out of the dirt like he was a shortstop picking up a ground ball. He could get the ball from his glove to his throwing hand so fast, it seemed like a card trick. He moved like a dancer around the plate on bunts.

And then there was his arm. His father's arm.

"Every time Johnny Bench throws," the legendary GM Harry Dalton said, "everybody in baseball drools."

Something happened that rookie year, something so absurd that it's almost beyond belief. It's my second-favorite Johnny Bench story. Bench was catching a veteran pitcher named Gerry Arrigo, and on this day, Arrigo didn't have anything on his fastball. Anyway, that's how Bench saw it. He kept calling for breaking balls and off-speed stuff.

Arrigo kept shaking off Bench.

They continued this dance for a while until finally Bench went to the mound to make his case. He explained that Arrigo's fastball was just not popping. Arrigo, in turn, explained that Bench was a rookie and that, considering the circumstances, he should just shut the hell up. This disagreement went on for a few seconds until finally, the two men understood that they were at an impasse and Bench shrugged and went back behind the plate.

He called for another curveball. Arrigo, furious at the impudence of this arrogant rookie, shook him off again. Bench only then called for the fastball, which Arrigo threw with all the fury he had inside him.

Bench reached out with his right hand and caught it barehanded.

"You should have seen his face," Bench would say. If we close our eyes we *can* see his face.

The next year Bench started in the All-Star Game. The next year he was the runaway winner of the MVP award—he set a record for catchers when he hit 45 home runs. Two years later, in 1972, he won another MVP, again leading the league in homers and RBIs. He led the league in intentional walks in '72, even though one of the game's most productive hitters, Tony Pérez, always hit after him.

Over his 13 prime years, he made every All-Star team, starting in 10 of them. He won 10 Gold Gloves. He retired with the most home runs for a catcher.

But with Bench, the numbers, the awards, the accomplishments only tell a part of the story. He was a pop culture superstar. He dated models. He sang in clubs. He hung out with celebrities. He was Captain of the Guards on *Mission: Impossible* and a pool waiter on *The Partridge Family* and he appeared on the Bob Hope Christmas Special from Vietnam. He wasn't just in the big leagues to become a baseball star. No, he intended to become the biggest star, baseball or otherwise, a hero for kids, Mr. America.

"We need more heroes, especially for our young people," he said in 1972, this after *Sports Illustrated* ran a cover photo of Dick Allen, cigarette in mouth, juggling baseballs in the dugout. "Even if we have to keep 'em a little naive, it's worth it. I was 17 before I knew that any major-league player smoke or drank. It didn't hurt me either."

Late in his career, he began hosting a baseball comedy show called *The Baseball Bunch.* Maybe you remember. In it, he played a Little League coach for a team that featured eight kids and the Famous Chicken mascot. Bench, along with Dodgers manager Tommy Lasorda, would break down the fundamentals of the game and the Chicken would provide the comedy—you know, when they talked about stealing bases, the Chicken would actually steal a base and run away with it.

"The show," Mark Bechtel wrote in *Sports Illustrated*, "made us feel good about looking up to Bench and his pals as role models."

That was what Bench was after. He never stopped trying to represent this old-fashioned idea of an American hero. "With Watergate and with politicians under attack and all kinds of investigations, it's important that the young people have someone to look up to," Bench said. "Maybe it sounds corny to people, but that's what made this country."

No. 29 **Eddie Collins**

You've no doubt heard the quote—often attributed to British prime minister Benjamin Disraeli or author Mark Twain, though it's likely neither came up with it—that there are three kinds of lies: lies, damned lies, and statistics. People often use that quote to bash all statistics, but I've always viewed it differently.

I've always thought it means, simply, that you can lie three different ways.

You can lie in such ways that are less direct—white lies, errors, minimizing things, exaggerating, etc. Most lies are probably like this.

You can lie in ways that are more direct—deceit, fraud, cheating, reinvention, fabricating something out of thin air.

And then, you can manipulate statistics—which is to say you can use small sample sizes or designer numbers or statistics formulated for other purposes—to make seemingly incontrovertible points that are, in reality, not true at all.

Take a look, for example, at the numbers for these four players:

Player 1: .375/.394/.563 with 1 home run, 5 runs, 6 RBIs, and 0 errors

Player 2: .324/.324/.500 with 1 triple, 4 runs, and 0 errors

Player 3: .233/.258/.300 with 1 triple, 5 RBIs, 1 steal, and 1 error

Player 4: 226/.273/.258 with 1 double, 2 runs, 1 RBI, and 2 errors

Now, I'm going to tell you: Those are the statistics of four players on the 1919 Black Sox team that threw the World Series. Three of those players were permanently banned from the game. Can you pick out the player who was not?

Because of the way I framed this—and because you know it wouldn't be a trivia question if it had an obvious answer—you might have guessed that the one player not banned has to be Player 3 or Player 4.

It is indeed Player 4.

Player 1: Shoeless Joe Jackson

Player 2: Buck Weaver

Player 3: Chick Gandil

Player 4: Eddie Collins

Nobody, not even Collins's greatest enemy—and as you will see, he collected enemies because his personality annoyed the bejeebers out of people—would have suggested that Collins was complicit in the Black Sox scheme. He was utterly incorruptible. Also, the eight players who conspired with gamblers loathed him as much as they loathed owner Charlie Comiskey.

But the stats . . . well, it's just a nice warning that we all could be a little bit more careful about using baseball stats to prove things they aren't meant to prove.

They called Eddie Collins "Cocky." It wasn't so much a nickname as it was a descriptor. There was nothing subtle about it. It was not ironic, like calling a chronically shy and quiet player "Gabby" Hartnett. But it was hardly celebratory. Collins could be quiet and reserved off the field; he was an Ivy League–educated man who went to church every Sunday; his oldest son, Paul, became an Episcopal minister who officiated his father's second wedding.

But on the field, he was all arrogance and bluster and condescension. He knew himself to be the smartest player in baseball. He probably wasn't wrong. He probably was the smartest player in baseball. But most other players figured he didn't have to be quite so loud about it.

It's unclear that Collins even understood that he was being obnoxious. He grew up in a different world from other baseball players. He attended boarding school, where he excelled as a student and as an athlete. At Columbia, he was the team's quarterback, their best ballplayer and the biggest man on campus.

But unlike his contemporary Christy Mathewson, Collins did not carry around his privilege gracefully. He was the best. And he wasn't going to act like he didn't know it.

Edward Trowbridge Collins's signing story is legend. He was playing semipro baseball in Vermont under the not-especially-persuasive pseudonym "Eddie T. Sullivan." He used the name in an attempt to keep his college eligibility (it didn't work). This was 1906.

One day a Philadelphia Athletics pitcher named Andy Coakley happened to be in the stands. He was in Vermont on his honeymoon. While we can only guess at the splendor of a honeymoon that ends up at a semipro baseball game in Montpelier, Coakley saw the 19-year-old Eddie T. Sullivan play and was dazzled. He immediately got word to Athletics manager Connie Mack, writing that Philadelphia had better get this kid signed quick because word was sure to get out.*

The entire Coakley story is quite famous—shortly after Coakley sent word, Mack sent out a backup catcher named Jim Byrnes to see Collins, and shortly after that Mack made the signing. But there's something about it that I had not known before: Coakley was barely older than Collins when he sent in the report. He was only 23 years old and was hardly established as a big-league star. Could you imagine a 23-year-old today going to a semipro game on his honeymoon and then calling the team's GM about a player? In any case, if Coakley's name sounds familiar to you, it is because he became the legendary longtime coach at Collins's alma mater, Columbia, where he developed a father-son relationship with many players, including a pretty good first baseman named Lou Gehrig.

---

* In fact, word already had gotten out—the Giants' John McGraw knew all about Collins but, for some reason, did not pursue him.

Collins signed with Mack and the Athletics on one condition: He never wanted to play in the minor leagues. The A's put it in writing and Collins learned at the big-league level. In his first full season, he hit .347/.416/.450 for a 170 OPS+. He stole 63 bases. He scored 104 runs. He played superb defense. He was a complete player. He really didn't have a lot to learn.

That was basically the player he kept being for the next two decades.

In his career, Collins did everything except hit home runs. He hit .333 for his career, knocked 3,315 hits, scored 1,821 runs, reached base 4,891 times (only Ty Cobb and Tris Speaker reached base more at their retirement—even now, he's 10th on that all-time list).

It was his baseball intelligence that left people awed. He walked three times more often than he struck out, something even Cobb didn't do. He was not particularly fast and yet he stole more than 700 bases, four times leading the league (he was one of the first to fully realize that you steal off the pitcher as much or more than the catcher).

He was almost certainly the greatest bunter in the history of Major League Baseball—his 512 sacrifice hits are the most in baseball history and nobody is even a close second. Collins used to say he would put a different kind of English on the ball depending on the sort of bunt it was.

People in and around baseball couldn't say enough about his game. Mack named Collins his all-time team captain. John McGraw, despite his own failure to recognize Collins's talent as a young man, called him the greatest second baseman ever—better than Rogers Hornsby or Napoleon Lajoie.

"Not only does he play the game, but he thinks it," Cobb said. "If anyone tells you he wasn't the greatest second baseman of all time, you argue with him."

"He was the greatest infielder I ever saw," Frankie Frisch confirmed.

"Eddie was the kind of guy you could count on any time," Casey Stengel said.

"That man is the best ballplayer I ever saw," Johnny Evers said.

Winning followed Collins, too. In 1908, the A's had a losing record. When Collins had his first full season in 1909, they went 95-58 and were narrowly beaten for the pennant by Cobb's Tigers. Then, for the next five seasons, Collins hit .344/.435/.447, led the league in stolen bases once, led the league in runs scored three times, finished top five in WAR each season, and won a Chalmers Award, which was that day's MVP.

The Athletics over those five seasons won four pennants and three World Series titles.

And what happened next? The Athletics sold Collins to the Chicago White Sox for $50,000.

"Say, for the love of Mike," wrote columnist Blinkey Horn in the *Nashville Tennessean*, "what is the matter with this fellow Connie Mack?"

What was wrong with Mack? Nothing except his finances. Mack built two of the great dynasties of early baseball—the 1910–14 A's and the 1929–31 A's. In both cases, the money ran out and Mack was left to sell off his team in parts.

The Athletics featured the famous $100,000 infield of first baseman Stuffy McInnis, Collins at second, Jack Barry at shortstop, and Home Run Baker at third.

They were not called the $100,000 infield because that is what the players were paid. Far from it. Collins made about $12,000, Baker about $8,000, and McInnis and Barry did not make 10 grand between them. The salary of the $100,000 infield wasn't even $30,000 a year.

No, the reason they were called the $100,000 infield is because that was the estimate of how much the four players would be worth if they were sold off as a group. And the estimate proved to be astonishingly good. When Mack realized that the team was in financial trouble, he sold Collins to the White Sox for the aforementioned $50,000. He sold Barry to the Red Sox for another $10,000. He got into a big salary fight with Baker— Baker sat out the entire 1915 season—but eventually sold him off to the Yankees for $37,500.

That's $97,500 for three-fourths of the $100,000 infield. Mack didn't sell McInnis but surely could have gotten more than $2,500 for him.

With Collins and others gone, the Athletics went from four-time pennant winners to the worst team in baseball. They lost 109 games in 1915 and 117 games a year after that.

And the White Sox after they bought Collins? They were the opposite story. They had not been good for a decade before Collins came along and then in 1915 they won 93 games, tied for most in team history. Two years later, they won 100 games and the World Series. Collins had fallen off a bit statistically—he didn't even hit .300 in 1917 or 1918 as he dealt with some injuries—but he was still so skilled, so smart, he drew so many walks, bunted so well, played such solid defense that he was a winning player and the White Sox team captain.

Collins had a renaissance season in 1919. He hit .319 and led the league in stolen bases and plate appearances. But his White Sox were a wrecking ball of bad blood, nasty feuds, and incessant greed. You might know that many of the near-universal beliefs about the Black Sox are probably not true—it's probably not true, for instance, that Comiskey was unusually cheap or that gamblers were the ones to conceive the fix—and so while the team was talented, it was also fundamentally broken.

"From the moment I arrived at training camp from service," Collins would say, "I could see that something was amiss. We may have had our troubles in other years, but in 1919 we were a club that pulled apart rather than together. There were frequent arguments and open hostility. All the things you think (and are taught to believe) are vital to the success of any athletic organization were missing from it."

"And yet," he would add, "it was the greatest collection of players ever assembled, I would say."

How much of the blame should Collins take for the White Sox's descent into baseball infamy? He certainly had nothing at all to do with the team consorting with gamblers or deciding to throw a World Series, but he was that team's captain. He fully admitted that there were two distinct cliques on the team, his group and the other group led by Chick Gandil. Collins did nothing to bring the team together—quite the opposite. While history has made owner Comiskey the villain of the story, many of the Black Sox hated Collins every bit as much, perhaps even more.

Also, Collins caught wind of the World Series fix early—he would say he suspected it for a long time before the World Series and knew for sure after the first inning of the first game—but seemed entirely paralyzed about how to deal with it. The following May, as a direct challenge to Collins, the *Sporting News* ran a story on its front page under the headline: "Why Do Honest Ball Players Stand for Crooks in Ranks?"

What did Collins do to try to stop the fix? It's unclear. He did have a meeting with Comiskey in early September and he always claimed that he warned Comiskey—but Comiskey denied that, saying only that Collins complained about the pitcher Eddie Cicotte. Either way, nothing came of it. The fix was in and Collins stayed on the sidelines.

Later, though, once it had all gone public, Collins attacked his eight teammates, the Eight Men, with unmatched fury. He never did forgive any of them, not even Buck Weaver, who claimed until his death that his crime was the same as Collins's crime—knowing about the scheme and not turning in his teammates. Collins believed Weaver was lying and never hesitated to say so. "If the gamblers didn't have Weaver and Cicotte in their pocket," he wrote, "then I don't know a thing about baseball."

Something interesting happened late in Collins's career—at age 33, rather suddenly, he began putting up better numbers than he ever had before. From 1920 to 1926, he hit an incredible .348/.435/.447—23 points higher than his career average at the time, 30 points higher in slugging—and he twice led the league in stolen bases, twice finished second in the MVP race.

You can look at those numbers and think that Collins actually got better as he got older.

Ah, but remember that part about lies, damned lies, and statistics. He didn't get better. It's just that 1920 is when Deadball ended, the spitball was banned, umpires started putting fresh new baseballs into games, and offense went up across the game. Collins enjoyed hitting in that new environment. So did every hitter.

You can also calculate that Collins's numbers—already legendary—would have undoubtedly been much better had he played his entire career with the live ball. If you neutralize his numbers and try to mathematically place him in a more neutral run environment, he adds 200 more hits and his runs push up to almost 2,000.

But again—lies, damned lies, and statistics—this doesn't take into account that Collins played in a segregated game.

Speaking of baseball integration: Collins played an unfortunate role in the game's segregation. After his playing days, he became an executive with the Boston Red Sox. He had his successes: When he died, the *Boston Globe* reported that he had only recommended two players to owner Tom Yawkey. One was Hall of Fame second baseman Bobby Doerr.

The other was a guy named Ted Williams.

"Eddie," Williams would say, "was my greatest friend in baseball."

But if he is remembered at all for his days in Red Sox management, it was for the sham Jackie Robinson tryout. This story is in the Jackie Robinson chapter, but let's tell it here from Collins's perspective. In 1945, when Collins was general manager of the Red Sox, he received an impassioned letter from Boston city councilman Izzy Muchnick demanding that the Red Sox give African-American players a chance. Collins, to his credit, responded.

But the response itself was certainly not to his credit.

"As I wrote to one of your fellow councilors last April," he replied, "I have been connected with the Red Sox for 12 years and during that time we have never had a single request for a try-out by a colored applicant. . . . It is beyond my understanding how anyone could insinuate or believe that 'all ballplayers regardless of race, color or creed have not been treated in the American way' so far as having an equal opportunity to play for the Red Sox."

He actually claimed the black players did not *want* to play major-league baseball. When Muchnick called him on this absurdity, Collins replied again, stating that the Red Sox would enthusiastically offer a tryout to talented black players if Muchnick could find any.

It seems certain that Collins did not think Muchnick could find such players. But Muchnick was working together with *Pittsburgh Courier* sports editor Wendell Smith, who suggested three players for such a tryout—a talented young infielder named Marvin Williams, a gifted and fast player named Sam "the Jet" Jethroe, and, yes, Jackie Robinson. Collins was cornered. He agreed to the tryout, and there Robinson—only just back from military service and having not played much regular baseball since college—crushed line drive after line drive.

The Red Sox manager Joe Cronin was duly awed and said so to reporters. Collins was mum. Nothing came of it—the Red Sox would be the last team to sign a black player—and when the Dodgers signed Robinson six months later, Collins said: "More power to Robinson if he can make the grade."

Was Collins a racist? Some, including Howard Bryant in his book *Shut Out*, believe so. Others have written he was not outwardly racist but instead a man of his time.

Still, it must be pointed out that for a person who held himself in as high regard as Collins did, he did find himself on the wrong side of history in the two biggest scandals in his baseball lifetime, the Black Sox scandal and segregation in baseball.

In late 1950, Collins suffered a cerebral hemorrhage that left him partially blind. His last public appearance was in February 1951, when he was among those in baseball being honored. Another of the honorees was the National League Rookie of the Year who had played across town from the Red Sox—the Boston Braves' Sam Jethroe.

Collins congratulated Jethroe—it's unclear if he remembered their previous encounter—and made an offhand remark about how the Red Sox could have used a player like him. Jethroe quietly but firmly said: "You had your chance, Mr. Collins. You had your chance."

The Red Sox had still not signed a black player and would not for another eight years.

Eddie Collins died a month later.

No. 28 **Randy Johnson**

The first time I saw Randy Johnson was also the first time I went on the road as a baseball writer. I was 20 years old and working as an agate clerk for the *Charlotte Observer*. My job as an agate clerk was answering the phone, putting together the daily standings, and taking high school and community results over the phone. I was not good at this job. Many people had to be sick, on vacation, or otherwise indisposed for me to get a chance to cover a ball game.

But that summer, thanks to a series of increasingly unlikely occurrences, I ended up being the only healthy and available person who could join columnist Tom Sorensen for a road trip to Jacksonville as the Charlotte O's and Jacksonville Expos battled for the Southern League Eastern Division title.

This is an aside—well, this whole story is an aside—but that O's team had one of the first great players I ever covered, a guy by the name of Tom Dodd. If you know the name now, it's probably because he was involved in one of the weirder things the New York Yankees ever did. They drafted him in the first round of the 1980 secondary draft, and two years later they traded him to Toronto for John Mayberry.

A few months later, they worked out a trade to get Dodd back. In exchange, this time they threw in soon-to-be Hall of Famer Fred McGriff.

In any case, by the time I wrote about Dodd and the O's, he was 28 and no longer a prospect. He'd already had his cup of coffee for Baltimore in the big leagues (going three for 13 with a home run off Toronto star lefty Jimmy Key). Instead he became a Charlotte minor-league legend. He hit 37 home runs that season with 127 RBIs in 1987; it just didn't make any sense to me at all that he wasn't good enough to hit in the big leagues.

I didn't fully understand then that baseball doesn't quite work that way. Dodd surely was good enough to hit in the big leagues, but it takes more than that. He didn't really have a defensive position; he tried to hold his own at first base but the Orioles had a pretty decent first baseman in future Hall of Famer Eddie Murray. Also, Dodd had blossomed late and, as such, had missed his window.

People don't realize that making it to the big leagues is about so much more than talent.

Anyway, Tom and I drove to Jacksonville for the big playoff game. And I saw Randy Johnson. I remember that part vividly. What I don't remember at all is that I also saw future Hall of Famer Larry Walker, who played for Jacksonville, too. It still boggles my mind that I saw two of the one hundred greatest player in Jacksonville, Florida, on my very first baseball road trip.

In any case, Randy Johnson stays powerfully in the memory. You don't forget your first 6-foot-10 pitcher. That's mainly what he was known for then: being the tallest pitcher in the history of professional baseball. He was drafted by the Expos in the second round out of USC, where he had gone on a joint basketball-baseball scholarship. Everyone knew he had great stuff, otherworldly stuff, but nobody knew if he would actually make it as a major-league pitcher. He was pretty awkward. He didn't have a windup and delivery in those days so much as he unfolded before your very eyes, like one of those inflatable people that flop around in front of car dealerships. He more or less had no idea where his dangerous fastball was going and it was not yet clear that he ever would.

When I asked someone in Jacksonville if Johnson would become a big-league star, the answer was as direct and memorable as such an answer can be:

"Johnson? Hell no. That guy could throw a pitch from the Eiffel Tower and not hit Paris."

Late bloomers in baseball are fascinating creatures. Phenoms, those people born with an abundance of talent and an apparent instruction manual logged in their heads, are somewhat easier to understand. But what about people like Johnson? He was already 24 years old when I first saw him in Jacksonville, and you would expect most gifted 24-year-old pitchers to already be in the big leagues. That year, he pitched 140 innings and while he struck out 163 batters, he also walked 128 batters. And this was two levels below the majors.

He went to Indianapolis the following year and somehow—it's unclear how he did this—managed to balk 20 times in just 113⅓ innings. He had three balks in one game in Louisville. He did combine with former U.S. Olympian Pat Pacillo on a no-hitter in Nashville, but even that wasn't ideal. Johnson lost the game by walking Lenny Harris in the first inning and then allowing Harris to steal second and third. Harris scored on a groundout for the only run of the game.

The Expos called Johnson to the big leagues five days after his 25th birthday. The papers trumpeted the fact that he had become the tallest player in Major League Baseball history, and in his second big-league start he was fantastic, throwing a complete game, allowing one run, striking out 11. He made quite an impression.

"You're one big unit, aren't you?" his teammate Tim Raines asked.

And that's where the Big Unit nickname came from.

But it wasn't going to be a smooth rise in the big leagues. Yes, he was a big unit, but he wasn't yet *the* Big Unit. Players sensed weakness. In a spring training game, several New York Mets players screamed insults at him. "We were on him pretty good," Mets manager Davey Johnson said at the time. Johnson tried to fight back by celebrating after every out he got.

"If they think they can intimidate me," he told reporters, "they're wrong."

But they could. They did. Even years later, Johnson remembered a time when Tony La Russa, then managing Oakland, began yelling for him to quit whining. It turned him inside out. "It was as if I was this California surfer dude who'd let you take advantage of him," he said. "People tried to rattle me. And it worked."

Johnson started just six games for the Expos in 1989. He walked seven batters in his first one. He lasted just three innings in his second and didn't make it out of the second inning the next time. In early May, the Expos made their decision: They weren't willing to wait and see what Johnson might become. They traded him to Seattle for a few months' worth of an established left-handed power pitcher, Mark Langston. Those Expos had delusions of grandeur; they believed themselves to be one pitcher away from glory.

Langston was every bit as good as they could have hoped—he pitched 176 innings, struck out 175, had a 2.39 ERA, and threw four shutouts. It didn't matter. The Expos went 81-81 for the second straight year and finished a distant fourth. Langston left. The Expos lost out on one of the greatest pitchers ever.*

But at the time of the trade, it seemed that nobody at all talked about Johnson, not even in Seattle. Most focused on the anger over the Mariners dumping fan-favorite Langston rather than paying him. Some complained that other teams had offered more for Langston. Heck, the Mets had offered Howard Johnson! Randy Johnson seemed more a baseball oddity than a potentially dominant pitcher.

But Johnson came to Seattle and promptly made an impression. He threw a no-hitter against the Tigers in his first full season with the Mariners. He also led the league in walks three years in a row—his 152 walks in 1991 are the most for any pitcher in the last 30 years. In 1992, he had a particularly strange year—he led the league in walks, strikeouts, fewest hits per nine, and hit-by-pitch—his 18 HBPs was the seventh-highest total for a pitcher since World War II.

And if all this sounds familiar—all those walks, all those strikeouts, all those intimidated hitters, all those wild pitches, a Polaroid windup that took forever to develop—well, yes, that's right: He was basically a left-handed Nolan Ryan. He was also 29 years old and it did not seem all that likely he would ever put everything together.

But Randy Johnson had something that the young Nolan Ryan did not have.

He had the older Nolan Ryan as a guide.

---

* Four years later, the Expos added a young pitcher named Pedro Martínez—whew, can you imagine what that Pedro-Unit one-two punch would have looked like?

"You've got to get your control," Ryan said to him, and it meant a lot because Johnson was more than just a gruff-looking Big Unit who scowled at everyone. He was a lover of baseball history. He was a guy who would occasionally—and without any warning at all—drop a Kid Nichols or Christy Mathewson reference in conversation. He had the numbers of Warren Spahn, Sandy Koufax, and Steve Carlton plugged into his phone, and he took them up on their offer to call and talk baseball.*

When Ryan talked to him about getting control of his stuff and thinking more on the mound and remembering that he was the intimidating one—not all those weak-ass batters and managers yelling insults—well, he took that to heart.

Then there was something else, something much more personal and painful. His father, Bud, died on Christmas Day of 1992. Randy had raced home to say good-bye, but his father was gone by the time he reached the hospital. He put his head on his father's chest and wept.

After that, life was different. At first, he thought about quitting pitching. But with his mother's encouragement, he resolved instead to focus on what matters in life. He turned to his faith. He turned to those words from Ryan. He turned inside. "From that day on," he would say, "I got a lot more strength and determination to be the best player I could be and not get sidetracked and not to look at things as pressure but as challenges. What my dad went through was pressure. That was life and death. This is a game."

It's always problematic to write about life like it's a movie, as if one Rocky Balboa workout montage can change everything. But Big Unit's transformation was unmistakable: Beginning in 1993, as a 29-year-old, Johnson was a different pitcher. He struck out 308 batters that season, becoming the first pitcher to strike out 300 since Nolan Ryan himself. The league hit just .203 against him. He finished second in the Cy Young voting to Jack McDowell, who did not have nearly as good a year (McDowell did win three more games—wins were everything in the award voting in those days).

---

* Big Unit particularly bonded with Carlton; they would talk about how a pitcher has to be the leader on the mound, has to take care of his teammates, and they shared trade secrets about throwing the slider. That must have been some conversation: When Rob Neyer and Bill James rated the greatest sliders in baseball history in their *Guide to Pitchers,* they rated Carlton's and Johnson's Nos. 1 and 2, respectively.

For the next decade, Johnson was profoundly different from any pitcher in the history of the game. He led the league in strikeouts in every full season he pitched but one from 1992 to 2004. The one full season he pitched when he did not lead the league in strikeouts? That was 1997. He struck out 291. Roger Clemens struck out 292.

From 1999 to 2002, four seasons, he left the known universe. He went 81-27 with a 2.48 ERA, a 187 ERA+, and he averaged—*averaged*—354 strikeouts per season. He won all four Cy Youngs, carried the Arizona Diamondbacks to a World Series title, and was named *Sports Illustrated*'s co–Sportsperson of the Year along with his teammate Curt Schilling.

He did all this from ages 35 to 38. It's the greatest four-year run for any late-30s pitcher ever.

He kept on going to age 45, and in time his fastball finally did lose some of its heat, his slider some of its tilt. But by pitching for so long—after such a late start—Big Unit managed to win 300 games, he's second all-time with 4,875 strikeouts, and he put himself in the stratosphere with Lefty Grove and Warren Spahn. One of those guys is the greatest left-handed pitcher ever.

He also hit 190 batters, more than any pitcher in 100 years. You did not crowd the plate against Randy Johnson.

This will sound strange, but I think Johnson is somewhat underrated. I mean, sure, everybody knows he's one of the greatest pitchers ever. He was elected to the Hall of Fame on the first ballot with 97.3 percent of the vote—he went into the Hall with Pedro, who could have been his teammate so many years before.

But because of the odd shape of his career, I'm not sure people quite grasp his place in baseball history. He came along at the very golden age of baseball pitching, when three other all-timers—Greg Maddux, Clemens, and Martínez—were at their height.

Johnson had the quirkiest of the four careers. He was traded before he even started. He was a misfit before he became an ace. He didn't play in a major market until he was 41 and spent only his declining years with the Yankees. While Maddux was beloved by fans in Atlanta and Chicago, while Pedro was idolized in Boston, while Clemens was a larger-than-life character, Johnson kept to himself. With all that, I'm not sure that his name naturally comes to mind when people argue about the greatest pitcher to ever take the mound.

But it should.

While he was hard to know when he played, Johnson has shown some of his fun personality since he retired. He appeared as himself on *The Simpsons* and he has done some entertaining commercials—like the one about how you don't ever really want to get into a snowball fight with Randy Johnson—and it does humanize him, which is great, because he always was more than just a guy who carried a scowl and a grudge and took the inside of the plate by force.

Randy Johnson is the most recent pitcher to win 300 games. Now the question is: Will Johnson be the last pitcher to ever win 300 games in a career? I don't think so. For one thing, it's probably good to follow the advice of Romeo Void (or Justin Bieber, if you insist on being more current) and never say never.

But, even beyond that, I don't think you have to work that hard right now to imagine a 300-game winner. I think Justin Verlander, for example, might have a shot. Sure, it's something of a long shot—he still has 75 wins to go and he's 38—but he has a shot just the same.

Heck, Johnson had 46 fewer wins at Verlander's age.

And that's the point. It is true that wins are harder to come by now because of the way starting pitchers are used, but it's also true that the game is in constant motion and something new will always come along to surprise us. Who could have imagined Randy Johnson before Randy Johnson?

No. 27 **Mike Trout**

M ike Trout has led the league in at least four major statistical categories every full year of his big-league career. We should take a
moment, or many moments, to appreciate just how absurd this
is. Many of the greatest players in baseball history—say Hall of Famers
Robin Yount or Ryne Sandberg or Ron Santo—rarely led the league in
any major statistical category.

Vladimir Guerrero, for instance, led the league in four major statistical
categories in his *entire* career. Robbie Alomar led the league in one.

But Trout leads the league in four major categories every single year.
Here, you can see it for yourself:

2012: Led league in runs, stolen bases, OPS+, and both versions of
WAR

2013: Led league in runs, walks, and both versions of WAR

2014: Led league in runs, RBIs, total bases, and FanGraphs WAR

2015: Led league in slugging, OPS, OPS+, and both versions of WAR

2016: Led league in runs, walks, on-base percentage, OPS+, and both
versions of WAR

2017: Led league in on-base percentage, slugging, OPS, and OPS+

2018: Led league in walks, on-base percentage, OPS, and OPS+

2019: Led league in on-base percentage, slugging, OPS, and OPS+

We'll not count 2020 because it was not really a season, but even in 2020 he was among the leaders in on-base percentage, slugging percentage, runs, total bases, homers, RBIs—over a full season he undoubtedly would have continued his absurd and wonderful streak.

By the way, we're not counting other, perhaps less recognizable stats like most intentional walks (led three times) or win probability added (led five times) or runs created (led four times) or times on base (led four times) or fielding percentage for center fielders (led in 2015 and 2018, when he made zero errors) or adjusted batting wins (led five times).

I'm throwing around a lot of statistics here, which can blur the point. The Black Ink system—which measures how often a player leads the league in a major category—is usually a good way of determining just how good a player was. Trout's Black Ink score is 33, already higher than the average Hall of Famer, and better than Willie McCovey, Ernie Banks, Ken Griffey Jr., Jeff Bagwell, Roberto Clemente, Frank Thomas, Cal Ripken Jr., and dozens of other legendary players.

And he's only played eight full seasons. The only players in baseball history who can compare are the greatest players in baseball history: Cobb, Hornsby, Mantle, Foxx, Aaron, Ruth.

But here's the thing I wonder: Do such statistical wonders do more to camouflage Trout's greatness than spotlight it? It's almost like so many people have become immune to these sorts of historical arguments. It isn't like Trout is a secret. It isn't like people miss the point that he's the best player in baseball, a player more easily compared to the Mantles and Mayses and Aarons and Griffeys and Cobbses than players of his own time.

No, it's more like, for so many, the Trout conversation has become too much brain and not enough heart. Have you ever tried to explain to someone what chocolate tastes like? It is a profoundly frustrating experience, as each word like "sweet" and "bitter" and "earthy" and "heavenly" takes you just a little bit further away from the actual taste.

So it goes with Trout and the numbers. There are always more dizzying and overwhelming statistics to talk about. He is already in the midst of surpassing the very best—DiMaggio! Rose! Ryan! Pedro!—on the all-time WAR list. If he can stay healthy and at the top of his game for another 10 years, he could challenge Babe Ruth himself.

But does that get us any closer to the taste? The most common questions asked in Trout stories are uncomfortable ones: Why is he not a bigger deal? Why is he not more famous? Why don't people appreciate him? What does Mike Trout have to do to capture America's attention?

The theories come in waves. The kids just don't dig baseball. Trout plays most of his games after half of America has gone to sleep. His Angels are a perpetual nonfactor; they have not won a playoff game since Trout arrived. And Trout's personality plays a role, too, the theories continue, because he steers clear of fame, best he can, preferring a quieter life.

Beyond that, he is so consistent—so metronome, Old Faithful, changing of the guards, bullets missing James Bond, Taylor Swift album to No. 1, Angela Lansbury finds the murderer, *Shawshank Redemption* is on television again, the sun comes up in the morning consistent—that it blunts our sense of wonder.

See a guy hit .300, walk 100 times, score 100 runs, drive in 100 runs, steal 30 bases, hit 40 homers, play fantastic center-field defense, and light up the ballpark with joy once, yeah, you can appreciate that.

See him do it every single year and what's left to be excited about? We all know it shouldn't be that way, but we can't help ourselves. We're human. How many gorgeous sunrises in a row can we appreciate? We get bored, even with greatness.

Jeff Trout was a good ballplayer. He won't tell you that because of course he won't—he's Mike Trout's dad, for crying out loud. Where do you think Mike got his humility from? But Jeff could really hit. Actually, it's better to say he could really switch-hit. Left-handed, right-handed, he pounded line drives all over the field, sort of a smaller Daniel Murphy, if you want a comparison. Before his senior year at the University of Delaware, he spent a summer in the Atlantic Collegiate Baseball League, which has sent dozens and dozens of players to the big leagues, from Jamie Moyer to Frank Viola to Craig Biggio to Dennis Leonard.

He hit .481 and was given every award the ACBL can give.

"He's unique," the sportswriter Jim O'Connell said; he was the league's official scorer.

Then, Trout went back to play his senior year—this even though the Cubs had offered him a shot—and he hit .518 with gap power. He was named an All-American. He was small (5-foot-8 or so), but the Minnesota Twins liked his bat and drafted him in the fifth round and sent him to the Wisconsin Rapids, where he hit .341 and slugged .511 and impressed his young manager. "He could really hit," that guy, Charlie Manuel, would say.

So why didn't Jeff make it to the big leagues? Well, it's never one thing, is it? He had knee injuries, a lot of them, which led to four knee surgeries. He had other injuries, too—a thumb injury, a hand injury . . . he just played the game so hard that it was hard for his body to keep up. He had no choice but to play the game hard; you think teams send limos for 5-foot-8 ballplayers? They do not. He had to play harder than anybody else just to be seen. As he told one reporter, he saw extra batting practice as a privilege.

But there were other reasons he didn't make it to the majors. He did not have a natural defensive position. Second base might have become his natural position, but the Twins thought he was a better fit at third. Then, third base might have become his natural position, but the Twins vacillated and moved him back to second. Back and forth he went, and he made a bunch of errors, he never really got comfortable, and he soon had a reputation as an all-hit, no-field player. Once you get that reputation, it's hard to break out of that prison.

Also, he was cursed with a worldview. He loved baseball, but he never saw it as his whole life. He got married to Debbie, and they had a daughter, Teal Marie. As he told a reporter, "I'm not getting younger. I have to think about my future."

And finally, there was just the nasty business of baseball. Through everything, Jeff Trout hit. In 1986, while playing for Double-A Orlando, he hit .321/.406/.451. When he told the Twins he needed to make progress or he would have to quit the game, they promised to promote him to Triple A in 1987 and give him that chance to make the big-league club. Anyway, that's how Jeff heard it.

But the Twins did not follow through. Instead, they told him they were going to send him back to Orlando and would promote him to Triple A only if he hit well again. Jeff wasn't going back to Orlando. He asked the Twins to release him so he could try to hook up with another club. But the Twins also refused to do that. "The Twins told my agent that they aren't going to release a big-league bat," Jeff told the *Millville Daily*. "And my agent told them that if that's the case, they should put me in the big leagues."

It never got better. Trout refused to report, the Twins suspended him without pay, and neither side budged. "I don't want to give up pro baseball," Trout said. "I don't think I've reached my full potential as a ballplayer, and I'd like to keep playing. But I don't want my career to continue down this path. I've taken my stand."

He held that stand. In August, he retired from baseball and dedicated himself to becoming a father, a teacher, and a coach. "It's time to do something else," he said. "There are a lot of other things to do besides play baseball."

Four years later, his youngest son, Mike, was born.

Are there times when Jeff wonders whether he left baseball too early? Sure, maybe, but not too many times. He has learned a lot about baseball and life in the years since then. He will concede he caught some bad breaks—all those injuries, an organization that wasn't supportive, some bad timing.

But now that his son Mike is one of the greatest players in baseball history, he understands there is a big difference between them. Talent? Sure. Mike is a lot more talented, too.

But there's something else . . .

"Confidence," he says. "I tried to be confident as a player; I tried to present myself as confident. But I wasn't confident. Not like Mike. Not like the great major-league players. I'd go 0-for-4 and I wouldn't sleep at all that night. I'd make an error and I'd be shaky for a while after that. I didn't believe as much as I needed to believe."

And Mike?

"Mike," he says, "doesn't have doubts."

Do you know why Mike Trout calls time-out in the box so often? It's because a thought creeps into his head sometimes. And he wants it out.

What thought creeps in, you might ask. But it's the wrong question. The thought doesn't matter. The way Trout views it, any thought in the box is bad. What he wants to feel, what he needs to feel for success, is something like emptiness. So, he calls time-out, he blanks out everything—"reset mode," he calls it—and he steps back in with his mind as clear as the sky in Phoenix.

"My philosophy," he says, "is 'keep it simple.'"

Trout is hardly the only hitter to take this approach. See the ball, hit the ball. *Ve la pelota, pegále a la pelota.* Hall of Famer Tony Pérez lived by the philosophy to the point that other players would laugh whenever a reporter asked about his hitting approach. "See the ball, hit the ball," they would say in unison. George Brett believed in it so deeply that he would practice various mind exercises to make sure he never had two thoughts going at the same time.

But Trout takes it to a different level. He doesn't guess at the plate. He doesn't think at the plate. He relies, instead, on his utterly unshakable confidence. He just knows that if a pitcher throws a pitch in his zone, he will hit the ball hard. As Jeff says, he doesn't have doubts. And if he misses it once, misses it twice, misses it 10 times, it doesn't have any impact on that conviction. He still has no doubts. Step out of the box. Reset. Step back in.

Where does that sort of supernatural confidence come from? Nobody knows. Even his dad doesn't know. Jeff did not raise Mike to be a ball-player; he never did the Mickey Mantle/Chipper Jones thing and teach his son to switch-hit (even though Jeff was a good switch-hitter himself and was more qualified than those other dads). Jeff had promised himself that whatever his own baseball ambitions had been, he would never place any of that on his kids—the thing he and Debbie wanted for them was to be able to live their own lives, follow their own passions, be their best at whatever they wanted.

Mike just took it from there. He deeply loved baseball right from the start. He always wanted to hang around his father's high school team. He always wanted to watch the games on television. He so completely fell in love with Derek Jeter that he insisted on wearing Jeter's No. 2 and copying his every move.

Confidence just came with it. He was talented, right from the start. He was so fast. He hit with power. He played defense. He grew much bigger than his father, too—he's now 6-foot-2, 235 pounds, and in family photos, you notice, he will usually stand a step behind so as not to tower over everybody else.

But more than anything, he just was so happy on the field, so at home, like it was the only place in the world to be. Everybody liked him. What a player. What a guy. As a pitcher in high school, he threw a no-hitter. In one state playoff game, he was intentionally walked every time he came to the plate, even with the bases loaded.

More than once, Jeff came home and said to Debbie a bit breathlessly, "Wow, he has a chance to be really good."

It's not fair to say Mike Trout was overlooked by scouts. He wasn't. They knew he existed. They knew he came from a great baseball family. They knew he was a first-round talent. This isn't a Kurt Warner story where he was stocking shelves at a supermarket when a scout happened to notice him.

They *knew* about him. But somehow they missed him, too. Somehow they missed that he was a once-in-a-lifetime player who, even as a teenager, was just about ready to star on a big-league field. It really is striking that people who get paid to scout baseball players could miss a talent that big.

Stephen Strasburg was the first pick in the 2009 draft—many were calling him the greatest pitching prospect in the history of the draft, so he took up most of the pre-draft conversation. Nobody seemed to care who was taken after him. A couple of center fielders—a college player named Dustin Ackley and a high school player named Donavan Tate—went after him, followed by a high school catcher. The next eight teams took pitchers.

Then came the Oakland A's, one of the smartest teams in baseball. They knew all about Trout. Their assistant general manager, David Forst, had seen Trout play. "He hit two home runs," Forst says somewhat sadly. "Then he came in to pitch and I saw him throw 95 mph to close the game out."

Why did he say that sadly? Because the A's took college shortstop Grant Green instead.

The Diamondbacks had back-to-back picks and took two position players, neither one named Mike Trout. The Astros took a high school shortstop, Jiovanni Mier, out of La Verne, California. The White Sox took an LSU center fielder, Jared Mitchell.

And then, finally, it was the Angels' turn and they took . . . Randal Grichuk.

But they had another pick right after that and selected Mike Trout.

Twenty-four players taken before him? Forst shrugs and says the A's probably leaned too heavily on their objective data on that one. "We probably didn't put enough art into that decision," he said.

J. J. Picollo, the Royals' assistant general manager, said the state of New Jersey undoubtedly played a role in the Royals taking pitcher Aaron Crow instead. "If there had been even one great prospect to come out of New Jersey in a while," he said mournfully, and he was right about that: New Jersey had not produced any big-league hitters in a long time. Who was the last great one to come out of New Jersey? Goose Goslin? Ducky Medwick? Eric Karros?

But Picollo readily acknowledges it's no excuse: He's *from* New Jersey. Heck, he's from a town not far from Trout's Millville. "That one will always hurt," he says.

There are plenty of reasons teams missed. There was the bad Jersey weather—Trout didn't play as much as prospects in warmer climates. There was the fact Trout was a little bit of a late bloomer—Baseball America had him as only the 80th-ranked high school player before his senior season began. And there were some mild questions about Trout's thick, football body type; some scouts thought he would not age very well.

But the bottom line is most scouts just missed on what makes Mike Trout so special.

"We knew he had talent," Royals general manager Dayton Moore said. "We knew he was a great athlete. The draft is filled with great athletes. But we didn't see the rest of it. We didn't see how much he wanted to be a big-league ballplayer. We didn't see that he had prepared his whole life to become a great ballplayer."

Everyone found out fast. At 17, Trout hit .360 in rookie league ball, so the Angels moved him up to Class A. At 18, he hit .362 in Class-A ball with power and had 45 stolen bases, so they moved him up again. At 19, he hit .326 in Double A with power and had 33 stolen bases, so they brought him up to the big leagues.

At 20, he was the best player in baseball.

That fast.

It has been written repeatedly that Mike Trout has never done a late-night talk show. He turned down *60 Minutes,* which wanted to do a piece on him, and he turned down HBO, too. He's not the type to spend his free time chasing celebrity endorsements. He has never participated in the Home Run Derby—it just doesn't interest him; he prefers watching it with his family—and if you type "Mike Trout controversy" into Google, you will get one hit. That's when the commissioner of baseball, Rob Manfred, awkwardly poked at Trout's indifference to fame.

"Mike has made decisions on what he wants to do, doesn't want to do, how he wants to spend his free time or not spend his free time," Manfred said. "I think we could help him make his brand very big. . . . But he has to make a decision to engage. It takes time and effort."

Yes, we live in a time when someone's reluctance to make his "brand very big" is controversial.

But it's unavoidable—this is the knock on Trout. He's boring. He doesn't interest the nation. He can't make baseball cooler. He doesn't try to be baseball's LeBron James or Tom Brady. He isn't in movies. He hasn't single-handedly made the Angels a contender.

And people will argue about how fair or unfair all this is, but really, I prefer to see what's left.

And here's what's left: Mike Trout is a small-town kid who every single day comes to the ballpark with a smile and the same joy he has felt for baseball since he was 12. He signs autographs. He hits home runs. He visits hospitals. He steals bases. He answers questions politely. He makes diving catches. He treats people with respect. He draws walks. He works with Big Brothers Big Sisters. He scores runs. And he's still just 29 years old.

And he's on his way to becoming the greatest player in the history of the game.

I mean, if that isn't enough, well, what does that say about us?

No. 26 Grover Cleveland Alexander

The *Winning Team* is a spectacularly bad movie. No, seriously, as bad as you think it might be, it is so much worse than that. Even if you are a devotee of bad old movies—and I like to think of myself as one of those—*The Winning Team* will break your spirit.

It shouldn't be this bad. The movie stars Ronald Reagan as pitcher Grover Cleveland Alexander. This is such a wonderful confluence of American history; it makes Alexander the only player in sports history to be named for one president and to have another president play him in a movie.

The Winning Team also features Doris Day, who would become Hollywood's biggest female star. There are also a few ballplayers in there, including Hall of Famer Bob Lemon.

Put all of that together and it's hard to believe that *The Winning Team* doesn't at least make for some fun kitsch watching.

But let me be clear again: It does not. Watch *The Winning Team* for even 10 minutes and you realize it's not just a bad movie. It's a Dementor from Harry Potter. "They drain peace, hope and happiness out of the air around them," J. K Rowling wrote of them—the Dementors, I mean—and while I'm not sure that watching *The Winning Team* is what inspired her to develop the characters, I'm also not sure it wasn't.

The biggest trouble with the movie—other than the writing, acting, direction, and such—is that it begins with these words: "This is The True Story of GROVER CLEVELAND ALEXANDER."

Spoiler alert: It is not.

Oh, there's some truth in it. In the most basic ways, *The Winning Team* hits some of the big events of Alexander's life. He grew up in a small farming community in Elba, Nebraska. He used to like throwing rocks. He was working as a lineman for the telephone company when he was recruited to play for a professional team in Galesburg, Illinois. He was sensational for Galesburg and showed incredible control, but he was hit in the head with a throw and was knocked unconscious for 36 hours. He woke up with double vision. His pitching days seemed over.

Then he regained his full vision and soon after became a successful major-league pitcher. Then he went to war, where he endured terrible things and began drinking, and then he returned home and suffered in so many ways, particularly with epileptic fits, but eventually he got a chance to pitch in the 1926 World Series against the Yankees, where he struck out Tony Lazzeri with the bases loaded to win the championship.

All of these are, to various degrees, true. So, you add in some impossibly corny jokes, a little Doris Day singing (because why else would you have Doris Day in the picture?), and some terrible dialogue, and you have a picture!

"If you wanna marry the boy," Aimee (Doris Day) hears from her father, "I'm not a-gonna stand in your way. But I ain't a-gonna help you do it, neither. . . . I know that boy ain't cut out to be any farmer. He ain't cut out to be anything but just what he is: a fella that wants to play!"

But even with all that, the movie *still* should not be as bad as it is. What takes it to a different level is that it is a terrible lie. It romanticizes a life that was starkly unromantic. It's a sunny movie, and Ol' Pete Alexander lived a dark life.*

---

* OK, one more point: The title of the movie tells you how bad it is. It's called "The Winning Team." No, really, it includes the quotation marks. It's not *The Winning Team*. The title is bracketed by quote marks so that, what, it's supposed to be ironic? And also: Why is a movie about Alexander called "The Winning Team"? I guess the point is that Alexander and his wife, Aimee, teaming up, they're the "winning team." This makes sense in that Aimee was a consultant on the movie. It doesn't make sense in that in real life Aimee did not grow up with Alexander and actually divorced him twice.

The movie begins in the Baseball Hall of Fame with a close-up of Grover Cleveland Alexander's plaque. You can read the words:

GREAT NATIONAL LEAGUE PITCHER
FOR TWO DECADES WITH PHILLIES,
CUBS AND CARDINALS STARTING
IN 1911. WON 1926 WORLD CHAMPIONSHIP
FOR CARDINALS BY STRIKING OUT
LAZZERI WITH BASES FULL IN
FINAL CRISIS AT YANKEE STADIUM.

That is, in fact, Alexander's plaque and this must be said: Wow, it's terrible. Here was one of the greatest pitchers in baseball history, and half of his plaque focuses on one at-bat? This would be a bit like doing a Tom Hanks Hall of Fame plaque like this:

GREAT AMERICAN FILM ACTOR
FOR FOUR DECADES STARTING WITH
ROLE AS "RICK MARTIN" ON
THE LOVE BOAT. WON 1995 OSCAR
FOR PLAYING FORREST GUMP
WHO PLAYED PING PONG REALLY WELL
AND ALSO RAN FROM COAST TO COAST

You see what I'm getting at? The plaque doesn't really give you a sense of the scope of Alexander's career or life. No mention of his impeccable control? No mention of his 373 wins? No mention of his nickname "Alexander the Great"? Compare the words on his plaque with those on the plaque of, say, Walter Johnson or Christy Mathewson and you wouldn't think he was in their league. You would think Pete Alexander* was a good

---

* I think the first time I saw him called "Pete Alexander" rather than "Grover Cleveland Alexander" was in Bill James's *New Historical Baseball Abstract* back in 2001. Bill ranked him the third-greatest pitcher ever, and I instinctively thought: "Who in the heck is Pete Alexander?" I had always heard him referred to as Grover. But, it's true, people did call him Pete (along with Alex, Alec, and Dode). It's also true that even now, the name "Pete Alexander" rings foreign to many baseball fans.

pitcher who happened to be in the right place at the right time in 1926. And that's just not how it was.

A few years ago, I traveled to Elba, Nebraska, the little town where Alexander grew up. I was doing a story on how many great pitchers had grown up in small midwestern towns. Walter Johnson was from Humboldt, Kansas; Bob Feller was from Van Meter, Iowa. Carl Hubbell was from Carthage, Missouri. And Pete Alexander was from Elba.

There wasn't much to see in Elba. The population is only about 200, and it wasn't any bigger in Alexander's day. Elba reminded me a lot of my wife's hometown of Cuba, Kansas. I recall two landmarks: the brick schoolhouse and a bar called "Grover's."

If you know the story of Grover Cleveland Alexander, you will feel the immense sadness of seeing a bar called "Grover's."

As I walked around Elba, it was easy to picture a young Alexander looking around for perfect rocks to throw. That's how it began for him . . . and so many pitchers. As Satchel Paige once said, "there wasn't anything else to throw." But even if that story is familiar, Alexander was particularly smitten with rock throwing. He used to keep the best throwing rocks in his pockets until they tore holes in his pants. It is legend (and perhaps even true) that when his mother wanted to cook a chicken, she would send young Alexander outside to kill one with a rock. Alexander said he always gave the chicken a running start.

Grover's father wanted him to become a lawyer like his namesake Grover Cleveland, but this apparently was never in the cards. Alexander did, reluctantly, graduate from high school and then he got a job digging holes for the telephone company. He pitched some ball around town for a couple of bucks and would have loved to play more, but he did not see himself as talented enough to make a living out of baseball.

"I can play with these farmers around here," he would tell the Galesburg manager Jap Wagner. "But that's about as far as I can go."

Wagner knew better. He had seen how hard Alexander threw with his quick, side-armed motion, but even more he saw Alex's pinpoint control. "Can you just throw it wherever you want every time?" Wagner supposedly asked, and Alexander simply nodded.

Well, he could. Among his many, many nicknames was "Down and Away Alexander" because he seemed to throw every single pitch down and away. "It's a good spot," Grover would say, "if you don't want the hitter to do anything."

He was an instant sensation. In 1911, as a rookie for the Phillies, Alexander led the league in wins (28), innings (367), shutouts (7), and fewest hits allowed per nine innings (7.0). He was just a natural pitcher. He mixed velocity and command in the timeless way that transcends the seasons.

His style is important to think about when trying to place him in history. When people wonder how someone like Alexander would pitch in today's game, they might try to estimate the miles per hour on his fastball (undoubtedly a disappointing number) or attempt to take him through a time machine to a moment when hitters study video and work out like tri-athletes and work their swings into perfect launch-angle feats of strength.

But it might be better to think that Alexander led his league in strikeouts six times, in fewest walks per nine innings five times, in WHIP five times, in shutouts seven times. From 1915 to 1917, Alexander the Great won the triple crown of pitching each year. He's the only pitcher to win it three years in a row.

In 1915, he went 31-10 with a 1.22 ERA and 241 strikeouts.

In 1916, he went 33-12 with a 1.55 ERA and 167 strikeouts.

In 1917, he went 30-13 with a 1.83 ERA and 200 strikeouts.*

In addition to all that, Alexander had a combined 36 shutouts in just those three seasons, which is more than Lefty Grove or Greg Maddux, more than Pedro Martínez and Clayton Kershaw have combined. He threw 16 shutouts in 1916, a modern record.

Hitters have become so much better, stronger, faster, more prepared . . . but they still can't hit pitches perfectly placed down and away. That, I suspect, will never change. In 2019, hitters batted less than .130 on pitches down and away.

After 1917, Pete Alexander went to war. He was so close to the action that the booming sounds caused him to lose hearing in his left ear. He took a shell to his right ear, which may have caused his later cancer. He badly hurt his right arm operating a howitzer. Most significantly, he had his first

---

* His 1917 season is no longer considered a triple crown winner because a starter-reliever for the Giants named Fred Anderson had a 1.44 ERA that year. Anderson pitched only 162 innings, which at the time did not qualify for the ERA title. However, since 1961, any pitcher with 162 innings—he hit the number on the nose—qualifies.

epileptic seizure; his epilepsy might have been sparked by the ball to the forehead he took back in his first year of professional baseball. He never overcame a chronic case of what was then called shell shock and is now known as post-traumatic stress disorder.

According to most versions of his story, he began drinking heavily in France to numb and forget the pain.

Actually, nobody can say for sure exactly when Alexander started drinking heavily. His father and grandfather were hard drinkers. Pete certainly would drink beer in his younger days. There is a belief that his drinking actually began earlier and that even in 1915 it played a role in his World Series performance. That's worth exploring.

Alexander was scheduled to pitch Game 5 of that 1915 World Series. His Phillies trailed the Red Sox three games to one in the best-of-seven series. Their only win had been when Alexander pitched Game 1.

"Alexander," the *San Francisco Examiner* wrote, "is their last, forlorn hope."

Alexander himself wrote in his syndicated column before the game: "We are backed up against the wall. We will fight back to the best of our ability, however, and we are not licked, not by a longshot. We will go to the limit today, using every possible means to win. It's make or break with us."

I mean, you know he was serious because otherwise there was no possible way for him to string together quite that many clichés. Later in the column, he made it clear that he would try his best because that was one cliché he had missed: "I will give our boys everything that is in this arm of mine," he wrote.

But Alexander did not pitch. The Phillies instead went with Erskine Mayer as their starter, and then they put Eppa Rixey in the game. They lost in the ninth when Boston's Harry Hooper hit the game-deciding home run. For many, many years there were theories that Alexander showed up to the ballpark drunk and that was why he didn't pitch. For years, I believed that, too.

But now, taking all things into consideration, it probably isn't true.

See, in the column he wrote before Game 5, he also said this: "Of course, I don't know that I will pitch in this critical game. When I warm up, if I feel good, I'll go in. If my arm doesn't feel right I am not sure that I can do justice to the job that is before me, I'll tell Pat [Moran, the manager] so and ask him to select another man."

It seems that was what happened.

"In my story yesterday," Alexander wrote the next day, "I said I would pitch if I felt right when I warmed up. I pitched quite a few before the game and developed a pain in my back. I believe I caught a cold on that damp day last Friday when I worked in the opening game. In any event, Moran looked me over and decided that it would be foolish for me to take a chance when I did not feel up to snuff."

It's possible that he was covering up for his drinking, but it makes more sense that his alcoholism really set in after the war, as his life began to fall apart.

His pitching did not deteriorate, however. Alexander led the league in ERA his first two seasons back—winning another pitching triple crown in 1920. And he kept on pitching pretty well for the Cubs. They loved him in Chicago, so much so that one year the fans just gave him a car—no special reason, no special occasion, they just announced a Grover Cleveland Alexander Day and gave him a car.

But in 1926, Chicago manager Joe McCarthy—the same Joe McCarthy who later would win seven World Series with the Yankees—grew sick of Alexander's drunkenness. McCarthy suspended him and then dumped him on the waiver wire and eventually sold him to the St. Louis Cardinals.

The Cardinals' manager and star was Rogers Hornsby, and you might know that he was a zealot about players not drinking or smoking or even going to movies. But Hornsby was even more of a zealot about winning, and he proved willing to ignore the drinking as long as Alexander pitched effectively.

Alex did, somehow, pitch effectively in 1926. He was 39 years old and his fastball was gone—he struck out just 35 batters in more than 148 innings—but his control was still impeccable. A pitcher, even one with no stuff, can do some pretty remarkable things by throwing the ball down and away every time.

And this led to the moment that takes up half of Pete Alexander's plaque: the famous World Series between the Cardinals and the Yankees. Remember this was 1926, one year before the Yankees would put on the field a team many still consider to be the greatest in baseball history. Well, the 1926 Yankees were exactly the same team with exactly the same lineup, featuring Babe Ruth, Lou Gehrig, Tony Lazzeri, Earle Combs, etc.

The Yankees won Game 1 when Gehrig drove in Ruth for the winning run. The Cardinals came back to win Game 2 behind Alexander, who had found his youthful spirit and pitched a complete game, striking out 10 batters. The Cardinals won Game 3, but Ruth smashed three homers in Game 4 to even the Series. Then the Yankees took the series lead with a 10-inning victory sealed by Lazzeri's sacrifice fly with the bases loaded.

Now it was up to Alexander. He was old. He was exhausted. He was in great pain. But he was a natural pitcher. He threw a complete game to win Game 6. And then, in Game 7, bottom of the seventh, the Cardinals led 3–2, but Combs singled, Ruth was intentionally walked, Gehrig was unintentionally walked, and the bases were loaded.

In came Grover Cleveland Alexander on zero days' rest to face Lazzeri.

Alexander, by all accounts, stumbled on his way to the mound. Was he drunk? That was how Hornsby would tell the story for the rest of his life. Was he hungover? Many others have told it that way. Was he dealing with issues leftover from the war? That's how the movie made it sound. But Alexander always insisted he was sober . . . and tired.

Whatever it was, he faced Lazzeri, who had driven in 117 RBIs as a rookie. Alexander may or may not have warmed up (several accounts said he did not, but Alexander himself remembered throwing a few warm-up pitches). Alexander walked around the mound for a minute to "let Lazzeri stew."

In the movie, Alexander fell behind in the count 3-1. But in real life, it was much simpler.

The first pitch was a curveball low and away. Lazzeri took it for a strike.

The second pitch was a fastball that did an unusual thing: It caught too much of the plate. Lazzeri turned on it and crushed it to deep left field. No one can say for sure how close it was to being a home run, but it did drift foul. Alexander would utter the classic line about it: "A few feet made the difference between a hero and a bum."

Third pitch, Alexander threw the low-and-away curve one more time. Lazzeri flailed at it for strike three. The inning was over.

But not the game. Alexander pitched the last two innings without giving up a hit. He did walk Ruth with two outs in the ninth, but then Ruth— in one of the more bizarre endings to any World Series—was caught stealing. Ruth would say he believed Alexander to be so dominant that the team's only chance was for him to try to get into scoring position.

Alexander pitched three more years for the Cardinals. In 1927, at age

40, he won 21 games and led the league in WHIP—he walked just 38 batters in 268 innings. At age 43, his life a complete wreck, he tried to pitch for the Phillies once more but made only three starts and then retired.

In all, Alexander is third all-time in victories (373, tied with Mathewson), fifth in pitcher WAR, and second with 90 shutouts. He's one of six or seven pitchers who have a viable argument as the greatest of all time.

Sadly, though, the Pete Alexander story does not end with that Lazzeri strikeout or even his last pitch with the Phillies. Life ain't like bad movies. Alexander lived two more heartbreaking decades—he died just before *The Winning Team* came out.

In those years, he was arrested numerous times. He was thrown in jail. He was sued for being a "love pirate." He and Aimee divorced and then got back together and then they got divorced again. He scraped for money any way he could, occasionally pitching an inning or two in exhibition games for the traveling House of David team. He was broke, he was usually drunk, and he was in agonizing pain. Alexander is at the heart of perhaps the saddest line in sports literature.

"Aren't you Grover Cleveland Alexander?" he was asked.

"Used to be," he said.

Alexander was elected to the Hall of Fame in 1938—he represented the third Hall of Fame class—and while he was honored, he also felt lost. "You can't eat a tablet," he said when asked about how it felt to see his Hall of Fame plaque. He died penniless in 1950.

At one point during those last years, he got a job telling his own story at a nickel theater show in New York. Night after night, he would tell the story of his career, finishing with his down-and-away fastball and his World Series heroics. The show was fairly popular but after a time, Grover Cleveland Alexander quit. Someone asked him why.

"I'm tired of striking out Lazzeri," he said.

We know so little about John Henry Lloyd. There is something truly heartbreaking about that.

I'll give you an example: When you start to research Lloyd, you will pretty quickly come across a guy named Ted Harlow. Who is that? Well, he was, by some accounts, a St. Louis sportswriter, but by many of the more recent accounts, he was more than that. He was a *legendary* St. Louis sportswriter. By all accounts, he was a white sportswriter, which is important.

Harlow called Pop Lloyd the greatest baseball player who ever lived.

"Legend has it," the *Press* of Atlantic City reported, "that in 1938 noted St. Louis sportswriter Ted Harlow was asked whom he considered the best player in the history of the sport. . . . He picked Lloyd."

"How great was Lloyd?" the *Orlando Sentinel* asked. "Well in 1938, St. Louis sportswriter Ted Harlow called Lloyd the greatest of all time."

"In 1938," SouthJersey.com wrote, "many years after Lloyd's career was over, Ted Harlow, a St. Louis sportswriter, paid Lloyd the ultimate compliment."

"St. Louis sportswriter Ted Harlow," a man named Ray Anselmo wrote in a story called "The Black Wagner," "when asked in 1938 who the best ever player in baseball was, replied, 'If you mean in organized baseball, my answer would be Babe Ruth. But if you mean in all baseball, organized or unorganized, the answer would have to be a colored man named John Henry Lloyd."

"He is generally considered the greatest shortstop in Negro Leagues history," is how Lloyd's Wikipedia page begins, "and both Babe Ruth and Ted Harlow, a noted sportswriter, reportedly believed Lloyd to be the greatest baseball player ever."

So, yes, Harlow's opinion about Lloyd is well known and has been shared with the world. There is just one small issue with Ted Harlow.

He never existed.

I'm going to take you down this rabbit hole to show you how all this came to be, but I don't want to get too far away from the point, which is: We know so little about Lloyd. And it is heartbreaking. Here was this extraordinary baseball player, this phenomenon, and he has been lost to history because of a hatred that has plagued America. Now, we try so hard to bring him back that it sometimes takes us to strange places.

In 1938, a rather extraordinary and unusual story appeared in *Esquire* magazine. What made it unusual and extraordinary is that it appeared nine years before Jackie Robinson crossed the color line and 10 years before Harry Truman integrated the military. There was no real momentum yet for including black players in the major leagues.

And then this story appears called "Unrecognized Stars." And then, in case you missed the point, the subtitle clarified things: "Some of the country's best baseball players are unknown because they are Negroes, barred from the major leagues."

The story was written by a writer named Alvin F. Harlow. He was not called Ted, and he was not a sportswriter, and he did not say that Pop Lloyd was the greatest baseball player who ever lived. But he is at the heart of the myth.

Alvin F. Harlow had a strange and wonderful career as a writer. He followed his interests wherever they led. You would be hard-pressed to find an American writer with such diverse interests. He wrote several books about railroad folklore, for example. But then he also wrote a biography of Teddy Roosevelt, another on Andrew Carnegie, another on vaudevillian Eddie Foy, and another on Joel Chandler Harris, who was best known for his Uncle Remus stories.

He wrote a book called *The Story of Sending a Letter in Ancient and Modern Times*.

He wrote a book about people in Cincinnati called *The Serene Cincinnatians*.

He wrote a book about the Ringling Brothers circus, two books about small-town teachers, and one about telegraphers during the Civil War. He wrote a book about the early days of the Bowery, another about stamp collecting, and another called *Murders Not Quite Solved*.

He wrote fiction, nonfiction, and poetry and was a regular author for a magazine called *Weird Tales*. You never knew where the muses would lead Alvin F. Harlow.

In 1937, he became fascinated by Negro Leagues baseball. Why? He said it had something to do with Jesse Owens's performance at the 1936 Berlin Olympics. He, like most Americans, was so taken and inspired by Owens winning four gold medals—even as Adolf Hitler watched from the stands—that it made him think about all the great black athletes in America who were being overlooked. Baseball was everything in those days, so he began to investigate by going to some Negro Leagues games. And what he saw left him breathless.

"I have seen some games in that league," he wrote, "which were distinctly superior in quality to not a few that I have witnessed in the National and American Leagues."

So, he wrote about the Negro Leagues. It was one of the first national stories—probably *the* first national story—to celebrate the excellence of black players. Harlow told the story of a Cuban pitcher named Ramón Bragaña, who had been so dominant in an exhibition series against the New York Giants that their manager, Bill Terry, said, "This Bragaña is just about as great a pitcher as I ever saw." He wrote about Martín Dihigo, whom John McGraw considered one of the greatest natural ballplayers who ever lived. He mentioned Oscar Charleston, who was aging but still one of the great draws in the Negro Leagues.

But one story stood out. He said that a longtime St. Louis sportswriter—no name was given—was a guest on a local radio show and was asked to name the greatest baseball player he'd ever seen. My best guess is that Harlow—who was from Missouri himself—just happened to be listening and probably didn't even know who the sportswriter was or how to confirm it with him. And that's where we get the familiar quote that people have wanted to attribute to the ubiquitous Ted Harlow.

"If you mean the greatest in organized baseball, my answer would be Babe Ruth," Harlow quoted the writer as saying. "But if you mean in all of baseball, organized or unorganized, the answer would have to be a colored man named John Henry Lloyd."

Somewhere along the way, that unnamed sportswriter became Ted Harlow.

There's one more part to this crazy story. Did you notice that the Wikipedia entry mentioned above had Ted Harlow *and* Babe Ruth call Pop Lloyd the greatest player ever? Where does the Ruth reference come from? That's even more baffling than the Ted Harlow part. Monte Irvin, in his book *Few and Chosen,* wrote that Babe Ruth said it when being interviewed on the radio by Graham McNamee. The exchange is strikingly familiar to the one Harlow heard.

McNamee asked Ruth to name the greatest player ever.

"You mean major leagues?" Ruth asked.

"No, the greatest player anywhere."

"In that case," Ruth said, "I'd pick John Henry Lloyd."

Did a sportswriter say that? Did Ruth say that? It would be so wonderful to have something tangible, something we can hold on to. There are, as you will see, a few definitive quotes about the greatness of Lloyd. There are a few statistics that have been uncovered and tell a story. But at the center of it all, we know so little about Pop Lloyd. If we want to know how great Pop really was, then, sadly—or perhaps happily, if you want to see the world with optimism—we must use our imaginations.

What *do* we know about Pop Lloyd? It's easier to mix it in with what we don't. We don't know for sure where he was born—Florida, somewhere, but the city remains unclear. We do know his father died when he was a baby, and he was raised by his grandmother in and around Jacksonville. We don't know how long he attended school, but it seems certain he didn't go for very long; his opportunities were limited, and he needed to find jobs to help support his family.

We don't know what led him to baseball or what convinced him to try professional baseball. There's a story, a fun story, that he played semipro ball in Macon, Georgia, for a team called the Acmes and that he began as a catcher. Unfortunately for him, the team could not afford any catching equipment, so he played without a mask or any protection for his knees or chest, and by the end of the day, he had two swollen eyes and bruises all over his body.

That's when he became a shortstop.

True? We don't know. We know so little. It is usually told that Lloyd was discovered as a baseball-playing waiter at one of the Palm Beach hotel resorts. Those hotels played an enormous role in early black baseball. The concept—and in many ways, professional black baseball itself—started on Long Island at the Argyle Hotel in the late 1880s, when a headwaiter named Frank P. Thompson put together a baseball team of black waiters to play ball and entertain the guests.

They were so good that soon after they re-formed as the Cuban Giants—they pretended to be Cuban and spoke broken English on the field—and quickly became the best black baseball team in the country.

In Florida, Henry Flagler—who cofounded Standard Oil—built the enormous Royal Poinciana Hotel (at one point the largest wooden structure in America) and the Breakers in Palm Beach. He built a couple of baseball diamonds there, and the baseball rivalry between the hotels became so competitive that soon extraordinary players—all-time greats like Charleston, Smokey Joe Williams, and Cannonball Redding—were recruited to play. Think for a moment how amazing it must have been to vacation at one of those luxurious places and then go outside and be offered some of the best baseball being played anywhere in the world.

The most common version of the story is that Lloyd was seen playing ball at one of the resorts and was signed and brought back to Philadelphia by Cuban X-Giants owner E. B. Lamar. But it's just as possible this isn't true; his widow told Robert Peterson for *Only the Ball Was White* that Lloyd was not recruited at all and actually went north on his own, staked with only $1.50 and a pocket watch.

So back to what we do know. We know he was great. We don't need to hear from Ted Harlow or even Babe Ruth. Everybody said so. The Giants' John McGraw loved him so much that he kept coming up with schemes to try to get Lloyd past baseball's color line—at different times hatching plots to pass him as Cuban or as Native American (none ever got very far).

The Athletics manager Connie Mack saw Lloyd play and was so overwhelmed that he immediately dubbed him "the Black Honus Wagner."

Wagner, upon hearing this, was so overwhelmed that he said, "It is a privilege to have been compared with him."

We know that in Cuba they called him "El Cuchara," or "The Spoon," for the way he scooped up every ground ball, no matter the condition of the field, no matter how many rocks littered the baseball's path.* Negro Leaguer Ted Page used to say that Lloyd's hands were so big and powerful that when he fielded a ground ball, his glove would actually dig a hole in the infield and he would come up with dirt and pebbles as well as the ball.

We know that Lloyd could really hit—.400 in several seasons in which some statistics have managed to break through the fog, somewhere in the .340 or .350 range over his long, long, long career. So many of the people who would talk about him in the years to come did not see Lloyd play until he was in his late 40s, but they would generally say the same thing: Even then, he could really hit.

At age 46, while playing for the New York Lincoln Giants, he hit .381.

We know he bounced around continuously in his baseball life as he tried to make his way. "Wherever the money was," he said, "that's where I was." James A. Riley, in his *Biographical Encyclopedia of the Negro Baseball Leagues,* had him playing for 13 different franchises, not to mention the games he played in Cuba, Mexico, the Dominican Republic, and anywhere else he was offered a chance.

We know he was a joyous and wonderful baseball character. As a young man, they called him "Just in Time Lloyd" because when opponents hit grounders to him, he would often wait until the last possible instant and then unleash that big bazooka of an arm of his and get the runner by a blip. Then he would laugh and say, "Just in time!"

"You could hardly see his feet move," Judy Johnson, a great Negro Leagues player himself, said of Lloyd playing shortstop. "He just looked like he would slide over to the ball."

We know that as an older man, they called him "Pop" because he was like your father.

He was the ultimate gentleman—a duplicate of Wagner in that way.

---

* Buck O'Neil had always heard he was called "the Tablespoon" for the way he would set the table by getting on base all the time. This, too, is fantastic.

He never swore. He never bragged. "You can never win a ballgame with your mouth," he used to say. Some years ago, I wrote a book about Buck O'Neil, and that meant spending so much time with that extraordinary man. I cannot tell you how many times people would come up to Buck and tell him how sad they were that he never got the chance to play or manage in the big leagues. "Oh, don't cry for me," he would say. "I was born right on time." That was even the title of his autobiography.

But do you know where he got that remarkable attitude from? Pop Lloyd. See, Lloyd lived long enough to see Robinson break the color line, long enough to see every team in baseball sign at least one black baseball player, and he was asked: Do you ever feel like you were born too soon?

And this is what he said: "I do not consider that I was born at the wrong time. I feel it was the right time. I had a chance to prove the ability of our race in this sport, and because many of us did our best for the game, we've given the Negro a greater opportunity now to be accepted into the major leagues with other Americans."

Lloyd, like O'Neil, did hope to be elected into the Hall of Fame before he died. In both cases, it was not meant to be. But O'Neil played a key role in getting Lloyd elected to the Hall of Fame in 1977, the same year that Buck's protégé, Ernie Banks, became the first major-league black shortstop to be elected.

A man named James Usry accepted the plaque in Lloyd's honor that day. Who was Usry? He was the assistant superintendent of the Atlantic City school system. He would later become the first black mayor of Atlantic City. He wasn't a ballplayer . . . the reason he was there to speak on Lloyd's behalf is that the two were great friends and had worked together in the school district. Lloyd became a school janitor once he finished playing ball.

Everybody at the school loved Lloyd. The kids called him Pop. And even though he would occasionally tell stories, they never knew just how great he was as a ballplayer. Usry did know. Sometimes Usry would drive by the school and see Lloyd mowing the lawn, and he would seethe. That, he believed, wasn't how it should end for one of the greatest baseball players who ever lived.

But he also noticed, with wonder, that Pop Lloyd would be smiling.

Rickey Henderson

When Rickey Henderson was elected to the Baseball Hall of Fame, 28 people did not vote for him. I realize you can play the rage game all day and all night; you can just point to so many of the all-time greats and count the number of people who did not vote for them, and get angry all over again.

Here are the closest to unanimous election:

0 votes shy: Mariano Rivera

1: Derek Jeter

3: Ken Griffey Jr.

4: Ty Cobb

5: Tom Seaver

6: Nolan Ryan

8: Cal Ripken Jr.

9: Henry Aaron; George Brett

10: Bob Feller

11: Babe Ruth; Honus Wagner

12: Chipper Jones

13: Tony Gwynn

15: Randy Johnson

16: Mike Schmidt; Greg Maddux; Johnny Bench

20: Ted Williams; Steve Carlton

23: Willie Mays; Stan Musial

24: Carl Yastrzemski

27: Reggie Jackson

28: Rickey Henderson

You will note that the list does not even include Mickey Mantle (43 shy), Al Kaline or Frank Robinson (45 shy), Sandy Koufax (52 shy), or Bob Gibson (64 shy, the same as Warren Spahn).

But a special word must be said for Rickey. He stole about 500 more bases than anyone. (You can add Lou Brock's stolen bases to active leader Rajai Davis's stolen bases and still not climb up to the top of Mount Rickey.) He scored more runs than anyone. He got on base more times than anyone not named Rose, Bonds, or Cobb, he hit more leadoff home runs than anyone, and on and on.

Bill James, when asked if Henderson was a Hall of Famer, gave the legendary answer, "If you could split him in two, you'd have two Hall of Famers." And that's right—really, you could divide him into three and get three Hall of Famers. He's a bona fide Hall of Famer just for the base stealing. He's a bona fide Hall of Famer for 3,000 hits. He's a bona fide Hall of Famer for being the greatest run scorer.

Beyond that, though, Rickey was Rickey. Has there ever been a player who was more fun, who is the centerpiece of more great stories, who made your heart sing the way he did? In the end, no, the 28 people who didn't vote for Henderson don't really matter. Rickey Henderson went into the Hall of Fame on the first ballot, like most of the great ones, and he had his day in Cooperstown, and his plaque begins with these words: "Faster than a speeding bullet." He didn't need those 28 votes to secure his legacy, and those 28 votes are nothing more now than pointless trivia.

But my point is: Why would you even want to vote for the Hall of Fame if not to vote for Rickey Henderson? Or in other words, if you love baseball, as a Hall of Fame voter surely does, why would you want to live the rest of your life knowing that you didn't vote Rickey Henderson into the Hall of Fame?

All right, the rest of this will be a series of Rickey stories. That's what you want. That's what I want. We can only assume that's what Rickey wants. Rickey loves a good Rickey story. We'll get the most famous one out of the way first because it isn't even true. The story goes that when Rickey joined the Seattle Mariners in 2000, he saw John Olerud taking some ground balls while wearing his batting helmet.

"Huh," he said, "I played with a guy in New York who did that."

"Yeah," Olerud said. "That was me. Last year."

As mentioned, the story isn't true. Olerud and Henderson have debunked it. Apparently, it was a gag the Mariners' assistant trainer came up with and it soon spread around the clubhouse, as good gags will.

But even an untrue Rickey story leads to a great tale. When Rickey was debunking the story, he made the point that while it was funny, it was also silly because he'd known Olerud years before they played on the same team. Of course he did. Olerud played first. Henderson always loved talking to first basemen when he got on base.

And, as Rickey said, "I was always on base."

Henderson was born on Christmas Day in 1958, in the backseat of an Oldsmobile speeding toward the hospital. "I was already fast," he said. He was named Rickey Nelson Henley Henderson after Ricky Nelson, the teen music sensation of the day who had grown up in front of America on the television show *The Adventures of Ozzie and Harriet* and at the time had more hits than Elvis.

Football was Rickey's game as a teenager, not baseball. He was, by all accounts, an awe-inspiring running back, which is easy to imagine. His dream was to play for the Oakland Raiders, and he very well might have done that; Hall of Fame defensive back Ronnie Lott grew up in California at the same time and saw Rickey at a few all-star games and said he was a serious handful as a runner.

But Rickey's mother, Bobbie, insisted he play baseball.

So did others. It's funny, looking back, at how many people in his life seemed to be conspiring to make him a ballplayer. Perhaps the most influential of those was his school guidance counselor, Tommie Wilkerson, who offered him a deal: She said that she would give him a quarter for every good thing he did on the baseball diamond.

"What qualified as a good thing?" he asked. She decided he would get a quarter for every hit, for every stolen base, and for every run scored.

Hits. Stolen bases. Runs scored. You think Wilkerson set Rickey on the right course or what?

Rickey, at his Hall of Fame induction, said that he quickly had 30 hits, scored 25 runs, and had 33 steals in high school. That's 22 bucks! "Not bad money for a high school kid," he said.

If Wilkerson had kept the deal going for his big-league career, she would have had to pay for 3,055 hits, 2,295 runs, and 1,406 stolen bases. If you're a math teacher, feel free to use this example for your classes. They'll love it.

Answer: It's $1,689.

Henderson led the American League in stolen bases every year in the 1980s except one. That one year was 1987. He was injured and only played in 95 games. He stole "just" 41 bases. That still would have led the National League in 2019.

The actual stolen base race went down to the final day. Seattle's Harold Reynolds had 59 stolen bases and Kansas City's Willie Wilson had 58. Wilson stole a base in the Royals' win over the Twins to tie, but Reynolds also stole a base off Texas knuckleballer Charlie Hough and won the title. It was a pretty big deal, as Reynolds says: It was the first time a Mariners player had led the league in a major category.

The next day, his phone rang. It was Rickey. Reynolds was expecting congratulations.

This is what he heard instead.

"Sixty stolen bases? You ought to be ashamed. Rickey would have 60 stolen bases at the All-Star break."

And then Rickey hung up.

———

Right, we'd better get the third-person thing out of the way: Rickey did indeed call himself Rickey. Now to be fair, Rickey didn't call himself Rickey quite as much as people claimed Rickey called himself Rickey. A lot of that stuff was for effect. A good Rickey Henderson story requires a good third-person reference. So, we don't really know if, during negotiations with the San Diego Padres and GM Kevin Towers, he left a message that said: "Kevin, this is Rickey. Calling on behalf of Rickey. Rickey wants to play baseball."

But isn't it pretty to think so?

"Listen," Henderson said, summing this whole thing up, "people are always saying, 'Rickey says Rickey.' But it's been blown way out of proportion. People might catch me, when they know I'm ticked off, saying, 'Rickey, what the heck are you doing, Rickey?' They say, 'Darn, Rickey, what are you saying Rickey for? Why don't you just say I?' But I never did. I always said 'Rickey,' and it became something for people to joke about."

This one has been told in different ways but here is the most likely version: In 1996, at 37, Henderson played his first game in the National League. It was a big deal then. He played the bulk of his career when the leagues were really separate entities, before interleague play, before easy passageway between them. So, while everybody in the National League obviously knew about Rickey Henderson, he was still something of a curiosity when he joined the Padres.

His first game was against the Chicago Cubs, and Jaime Navarro was pitching.

Henderson stepped into the box and then he started talking to himself. Everyone knew about that routine in the American League; Henderson would constantly talk to himself, pump himself up, "Rickey gonna hit this guy! This guy's got nothing! Rickey's good, Rickey's getting a hit, Rickey's going to steal second and then steal third . . ." and so on.

He was going through that whole routine and behind the plate, Cubs catcher Scott Servais and home plate umpire Jim Quick were trying hard not to laugh. Nobody put on a show quite like Rickey . . . but with the count 2-2, Henderson swung and missed. And then he turned around toward Servais and Quick and he said this:

"That's OK. Rickey still the man."

The *Athletic's* Jayson Stark was once doing a story on Lenny Dykstra—this was when the player everybody called "Nails" was evolving into the best leadoff hitter in the National League while Henderson continued to dominate the American League. So naturally, Jayson wanted to ask Rickey about Lenny.

Jayson: So I'm writing this story about how Lenny Dykstra is becoming the National League version of you. . . .

Rickey: Who is Lenny Dykstra?

Jayson (laughing): He's the other leadoff hitter.

Rickey: There ain't no other leadoff hitter but me.

Alex Rodriguez can remember times when Henderson would strike out looking. It didn't happen often. As Jim Murray famously wrote of Henderson, "He has a strike zone the size of Hitler's heart." Henderson would get into that familiar crouch, and he had the most discerning eye of anyone west of Ted Williams, and over his career, he walked about 500 more times than he struck out.

So, no, pitchers didn't often slip that third pitch past him while he watched.

But every now and again they did, and when he would get back to the dugout, Rodriguez would ask, "Hey Rickey, was that a strike?"

And Henderson would say: "Maybe. But not to Rickey."

It seems to be true that in 1996 or 1997, the San Diego Padres' payroll department freaked out because they had a million-dollar surplus that they couldn't identify. They kept looking and looking and finally came to understand that there was something wrong with the million-dollar bonus check they had given Henderson. So they went to Henderson and asked if there was any problem with it.

There wasn't. Rickey hadn't cashed it.

He'd framed it instead.

No player in baseball history had such an unusual relationship with money. On the one hand, he always felt desperately underpaid and was constantly fighting for more. It wasn't spring training unless Henderson was holding out. As Don Mattingly once said when Henderson was not there on the first day of camp, "You have to say Rickey's consistent. That's what you want in a ballplayer: consistency."

Yes, Rickey negotiated hard. Once, during one of those disputes, he said, "If they want to pay me like [Mike] Gallego, I'll play like Gallego."*

So, OK, yes, he wanted money. On the other hand, money seemed to mean nothing to him. There are so many stories of him not cashing checks. And he never spent a penny of his per diem meal money. He would instead stuff the cash in shoe boxes and whenever one of his daughters got good grades in school, he would let her go up and choose a shoe box, like an educational version of *Let's Make a Deal*.

Rickey, much like Yogi Berra, sees the world through his own wonderful prism. Someone asked Henderson what he thought of a *Sports Illustrated* article in which Ken Caminiti said 50 percent of the players in baseball were using steroids (he actually said "at least half," but that's close enough). Rickey's response? "The article said 50 percent? Well, I'm not one of them. So that's 49 percent right there."

Then there was the time Henderson went on the Padres' team bus and there were no open seats near the front. He looked around for a moment when someone—Steve Finley or Brad Ausmus seem to be the most likely candidates—said, "Just make them move and take any seat you want, Rickey. You've got tenure."†

To which Henderson responded, "Tenure? No, Rickey got 15 year."

Then there's the famous sign story. I have heard it told several different ways by several different people, so it might just be legend. But my favorite

---

* Gallego did not take that personally. He, like everyone else, loved Rickey. "When we were kids," he told the *San Francisco Chronicle*, "we played in the backyard emulating Pete Rose's stance or Joe Morgan's. I believe Rickey emulated Rickey. He was his own star. He was the best at being Rickey."

† The two men, Rickey and Yogi, connected briefly in 1985. Henderson signed with the Yankees and Berra was the manager before getting fired after only 16 games. There was enough time for this: Berra was asked by reporters how he would handle Henderson's baserunning. "He can run anytime he wants," Berra said. "I'm giving him the red light."

version is one Tony La Russa tells, of how when Henderson was traded from the Yankees back to Oakland in 1989, some of the newspapers were pretty ruthless. It's true.

"The A's manager," Frank Blackman of the *San Francisco Examiner* wrote, "will have to apply his considerable skills to the care and feeding of one of the game's most gifted—but reportedly most temperamental—players, Rickey Henderson."

"Did A's acquire Jekyll or Hyde?" asked the *Sacramento Bee*.

"I don't care if the Yankees got three dogs and a rat for him," one Yankees fan told a reporter in New York.

So Henderson was pretty ruffled when he met with La Russa for the first time. "Rickey's a team player," he kept saying again and again. La Russa said he was happy to hear that. And then they began discussing signs, and La Russa said that Henderson didn't have to worry about all that because he would have a perpetual green light—steal at will.

"Does anybody else get the green light?" he asked. When La Russa shrugged, Henderson shook his head and said he didn't want a green light. He wanted signs like everyone else. "Rickey's a team player," he said again. So La Russa, thrilled by the gesture, went over the signs, which included a swiping of the arms that would be used to take off all other signs.

In Henderson's fourth game, the A's were playing Toronto, and in the fifth inning, Henderson singled to right. The Blue Jays had a two-run lead and Jimmy Key on the mound. Key had a good pick-off move, so La Russa didn't want Rickey running. He had his third-base coach go through all the signs and then swipe the arms to take off everything—the no-go sign. But on the next pitch, Henderson took off anyway and swiped second base. He scored on a single by Dave Henderson, and La Russa figured Rickey just missed the sign.

A little later, though, Rickey singled to put the A's up 6–2. David Wells entered to pitch for the Blue Jays, and Wells also had a great pick-off move. So, again, La Russa wanted Rickey staying put. He had his third-base coach go through all the signs and then wipe the arms to take off any play. And once again, Henderson stole second on the next pitch.

Now, La Russa was hot. "Hey Rickey," he said, "all that stuff about being a team player, what gives?"

Henderson looked at La Russa as if he had no idea what he was talking about.

"We gave you a sign," La Russa continued. "Did you not see it?"

Henderson said, "Yeah, I saw it. You said if you wipe the arm, that means take off. And so Rickey took off."

Rickey Henderson loved the game, absolutely loved it. It's funny to think that there ever was a time when baseball left him cold, because by the end, well, he didn't want it to end. He just kept playing and playing for anyone who would give him a uniform. Heck, when he was 44, he was kicking it around for an independent team in Newark in the hope that he could get just a few more at-bats.

He loved the game within the game. He loved to challenge players. He used to go up to catchers before games and say, "You think you can throw me out? Well, I'm gonna give you that chance." Once against the Orioles, he was on first base and looked over at third baseman Floyd Rayford and held up a peace sign. Rayford didn't know what he meant. That's because it wasn't a peace sign—Rickey was holding up the number two. And two pitches later, he was standing on third with Rayford after having stolen two bases.

Lord, did he love stealing third—he always told people it was easier than stealing second. Nobody else really believed that, but it was for Rickey: He stole third base 322 times, the most ever. Base-stealing stats for older players like Cobb are not complete, but we don't know of anyone else who stole third even 200 times. Lou Brock stole third just 79 times, for instance.

Rickey loved sliding headfirst. He used to say that he patterned his headfirst slide not after any person but after a passenger airplane. He was on a plane that had a rough landing, lots of bumps, and it occurred to him that this is what would happen to the body if he dove too high off the ground on his slide. And when the next plane landed without a bump, he developed that low-to-the-ground, graceful slide that he made famous.

He loved making people laugh and cheer and smile and just feel things. "I am a performer," he used to say. "I give entertainment."

He loved getting into a pitcher's head and drawing walks. For Rickey, a walk wasn't just as good as a hit, it was better. One of my favorite baseball statistics is that Henderson led off an inning with a walk 796 times in his career. That is just an impossible number. Think about it from the perspective of a pitcher: Henderson comes up first in an inning, what is the absolute last thing you would want to do? Right: walk him.

And yet he walked 796 times leading off an inning—that's more walks than Ryne Sandberg, Ernie Banks, Gwynn, Brock, Vladimir Guerrero, or Berra had in their entire careers, and those include intentional walks. What a force of nature Rickey Henderson was.

There are so many great quotes about Rickey Henderson and so many great quotes Rickey Henderson said—who can forget how on the day he stole the base that broke the big-league record, he thanked a bunch of people and then said, "Lou Brock was the symbol of great base-stealing. But today, I am the greatest of all time!"

But my favorite Rickey Henderson quote is a simple one, offered by his old teammate Mitchell Page. He said, "Rickey Henderson is a run, man." Yes, he was. Yes, he was.

No. 23 Albert Pujols

L et's begin with the story about "Buddy Walk in the Park" because there is a whole generation of people who are too young to remember Albert Pujols as he really was. This is not to blame anyone. Time passes. Pujols came to play ball for the Los Angeles Angels way back in 2012, and that's a long time ago. I mean, that was the year of the *first* Avengers movie.

So if you are a teenager or relatively new to baseball fanhood, there really is no way for you to remember Pujols before he joined the Angels, back when he played in St. Louis, before his bat slowed, before his body broke down, before he had to make the depressing but necessary calculation that he could be most useful and effective by trolling for mistake pitches and hitting as many of them as he could over the fence.

So how good was the young Albert Pujols?

We'll get to the numbers, the achievements, the jaw-dropping consistency ... but if you really want to know how good he was, you need to know about the Buddy Walk.

Every year in St. Louis there is a special day at Busch Stadium to raise money and awareness for the National Down Syndrome Society. On that day, children with Down syndrome are invited to walk on the field with their favorite Cardinals players: the Buddy Walk. It's a meaningful day for everybody, obviously, but it was something more for Pujols and his wife, Deidre—they have a daughter with Down syndrome. They have dedicated an enormous amount of time and money to, in their own words, "promote awareness, provide hope and create supportive and memorable events for the families and children who live with Down syndrome."

Notice their words about creating memorable events—that's what touches the hearts of the Pujols family. And that is what we are talking about here. In 2002, a 10-year-old girl with Down syndrome named Kathleen Mertz threw out the first pitch to Pujols. When he walked back over to give her a signed baseball and a hug, she spoke in his ear: "Albert, please hit a home run for me."

He looked at her and smiled. This is the ultimate baseball request, right? How many stories have we heard through the years of a kid asking her favorite player to hit a home run? It started with Babe Ruth and it has never stopped. And every now and again, if the timing works, the player will connect just so and make the dream real.

In the first inning of that 2002 game, Pujols launched a long home run off Houston's Kirk Saarloos, and Kathleen Mertz felt a joy that she knew would last for the rest of her life.

Nice story, right? Well, buckle up. We have only just begun.

One year later, on Buddy Walk day in 2003, Kathleen Mertz was back at the ballpark. This time she walked out to second base with Pujols's teammate Fernando Vina, but she saw Pujols and waved and he smiled and waved back. The two had become friends over the previous year (she brought a sign to the ballpark that read "Albert Pujols is my best friend in the whole universe!").

"Hit me another home run, Albert!" she shouted out, and he grinned. Then he went to catch the first pitch from a girl named Niki Cunningham. When he gave her the ball and a hug, she asked if he might be kind enough to hit a home run for her, too.

In the 13th inning of the game, facing Dan Miceli, Pujols pulled a long walk-off home run.

So that's two children whose request he fulfilled.

That's probably more than any ballplayer should expect. Home runs are, as we all know, rare birds. The pitch has to be right. The swing has to be right. The ballpark, the weather, the altitude, all of it has to be just right.

In 2004 and 2005, Pujols tried to hit a home run on Buddy Walk day. It just didn't happen.

But on Buddy Walk day in 2006, Pujols found himself swarmed with an unusual flurry of home run requests. It seemed like every direction he turned, there was another kid asking him to hit another home run. " 'Hit one for me! Hit one for me! Hit one for me!' " then–Cardinals manager Tony La Russa recalled the kids shouting out, "and Pujols smiled and nodded at each one of them."

In the first inning, against Pittsburgh's Ian Snell, Pujols smashed a fly ball to deep left field for a home run. He'd done it! Three home runs for three kids . . . but this time, remember, he didn't promise a home run to any specific child. He just nodded at everybody. You could imagine the kids arguing with each other about which of them could claim the homer.

Pujols fixed that. In the third inning, facing Snell again, he hit a blast to almost the exact same spot for his second home run of the day. Remember the classic *Seinfeld* episode where Kramer asked Paul O'Neill to hit not just one but two home runs for a sick kid in the hospital?

"Where the heck did you get two from?" O'Neill asked him.

"Two is better than one," Kramer replied.

Yes. Two is better than one.

"I'll say this," Pujols's teammate Adam Wainwright told reporters. "Albert is the one guy I know who can tell a kid he'll hit two homers for you and you know he's good for it."

So that's a pretty good story. But, yeah, we're not done.

In the fifth inning, Pujols came up to face Ian Snell again. And this time he didn't just hit a home run. He hit a blast to center field that was so majestic, so absurd, so wonderful that Snell himself told reporters after the game: "I thought it was going to hit the St. Louis Arch out there. I wanted to go high-five him."

Believe it or not, the story still doesn't end.

Pujols sat out 2007's Buddy Walk day with a bad elbow. In 2008, Pujols was again hurting but there was never a question about him playing, not once he saw all those kids flowing into the ballpark. He met with a large group of them before the game. They asked him to hit a home run. He nodded.

In the first inning, he crushed a long home run off Florida's Josh Johnson.

"Let me tell you something about Albert Pujols," Wainwright said. "There is nothing he can't do."

It seems to me that no player in baseball history has gone from being a total nonprospect to a baseball superstar quite as fast as Albert Pujols.

Pujols was a 13th-round selection by the St. Louis Cardinals in the 1999 draft. Thirteenth-round draft picks rarely make it—I do not say this lightly. Since the first year of the draft, only 13 percent of all 13th-round picks have made it to the big leagues at all, and less than 8 percent have posted even one win above replacement.

Actually, the numbers are even smaller than that because some of the players who were drafted in the 13th round actually refused to sign and went back into the draft. A handful of 13th-round picks have made it—Jim Thome, Jack Clark, Matt Carpenter, and so on—but all of them needed time to develop.

That's what was supposed to be the best-case scenario with Pujols. He came out of Maple Woods Community College in Kansas City. He didn't have a defensive position. He couldn't run. Scouts didn't like his body type. And there were whispers that he was considerably older than his stated age of 19—whispers that had been following him around since he and his father came from the Dominican Republic to Independence, Missouri, when he was 14. In high school, opposing teams would walk him not only because he was such a good hitter but because managers believed he was an adult passing for a high school student.

So, the Cardinals took him in the 13th round with the hopes that maybe someday . . .

Two years after that draft day, Albert Pujols was one of the five best players in baseball.

How? What? Well, look, the obvious part of this was that scouts simply missed Pujols's once-in-a-lifetime hitting talent. It was there. Pujols was an absurd hitter at Maple Woods; it is believed that he didn't strike out a single time. He hit .461 with 22 home runs. "I put up sick numbers," Pujols says. "I was a monster." Needless to say, Pujols remains pretty unimpressed with the scouts who missed his talent.

But it was more than just that: There was transformation, too. In 2001, when Pujols arrived at spring training, nobody was thinking about him actually making the team. Sure, he'd been sensational in his one year of minor-league ball, hitting .324 and slugging .565 in Peoria and then hold-ing his own for three weeks in High-A. He had even made his way to the No. 2 spot on the Cardinals' prospect list behind Bud Smith. But he was still a Class-A ballplayer.

"He's still young but has the approach of a veteran," Baseball Amer-ica gushed, though they quickly pointed out that the Cardinals still didn't know how his defense would hold up. "He'll start at Double-A New Haven," they wrote confidently.

And that was indeed the plan . . . only then La Russa actually saw him play. And what La Russa saw, even only after a day or two, left him aston-ished. "Impressive," he said, much in the same way that Darth Vader said "Impressive" after watching Luke Skywalker jump out of the carbonite freezing chamber.

"Pujols shouldn't make the club," he told reporters that day, "but I didn't think [Mark] McGwire was going to make the club in 1987. And he became Rookie of the Year."

Well, this was quite the statement. McGwire's situation in 1987 was quite different. Pujols was a 20-year-old late draft pick with one year of A-ball under his belt. McGwire was the 10th overall pick in the 1984 draft, and by 1987, he was one of the game's best prospects—he'd even had a little time in the big leagues at the end of the 1986 season.

The fact that La Russa, just days into camp, was comparing Pujols to McGwire tells you just how wowed he was.

"Balls he swings at, balls he takes, the way the ball comes off his bat," La Russa swooned when asked about a week later what so impressed him about Pujols. Pujols hit a homer and a triple in the Cardinals' first intrasquad game. Privately, La Russa began telling people that he'd never seen anyone quite like Pujols before.

It got to the point where La Russa was afraid to play Pujols because he was afraid that he would be overtaken by emotion and rush Pujols to the big leagues. "La Russa has been playing Pujols sparingly, perhaps trying not to fall in love with him too soon," the *St. Louis Post-Dispatch* wrote.

But it was too late. La Russa was in love. Cardinals GM Walt Jocketty, if anything, was more in love. No, they didn't want to rush Pujols. But every now and again, a player comes along who is an exception to the rule. The Cardinals went back and forth and back and forth . . . and decided that as good as Pujols looked, they would send him to the minors for a little while anyway. It couldn't hurt. Let Pujols get a little more seasoning.

Then Bobby Bonilla pulled his left hamstring and the Cardinals brought Pujols to Colorado for Opening Day, and he singled off Mike Hampton. Four days later, in Arizona, he went three-for-five with a double and a homer. At the end of the first month, he was hitting .370 and slugging .807 with eight doubles, a triple, and eight home runs in just 21 games.

And for the year, he hit .329/.403/.610 with 47 doubles, 37 homers, 112 runs, and 130 RBIs. It's one of the greatest rookie seasons in the history of baseball.

Eight of his next nine seasons would be even better than that.

Albert Pujols was driven by rage. Some players are just like that—Tom Brady, Michael Jordan, Kobe Bryant, Jimmy Connors, Roger Clemens, Patrick Reed. They need enemies. They need hostility. They need doubts to feed them.

With Pujols, the doubts were always there. When he and his father came to America, Pujols struggled to learn English. People made fun of him for that. They made him feel dumb. The baseball diamond was not only his sanctuary, it was the one place where he could fight back, where he could win. When he showed up to play high school baseball at Fort Osage High, his coach David Fry tried to communicate using Pujols's cousin as an interpreter. After a halting few minutes, Pujols finally told his cousin to say this: "I am here to play baseball. Let's go play. I'm not here to talk about anything."

That never changed. Pujols wasn't interested in talking. He came to hit, he came to win. To see him work out in the batting cage was to see Ali work over the heavy bag. Every move, every swing, every step had purpose. He wasn't interested in talking or playing or just getting his swings in. He had to get better. Every day. Every minute.

In 2003, Pujols led the league in hitting at .359 and also led the league in runs, hits, doubles, and total bases. He had arrived! Only, no, Pujols realized he was just an average fielder and that wouldn't do.

So in 2004, he hit .331/.415/.657 and led the league in runs and total bases again, but now he was suddenly an above-average first baseman. His Cardinals won 105 games and went to the World Series (he hit .500 with four home runs in the NLCS to get them there). He had arrived! Only, no, Pujols decided he was only an average baserunner. And even though Pujols always had below-average speed, that simply wouldn't do.

So in 2005, he hit .330/.430/.609, again led the league in runs, played an even better first base—probably should have won the Gold Glove—but now he also became a base-running threat, too. He worked on his jump. He pushed himself to be more aggressive. He stole 16 bases and was caught just twice and he became one of the league's best at going from first to third or second to home on a single. He won the MVP award. He had arrived!

But no. He never would arrive. In 2006, he hit .331/.431/.671, led the league in slugging and OPS for the first time, did win his Gold Glove, and, though he missed some games with injury, he carried the Cardinals to the World Series, where this time they won against the Tigers.

Albert Pujols led the National League in Wins Above Replacement in 2005, 2006, 2007, 2008, and 2009. Do you know who was the last National Leaguer to lead the whole league—pitchers and hitters—in WAR five straight years? Nobody. Not Willie Mays. Not Barry Bonds. Not Henry Aaron. Not Stan Musial or Rogers Hornsby or Honus Wagner. Nobody.*

Pujols won three MVPs, but he should have won more—he finished second four times and in 2007 he somehow finished ninth despite (as always) leading the league in WAR. That year is Exhibit A of just how good Pujols was. He hit .327/.429/.568 with 32 homers, 103 RBIs, 99 runs, he was phenomenal defensively . . . and there were questions along the lines of "What's the matter with Albert?"

Pujols's decline probably began in his last year in St. Louis. He still had a great year, but it wasn't quite a Pujols year. He failed to hit .300 for the first time (he hit .299), failed to drive in 100 RBIs for the first time (he drove in 99), and he was just not quite as sharp at age 31. Even so, he was ridiculous in the playoffs, hitting .350 and slugging .500 in the Cardinals' rather stunning upset of Philadelphia in the Division Series, then torching Milwaukee in the NLCS (.478/.556/.913 with four doubles and two homers in six games). He also hit three homers in the World Series against Texas as the Cardinals won the World Series again.

Those playoff games made it a bit too easy for baseball people to con-

---

* In the American League, Mickey Mantle, Babe Ruth, and Walter Johnson did it.

vince themselves that Pujols was still the same player. Looking back, we know that he wasn't . . . but even at the time, it was probably a bad bet. He was turning 32 years old, and he'd been in the league for 11 grueling seasons. In general, players like Pujols—big right-handed power hitters who excel by hitting sizzling line drives into gaps and over fences—do not tend to age well. Frank Thomas had his last great season at 32 and so did Vlad Guerrero. Miguel Cabrera probably had his last great season at 32 or 33. And so on.

When Pujols went to the Angels for that 10-year, $240 million deal—which still, impossibly, has two seasons to go—everybody, including the Angels, I assume, knew that it wouldn't end well. What nobody knew is that it wouldn't even start well. In his first season, he hit .285/.343/.516 with 30 homers. He played first base well but not like he once had. He was an average baserunner. He unintentionally walked just 36 times all season. It was fine. But it wasn't Pujols.

And that has been Pujols's best season in Anaheim by quite a bit.

He did hit 40 homers in 2015, but he had a .307 on-base percentage. He did drive in 101 runs in 2017, but with an anemic .672 OPS. He has hit .245 or less in four of the last five seasons. He has not had even an average OPS+ since 2016.

His career batting average, which stood at .328 when he left St. Louis, undoubtedly will drop below .300 this year.

Pujols does keep adding to his astounding career batting totals—he's up to 661 doubles (7th all-time) and 656 homers (6th) and 5,863 total bases (5th) and 2,075 RBIs (4th). The last of these is particularly compelling: If he can just stay healthy the next two seasons to match his typical Angels pace, he would move ahead of Babe Ruth into second place on the RBI list, and he might even think about playing one more year to catch Henry Aaron at the top.

It has been so hard to watch one of the greatest players in the history of baseball fade like this. Each year, I hope against hope for Pujols to be Pujols one more time. Sadly, that just isn't how time works. He is 40 now and a decade past his prime. It hasn't been a sad career, though; far from it. It has been extraordinary. It has been an inspiration. I think now of that moment in Houston, that unforgettable moment in 2005, with the Astros (still a National League team!) up 4–2 in the ninth, their dominant closer

Brad Lidge on the mound, all of Houston going out of their minds because finally, after 40 years, the Astros were going to the World Series!

The Cardinals put two on. Pujols came to the plate. The sound was a jet engine meets a NASCAR race meets Disney World when Elsa and Anna from *Frozen* come out meets Arrowhead Stadium with the opponent trying to call a play in the red zone meets a volcano erupting meets pretty much any sports talk show on television.

And Pujols swung the bat and connected.

And there was silence. It was not a normal silence. It was the sort of silence that has its own weather pattern. You know that goofy old threat about knocking someone into next week? Albert Pujols had knocked the ball into next week. And it was so silent you could hear his cleats pounding on the dirt as he ran around the bases.

He'll never be that player again, no. But maybe he will connect like that one more time. That would be nice. It would be great to say to our kids, "Yeah, that's Albert Pujols."

No. 22 **Lefty Grove**

Lefty Grove was only just barely elected to the Hall of Fame in 1947. He made it by two votes. Nobody from the Hall of Fame even bothered to call him—he got word from a *Cumberland News* reporter who was calling to get his reaction. "It's news to me," Grove said, "but I'm tickled to death."

Grove was one of four players elected to the Hall of Fame that year. There had been a pretty big backlog because of World War II and because the sportswriters were generally reluctant to believe that anyone belonged in the Hall of Fame—they did not come close to voting for anyone in 1945 or 1946. But that year, 1947, they elected Carl Hubbell, Frankie Frisch, Mickey Cochrane, and Grove.

We look now and Grove was clearly, unquestionably, and vividly the best of those four players. Just look at Jay Jaffe's JAWS system, which measures a player by career WAR and peak WAR.

1. Grove, 86.3 JAWS

2. Hubbell, 57.9

3. Frisch, 57.4

4. Cochrane, 42.1

Of course, they didn't have JAWS back then. But they certainly had pitcher wins, which was then the most important pitching statistic, and Grove won 300 games. At the time only four other modern pitchers—the other three being Deadball Era pitchers—had won 300.

And of the group, Grove had the best winning percentage. He lost only 141 games—his .680 winning percentage is not just the highest for any pitcher with 300 wins, it's also the highest for any pitcher with 275 wins, the highest for any modern pitcher with 250 wins, and only Whitey Ford, while playing for those invincible New York Yankees, has a higher winning percentage among those pitchers with 225 wins.

But beyond numbers, beyond awards, beyond everything, Grove was a legend who threw one of the hottest fastballs the game had ever seen. "Lefty Grove," Westbrook Pegler famously wrote, "could throw a lamb chop past a wolf."

"Sometimes," Joe Sewell said, "when the sun was out, really bright, Grove would throw that baseball in there and it looked like a flash of white sewing thread coming up at you."

So why did Lefty Grove just barely make it into Cooperstown in 1947 with the fewest votes of the four players who were elected? Why, a year earlier, did he receive just 23 percent from the BBWAA in their chaotic Hall of Fame vote?

How in the world did they miss his all-time greatness?

I can't say for sure, but I do have a theory. I think it has something to do with what you might call price conditioning. You know how merchandise almost always ends with a 99? How a gallon of gas at $1.99 will sell so much more than a gallon of gas at $2.00 . . . Or a car priced at $19,999 just seems like so much more of a bargain than a car with a $20,000 sticker price. There is a lot of science that explains why the human brain falls for this.

And it's the same thing between a pitcher with a 2.99 and 3.00 ERA.

They called him Lefty Groves for a startlingly long time. Yes, for five years the *Baltimore Sun*, when referring to the greatest pitcher to ever throw for the Orioles or perhaps anyone else, wrote "Lefty Groves" with an *s*. Did he not correct them? Did he not care? Did they not care? Nobody knows. It's one of the weirder aspects of a weird life.

Robert Moses Grove was a driven, volatile, profane, and talented son of a gun. Boy, did he hate losing. He was born that way. Bobby Grove, as he was called, grew up poor in Lonaconing, Maryland, where his father and older brothers were coal miners. He didn't see that as any kind of life. As the story goes, Bobby worked in the mines for just two weeks before quitting for good.

"Dad," he famously said, "I didn't put the coal in here and I don't want to take no more of it out."

He attended a little red schoolhouse for about as long as he could—he might have reached the eighth grade—before seeking nonmining work around town. He worked at the big glass factory. He put down rails for the railroads. He worked in a textile mill that made silk thread. There wasn't much time for baseball; Grove did not play on an organized team until he was 19 years old.

But he did throw things a lot. Rocks mostly. Yes, another rock thrower. Bobby Grove drew a home plate in the dirt on the side of his father's barn and 60 feet, 6 inches away, he drew a line to represent a pitching rubber. Then he would throw rocks as hard as he could over that home plate (or anyway, considering his wildness in the early days, as close as he could get).

His father used to say he could tell how much his son's fastball was improving by the size of the dents on the side of the barn.

There were neighborhood games, too. According to Jim Kaplan, author of *Lefty Grove: American Original,* the kids would sometimes fashion balls out of cork stoppers, wool socks, and black tape and use picket fence slats as bats. Grove would say that he was nothing special in these contests—the other kids pitched better and hit better. But none of them could throw as hard. He would pretend to be his hero, the Washington Senators' Walter Johnson.

Grove just oozed pitching talent. He didn't need training. When he was 19, he was signed to play for his first team—a semiprofessional team at that. Dick Stakem ran the general store in a nearby town, and he loved baseball so he put together a team. It cost a quarter to see Stakem's team play, but the crowds were pretty large—Grove made $193 pitching for the team. He was great from the start. In his first game, he pitched seven innings and struck out 15.

And then came his first big game against the powerful Baltimore & Ohio Railroad team (B&O Railroad for you Monopoly fans). Bobby

Grove threw a no-hitter, struck out 18, and was so cocky about things after a walk that he told the baserunner to just go ahead and steal second and then go ahead and steal third. The runner obliged. "You can stop right there," Grove said, and he struck out the next batter to end the inning and the threat.

Needless to say, Grove was working for the B&O Railroad the next year.

But he never played for the B&O baseball team. No, before the season began, he was recruited to play for a real professional team in Martinsburg, West Virginia, about 90 miles away. According to legend, he bicycled the whole way even though there weren't particularly good roads (or any roads) between the towns.

Grove wasn't in Martinsburg long but he was there long enough to leave an impression. Apparently, in one game, he walked 16 batters and struck out 23.

That's when he drew the attention of a classic baseball character named Jack Dunn, who had an enormous (but not entirely positive) impact on his life and on baseball history. Dunn was a ballplayer from his earliest memory, but at age nine—according to Leigh Montville's fine book *The Big Bam*—a train car ran over his left arm. Doctors at first suggested amputating the arm, but Dunn said, "I'd just as soon die with my arm on." He recovered without surgery but his left arm was never quite the same; he couldn't lift it above his head.

This did not prevent him from playing ball—as Dunn often said, there was nothing wrong with his right arm. He was a pitcher first; not a hard-throwing one, but he had impeccable control and he knew every pitching trick imaginable (and invented a few of his own). He won 64 games as a pitcher, most of them for Brooklyn (he was one of the few pitchers who did not wear a fielder's glove). Even after he hurt his right arm, he still played ball—he became a third baseman and a shortstop and in his last year, at age 31, he hit .309 in part-time duty.

Dunn always knew he would spend the rest of his life in baseball. He considered starting a school for pitchers. Instead, he became a minor-league manager and—after borrowing every penny he could—bought the Double-A Baltimore Orioles. This turned out to be a fantastic investment because it just so happens that Dunn was an almost supernatural judge of talent.

For instance, according to my favorite version of the story, he once got a tip about a local Baltimore kid who could hit and pitch. The kid was a bit troubled; he was at a local reform school. Dunn went to see the kid, who was wearing overalls and rings on three fingers, and was so taken by the boy's look, his physique, and the way he carried himself that, without even watching him throw a single ball, he offered the kid a contract.

Yes, that's right. The kid's name was George Ruth. They would soon call him Babe.

Then, only five years later, he heard about this left-handed whirlwind throwing in West Virginia. He sent his son, Jack Jr., down to see what the fuss was about. Jack Jr. was profoundly impressed and wanted to make a deal. It turned out that the Martinsburg team owner had a problem: His stadium didn't have any outfield fencing. Jack Jr. offered about $3,000, enough to cover a new fence for the ballpark.

And just like that, Dunn's Orioles had signed the greatest hitter and greatest pitcher of the next era within a five-year period.

"I'm the only man traded for a fence," Grove would say.

Grove was extremely nervous about going to Baltimore. He'd never been anywhere. He took his first train ride after signing and was so jittery about it that he didn't eat the whole way. When he arrived, he saw his name (sort of) in the paper:

"Lefty Groves Latest Addition to Team, Has All the Earmarks of Clever Twirler," the *Baltimore Sun* reported.

Yes, they called him Groves right from the start.

Grove was fantastic for Baltimore. He was still wild in those days—he averaged 156 walks a year his four full seasons in Baltimore—but he struck out everybody and he gave up so few hits. His record over those four full seasons was 96-34.

You will ask then: If he was so great, why did he spend four seasons playing for the Double-A Baltimore Orioles? And the answer is: Jack Dunn. He simply wouldn't sell Grove (or Groves) at any price. Major-league teams were salivating. Philadelphia Athletics manager Connie Mack saw Grove pitch and said, "When he is right, he's unbeatable." When Brooklyn Dodgers manager Wilbert Robinson saw him, he said: "He makes Dazzy Vance look silly," which meant something since Vance was Robinson's best pitcher.

In 11 exhibition at-bats against Ruth, Grove got 10 outs, nine by strikeouts, and shouted: "I'm not afraid of you!"

"Groves is a young fellow, always in training, never has a sore arm," Dunn wrote. "He is getting better and better. Wild as a hawk sometimes, but when that fellow has a fair amount of control he can sure throw them through a batter. I believe his smoke ball is just about as fast as that of Walter Johnson's at his best."

The more desperate teams were to get Grove, the more Dunn played hard to get. "Why," he would ask suitors, "would I ever trade away the greatest pitcher in the world?" Dunn's recalcitrance kept Lefty Grove from getting to the big leagues until he was 25 years old—by then, in Dunn's own estimation, he had already been the greatest pitcher in the world for three years.

Finally, in 1924, Dunn relented. He sold Grove to Philadelphia for the unheard-of price of $100,600—the $600 was tacked on so that the Grove sale could surpass the $100,000 the Boston Red Sox got for Babe Ruth.

When Grove got to Philadelphia, the newspapers welcomed him by, yes, calling him Lefty Groves. Maybe Lefty himself thought that was his name. The Groves thing did finally end after the 1926 season.

First came 1925 and Grove's worst season. He did lead the American League in strikeouts, but he also led the league in walks and wild pitches. He had his only losing season, going 10-12 with a 4.75 ERA. He might have been hurt. It might also have just been a case of nerves. People began calling him the $100,600 lemon.

On July 4 of that year, however, the $100,600 lemon gave a sign of what was to come. On that memorable day, he dueled with Herb Pennock in New York, with 50,000 or so fans in the crowd. The two men just kept throwing shutout innings at each other. Pennock was more dominant—he would allow only four hits all game long—while Grove proved more resourceful. The game was 0-0 in the fifth when the Yankees put runners on first and third with one out. But Grove wiggled out of the jam, with a groundout and a deep fly ball.

In the bottom of the ninth, still scoreless, the Yankees put runners on second and third, and Grove got the inning-ending strikeout.

In the 10th, with a runner on first, he struck out Earle Combs and Ruth.

And on it went—12th inning, 13th inning, 14th inning. Finally in the 15th, with the game still scoreless, the Yankees got the run when Bobby Veach scored from second on a single. Thus ended one of the most famous pitching duels in baseball history.

Still, even with that, 1925 was mostly a washout for Grove. The talk was that his wildness would prevent him from ever becoming a great pitcher. Grove's famous temper boiled over that. "Huh, so I'm the wild guy in the league?" he asked John J. Nolan of the *Philadelphia Evening Bulletin.* "I'll show them something next year."

He did show them something. What Grove did that offseason before the 1926 season would become the stuff of fables. He went back to his father's barn, where he had drawn a home plate and a pitcher's rubber. On the barn itself, he drew a tiny little circle. And for hours every morning, he would throw until he hit that circle 20 times in a row.

Yes, he would show them something next year.

In 1926, he led the league in ERA, strikeouts, fewest hits per nine, and, surprisingly, strikeout-to-walk ratio. He only went 13-13 but that wasn't his fault—he lost 1–0 three times, 2–0 once, and 3–0 once—and so not everybody realized just how good he was. Using today's measures, he would finish in the top two in the Cy Young voting.

And then, Lefty Grove went on to dominate the league like no pitcher ever has or probably ever will.

This is not hyperbole. Grove led the league in ERA nine times, that's a record, and it has never been approached. Roger Clemens is second on the list with six ERA titles.

There was no such thing as FIP (Fielding Independent Pitching) in Grove's day, but we figure it now based on strikeouts, walks, and home runs allowed. Grove led the league in FIP eight times, again a record unlikely to be matched.

Back to the more traditional stats, he led the league in wins four times, in winning percentage five times, and from 1925 to 1931, he led the league in strikeouts every single year. His 1931 season—he went 31-4 with a 2.06 ERA and a 217 ERA+—was good enough to win the first MVP award handed out by the Baseball Writers' Association of America (he beat out Lou Gehrig, who had 185 RBIs). It is considered one of the greatest pitching seasons ever but, in truth, it might not even have been his best. Grove had four or five other seasons that were every bit as good but didn't quite have the same counting numbers.

Grove just did remarkable things all the time. In August 1928, facing Cleveland, he struck out the side on nine pitches. Barely a month later, this time against the White Sox, he did it again. For 90 years, he was the only pitcher to pull off two immaculate innings in the same season (Chris Sale did it in 2019).

Grove had 10 seasons with a 150 or better ERA+. This is more than Tom Seaver. This is more than Sandy Koufax. OK, that was a setup. Grove had more seasons with 150-plus ERA+ than Seaver and Koufax *combined*.

So let's ask the question again: Why did Lefty Grove struggle to get into the Hall of Fame? Why is his name so rarely mentioned today, while Cy Young and Walter Johnson and others remain legendary? Why is it if you ask people to name the greatest pitcher ever, Grove's name will almost certainly not come up?

My theory is this: Grove's career ERA is 3.06.

That's it. That to me is where the story begins and that's where the story ends.

Grove's 3.06 ERA kicks in an instant reaction. What do you think when you see a pitcher with a 3.06 ERA? Good but not great, right? We all have a chart in our heads, one that developed over years and years of baseball fanhood.

Sub-2.00 ERA: otherworldly.

Sub-3.00 ERA: great.

ERA between 3.00 and 4.00: pretty good.

ERA over 4.00: not so hot.

ERA over 5.00: Get the hook.

We know, instinctively, that not all ERAs are created equal. But the numbers still register a reaction. In 1947, you had Hubbell and Grove up for the Hall of Fame. As great as Hubbell was, he surely wasn't Grove—but his ERA (2.98) was below the line. Grove's was above. And Hubbell was elected with a much higher percentage.

I think Grove's ERA has never stopped throwing people off the trail. When SABR did its top 100 players, they listed *10* pitchers ahead of him. Only one of them—Walter Johnson—had more modern-era Wins Above Replacement.

But here's the deal with Grove's 3.06 ERA. It's absolutely incredible. In context, it might be more impressive even than Johnson's career 2.17 ERA or Christy Mathewson's 2.13 ERA. Look:

Best Career ERA+ for Modern-Day Starters*

1. Pedro Martínez, 154

2. Grove, 148

3. Johnson, 147

4. Ed Walsh, 146

5. (tie) Smoky Joe Wood, 146

Yes, if you incorporate time and place, Grove's 3.06 ERA looks very different. Well, you know this has to be true because you know that nobody won as many ERA titles as he did.

Grove played in a time when offenses scored runs at will. In 1936, Grove had a 2.81 ERA, which seems good but hardly historic. It was historic, though. It was a half-run better than any other pitcher in the league. That year, American League teams averaged 5.67 runs per game, the most for any year in league history.

In 1928, Grove went 24-8 with a 2.58 ERA and led the league in strikeouts. Great year. But again, it was better than it looks because teams averaged 5.41 runs per game, the second most in league history.

In 1938, Grove finished with a 3.08 ERA, pretty close to his career ERA. Special? Yes. It led the league. AL teams averaged 5.37 runs per game, the fourth most in league history.

You can see the trend. And now add this: Grove pitched his home games in two of the most extreme hitters' parks in baseball, Shibe Park in Philadelphia and Boston's Fenway Park.

And then add this—throughout his career, Lefty Grove was used in just about every role imaginable. He was a starter. He was a reliever. He was a closer. He was an emergency guy. He was everything. In 1930, he led the league in wins *and* saves (though it would be decades before the save became an official statistic). From 1931 to 1933, he led the league in complete games each year *and* he had double-digit games finished each year on top of that.

---

* We are not including active starters like Clayton Kershaw (157) or Jacob deGrom (148) because they still have some years to go.

Put it all together, and there's a powerful argument for Grove as the greatest pitcher of all time, even if his ERA was higher than 3.00.

Lefty Grove was a legendary hothead. "On the mound," Red Smith wrote of him, "he was poetry. He would rock back until the knuckles of his left hand almost brushed the earth behind him, then come up and over with the perfect follow through."

Off it? He was hellfire. He threw tantrums repeatedly. He kicked water buckets. He swore often and loudly. He threw chairs and bats and gloves in the clubhouse when he lost. Once, he was in the middle of one of his spells and everybody was silent until Connie Mack finally tried to get Grove to quiet down. This was a mistake. As Doc Cramer used to say: "You had to wait 'til the steam went out of him."

"To hell with you, Mack! To hell with you!" Grove shouted.

Mack watched Grove walk away sadly and then softly said, "And to hell with you too, Robert."

But my favorite Grove hothead story came after he retired. He was in a clubhouse when he saw a young player kick the water bucket after a poor inning—the very thing he had done so many times in his career. Grove shook his head.

"Kid," he said, "when you kick a water bucket, never kick it with your toes. Always use the side of your foot."

No. 21 **Joe Morgan**

I n 1971, the Cincinnati Reds traded one of the league's great sluggers, Lee May, along with their Gold Glove second baseman Tommy Helms to Houston, a division rival. It was a risky move. The Astros were an up-and-coming team. That season, for the first time in their history, they had pulled even with the Reds in the standings. They had started to brag that they were going to race past Cincinnati and become the dominant team in the league.

Around Cincinnati, people asked: Why in the world was Reds general manager Bob Howsam trying to help the Houston Astros do that?

"Power for speed," Howsam told reporters. That was his explanation for the deal.

Power for speed? What does that even mean? Nobody knew. Power was, you know, tangible. It was vital. In 1970, when the Reds won the pennant, they were loaded with power; that was why they won. May hit 34 home runs and Tony Pérez hit 40 home runs and Johnny Bench hit 45 home runs. They led the league in home runs. They were the Big Red Machine.

They were not the Fast Red Machine.

Power for speed?

"What does the general public think of the trade?" *Hamilton Journal-News* columnist Bill Moeller asked the day after the deal. "It seems the majority of the fans feel it was the Reds' worst trade since they let Frank Robinson go."

No, it didn't take long for the fans to be outraged. May had hit 34 or more home runs each of the previous three seasons. Helms had established himself as the best defensive second baseman in the National League. Those two had been core players for the Reds' pennant-winning team. More than that, they were leaders. They were fan favorites. And they didn't want to get traded.

"You go out and give all you can, even on a lot of days when you shouldn't be playing," May told reporters. "And this is the appreciation you get."

"Hello, you have reached the residence of Tommy Helms of the Houston Astros," was how Helms answered his phone for a while.

Heartbreaking, that's what it was.

And what did the Reds get back in the deal? They got a pitcher, Jack Billingham, who had just gone 10-16. So, that didn't seem too great. They got a fourth outfielder with a fun name and a .228 career average, César Gerónimo. They got a 30-something former All-Star in Denis Menke. They got a pinch-hitter named Ed Armbrister.

But the main person they got in the deal, the key to the whole thing if you listened to Howsam talk, was a second baseman named Joe Morgan.

And nobody in Cincinnati particularly wanted Joe Morgan.

"What are the Reds doing?" one person wrote in a letter to the editor. "I wouldn't have traded Tommy Helms for Joe Morgan straight up. Helms is a Gold Glove winner! What has Joe Morgan ever done?"

There have been a handful of players in baseball history whose genius was hidden in plain sight. Morgan was such a player. More than one person has pointed out the great irony that envelops Morgan's baseball life: Joe Morgan the broadcaster never seemed to understand exactly what made Joe Morgan the ballplayer so electrifying and wonderful.

No, to explain Morgan, new stats had to be invented and configured. Stats like Wins Above Replacement. Morgan made abundantly clear his disdain for WAR. He never hid his disdain for all the analytics gurus, those people who never played the game at the highest level, coming up with complicated statistics and novel approaches to measuring a player's value.

And yet, those analytics gurus were the ones who fully saw Morgan's greatness on the field.

I suspect all of this drove Joe Morgan more than a little bit crazy.

But it shouldn't have bothered him. Morgan was raised to be a sabermetric dream of a ballplayer. He learned the game from his father, Leonard, who had played semipro ball in Texas. Leonard was several inches taller than his son would become and he did everything on the baseball diamond. He pitched. He caught. He played short. He hit. He stole bases. He bunted.

And Leonard always preached versatility to his oldest son. Leonard and Joe would go to Oakland Oaks ball games back in the 1950s when that team had some terrific players. Joe was partial to a lefty slugger named Jim Marshall (who got a few years in the big leagues). Leonard preferred former Negro Leagues star Piper Davis. But what Joe would always remember was the dialogue between father and son—he never got over how astute his father was at scouting players' strengths and weaknesses.

"See there," Leonard would say. "That guy is fast. But he doesn't know how to steal bases."

"Look at him," Leonard would say. "He's not much at the plate but he always gets down the bunt."

"That third baseman has good feet but he can't throw a lick," Leonard would say.

Leonard could do this with every player, even after watching only an inning or two. And there was a theme behind his scouting reports: You had to do everything well to impress him. He wasn't interested in a slugger who hit a three-run homer, then gave up two runs the next inning with an error. He wasn't interested by a fast baserunner who routinely got terrible jumps and wasn't able to pick up the extra base. No, you had to do it all or else you were hurting the ball club.

"What he'd emphasize over and over again," Joe explained, "was the value of being a complete player, one who could do it all. He stressed how much a complete player added to his team—and how much he took away when parts of his game weren't there."

And this was how Joe Morgan lived and played baseball.

That's what all those Cincinnati fans missed after the trade was made. What did they see? They saw a 5-foot-7 infielder who weighed maybe 160 pounds, one of the smallest players in the game. "Little Joe," they called him (Morgan loathed that). Lee May was a giant; 6-foot-3, 200-plus pounds. They called him the Big Bopper.

The Big Bopper for Little Joe? Of course fans rebelled against the deal.

But there was more. Little Joe had hit .253 the previous three seasons. Heck, Helms had hit .253 himself, and he was a defensive wizard. Sure, Morgan was fast, and he stole some bases, but he wasn't stealing 50 or 60 bases a year like Lou Brock. His second base defense, according to scouting reports, was average at best.

And let's not kid anybody: He had a rep for being moody and difficult. True, this reputation mostly came from clashes he had with Astros manager Harry "the Hat" Walker, whom Morgan would later call "possibly the biggest fool I have ever known in the game" and "the most blatant racist I ever met in baseball." But in the moment, Morgan was seen as the problem.*

"I got the reputation of being a troublemaker," Morgan would say, "although I wasn't then or ever."

You put it all together—Morgan's size, his low average, his average defense, his reputation as a troublemaker—and you can see why people in Cincinnati were so down on the deal.

But, again, this was because Morgan's greatness was hidden in plain sight. True, he would become a better player in Cincinnati, but he was already a tremendous player in Houston.

---

* Harry the Hat was somewhere in the middle of one of baseball's darkest stories—a story that still causes controversy today. In 1947, just after Jackie Robinson broke the color barrier in baseball, Stanley Woodward of the New York Herald Tribune broke the story that a few St. Louis Cardinals plotted to strike. The league stepped in and stopped them. Harry the Hat was on that Cardinals team and was undoubtedly in the middle of things—Woodward reported that it was Harry's brother, Dixie Walker of the Dodgers, who had started the whole idea. All of this is controversial today because some baseball historians think that Woodward overstated the threat to make it a bigger story—the players involved said that it was just idle talk and they never intended to actually go through with it. Harry the Hat always said that he and his brother may have been originally against the idea of Robinson because of the way they were raised, but over time they had changed and sought to treat everyone equally. Harry Walker's insistence that he changed is powerfully contradicted by Morgan, who remembered how often Walker would say things to him like, "It will be a black day . . . oh, ha ha, didn't mean to say that, pardner!"

And people missed it because, in 1971, batting average was more or less everything in baseball analytics. And batting average missed the fact that Morgan walked 100 times a year.

They missed it because they saw his power numbers—he hit 13 homers in '71—and didn't appreciate that he played half his home games in the hitters' dungeon that was the Houston Astrodome. Morgan had hit nine of those homers on the road. And homers aren't everything: Morgan had led the league with 11 triples—again, he had more on the road than at home.

They missed it because they looked at his seemingly good stolen-base numbers—40 steals that year—and didn't appreciate that they were actually fantastic numbers. He was caught only eight times. All of this suggested that his stolen-base numbers could skyrocket if he was on a team that let him run more (hint: this happened in Cincinnati).

They missed it because they looked at his fielding only through the prism of errors and didn't appreciate that there is so much more to the art form. Morgan was developing into one of the best second basemen in the league.

In other words, they missed it because Bill James and Baseball-Reference and FanGraphs and the Moneyball gurus and others had not come along yet to ask some hard questions and offer some fascinating new data that gives people a new way to look at baseball.

Morgan had a 3.4 WAR or more in every full season he played for the Astros. He finished in the top 10 in WAR in 1965 and '71. He was already terrific and was about to take off Apollo 11 style.

Of course, we must point out again that Joe Morgan really doesn't like WAR.

Enter Pete Rose.

Yes, he plays a big part in the story. When Morgan arrived in Cincinnati, Reds manager Sparky Anderson—an admitted Morgan skeptic—pulled his new player aside and said: "I just want you to know that whatever happened in Houston is over. You get a fresh start here."

And then he made sure that Morgan's locker was next to Rose's locker.

It was one of the most remarkable bits of matchmaking in baseball history. There seems no obvious way, looking back, to think that Morgan and Rose would hit it off. Their personalities were entirely different. Their temperaments were entirely different. Their stature in the game was entirely different. It's hard to imagine meeting Joe Morgan and Pete Rose and thinking that they would become the best of friends.

And yet that's exactly what happened. They just got each other. They made each other laugh. They loved insulting each other. They confided in each other. Rose was a white guy who Morgan felt comfortable joking with about race. Morgan was so baseball brilliant that Rose felt comfortable getting advice from him.

They fed off each other's brilliance. For five years, they played the best baseball of their careers side by side.

1972: Morgan, 9.3 WAR (led league); Rose, 6.1 WAR (5th)

1973: Morgan, 9.3 WAR (led league); Rose, 8.3 WAR (career-high, won MVP)

1974: Morgan, 8.6 WAR (2nd); Rose, 5.9 WAR (6th)

1975: Morgan, 11.0 WAR (led league, won MVP); Rose, 4.1 WAR

1976: Morgan, 9.6 WAR (led league, won MVP); Rose, 7.0 WAR (3rd)

What exactly did they do for each other? My theory: Morgan helped Rose be more disciplined. Joe Morgan was all about efficiency—he did all those little things well, he walked twice as often as he struck out, he stole bases at a very high percentage, he scored 100-plus runs every year, he played sound defense. Morgan helped Rose become more efficient himself. Rose began walking more (in 1974, for the first time in his career, Rose drew more than 100 walks). Rose began taking extra bases more (he led the league in doubles in 1974, 1975, and 1976). And so on.

And what did Morgan get from Rose? That's easier: relentlessness. Morgan had always played the game hard and played it to win. But in Rose, he saw something else, something unusual: Rose didn't just play hard. He didn't just play to win. He played to *play*. That is to say, Rose saw every game, every at-bat, heck, every round of batting practice and fielding practice as a one-of-a-kind opportunity to do something special.

Morgan wasn't like that before. He wanted a few days off during the year so he could stay fresh. He didn't see any reason to be in games that were out of hand. He certainly didn't follow his own statistics with any particular passion.

And then he would watch Rose . . . particularly on days that Pete had four hits. Yes, that was the telltale sign. Rose would get four hits, and then he would come up again in the late innings, and maybe the game was in hand, maybe the game didn't matter in the standings, whatever, Pete Rose *hungered* for that fifth hit. In some ways, he wanted that hit more than he'd wanted the first four.

Why? What drove this guy? He knew his batting average to the fourth decimal point every single day. He never allowed himself to get taken out of a game, not ever. "Pete, I'm resting you this week," Anderson once told Rose. "I'm not arguing with you. You just tell me what day and I'm sitting you down and giving you a rest."

"OK, Sparky," Rose said. "How about Thursday?"

"Thursday's an off-day," Anderson said, but by the time he said that Rose was already on the field chattering like a kid skipping school.

Morgan started wanting some of that action. No, he was never going to be Pete Rose; there was only one of that guy. But he didn't need to be Rose. He just wanted to take his own game to a new level. And, in Cincinnati, he became the best player in baseball.

"Pete," Morgan would say, "helped make the player that I am."

From 1972 to 1977, six years, Joe Morgan was impossibly good. Over those years, he hit .301/.425/.495. He led the league in runs once, in walks twice, in on-base percentage four times. He averaged 22 homers and 60 stolen bases a year. He won four Gold Gloves and two MVP awards. He scored 100 runs and walked 100 times each season.

In just those six years, he had 53.6 WAR—more than seven Hall of Fame second basemen had in their entire careers.

But beyond that, he just did incredible things all the time. My favorite happened in 1975 in an early-season game against the San Francisco Giants. It was the bottom of the ninth inning and the score was tied and Morgan was at second base. There were two outs and Morgan saw Giants pitcher Charlie Williams throw the ball in the dirt.

Nobody in baseball anticipated the wild pitch better than Morgan. He took off toward third, but all along he watched the Giants' catcher, Marc Hill. This was Hill's rookie year. And there was something about the way Hill went after the ball, something imperceptible to everyone in the ballpark except Joe Morgan.

About 20 feet from third base, Morgan essentially stopped.

Hill looked over at Morgan in utter disbelief. Why was he stopping? Hill's next move was pure instinct. He fired to third base. Morgan took off for the bag at exactly the same time. The ball and runner reached the bag simultaneously, but the runner was under control while the ball was not. It was a wild throw and it skipped into left field. Morgan raced around and scored the winning run.

"I could have made third easily," Morgan told reporters. "But I deliberately held back. I was hoping Hill would do just what he did."

It was impossible. Morgan had all but hypnotized Hill and prompted him to throw the ball away. He was a warlock as much as a ballplayer.

"If Joe Morgan keeps up his current pace," Anderson said, "he'll be dead in a month."

A few months after I wrote this, Joe Morgan died after a long battle with polyneuropathy. And I found myself remembering a moment when I was driving through Indiana and was pulled over for speeding. The officer had me, I definitely had been speeding, but as he came up to the car he noticed in the front seat a copy of my book *The Machine*, about the 1975 Cincinnati Reds. He asked about it, and I told him that I had written it.

Without hesitation, he said: "Johnny Bench, Tony Pérez, Joe Morgan, Dave Concepción, Pete Rose, George Foster, Ken Griffey, and César Gerónimo."

That is the complete lineup of that Reds team, a group of players still known around Cincinnati as "the Great Eight."

I nodded approvingly, and then he asked me a question: "Who was the best of the eight?" I am embarrassed to say that I hesitated for a moment because here was a white police officer who had pulled me over for speeding and based on that alone the thought occurred to me that my best chance to escape the ticket would be to name a white player, Pete Rose or Johnny Bench.

But I couldn't lie to the guy.

"It's Joe Morgan," I told him. The officer nodded.

"That's right," he said, and he let me go with a warning.

No. 20 Frank Robinson

Frank Robinson, for me, will always represent what it feels like to be eight years old. When you're eight years old, time stretches like an endless rubber band, and the sun glows a brighter yellow than it ever will again, and every stone stoop and brick wall seems built for you to throw a ball against, and the mind teeters between what's real and what is magic.

I was eight years old when Frank Robinson became the first African American to manage a Major League Baseball game.

No, I didn't understand the full scope of the thing. All I knew was that it was big. For people who are just a few years older than me, eight years old might mean gathering around a static-touched black-and-white television and watching Neil Armstrong land on the moon and say those forever words: "(GARBLE) (GARBLE) STEP (GARBLE) MAN. (GARBLE) (GARBLE) LEAP FOR (GARBLE) (GARBLE)."

But for me, it was Robby. I was a developing baseball fan then, but most of what I knew about the game I picked up from overheard adult conversations. It was clear from those conversations that my hometown baseball team, the Cleveland Indians, was not just poor but something of an embarrassment. Adults talked about them in the same hushed tones they used when talking about ne'er-do-well relatives who always asked for money.

One of my earliest memories, it had to be around the same time, was going to an amusement park called Cedar Point in nearby Sandusky, Ohio. This was our annual summer vacation trip and there was this Old West Riverboat Ride we loved. We'd be floating down the river, Mark Twain style, and then suddenly we would hear gunfire. "Oh no!" the boat captain would shout out. "We're being attacked by Indians." Right, you'd have to say the ride hasn't aged well.

But the point is that then the boat captain would say: "Oh, don't worry folks. Those are Cleveland Indians. And everyone knows they can't hit anything."*

Then, in September 1974, Frank Robinson arrived. Well, *arrived* might be too grand a verb; Cleveland had picked him up off the waiver wire. As an eight-year-old, you have no sense of age—the fact that Robby was thirty-eight and in full decline meant nothing at all to me. Here was a superstar of the highest order. I was unaware that the California Angels, who had put Robby on the waiver wire in the first place, were shocked and thrilled that someone had picked him up. This was an easy way for them to dump his enormous salary ($173,000).

The teams worked out a deal, and Robinson put on a ridiculous all red uniform with INDIANS written in capital letters across the chest in some sort of bizarre font.

It soon became apparent why Cleveland had made this deal: They intended to make Frank Robinson the first black manager in baseball history. For a time, Tribe management—led by general manager Phil Seghi—played it off, kept denying it, but it was too obvious to miss. Two weeks after Robby got to Cleveland, Seghi thanked his manager Ken Aspromonte and told him that there would be a new manager in 1975. He asked Aspromonte to keep it quiet until the end of the season.

Aspromonte did keep it quiet . . . for about 38 seconds, at which point he called a team meeting and raged about how the team had just fired him. This may or may not have led to the verbal fight between Robinson and Cleveland's ace Gaylord Perry, who quickly told reporters that he abso-

---

* Starting in 2022, the Cleveland baseball team will have a new name. This is long overdue.

lutely could not and would not play for Cleveland if Robinson was the manager.*

So, yes, Cleveland screwed up the whole thing. That was more or less inevitable for this organization. The next day was one of the most shameful in Cleveland sports history as fans booed Robinson relentlessly and someone unfurled a bedsheet banner that read: "Sickle cell anemia: The great white hope."

This was America—and Cleveland—in 1974 before there had ever been a black manager in baseball. It wasn't so long ago.

As a little kid, I must say, I was only vaguely aware of such things. The world felt to me a blur of so many things—Watergate, Vietnam, Rock'em Sock'em Robots, Muhammad Ali fighting George Foreman, Henry Aaron passing Babe Ruth, McDonald's burgers, fat Elvis wearing capes, *The Tonight Show with Johnny Carson,* Sinatra coming out of retirement, Redd Foxx having perpetual heart attacks on *Sanford and Son.* It felt impossible to keep up.

But I remember my father telling me on the day Cleveland hired Frank Robinson to be manager that something important had happened, something historic, something that people would write about in books.

And I remember a few months later, when the 1975 Topps baseball cards came out, the first Topps baseball card set I ever collected in earnest. Early on I got a Frank Robinson card. I loved that card so much I kept it under my pillow when I slept. It was purple and pink—Topps was going for something funky in those days—and it put his position as "Des. Hitter" and it had a facsimile autograph written across the bottom (perfect penmanship!). Robinson himself was wearing a Crooked C cap that was probably painted on by the Topps "artist."†

The most compelling part of that baseball card, though, is the inscrutable look on Frank Robinson's face. He isn't exactly smiling, and he isn't

---

* Perry had told the press that since he was the team's star, he deserved to make at least the $173,000 that Robby was making. Robinson didn't like that one bit.

† Topps would have an artist paint new baseball caps onto players who had switched teams after they took photographs. I always assumed it to be a precocious 13-year-old who had impressed the company with an eighth-grade art project. They weren't particularly convincing.

exactly *not* smiling. The look is something else, something profound; at least I always thought so.

It's a look that says: "Yes, I've accomplished a few things in my life."

Robinson grew up playing sports with Bill Russell and Curt Flood. I'm not sure what was happening in West Oakland at the time but think of the extraordinary confluence of not just athletic talent but pioneering spirit. Here you had the first black manager in baseball, the first black coach in the NBA (and the greatest winner in the history of sports), and the man who fought the system to break free in baseball, all playing on the same playground.

Robinson's pro baseball career began with pain, and I feel pretty certain that the pain never quite dissipated. He signed for $3,500 with the Cincinnati Reds, but let's get the timing right: This was 1953. This was two years before Rosa Parks refused to go to the back of the bus. The Reds had not yet played a black player. This didn't actually put the Reds behind the curve; only six teams at that point had played a black player.

As such, the Reds had absolutely no idea how to develop an African-American baseball player. They did everything wrong with Robinson. Right away, they sent him to Ogden, Utah, a city and state heavily influenced by the Mormon Church, which at the time proclaimed African Americans to be inferior to whites. Robinson was just 17 years old and had only known life in West Oakland. He was surely aware of racism but, as he would say, at that point it was still mostly theoretical in his mind; the racism he came across in California was mostly undercover, cloaked with whispers.

In Ogden, however, racism was palpable and very much a part of daily life. It goes without saying that the Reds did not prepare him for this. On one of his first days in Ogden, Robby went to a theater to see a movie.

"We don't serve your kind here," the person taking tickets said to Robinson.

Robinson did not comprehend what the man was saying. Wondered if he misheard. His kind? Was he too young? He tried again to give the money and get a ticket.

"We don't serve n——here," the man said more clearly.

Something broke inside Robby at that moment. Every fiber of his being wanted to lash out; Robinson, even at that age, was a man, a force. But he knew that he could not lash out. He knew that he could only go back to the hotel quietly, and he felt dizzy, like the world had started to spin out of control. He no longer felt like he knew the rules of living.

"It bothered me so much," he would say, "that I never let anything like that happen again. I stayed in my place. I went only where there was no problem. All I knew to do then was withdraw."

Remarkably, this did not impact him on the field. He was such a great ballplayer right away. I think now about not only the courage of those incredible baseball pioneers but the extraordinary discipline. In 72 games for Ogden, Robinson hit .348 with 17 home runs and a .656 slugging percentage. He played his way right out of Ogden and hoped to never return.

But the Reds . . . it really is startling how bad teams were in those days in developing young African-American players. They sent him to Columbia, South Carolina, this a decade or so before the University of South Carolina enrolled its first black student since Reconstruction. Robinson actually found the South to be less hateful than Ogden—perhaps because his expectations were different—and he hit .336 with 66 extra bases in 132 games.

So what did the Reds do? They sent him *back* to Columbia.

It's almost as if the Reds were trying to ruin Frank Robinson before he ever got started.

But he was too strong for that, too driven, too talented, too committed. One year later, he came to spring training and played his way onto the team. The Reds' manager, Birdie Tebbetts, was a hard character, but so was Robby, and the two got along splendidly. "I'd be happy if Frankie bats .250 and hits 15 home runs," Tebbetts said when announcing that the 20-year-old Robinson had made the ball club.

There was no chance of Robby hitting .250 with 15 home runs. Instead, he hit .290/.379/.558 with 38 home runs and a league-leading 122 runs, one of the great rookie seasons in baseball history. He could do everything then. He hit. He slugged. He ran. He fielded. He even threw well, though he had an arm injury that sometimes made him yelp after throwing. He was so good, so fast, that fans voted him into the All-Star Game barely three months into his career.

"He has the potential to become another Ted Williams," Tebbetts gushed to reporters.

Soon, people would find there was so much more to Robinson than just his baseball talent. At the end of his first year, he attended Xavier

University to study psychology. He quickly became a team leader and his aggressive style of play—crashing into second to break up double plays, dusting himself off after brush-back pitches, and pounding line drives up the middle, never backing down—influenced an entire generation of future players, from Pete Rose to Hal McRae.

He was so good, too. Over the next nine seasons with the team, Robby hit .304/.390/.554, won an MVP, won a Gold Glove, led the league in OPS three times, led the team to a pennant, and became the most feared player in the game. Nobody played harder.

You probably have heard the expression: "Close doesn't count except in horseshoes and hand grenades." Well, it has been written in many places that it was Robinson who came up with that expression (in particular, the second part about hand grenades—the horseshoes part goes back to at least the 1930s). And while I don't know if that's true,* it certainly is fitting. That's how he played baseball. Close was not good enough.

In 1966, as baseball fans know, the Reds traded Robinson to Baltimore for Milt Pappas. "Bad trades are a part of baseball; who can forget Frank Robinson for Milt Pappas for godsakes?" Annie says in *Bull Durham*. It seems that there was a feud going on between Robinson and the Reds' Bill Dewitt, which seemed destined to lead to a sour ending.

"Robinson is an old 30 years of age," Dewitt told reporters after the deal. "He has an old body."

Robinson didn't need added motivation like that. But he took it. In 1966, he was unstoppable. At first, he did worry a bit about going to the Orioles, another team that had not really had a black star before. But his concerns faded almost immediately. A few minutes after he arrived, another Robinson, an Arkansan named Brooks, pulled him aside and said: "I think you're exactly what this team needs."

They would become as close as brothers (they were often photographed as "the Robinson Brothers"). Once, a reporter talked about the

---

* Robinson was quoted saying this in *Time* magazine in 1973, which is one of the earliest references. But I can find it a few times before then; the earliest reference, interestingly enough, was actually offered by then–Minnesota Twins pitcher Jim Kaat in 1967. He had just pitched very well against Cleveland, striking out 10, but he lost the game after he made a throwing error in the ninth. "The only thing that would make me feel better would be to have won," he said. "But close doesn't count except in horseshoes and hand grenades."

confusion of seeing two Robinsons on the field, and Frank said: "We're easy to tell apart. He wears a different number."

In 1966, a determined Frank Robinson won the Triple Crown and also led the league in runs scored, OPS, and total bases. He carried the Orioles to their first pennant and their first World Series title. When people asked him afterward if Dewitt's statement had anything to do with it, he would offer that half smile and half frown and say, "Damn right."

"Pitchers did me a favor when they knocked me down," he often said. "It made me more determined. I wouldn't let that pitcher get me out. They say you can't hit if you're on your back. But I didn't hit on my back. I got up."

So he did. Pitchers plunked Frank Robinson 198 times over the years, and he remembered every last one of them. Lew Burdette hit him four times; Robinson slugged nine homers off him. Sandy Koufax got him twice, Robinson hit seven homers off him. Robby and Don Drysdale had epic battles; same with Bob Gibson. Robinson leaned over the plate and dared. He didn't always win. But he always got up.

In all, Robinson hit .294/.389/.537 despite playing in an era utterly dominated by pitching—his career 154 OPS+ is essentially the same as Henry Aaron, Willie Mays, and Joe DiMaggio. As for the rest of his career numbers . . . well, there's a story that goes along with that.

If you want to understand Robinson—the pride, the ferocity, the class, and the hunger to win—I don't think there's a better way to do it than to look at what happened after he became the first black manager in baseball history.

He turned 39 his first year as Cleveland manager in 1975. And, this is important, he could still hit. No, he wasn't close to the hitter he had been—he hit only .251 playing in 1974 for the Angels.

But look beyond batting average and you can see: He walked 75 times that year (led the team), he hit 26 doubles (led the team), he hit 20 homers (led the team), he drove in 63 RBIs (led the team), he scored 75 runs (led the team), and he had an outstanding 146 OPS+ (led the team).

He was, unquestionably, the best hitter on the Angels.

At the end of the 1974 season, Robinson had 2,900 hits and 574 home runs. You can see the point here: He was less than a season away from 3,000 hits and 600 home runs was in range, too. He'd hit 30 home runs in 1973.

Yes, he was so close to two of the biggest and most meaningful numbers in baseball. Even now, only four players—Henry Aaron, Willie Mays, Albert Pujols, and Alex Rodriguez—have 3,000 hits and 600 home runs. In Robinson's time, it was only Aaron and Mays, his two great contemporaries and rivals. Robinson was hardly unaware of where he stood. "Those are personal goals," he admitted in his press conference to take the managerial role.

But personal goals, for Robinson, were just that: personal. They were not important. Winning was important. Playing the game right was important. When he became Cleveland's player-manager, he could have played himself every day. Who would have complained? He was Frank Robinson, for crying out loud, *and*, as mentioned, he could still hit. That season, his .508 slugging percentage was second on Cleveland behind only Robby's longtime pal Boog Powell.

But Robinson didn't play himself every day.

In fact, he hardly played himself at all.

Compare this with a Robinson disciple named Pete Rose. Pete idolized Robby back when he was first called up to Cincinnati. They spent many dinners together where Rose picked Robinson's brain for tips and ideas about how to play the game. When Rose became manager of the Cincinnati Reds, he was 43—and you'd better believe he played himself as often as he could until he broke Ty Cobb's all-time hit record.

But Robby wouldn't do that. He was still a viable hitter, but Cleveland already had a designated hitter named Rico Carty (who was only four years younger than Robinson) and he was a good hitter. So he played. "I'm here to win games," Robinson said. He'd put himself in there every now and again, sometimes as a pinch-hitter, but that was it.

And you know what? He never did get to 3,000 hits—finishing instead with 2,943. He never did get to 600 homers, finishing instead with 586. Just about any other team in baseball would have put Frank Robinson in the lineup.

But Robinson himself cared about something larger. So when you look at his career numbers, you see more than production. You see who he was.

For a moment, I want to talk about Frank Robinson as I remember him from when I was eight years old. The date was April 8, 1975. It was a Tuesday. The Academy Awards were that night—*The Godfather Part II* won

Best Picture. Most of the big sportswriters in America were in Cleveland for the big day. It was chilly, as April days in Cleveland tend to be.

This was the day Frank Robinson managed his first game.

"Frank Robinson wrote down 10 names," Dick Young wrote in the New York *Daily News* and more than 100 syndicated newspapers across America, "took the list up to the plate and handed it to the umpire. For the first time, a black manager had made out a lineup for a big-league ballgame. The stadium did not fall down."

Almost 57,000 people poured into Cleveland Municipal Stadium for the game, Cleveland versus New York, Opening Day. But here's how we knew it was different: They put the game on the radio at school. This was history! This was a learning experience! There were a few pregame speeches, one more special than the others: Rachel Robinson spoke. We were told that she was Jackie Robinson's wife.

This seemed impossible to eight-year-old me. Jackie Robinson was, like, a historical figure that we read about in books. At that age, you have no sense of time; the fact that Robinson had died less than three years earlier (at the age that I am now) was simply beyond my understanding.

"It has taken too long to get here," Rachel said that day—it had been Jackie's great wish to live to see a black manager in Major League Baseball.

"I so wish Jackie could be here," Frank said. "But, you know, since Rachel is here, I feel that Jackie is, too."

Robby tried to hide his nerves . . . but he really couldn't. He walked around anxiously. He would say that he felt like Alice in Wonderland. "I've watched Robby before games for years," Powell would say. "This one was different."

Robinson's ace pitcher and nemesis Perry started for the Tribe—he would soon demand and receive a trade because he and Robby just couldn't get along—and Perry worked around a leadoff walk to Sandy Alomar to pitch a scoreless inning.

That brought up the Tribe lineup to face the Yankees' Doc Medich. Robby batted himself second. Leadoff hitter Oscar Gamble fouled out. And Robinson stepped into the box. He felt as if in a daze. Medich's first pitch was low, at least Robinson thought so, but the umpire called it a strike. The second pitch was a fastball that caught the outside corner. "I couldn't pull the trigger," Robby would say. He was down 0-2. And he felt uneasy.

But on the third pitch, Medich tried to get Robby to chase by dropping down and throwing a sidearm slider. Robinson fouled it away and suddenly, for no reason he could pinpoint, he felt at ease again. This was just hitting. Few in the history of baseball had ever been better at it. He fouled off another pitch, took a ball, fouled off another pitch, and took a second ball. The count was even, 2-2, and Robinson now felt fully engaged.

Medich threw the next pitch down and away, right where Robinson expected it. Robby turned on the pitch and launched it deep to left field. He began running as hard as he could. He did not think it was gone. But then as he got to second, he looked over at the third base coach, Dave Garcia, who was clapping and smiling and jumping around.

It was gone.

And, in my memory, we eight-year-olds all jumped up out of our desks and screamed. I don't know. Maybe it didn't happen quite that way. We were all so young. It might have been a dream.

No. 20 (tie) **Mike Schmidt**

Before that game in Chicago began, Mike Schmidt was feeling out of sorts. This was and always would be a common feeling for Schmidt. This was 1976, and it was still April, but it was never too early for Schmidt to start getting into his own head.

He was hitting .167 for the season, and sure, the season was only a week old, but he hadn't felt right during spring training, either. In fact, he had not felt right for much of the 1975 season, though he ended up leading the National League in home runs. And if you wanted to go back even further, well, yeah, you might say Schmidt had never felt quite right.

"As a player," he would write in *Clearing the Bases,* "I studied swing mechanics to the extent that I actually hindered my own development as a hitter. I experimented with every stance, position in the box, grip pressure, swing plane, stride distance and size of bat known to man."

Schmidt saw how other hitters did it, hitters like Tony Pérez and Rod Carew and his teammate Greg Luzinski. They didn't worry about anything, didn't mess around with their swings, didn't carry the pressure of mankind on their own shoulders with every single at-bat. They didn't hear the crowd. They didn't think about their last at-bat. They didn't wonder what might happen if they changed their stride by an inch or two.

Maybe Schmidt envied that about them.

But he couldn't *be* like them. He just couldn't. "Schmidty," his manager Danny Ozark once said to him, "if you were dumb, you'd be better off." But Schmidt couldn't be dumb. He couldn't stop thinking. And that day in Chicago was worse than most because Ozark, seeing how Schmidt was torturing himself, dropped him from third to sixth in the lineup. He hoped that would relieve some of the pressure, but for Schmidt, it only added to it. *Why did they drop him to sixth? Did they think he wouldn't hit again? Was this a permanent move? Would he ever be in the middle of the lineup again?*

But something different happened before that game: Dick Allen called Schmidt over. At that point, Allen was a particular kind of legend—he was one of the great sluggers of his time, a former MVP and Rookie of the Year and two-time home run champion, but he was something more than that. He was a badass, with all the good and not so good that comes with that. He had appeared on the cover of *Sports Illustrated* juggling baseballs with a cigarette dangling out of his mouth. He'd been traded five times because teams loved his hitting but didn't really know how to deal with him. He was his own solar system.

"You've got to relax, man," he said, "it looks like you're having no fun at all." Schmidt nodded. He wasn't having fun. He didn't even know how baseball *could* be fun, not when there was so much pressure and so much expectation and so much responsibility and . . .

"Listen, man," Allen said. "Today, just today, I want you to do nothing but have fun, all right? Don't think about anything else. Just play the game like you're a little kid. Just play. Just enjoy it, man."

Schmidt nodded again—hey, he would try. Between innings, Allen and Schmidt threw the baseball around like it was a football, with each running wide receiver patterns. They clowned around in the dugouts. Schmidt liked it. And it was a silly day anyway; the wind was blowing at Wrigley Field, and the Cubs started whacking the ball all over the park. The Phillies were soon down 12–1. Fun!

Schmidt felt no pressure at all as he came up to face Chicago's Rick Reuschel down 11 runs. And he lashed out an RBI single. It felt pretty darned good.

In the fifth inning, the Phillies were still down 11 runs, now it was 13–2, and Schmidt came up to face Reuschel again with a man on. Reuschel threw a curveball that hung like an air freshener tree dangling from a taxi driver's rearview mirror, and Schmidt pulverized it, pulling the ball to left, out and over the wall and the bleachers and onto Waveland Avenue.

Now, that really was fun.

When Schmidt came up in the seventh, the Phillies were still down by nine runs. It was still Reuschel on the mound. Reuschel threw a fastball that he tried to back up over the outside part of the plate, but it backed up too much, caught too much of the plate, and Schmidt turned on it, pulled it down the line and over the net for another homer.

Schmidt came up again in the eighth inning, this time with the score 13–9 and two runners on. Reliever Mike Garman was on the mound for the Cubs, and he fired a fastball that was probably four or five inches outside. But Schmidt reached out and got all of it, driving the ball some 450 feet to straightaway center.

Allen wondered if maybe his pep talk had been too good.

Finally, 10th inning, score tied at 15. Allen drew a walk, and he had this full grin on his face as Schmidt stepped to the plate again. On the mound was Reuschel's brother, Paul, who was sent into the game specifically for Schmidt. Paul Reuschel threw a fastball that analysts now call "middle-middle." In those days, they would say it was right down Broadway. Schmidt did not get all of it. He did not have to get all of it. The ball jumped to left field and hopped into the basket at the top of the left-field wall.

With that, Schmidt had become just the eighth modern player—joining legends Lou Gehrig and Willie Mays, sluggers Chuck Klein, Gil Hodges, Rocky Colavito, and Joe Adcock and outlier Pat Seerey—to hit four homers in a game.

"When you get behind 13–2 like we did," Schmidt told reporters, "most guys would have quit and thought about tomorrow. But it made me more relaxed. And I started swinging away."

This is how it was. When he relaxed, there simply wasn't anyone quite like him.

But relaxing . . . for Mike Schmidt that was the hardest thing of all. He hit .208 over the next week.

"Any time you think you have the game conquered," he said, "the game will turn right around and punch you in the nose."

There's a game Mike Schmidt played in high school—a game he played on the day he graduated from high school, in fact—that perhaps tells his story as well as anything. Schmidt actually switch-hit in high school. Perhaps that shouldn't be too surprising since he was a chronic tinkerer at the plate, but if you think about the Schmidt swing, that short and perfect right cross of a swing, it's hard to imagine why he ever hit left-handed.

But he did. Or maybe it is better to say he tried.

Schmidt was a fantastic athlete at Fairfield High School in Dayton, Ohio. He would have been the team's quarterback—and a likely Division I college prospect—except he blew out his knee as a junior and gave up the sport. He was an all-city basketball player. He was 6-foot-2, close to 200 pounds, and was quite fast. He had natural power, and he threw hard enough to be the baseball team's top pitcher.

His baseball tools were impressive enough that Philadelphia Phillies legendary scout Tony Lucadello would check in on him from time to time.

Nobody else did. No other scouts. No college recruiters. Nobody. And there was a very specific and logical reason for this: Schmidt couldn't hit. He was, essentially, a switch-hitting out. He hit .176 his senior year going into the playoffs, and do you know how many home runs he hit all season? One. All year. We'll get to that in a minute.

Schmidt obviously did not get drafted out of high school. Heck, he didn't even get one Division I college scholarship offer. He chose to go to Ohio University because he wanted to become an architect and they had a good program there in Athens. He hoped he could walk on to their very good baseball team. The idea of becoming a pro baseball player was completely out of the question.

Ah, but now we come back to that one home run he hit his senior year.

It was in the Dayton City League semifinal against Meadowdale. Schmidt was having a typically awful day. He managed one broken-bat single in his first five at-bats. He batted lefty three times and managed only to lift harmless and short fly balls. But the game went on and on and into the 13th inning. Schmidt came up with a man on and his team down a run.

The man on the mound was a right-hander. Schmidt headed up to the plate to hit left-handed.

And then he changed his mind. He made a calculation: The ballpark at Fairview had a big hill in right field; it was almost impossible to hit a home run that way. But the fence was reachable in left field. So Schmidt switched around and chose to bat right-handed, and in that moment he made a determination that would fundamentally change his future.

"I knew," he would say, "I was either going to strike out or homer."

Those were the only two options he put on the table for himself: strike-out or home run. He took all other options out of play. A strikeout would lose the game. A home run would win it. There was nothing else to do.

And Schmidt launched the only home run of his senior year, a mammoth bomb that soared high over the 360-foot wall in left field.

With that, Mike Schmidt had his baseball direction, his baseball purpose. He went to Ohio University, where coach Bob Wren told him to immediately drop that switch-hitting nonsense and just focus on being the right-handed force he was meant to become. "He has big-league power," Wren told reporters during that freshman season. In his second year at OU, he hit .310, was named an All-American, and led the team to the College World Series. The next year he was even better.

And with that he became an extraordinary prospect: 6-foot-2, 195 pounds, brilliantly fast, a bazooka for an arm, and what the scouts like to call light-tower power. "To have his body," Pete Rose once said of Schmidt, "I'd trade mine and my wife's and I'd throw in some cash."

Scouts were interested, but none of them as much as Lucadello, the Phillies' area scout who had been watching Schmidt on and off since high school. He told the Phillies that Schmidt was the best player in the 1971 draft, but he also told them no other team knew quite how good he was and they could get him in the second round.

The Phillies took a pitcher named Roy Thomas in the first round.

And then, in the second round, with the 30th overall pick, the Phillies took Mike Schmidt. This was one pick after the Kansas City Royals chose a high school third baseman named George Brett.

Schmidt was in the big leagues two years later.

We must pause in our Mike Schmidt tale to tell the heartbreaking story of Tony Lucadello. Well, it isn't all heartbreaking. Baseball's color and wonder comes from people like Lucadello. He was a baseball character, the sort you make movies about. (My friend Mark Winegardner wrote *Prophet of the Sandlots*, an extraordinary book, about him.)

He used to come to games wearing a houndstooth hat, like he was Alabama coach Bear Bryant. This would seem to make him stand out, but he actually never liked being seen at games because that would give away his interest level in certain players. So he would find a spot behind a tree or behind an outfield fence or, most often, in his car to watch the game.

He thought he was fooling people. But the other scouts would see that houndstooth hat. And they would know he was there.

They also knew that if they came early enough, they would find him under the bleachers looking for loose change. The story goes that over the years, Lucadello collected more than $3,000 in nickels, dimes, and quarters, which he used for his goddaughter's college education.

Lucadello was a lovable guy—didn't drink, smoke, swear, or carouse—and baseball meant everything to him. He really did have a sixth sense for finding ballplayers; he signed more than 50 of them who made it to the big leagues, including Schmidt and Hall of Famer Fergie Jenkins. He worked with Kansas City Monarchs manager Buck O'Neil to sign Ernie Banks to the Cubs. He didn't just sign players; he spotted them for other scouts, too. Lucadello saw a 15-year-old Orel Hershiser and told a fellow scout, "Someday that kid is going to be a big-league star."

He was irresistibly drawn to Schmidt. Somehow, even when Schmidt wasn't hitting at all, Lucadello just had this sense that someday it would click for the kid. He was thrilled when the Phillies drafted him, and he came to Schmidt's house to make the offer. You know that cliché of someone writing down an offer on a piece of paper and sliding it across the table? (As Michael Scott once said in The Office, "This is how it's done . . . in the movies.")

Well, Lucadello did it with his own distinct style. He went to the trunk of his car and pulled out a typewriter. Then he came in the Schmidt home, put the typewriter on the table, and told the Schmidts to look at the paper that was wrapped inside the roller. There, these words were typed out: "We're prepared to offer Mike $25,000 if he'll sign with the Phillies right now."

Eventually, Mike Schmidt signed for $37,500.*

In 1989, which actually ended up being Schmidt's final season in the big leagues, Lucadello became convinced he was no longer wanted as a scout. Baseball was moving away from him, he told friends, and it made

---

* He used about a third of that money to buy a yellow 1971 Corvette Stingray fastback. This is one of those almost meaningless facts that I love.

him feel lost. He was 75 years old, and baseball was everything. "Tony," former Phillies GM Paul Owens told him repeatedly, "you're hired for life. You know that."

But Owens was no longer the GM, and Lucadello was sure the new regime was ready to let him go. "It used to be that way," he told Owens sadly. "But it's different now."

On May 8, 1989, Lucadello went to a high school baseball field in Toledo and shot himself. He was found dead on the field before the game that night. When Schmidt heard the news from his mother, they cried together.

"Without Tony Lucadello," Schmidt said, "I wouldn't have been a Philadelphia Phillie. I might not be in the major leagues. . . . You can't make it in baseball by yourself. There are so many people who nobody knows who make all the difference."

Many Philadelphia fans never warmed up to Mike Schmidt. Or if you prefer a more direct approach, a subsection of Philadelphia fans booed the hell out of Mike Schmidt at various points throughout his career.

It wasn't everyone. It wasn't close to everyone. But it was a large enough group that it led to one of the strangest player-city relationships in baseball history. Schmidt is the greatest Philadelphia Phillies player ever, and it isn't close at all.

Phillies Position Players by WAR

1. Mike Schmidt, 106.8

2. Chase Utley, 61.8

3. Ed Delahanty, 61.0

4. Richie Ashburn, 57.7

5. Sherry Magee, 48.1

Schmidt won three MVP awards—all other Phillies position players combined won three MVP awards (Chuck Klein in 1932, Ryan Howard in 2006, Jimmy Rollins in 2007).

Schmidt won eight home run titles, led the league in on-base percentage three times, led the league in slugging percentage five times, led the league in RBIs four times, won 10 Gold Gloves, and was the World Series MVP for the only Phillies championship team between 1883 (when they were still the Philadelphia Quakers) and 2007. He is, in my view and the view of many others, the greatest third baseman in the history of baseball.

He is the Phillies' best player, their second-best player, and their third-best player.

He is what George Brett is for the Royals, what Cal Ripken Jr. is for the Orioles, what Stan Musial is for the Cardinals.

And yet, Philadelphia—at least a substantial piece of Philadelphia—just never quite loved him.

It became a cottage industry in Philadelphia to explain exactly *why* some fans never embraced Schmidt. Some thought it had to do with Schmidt's three-outcome style: He homered, walked, and struck out about 40 percent of the time, which was a very high number in those days. (And it could lead to monumental slumps—he went 1-for-20 in the 1983 World Series, for instance.) Some thought it was simply Philadelphia being Philadelphia; it's a town that feels deeply in victory and defeat. Maybe Phillies fans boo. But they cheer loudly, too.

The prevailing theory was that they couldn't read him. Schmidt just didn't show much. He carried himself so unemotionally—"Captain Cool," they would call him, though not with affection—and Philadelphia is a town that runs hot, a town drawn to fire, a "Rocky" kind of town, a "Broad Street Bullies" kind of town, a Larry Bowa slamming his batting helmet kind of town.

"Captain Cool," Dan Sernoffsky wrote in the *Philadelphia Daily News,* "according to popular belief, played the game with what manager Dallas Green would call a 'laissez-faire' attitude, devoid of all emotion and unwilling to work hard once things were out of reach. He was the kind of guy, everyone felt, who would send ball after ball over fences in a meaningless series against the likes of the Chicago Cubs or New York Mets but would strike out with the bases loaded in a crucial series against the likes of the Pittsburgh Pirates or Montreal Expos."

The charge was largely false—throughout his career, Schmidt hit better in high-leverage situations than low ones. Schmidt did have epically bad moments (he hit .063 in the 1977 NLCS in addition to that 1-for-20 slump in the 1983 World Series), but they did not come from Schmidt trying too little. He was that sort of player, one who would get particularly hot or particularly cold for various stretches. If anything, the hard times came from him trying too hard.

He heard all the boos. He felt them. "I act like it doesn't bother me," he would say, "like I don't hear anything the fans say. But the truth is I hear every word and it kills me."

The booing created a vicious circle; the fans would boo, he would hear them, he would struggle more, the fans would boo more—it got to the point that he would be on the field thinking about what would happen if he struck out or booted a ball. This is the last thought a ballplayer needs. "'Blow this one,' I'd think, 'and I'll need cops to guard my house.'"

As mentioned, this wasn't everybody. He heard plenty of cheers. Some fans stayed with him through it all; and you will hear them say that Philadelphia's rejection of Schmidt has been dramatically overblown.

But that isn't quite right. It wasn't overblown, because Schmidt felt it profoundly. His style—great defense, lots of home runs, lots of walks, lots of strikeouts, relatively low batting averages, a reserved presence on the field, a breezy confidence off it—did not fully connect with the fans. And I suspect Mike Schmidt heard hometown boos more than any other all-time great player.

"It's hard for me to be positive," Schmidt said of Philadelphia as he prepared to go into the Hall of Fame, "to have real good things to say about a town that never did anything for me and, in general, made life miserable for me."

He apologized later for saying that. When Philadelphia threw him a Hall of Fame celebration, he worried that he might get booed again. But he didn't. This time it was nothing but cheers.

"What a great day," Schmidt shouted out as he looked over the adoring crowd. "I only wish that all of you could stand right here and see what I'm looking at!"

No. 18 Tris Speaker

There are so many wonderfully unexpected origin stories in baseball, but I think Tris Speaker's may be the best of them all.

Before we get to that, Tristram E. Speaker—the "E" did not stand for anything—was born in 1888 and grew up in Hill County, Texas, in a family that often still seemed to be fighting the Civil War on the side of the Confederacy. His father, Archie, had been too young to fight in the war, but both of Archie's brothers were Confederate soldiers, as was his mother Nancy Jane's brother. Tris embraced the Confederacy himself. For the rest of Tris's life, he engaged in titanic arguments over the fight he never stopped calling "the War of Northern Aggression."

Speaker was a natural right-hander and began playing baseball as such, but when he was 10—the same year that his father died—he was thrown from a horse and broke his right arm in several places.

"I feared my days in athletics were over," Speaker wrote in a series of autobiographical newspaper columns. "But even before the fractures knitted, I was out practicing to peg with my left hand. Weeks of hard practice finally brought the desired result, and I found I could throw left-handed even more accurately than I could with my right."

Speaker's switch to left-handed thrower and, shortly afterward, left-handed hitter is one of the more stunning transformations in baseball history; he would later thrill crowds by catching fly balls with either his gloved right hand or bare left hand. But that's not what I'm referring to as his origin story. That part comes a little later.

Speaker played football and baseball in and around Hill County; he gave up football after a nasty injury. He began kicking around as a semipro baseball player and was discovered by Doak Roberts, owner of the Cleburne Railroaders in the old Texas League.

He quickly developed a reputation as a hard-nosed, stubborn cowboy of a ballplayer. And by "quickly," I mean his first game. He was a pitcher then, and he lost that first game in part because of an error committed by the team's player-manager, Benny Shelton. Speaker loudly cussed out Shelton and then, when other players stepped in, he challenged them all to fight him. In later years, Speaker defended himself like so:

"All I said was that he was a splay-footed, butter-fingered tramp that ought to pay his way into the ballpark. He booted an easy grounder that made me lose my game . . . and that monkey-faced second baseman stuck his nose into it, and I told him I could lick him. Which I can."

Splay-footed, butter-fingered tramp.

Maybe that's what the players are saying when the benches clear.

So, yes, Speaker was a charmer right from the start. But one thing he was not was a pitcher—he would say he lost all seven of his starts and, according to a legend, in one of them he gave up 22 consecutive hits. Then he caught a break: The team's right-fielder was conked in the head with a pitch, and Speaker was put in right field. He showed some promise. The next year, he became a full-time outfielder for the Houston Buffaloes, and he hit .314 to lead the league. The Boston Red Sox bought his rights and brought him to town. "He is a left-handed batsman," the *Boston Globe* wrote, "and a likely looking youngster."

As likely looking as he might have been, Speaker only hit .158 in seven games for Boston, and in those days teams didn't fret over small sample sizes. The Red Sox did not ask him to come back the following year.

Speaker was frantic all off-season. He sent telegrams to every club he knew and got no responses. Then, he grew even more desperate. He just showed up at Giants spring training two days in a row in the hope of catching the eye of Giants manager John McGraw. But McGraw wouldn't even look at him.

And yes, if you've been following along, reading every chapter, you will note this means Speaker is another on the list of all-time greats—Hank Greenberg and Eddie Collins among them—that McGraw whiffed on. He would say later in life that Speaker was his biggest miss of all.

After the Giants fiasco, Speaker just got a train ticket and showed up uninvited at the Red Sox camp in Little Rock, Arkansas. The Red Sox, perhaps taking pity on him, let him train with the club but they did not seem any more impressed by him than they had been the year before.

And here's where the origin story comes in. When spring training ended, the Little Rock Travelers owner—a baseball writer, scout, promoter, and all-around character named Michael J. Finn—expected the Red Sox to, you know, pay $500 for the use of their facilities. That's how it was supposed to work. But the Red Sox were broke. A deal needed to be struck.

And the deal was this: The Red Sox gave Tris Speaker to the Little Rock Travelers.

The papers called Speaker "ground rent."

And people think the Red Sox are cheap now because they didn't keep Mookie Betts.

That's when Speaker came of age. In Little Rock, he hit .350, leading the league again, and he stole 28 bases, and he played center field defense that left everyone awestruck. The legendary sportswriter Grantland Rice would later say he saw Speaker play that summer and wrote, "He was all over the lot—six or seven putouts and three hits. He was the smoothest looking minor-league outfielder I ever saw." Finn called him "Ty Cobb the Second."

Well, now the Red Sox wanted Speaker back. Thing is, everybody, including McGraw, wanted Speaker now. McGraw reportedly offered $5,000 for him. Another unnamed team offered $7,500. But Finn and the Red Sox had a handshake agreement that if Speaker did turn out to be a real ballplayer, the Travelers would sell him back to the Red Sox for the $500 it cost to lease the facilities.

And Mickey Finn, man of his word, did just that.

In 1915, Tris Speaker might have made the greatest catch in World Series history. Then again, he might have made a very good catch but not one you would call an all-timer. Then again, he might have made a fine but not particularly special catch that has been exaggerated because of its timing. It's so hard to tell with old baseball stories.

What is certain is that Speaker was a breathtaking outfielder, maybe the first such creature in the American League. He played center field the way he lived—aggressively, dangerously, boldly. Speaker would play so absurdly shallow that baseball writers in the day would sometimes call him a fifth infielder.

This was no exaggeration. He turned six unassisted double plays, to give you an idea of just how close he was standing to the infield. He also led American League center fielders in assists eight times and his 450 assists is a record for all outfielders that will never be broken. It is more than *double** the assist total of Willie Mays. And this was because Speaker played so close to the infield that several times a year he would throw out the hitter at first base.

Speaker's defense was so utterly wonderful that you could argue it made him underrated as a hitter. This seems impossible: Speaker hit .345/.428/.500 for his career, his 792 career doubles is a record that might never be broken (even Pete Rose couldn't catch him), and his 3,514 hits is fifth on the list (even Derek Jeter couldn't catch him). In 1912, he became the first player to hit 50 doubles and steal 50 bases in a season (only Craig Biggio has done it since) and he also led the league in homers (10) that season. He won the Chalmers Award, which was the MVP award of the day.

How do you underrate that?

But simple narratives do tend to carry the day . . . and in Speaker's time, the simple narrative was that Ty Cobb was the hitter (along with Joe Jackson) while Tris Speaker was the fielder. Speaker's Hall of Fame plaque barely mentions his offense—almost in passing, it includes his .344 career batting average (now known to be .345) and states that he managed Cleveland to the 1920 World Series title.

---

* There's a famous Joe DiMaggio story that gets at the point: When DiMaggio came up to the Yankees in 1936, he too played an absurdly shallow center field. After one game, pitcher Lefty Gomez heard DiMaggio in the clubhouse bragging about how he would make everyone forget all about Tris Speaker, to which Gomez said: "Yeah, that's great, Joe, but let's not make them forget Lefty Gomez. Play deeper."

But it begins: "GREATEST CENTREFIELDER OF HIS DAY."*

Speaker really was the most celebrated fielder of the day, which takes us to the 1915 World Series, Game 2, Reds Sox versus Phillies at the Baker Bowl. You can look at the Grover Cleveland Alexander essay for a fuller recap of the Series but suffice it to say that Philadelphia won Game 1 and the Red Sox needed to win Game 2. President Woodrow Wilson and his fiancée were in the crowd. The Red Sox led by a run going into the ninth inning. A little right-hander from Oklahoma called Rube Foster (not the legendary Rube Foster who founded the Negro Leagues) had pitched the game of his life for Boston, and he got the first two outs of the inning.

Then Foster faced the Phillies' No. 3 hitter, a guy named Dode Paskert, who many people called the National League's Speaker. They did not call him this because of his offense; Paskert was nowhere near Speaker's league at the plate. But Paskert was also acclaimed as a defensive wizard in center field.

Paskert pounded Foster's pitch to deep center field, far enough that just about everyone in the ballpark felt sure that it was going to be a home run.

That's how the *New York Times* reported it, anyway.

"Everyone (but the Red Sox center fielder) knew the ball was gone for a Philly victory."

It's unclear how much faith we should be put into this account, however, since the most basic fact is wrong: A home run would not have meant a Philly victory. It would have only tied the game. But ignoring that: It seems certain that Speaker was playing his usual shallow center field, and he got a sensational jump on the ball, and he raced back to the wall. And he reached over the fence. And he caught it to save the game for the Red Sox.

Incredible, right? Yes. But *how* incredible?

Here's how the *Times* described it: "Off with the crack of the bat from his normal shallow position, reached the center-field fence, leaped and,

---

* Yes, that's right, on Tris Speaker's Hall of Fame plaque, it spells center fielder as "centrefielder," making Canadian baseball fans very happy. I don't know if this was an error or simply an outdated spelling. Speaker's plaque has other errors, too. It says his career began in 1909 when it actually began in 1907 and, as mentioned, his batting average has been adjusted since then. You know how baseball cards and postage stamps with errors are worth more? Speaker's plaque should be the most valuable one in Cooperstown.

half his body over the wall, came down with the ball clutched in his tiny mitt."

Well, that sounds incredible. Frank G. Menke, the Hearst newspaper reporter, made it sound even more dramatic.

"Paskert connected with one of Foster's twisters and sent it soaring toward the center field bleachers. A roar went up from the crowd as the ball left the bat, and it increased as the ball went on and on. Could Speaker make it? Could he stop it in flight? For three or four seconds the crowd waited for the answer and Speaker answered by making one last lunge for the bleacher rail, whirling around and grabbing the ball just about to drop into the stand for a home run drive."

So that seems clear . . . except that others only mentioned the catch in passing. One scribe didn't mention the catch until the twentieth paragraph and only that Speaker plucked the ball from the crowd, like it was a grape. A couple of the writers didn't mention the catch at all. This included a sportswriter named Tris Speaker who was writing a syndicated column about the series. The only thing he wrote about the catch was "It was a relief when I caught Paskert's fly in the ninth inning because you are never sure a game is over in that park."

Best guess: It was probably a good catch but a couple of writers exaggerated it for effect. The game was almost immediately declared one of the best—perhaps even the best—World Series game ever played, and so it fit the story better for Speaker's last catch to be otherworldly. We'll never know for sure.

Tris Speaker was a member of the Ku Klux Klan. This has sometimes been explained away by some as a consequence of his racist upbringing (another man from Hill County, Hiram Wesley Evans, became the imperial wizard of the KKK) and by others who say that for a brief time the KKK managed to boost its membership exponentially by publicly downplaying the hatred and trying to present themselves as a legitimate pro-America group.

These explanations are too forgiving. Tris Speaker was certainly a bigot. He spent countless hours railing against the North over the Civil War. He was also fiercely anti-Catholic, sometimes getting into vicious fights about it. He had other issues. He was, in the words of his biographer Timothy M. Gay, "an inveterate gambler who was befriended by hustlers and bookies," and he unquestionably gambled on baseball games and probably threw a few of them. He was actually thrown out of baseball by American League president Ban Johnson after a convoluted gambling scandal that also involved Ty Cobb, though both were reinstated by Commissioner Kenesaw Mountain Landis. He got into numerous fights. He was, as the kids say, problematic.

But he was also complicated. Speaker was a charmer who would sometimes go on the road with comedian Will Rogers, and he would do various rope tricks for the crowds. He was beloved on the speaker's circuit and one of those guys reporters would call all the time just to get a story.

Finally, there is one last surprising and happy twist. In 1947, as he approached 60 years old, Speaker was kicking around, doing various jobs around Cleveland, when Tribe owner Bill Veeck asked him to come back to the team to work on defense with the young outfielders, particularly rookie Dale Mitchell. Veeck might have meant it as a publicity stunt—Tribe manager Lou Boudreau told reporters, "I don't know whether to ask him for batting tips or an autograph"—but Speaker took it seriously.

Look at that year again: 1947. What happened in 1947? Right, that was the year Jackie Robinson broke the color barrier in the National League. And it was also the year that Larry Doby broke the color barrier in the American League, for Cleveland. Doby was a natural second baseman but Veeck and Boudreau wanted to turn him into a center fielder.

Enter: Tris Speaker.

Speaker *loved* working with Doby. He would later call it one of the great thrills of his life, working every day with Doby on the finer points of defense. "I've never seen a young ballplayer with such a high potential," he told Shirley Povich at the *Washington Post*. "I get a personal pleasure out of working with a kid who can do so many things so well."

Every day they would work together, and their friendship grew to the point that when Larry Doby was elected to the Hall of Fame, he took a moment to thank Tris Speaker, his mentor.

None of this changes Speaker's history, obviously. But perhaps it does offer hope. It's like Buck O'Neil, the great Negro Leagues player and manager, used to say all the time: People aren't one thing.

No. 17 **Rogers Hornsby**

L et's check in and see what people through the years have had to say
about Rogers Hornsby:

Sportswriter John B. Sheridan: "He is, as the French say, deficient in the social relation."

Hall of Famer Travis Jackson: "He cares little for what anyone says, and still less what they think."

St. Louis Browns pitcher Les Tietje: "Now there was a p-r-i-c-k."

Sportswriter Lee Allen: "Subtle as a belch."

Journalist Westbrook Pegler: "He has go-to-hell eyes."

Hall of Famer Satchel Paige: "If Mr. Hornsby had known as much about hitting as he thought he knew about pitching, he'd have held all the records."

Jimmy Dugan in *A League of Their Own:* "Rogers Hornsby was my manager, and he called me a talking pile of pig @*($#*. And that was when my parents drove all the way down from Michigan to see me play."

Hall of Famer Billy Herman: "He was a very cold man. I broke in with the Cubs under Hornsby in 1931. He ignored me completely, and I figured it was because I was a rookie. But then I realized he ignored everybody."

Sportswriter Gordon Cobbledick to St. Louis Browns team owner Bill

Veeck before he hired Hornsby: "Don't get involved with that guy. You've got enough troubles already."

Sportswriter J. Roy Stockton: "Hornsby wanted to win so badly that he was a sourpuss about it."

Bill Veeck: "A man who would call Hornsby a sourpuss would wonder why everybody was complaining about Attila the Hun's table manners."

Inscription of a silver loving cup from St. Louis Browns players after Veeck fired Hornsby: "To Bill Veeck: For the greatest play since the Emancipation Proclamation."

Writer Bill Surface: "His apparent prejudices against Jews and Negroes were shocking but, on examination, turned out to be simply two items in a long accounting against the world. He was equally capable of sneering at anyone who liked baseball general managers or ate lunch."

Writer Bill James: "Rogers Hornsby is rated in the top 10 by most people, who apparently don't feel it is important to have a second baseman who can field."

Rogers Hornsby himself: "I'm a tough guy, a gambler on horses, a slave driver and, in general, a disgrace to the game. I wish I knew why. I only wanted to win."

Looking back, it's fair to ask why Hornsby, rather than Ty Cobb, is not baseball's ultimate villain. He had all the attributes. To start with: Nobody liked him. The players didn't like him. The writers didn't like him. Baseball management hated him like no one else. The people running baseball didn't like him; he was probably blackballed from baseball for decades because of his addiction to gambling on horses.

He was divorced twice, and his second wife said that numerous times he "laid violent hands on her" and "threatened to do her bodily harm." His secretary, a woman he was having a secret affair with, killed herself one night after going to dinner with him. Police found a safety deposit box they held jointly with $25,000 in cash. This was about the time the government went after him for tax evasion.

He was a known racist, probably an anti-Semite (though he did have Jewish friends who denied that specific charge), and no player in baseball history—not Cobb or anyone else—had as many detractors jumping in line to talk about just how terrible a person he was.

In 1924, Hornsby had one of the most remarkable seasons in baseball history. He hit .424, still the highest batting average record for any modern player. He led the league in hits, runs, doubles, on-base percentage, slugging percentage, OPS+, total bases, and so on. He posted an incredible 12.1 WAR, though obviously he did not know that.

He did not, however, win the MVP award. Instead, that went to pitcher Dazzy Vance, who did have a spectacular season himself (won the pitcher triple crown, 28-6, 2.16 ERA, 262 strikeouts, etc.). Still, there were those who wondered how a man could hit .424 and still not be elected MVP.

Well, only eight sportswriters voted that year—six voted Vance No. 1, two voted for Hornsby.

And one of those writers, Jack Ryder, left Hornsby entirely off his ballot. It wouldn't have made a difference—Vance won by 12 points, so even if Ryder had put him first on his list (which he obviously would not have), Vance still would have won. Still, people wondered how Ryder could have done that, could have voted for *10* other players but not Hornsby.

When they asked Ryder, he did not back down one bit.

"I will concede," he said, "Hornsby is a most valuable player to himself."

There's a postscript to that story. The next year, 1925, Rogers Hornsby put up a year that really has no equal. He won the Triple Crown, but that's really only the start of it. Look at the margins by which he led:

Batting average: .403 (led by 36 points)

On-base percentage: .489 (led by 43 points)

Slugging percentage: .756 (led by 158 points)

OPS: 1.245 (led by 224 points)

Home runs: 39 (led by 15 homers)

RBIs: 143 (led by 13)

Runs created: 185 (led by 31 runs)

The writers damn well named him MVP after *that* season. They did not want to but he left them no choice.

Children loved him. That is the one good thing people unanimously said about Rogers Hornsby. There had to be something nice to say, and it was true that Hornsby had this Pied-Piper spirit that entirely eluded adults but captured the imagination of young people. "Hard-boiled Hornsby," sportswriter Bob Broeg said, "was a pushover for kids."

Hornsby worked with tens of thousands of kids through the years in various youth baseball programs. And when he was teaching hitting or pitching to a kid, he displayed patience and warmth that were missing in every other dealing in his life (even, alas, with his own kids). He loved it. He never seemed more at home than when teaching baseball to kids. He would sign autographs for hours. "Any ballplayer that don't sign autographs for little kids," he used to say, "ain't an American. He's a communist."

And this gets to an important part of understanding Hornsby: He didn't think of himself as the bad guy. Few people do, of course—most people see themselves as the hero of the story—but Hornsby was particularly certain that he was misunderstood. The way Hornsby looked at life, he was devoted to the two things that mattered: baseball and truth. He just couldn't see why that bothered so many people.

His religious devotion to baseball led him to never drink, never smoke, never read or go to the movies (bad for the hitter's eye). He believed a hitter should get as much sleep as possible, and he would routinely sleep 12 hours a night (often sated by huge portions of red meat and ice cream). He had no interests other than baseball whatsoever, except betting on the horses. For fun when on the road, he apparently would go to a hotel lobby and just sit there for hours and watch people go by.

His insistence on telling the truth (as he saw it) led him to say all sorts of hurtful, vicious, and cruel things, even if he didn't see it that way. Charles Alexander, who wrote the definitive Rogers Hornsby biography, remembered being a boy and seeing a long-retired Hornsby after he became manager of the Beaumont Double-A team. The city was so appreciative of the legend that they held a Rogers Hornsby Day and presented him before the game with a Texas Stetson and the keys to a Cadillac sedan.

"It's nice," Hornsby said to the crowd. "Now, get it outta here so we can start the game." And he walked off.

"My parents," Alexander wrote, "who always put a considerable store in appearance, simply didn't know what to make of Hornsby's graceless response to a genuine, openhanded expression of civic gratitude."

But Hornsby undoubtedly didn't see his response as graceless. He never thought about it that way. He was just being *honest*. He didn't give a damn about the car.

Honesty—always. In 1918, Hornsby repeatedly ticked off manager Jack Hendricks with his attitude; he played exactly the way he wanted to play, no more, no less. Once when he was tagged out standing up at home plate, he told his teammates, "I'm too good a ballplayer to be sliding for a tail-end team." Hendricks fined him $50, which Hornsby paid with a bagful of silver dollars he'd picked up the night before, special for the occasion.

Honesty—always. There's a story that in 1927, Hornsby was doing something he almost never did—having dinner with another ballplayer. In this case, it was his young Giants shortstop Doc Farrell (so called because he had a degree in dentistry and would, in fact, become a dentist after he retired). A reporter came up and asked Hornsby if the Giants could take the pennant.

"Not with Farrell playing short," Hornsby grumped, and if that sounds like a punch line, a fun little stab by a manager, it was not. Hornsby did not make lighthearted jokes. He traded Farrell away to the Boston Braves a few weeks later, even though Farrell was hitting .387 at the time.

Honesty—always. When asked later in life about some specific players who were not yet in the Hall of Fame, Hornsby grunted: "The big trouble is not really who isn't in the Hall of Fame, but who is."

"I've never taken back anything I ever said, and I've never failed to say exactly—and I mean exactly—what I was thinking," Hornsby said. "To everybody, from the owner to the bat boy."

Here's a fascinating Hornsby story that fits our time. In 1923, Branch Rickey was managing the St. Louis Cardinals, and it seems that he came up with a foolproof system to steal catcher signs and relay those signs to hitters. It is unclear exactly what that system was, but it was apparently one that Rickey took with him wherever he went, because, in later years, his Cardinals and Dodgers were both considered top-notch sign stealers. This was, in those days, a compliment.*

In any case, Rickey wanted Hornsby to take part in his sign-stealing scheme. He figured Hornsby was already the best hitter in the National League. Think how much better he'd be if he only knew what pitch was

---

* It is striking how often sign stealing comes up when digging into old baseball research. The other day, I fell into a rabbit hole about how the San Francisco Giants were charged with stealing signs the day Willie Mays hit four home runs. We'll save that for another book.

coming! Rickey supposedly nagged at Hornsby about it a few times to no avail; Hornsby wasn't interested. It's not that Hornsby was a puritan when it came to baseball rules; he'd cheat as much as the next guy. But he was a hitting purist. And he didn't want Rickey or anybody else in his head when he was at the plate.

"Why don't you use 'em, Rog?" Rickey asked. "It can't hurt."

"Hornsby'll decide what Hornsby'll swing at," Hornsby said, a classic Rickey Henderson–type line that he probably assumed would end the conversation.

But it did not. In a game against the Giants, Hornsby was on third when he saw Rickey give a sign to a hitter—Rickey would say it was a take sign, but it's quite likely that it was a sign for what pitch was coming next—and Hornsby visibly lost his cool, making wild gestures that everybody in the crowd could see.

When Hornsby got back to the dugout, Rickey confronted Hornsby, who unleashed a blue streak of words that Rickey would call "vile and unspeakable." Then Hornsby belted him. The two fought for a few seconds before the mini-fight was broken up. Shortly after that, Hornsby was briefly suspended and newspapers were filled with rumors that Hornsby was going to be dealt, possibly to John McGraw's Giants, possibly to the Cubs.

In the end, Hornsby was not traded. In fact, less than two years later, he took over for Rickey as manager of the Cardinals.

Rogers Hornsby was not just a great hitter. He was a revolution. He was for the National League what Babe Ruth was for the American. Baseball fundamentally changed in 1920, the end of Deadball. It is actually not that easy to pinpoint exactly *why* that was the year that Deadball ended. It probably comes down to three things.

1. Livelier baseballs were probably introduced in 1920. MLB angrily denied this, but, you know, MLB always angrily denies any change in the baseball. There is plenty of reason to believe that the baseballs after 1920 were better made and much livelier.

2. More baseballs were used in each game; this was a direct response to that year's tragic moment when Yankees pitcher Carl Mays beaned Cleveland's Ray Chapman, who died 12 hours later.

3. The spitball was outlawed, again a response to the Chapman beaning.

These three items, perhaps, do not seem like big enough changes to entirely transform baseball . . . but baseball was transformed. In 1920, Babe Ruth hit 54 home runs, double the old record.

And in 1920, a 25-year-old Hornsby—a lifetime .310/.370/.440 hitter to that point—hit .370/.431/.559, leading the league in all three splits, and he also led the league in hits, doubles, RBIs, and total bases.

Over the next five seasons combined—this is so ridiculous—Hornsby would hit .402.

Nobody, not even Ty Cobb, hit .400 over five full seasons.

Hornsby's game was just made for the new live ball. Before he and Ruth came along, the dominant style of hitting was for the batter to choke up on thick bats for ultimate control. But Hornsby, even when the ball was dead, refused to do that. He held the bat at the very bottom, swung through with force. "It was impossible to get him to swing at anything but strikes," Grover Cleveland Alexander said. Hornsby's batting eye was so renowned that he is the true protagonist of a legendary baseball story that has been attributed to so many others.

A young pitcher, facing Hornsby, complained about a pitch being called a ball.

"Son," umpire Bill Klem said, "when you pitch a strike, Mr. Hornsby will let you know it."

Hornsby's .358 batting average is second all-time behind Ty Cobb, but even that is deceptive because that includes his time in the Deadball Era. If you start in 1920, Hornsby's batting average has no equal.

Batting Average from 1920 On (minimum of 5,000 plate appearances)

1. Rogers Hornsby, .374

2. Harry Heilmann, .362

3. Tris Speaker, .354

4. Babe Ruth, .347

5. Ted Williams, .344

How was he as an all-around ballplayer, though? Bill James believes he was a mediocre second baseman at best, grading him a C. He did make a lot of errors, particularly as a young man, and his range was usually below average, and he was known, even in his day, as being shaky on fly balls. "Flies," he used to say, "are the right fielder's job. I'll do the hitting." But it should be said that his overall defensive numbers are not bad and there have been those who were kind about his fielding. "He was one of the finest fielding second basemen of his times," Joe Reichler wrote on the day Hornsby died.

He was quite fast—he led the league in doubles four times and triples twice—but he was not a particularly good or committed baserunner.

But the big thing is that he was, by all accounts, a pain in the neck to deal with—he was traded three times and released twice more. He was the most loathed manager of his or any other time. He only played in two World Series, but he hit poorly in both of them.

Would you want him on your team? It's one of the great questions of baseball history, one that defies any easy answers.

Hornsby's post-baseball life was sad—he lost so much of his money gambling. There was a long stretch of time when he was away from the game, again, probably because the commissioner had quietly banished him over that gambling. He tried for a time to manage in an outlaw league in Mexico, and when asked why he would do that, he replied: "Baseball has forgotten me."

On the day he died—January 5, 1963—there was no parade of glowing remembrances from people around baseball. The nicest things anyone could think to say was that he loved baseball, he was good around kids, and he generally didn't complain to umpires.

"But when you hit .400," Casey Stengel said, "you don't have much to complain about."

No. 16 Alex Rodriguez

L et's begin with how Allard Baird saw him.

    Baird is one of the most admired and remarkable talent evalu-
ators in all of baseball. He worked with the Mets in scouting and
player development and before that did the same for the Boston Red Sox
as they won three World Series titles. He worked his way up from a low-
level scout who lived out of his car to the general manager of the Kansas
City Royals.

Baird saw him in the early days, those 200,000-mile-a-year days when
Baird fueled on fast food and hope and followed the lights from small
town to small town in search of a ballplayer. He didn't fully know what he
was doing yet. He was still learning how to judge a young player's potential, and he was learning the subtleties of the famous 20-to-80 scouting
scale. The way that works, scouts rate players on five tools (hitting, power,
defense, speed, and arm) on a 20-to-80 scale.*

The scale itself works like so:

---

* Scouts do more than this, particularly now, but the 20-to-80 scale on five tools is remarkably durable.

20 means poor. There are not many players with 20 tools in the big leagues. Maybe the single slowest player in the big leagues (Albert Pujols now?) would be a 20 speed.

30: Well below average. Someone who would hit fewer than five homers in a full season has 30 power.

40: Below average. Pretty self-explanatory.

50: Average. Pretty self-explanatory.

60: Above average or in scout terms, "Plus." If someone is an above-average defender but perhaps not quite Gold Glove elite, you might put a 60 on their defense.

70: Well above average, or "Plus-Plus." Walker Buehler has a plus-plus fastball. Cody Bellinger has plus-plus power. And so on.

80: OK, now we're getting into some inexact territory. I've heard some scouts refer to an 80 tool as "Hall of Fame" level. I've heard others say that it's even better than that—it's the best of the best of the best. So basically an 80 for each tool would be:

Hitting: Ted Williams

Power: Babe Ruth

Speed: Rickey Henderson

Defense: Ozzie Smith

Arm: Roberto Clemente

The point I'm trying to get at is that, for someone scouting a high school game, an 80 is no-go territory. You just don't give out eighties. What is the likelihood that you're going to see a high school player who could throw like Clemente or hit like Williams? Baird had been scouting for a while, and he had never once given out an 80. He'd hardly ever given out any 70s.

And then came the day he went to see Westminster Christian School play so he could get a look at the junior shortstop they had there. Baird didn't go unprepared: He knew that this kid was talented. He was the talk of the scouting community and had been for a while. But Baird had not yet seen him up close.

And what he saw? He's never forgotten it. He never will.

First, Baird watched the kid take some ground balls before the game . . . and he couldn't believe his eyes. That balance! That range! That quickness! The ball just seemed to stick to his glove, and then he would transfer it to his throwing hand so fast that Baird felt like a sucker in a three-card monte exhibition. It was utterly incredible. This 16-year-old kid, Baird thought, could hold his own at shortstop in the big leagues immediately.

Then there was that arm! It was more amazing than the fielding. Baird had never seen anything like it. This kid just flicked his wrist and the ball turned into a laser beam shooting across the infield.

That was the first time Baird thought: Holy cow, this kid has an 80 arm.

Hitting? That's Baird's specialty. He has studied the human body, looked hard into movement and rhythm and weight shifts; man, that stuff thrills him. How the arms come through. How the legs power the swing. The hands. Baird could talk all day and night just about the hitter's hands.

He watched this kid swing the bat and . . . his jaw dropped. It was perfect. He had never seen a better high school hitting stroke. He had never dreamed of seeing a better high school hitting stroke.

The power was easy. The kid hit two home runs that day, both of them absolute bombs.

The speed was easy. The kid stole two bases that day, one of them standing up (this after one of two intentional walks). The kid was 35-for-35 in stolen bases that season.

It didn't seem real. But as impressive as those tools were, there was something else that Baird saw, something that blew his mind: The kid played baseball with such infectious delight. Scouts, if they're good, look for so many things. They look to see how a player responds to teammates (this kid was in the front of the dugout cheering them on). They look to see how teammates respond to the player (they so obviously loved this kid, they met him at home plate happily after each home run). They look to see if the player is coachable. This kid seemed utterly coachable.

You just don't see a player like this. Not ever.

Baird left that game and headed back to send in his report. But he felt dizzy. No, he felt like Jack from the beanstalk story—who would ever believe he'd seen an actual giant? As he looked at the report where he was supposed to fill out those numbers, he honestly did not know what to do. And then he realized that he had no choice: If he wanted to be a good scout, he had to be entirely honest.

And so he put an 80 on the kid's arm, an 80 on the kid's power, and an 80 on his hitting talent.

He put 70 on his speed and defense.

He had never expected to send in a report like that. And he never would again.

And when Allard Baird finally faxed in his scouting report on Alex Rodriguez, he was literally shaking.

There's no point in trying to clean up Alex Rodriguez's brilliant, infuriating, dazzling, inauthentic, breathtaking, destructive, and altogether messy baseball career. No point at all. It's all there. And it's everything.

A-Rod is the power hitter of his time. For 20 years, he seemed certain to break the all-time home run record. Even in falling short, he hit 696 home runs.

He's also a liar who was suspended for an entire year for using PEDs (this after threatening to sue Major League Baseball).

A-Rod is a Yankees postseason hero, a guy who carried the Yanks to their last World Series title in 2009, almost by himself.

He's also a multitime Yankees postseason goat who inspires more fury among New York baseball fans than any great player in the team's history.

A-Rod is a player who broke the bank and also a player who tried to give up the money to try to win some love. He's a Gold Glove shortstop who gave up the position for a player who was not, by any measure, his defensive equal.

He's a three-time MVP who spent a baseball lifetime hitting lazy-looking fly balls that sent outfielders to the wall with hope, only to keep on going and going, like children leaving for college, soaring far out of reach. Nobody hit a baseball quite like him, balls that would never come down, balloons being taken by the wind.

He's also a tabloid back-page punch line, being fed popcorn by Cameron Diaz, hobnobbing with Madonna, being labeled "A-Fraud" in headlines so often that at some point that became his name.

He's a player who talked again and again about how much he loved the game.

He's a player who so rarely seemed to be enjoying himself on the field.

He's a player with more Wins Above Replacement than any position player of the last 50 years who is not named Barry Bonds.

He is a player who, it has been reported, has not one but two paintings of himself as a centaur.

How can you clean up the A-Rod story? Which parts would you leave out?

Sure, the people who loathe him—so, so many of those—would happily leave out the extraordinary ballplayer, the incredible defense, the untouchable arm, the breathtaking power, the stunning speed. They would happily write him out of baseball history. That would be convenient . . . but impossible. Try this experiment: Think of the first person who comes to mind when I say: "Five-tool player."

I tried this on Twitter and maybe 50 or so names came up, not counting various jokey choices like lovable slugger Steve Balboni.

The players named most: Willie Mays, Ken Griffey Jr., Mike Trout, Mickey Mantle, Barry Bonds, Clemente, Henderson, Henry Aaron, Larry Walker, Bo Jackson, Eric Davis.

All of them are wonderful choices, wonderful players, but you do notice the thing they all share, right? They were all outfielders. And that makes them fundamentally different from A-Rod. Could Bo or Davis hit like A-Rod even at their best? Could Bonds throw like A-Rod? Could Griffey or Aaron or Walker run like A-Rod? Could Rickey or Clemente slug like A-Rod? Could Mantle or Trout field like A-Rod?

Even Mays, the ultimate of the ultimate five-tool players—could he play shortstop like A-Rod?

No, Alex Rodriguez is alone in this game. There has never been a player with so much breathtaking skill.

But you can't just tell that story, either. Sure, the people who love him—not quite as large a group, I suspect—might want to downplay the rest of it, the grotesque way he kept denying and admitting and denying and getting caught using PEDs, the nasty fight he had with baseball over PEDs after he was caught, the multitude of ways so many of his teammates loathed him, the way he warred with Yankees manager Joe Torre, the way he got benched in the playoffs because he seemed so overwhelmed by the moment, the way he distracted Toronto third baseman Howie Clark by shouting "Mine!" while on the basepaths, the way he slapped the ball out of Bronson Arroyo's hand during that playoff game, the way he freaked out Oakland pitcher Dallas Braden by walking across the mound after a foul ball, the way he took shots at his friend Derek

Jeter in a magazine article (years before they became teammates), and so on and so on and so on.

Can you really leave that out? No. Of course not.

And so what are you left with? A cloud. A blur. A baseball Rorschach test. Who, after all, sees A-Rod the same way?

Alex Rodriguez was 20 years old when he had a season for the ages. He hit .358 and led the league in runs (141), doubles (54), and total bases (379). He also hit 36 home runs, drove in 123 runs, stole 15 bases, and played a superior shortstop.

He created 157 runs that season. It was the most runs created for a shortstop since . . . ever.

Most Runs Created for a Shortstop Through 1996

1. Alex Rodriguez, 1996, 157

2. Arky Vaughan, 1935, 147

3. Alan Trammell, 1987, 137

4. Robin Yount, 1982, 136

5. Ernie Banks, 1958, 135

It was also the most runs created in a season for a 20-year-old—and it still is. Even Mike Trout at 20 did not surpass it. A-Rod just lost the MVP that year to Juan González in one of the worst MVP voting blunders in baseball history (though you could make a solid argument that Griffey should have won it over González, too).

Two years later, at age 22, A-Rod became the first—and still the only—player in baseball history to have a 42-42 season, that being 42 homers and 42 stolen bases. He also led the league in hits; in WAR; he scored 123 runs; drove in 124 runs; he played superb defense again; and this time he finished ninth in the MVP voting, which again, bizarrely, went to González—voters loved Juan Gone and his RBIs.

González's *combined* WAR in his two MVP years was not as high as A-Rod's WAR at age 20.

Two years after that, A-Rod had perhaps his best season. He hit .316/.420/.606 with 41 homers, 134 runs, and 132 RBIs; he should have won the Gold Glove at shortstop and was by all the measurements one of the best baserunners in the game.*

That's exactly why A-Rod and the most zealous agent in the business, Scott Boras, went to market. They did not hide their intentions. They unabashedly went after the biggest contract in the history of sports. And they got it from a surprising source: the Texas Rangers.

The Rangers didn't just make A-Rod the highest-paid American athlete ever. They Usain Bolted past everybody else. Here were the highest salary packages in team sports at the time:

Football: Troy Aikman, 9 years, $85.5 million

Basketball: Kevin Garnett, 6 years, $126 million

Hockey: Jaromir Jagr, 7 years, $48 million

And here was A-Rod.

Baseball: Alex Rodriguez, 10 years, $252 million

As you might imagine, everybody was pretty chill about the whole thing. Or not.

"Baseball has just signed its death warrant," was the headline of Bill Plaschke's column in the *Los Angeles Times*.

"The Texas Rangers signed him to a contract worth $79 million more than what Peter Angelos paid for the Orioles—a contract that isn't just bad for baseball, but disastrous for baseball," wrote John Eisenberg in the *Baltimore Sun*.

"Folks, this is nuts," Gary Mason wrote in the *Vancouver Sun*. "This is madness. And if you care about the future of sports, you should be enraged."

"I'm stupified," former A's GM Sandy Alderson said. "We clearly have a crisis situation at hand."

"It just speaks to the insanity of the economics of baseball today," said Dean Bonham, head of a sports marketing firm.

---

* A-Rod's speed and baserunning savvy always were wildly underappreciated. He took the extra base like few others. He scored from second on a single 16 out of 19 times that year. He scored from first on a double 11 out of 19 times. These are elite numbers.

Papers ran all sorts of charts to show just how much money A-Rod would get per game, per inning, per at-bat, per strikeout. They offered very odd calculations to show just how many airplanes, Porsches, rounds of golf, Microsoft shares, and McDonald's Happy Meals his salary could buy.

"This wasn't about winning," Mike Lupica wrote of A-Rod and Boras in the New York *Daily News*. "It wasn't about finding the best possible stage. . . . Agents like Scott Boras run baseball without any love of the game, any respect for it. Or any soul."

"What's breathtaking," Thomas Boswell wrote in the *Washington Post*, "is the majestic size of the blunder the Rangers have pulled. . . . Don't they show Sesame Street in Texas? Can't anybody count?"

And the most prophetic take came from the brilliant Dan LeBatard in A-Rod's hometown of Miami: "Rodriguez has always conducted himself with uncommon grace and dignity. But now he has sold a slice of his soul for that $252 million, becoming a little more like all the rest of the athletes keeping score with money. It isn't just that he went after the money. If Oprah and Jim Carrey and Ricky Martin get paid like that, Rodriguez is entitled too. It's that he took it from a team that is equal parts loser and sucker, and he's far more likely to be swallowed by the quagmire in Texas than he is to lift the Rangers out of it."

A-Rod did indeed get swallowed up by the quagmire in Texas to the point where after three years, he was willing to do *anything*, even giving up much of the money, just to get the hell out.

You could understand. Before the deal, Rodriguez was seen as one kind of player—bright, fun, lovable, incredible. Maybe he didn't get his due in Seattle because of the time zone, or because the team was only good enough to break a city's heart. But his game was just so exuberant and wonderful. He was not yet 25, and he had 189 home runs and he could do it all and so many baseball fans adored him.

After the contract, all of that melted away. He wasn't exuberant or wonderful. No, he was a dollar figure. He was a mercenary. He had three extraordinary seasons in Texas. In 2001, he played every game and shattered the shortstop home run record, becoming the first in baseball history to hit 50 (he finished with 52, breaking Banks's record by five).

Then next year, A-Rod played every game again and he broke the home run record again, this time hitting 57 home runs. He also led the league in RBIs and total bases, and he won his first Gold Glove.

And the next year, he played every game but one, led the league in runs, homers, and slugging percentage, won another Gold Glove, and finally took his first MVP award. All of this stuff was unprecedented and unheard-of and remarkable.

And . . . so what? Who cared? The Rangers finished fourth all three years. A-Rod got booed everywhere for chasing money to the exclusion of all else. Whispers began leaking out about how much his teammates did not like him. He became the very symbol of the out-of-touch ballplayer. "Somebody wins a lottery and they're a national hero; somebody works their butt off, and he's the devil," he complained, which only made people boo him louder.

How much of it was fair? Who can say for certain? Fair or not, it was real. A-Rod played every card he had to get out of Arlington and get a reset on his career. He tried going to the Red Sox by taking a big salary cut, but the players' union understandably wouldn't let him do it. So the path eventually took him to New York, where he agreed to move to third base for Derek Jeter. He won two MVP awards for the Yankees and, in 2007, had one of the greatest offensive seasons in team history when he hit .314/.422/.645 with 54 homers, 143 runs, and 156 RBIs. Only Babe Ruth, Lou Gehrig, and Joe DiMaggio among Yankees greats produced more runs (runs + RBIs - homers) than A-Rod that season.

Then the PED stuff started coming out—first when José Canseco called him a hypocrite and a liar, then when what was supposed to be an anonymous 2003 test result was leaked, and then when the Biogenesis scandal broke with A-Rod front and center. He humiliated himself again and again through these years with his angry denials and humbled admissions swirling together so seamlessly you could hardly tell one from the other.

By the end, his career was a broken trail of anger and regret and lost promise. When he got his 3,000th hit, almost nobody cared. When he got his 600th and 650th home runs, almost nobody cared. He had something of a revival season at age 39 as he tried to make things right, and America loves a comeback story. Almost nobody cared.

"I do want to be remembered as someone who was deeply in love with baseball," he said at his retirement, but he knew full well, even as he said that, that this would not be at all how people remembered him. There was no coming back for Alex Rodriguez.

The way Alex Rodriguez has come back in retirement is one of the more stunning stories in sports. The only comparison I can come up with is George Foreman, who was as menacing a figure as anyone in the history of sports as a boxer. Then he became happy George Foreman, the grill guy. It was quite the transformation.

A-Rod's is not quite to that level in that I don't think he's nearly as popular as Foreman. But it's unquestionable that many people now adore him. He's the lead broadcaster for ESPN's *Sunday Night Game of the Week*. He's a regular guest on all the talk shows. He's been a shark on *Shark Tank*. He's an Instagram star. He was engaged to the incomparable singer and actress Jennifer Lopez. He's the guy players all around baseball look to for advice—and not just about baseball.

He even hosts a show on CNBC about helping former athletes make comebacks in life.

"Can you believe this?" he told *USA Today* as he was sitting at center court of Wimbledon with John McEnroe watching Novak Djokovic play. "I could never have dreamed this five years ago. I'm so grateful for where I am . . . it's crazy how this has worked out."

It is crazy. Yes, there are still many, many, many people who loathe A-Rod and always will. As of this writing, A-Rod has not yet appeared on the Baseball Hall of Fame ballot, but the general feeling is that he will not be elected.

But who knows? This comeback: It's something quite remarkable. How did it happen? Well, I think he's a smart guy who has come across as sincerely contrite for the mistakes he made and managed to get across his true love of baseball. This alone is incredible; so few athletes have managed to do it. Think Pete Rose. Think Barry Bonds. Think Roger Clemens. Think about their failures.

But I think there's something else, too. It goes back to what Allard Baird saw all those years ago on a high school baseball field: A-Rod was destined for greatness, perhaps more than anybody who ever played the game of baseball. And he was great, truly great, but it never quite felt that way. It always felt corrupted. It always felt disappointing. He did that to himself.

And now, A-Rod stands before America and says that he wishes he'd done it all differently. He wishes that he could go back to that high school day when he hit two home runs and stole two bases and inspired a young scout to send back a report with 80s on it. He can't go back. He knows that. We know that, too. And maybe we all understand that feeling too well.

No. 15 **Josh Gibson**

ometimes I play this game and imagine what it would be like if I was one of only a few people in America who got to see Mark McGwire hit baseballs from 1996 to 2000.

The question: How would I tell that story?

Forget the records. Nobody is keeping records. Forget the numbers. There are no numbers, at least no numbers anybody trusts. Forget the PED part. Nobody cares enough to even look. Forget everything. There is no video footage. There are no newspaper stories. There are only a handful of grainy posed photographs that show nothing at all except that someone named Mark McGwire once existed.

How would I tell that story?

Or more to the point, how would I tell that story so that you believed me?

Would I try to tell you how he routinely hit the longest home runs that anyone had ever seen? These home runs were like optical illusions. These baseballs would go to parts of stadiums nobody had ever hit before. Would you believe me? Wouldn't you just say: "Well then, how come I never heard of him?"

Would I tell you that he undoubtedly hit more home runs than Babe Ruth hit in a season, more home runs than Roger Maris hit in a season, more than Mickey Mantle or Willie Mays or Jimmie Foxx or Hank Greenberg or any of those guys?

You would then ask: "How many?"

"Oh, he probably hit 65 or 70 in a year," I'd say.

"Sure he did," you would respond.

Would I tell you these incredible and unbelievable stories about him? McGwire used to show up for batting practice before games and put on such a show that opposing teams' players would come out just to watch. He would hit 475-foot home runs, 500-foot home runs, 525-foot home runs with such regularity—he'd hit one every other day, it seemed—that after a while you would just expect them, and when he hit a normal-sized home run it almost felt like a disappointment.

How could I convince you just how remarkable Mark McGwire was if you didn't see him, didn't read about him, didn't know about him?

The answer: I couldn't. Not unless you were willing to believe.

On September 27, 1930, the *Pittsburgh Courier* ran a grainy black-and-white photograph of an 18-year-old Josh Gibson. Above the photo, there was one word: "Sensation." That is all it said. Below the photo, there was a brief caption about how Gibson's "terrific hitting and fine receiving" was one of the sensations of the Homestead Grays' season.

That is the only time in 1930 that Gibson was mentioned in his hometown newspapers.

A journey through the Pittsburgh papers to learn about Josh Gibson is certain to end in disappointment. He is there . . . and also he isn't there at all.

"I am an invisible man," Ralph Ellison wrote in his 1952 classic. "No, I am not a spook like those who haunted Edgar Allen Poe; nor am I one of your Hollywood-movie ectoplasms. I am a man of substance, of flesh and bone, fiber and liquids—and I might even be said to possess a mind. I am invisible, understand, simply because people refuse to see me."

We know some things about Gibson now, know them because of the insistent research of people who refused to let him die. You can try to see the small part of Gibson visible on his Hall of Fame plaque:

CONSIDERED GREATEST SLUGGER IN NEGRO
BASEBALL LEAGUES. POWER-HITTING CATCHER
WHO HIT ALMOST 800 HOME RUNS IN LEAGUE
AND INDEPENDENT BASEBALL DURING HIS
17-YEAR CAREER. CREDITED WITH HAVING
BEEN NEGRO NATIONAL LEAGUE BATTING
CHAMPION IN 1936-38-42-45.

You can see the small part of him that comes through in the glowing quotes:

Monte Irvin: "I played with Willie Mays and against Hank Aaron. They were tremendous players. But they were no Josh Gibson."

Walter Johnson: "His name is Gibson. He can do everything. He hit the ball a mile. He catches so easy he might as well be in a rocking chair. Throws like a rifle. Too bad this Gibson is a colored fellow."

Buck O'Neil: "Greatest power hitter I ever saw."

Satchel Paige: "You look for his weakness, and while you're looking for it he's liable to hit 45 home runs."

Carl Hubbell: "He's one of the greatest backstops in the history of baseball, I think. . . . Boy how he can throw. And you know how he can hit. But with all that, the thing I like best about him is that he's as fast as greased lightning."

Waite Hoyt: "Josh Gibson is the most valuable player in colored ball. Gibson earned his clouting reputation. He has one of the greatest throwing arms in any league."

Bill Veeck: "Josh Gibson was, at the minimum, two Yogi Berras."

Barry Bonds on breaking the home run record: "No. In my heart, it belongs to Josh Gibson."

You can try to find him in the numbers that make it through the fog. You see on his Hall of Fame plaque that he hit almost 800 home runs. James A. Riley, in his *Biographical Encyclopedia of the Negro Leagues,* says Gibson was credited with 962 home runs, a titanic and oddly specific number. Seamheads, which is trying so desperately to rebuild the statistical records of Negro Leagues players, has found 238 of them as well as a lifetime .365 batting average.

You can try to find him in the legends. The best of these comes from

Robert Peterson's classic *Only the Ball Was White*. Gibson was playing for the Pittsburgh Crawfords then and he hit a ball so high that nobody saw it land. After looking at the empty sky for a few moments, the umpire finally ruled that if the ball wasn't going to come down, it had to be ruled a home run. The next day, the Crawfords were playing in Philadelphia, when, in the middle of the game, a ball came falling out of the sky and was caught by the center fielder.

"Gibson!" the umpire shouted. "You're out! Yesterday! In Pittsburgh!"

There's another one, maybe slightly better sourced, about how he came to be a professional baseball player. One evening in 1930, the Kansas City Monarchs came to play a night game against the Homestead Grays in Pittsburgh. Night baseball was brand-new—this was five years before the Cincinnati Reds played the first night game in the major leagues. A curious crowd gathered.

The game was played under the primitive light set that Monarchs owner J. L. Wilkinson had mortgaged everything to buy—he believed in the future of night baseball. Unfortunately, those lights had various problems, the main one being that they didn't actually provide much light. Hitters were often helpless. Also, the light poles were not very tall so pop-ups routinely flew over them into a dark void, leaving outfielders in danger at all times.

But catchers were in even more danger. As it goes that night, Smokey Joe Williams was pitching, a challenge for catchers even under the best of conditions, and the catcher that night broke a finger. The Grays' other catcher, Vic Harris, was in the outfield, which was scary enough; he wanted nothing whatsoever to do with catching duties under the light.

So owner Cumberland Posey went into the crowd and plucked out an 18-year-old kid who had been making a name for himself by hitting any number of long home runs in the Pittsburgh Industrial League. "Son," Posey said, "you are now our catcher."

And that was Josh Gibson.

There are many more stories, legends, most of them about his longest home runs. He may or may not have hit one entirely out of old Yankee Stadium (a more moderate version is that he hit one off the wall behind the Yankee Stadium bleachers, some 580 feet from home plate). He may or may not have hit one out of Washington's Griffith Stadium. He hit one at Cincinnati's Crosley Field that locals called the longest one ever hit there, same with Cleveland Municipal Stadium, same with Pittsburgh's Forbes Field.

Many of his longest home runs, interestingly, were to right field. He apparently had ridiculous and even unprecedented opposite-field power. Chester L. Washington of the *Pittsburgh Courier* told one story about how Gibson hit a ball in Washington to right field that soared over the stands and crashed into a sign advertising hot dogs.

"Hit the sign so hard," Washington wrote, "that a fan hollered, as dried paint and dust flew from the board, 'By gosh, Josh knocked the mustard off that hot dog.'"

How can we go back in time and see more of Gibson? How can we make him feel more real than the legends and hidden numbers make him? We can go through the newspapers, of course. There isn't much. But there is something.

In April 1931, for instance, the *Pittsburgh Courier* had this line: "Posey believes Gibson will develop into one of the best that ever played in colored baseball." Gibson was 19 at the time. So he was already showing the extraordinary promise for what followed.

We can look at the incomplete box scores and try to piece him together. That year, the *Pittsburgh Post-Gazette* actually ran some of the Homestead Grays' box scores. It was sporadic, but from May 29 to June 29, one month, I was able to find partial box scores for 23 games. These games were against all competitors, including local town teams. But Gibson was 19 years old, and he was playing catcher every day, and he was just beginning to make a name for himself.

In one game, he hit three home runs. In another, he hit two. In yet another, he hit a double and two triples (one of the underrated elements of Gibson, as Hubbell referenced above, was his speed). Totaling it up, Gibson hit about .435 and slugged well over 1.000 for that stretch. He hit 13 home runs in the 23 games, so many that the *Post-Gazette*'s chronicler clearly got bored and just kept rewriting "Josh Gibson hit another home run."

We can pick up scattered bits of information here and there. In 1932, the New York Black Yankees intentionally walked him twice in both the ninth and tenth innings, once with the tying run on base, once with the winning run on base. That same year, he competed in a skills competition before a game against the Baltimore Black Sox and he won the long-distance throwing competition. This is no surprise. Everyone marveled at his arm.*

The *Pittsburgh Courier,* for reasons that elude me, kept referring to him as "Josh" Gibson in those early days, with the quotations, as if it was a nickname, as if he was called that because of the way he liked to josh people. But it was his name. He was born Joshua Gibson, and while we aren't sure, it seems likely that he was named for his great-grandfather.

In 1933, the *Courier* wrote in its "Melting Pot of Sports" column: "Josh Gibson led the Crawfords with a rating of .467, including 55 home runs. Oh boy, oh boy, oh boy, can that guy hit?"

It was roughly around that time that people started directly comparing Gibson to Babe Ruth. The famous quote about this, uttered by many different people, goes like so: "They called Josh Gibson the black Babe Ruth, but many believe that if the world had been different, they would have called Ruth the white Josh Gibson."

This quote, while powerful and thought-provoking, isn't exactly right. Ruth came along years and years before Gibson, and he had established himself as baseball's greatest hero long before Gibson was pulled out of the stands in Pittsburgh. To compare Gibson to Ruth was the single greatest compliment anyone could offer any ballplayer, and for that tag to be placed on Gibson—who was called at various times the Brown Bambino, the Bronze Bambino, the Babe Ruth of Colored Baseball—shows he separated himself from even the greatest players in the Negro Leagues.

But the bigger question: Was Gibson as great a hitter as Ruth? Buck O'Neil, who saw both, believed so, believed that Gibson was even a little bit better because he didn't strike out as much. Others of the time pointed out that Gibson hit baseballs to spots only Ruth could hit, but it was more incredible in Gibson's case because, as mentioned, he was hitting the ball the opposite way. A writer named Rollo Wilson wrote that Ruth had never hit a ball as far as Gibson's longest shots, and the *Pittsburgh Courier* ran a

---

* Gibson's defensive talents are in some dispute. He had a bazooka for an arm and was an incredible athlete—some have said that he was one of the greatest defensive catchers ever. Others have said he was a very good catcher but not quite in the league of Negro Leagues defensive stars like Biz Mackey and his teammate Bill Perkins (whom Paige called the greatest defensive catcher he ever saw).

photo of Gibson with that story under the headline: "Better than Babe Ruth?"

In 1937, the *Courier* sent a Western Union telegram to the Pittsburgh Pirates and their manager, Pie Traynor. It read as follows:

KNOW YOUR CLUB NEEDS PLAYERS.

STOP

ANSWER TO YOUR PRAYERS RIGHT HERE IN PITTSBURGH

STOP

JOSH GIBSON CATCHER BUCK LEONARD FIRST BASEMAN AND RAY BROWN PITCHERS OF HOMESTEAD GRAYS AND SATCHEL PAIGE AND COOL PAPA BELL OUTFIELDER OF PITTSBURGH CRAWFORDS ALL AVAILABLE AT REASONABLE FIGURES

STOP

WOULD MAKE PIRATES FORMIDABLE PENNANT CONTENDERS

STOP

WHAT IS YOUR ATTITUDE? WIRE ANSWER

This was mostly a stunt but, perhaps to the paper's surprise, they got a response from Pirates owner William E. Benswanger—son-in-law of the Pirates' founder, Barney Dreyfuss. And then, I imagine, to their even greater surprise, Benswanger said: "I think that colored people should have an opportunity in baseball just as they have an opportunity in music or anything else," he said.

He added that he'd seen Gibson play and "he certainly looked like big-league timber to me."

Benswanger did seem to believe this. He brought up integrating the game on numerous occasions during owners' meetings (where he said he was generally shut down by Commissioner Kenesaw Mountain Landis). He also tried to sign Gibson in 1942, though in retrospect this seemed more of a halfhearted attempt. Benswanger's heart might have been in the right place, but he lacked conviction and courage and the Pirates did not play an African American until 1954, seven years after Jackie Robinson.

We do not often hear directly from Gibson himself; there are so few quotes in the newspapers. There is one in 1938. The Grays had gone on a five-day, eight-game road trip, and the only time to get sleep was on the bus between cities. Gibson famously could not sleep on buses. Still, he hit .600 in the eight games with five home runs. "That ain't nothin'," he said. "If only I had a little sleep, I'd have shown you how to bust that apple."

In 1939, Wendell Smith began to write for the *Courier*—he was the Jackie Robinson of sportswriting. He was sharp and combative, and he directly challenged Major League Baseball in ways that few had done before him. He wanted to know "how in the hell the Detroit Tigers wouldn't sign Josh Gibson," when the team was so desperate for catching help. He wanted to know how Ford Frick, president of the National League, could claim that people would "not stand for a guy like Josh Gibson slamming one of Vernon Gomez's pitches out of Yankee Stadium."

Gibson's later years were agonizing. In 1943, when Gibson was just 31, he was admitted to the hospital after suffering what the papers called a nervous breakdown. In truth, he was diagnosed with a brain tumor. He came out of the hospital after 10 days, but the pain never dissipated. For the rest of his life, he drank heavily and smoked marijuana to ease that pain.

But he also never stopped hitting. In fact, his greatest offensive year might have been 1943. Seamheads estimates he hit .441 with 112 RBIs and 101 runs scored in 78 games. The next year, he smashed a 440-foot double in the East-West All-Star Game. In 1945, he is credited with winning his final batting title. And even in 1946, when he was a shell of himself (this after he spent weeks in a sanitarium in Puerto Rico), he still crushed several home runs of such length that the white newspapers mentioned them—a 450-footer at Forbes Field, 500-footer in St. Louis, a ball that went over the roof in Philadelphia's Shibe Park.

He died a few months later, in January 1947, at his mother's home. He was just 35 years old. "Gibson's career," the *Pittsburgh Sun-Telegraph* wrote, "was a story of ponderous hitting of home runs and line drives which broke up many games."

"Josh Gibson," the *Pittsburgh Post-Gazette* wrote, "was one of the greatest distance hitters in the history of baseball."

"A tremendous power hitter," the *Pittsburgh Press* wrote, "Gibson once hit four home runs against the Memphis Red Sox. In 1938, he was credited with a 513-foot home run at Monessen, Pa."

"The Great Umpire," Smith wrote in the *Courier*, "has silenced the mighty bat of one of baseball's greatest sluggers of all time, Joshua (Josh) Gibson, the peerless of Negro catchers, and the man whose prodigious feats at the plate have thrilled baseball fans across the nation and on the sultry soil of Latin America for the past 19 years. The king of sluggers is dead . . . long live the king!"

Perhaps you have heard the story of Pete Gray. It has long been one of baseball's most inspirational stories. Gray was from a small town just outside Scranton, Pennsylvania. He was about three years older than Gibson, and like Gibson he adored baseball. When he was six years old, Gray was hitching a ride on the side of a produce truck when the driver suddenly stopped, and Gray fell off the truck. His right arm got caught as he fell. Doctors had to amputate the arm just above the elbow.

Gray learned to do everything with his left arm. This included baseball. He taught himself to hit by hitting a rock with a stick for hours at a time every day. He taught himself to field using an extraordinary technique: "I'd catch the ball in my glove and stick it under the stub of my right arm," he said, "Then I'd squeeze the ball out of my glove with my arm, and it would roll across my chest and drop to my stomach. The ball would drop right into my hand and my small crooked finger prevented it from bouncing away."

Gray often said that he saw Babe Ruth call his shot in the 1932 World Series, and that is what inspired him to believe that he could play in the major leagues someday. And in his late 20s, with World War II going on, he worked to do that. He played well in the minors for a couple of years when, in 1945, the St. Louis Browns paid $20,000 for his rights. The Browns were no joke—they had won the pennant in 1944.

Still, teams needed to do anything they could for attention during the war, and this was particularly true of the Browns, who weren't drawing flies. Gray was a proud ballplayer and refused to see himself as a publicity stunt—he was, by his teammates' accounts, an ornery guy who hated the very idea that anyone would feel sorry for him—but it became clear that as extraordinary as he was, he was not a major-league ballplayer, not even in 1945 with most of the players at war.

He did have some nice moments early, including a three-hit game against Philadelphia on July 4, but then pitchers started throwing him exclusively breaking balls and he hit .165/.189/.204 the rest of the way and was sent to the minors at year's end, never to return. Gray's achievement, however, has been much celebrated. There have been books written. There was a television movie made. There have been countless stories celebrating him.

Now, reread that—but try to do so through the eyes of Josh Gibson, the Black Babe Ruth.

Think of Gibson in 1945, in so much pain. He wants to play in the major leagues. Of course, he does. He wants to be seen. He wants to be cheered. But they will not give him a chance. They will not even give him a tryout.

How does that Pete Gray story sound now?

"Does this story help your morale?" Smith raged. "The St. Louis Browns have signed Pete Gray, a one-armed outfielder, for next season. This proves further that Organized Baseball will take anybody rather than have a Negro player in its ranks."

Smith wrote several times about Pete Gray and Josh Gibson and the cruelty of fate.

There is one final Josh Gibson story to tell. That same year as Gray, 1945, Gibson wrote a column about his greatest thrill in baseball. Think about what that might have been. The longest home run at Yankee Stadium? Facing Satchel Paige? Throwing out Cool Papa Bell on the basepaths?

No.

His greatest thrill in baseball was winning the MVP award in Puerto Rico in 1941. He loved Puerto Rico. He was stunned at how well he was treated there, how different the experience was compared to playing at home. In Puerto Rico, people treated him like a hero.

But it wasn't the MVP award itself that thrilled him. Read his words:

"Receiving the cup symbolic of the most valuable player award at the end of the season," he wrote, "was a highly significant and pleasing event in my life. The fanfare, the cheering of the fans and the many congratulatory speeches from league officials and other dignitaries gave me a thrill unequaled in my career."

Think of that. Perhaps the greatest catcher in the history of baseball, perhaps the greatest home run hitter in the history of baseball, perhaps the greatest player in the history of baseball, and the thrill he remembered was that one day in another place when people celebrated him.

"I will never forget it," he said.

No. 14 **Lou Gehrig**

M any people believe Lou Gehrig's story—and his life—ended on that Independence Day in 1939 when he gave the most famous speech in the history of baseball, the history of sports, and one of the most famous speeches in the history of America.

At first, it seemed, he would not speak at all that day. The Yankees had declared it Lou Gehrig Day, and more than 61,000 people came to the ballpark. Gehrig was so utterly overcome with emotion that Babe Ruth, his friend and rival, came over to him and whispered in his ear: "C'mon, kid. C'mon, kid, buck up now. We're all with you."

"Ladies and gentlemen," the master of ceremonies announced to the crowd, "Lou has asked me to thank you all for him. He is too moved to speak."

The crowd roared, louder and louder, shrieks of support and love until Gehrig took steps forward. "I knew he would speak," his wife, Eleanor, told a reporter as she watched him from the stands, and sure enough, Gehrig braced himself and stepped to the microphone.

"For the past two weeks," Gehrig said after a moment of reflection, "you've been reading about a bad brag." He meant "break" but was so overcome by emotion that he could not finish the word. He stopped again to compose himself.

"Today," he continued, "I consider myself the luckiest man on the face of the earth."

The crowd cheered loudly as he looked down.

"I have been in ballparks for 17 years and have never received anything but kindness and encouragement from you fans. When you look around, wouldn't you consider it a privilege to associate yourself with such fine-looking men as are standing here in uniform in this ballpark today?"

Again, the fans nodded and shouted. Gehrig thanked everybody who came to mind: his teammates, his manager, the Yankees' owner, the groundskeepers, the office staff, the sportswriters, the people running the concession stands. He even thanked the New York Giants—"a team you would give your right arm to beat, and vice versa"—for sending a gift.

"When you have a wonderful mother-in-law who takes sides with you in squabbles against her own daughter, that's something," Gehrig said. "When you have a father and mother who work all their lives so that you can have an education and build your body, that's something. When you have a wife who has been a tower of strength and shown more courage than you dreamed existed, that's the finest I know."

He took in the crowd's love, and one last time he braced himself.

"So I close in saying I might have had a bad break. But I have an awful lot to live for. Thank you."

Gehrig broke down after that, but so did everyone. Ruth cried, too. So many things happened in a flurry after that. By the end of the year, the Baseball Writers' Association of America voted unanimously to simply put Gehrig into the Hall of Fame immediately without a standard election or waiting period. That's good to remember when people say Mariano Rivera was the only player elected unanimously to the Hall of Fame. (Roberto Clemente received similar treatment after his untimely death in that the BBWAA waived his five-year waiting period. But his vote was not unanimous.) Soon after, Gehrig became the first player in American sports to have his number retired.

And most people think the story ends there.

But, in fact, Gehrig lived for almost two years after his Luckiest Man speech. They were a difficult and painful two years, as his body rebelled against him, and he teetered between hope and despair while doctors tried to figure out what his disease was. There were times he felt sure he would recover. And there were more times when he knew he would not.

And then there was the story in the New York *Daily News* that crushed his spirit just months before he died.

Jimmy Powers was the acerbic, passionate, staunch, principled, and fiery sports editor of the New York *Daily News*—"America's Foremost Sports Editor," as it said on the side of *Daily News* trucks. He grew up in Cleveland and worked at papers in the Midwest before coming to New York in 1928 (three years after Gehrig became a regular) with the intention of changing the sports world.

Powers fought for things. He fought for little things—he was one of the first to insist that stadium scoreboards alert the fans as to whether a ball was a hit or an error. He also fought for big things. It's fair to say that no white sportswriter in America pressed harder in the early days to integrate the major leagues. In the 1930s and into the early 1940s, he wrote column after column railing against baseball's secret agreement to keep African Americans out of the game. He wrote about how great many of the black players were—he said he personally had seen at least 10 who were good enough to play in the majors—and he encouraged white baseball fans to go to Negro League games so they could see the players they were missing.

"How would you like your sister being married to one?" one reader wrote in. Powers responded that indeed he wouldn't want his sister marrying a ballplayer, if that's what he meant by "one." "They're too grouchy," Powers said.*

Powers loved to inflame, to stir things up. When he wrote his book, *Baseball Personalities,* he purposely chose to avoid writing about those

---

* Ironically, when integration came to baseball it was through one of Powers's least favorite people in the world: Brooklyn's Branch Rickey. Powers loathed Rickey unconditionally, and so after Jackie Robinson was signed, Powers's integration columns shamefully went silent. According to Jimmy Breslin's book about Rickey, in a three-month span in 1946, Powers wrote 80 anti-Rickey columns but not one about Robinson or the cause that Powers had fought so hard for a few years earlier. To be fair, Breslin hated Powers as much as Powers hated Rickey, so he was definitely overstating things to settle some old scores with his longtime newspaper rival. But it's true that Powers's aim wasn't always true.

great players who were not quite colorful enough for his taste. He chose instead to write about the egotists, the cheaters, the liars, the showmen, the big-mouths.

And as for the more genial and upstanding Gehrigs and Joe DiMaggios and Jimmie Foxxes?

"Those players were worth more to their teams than a dozen showoffs and blowhards," he conceded. "Yet something was missing—something indefinable."

As for Gehrig explicitly, Powers explained his absence from the book like so: Gehrig was "nice to kids, a swell person." For him, those were disqualifying qualities; his book, he explained, was about the rogues, not the sweethearts.

But there was actually another reason Powers did not include Gehrig in his book.

In 1940, the Yankees were unexpectedly mediocre for most of the season. They had won four straight World Series titles—including 1939, after Gehrig retired—and everybody thought 1940 would be the same. But the Yankees got off to an atrocious start, losing eight in a row in early May, and on August 9, they still had a losing record and were stuck in fifth place, 10½ games back. As it turns out, the Yankees were almost unbeatable for the rest of the season—they went 37-15 and nearly caught the Tigers for the American League pennant.

But in mid-August, nobody knew that was going to happen. All was disgust and panic around the Yankees. Nobody could figure out what had gone wrong. Powers decided he had the winning theory.

He suggested (in great detail) that Lou Gehrig had infected the rest of the team with polio.

This really happened. The date was August 18, 1940, and it came at a specific moment when Gehrig was beginning to understand in a deeper way that the end was near for him. "Please don't judge me a crybaby or believe me to be losing my guts," he wrote to his doctor. And he went on. "There is definitely something going on within my body which I do not understand."

"Our boy," his wife, Eleanor, wrote to a friend, "is pretty discouraged."

As he tried to come to grips with the terror that he undoubtedly felt in having the disease that would eventually bear his name, Gehrig woke up that day to a headline: "Has 'Polio' Hit the Yankees?"

Powers went all-in on this theory. He drew a dystopian illustration of an aging (dying?) Yankees player surrounded by clouds of doom. He included a sidebar box with the headline "Slumping Yanks" that went through the Yankees, player by player, along with the odd troubles they were having. Some lowlights:

RED RUFFING: "Has unexpectedly lost his overpowering fastball."

LEFTY GOMEZ: "Has been able to throw with hardly any power at all."

BILL DICKEY: "Has little of his once-great hitting power."

JOE GORDON: "Inexplicably off form."

STEVE SUNDRA: "Strangely ineffective after the best season of his career."

RED ROLFE: "In and out of the lineup with a recurring eye ailment."

And then at the bottom of the box was this statement: "CAN CO-INCIDENCE EXPLAIN THESE SIMULTANEOUS AILMENTS? COULDN'T THE 'POLIO' GERM BE THE COMMON CAUSE?"

It was a staggering display of irresponsible journalism. Powers wrote a long, long story that covered two pages. "According to overwhelming opinion of the medical profession," he wrote, "poliomyelitis, similar to infantile paralysis, is communicable. The Yankees were exposed to it at its most acute stage. They played ball with the afflicted Gehrig, dressed and undressed in the locker room with him, traveled, played cards and ate with him. Isn't it possible some of them also became infected?"

No doctor had ever said Gehrig had polio. His disease was relatively new and rare but not entirely unknown—doctors had already named it amyotrophic lateral sclerosis, or ALS. Powers had built his entire premise on the poorly chosen words of one doctor who was asked by Gehrig to "put what this is in layman's terms so people can understand it." The doctor then said—incorrectly—that it was similar to chronic poliomyelitis.

Powers continued on his rampage, quoting liberally from Robert Bing's *Textbook of Nervous Disorders* and continually referring to unnamed players and Yankees officials who were "worried."

He did quote one doctor who made the obvious counterargument: "There is no similarity between the symptoms of these individual [Yankees'] cases and Gehrig's. Lou suffered from deterioration of the nervous system. The trouble with these other boys is something entirely different."

But instead of using that quote to scrap the story, Powers doubled down. "Something has happened to the Yanks!" he insisted. "If Gehrig passed through a stage in which the cause of his ineffectiveness was undetermined, isn't it possible such is also the case with many of the Yanks today?"

It was one of the most reckless and damaging stories ever printed in the sports section of a newspaper. When Gehrig read it, he was overcome with fury and a deep depression. In a letter to his doctor, according to Jonathan Eig's superb book, *The Luckiest Man,* he called Powers "a yellow so and so who hasn't got a gut in his body." Gehrig promptly sued the *Daily News* for $1 million, stating he was "greatly injured in his credit and reputation and in the social intercourse with his friends and suffered great pain and mental anguish."

Powers and the *Daily News* initially tried to fire back. They said it was Gehrig's own doctor at the Mayo Clinic who had misidentified the disease initially as a form of poliomyelitis. But as it became clear just how wrong they were, Powers quickly wrote not one but two apology stories, the bigger one on September 26 under the headline "Our Apologies to Lou Gehrig and the Yankees."

It was, looking back, not a particularly strong or heartfelt apology. Powers spent half the column explaining why he came up with the theory in the first place, and in doing so he basically rehashed the entire bit of nonsense.

"I suddenly posed a natural, logical question," he said. "Could a 'polio' germ be responsible for the Yankee collapse? Gehrig's feelings were hurt by that process of thought. I am sorry."

Powers then went on to write about how much he liked Gehrig, how often he'd had dinner with him and Eleanor, how he had gone fishing with him, etc. "Hurting Lou Gehrig's feelings were far from my mind," he wrote. "I was primarily occupied with the Yankee collapse, trying to find a logical explanation for it. I suppose a sportswriter has no business getting snarled up in medical controversy, and tossing about triple-jointed, jaw-cracking, disease terms, in an effort to explain a puzzling reversal of baseball form."

If that seems pretty flat for an apology, it should be said it probably was intended to be something slightly different than an apology. Gehrig had sued the *Daily News* for libel, and to win a libel case, you have to prove malice. Gehrig's lawyers knew malice would be impossible to prove here. Powers did adore Gehrig; all of the New York sportswriters did. Powers had written countless positive words and nary a negative one about Gehrig in more than a dozen years.

Powers had been incompetent. Powers had been irresponsible. But there was a clear absence of malice.

Gehrig wanted to keep going with the lawsuit, though. He was dying, and in unbearable pain. But there was really no way to win and, sadly, no way for him to endure a court fight. The *Daily News* finally agreed to pay Gehrig $17,500 and the case was settled.

"Gehrig," Eig would write, "signed the one-page agreement in a hand so shaky it would appear to have been written by the passenger of a car rumbling down an unpaved road."

Gehrig was gone less than six months later.

Lou Gehrig was baseball. Those are the words New York mayor Fiorello La Guardia said the day Gehrig died. "Lou Gehrig was baseball and everything it stands for," La Guardia said in full.

And that is about as well as it can be said. Gehrig came into America's consciousness in 1920 when he was 17 years old. He played in a New York *Daily News–Chicago Tribune* exhibition game arranged between the high school champions of New York City and Chicago. It was a pretty big deal. The game was played in the ballpark that would soon be named Wrigley Field. More than 10,000 people showed up to cheer.

And Gehrig came up in the ninth inning with the bases loaded and the game still close.

Over time, he would become known for hitting with the bases loaded. He hit 23 grand slams in the big leagues, a record for 70-something years until it was broken by Alex Rodriguez. Something inside Gehrig lit up when he saw the bases filled. On this day, he saw a pitch high and inside and turned on it. He ran as hard as he could to first base; the idea that he could hit a ball out of a major-league stadium didn't even occur to him. The first-base coach told him to settle down.

The ball flew out of the park and onto Sheffield Avenue.

The next day 5,000 or so people were waiting for his Commerce High team at Grand Central Terminal. The *Daily News* ran a series of photographs of the reunion, including one of the hero. "The bright star of the inter-city high school championship game, played in Chicago," the *Daily*

News wrote under his photo, "was Louis Bunora, the first baseman of the High School of Commerce, who made a home run with the bases filled."

Yeah. Louis Bunora. That's how he was introduced to New York—mixing up his name with Commerce shortstop Bobby Bunora. But in the main story, they got his last name right. They called him "Babe Gehrig."

He grew up loving the Giants, and if you've been following along in this series, this brings John McGraw back into the mix. McGraw through the years blew his chances with Hank Greenberg, Tris Speaker, and Eddie Collins. Go ahead and add Gehrig, too. He tried out for the Giants when he was 18, and he reportedly hit six consecutive home runs in batting practice. But then he went into the field, where he bombed. After he let another ball go through his legs, McGraw reportedly said: "Get this fella outta here. I've got enough lousy players without another one showing up."

Gehrig went to Columbia instead and starred as a hitter and pitcher. He struck out 17 batters against Williams College in one game (though Columbia lost 5–1; "I must have walked everybody else," Gehrig would say). He hit two long home runs against Rutgers; Yankees scout Paul Krichell, who was in the stands that day, would say he immediately sent word to General Manager Ed Barrow that he had discovered the next Babe Ruth. Gehrig was signed almost immediately.

He played 13 games for the Yankees in 1923 and hit his first big-league home run off Boston's Bill Piercy at Fenway Park. In that game, he was already batting cleanup behind Ruth. That is where they would spend the next decade together, with Ruth hitting third and Gehrig fourth.

That's how they got their uniform numbers—Babe Ruth at 3, Gehrig at 4.

Gehrig was a genius as a hitter—a Ted Williams type of genius. This can get overlooked because Gehrig is known for so many other things. He's known most for how his career ended and for Lou Gehrig's disease. He is known for being indestructible and playing in 2,130 consecutive games. He's known for pairing with Babe Ruth on some of the greatest Yankees teams of all time.

But Gehrig's OPS of 1.080 is third all-time, behind only Ruth and Williams. He hit .340/.447/.632, walked about twice as much as he struck out, and led the league at different times in doubles, triples, and home runs. His 185 RBIs in 1931 is an American League record, and his 167 runs scored in 1936 is second only to Ruth's 1921 season, a number even more incredible when you realize Ruth wasn't on that 1936 team.

At one point or another, Gehrig led the league in just about everything: runs, hits, doubles, triples, home runs, RBIs, walks, batting average, on-base percentage, slugging percentage, and total bases. As a fielder, the reviews are more mixed—he was probably about average as a first baseman. As a baserunner, same thing—he was probably about average.

But there was nothing beyond his reach as a hitter.

Or as a man. Gehrig's July Fourth speech will be remembered forever. But perhaps we should also remember his response when asked about players in the Negro Leagues. Gehrig was a profoundly decent man, and he played many games with Negro Leagues players in various exhibitions. He talked often about the greatness of so many of those players, like Satchel Paige and Josh Gibson and the man they so often compared to him, Buck Leonard.

When asked if those players should be allowed in the major leagues, he did not hesitate or equivocate. "There is no room in baseball for discrimination," he said. "It is our national pastime and a game for all."

No. 13 **Roger Clemens**

R oger Clemens once threw a bat at Mike Piazza during a World Series game. It's true, kids. Well, to be technical, he threw the barrel
of Piazza's bat, which had just shattered on a foul ball. Clemens
might not have intended to actually hit Piazza with the bat. But what is intention, anyway? He definitely threw it in Piazza's direction, and he threw
it hard—the bat tumbled, end over end, all the way to the dugout—and it
came fairly close to getting Piazza.

The thing felt strange and grotesque at the time. But as the years go
on, it feels stranger . . . and less real. Did that really happen? Did a baseball
pitcher really throw a bat at a hitter during the World Series?

Yes. And not only that: Clemens's later explanation did not exactly fill
the heart with thoughts of Christian charity. "I thought it was the ball," he
said of the bat.

Much has been written about this incident and bizarre explanation.
The very idea that Roger Clemens could have mistaken a baseball bat for
a baseball is obviously nonsensical. But, even if you somehow bought
into it—as a surprising number of Yankees apparently did—Clemens

left blank why he would throw a *baseball* full speed into the ground toward Piazza.*

Here is the bigger point, not only of this curious moment but of the chaotic career of William Roger Clemens: He got away with it. He got away clean. In the NFL in 2019, a player conked another with a helmet. The player was suspended for the rest of the season. Clemens threw a bat at a baseball player in front of the entire country, in a World Series game, and yes, the benches cleared, and yes, he and Piazza had a brief back-and-forth about it, and yes, on television Tim McCarver called it a "blatant act."

But then the game went on like nothing had happened. It's not just that Clemens wasn't suspended for like six months. He was not even ejected from the game. Not just that: He stayed in to pitch the best World Series games of his life. He was a force of nature that night, snarling, grunting, throwing the ball as hard, surely, as any 37-year-old ever had. He pitched eight innings, allowed just two hits, both singles, struck out nine, didn't walk anybody, did hit somebody with a pitch, didn't allow a runner to reach third base. The Mets hit that night as if they were frightened; and why wouldn't they be? The guy *threw a bat* at Mike Piazza.

After all of that, what is the takeaway?

Is it that Roger Clemens might just be the greatest pitcher who ever lived?

Is it that Roger Clemens did not even deserve to be out there at all?

Or, somehow, are we left trying to make sense of both thoughts at the same time?

There's a line from Roger Clemens's autobiography, *Rocket Man,* that stays with me. The book was written in 1987, so this was when Clemens was still 24 years old and establishing himself as a big-league star—just one year after he won his first Cy Young Award.

"I never wanted for anything," he wrote of his childhood, "except possibly a father in the stands watching me pitch."

Every single day while writing this book, every day, I have been re-

---

* "Why would he throw it at him?" Yankees manager Joe Torre raged at reporters after the game. "So he could get thrown out of the game in the second game of the World Series? Does that make sense to anyone? Somebody answer me!" Nobody answered him.

minded that so much of baseball—and not only baseball—is about fathers and sons. So many of these men found greatness in the game because they were inspired by their fathers, pressured by their fathers, intimidated by their fathers, taught by their fathers.

Roger Clemens never knew his natural father, a World War II veteran and chemical plant truck driver named Bill Clemens. His mother, Bess, moved the family away from Bill when Roger was less than six months old. In Roger's memory, he and his father had exactly one conversation, and it was when he was 10 years old. Bill called the house, upsetting his mother. "I got on the phone," Roger remembered, "and said, 'There is no need for you to call here anymore.' "

They never spoke again. Bill Clemens died when Roger was 18.

Roger Clemens adored his stepfather, Woody Booher. Bess married Woody when Roger was two years old. By family accounts, Woody was a sweet man, a tool-and-dye maker, who never raised his voice and adored being a father to all of Bess's children. According to Jeff Pearlman's *The Rocket That Fell to Earth*, Booher's actual marriage proposal included these words: "I love you, but I'll always look after your children first."

"Woody was the one," Bess said, "who gave Roger all his extra pushes."

But Woody died of a heart attack when Roger was just eight; Clemens would never forget the moment. He was sent to the basement when the ambulance arrived. He then put down a stack of books and climbed up so he could see the scene through the tiny window near the ceiling. He saw his stepfather on a gurney, covered by a sheet, and a crowd of hopeless people surrounding him.

"After my stepfather died," Clemens said, "I had doubts God was fair."

No, Roger Clemens did not have a father in the stands as baseball began to consume his life. He did, however, have his brother Randy, who was nine years older. As Roger came of age, Randy was the coolest guy in the world. He was a high school baseball star. He was a high school basketball star. He was dating the captain of the cheerleading squad, and they were the king and queen of the prom. "Randy was the star," Roger would write. Randy was all that the young Roger Clemens could ever hope to become.

And Roger felt like the opposite of that. He was chubby then, awkward, filled with the rage of a boy who had lost not one but two fathers in his life. He looked to Randy to tell him how to live.

And Randy's philosophy was simple. There are two options in life.

1. You win.

2. You fail.

That was it. There was no middle ground in the belief system of Randy Clemens. This would end up doing more than driving Roger Clemens's life ("When I lose," Roger would say many years later, "I feel so badly that I can't go out and face the public"). It would also end up haunting Randy Clemens's own life.

Roger Clemens was not a baseball natural. He competed hard, but he didn't throw hard. He lacked athleticism. His most noteworthy achievement when he was young was being the other pitcher on a team that featured Kelly Krzan, the first girl to play Little League baseball in Dayton and perhaps even the state of Ohio ("Cute Batter Up," the *Dayton Daily News* headlined their story about her). Krzan dealt with all of the misogyny you would expect, but she told Pearlman that it was Clemens who somehow felt most aggrieved by her just wanting to play ball.

"Whenever Kelly was pitching," Kelly's mother, Patricia, said, "he'd get mad and throw things. He'd stomp around and tell people that a girl shouldn't be pitching."

At 15, Roger left Ohio to move in with Randy, who had gotten married and found a job in Sugar Land, Texas, just outside of Houston. Life had already proven a disappointment to Randy. He had played college basketball but was thrown off the team after being caught using marijuana on a road trip. He was already struggling with substance abuse issues that would grow worse with the years. But he was by all accounts a devoted brother who wanted to help Roger find his way. In Randy's mind, that would mean pushing Roger to the very limit.

Roger wanted to be pushed. He had a hunger that he could not explain to anyone but Randy. As a high school junior, Clemens wasn't good enough to start regularly; he filled in as a spot starter and reliever. As a senior, he won some games but he was no prospect. His fastball barely touched 80. Even so, at Randy's insistence, he was putting himself through the excruciating workout routines that would later be almost as celebrated as his pitching. He ran nonstop. He threw continuously.

He also became what one of his youth coaches called "a real pain." He yelled at opponents from the mound (he would say that he picked this up from his hero, Nolan Ryan). He refused to accept coaching from anyone but Randy. He often seemed at the very edge of losing control, and this is because—as he would admit—he *was* at the very edge of losing control.

"They never said I was a can't-miss prospect," Clemens would say. "I didn't open anyone's eyes. They doubted my ability. I always had to overcome the doubts others had in me. But I've made myself thrive on that. I decided to prove them wrong. That's what got me to the big leagues. That's what made me a power thrower."

He had no Division I scholarship offers out of high school. Heck, he barely had any offers at all. The greatest break of his young life happened when his high school coach, Charlie Maiorana, called San Jacinto College coach Wayne Graham on Clemens's behalf. Maiorana did not call Graham to get an offer. Clemens wanted more than San Jacinto. The coach called to ask Graham if he could pull a few strings and help get Clemens to the University of Texas.

Graham was connected—he'd been a star at Texas—but he was not *that* connected. Still, he took a liking to Clemens and did end up offering him a scholarship to San Jacinto. It's hard to know what Clemens thought about that. But it turned out to be the turning point.

Wayne Graham lived a baseball life. He began as a bat boy for his father's team, the Finger Furniture Nine, which finished second in the prestigious *Houston Post* tournament one year. After he starred at the University of Texas, he was a line-drive hitting minor-league third baseman for more than a decade. He twice got big-league cups of coffee, once with the 1963 Phillies and again with the 1964 New York Mets.

More than anything, Graham was a brilliant student of baseball. At San Jacinto, his teams won five National Junior College championships. He later coached at Rice, where he mentored several future big leaguers (Lance Berkman and Anthony Rendon among them) and won a national championship.

Graham saw potential in Clemens when so few did. "Why did you recruit this fat boy?" Graham remembered one of his assistant coaches asking. Graham had his reasons. On the one hand, he saw how badly Clemens wanted to succeed, how hard he was willing to work, how much rage he had inside him. On the other, though, he couldn't help but notice that none of that rage seemed to come through in Clemens's actual pitching. Where was the velocity? Where was the force? Randy had taught his younger brother to be smooth on the mound, to be graceful, and Graham had to break the kid of that habit. He wasn't dancing out there. He was pitching.

"ROGER!" Graham would shout every time he watched Clemens pitch. "FINISH!"

That was the word between them. Finish. If you ever watched Clemens pitch in the big leagues, this was the part that would stand out. There was still a gracefulness to his motion, a fluidity, yes, but when it came to the end, the part when he threw the ball, he brought violence. There was no holding back with Roger Clemens, and he got that from Wayne Graham.

By the end of his freshman year, Clemens's fastball was not only topping 90 mph, it was getting closer to the mid-90s. He was dominating hitters. It was such an incredible transformation that suddenly scouts became quite interested. The New York Mets took him in the 12th round of the draft. But Clemens's dream was still to pitch for the University of Texas, and that's what he did instead. He left San Jacinto, went to Texas, became a superstar, and was on the mound when Texas won the College World Series.

Boston took Clemens with the 19th overall pick in the 1983 draft and then came the rest.

But, yes, there is a postscript to the story, not a particularly happy one. Clemens left for Texas without telling Wayne Graham. He never called. He never wrote. He never thanked Graham for changing his life. He never even said good-bye. The two men didn't talk for years after that.

How should we look at Roger Clemens's career? Should we look at it at all? This is the baseball question, and different people will give you different answers. In MLB's Mitchell Report, Clemens was charged with using steroids later in his career. The charge mostly came from a strength coach named Brian McNamee. Clemens was so enraged by the charge (and was so driven to win, the defining quality of his life) that he demanded his day in court, his day before Congress, where he vehemently denied ever using steroids.

Then he was indicted by a federal grand jury on counts of perjury and contempt of Congress.

And that led to two trials, one that ended as a mistrial, the other where he was found not guilty on all counts.

But, guilty or not guilty in court, he was found guilty in the court of public opinion, where he now lives a sort of baseball half-life as either a legend or a scoundrel. He has not been elected to the Baseball Hall of Fame. There is no indication he ever will be.

As such, his baseball career is, to many, nothing more than a mirage. You can talk about the achievements, the awards, the numbers. You can talk about seven Cy Young Awards and a 354-184 record and 4,672 strikeouts and seven ERA titles, and numerous people will not argue about what any of that means because they don't even see it.

But Clemens's career happened, and as Tom Tango once pointed out, it is beyond belief. Roger Clemens's career is a staggering combination of Pedro Martínez's entire career and Sandy Koufax's entire career.

How's that? Well, look at Clemens's career in Boston:

Clemens in Boston: 192-111, 3.06 ERA, 144 ERA+, 1 MVP, 3 Cy Youngs, 81 WAR, 56 Wins Above Average.

And now look at Martínez's career total: 219-100, 2.94 ERA, 154 ERA+, 3 Cy Youngs, 86 WAR, 61 Wins Above Average.

Clemens wasn't *quite* all of Pedro in those years, but he was pretty darned close. Clemens never had a season in Boston as good as Pedro in 1999 or 2000, but his 1990 season was in the ballpark, his 1987 season was astounding, and his 1991 and 1992 seasons were incredible and we haven't even yet mentioned his 1986 season, when he went 24-4 with a league-leading 2.48 ERA and did something even Pedro failed to do: win an MVP.

I thoroughly believe Clemens was underrated as a young pitcher and overrated as an old one. By 1998, when he allegedly began working with McNamee, he was already a fully qualified Hall of Famer and one of the greatest pitchers in baseball history.

Clemens's years after Boston: 162-73, 3.21 ERA, 140 ERA+, 4 Cy Youngs, 58 WAR, 39 Wins Above Average.

And Koufax's career total: 165-87, 2.76 ERA, 131 ERA+, 1 MVP, 3 Cy Youngs, 53 WAR, 31 Wins Above Average.

It's pretty incredible if you look at it that way. He wasn't Pedro. He wasn't Koufax. He was both.

How much of it was authentic? And, even beyond that, how hard does anyone want to work to stand up for Clemens and his legacy? He was hardly an admirable figure. There's a pretty good argument that the PED allegations pale in comparison with his problematic relationship with the late country music star Mindy McCready. The New York *Daily News* reported that Clemens started seeing McCready when she was just 15 (he was in his 30s and married). McCready confirmed to the *Daily News* that the two had an affair, though she later said that it didn't begin until she was 18.

Clemens, meanwhile, denied that the affair happened at all and publicly attacked McCready, calling her a liar. His lawyers briefly threatened a defamation case. When McCready died by suicide at age 37, Clemens made it sound like he barely knew her, even as his agent conceded that they were close friends. "The few times that I had met her and her manager/agent," Clemens said, "they were extremely nice."

How can you think good thoughts about a person like that?

On the other hand, it is also true that most people probably do think he does belong in the Hall of Fame. Clemens got 61 percent of the Hall of Fame vote from the Baseball Writers in 2019, and baseball writers are famously staunch on the subject. Most informal polls I've seen (or conducted) have Clemens's Hall of Fame support closer to 75 percent.

One thing is sure: It's almost impossible to have a pure baseball conversation about Clemens. And he brought that on himself. Any attempt to discuss his power pitching, his control, his multiple 20-strikeout games, his incredible split-fingered fastball, will fade off into a discussion of his ethics, his rage, his bullying, and various uncertain things. And here's the big reason: All his life, Clemens got away with it. Whether it was throwing a bat at Piazza, taking PEDs to dominate, or allegedly doing shameful things in his private life, well, we don't know it all. But we know he got away with it. We know that he never admitted any of it, much less expressed any remorse.

And if there's one thing so many people cannot abide, it is someone getting away with something.

He was one helluva pitcher, though. He really was. On the mound, he was the best of his time, and his time happened to include Randy Johnson and Greg Maddux and Pedro Martínez, three of the greatest who ever lived. What separated him was a hunger and a fury and a thunderous unwillingness to lose that swelled from somewhere deep inside. He couldn't turn it off when the game ended. Maybe it had to do with an empty seat where his father was supposed to be. Maybe that was just how it had to be.

No. 12 **Honus Wagner**

The most famous baseball card ever printed is the Honus Wagner T206. In mint condition—or as close to mint condition as you can get for a card that appeared in cigarette packs more than 100 years ago—it has sold for more than $3 million. There has been a book written about it, a movie made about it, there have been numerous scandals surrounding it (with one dealer going to prison). Various Wagner cards have been owned by hockey legend Wayne Gretzky and mercurial actor Charlie Sheen. The card has been auctioned off by nuns to raise money for their ministries.

The T206 Wagner is not the rarest of all baseball cards, though it is rare. It is certainly not the most unusual of all baseball cards—there's a plainness about it with its orange background and photo of an unsmiling Wagner posing stiffly while wearing a collared uniform, the words "Wagner, Pittsburg" typed below.

But it is the most famous because it comes with a story, a story that goes beyond the card itself, a story that goes a bit beyond baseball itself, a story that just might (or might not) get to the heart of one of the greatest heroes to ever play the game.

———

Baseball cards go back more or less to the start of professional baseball. There were various cards celebrating baseball even before the 1869 Cincinnati Redlegs became the first openly professional team, but recognizable baseball cards—photographs of Major League Baseball players on cardboard that you can trade or flip or put in the spokes of your bicycle—began ten or so years after the birth of the National League. They first appeared in packs of cigarettes. According to *The Card,* Michael O'Keeffe's book about the T206 Honus Wagner, the first distinct baseball card was probably a 25-card set put out by the cigarette manufacturer Goodwin & Company in 1886.

The idea, looking back, was quite brilliant. In addition to connecting tobacco to the sport that was rapidly becoming the national pastime, and in addition to giving consumers an extra reason to stick with one brand of cigarettes, the baseball cards themselves helped keep the cigarette packs rigid and firm, preventing cigarette breakage. It was such a breakthrough idea that soon other cigarette companies began creating their own baseball card sets.

These days, it seems incongruous to have baseball cards in a cigarette pack, not least because now it is illegal for anyone younger than 21 to buy cigarettes. But in those days, tobacco companies openly and unabashedly marketed cigarettes to minors. That might seem vulgar now, but it's important to remember how different those times were. Less than 40 percent of all teenagers were in school. Children were working in factories and on farms, working long hours. The Keating-Owen Child Labor Act did not pass until 1916.

When the American Tobacco Company bought out everybody and became a monopoly—under the ferocious leadership of a man named Buck Duke, who later endowed a university that would take on his last name and go to a bunch of Final Fours—it took the baseball card business to another level. The crescendo came from 1909 to 1911, when they put out a gigantic set of 524 baseball cards, the set now known at T206.

The set wasn't called T206 at the time. No, that is a whole other rabbit hole, but one we must go down because it takes us all the way back to Honus Wagner. The set was classified as T206 by a fascinating, strange, and utterly devoted man named Jefferson Burdick, known by many as the Father of Card Collecting.

We don't know too much about Burdick's life. He was born around 1900 and grew up in upstate New York, in a little town called Central Square, just outside Syracuse. He fell in love with cards early—he once said that he and his friends would ask their fathers to change cigarette brands periodically so they could collect cards from different sets.

Burdick, however, was not a particularly big baseball fan—it is believed he never once attended a baseball game. No, he was an obsessive fan of *cards*—"I have an inherited love of pictures," he said—and baseball cards just happened to be a big category in his much larger obsession. Burdick's definition of what made a card was pretty liberal. He collected postcards, playing cards, greeting cards, business cards, advertising cards, as well as baseball cards, yes, but he also collected chewing gum wrappers, cigar wrappers, vaudeville flyers, and political posters.

"Some ask how anyone becomes interested in cards," he said in one of the few interviews he ever gave. "You don't. Collectors are born that way."

He collected obsessively. In his lifetime, he accumulated more than 300,000 items, which he painstakingly categorized and mounted and donated to New York's Metropolitan Museum of Art. To say this was his life's work would be to understate things. He walked into the museum for the last time on January 10, 1963, worked a full eight hours on his cards, and then stood up and announced: "I shan't be back." He checked into the hospital the next day and died two months later.

Burdick is the one who named the famous set T206, with the *T* standing for "Tobacco." But more to the point, he is the man who first alerted the world about the specialness of the T206 Wagner. He put out the first version of his American Card Catalog in 1933 and listed the values of the cards. Most were a nickel. Some were a dime.

But the T206 Honus Wagner card he listed as the most expensive and valuable card of them all—worth $50, about $1,000 in today's money.

Why? Burdick had his reason. And finally, we get to our hero.

Honus Wagner was the greatest and most beloved player of his day. His full name was Johannes Peter Wagner, and during his playing days he was called Hans Wagner much more often than he was called Honus. The Honus name really took hold after his playing days were over, after he had become a larger-than-life legend. I guess people thought "Honus Wagner" sounded more regal.

There are those, as Bill James first pointed out, who sometimes confuse Rogers Hornsby and Honus Wagner. It's a bizarre thing. Maybe it's because both of them were right-handed middle infielders who won a lot of batting titles. Maybe it is because their names, though they seem to have no obvious similarities, do seem to reflect off each other.

But the comparison could not be more inapt. They were, in all ways that mattered, polar opposites. Hornsby was the worst in just about every way—a racist, a bully, a rogue, a terrible teammate, a defensive liability, a selfish son of a gun—while Wagner was friendly, admirable, openhearted, brilliant defensively, and beloved.

Wagner was the best defensive player of his day. From Ogden Nash's famous "Line-Up for Yesterday":

> *W is for Wagner*
> *The bowlegged beauty*
> *Short was closed to all traffic*
> *With Honus on duty**

Wagner was, despite his famous bowed legs, breathtakingly fast, and he led the league in stolen bases five times and triples three more.

And he was universally admired. Don't mistake that for softness: Wagner was not exactly a sweetheart. He could drink with the best of them, and he was a furious competitor. He jawed at umpires—once he was charged with throwing a ball wildly on purpose to hit an umpire. He vehemently denied it but was still suspended for three days.

One Wagner story, probably apocryphal but certainly indicative of Wagner's relentlessness, goes that Ty Cobb insulted his German heritage, and Wagner responded by slamming down a tag so hard on Cobb's face that it almost knocked out his teeth. Baseball was a tough game and Wagner—who was a sturdy 5-foot-11, 200 pounds and came from Pennsylvania coal country—was as tough as he needed to be.

But he treated people with grace and respect. When told that people were calling a Negro Leagues star, Pop Lloyd, "the Black Honus Wagner," he responded: "It is a privilege to have been compared with him."

And he was smart. So smart. "I never saw Honus make a mental mistake, and I never heard of a person who saw him make one," Wagner's

---

* This couplet is quite terrible.

longtime teammate and, later, Hall of Fame manager Bill McKechnie said.

Burleigh Grimes told a great story of seeing an older Wagner facing a rookie pitcher. Wagner was a great old player. He hit an astonishing 20 triples at age 38 and 17 triples at age 41. The story goes that near the end, Wagner faced a rookie pitcher with a terrific curveball. The kid threw that curve and Wagner swung and missed so hard that he fell to his knees.

"Watch this," Grimes said to a teammate. The pitcher, no doubt filled with boldness after making the legend look silly, threw the curve again. Wagner drilled the ball off the wall so hard that Grimes said the wall shook for five minutes.

Wagner truly had no weaknesses. He won eight batting titles and led the league multiple times in every major category except home runs, which wasn't a significant part of baseball in his day. There is a good argument to make that the Gold Glove should be named for him; that's how revolutionary his defense was (he cut a hole in his glove so he could get the ball out more quickly on the exchange). He was a great bunter, a great handler of the bat—using a batting style where his hands were a few inches apart and a bat roughly the size of a telephone pole—and, as mentioned, an aggressive and spectacular baserunner.

He was elected with the first class into the Baseball Hall of Fame. And his plaque is more impressive than most:

> THE GREATEST SHORTSTOP IN BASEBALL
>
> HISTORY. BORN CARNEGIE, PA, FEB. 24, 1874
>
> KNOWN TO FAME AS "HONUS," "HANS" AND
>
> "THE FLYING DUTCHMAN." RETIRED IN 1917,
>
> HAVING SCORED MORE RUNS, MADE MORE
>
> HITS AND STOLEN MORE BASES THAN
>
> ANY OTHER PLAYER IN THE HISTORY
>
> OF HIS LEAGUE.

It should be added here—for the purposes of our story—that Wagner was also one of the great negotiators of his day. He "retired" several times in his career, most significantly before the 1908 season. He was just 34 then and coming off a typically great season: He led the National League in batting average, doubles, stolen bases, on-base percentage, slugging percentage, and total bases. But he said he was through. His body was too beat up to keep going.

It became a daily story: Would Wagner actually quit? Soon there were rumors that he was really quitting because he was sick of the way fans (particularly gamblers) in the crowd booed him and gave him a hard time for not getting a hit every time up. He talked about going into show business—starting a circus, was the way he described his plans. The Pirates' owner, Barney Dreyfuss, pleaded with him to come back. So did the president of the National League, who said professional baseball would collapse without him.

In the end, yes, Wagner returned and had perhaps his greatest season in 1908, finishing two home runs shy of the Triple Crown.

But in the years since, it has become canon that the whole thing was a negotiation. Wagner denied it ferociously ("There was no financial trouble or any other misunderstanding between the club and myself," he said), but it's pretty meaningful that he doubled his salary. It was not the only time Wagner played hardball.

This too is part of the T206 Wagner story.

In 1909, Wagner was far and away the most famous and beloved baseball player in America. As such, when the American Tobacco Company decided to put together its baseball card set, he was the most important player for the company to secure. It's unclear how the ATC negotiated with players for photo rights. In most cases, they probably didn't. A few players might have gotten a nominal fee, but most probably got nothing at all.

Wagner, though, was in a different category entirely, so much so that the ATC paid $10 to Pittsburgh's most-read and influential sportswriter, John Gruber, to get Wagner's permission. Ten dollars was not insubstantial in 1909. It was a weekly salary for most families.

Gruber did not get Wagner's permission. He did, however, get the most celebrated letter in baseball card collecting history.

Dear John,

I don't want my picture in cigarets, but I don't want you to lose the $10, so I'm enclosing my check for that sum.

Hans Wagner

Gruber never cashed the check. He framed it and kept it on his wall for the rest of his life.

By the time Wagner declined, the ATC had already printed some Wagner cards—estimates range from 50 to 200 cards. But after getting word from Gruber, they immediately stopped. That's why Jefferson Burdick priced the card so high. In 1955, he said, "Only three or four copies have been found."

To give you an idea of the rarity, baseball card historian Scot A. Reader estimates that there were 370 million T206 cards printed from 1909 to 1911. That would be about 700,000 copies per card. With so few Wagners out there, you can understand why it might be so valuable.

But it should be added: The Wagner is not the rarest of the T206 cards. No, that designation is reserved for a mediocre pitcher named Slow Joe Doyle—called that because apparently he took *forever* between pitches. Doyle's original card mistakenly placed him on the New York Giants instead of the New York Highlanders. It's believed the company caught the error after only a dozen or so got out. That card has sold for more than $300,000.

But that still doesn't put it in the range of Wagner's card . . . and that's because it isn't just rarity that sets Wagner's card apart. It's the story. Why did Wagner refuse to be a part of the T206 set?

"It is because Wagner was a nonsmoker," Burdick said, "who wouldn't allow a picture on a cigarette card, as it would imply his approval of smoking."

Yes. That's the story that emerged: Wagner had refused to have his photo placed on a cigarette card because he did not want to play any role in encouraging kids to buy cigarettes. He loved kids; he was famous for going through the outside clubhouse entrance down the right-field line of Exposition Park and holding the door open just long enough for a few kids to get in and see the game.

In other words, the Wagner card came to represent the moral principles of the great Honus Wagner.

But is that really why Wagner refused to allow his card in the T206 set? Well, that's an interesting question. Several people—including collector and baseball historian Keith Olbermann—have looked deeply into it and determined it probably isn't true. There are a couple of reasons to doubt. One, Wagner himself was a tobacco user. He chewed tobacco on and off the field. His granddaughter Leslie Blair recalled him always having a mouth full of chew. He loved few things in life more than he loved a cigar. He was so devoted to cigars that he agreeably appeared on a cigar trading card and on multiple occasions let his photo appear on the box cover of a particularly favored brand of cigars.

Two, well, we already told you: Wagner fought for his money. It seems every bit as likely as any other theory that he turned down the ATC offer because it was too low.

What do we go with here? Well, I prefer the romantic version of the story. We can never be sure, obviously, but the money motivation seems less convincing because Wagner gave his friend Gruber a $10 check, suggesting that he felt bad about letting his friend down. If it had been a situation in which he felt like the company was trying to take advantage of him financially, would he really have given that check?

Second, we do know that he really *was* worried about children using tobacco. How do we know that? Well, in 1914, a short but wonderful letter from Wagner appeared in the *Pittsburgh Press*. It was filled with advice for a friend who was giving a talk to boys. The letter was headlined "Wagner's Advice to Boy Friends."

"I don't think you could use a better line of talk," Wagner wrote, "than to tell a boy not to use tobacco and to let drink and lies alone; keep good hours, take plenty of exercise and not over-exert. And when a boy sets out to do a thing he should make up his mind to do it well, for a job not completed is no job at all. Tell 'em to take the advice of their parents on all things. When in doubt, a boy should curt his temper and count a hundred when he speaks when he feels mad over something."

Tobacco was the very first thing he mentioned.

No, we will never know for sure. But here's the thing about legendary players: So many of them, the closer you look the more disappointments you will find.

But it isn't so with Honus Wagner. The closer you look at Wagner, the better he looks.

Here's one more Wagner story, one I told in the Arky Vaughan chapter. This time let's tell it from the perspective of Wagner. Honus was a natural ballplayer. There doesn't seem to be much coaching in his early life; he learned the game on his own. His most famous quote is simply: "There ain't much to being a ballplayer if you're a ballplayer."

Fifteen years after Wagner retired as the greatest shortstop in the history of the game, Vaughan came along for the same team—this is the shortstop version of Sandy Koufax and Clayton Kershaw story coming along as Dodgers left-handed pitchers. Vaughan was immediately a great hitter, but he was an erratic shortstop. He made a lot of errors—46 in each of his first two years. The Pirates brought in Wagner to teach the kid a few things. "They said if I couldn't make a shortstop out of Arky Vaughan, nobody could," he told reporters.

The two men became as close as a father and son. They roomed together for the next nine years. Vaughan would later say that from Wagner, "I learned more baseball than I ever dreamed existed."

And Wagner had a deep love for his protégé: "Vaughan is such a fine hitter and such a whirlwind on the bases. Of all the players I tried to help, he's the best."

But the funny part is that while Vaughan undoubtedly learned so much from Wagner by simply being around the great man, Honus was not what you might call a gifted teacher. Yes, Wagner worked with Vaughan for hours on the field, but when someone asked Vaughan how it was progressing, he smiled.

"I'm not sure," Vaughan said. "When I asked Mr. Wagner what to do, he said, 'You just run in fast, grab the ball and throw it to first base ahead of the runner.' But he didn't tell me how."

No. 11 **Mickey Mantle**

There is a famous Mutt Mantle story you may have heard, a story about how Mutt found his son at a low point, ready to quit baseball forever, and promptly kicked his son's butt, threatened to drag him back to work in the Oklahoma mines, and, through a heavy dose of tough love, launched his son's legendary baseball career.

The story, best we can tell, is absolutely true.

But inside the story is something else, something hard, something painful. Mickey Mantle's baseball career was a glorious triumph. Nobody, other than perhaps Babe Ruth himself, launched more dreams. Mickey Mantle was unlimited—the perfect baseball name, the perfect baseball body, a switch-hitter who hit titanic home runs from either side of the plate (they invented the "tape-measure home run" for him), a hitter with an incredible eye, a blazing fast baserunner, a stunning force of nature standing in center field at Yankee Stadium.

He won the Triple Crown in 1956. He was even better in '57. He played 18 years in the big leagues, and his Yankees went to the World Series in 12 of them. He hit 536 home runs and won three MVPs and along the way, he inspired the hopes of countless kids. Singer/songwriter Paul Simon was one of those kids, and when he wrote "Mrs. Robinson," he really was thinking, "Where have you gone, Mickey Mantle." But "Joe DiMaggio" had the right syllables.

"For a huge portion of my generation," one of those kids, Bob Costas, said at Mantle's memorial, "Mickey Mantle was that baseball hero. And for reasons that no statistics, no dry recitation of the facts, can possibly capture, he was the most compelling baseball hero of our lifetime. He was our symbol of baseball at a time when the game meant something to us that perhaps it no longer does."

Mantle himself couldn't understand it. I saw Mantle a few times late in life—at events, at baseball card shows—and his body was destroyed by injuries and alcohol and all those late nights, and people would approach him with tears in their eyes as they tried to find the words to explain the role he had played in their lives. And, more often than not, he would turn away from them, as if he couldn't tolerate their affection or, more likely, as if he felt entirely unworthy of their love.

For Mickey Mantle, living was the hard part.

Charles Mantle was a ballplayer. His son Charles "Mutt" Mantle was a ballplayer. His son Mickey Mantle was a ballplayer. Of the three, though, none loved the game like Mutt. Baseball consumed him. Mickey always thought Mutt had the talent to play the game professionally, but that was never really an option. Mutt got married at age 17 and worked the fields as a tenant farmer.

Mutt knew with a chilling certainty that his future son would be called Mickey, after his favorite ballplayer Mickey Cochrane, and that Mickey Mantle would be the best ballplayer of them all.

Mutt could not support his family by farming and by the time Mickey was three, Mutt was working in the lead and zinc mines of Oklahoma. The work killed him daily. "Every time he took a breath," Mickey remembered, "the dust and dampness went into his lungs. Coughed up gobs of phlegm and never saw a doctor. . . . He realized that if he didn't die of cancer, he'd die of tuberculosis. 'So what the hell, live while you can,' he'd say and light another cigarette."

Mickey was his father's life's work. His mother, Lovell, would say that when Mickey was 12 hours old, Mutt showed him a baseball for the first time and felt just a little bit heartbroken when Mickey turned toward milk instead. Mickey said he was taught baseball player positions before the alphabet and his nightly lullaby was the radio broadcast of St. Louis Cardinals games.

Mickey told his wife, Merlyn, that at five years old he already knew that he would not be able to face his father's disappointment if he did not become a great big-league ballplayer.

There's an extraordinary moment in the film *Searching for Bobby Fischer.* The movie is about a chess prodigy, Josh Waitzkin, but it is also about his parents' struggle to figure out exactly what they were supposed to do. Josh's father, played by Joe Mantegna, is a sportswriter who can't help but think from his own experiences that he must push his son to greatness. Josh's mother, played by Joan Allen, meanwhile fights to let Josh be a child.

"How many ballplayers grow up afraid of losing their father's love every time they come to the plate?" Allen asks Mantegna in the crescendo scene.

"All of them!" Mantegna roars. The scene was so powerful that Mantegna, who has been an actor for closing on 50 years and has performed in hundreds of thousands of scenes, remembers the specific power of the moment. "I thought it was a terrific statement," he says, "especially for baseball fans."

Yes. Well, it's Mutt Mantle's scene.

Every day throughout Mickey Mantle's childhood, he played baseball with Mutt—though *play* is probably the wrong verb. Mutt did not believe in play. Everything in his dark and harsh life had told him that to get ahead in life, you needed to beat the system. So he came up with a plan, and the plan definitely did not involve play.

No, instead, he would make Mickey a switch-hitting, switch-throwing phenomenon. He guessed that with baseball becoming more specialized, the ability to hit from both sides of the plate and the ability to pitch with both arms would be an enormous advantage. He had Mickey throw for a half hour with his right arm and then a half hour with his left. Mutt would have Mickey hit left-handed against his pitches and right-handed against his father, Charles, who was a lefty.

Mickey hated it at first. All of it. But he mostly hated the switch-throwing part; throwing lefty drove him crazy. And so, for perhaps the only time in his childhood, he rebelled and refused to do it. A deal was struck. Mutt would stop making Mickey throw left-handed.

But Mickey had to promise to hit left-handed against every righty pitcher he faced for the rest of his life.

As it turns out, Mickey Mantle broke the promise twice. The first time came three or four years later when playing in a neighborhood game. Mickey had struck out two or three times against a righty pitcher, and he was furious, and so the next time he stepped in righty. But before the first pitch was even thrown, he heard the voice: "Go on home!" That was Mutt Mantle, who was watching, who was always watching, and that evening Mutt made it clear that if Mickey didn't hit left-handed the next time, he would never be allowed to play ball again.

The next time he batted righty against a righty pitcher was when Mickey was 25 years old. It was May 30, 1957, five years almost to the day after Mutt Mantle died. The Yankees led Washington 9–0, and Senators pitcher Emilio Hernandez was on the mound. Mickey had twice that day come close to homering left-handed but his shots died at the warning track, and he wanted a home run, so he took a crack from the right side, his better power side. "He doesn't have much of a curve," Mickey would say of Hernandez. "I figured I might get a high fastball which I could hit into the left-field seats." Mantle hit into a double play instead, the first time he'd done that all season. Later, he tried the switch again against Hernandez and hit a soft ground ball.

The headlines across America read: "Father knows best."

There's another thing about the movie *Searching for Bobby Fischer* that is worth mentioning here: There was no Joan Allen character in young Mickey Mantle's life. His mother, Lovell, was distant and detached. Neither of Mickey's parents said "I love you" throughout his childhood.

The love, as it was, came through daily baseball workouts. Mickey would come home from school, and Mutt would come home from the mines, a cigarette dangling from his mouth, exhausted from his day, and the sessions would begin. They were long and intense and inescapable, no matter the weather.

"Dad, I'm hungry," Mickey would say when dinnertime hit.

"Your belly can wait," Mutt would growl, and that's when he might throw one at his son's head to get the point across.

"When his Dad would pitch to him for hours," Merlyn wrote, "out of a hundred pitches, Mick would be in terror of missing one and looking bad and having his father frown or criticize."

Mickey Mantle wet his bed until he was 16 years old.

There was a time when people told the Mantle story like it was a fairy tale; here was an Oklahoma miner who, through sheer stubbornness, raised baseball's greatest star. It was no fairy tale, however, and these days it's hard to find much affection for Mutt Mantle, who raised a legendary ballplayer but also a son who became an alcoholic, an absentee father, an unfaithful husband, and a deeply depressed man.

Mutt's pressure on his son was unrelenting. Nothing was good enough. Nothing could be good enough. When Mickey was in high school, he played for a semipro team called the Baxter Spring Whiz Kids, and he once had a game where he hit three long home runs, a performance so awesome that the crowd passed around the hat and raised more than $50 in coins to give to him in appreciation. That was as much as Mutt Mantle made in a week working in the mines.

"He coulda done better," was Mutt's summation of the performance.

How much of Mickey Mantle's greatness was due to his father's single-minded focus? It's impossible to know, but it must be said that Mickey was an extraordinary athlete, one of the greatest to ever play baseball. It's possible that his youthful combination of speed and power is unmatched in major-league history. The power is obvious. The speed—the legend has always been that he was timed at 3.1 seconds to first base, the fastest time ever recorded.

Let's say for the record: That didn't happen. Not 3.1 seconds. No way. I asked Tom Tango—who spends his days breaking down Major League Baseball's Statcast data—to think about someone going in 3.1 seconds to first base, and he pointed out that in 2009, when Usain Bolt set the world record in the 100, he ran the first 30 meters in 3.78 seconds.

Translate that to yards and it's roughly 3.5 seconds. If you want to say that maybe the stopwatch didn't start until the batter was out of the box, maybe cutting it down to 88 feet, you *might* be able to get it down to 3.2 or 3.3 seconds.

But again, this is comparing Mantle to *USAIN BOLT* running with perfect form on an ideal running track with the best equipment a runner can have.

So, no, Mantle did not actually run a 3.1 to first unless the stopwatch didn't click until he was three or four steps down the line.

But the time doesn't matter: The point is Mantle was blazing fast. People miss this because he badly hurt his knee as a rookie, and because he stole only 153 bases (compared to Willie Mays' 338, for example). But the stolen base number is misleading; the Yankees didn't steal bases. And Mantle's 80 percent success rate is fantastic; it ranks sixth among Hall of Famers with more than 100 stolen bases. He undoubtedly could have stolen many more bases if asked.

Mickey was a football phenomenon, once scoring four touchdowns of 80, 75, 45, and 20 yards in a single game. He was a basketball phenomenon, the best player on his high school team. He had world-class speed. He was impossibly strong.

The point: It seems more than possible that he would have turned into a great ballplayer even with a father who stayed back and just cheered from the little wooden bleachers by the fields.

But Mickey himself never thought so.

"My father is the only reason I became a ballplayer," he would say.

He became a ballplayer. The Yankees signed him with some fanfare. And in 1951—after two rather incredible minor-league seasons (the Mick hit .383 in Joplin, Missouri, with 26 home runs in 1950)—Mantle came to Yankees spring training as the next Yankees star. The team was so sure about it that they gave him uniform No. 6, to put him next in line in Yankee royalty.

Uniform No. 3: Babe Ruth

Uniform No. 4: Lou Gehrig

Uniform No. 5: Joe DiMaggio

Uniform No. 6: Mickey Mantle

Sportswriters loved the Mick right away. What a story! They kept finding new and ever-more-glowing ways to celebrate Mantle's talent. He was "the fabulous kid," the "eye-popping Oklahoman," "the infant phenom," "Miraculous Mantle," the "Colossal Kid," "the next Mel Ott," and, most directly, "the Future of Baseball."

This is what Mutt had prepared him for all his life, and Mickey hit right through the pressure. That spring, he hit .400 and cracked nine home runs. Yankees manager Casey Stengel said, "He should lead the league in everything."

He made the club. How could they leave him off? And after the season began, he kept on hitting. He crushed a 440-foot home run at Comiskey Park. He scored three runs and drove in four against Bob Lemon and Cleveland. He was still hitting .300 on May 22.

It's hard to say exactly when things started going south. It wasn't one thing. There was no obvious slump. He just began to lose confidence. He went a month without homering. He began to strike out more. He felt isolated, alone, particularly because the great Joe DiMaggio was so cold toward him. The draft board rejected him because of a bone disease, but people still called him a draft dodger. For a few weeks, there were rumors that he would get sent down. The newspaper reporters who had so loved him took cheap shots. "The next DiMaggio," one wrote bitingly, "struck out on three pitches."

"He is lacking a bit," Stengel admitted. Stengel adored the kid and didn't want to send him to the minors. He fought it for as long as he could, but on July 13, Mantle struck out three times and made a poor throw home and Stengel benched him.

"There is a possibility," the New York *Daily News* wrote with perhaps too celebratory a tone, "that the front office will send him to Kansas City at long last."

And so they did, the very next day. Mantle fought tears when he heard the news.

"He'll be back," Stengel assured reporters. "And he'll be a great ballplayer."

Mantle was not so sure.

Mickey Mantle told the story this way: He went to Kansas City and went 1-for-22—his one hit was a bunt—and he was so beaten down that he told his father he was quitting baseball.

The truth—as truth tends to be—is tougher to get at. Mantle did not go 1-for-22. He did start out 3-for-18, but he quickly turned himself around and started mashing baseballs all over the place, including one game where he went 5-for-5 with a single, double, triple, and two home runs. It's unclear when he met with his father. According to one story, it was July 22 before Mickey's first home game with the Kansas City Blues. According to another, it was quite a bit later, August 11, on the day that was supposed to be "Father-Son Day" at Kansas City Municipal Stadium (the game was rained out).

Whatever the case, it seems that Mickey did turn to his father back in the hotel after the game and say, "I can't take it anymore. I'm going to quit."

"I thought he was going to give me a pep talk," Mickey would later say, which is odd because there is nothing whatsoever I can find in Mutt Mantle's life to suggest he was the pep talk kind of dad. This was also at a time when Mutt Mantle had to be in great pain. He was dying of cancer.

As best we can reconstruct the scene, Mutt never raised his voice. He might have even nodded as his son spoke. And then he began grabbing Mickey's clothes and throwing them into a suitcase.

"What are you doing?" Mickey asked.

"I thought I raised a man," Mutt said. "I see I raised a coward instead. You can come back to Oklahoma and work the mines with me."

"No, wait a minute," Mickey said.

"Bullshit. You come and work the mines with me. I didn't raise a man. I raised a baby."

Mantle would say that both men were crying at this point.

And then Mutt Mantle just left. On the way out the door, he said, "If you can't play, get a bus and come home."

"It was as though," Mickey would say, "Mutt had leveled a double-barreled shotgun at my head."

Mickey stayed in Kansas City, of course, and he was back in the big leagues by late August. He hit .267 for the season and then got just seven plate appearances in the World Series before getting hurt—this was when he gave way at the last possible second on a fly ball hit between him and DiMaggio. Mutt was there for the game—it was the last game Mutt Mantle saw his son play—and he personally took Mickey to the hospital. Mickey's knee was never the same. Mutt Mantle died seven months later.

Many years later, when Mickey Mantle was at the Betty Ford Center trying to deal with his alcoholism, they asked him to write what they call a "grief letter" to his father. He told *Sports Illustrated* that in the letter he apologized to his father for not living up to expectations. He wrote about his desperate wish that Mutt could have seen him become a star. He wrote about his four sons.

And, yes, he wrote, "I love you, Dad."

But to close friends—according to Jane Leavy's seminal biography—the Mick explained that he also wrote about the pain of expectations, and how he wanted Mutt to stop running his life, and how much better off he would have been had he not tried to be all that Mutt Mantle wanted him to be.

When I was 20 years old, I sat next to Mickey Mantle in a baseball dugout. He was in Salisbury, North Carolina, for a celebrity baseball game arranged by Costas, and I was there to write about the game and him. It was the first big assignment of my life. I was deeply nervous.

And as I sat next to him, he was slouched over, his eyes half-open, and he so clearly did not want to talk, which was good because I had no idea what to ask him. We just sat there next to each other for 10 minutes, 15 minutes, 20 minutes, in complete silence. I kept looking over at him, this Great American Hero, and he looked so old, so tired, so beaten by life. I was just a kid with the hope of being an actual writer someday, and I remember wishing I had the words to capture all of him, all those home runs, all those great catches, all those World Series moments, all the pain he endured, all the blurry nights that wrecked him.

But I didn't. And I still don't. Life is so much more complicated than it should be. I just sat there silently until finally he stood up and limped away.

No. 10 Satchel Paige

L et's take a moment at the start to appreciate the sheer unlikeliness, the fantastic improbability, the pure impossibility of Satchel Paige. He is not like any other ballplayer, not even Babe Ruth. He is closer to the American folk heroes, fictional and non, closer to Johnny Appleseed and Harry Houdini and Marilyn Monroe and Casey Jones and Muhammad Ali and Paul Bunyan and Calamity Jane and Huck Finn.

"I want," Paige said not long before his death, "to be the onliest man in the United States that nobody knows nothin' about."

Ol' Satch became just that, if you follow the syntax: a man that nobody knew nothing about or, more directly, a man that everybody knew something about. He made himself a star.

Now: Think of the dizzying odds against that happening.

Leroy Page (the *i* in the middle of Paige was later added by his parents to, in Satchel's words, "make themselves sound more high-tone") was born in some unknown year, perhaps 1906, in the Deep South. What chance did he have then?

He grew up in "Mobile, Alabama, hiding from truant officers and cops, from reform school." He barely knew his father. He had so many brothers and sisters (10 in total) that he would often say he didn't even know all their names. He chose to become a baseball player at a time when the very idea of African Americans playing in the major leagues was a million miles away. He started in the Negro Leagues at a time when that was a sure way to become invisible to the American public.

But Satchel Paige—he couldn't be invisible. It wasn't in his nature.

He was first called Satchel at age seven or so. His mother had put him to work at the train depot, where he could pull in a few coins carrying around people's satchels and bags. He realized that he could make more money by carrying more bags at once so he fashioned a contraption using a pole and some rope and it allowed him to carry three or four bags at a time. Paige was always mechanically inclined like that.

"You look like a satchel tree," one of the other boys yelled, and then they were all yelling it, and that became his name.

Satchel Paige told a lot of charming stories like that. He romanticized his childhood for the laughs; that was his natural inclination. "Laughing is a pretty sound," he once wrote. But the truth is that he felt real pain as a boy. He grew up poor. He grew up hungry. He grew up with Jim Crow and racism surrounding him, like air.

"Even if you're only seven, eight, or nine, it eats at you when you know you got nothing and can't get a dollar," he said. "The blood gets angry. You want to go somewhere, but you're just walking. You don't want to but you got to walk."

Paige didn't just walk. He threw rocks. He threw them at birds. He threw them at squirrels and rabbits. Mostly he threw rocks (or bricks) at other kids in other gangs around the neighborhood. "Rocks made a real impression on a kid's head or backside," he said.

Paige didn't throw rocks in the expectation that it would take him anywhere. He threw rocks because he was naturally good at it, and there wasn't anything else to do and, yes, the idea of inflicting pain for a young man without hope was powerful and irresistible.

"Those fights," he wrote, "helped me forget what I didn't have. They made me a big man in the neighborhood instead of just some more trash."

When he was 12 years old, Paige was caught trying to steal toy rings and gems from a store in the neighborhood. Why toy rings? Even Paige couldn't explain it. Police already knew him as a fighter and as a boy who had been skipping school for years. They showed no mercy. He was taken from his home and sent to the Industrial School for Negro Children at Mount Meigs, Alabama.

Yes, perhaps the two most celebrated legends in baseball history—Satchel Paige and Babe Ruth—both began their baseball journeys in reform school.

Paige and Ruth were naturals. Paige's rock-throwing skills transferred perfectly to the pitcher's mound. He threw hard. He threw with purpose. And—we will come back to this again and again—he had impeccable control.

"A musician is born with music," Paige said. "A pitcher is born a pitcher."

At reform school, a coach, Edward Byrd, offered a few adjustments to Paige's pitching style. "He showed me how to kick up my foot so it looked like it blacked out the sky," said Paige, and when he got out of reform school at age 17, he was already a great pitcher. He immediately tried out for a semipro black team, the Mobile Tigers, and he threw astoundingly hard. This led to one of the greatest exchanges in baseball history.

"Do you throw that fast consistently?" the team's manager asked.

"No, sir," Paige said. "I do it all the time."

Paige soon graduated to the Negro Leagues. He would bounce from team to team, wherever the money happened to be—and there was always money because he almost immediately became the biggest draw in black baseball. Not long after, he was getting a percentage of the gate. Much of this was due to his amazing pitching; there is every reason to believe he was the greatest pitcher on earth.

But, beyond that, Paige was a natural showman. You just had to come to the ballpark and see what he might do next. Sometimes, he would catch fly balls behind his back. On occasion, when he was feeling puckish, he would tell his outfielders to sit down because he was just going to strike out this sucker anyway. Sometimes he would purposely load the bases and then strike out the next three batters, just to give the fans a thrill.

He guaranteed to strike out the first six or first nine or first 12 batters he faced. The first time he made the guarantee, it was in Birmingham. He announced that he would strike out the first six, and there was much shouting and abuse from the Birmingham Barons' bench. But after he struck out the first five—while the crowd lost their minds—the Barons players stood up in unison and waved their white towels in surrender.

Ol' Satch took pity on them and let the sixth guy pop out.

So many stories. We can't get to them all. You might know Paige was famous for speeding. You might think it odd that the man who famously said, "Avoid running at all times," would have such a lead foot, but he loved cars, and he loved moving fast, and he was always late. The story goes that he was once flying through a small town and he was pulled over. The police officer fined him $5 on the spot. Paige gave him $10 instead.

"No, it's five dollars," the officer said.

"I'll be coming back in a few hours," Paige said.

Wait, here's another Paige story, one you might remember from the Robin Roberts chapter. Roberts faced Paige in an exhibition and, in Roberts's memory, he got a hit. Years later, when Roberts was inducted into the Hall of Fame (as a pitcher; he actually couldn't hit much), he saw Paige and reminded him of the hit.

Paige shook his head. "Roberts," he said, "at home, I have a book with the names of all the great hitters who got a hit off me."

He paused.

"You ain't in it," Paige said.

Wait, here's another. Satchel Paige was pitching in an exhibition game when he gave up a long home run to a teenaged Ralph Kiner. Paige was perplexed. He called over Buck O'Neil, who was playing first base at the time. "Who was that?" Satchel asked. O'Neil said it was a terrific high school player named Ralph Kiner—after the war, Kiner would lead the National League in home runs seven years in a row.

"You tell me the next time he comes up," Satchel said. O'Neil did, and Paige struck Kiner out on three pitches.

Wait, how about one more. A white team in his hometown of Mobile once tried to get Paige to pitch for them. Paige would pitch for white teams now and again. He periodically pitched for the House of David team—a religious commune where all the men wore long beards. Paige wore a long beard for the occasion. The difference here was that the Mobile team actually wanted Paige to wear whiteface. They offered $500.

"I think I'd have looked good in whiteface," Paige said, but he didn't do it. Why not?

"Nobody would have been fooled," Paige said. "White, black, green, yellow, orange—it don't make any difference. Only one person can pitch like me."

A few Satchel Paige quotes you can live by:

"Ain't no man can avoid being born average, but there ain't no man got to be common."

"Ya gotta keep the ball off the fat part of the bat."

"If your stomach disputes you, lie down and pacify it with cool thoughts."

"It ain't gambling if you know. It ain't bragging if you can do it."

"Ain't nothin' better in the world than baked catfish."

"Don't look back. Something might be gaining on you."

Probably the most famous Satchel Paige legend was the time he intentionally walked a batter (maybe even two batters) to face Josh Gibson with the bases loaded and the game on the line.

Buck O'Neil loved telling that story . . . and he told it this way: He said it happened during the 1942 Negro Leagues World Series. It was late in the game. Paige's Kansas City Monarchs were winning, and he called Buck over to say what he wanted to do. Buck flipped out and motioned for Monarchs manager Frank Duncan to come out.

"Frank," Buck said, "listen to what this fool wants to do."

Satchel explained that he wanted to walk two batters so that he could face Josh Gibson with the bases loaded. Duncan just nodded. He had known Satchel for almost 20 years. "Buck," he said, "you see all these people out here? They came to see Satchel pitch to Josh."

Paige walked the batters and up came the great Gibson. Apparently the two men—who had been teammates as well as rivals—had spent years preparing for this moment. On the first pitch, Paige fired his fastball over the outside corner and Gibson watched it go by for strike one.

"OK, Josh," Paige said as Buck O'Neil remembered, "now I'm gonna throw you another fastball, just about the same place. But it's gonna be a little harder than the last one."

Again, fastball, outside corner, Gibson watched it, strike two.

"Josh," Paige shouted out, "I got you oh-and-two, and in this league, I'm supposed to knock you down. But I'm not gonna throw smoke at yo yolk. I'm gonna throw a pea at your knee."

And that was one more fastball, blinding fast, and Gibson looked at it for strike three and walked quietly back to the dugout.

Paige remembered the episode a bit differently. He remembered telling Gibson before the at-bat even began that he was going to throw two sidearm fastballs at the knees on the outside corner and Gibson watched them both go by for strikes.

"Josh," Paige said, "you're too good for me to waste any pitches so I'm going to finish you off with a sidearm curve. That's your weakness." Paige threw the curve, Gibson buckled, and the ball broke over the heart of the plate for strike three.

"They had to halt play for about an hour to clear the field of straw hats," Paige said.

Are either of these versions right? Maybe not. There's a newspaper account that suggests that Paige *did* once walk a batter to face Gibson with the bases loaded, but it wasn't in the Negro Leagues World Series. The paper reported it happening in July 1942. Gibson had hit two long home runs during batting practice and told everyone that he was going to hit one off Satchel that very day. He started out 0-for-3, and in the ninth, with Paige's Monarchs leading 5–4, Satchel walked George Easterling to load the bases for Gibson.

And Gibson flew out harmlessly to center.

"I's regusted," the *Pittsburgh Press* quoted Gibson saying after that.

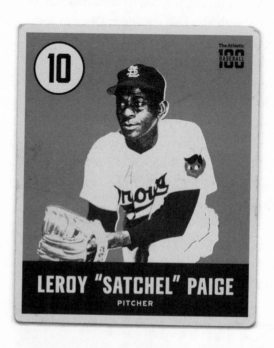

LEROY "SATCHEL" PAIGE

PITCHER

How about a few Satchel Paige quotes about age? As you might know, people always thought that Paige was lying about his age, that he was much older than he claimed. His original tombstone had a question mark where his birth year was supposed to be.

"If I've said it once, I've said it a thousand times. I'm 44 years old."

"Age is a question of mind over matter. If you don't mind, it don't matter."

"How old would you be if you didn't know how old you were?"

"If you keep moving, Old Age ain't got a chance of catching you. He moves mighty slow."

"When you come down to it, it's my fault everybody thinks I'm so old. They want me to be old. So I give 'em what they want."

"My birthday was September 18. That made me 40. Isn't that where life begins?"

"What does age matter if you can produce the goods?"

And, as long as we're offering quotes, here's what a few Hall of Famers said about Paige:

"Satchel's a better pitcher than I ever hope to be," Dizzy Dean said.

"It starts out like a baseball and when it gets to the plate, it looks like a marble," Hack Wilson said of his fastball.

"Satch was the greatest pitcher in baseball," Ted Williams said. Later, Williams took a moment in his own Hall of Fame speech to call for Paige's induction into the Hall.

"The best and fastest pitcher I've ever faced," Joe DiMaggio said.

"The best right-hander baseball has ever known," Bill Veeck said.

"In his prime," Lou Boudreau said, "he must have ranked with the Walter Johnsons, Christy Mathewsons, and Bob Fellers among the best pitchers of all time."

"Paige was the best pitcher I ever saw," Feller said.

OK, I want to get to something else, something people don't talk much about with Paige. But first, yes, we have to tell Bob Kendrick's favorite Paige story. Kendrick, who is president of the Negro Leagues Baseball Museum, first heard the story from Vin Scully, but he quickly confirmed it with the originator: Hall of Fame manager Whitey Herzog.

In 1957, Herzog and Paige were playing for the Miami Marlins Triple-A club. When the team was in Rochester, Herzog noticed a small hole in the outfield wall that looked to be almost exactly the size of a baseball. He went over to it and realized that it *was* almost exactly the size of a baseball; a baseball would *just* fit in it. So, he went to the dugout, got a bunch of baseballs, and tried throwing a ball through the hole. He never ever came close.

That's when he decided to issue the challenge to Satchel Paige. At the time, Satch was (at least) 51 years old, and though he didn't have the stuff, he still had that control. He still warmed up by throwing pitches over a chewing gum wrapper.

"Hey Satch," Herzog said, "you're always talking about how you can throw a baseball through the eye of a needle. You see that hole out there in center field? Bet you a bottle of bourbon you can't throw a ball through it."

Paige smiled. He was nobody's fool; Paige worked cons, he didn't fall for them. Robert Paige, Satchel's son, remembered a time his father gave him a lock and a bucket of keys and said, "You want to make a dollar? Go through this bucket and find the key that opens the lock."

Robert spent hours on this and finally found the key. Satchel nodded approvingly and handed over a blank piece of paper.

"What's this?" Robert asked.

"It's a piece of paper," Satchel said. "Make as many dollars as you want."

Eventually, Satchel did pay the dollar. But not until he convinced his son that he wouldn't. The point being, Satchel Paige was nobody's sucker.

"Wild Child," he asked Herzog, "is that hole big enough for a ball to fit through?"

"It's big enough," Herzog said.

"Then I'll take your bourbon," Paige said. Herzog stepped off 60 feet, 6 inches, and tried to hand Satchel a bag of baseballs. Paige shook his head. "No, Wild Child,* I don't believe I'll need all of those baseballs. I believe I'll need only three."

Paige threw the first ball, and it hit the hole, rattled around like a golf putt that seems sure to drop, and then popped out. Herzog could not be-

---

* Paige called Herzog "Wild Child." He had nicknames for everybody. He most famously called Buck O'Neil "Nancy." There's an incredible story that goes with that. I'll get to in a minute.

lieve what he just saw. On the first try, Paige had come as close as humanly possible to throwing a baseball through that hole.

Second pitch, Paige threw, and the ball whistled clean through the hole without even touching the sides.

"I'll take that," Paige said as he grabbed the bottle of bourbon and walked off.

Kendrick asked Herzog if the story was real. Herzog lit up. "Absolutely true!" he shouted.

OK, the Nancy story. Buck O'Neil told it thousands and thousands of times in his life, and there's a long version and a very long version and an even longer version than that. It only got better as he went into detail but for the sake of time, I'll give you the short, which we pick up already in progress. While playing in North Dakota, Paige had met a beautiful young woman named Nancy—Satch invited her to come see him play in Chicago. We'll let Buck take it from here:

"We're at the Evans Hotel in Chicago. Satchel and I are in the lobby, in front of a bay window, sipping on a little tea. A cab drives up, and out steps Nancy, pretty as a picture. Satchel gets the bellman and they take all her stuff up to Satchel's room. I go back to sitting at the table.

"I wasn't there 20 minutes, when another cab drives up. And out steps Lahoma . . . Lahoma was Satchel's fiancée. I said, 'Uh, oh.' I greeted Lahoma, and I said, 'So good to see you, Satchel stepped out with some reporters, but he will be back presently. Come sit down and have whatever you want.' She ordered a drink, and I excused myself for a moment and went to the bellman and said, 'Hey man, you better go upstairs and tell Satchel that Lahoma is here.' I was in the room next to Satchel, and next to me was a vacant room. I said: 'You go put Nancy in that vacant room and come back when you're done.'

"We were staying on the second floor of the Evans Hotel, so if Satchel comes down the elevator or the stairs we're going to see him. He goes down the fire escape, walks around the building, walks in the front door. And he says, 'Oh, Lahoma, what a pleasant surprise.'

"We had a good time that night. Joe Louis came by and spent some time with us. Now it's 11 o'clock, and I say, 'Well, we got a game tomorrow, better get some sleep.' But I can't sleep because I know Satchel's got to go see Nancy, give her some money so she can go home.

"After about an hour, Satchel's door opens, and I say, 'Uh huh, it's going down right now.' Satchel goes to Nancy's door and knocks lightly. He whispers, 'Nancy.' No one answers.

"He knocks a little louder—'Nancy!' No one answers.

"He knocks loud now. 'NANCY!'

"When he yelled that, Satchel's door opened. I know that has to be Lahoma, so I jump out of bed and open my door and say, 'Satchel, are you looking for me?'

"And without missing a beat he says: 'Yes, Nancy, what time is the game tomorrow?'

"And I've been Nancy ever since."

Here we go: Let's talk about something else, something people sometimes miss. Let's talk about *why* Satchel Paige was such a great pitcher. You know the stories. You know the legends. You might know some of the numbers—Paige estimated that he pitched in 2,600 games in his career, threw 300 shutouts, and pitched 55 no-hitters (his Hall of Fame plaque modestly states that he won "hundreds of games").

But what made him so great on the mound? Paige was a showman, sure, a philosopher, yes, a comedian and a pioneer and a folk hero. But he was, at heart, a very serious pitcher.

"I never joked when I was pitching," he said. "Between pitches, OK. But that ball I threw was thoughtful stuff."

He began as the purest of power pitchers. He didn't even have a curveball in those days. Paige had a funny way of explaining the curveball: "A curveball is throwed with spin. And the spin does somethin' to the air which makes the air get mad at the ball and push it away and that's a curve."

The young Paige didn't feel the need to anger up the air. "If you have a real fastball," he said, "that's all you need."

How hard did he throw in his prime? Kiner said he didn't throw quite as hard as Feller, the hardest thrower in the major leagues, but he threw plenty hard and because he threw "kind of sidearm," the ball had serious movement. But it's important to remember that by the time Kiner stepped up, Paige was already in his mid-30s and had dealt with some arm trouble.

I imagine in his heyday Paige hit triple digits with his fastball.

But it wasn't the pure speed that made that fastball so unhittable. It was the control. It was the command. He would throw that fastball low and away, that outside corner that Ted Williams always said turned .300 hitters into .230 hitters.

"Nobody," Paige said, "likes the ball low and away."

Satchel didn't just hit that corner consistently; he hit it all the time. "He threw the ball as far from the bat and as close to the plate as possible," Casey Stengel once said.

Then, when he got two strikes on a hitter, Paige liked to throw his "be ball." He called it his "be ball" because "it be where I want it to be," which was up and in. The be ball surely hopped over more bats than any pitch in baseball history, even more than Nolan Ryan's rising fastball.

Paige's control was so reliable that he could waste pitches all the time in an effort to get hitters to chase. It never bothered him to get three balls on a batter. The way he figured it, "When I got three-and-two on a batter, I ain't in the hole. The batter is. He knows the next one is gonna get a piece of the plate, and he's gotta swing.

"Now, I ain't braggin' about my control," he would add. "It ain't my fault I have it."

Later, when the fastball slowed some, Paige did add a curveball. He added a lot of pitches and he gave a name to every one of them. "I got bloopers, loopers and droopers. I got a jump ball, a be ball, a screwball, a wobbly ball, a whipsy-dipsy-do, a hurry-up ball, a nothin' ball and a bat dodger." He also had the midnight crawler, the midnight rider, the trouble ball, Long Tom, and his famous hesitation pitch, where he would stop his windup in the middle, hold it for an instant, and then throw. He said he learned that when throwing bricks as a child.

But, really, you got the sense that he was putting people on with half of that stuff. Yes, Paige changed arm angles and attacked hitters' weaknesses and messed around with some different grips. But to the end, Satchel Paige threw a fastball, and he threw it just where he wanted, and a pitcher can get a lot of outs doing just that.

In 1965—at age 58 (at least; the papers called him 60 years old)—Satchel Paige pitched one last time in the major leagues. You know, Paige had a pretty successful big-league career even if he didn't get there until he was 41 (at least). He posted a career 124 ERA+. He was 10 Wins Above Replacement.

To give you an idea of how good that is, he ranks eighth all-time in WAR after age 41, ahead of many other celebrated old pitchers including Jamie Moyer, Warren Spahn, Gaylord Perry, and Grover Cleveland Alexander.

How good must the young Satchel Paige have been?

His last game was a publicity stunt. Paige knew it. "I'm a gimmick," he said. Kansas City A's owner Charlie Finley was looking for a big gate at the end of another dismal season, and most people were not impressed—there were fewer than 10,000 people at the ballpark in Kansas City that day. A rocking chair was set up for Paige and there was a woman dressed as a nurse who stood by him as he rocked.

Paige never minded a little showmanship. And he felt like he had a surprise left for people. "I got my fastball and my famous hesitation pitch," he said. "I can go three innings for sure. I got as good a chance as any of those young boys out there."

He did just that. He pitched three scoreless innings, allowing one hit, a double off the center-field wall. Here's a good bar bet: Who got the one hit in Satchel Paige's last big-league game? It was Carl Yastrzemski, who celebrated after the game by hugging Paige tight.

"I don't know how old he is," Yaz said. "But that man can still pitch."

Paige retired the last seven batters he faced that day, even striking out opposing pitcher Bill Monbouquette. Sure, there have been those who said that the Red Sox backed off out of respect for Paige, but the Red Sox never said that. Young Tony Conigliaro had bragged before the game that he would smash a hit off Paige and tell his grandkids about it. Instead, he lifted a harmless fly ball to left. (Later in the game, against John Wyatt, he hit an inside-the-park home run.) Monbouquette estimated afterward that Paige was still throwing 88 mph.

And, yes, he was still putting the ball wherever he wanted. In his last game, Satchel Paige didn't walk anybody.

"How do you do it?" he was asked many times, and he always shrugged. Of all the extraordinary things he did in his life, working up through poverty and racism and becoming a legend, throwing strikes seemed like the easiest part of all.

"Home plate don't move," he said.

No. 9 **Stan Musial**

"He was born under a lucky star. He'd play poker and draw inside straights."

—Tim McCarver on Stan Musial

On May 6, 1938, Stan Musial—a 17-year-old boy with big dreams—skipped school for perhaps the only time in his life. Stash, as his family and friends called him, was not the sort to skip school or do any sort of irresponsible things; it just wasn't in his nature. But that day, the young sports editor of the *Donora Herald*, a guy named Johnny Bunardzya, offered to take Musial to his first big-league ballgame, Pirates versus Giants at Forbes Field. And Stash couldn't resist.

Musial had almost attended a game in Pittsburgh three years earlier. Braves versus Pirates. He was so excited: A 40-year-old Babe Ruth was playing for the Braves! Pittsburgh was only about 28 miles away from Musial's hometown of Donora, and he saved up enough money for a bus ticket and a game ticket. He even thought he'd have a bit left over to buy a hot dog and a souvenir of some kind. But then, being Stan Musial, he lent the money to a buddy, and the guy didn't pay him back in time, and Musial had to cancel at the last minute. It broke his heart.

Then Babe Ruth hit three home runs in what turned out to be his final week in baseball.

Musial would never forgive himself for missing that game.

But there was another reason Musial was so excited about going to see his first game: He was about to become a ballplayer himself! Almost nobody knew it—even the reporter Bunardzya didn't know it—but Stash had spent the previous year setting the stage for a baseball life. The baseball part of that, interestingly enough, was the easy part. Teams came after him. Cleveland. New York. St. Louis. Musial showed promise as a ballplayer. In those days, he was a pitcher, and he had a rocket left arm, and he dreamed about being like his hero, Lefty Grove.

He could hit a little bit, too.

The Cardinals showed the most interest. They came to see him and asked if he wanted to become a ballplayer. He most definitely did . . . but, he told them, he could not become one because of his father.

Lukasz Musial had emigrated to America from Galicia in what is now Poland when he was 19 years old. Lukasz, like millions of others in Eastern Europe, had come to America in search of freedom and hope and a dream. He landed at Ellis Island and chased after work until finally settling in Donora, where he labored for $4 a day at the U.S. Steel Zinc Works factory.

Lukasz was not opposed to baseball. Far from it. He loved watching his son play. He developed a personal attachment to Babe Ruth and often told his son stories about the big man.

But Lukasz was vehemently opposed to his oldest son working in the mines.

What does one have to do with the other? Well, baseball as a career frightened Lukasz. He knew that Stash was good at this game, but good enough? What if he wasn't? What if he got hurt? What if he wasn't given a fair shot? Lukasz could not get that image out of his head, that image of his son back in Donora, heartbroken, working until bone-tired, slowly dying the way that he was slowly dying under the factory's black smoke. No, that was no life for his Stash; baseball was too much of a risk. Lukasz wanted his son to go to college and make something of himself.

Yes, he also knew that Stan had not shown an abundance of promise as a student. He got strictly Cs and had not gotten an A since his junior high electrical shop class—but he was a good boy and, Lukasz hoped, a late bloomer.

The Cardinals tried to talk Lukasz into letting the boy sign. No dice. Stan tried to talk his father into letting him sign. No dice. Stan was devastated, but he was also not going to defy his father's wishes. That, too, was not in his nature. The closest thing to rebellious he'd ever been was as a small boy whenever Lukasz and his mother, Mary, were about to paddle him. He threatened to hold his breath until he died. He must have made a compelling case because he escaped the spanking.

He was ready to go to college. But the Cardinals made one more attempt—their last try. Lukasz said no again, and Stan, realizing that his baseball dream was over, broke down in tears. That's when Mary stepped in and put an arm around her son.

"Lukasz," she suddenly said with some force in her voice, "why did you come to America?"

"Why?" Lukasz said. "Because it's a free country!"

"That's right," Mary said. "It's a free country. In America, a boy is free to not go to college, too."

Lukasz knew when he was beaten. He signed the contract; the Cardinals would pay the boy $65 per month. It was a pitiful amount of money, even then; Stan could make as much working at the local gas station. But this was what his boy wanted, and Lukasz knew that Mary was right: America was the place where you were free to chase dreams.

Musial had to wait an entire year—his junior year in high school—before actually getting to play pro ball. And during that year, Lukasz began having second thoughts. He persuaded Stan's high school baseball coach and his gym teacher to try to talk Stan out of playing pro ball. The gym teacher tried to convince Musial's girlfriend, Lil, to talk to him as well. (Lil refused.)

Maybe Stan had some second thoughts himself. Was baseball the responsible thing to do? He wanted to marry Lil (and he did—they were married for 70 years). He wanted to have a family. He wanted to do the right thing. Was he being selfish? Was he really good enough to make a life out of this game? What would he do if he failed?

Musial was thrilled to put all of these thoughts out of his mind as he went to his first big-league game on that May day in 1938. Bunardzya would never forget the look on Stan's face as he walked into Forbes Field for the first time, saw how green the grass looked, saw all those seats, saw some of his heroes on the field, people he'd only read about. There was the great Mel Ott playing for the Giants. There were the Waner brothers—Paul and Lloyd—playing for his beloved Pirates, as well as their manager Pie Traynor (who never scouted him; he never really forgave Traynor or the Pirates for that).

"What a beautiful park!" Musial shouted out.

The game itself was nothing special. Ott did play third, and he got two hits and a couple of RBIs. The Pirates managed to knock 14 hits off Giants starter Cliff Melton, a tough left-hander who had won 20 games as a rookie in 1937. The Giants won 11–7, though Musial would never remember the score of the game. Truth is he remembered almost nothing of the particulars.

But one thing he did remember was that after a few innings, he turned to Bunardzya.

"John," he said as seriously as he'd ever said anything, "I think I can hit big-league pitching."

Have you ever noticed how close "Musial" is to "Musical"?

Let me step out of the background for just a moment here. We are down to the final 10 now. In all, this book is about 300,000 words. That's a lot of words. When I first wrote this as a daily project, I joked that if I wasn't careful, I would pass the word count of *Moby-Dick,* which I recall being the longest book ever written when I was forced to read it in school.

Truth is, we passed *Moby-Dick* back around Rickey Henderson.

I wrote so much of this book in the late winter and spring of 2020, just as the COVID-19 pandemic began to sweep through America. There was something particularly haunting about those early months when we could no longer see family and friends, when Opening Day was canceled, when we truly wondered if life could ever return to something like normal. . . . I spent almost every hour of every day thinking about ballplayers. I read books about them. I researched them. I watched movies and documentaries about them. Mostly, I remembered them, the ones I had seen, the ones I had spoken with, the ones I had heard so much about. Every night, and this is absolutely true, scoundrels like Rogers Hornsby or nice guys like Tony Gwynn, pioneers like Jackie Robinson, or rageful geniuses like Roger Clemens would invade my dreams.

And I never got nervous writing about any of them.

But I got nervous writing about Stan Musial.

We had been connected, Stan and me. I am not entirely sure how that happened. I guess it began many years ago when I was writing a blog as sort of a side gig, and I chose to write something about how Stan Musial had never been thrown out of a game. I had met Stan just once, in Cooperstown, so my admiration for him was very much from afar. But something about that piece touched a nerve in people; I received thousands of responses—this at a time when I felt sure my blog reached only a few dozen readers. St. Louis Cardinals manager Tony La Russa printed out copies and passed them out to his entire team during spring training, and then held a discussion about it.

I was even told by a family member that the piece was read to Stan himself.

A few years later, I wrote a cover story about Musial for *Sports Illustrated*'s "Where Are They Now" special edition. I was told that it sold more newsstand copies than any other in the magazine's long and storied history.

When Musial died in January 2013, I wrote a long obituary that, once again, seemed to capture the nation's attention.

There was something about Musial, I think, that somehow brought out the best in me and my writing. I don't think this had much to do with me. I assume it was his basic goodness, his consummate brilliance as a ballplayer, his devotion to making people happy. You know, sometimes Stan Musial would walk up to a restaurant table where a family or group of friends would be celebrating something, a birthday, an anniversary, a job promotion, whatever. He would be drawn to their joy. And then he would ask someone if he could borrow a dollar bill. He would then take the dollar bill and fold it in various ways until he had transformed it into a ring.

He would then slip the ring on a fan's finger, giving them a lifetime memory.

And I thought not only about the sweetness of the gesture but of the fact that at some point Stan Musial had to teach himself how to fold a dollar bill into a ring. Why would you teach yourself such a trick unless you planned to use it to bring joy to people?

Yes, there was something about Musial that lifts the heart, and I loved writing about that as much as I loved writing itself.

But as this countdown reached No. 9, I found myself so nervous.

Why? Because I wondered: What did I have left to say about Stan the Man Musial?

And then I remembered Stan Musial's famous advice about hitting. "You wait for a strike," he said. "Then you knock the *&#%^ out of it."

In other words: Don't complicate things.

It is true that Stan Musial was never thrown out of a game. There was a game in 1954 that best tells that story. The Cardinals were playing the Cubs and Chicago took a lead. But the Cardinals came back and in the seventh inning, with Cubs lefty Paul Minner on the mound, Musial stepped in with his joyously named teammate Wally Moon on first base.

Musial promptly doubled, scoring Moon and putting himself in scoring position.

Only he didn't. The first base umpire, Lee Ballanfant, called it foul. The ball, in the eyes of pretty much everybody else at Wrigley Field, had been clearly fair. But Ballafant saw it as a foul ball and appreciative Cubs fans cheered wildly in support of Ballafant's view.

The Cardinals on the bench, as one might imagine, were not as supportive. Shortstop Solly Hemus was the first to charge the field and the first to get himself thrown out of the game. He was quickly followed by manager Eddie Stanky, who quickly and colorfully managed to get himself thrown out of the game, too. Pinch-hitter Peanuts Lowrey* charged after home plate umpire Augie Donatelli and was about to get thrown out, too. Then a slightly dazed Musial wandered over.

Musial asked Donatelli what had happened.

"Lee called it foul," Donatelli said.

"Well, there's nothing you can do about that," Musial said instantly. No

---

* I have to interrupt this to tell you that there are two great stories about how Peanuts Lowrey, a 13-year big-league player who hit .273 with more than 1,000 hits, got his nickname. One is that his grandfather once said he was "no bigger than a peanut," which is good enough. But the better story is that Lowrey, as a child, used to play as an extra in the old *Little Rascals* movie shorts. And apparently he was pretty rambunctious on the set, so the actress Thelma Todd—known as "the Ice Cream Blonde"—used to give him peanuts to quiet him down. Thelma Todd has her own incredible story; she died at 29 under mysterious circumstances. But as mentioned above, we long ago passed *Moby-Dick* in word count and have to get on with things.

complaining. No screaming. No regrets. "Stan," the umpire Tom Gorman said, "is in a class by himself."

Instead, Musial stepped back in the box and promptly rifled another double to almost the exact same spot.

Don't complicate things. Stan Musial stretched out 902 doubles and triples in his career. That's 725 doubles and 177 triples. Only Tris Speaker stretched out more combined doubles and triples, but Speaker played in a very different time. It's better to look at players over the last 100 years.

Most Combined Doubles and Triples

1. Stan Musial, 902

2. Pete Rose, 881

3. George Brett, 802

4. Paul Waner, 796

5. Craig Biggio, 723

You know what that means? It means that nobody broke out of the box harder than Stan Musial.

Don't complicate things. Musial famously had exactly the same number of hits at home as he did on the road. He had 1,815 in St. Louis and 1,815 hits out of St. Louis. It might be more a mathematical curiosity than it is an expression of Musial's particular baseball genius, but it does speak to the Man's superhuman consistency.

"I wonder if he did that on purpose," Albert Pujols once said.

Don't complicate things. Musial won three MVP awards and finished second four other times. He won seven batting titles and led the league in runs (five times), hits (six times), doubles (eight times), triples (five times), RBIs (twice), total bases (six times), and OPS (seven times).

Here's what people said about Stan.

"I could have rolled the ball up there against Musial, and he would have pulled out a golf club and hit it out," Don Newcombe said.

"I had success with Musial by throwing him my best pitch and backing up third," Carl Erskine said.

"There is only one way to pitch Musial," Leo Durocher said. "Under the plate."

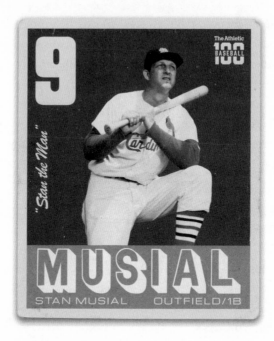

"Stan comes up to the plate and asks me how my family's making out," Joe Garagiola said. "Before I can answer him, he's on third."

One year, at the All-Star Game, American League pitchers and catchers gathered with coaches and talked about strategies for pitching each hitter in the National League. They spent an especially long time talking about Musial until Yogi Berra said disgustedly: "You guys are trying to stop Musial in 15 minutes when the National League ain't stopped him in 15 years."

Here was Stan's batting stance. How many times have people talked and written about his glorious peekaboo batting stance, the one Hall of Fame pitcher Ted Lyons always said "looked like a small boy looking around a corner to see if the cops are coming." His legs would be straight, and he would bend at the hip—his back at a 45-degree angle—and he would point the bat straight up to the sky. It looked so awkward and funny. But it only looked that way *before* the pitch was thrown. Afterward, Musial's body unfolded into a perfect hitting machine.

"Now the ball has been pitched," Branch Rickey said, "and Stanley takes his true position. He is no longer in a crouch and his bat is full back and so steady a coin wouldn't fall off the end of it. Then the proper stride and level swing. There is no hitch. He is ideal in form."

Here was Stan's harmonica. Remember how Musial is so close to "Musical"? He carried that harmonica with him everywhere and didn't need a second request to pull it out and start playing. He only knew four songs, as far as anybody knows. "Wabash Cannonball." "Take Me Out to the Ballgame." The national anthem. And "Happy Birthday." But those four songs were all he needed; they got him through every occasion.

Here was Stan's kindness. Harry Caray famously told a story about an obscenely hot St. Louis Sunday when the Cardinals played a doubleheader, and Musial played both games. Afterward, he was dead tired. He slumped over as he walked out of the park—he was barely even moving, and Caray watched him and wondered if he might just fall over. Then Musial got to his car, where 50 or 100 kids waited anxiously.

"Watch this," Caray said to the person walking with him, and just then Musial rose as if he had been inflated with air and he shouted out, "Whaddya say! Whaddya say!" And he signed every last autograph.

The kindness was always there with Musial. "Nicest man I ever met in baseball," Bob Gibson said. The Dodgers' pitcher Joe Black—one of the first African-American pitchers in the National League—said that the first time he pitched against the Cardinals, he heard racist taunts. After the game, he was sitting by his locker when he felt a hand on his shoulder. He looked up and it was Musial.

"I'm sorry that happened," Musial said. "But don't you worry about it. You're a great pitcher. You will win a lot of games."

Chuck Connors, who later became an actor and the star of the show *The Rifleman*, was briefly a big-league ballplayer. In 1951, he was playing for the Cubs and hitting so poorly that he couldn't sleep at night. He asked everyone he knew to help, but nobody knew how to help him. So he did the unthinkable: He asked Stan Musial of the rival Cardinals. And you know what Musial did? He went with Connors to the batting cage and worked with him for a half hour.

"You keep swinging," Musial said at the end as he slapped Connors on the back, and even though the batting lesson didn't save his career, Connors never forgot it.

"Stan was a better player than me," Mickey Mantle said, "because he was a better man than me."

Stan Musial and Ken Griffey Jr. are two of the greatest left-handed-hitting, left-handed-throwing outfielders in baseball history. They were both born on November 21 in Donora, Pennsylvania. Musial actually played with Griffey's grandfather in high school.

Don't complicate things. "You want to tell my story?" Musial said to me once. He smiled. "My story is easy! I'm the luckiest guy in the world."

Yes, let's go back to that quote at the top, the one from Tim McCarver: *"He was born under a lucky star. He'd play poker and draw inside straights."*

This is the thing you would hear again and again from Musial's friends: He was deeply lucky. Good things just happened to him. The world bent to his goodness. He would be the worst poker player at the table, and he'd walk away with the money. He'd hit golf shots that should have raced over the green but the ball would hit the flag stick and drop instead. In bowling alleys, the seven-pin would wiggle and fall to prevent the seven-ten split. In restaurants, he would order chocolate cake and it would be the last slice left.

There was something right about it all, something that made you think that there must be order in the universe after all. Stan Musial was not perfect. He made his mistakes like everyone else, he had his regrets like everyone else. There are surely people out there who will tell you he didn't sign an autograph for them. There are fights he wished he'd fought harder. He didn't get a hit every time.

"It's ridiculous," the announcer Bob Prince said at a dinner for Musial, "that we are gathered to honor a man who made more than 7,000 outs."

But he was a profoundly decent man. He tried to be a role model. He tried to be a hero. He tried to run out every ground ball and tried to put a smile on the face of everyone he ever met. All you can wish for someone like that is luck. And Stan Musial was lucky.

In 1962, when Musial was 41 years old, he had one final season in the sun. He had been injured and a shell of himself for three years, hitting just .273 from 1959 to 1961. He felt so bad about it that he actually demanded a pay cut. But he kept playing ball because he loved it so.

And in 1962 he was reborn—he hit .330/.416/.508, finishing third in batting and second in on-base percentage and he made his 23rd All-Star Game (the next year, his final year, he made his 24th All-Star Game but hit just .255 for the season).

But the thing he remembered most about that last great season was a game at Connie Mack Stadium in Philadelphia. He got to the ballpark, and he saw the woman who had changed his life. Helen Kloz had been the librarian at Donora High School. When his father and his coaches and a bunch of other people were trying to talk him out of playing professional baseball, Kloz told him that if he loved baseball that much, he should play baseball.

"You can't afford to lose your head," she told him, "but you can afford to follow your heart."

That line had an enormous impact on his life, and he always remembered to try to follow his heart without losing his head. After they embraced and caught up, Kloz asked him a favor, the favor everyone asks of a great ballplayer. "This is probably the last time I'll see you play, Stan," she said. "Won't you hit a home run for me?"

"By this time," Musial wrote of the moment, "home runs had become fewer and farther in between. And no one hits home runs on order, anyway, except in fiction. And to crown it all that night at Connie Mack Stadium with Miss Kloz in a box seat behind the Cardinals dugout, a strong wind blew in from right field."

No one hits home runs on order except in fiction. What a wonderful line. Leading off the second inning, facing Philadelphia rookie Paul Brown, Musial crushed a long home run for the woman who had most inspired him to play ball. That homer tied him with Ty Cobb for the all-time total-bases record (he broke the record later in that very inning with a single). Fact and fiction swirled together. And as he rounded the bases, Musial thought about Helen Kloz and how happy he was to give her this small gift, and he actually started laughing.

"I got lucky," he would say. He always did.

"How good was Stan Musial?" Vin Scully asked. "He was good enough to take your breath away."

No. 8 Ty Cobb

"On July 17, 1961, Tyrus Raymond Cobb, seventy-five, the greatest baseball player of his generation—and certainly the meanest, cruelest and richest—was put to rest in the red clay of his native state of Georgia. There were only three ballplayers on hand to pay their last respects to him. Why former catchers Mickey Cochrane and Ray Schalk and pitcher Nap Rucker bothered to show up is anybody's guess. Perhaps they wanted to make certain that Cobb was dead."

—sportswriter Ray Robinson

"Perhaps the meanest lie told about Ty Cobb is that nobody came to his funeral—or even more heartbreaking because it is more specific—that only three people did. . . . In fact, there were very few baseball players there, but that was because Charlie Cobb and her children had announced that it was a private service meant only for family and close friends. . . . It misses the phenomenon of all the little spontaneous memorial services that broke out across the country."

—author Charles Leerhsen

Ty Cobb works best as an extreme. That is to say, he seems of little use to us if he wasn't the BIGGEST RACIST IN BASEBALL HISTORY or THE MOST MISUNDERSTOOD MAN EVER TO WEAR BASEBALL SPIKES.

THE WORST PERSON IN THE HISTORY OF THE WORLD or A SYMPATHETIC FIGURE WHO NEVER OVERCAME HIS FATHER'S TRAGIC DEATH.

A HORROR MOVIE LUNATIC WHO SHARPENED HIS SPIKES TO SLASH or THE GEORGIA PEACH AND THE GREATEST BALLPLAYER OF THEM ALL.

Cobb, it seems, only makes sense to us in all capital letters.

As a ballplayer, Ty Cobb was his own species, his own category, a snarling, whirling, cunning, brilliant hit machine who won 11 or 12 batting titles back when that was more or less the only thing that mattered in baseball. He stole home 54 times in his career. Fifty-four! He retired with a .367 batting average (since adjusted to .366 after a couple of hits were found to be phantoms) and it is not just a record that will never be touched, it is an absurdity. Nobody has hit .367 in a season for 15 years.

In 2019, Christian Yelich won the National League batting title at .329. For 19 seasons, from 1909 to 1927, Cobb never hit as low as .329.

But that's not even the whole thing. From 1909 to 1919, Cobb never hit as low as .367 in a season.

He was not just the dominant ballplayer of Deadball. He was the only ballplayer of Deadball who mattered. He determined exactly how the game was to be played, how the bases were to be run, how a batter was to swing, how a ballplayer was to compete, and all anyone else could do was follow. In 1920, when the baseballs were boosted and the spitball was outlawed, a big lug named Babe Ruth took the game away from Cobb, made it more about hitting baseballs over fences. Cobb never quite forgave him (or the baseballs) for that.

"Nothing means much today," he grumbled years after he retired. "Some second-rate hinky-dinky can come up and pop a ball clear to the fence, a hit that with the old ball would have barely got out of the infield."

Cobb retired in 1928 with pretty much every baseball record that mattered. In 1955, Cobb appeared on the game show *I've Got a Secret,* and his secret that the panelists were supposed to guess was "I have the highest lifetime batting average in baseball."

"The reason it was hard to choose that one," host Garry Moore said after the panelists failed to guess the secret, "was because he also held the following records: the highest average in one American League season (.419 in 1911); most bases stolen in one season (96 in 1915); most total stolen bases (897); most seasons played in majors (24); most games played (3,034); most times at bat (11,440); most hits (4,191—with two hits later taken away); scored most runs (2,245); most years batting champion; most years hit over .300 (23, though that includes some partial seasons); most years hit over .400 (3), and that's only the beginning!"

The panelists were duly impressed. Then one of them, Bill Cullen, added, "Spiked a lot of second basemen, too!"

Cobb's game would not be easily recognized today. It was a different time, and not just because it was whites only. Every game was a day game. Travel was by train. And the game was brutal. Baseball was all about intimidation and nobody intimidated like Cobb did. He held the bat with hands apart, and he slashed at the dead ball, which was often black, torn, waterlogged from tobacco juice, and sometimes even warped.

Cobb ripped line drives and ground balls between fielders, who wore gloves not unlike the small pillows that wedding ring bearers carry, and then he ran and ran until somebody had the gall to stop him. The line about Cobb was that if you saw him racing toward second, the smart play was to throw the ball to third.

"He didn't outhit them, and he didn't outrun them," Wahoo Sam Crawford said. "He out-thought them."

There is a baseball in the Negro Leagues Baseball Museum in Kansas City that was signed by Jackie Robinson and Ty Cobb. It is a baseball oddity and a favorite of museum patrons because, of course, Cobb had long held the reputation as baseball's singular racist, surpassing even Cap Anson, who played a significant role in actually segregating the game. Cobb's racism—and general viciousness—is a subject we will dive into shortly.

But there's something oddly poetic about that baseball: The player closest to playing the way that Cobb did was probably Jackie Robinson. And vice versa. They were a pair. Each played with an inextinguishable fire. Each ran the bases with a daring that startled and awed the players of their day. Each had an athletic genius that eluded others. Each was driven by pain, by fury, by his own view of the world. Each received death threats. Each triumphed.

"I never thought," the tap dancer and Negro Leagues team cofounder Bill "Bojangles" Robinson said in 1947, "I'd live to see Ty Cobb in Technicolor."

Jackie Robinson, though, triumphed for a noble cause.

"A life is not important," he said, "except in the impact it has on other lives."

And Cobb triumphed for something else, something mysterious, something dark and harsh and bleak.

"They were all against me," Cobb said. "But I beat the bastards and left them in a ditch."

William Herschel Cobb might have invented the name "Tyrus." As Charles Leerhsen writes, Cobb named his oldest son after the ancient Phoenician city of Tyre, a city that bravely and hopelessly held out for seven months against a siege conducted by Alexander the Great. "Tyrus" did not appear on any national boy name charts until 1912, the year after Tyrus Cobb hit .419 with 148 runs, 127 RBIs, and 83 stolen bases.

The Cobbs named all their children with greatness in mind. They named their second son after John Paul Jones and their only daughter after Florence Nightingale.

William was a schoolteacher, a high school principal, a state senator, and a newspaper editor—he was called "Professor" around town. His wife, Amanda, seven years younger, was known as a great beauty who came from a notable Georgia family. She was 15 when she married William, who might have been her teacher.

Young Tyrus was a handful right from the start. He fought constantly. He raged uncontrollably. One story goes that Ty pummeled a classmate unmercifully after he misspelled a word that cost Cobb's team a spelling bee. "For decades," Leerhsen wrote in *Ty Cobb: A Terrible Beauty*, "Cobb's former neighbors . . . loved to tell how they had fought with him at various locations around town."

"My temper has always been quick," Cobb wrote of himself in 1914, "and, when younger, it got me in a lot of trouble."

Why was young Ty Cobb so restless, so angry, so possessed? Even his father did not know. "Conquer your anger and wild passions that would degrade your dignity and belittle your manhood," W.H. wrote to his son. "Cherish all the good that springs up in you. Be under the perpetual guidance of the better angel of your nature."

Ty idolized his father . . . but he struggled to find his better angels. And, because of that, he fought with his father for years. W.H. wanted his son to get an education and become a doctor. Ty wanted to play ball. W.H. wanted his son to make something of himself. Ty wanted to play ball. W.H. wanted his son to make a difference in the world. Ty wanted to play ball.*

The war between father and son went back and forth until, at age 17, Ty left home to become a ballplayer. By then, his father had accepted that his strong-willed son would not be dissuaded.

"Don't come home a failure," W.H. said.

Those words have become a dark legend because of the tragic event that soon followed, but it seems unlikely that W. H. Cobb meant them as an overarching decree. He was probably just trying to persuade his son not to quit baseball after he was released by the Augusta Tourists during the 1904 season. But William would be killed within the year, and "Don't come home a failure" became part of the pounding echo that drove Ty to baseball greatness and his place as the game's great villain.

There has long been a legend that Cobb was playing outfield in Augusta when he was called to the dugout and handed a telegram that said his father had been shot dead and his mother had pulled the trigger. That part of him being in the outfield probably isn't true. But it is true that on August 8, 1905, at 11 p.m., W. H. Cobb unexpectedly returned home. He had told Amanda and others that he was either going on a work trip or heading to the family farm for the night.

W. H. Cobb did not come through the front door, however, but instead went around the side of the house near the window. It has long been believed that he suspected Amanda of having an affair and was trying to catch her in the act. Amanda shot him twice, once in the abdomen and once in the head. She would say that she believed him to be a burglar. W.H. was, in the words of the *Atlanta Constitution*, "totally unconscious until his death."

---

* W.H. had been the first member of the family to graduate from college when he got a bachelor of arts in liberal arts from North Georgia Agricultural College. Ty was six years old and at the commencement.

People still argue about exactly what happened that night. Leerhsen, in his biography, makes the case that W.H. might not have been spying. For the story of Ty Cobb, though, the details don't matter much. His mother killed his father, and he was 18 years old and a ballplayer—"a crack outfielder and a sure hitter," the *Constitution* had called him just six days before the shooting.

Life came fast after that. Three weeks after the shooting, Cobb was in Detroit wearing a Tigers uniform for the very first time. A couple of days after that, he played in his first game and doubled in his first big-league at-bat.

Then Amanda Cobb was arrested for manslaughter. Then Cobb hit .238 in 41 games, the only time in his career he failed to hit .300. Then the court trial for Amanda began. Then Ty showed up for spring training and was cruelly hazed by Tigers players. "It was the most miserable and humiliating experience I've ever been through," Cobb would write. Teammates prevented him from taking batting practice. They sawed his bats into pieces. They stole his uniform and tied his clothes in knots. They locked him out of the hotel bathroom. They beat him up regularly.

Later, Sam Crawford would say that the treatment wasn't all that bad and that Cobb took it the wrong way. "Every rookie gets a little hazing, but most of them just take it and laugh," Crawford said. But Crawford was certainly underselling what happened and, anyway, Cobb wasn't every rookie. He was a deeply sensitive, fiercely proud, easily offended, volatile creature of rage—"I have never been able to see the humorous side of baseball," he admitted—and he was still processing a tragedy that would wreck anyone. In the middle of the 1906 season, Cobb left the team. It's almost certain he had suffered a nervous breakdown.

When he returned, he went to war with the whole world.

Ty Cobb was a ruthless, contentious, unreasonable, unyielding son of a gun. Of this, there can be no doubts.

"He would climb a mountain," the writer Bugs Baer said, "just to take a punch at an echo."

"He was possessed by the Furies," wrote another sportswriter, Bozeman Bulger.

"Cobb is a prick," Babe Ruth said. "But he sure can hit. God Almighty, that man can hit."

"Let him sleep; if you get him riled up he will annihilate us," Connie Mack said.

"When he's at bat, you can hear him gritting his teeth," Rebel Oakes said.

"The greatest of all ballplayers," Ernest Hemingway called him in a letter to Lillian Ross. "And an absolute shit."

"Ty Cobb wanted to play," Shoeless Joe Jackson's character says in the movie *Field of Dreams*. "But none of us could stand the son of a bitch when we were alive so we told him to stick it."

There was the time he slashed Home Run Baker when sliding into third and received death threats over it. "I would not have him on my team for nothing," Mack said of Cobb after that game, and American League president Ban Johnson wrote a letter telling Cobb to knock it off or he would have to quit the game.

There was the time he got into a fight with a black groundskeeper (and possibly the groundskeeper's wife) in Augusta, and another time in Boston he got into a fight with a black street worker who asked him to walk around wet cement (Cobb settled with him for $75), and the time he was arrested for assaulting a hotel bellboy in Cleveland (it has been reported countless times that the bellboy was black but Leerhsen rightly pointed out that there is no proof of this and it's more likely the bellboy was white).

Most famously there was the time in New York when he jumped into the stands and assaulted a disabled fan named Claude Lueker (Leerhsen says the man's name was actually "Lucker" but he was been called "Lueker" by everyone else, including Cobb, so we will use that spelling). Lueker had been berating Cobb for years and was particularly vicious that day. In Cobb's version of the story, Lueker called him the N-word, and at that point, his teammate Sam Crawford told Cobb he had to fight.

"If you don't do something about that guy," Cobb recalled Wahoo Sam saying, "you're a gutless no-good."

Cobb probably didn't need the encouragement. But he took it. And he went into the stands.

"The next thing I remember," Cobb said, "they were pulling me off of him."

It turned out that Lueker was missing his right hand and three fingers from his left hand after a printing press accident. "I don't care if he has no feet," Cobb reportedly yelled as he beat the man senseless. Lueker said,

"He hit me in the face with his fist, knocked me down, jumped on me, kicked me, spiked me and booted me behind the ear."

Cobb felt no guilt about it at all. "I'm pleased to note," he wrote in his autobiography, "that I didn't overlook any important punitive measures."

There are more stories, lots more. His wife divorced him on the grounds of "cruel treatment." Johnson tried to throw him out of the sport for betting on a game his team purposely lost. Other players hated him so much that in 1910, the St. Louis Browns tried to swing the batting race to Napoleon Lajoie; lots more on that in the Lajoie chapter. His alcoholism grew so bad at the end of his life that even his friend and lifelong defender, sportswriter Furman Bisher, said, "He lost his mind."

For 50 or so years, this was more or less the only story anyone told about Ty Cobb. Yes, he was a great ballplayer. But, more than that, he was mean. He was cruel. He was a racist. He sharpened his spikes and slashed for extra bases. He probably physically abused his wife. He would punch any black man who dared speak to him without what he deemed the proper respect. He might even have been a murderer.

The last of those comes from Cobb's biographer Al Stump, who wrote (not in Cobb's autobiography but in a later, more critical book called *Cobb: A Biography*) that Cobb claimed to have pistol-whipped to death a man who had tried to mug him. Whether Cobb actually claimed to do that, we will never know for sure, but we do know—thanks to the thorough research of a former prosecutor and baseball fan named Doug Roberts—that Cobb absolutely did not kill any muggers in Detroit on the day in question.

It didn't matter. People believed it. People would believe anything evil about Cobb. Exaggeration was Cobb's curse, and over the years he grew more brutal, more homicidal, more cold-blooded, more racist, more heartless in every telling. This probably peaked in 1994 with the movie *Cobb*, starring Tommy Lee Jones, a movie that painted Cobb as such an evil cartoon character that even baseball people eager to despise him felt a bit sheepish about it.

That's when the backlash began. In Cobb's hometown of Royston, Georgia—where Cobb built the city's first hospital—they opened up the Ty Cobb Museum to "show the other side of Cobb." The museum still exists and there they talk about Cobb's quiet generosity (he supported several down-on-their-luck players), the fact that he did have quite a few friends in the game, the many stories that show his humanity.

Others have followed, writing stories trying to correct the record on Cobb. For instance, the Cobb "sharpening of the spikes" stories are undoubtedly overblown and perhaps entirely fictitious (Nap Lajoie, a beloved figure, was a player who actually *did* sharpen his spikes). People also brought some counterweight to all of those stories of Cobb's fighting. For example, the story of Cobb assaulting that fan was usually told without pointing out that when Cobb was suspended, his teammates—who we are repeatedly told hated him—went on the first players' strike on his behalf.

Then in 2015, Leerhsen wrote a book that challenged more or less every negative thing that anyone has ever said or written about Cobb. It's a fascinating and valuable book that has flipped the way many people look at Cobb. In Leerhsen's book, the true villain of the story is not Cobb but Al Stump. Ironically, Cobb had brought on Stump to write a biography that would correct the record. "The fights and feuds I was in have steadily slanted to put me in the wrong," Cobb wrote in the introduction to his autobiography. "My critics have had their innings. I will have mine now."

But he did not. Leerhsen insists Stump repeatedly and cruelly made up almost everything in an attempt to cash in on Cobb's name and get revenge for some perceived slights.

And so where are we now? Can we find the real Ty Cobb somehow after all these years? It's not that easy. As important and beneficial as Leerhsen's book has been in halting the Cobb runaway train, I believe it goes to some difficult-to-believe extremes to clear Cobb of being some things that he undoubtedly was—a bully, a manic competitor, a deeply unpopular player, a violent man who often teetered on the edge, an alcoholic, and, yes, surely, a racist. It was on Cobb's racism that Leerhsen was, in my view, particularly unconvincing. "Yes, one Cobb biographer—sportswriter Al Stump, Cobbs ghostwriter for his final autobiography—exaggerated Cobb's racism," writes Steven Elliott Tripp, author of the excellent book *Ty Cobb: Baseball and American Manhood*. "And yes, some subsequent Cobb biographies unwittingly repeated some of Stump's fraudulent claims.

"But it does not follow that all accounts of Cobb's racism are false. In trying to debunk Stump and restore Cobb's reputation, Leehrsen pushes back too far."

I think Leehrsen's efforts are unquestionably valuable in that they show Cobb's racism was of his own design and, so, not as easy to pin down as many might think. He grew up in a family of abolitionists, at least on his father's side (his mother's side was staunchly pro-Confederacy; his grandfather Caleb Chitwood served as a captain in the Confederate army). His great-grandfather William was a preacher who was run out of Haywood County, North Carolina, for repeatedly preaching against slavery. His grandfather Johnny was a Republican who tried to stay out of the Civil War because of his objections to slavery. His father, as a state senator, wrote, "History teaches us that three systems of controlling the people have been tried: slavery, serfdom, and education, and the first two have been dismal failures."

Ty Cobb himself did throw out first pitches at Negro Leagues games (though, notably, he only played in one exhibition game against African-American players, when he was 24 years old, and never did again). He also, late in life, praised Willie Mays and Henry Aaron, and in 1952, as Leerhsen points out, he came out for integration in baseball: "I see no reason in the world why we shouldn't compete with colored athletes as long as they conduct themselves with politeness and gentility." He went on to say that white players should also conduct themselves the same way, which is kind of funny since politeness and gentility were hardly in his toolbox.

Anyway, it seems to me, it's easy to make too much of this. This was 1952. Jackie Robinson had been in the major leagues for five years, and Cobb had been notably silent on integration that entire time. Roy Campanella had just won the MVP award. America had seen Willie Mays. There was no going back by that point. Beyond that, Cobb's statement doesn't really contradict the way he lived his life. He certainly did not see himself as a racist and fought back against such charges by pointing out that he understood the black man in a way that many others could not because he had grown up with a "Negro mammy," and had "lived most peaceably with colored folk for years."

It was true—Cobb was kind to some African Americans. But, as Tripp explains, the one thing they all had in common was that they were, in Cobb's view, respectful of their place in society . . . and even more to the point, properly respectful and servile to Cobb himself.

"Cobb could be downright brutal toward African Americans who refused to conform to his preconceptions of how a black person ought to behave," Tripp wrote. "It did not happen often, but on occasion, he violently assaulted blacks who failed to show him the deference and honor he believed a black man or woman should always show a white man."

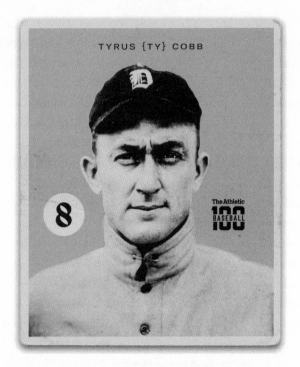

Whatever we may think of Leehrsen's perspective, he unquestionably brought much-needed balance to the story of Ty Cobb.

The only trouble is: Does anyone want balance in Ty Cobb's story?

Cobb played his last game on September 29, 1947. He was 60 years old at the time; he played in an Old-Timers' Game at Yankee Stadium. Cobb was still somewhat in the public eye. He was often quoted by newspaper reporters who wanted to know why Ted Williams couldn't hit .400 every year ("He waits too long for a good pitch," Cobb said) or what Cobb would hit in modern baseball ("About .300," he said, "but you've got to remember I'm 73 years old").

Nobody had any confusion about who Ty Cobb was then. He was the fiercest competitor the game had ever known. He was the greatest pure hitter the game had ever known. He was a cookie full of arsenic, like the quote from *Sweet Smell of Success*. And if it's true that a whole lot of people didn't like him—and it absolutely was true—then Cobb's response seemed to be the same as Mr. Potter from *It's a Wonderful Life*: "I don't like them either so that makes it all even."

"When my toes were stepped on," Cobb said, "I stepped right back."

When asked by his friend, sportswriter Grantland Rice, if he missed playing baseball, Cobb insisted that he did not. "I've almost felt like a prisoner who was set free," he said. "Baseball to me was more work than play. In fact, it was all work."

Only once in that rather extraordinary interview did Cobb sound at all like someone who loved baseball. He remembered a game from 1907, when he was just 20 years old. The Tigers were playing Philadelphia, and the Athletics led by two runs in the bottom of the ninth. There were two outs. Cobb came up with a man on against the great Rube Waddell, who had been pitching in the big leagues since Cobb was a boy.

Cobb hit a two-run homer to tie the game.

He sounded genuinely thrilled reliving that hit. And for a moment you could see him as he was then; young, hungry, still a little unsure, ready to show the whole world what Ty Cobb could do. Nobody had ever played the game quite like Cobb. And nobody ever will again.

"To see him," George Sisler famously said, "was to remember him forever."

All of this brings us to the end, his last time up in that Old-Timers' Game in 1947. When he stepped to the plate, he turned back to catcher Wally Schang and said, "Would you mind backing up a step? I'm an old man now, and I can barely hold on to this bat. I am worried I will hit you with it."

Schang had played against Cobb countless times through the years and had great respect for him. "Cobb never cut me up," he said. "He was too pretty a slider to hurt anyone who put the ball on him right."

Schang took a step back as Cobb had requested. It was the least he could do for a legend.

And, at age 60, Ty Cobb promptly laid down a bunt and tried to beat it out. For the rest of his life, he still felt some anger because he was thrown out by a step.

No. 7 **Walter Johnson**

Now I'm in Weiser, Idaho on a wild goose chase here to look over some palooka who was burning up the Snake River Valley Semi-Pro League. Someone sent the Senators a telegram, said there was a kid, Johnson, threw so fast you couldn't see 'em, and that he knew where he was throwing it too because if he didn't, there'd be dead bodies buried at home plates all over Idaho.

I get to the field just in time to see him shamble out to the mound, all arms and legs, eyes down like he doesn't even want to be there. Then, holy smoke, 19 years old and no one in big league ball ever had a fast one like this. So I offer the kid $500 to join the Senators. You know what that hayseed said? If I promise him train fare home in case he don't make it, he'll come. I say, "Kid, a one-way ticket's all you're gonna need."

—former catcher Cliff Blankenship on
his signing of Walter Johnson

This will sound corny, absolutely, but there's something sacred about the fastball. At the heart of this American game, beneath the strategies, the analytics, the statistics, the sacrifices, the shifts, the legends, the movements, the infield fly rule, there's a player with a ball and there's a player with a bat, and they stand 60 feet, 6 inches away from each other.

The player with the ball throws it as hard as he can.

The player with the bat tries to hit it.

That is the spark of baseball, that little piece of magic that rises above and grabs the heart and gives this game something that resembles time-lessness. You don't have to understand anything about stealing signs or linear weights or launch angles or tunneling or working the count to grasp and feel awed by what my friend, director Jon Hock, calls "a primal battle between a man with a stick and a man with a rock."

And to think that the pitcher who might have fired the most mind-blowing fastball of them all was just a nice guy from Humboldt, Kansas, who threw sidearm more than 100 years ago—well, yes, it sounds corny, but that's OK because if you can't say something corny about baseball, what's the point of even caring?

There have been many, many pitchers with great fastballs. I keep an up-dated list on my computer of the 50 I believe threw the hardest fastballs of them all.

You will recognize most of the names: Rube Waddell, Smoky Joe Wood, Smokey Joe Williams, Lefty Grove, Van Lingle Mungo, Ryne Duren, Sandy Koufax, Herb Score, Sudden Sam McDowell, Goose Gos-sage, Roger Clemens, Rob Dibble, Randy Johnson, Billy Wagner, Justin Verlander, Joel Zumaya, Noah Syndergaard, Jordan Hicks, and so on.

But I believe there are seven fastball pitchers who transcended the rest, seven pitchers who blew up the conception of what a fastball looks and sounds like. These are pitchers I like to think of as "X" in the algebraic equation: "Wow, this pitcher throws even harder than X" or "Nobody ever threw harder than X."

The first of these was Amos Rusie, the Hoosier Thunderbolt, who pitched in the 1890s and inspired the famous line, "You can't hit 'em if you can't see 'em." John McGraw said that of Rusie's pitches. There are those who believe that Rusie, more than any other player of the time, was responsible for the National League moving the pitcher's box from 50 feet away to 60 feet, 6 inches. Hitters were that frightened of his fastball at such close range.

For more than 20 years after Rusie arrived, he was the standard; newspaper writers would compare other pitchers to him. The list of comparables included Waddell, George Meakim, a Yale pitcher named Carter, a Philadelphia area semipro pitcher named Stein, Harry "Beans" Keener, Pink Hawley, Archie "Lumbago" Stimmel, Doc McJames, and no, I have not made up any of these names. Each of them, the writers claimed, "has as much speed as Rusie."

None of them, obviously, did have as much speed as Rusie. It's just that they threw pretty hard and Rusie's fastball was as far as the imagination went.

Those comparisons continued until the mid-1910s, when Walter Johnson came along. He's second on the list.

Third was Bob Feller, who just showed up as a high school pitcher from little Van Meter, Iowa. How hard did Feller throw? Well, nobody in baseball history worked harder to find out. Feller's fastball had a race with a motorcycle. Feller threw his fastball through numerous contraptions. His most famous reading was 98.6 mph, which seemed perfect since 98.6 is also supposed to be the temperature of the human body.*

Satchel Paige, fourth on the list, had a mythical fastball. It wasn't just breathtakingly fast, it was also perfectly placed where Ol' Satch wanted to throw it. That combination of power and control is probably unmatched in baseball history. "I never threw an illegal pitch," Paige once said. "The trouble is, once in a while I would toss one that ain't never been seen by this generation."

Fifth on the list is a folk hero, Steve Dalkowski, who never threw a single pitch in the major leagues and, in fact, only managed to get into 15 games in Triple A. But he threw so impossibly hard that he was the inspiration for both Nuke Laloosh of *Bull Durham* and George Plimpton's April Fool's Day pitcher Sidd Finch. Dalkowski was a real-life fictional character with a lightning-bolt fastball that he could not throw for strikes. In 1960, in Class-C ball, he pitched 170 innings, struck out 262, and walked 262. People who saw the pitch said no one ever threw it faster, and the witnesses

---

* The trouble with the 98.6 mph reading is that the speed of the ball was measured at home plate. Today, radar guns detect the speed of the ball out of the pitcher's hand. In Hock's movie *Fastball*, physicists made the mathematical adjustments and determined that, by today's methods, Feller's pitch was actually an almost unfathomable 107.6 mph.

included Ted Williams, who faced Dalkowski just once in batting practice, dropped his bat, and promised that he would never face that guy again.

Sixth is Nolan Ryan. His fastball needs no introduction or explanation. Nobody will ever strike out more batters. No one will ever walk more batters either. No one will ever throw more no-hitters. In *Fastball,* physicists concluded that Ryan most likely threw the ball harder than anyone in baseball history (his renowned 100.9 mph pitch, which for years was declared the fastest pitch ever by the *Guinness Book of World Records,* was, again by today's standards, adjusted to 108.5 mph).

And, seventh, at last, is Yankees closer Aroldis Chapman, who has thrown 17 of the 20 fastest pitches ever recorded by MLB's Statcast measuring system, including the top seven. He was clocked at 105.1 mph.

We can argue forever—and with no possibility of consensus—which one really threw the ball the hardest.

But it seems to me that, pure speed aside, none of them had a fastball that was quite as revolutionary, quite as heart-stopping, quite as new as the one thrown by that 6-foot-1, 200-pound Kansan who went to high school in Southern California and was discovered in Idaho, that friendly hayseed Cliff Blankenship gave train fare to in 1908, Walter Perry Johnson.

Walter Johnson won 417 games, far and away the most in modern baseball—meaning since the American League was founded in 1901. He threw 110 shutouts, far and away the most. His 3,509 strikeouts still rank ninth all-time, even though hitters rarely struck out in his day.

His 147 career ERA+ is third all-time among starters (not including active pitchers like Clayton Kershaw and Jacob deGrom, who have a lot of career left), behind only Pedro Martínez and Grove—but Martínez pitched fewer than half the innings Johnson pitched, and Grove's raw ERA is almost a full run higher than Johnson's 2.17.

His 164.5 Baseball-Reference Wins Above Replacement ranks second in baseball history behind only Babe Ruth.

Now, it's true, you can't really compare the pitching Johnson did during Deadball—or even in those early years after Deadball—with baseball 100 years later. Different games. Different times. We have nothing at all to compare that seems in the same category as Johnson's pitching from 1910 to 1915, when he went 174-80 with a 1.51 ERA, 1,494 strikeouts, 390 walks, and 24 homers allowed in more than 2,100 innings.

In 1916, Johnson pitched 369 innings and gave up zero home runs. Zero.

There's no conversion chart that can tell us how Johnson's stuff would hold up today. All we have are the stories and the quotes—but even from those, you can understand the awe that people felt when seeing how impossibly hard Johnson threw.

"When you see the arm starting forward," Birdie McCree said, "swing."

"The thing just hissed with danger," Ty Cobb said.

"He's got a gun concealed about his person," Ring Lardner wrote, "and he shoots them."

"On a cloudy day, you couldn't see the ball half the time it came in so fast," Jimmy Austin said.

"Most of the time you couldn't see the ball," Fred Snodgrass said.

"You batted against him for the first time," Dutch Ruether said, "and that easy sweep of the arm, with a bullet coming out of it, made you blink and wonder if your eyes were failing."

"I've thought about it a lot and I've come to one inescapable conclusion," George Sisler said. "If Ol' Walter Johnson had a curve, no one ever would have gotten a hit off him. Every game he pitched would have been a no-hitter."

Yes, he was purely a fastball pitcher until his later years. And it was enough. Legends? Oh, there are plenty of Walter Johnson legends. A former big-league pitcher named Al Schacht said that Johnson threw so hard, he once got a game called for darkness in the middle of bright sunshine. How'd that happen? The Senators' regular catcher was injured, and the new catcher simply wasn't up to the moment. On the first pitch of the game, the ball ticked the top of his glove and smashed into umpire Billy Evans's shoulder. He howled in pain but after a moment or two, he was able to get back to work.

The next pitch was low, the catcher never saw it, and it smashed into Evans's left shin.

"That's it," Evans shouted out. "Game called because of darkness."

Evans himself told another story, one about a batter who faced Johnson, saw (or didn't see) two fastballs go by for strikes, and headed back to the dugout.

"You've got another strike coming," Evans shouted to the player.

"I don't want it," the hitter said. "I've seen enough."

So many stories. Johnson said he once pitched for a Negro Leagues team—he didn't know it was a Negro Leagues team until he showed up, but $800 was $800—and the first batter he faced was a great slugger called Home Run Johnson.

"Come on, Walter Johnson, let me see that fastball," Home Run shouted out as he stepped to the plate. "I'm going to hit it out." And then he *did* hit it out. Big Train was impressed by that—he often talked about how great so many of the Negro Leagues players were—but he was not impressed by the way Home Run Johnson kept jawing after hitting it. In fact, he was so angry that he did something he never did: He began throwing the ball high and inside to Johnson. This sent Johnson tumbling to the ground time and time again. Walter threw it high and inside so many times and with such speed, that the last time Home Run Johnson came up, facing no balls and two strikes, he hit the dirt before Big Train even let go of the pitch.

The ball curved over the center of the plate for strike three.

Clyde Milan, a fine center fielder who twice led the league in stolen bases, remembered an exhibition game Washington played against Boston. The first time up, Johnny Evers cracked a hit off Johnson.

Evers was famously cocky, and so when he got to second base he shouted to Milan in center field: "So that's the great Walter Johnson. Listen, we've got a half-dozen pitchers in our league who are faster than he is."

Milan relayed exactly what Evers said to Johnson, who didn't say a word. But the next time Evers came up, Johnson threw three rocket fastballs by Evers, who didn't move his bat, he was so paralyzed. "Johnny hasn't seen any of them yet," Milan said.

At the end of that inning, Evers made sure to find Milan. Evers was still pale.

"You big blabbermouth," Evers screamed. "You told Johnson what I said, didn't you?"

How fast did Johnson actually throw? Let's go down that rabbit hole for a minute, even though we can't know for sure. Johnson always said that his ability to throw hard was just natural. "From the time I held a ball, it settled in the palm of my right hand as though it belonged there," he said.

And while we can't tell you exactly how fast the ball went, we do have a clue. Johnson was the first pitcher to have his fastball's speed measured. True, it was measured by an archaic (and ingenious) apparatus developed

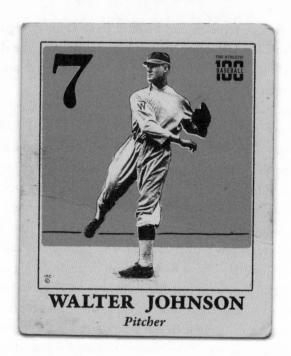

WALTER JOHNSON
Pitcher

by the Remington Arms Company. But it's still something. Remington had developed the machine to time the speed of bullets. Johnson's fastball seemed the obvious next thing.

Johnson and another pitcher, Nap Rucker, showed up in a large room at the Remington lab in Connecticut. The scientists had him stand 60 feet, 6 inches away and throw his fastball through a mesh square. The ball would brush through the mesh, triggering the clock. Then, 15 feet later, the ball would slam into a metal plate, stopping the clock. Johnson's fastball covered that distance in .1229 seconds, which means that it traveled 122 feet per second.*

This became a pretty famous measurement of the time: 122 feet per second! That's fast! As newspapers reported in the day, "The Twentieth Century Limited, flying at a mile a minute gait over the rails, makes only 88 feet per second!" He threw it faster than a train!

This was not the reason Johnson was called Big Train, by the way. We'll get to that.

---

* Rucker topped out at 113 feet per second.

What is 122 feet per second as we would understand it now?

It is 83.2 miles per hour.

It's OK to feel let down. But the story isn't over yet.

First, there's the measurement point. As mentioned above when talking about how fast Feller and Ryan really threw, the speed of today's pitchers is measured out of the hand. Feller's pitch was measured as it crossed the plate. But Johnson's pitch was measured seven and a half feet *after* it crossed the plate.

So, that requires a major adjustment. The *Fastball* physicists did the calculations and found that today Walter Johnson's pitch would actually be measured at 94 mph or so.

That's obviously very fast, though it certainly would not make anyone in today's game back away. But there's more: Johnson threw the ball with a shirt and tie on. He did not throw off of a mound. And most of all, he did not throw as hard as he could, because he was trying to guide his pitches through the target. It was an awkward thing, and it took him numerous tries to get it right.

"He didn't throw full speed or anything close," Rucker said after the experiment. "If he had, he would have thrown over 150 feet per second."

For the record, 150 feet per second is more than 102 mph. In church clothes. On flat ground.

Let's talk for a moment about the nickname: the Big Train. Few nicknames have ever fit a player better. Johnson actually had a lot of nicknames— Barney, the Coffeyville Express, the Kansas Cyclone, and, in 1907, the *Washington Post* briefly tried to call him "Jingles" because "he certainly has the bells on." Whatever that means.*

But "Big Train"—that's the nickname. It perfectly represents his fastball and his time, when a train symbolized the very pinnacle of speed and

---

* The Barney nickname comes from a time when Johnson was pulled over for speeding. He was in the car with his teammate Germany Schaefer, who said to the officer, "Don't you know who this is? Why, this is Barney Oldfield!" Barney Oldfield was the most famous race car driver of the day, a man whose name, according to the *Encyclopaedia Britannica*, "was synonymous with speed." The officer let the ballplayers go. And Walter Johnson became known as Barney.

power—you'll remember that Superman, created a decade after Johnson retired, was more powerful than a locomotive.

Here's the funny part: Walter Johnson was not the original Big Train, not even close.

No, it was a horse's nickname first.

When Johnson first got to the Washington Senators in 1907 at age 19, one of the most popular racehorses in the country was an enormous Thoroughbred named Roseben. The horse was so huge and strong that he routinely raced under monumental weight handicaps, meaning Roseben would carry 40 or 50 pounds more than the other horses. And he still won all the time, thrilling the nation.

As you guessed: Everybody called Roseben "Big Train."

So how did that nickname get passed on to Johnson? Well, it didn't at first. Other ballplayers were called Big Train before him. Sometimes, sportswriters called Christy Mathewson "Big Train." Lefty George, a large left-handed pitcher, was called "big train" for a year or so, though it was usually in lower-case letters as if he wasn't *that* big a train.

Most of all, that was the nickname for Ed Konetchy—a 6-foot-2, 200-pound first baseman who led the league in doubles and total bases in different years. Konetchy was particularly fast for a player so big, so you could see how he compared with Roseben . . . and big trains.

Best we can tell, *Washington Herald* sports editor William Peet was the first to call Johnson "Big Train," on September 6, 1913. This was after Johnson had pitched a three-hit shutout. It didn't catch on, though Peet stubbornly continued to call Johnson "Big Train" even as few others did.

No, Johnson didn't really become "Big Train," until a decade or so later, when he was nearing the end. Everybody admired Johnson by then, but until 1924 there was something important missing from his record: a championship. Johnson had played just about his whole career for bad teams. From 1907 to 1923, his teams finished an average 25 games out of first place—only once finishing within five games of the pennant.

Those Senators were famous for being "first in war, first in peace, last in the American League." And as unfair as it was, yes, this affected the way people looked at Johnson. Great pitcher? Absolutely! Nice guy? The nicest! Good fastball? The fastest! But if he was so great, why did his teams never win anything?

In 1924, finally, the Senators put together a competitive team with

Hall of Fame outfielders Sam Rice and Goose Goslin each having excellent years. Johnson was 36, and this was no longer Deadball, but he put together one more season for the ages. He won the last of his three pitcher triple crowns by leading the league in wins (23), ERA (2.72), and strikeouts (158). He also led the league in WHIP, hits per nine innings, and strikeout-to-walk ratio. The Senators won the pennant. And Johnson was named the league's MVP.

That was when everybody started calling him the Big Train. In the World Series against the Giants, he started Game 1 and was off his game. He kept getting out of jams, but the Giants got him in the 12th inning for two runs on a couple of walks and singles, and he took the loss.

He also took the loss in Game 5, giving up six runs in eight innings.

But in Game 7, on one day's rest, he came into a tie game in the ninth. He promptly gave up a triple to Frankie Frisch and it seemed like he might be the goat of the Series. But he got out of the jam, striking out future Hall of Famer High Pockets Kelly along the way.

In the 11th, he got into another situation, putting the winning run on second with one out. But he struck out Frisch and Kelly to end the threat.

He gave up a leadoff single in the 12th, too, but he got the next three batters, and the Senators scored in the bottom of the inning to take the World Series title. Walter Johnson pitched four scoreless innings when the team needed them most. That was the only World Series victory in the history of the Washington Senators, and the only title in Washington until the Nationals' win in 2019. The Big Train was finally the hero.

When Johnson died, more people talked about his decency and his kindness than his fastball. In a game where so many all-time great players are also supremely nice people—Honus Wagner, Stan Musial, Roy Campanella, Brooks Robinson, Tony Gwynn, Mike Trout, on and on—Walter Johnson might just have been the nicest of them all.

He was so nice that many people in his day saw it as his one fatal flaw. Ty Cobb used to crowd the plate against Johnson, knowing full well that he was too nice to throw at him. Babe Ruth used to talk about how he liked facing Johnson for the same reason (Ruth hit .350/.495/.675 against Johnson by the best stats we have).

"If he had been born a mean cuss and tried to dust off the hitters," Joe Sewell said, "nobody would have had a chance."

But he just couldn't be mean. It wasn't in him. He loved people, especially kids. He signed all the autographs. He talked baseball with anyone who wanted to talk baseball. He refused to question umpires. The umpire Billy Evans had another favorite Johnson story. Johnson had worked a 3-2 count against a hitter and then threw a clear strike three, but Evans called it a ball. "Sometimes," Evans would say, "we as human beings just make mistakes."

Evans felt terrible because the walk cost Johnson a couple of runs, so he gave Johnson an opportunity to complain. "How'd that one look to you, Walter?" he asked.

"Maybe a trifle low?" Johnson said kindly, and he smiled, and Evans later said, "A better man has never played the game of baseball."

Here's another one: You know the story about Wagner's refusal to appear on a tobacco card—that's why his T-206 card, the few that were printed before he made his refusal known, is the most valuable baseball card in the world.

Johnson had what might be an even more compelling story. A cigarette company offered him $10,000—more than $250,000 in today's money—to appear in an advertisement, and all he had to do was say he smoked that brand. Unfortunately, he could not do it because he did not smoke at all.

"I needed that money badly," he would say. "But I couldn't take it. I don't object to cigarette smoking. But I don't use them. And I believe it would have been worse than thievery if I had urged the kids to buy a package of my 'favorite' brand and helped to increase the habit of smoking among our youngsters."

There are countless examples. My favorite might be this: People often called Walter Johnson the "Big Swede." This was somewhat disconcerting in that Johnson was not Swedish. He had, as far as he knew, no Swedish ancestry whatsoever. And yet he accepted the nickname with the same gentle equanimity he accepted all well-intended things.

And when asked why, he simply said: "I didn't want to offend anybody. There are a lot of Swedes I know who are nice people."

No. 6 Ted Williams

Perhaps the most joyous poem about Ted Williams was written by an English poet named Wendy Cope, who, almost certainly, has never seen a baseball game in her entire life. She certainly never saw Ted Williams play. She writes for a British audience that, with rare exception, knows nothing and cares nothing about baseball.

But she wrote the poem, just the same, "The Ted Williams Villanelle"—a villanelle being an Italian song with a quick rhythm. Here is how that happy poem ends:

> *Enjoy your talents. Have your fling.*
> *The seasons change. The years advance.*
> *Watch the ball and do your thing,*
> *And don't let anybody mess with your swing.*

How did this even happen? A friend, Becki, told me about Cope's wonderful poem a few months ago—see, the poem was written for Becki's father, Ari Badaines, a clinical psychologist who grew up in the United States idolizing Williams. Badaines had been part of Cope's writing group for years and apparently he just kept nagging her with so many stories about

Williams's genius, his stubbornness, his singular focus, that eventually she wrote the poem for him.

I love so much about this. How many people have carried around the larger-than-life story of Ted Williams wherever they went? How many works of art has that story aroused? Joe DiMaggio may have inspired more songs, Sandy Koufax more bits of radio magic, Babe Ruth more biographies, Jackie Robinson more movies, and Satchel Paige more myths.

But Ted Williams inspires poetry. He inspires prose. He inspires nicknames—the Kid, the Splendid Splinter, Thumper, Teddy Ballgame. Cope's poem pulls from Williams's pure and absolute stubbornness. And what of Donald Hall's haunting "Couplet," written about Williams at an old-timers' game? A portion:

> *When the tall puffy*
> *figure wearing number*
> *nine starts*
> *late for the fly ball,*
> *laboring forward*
> *like a lame truckhorse*
> *startled by a gartersnake,*
> *—this old fellow*
> *whose body we remember*
> *as sleek and nervous*
> *as a filly's—*
> *and barely catches it*
> *in his glove's*
> *tip, we rise*
> *and applaud weeping*

The late Richard Ben Cramer wrote perhaps the best American magazine piece ever written, called "What Do You Think of Ted Williams Now?" about Williams's white-hot ambition. "Few men try for best ever," he wrote, "and Ted Williams is one of those."

Ben Bradlee Jr., in his marvelous biography *The Kid*, tried to find—in his perfectly chosen contradiction—"a man who wanted fame but not celebrity."

My friend Leigh Montville, in his equally marvelous *Ted Williams*, looked for a player and a man who was not any single adjective but was, instead, *all* the adjectives, cruel and generous, furious and jovial, aloof and friendly, cynical and naive, self-pitying and heroic. "He was a little kid," Leigh wrote. "Always. In a million ways. That was what made him fascinating."

And then there are the most famous words written about Williams, probably the most famous words ever written about any ballplayer, the words that come from his last day in the big leagues, from his last time at bat. We'll end with those words because they are probably still the closest we can get to this big, messy, brilliant, difficult, and remarkable American hero, Theodore Samuel Williams.

By the way: That's not even his real name.

Chapter 1: "There goes Ted Williams, the greatest hitter who ever lived."

No, he wasn't actually named Theodore. He was named "Teddy" after Teddy Roosevelt. The story went that Ted Williams's father, Sam, had been one of Teddy Roosevelt's Rough Riders, a story that was probably untrue—which was usually the story with Sam Williams. He was many things and nothing, Sam Williams, a soldier, pickle salesman, a photographer. Truth is, Ted barely knew his father; Sam was, most of all, an alcoholic who, in Williams's memory, rarely seemed to come around unless there might be a little money to be made in the deal.

Ted's mother, May, meanwhile, was also gone but for an entirely different purpose. She was out saving souls. She was—as Nick Davis described her in his superb PBS American Masters documentary on Williams—a foot soldier in the Salvation Army. She spent her days "bringing sunshine," according to the *San Diego Union*, and this meant feeding orphans in Tijuana and helping homeless people along the streets of San Diego and giving hope to those who had lost all faith.

Unfortunately, her sunshine did not often spread to her two sons, Teddy and Danny. Young Ted Williams—and old Ted Williams for that matter—could not understand how St. May could have so much love for all those strangers and so little leftover for her sons.

Teddy was alone, and if that created wounds inside him that never healed, it also gave him all the time he wanted to hit baseballs. He was a hitting prodigy. That is not to say he was a natural hitter—though Reds star

Joey Votto has marveled "it was like he was carved out of stone for hitting; he was made like David just for this particular endeavor"—but instead to say that like Bobby Fischer with chess or Larry Bird with basketball or Charlie Parker with the saxophone, he simply pushed all boundaries of obsession.

Ted Williams spent all of his time hitting baseballs. A few people were there to aid his obsession. A playground director named Rod Luscomb—who had played for a year with the old San Diego Aces in Class-D ball—would throw him batting practice for a few hours. A friend named Wilbert Wiley shared Williams's obsession for a time and they would take turns pitching to each other. An uncle, Saul Venzor, would throw him some pitches, too, and offer advice.

But Williams took more swings alone, in front of a mirror, in his driveway, on the playground. He was his own teacher. He would swing at baseballs that were invisible to everyone else, baseballs thrown by major-league ghosts with blinding fastballs and exploding sliders and breathtaking curves, and he would swing and swing until he hit them all because, damn it, when he walked down the street he wanted people to say those magical words: *There goes Ted Williams, the greatest hitter who ever lived.*

"Don't let anyone mess with your swing," the great hitter Lefty O'Doul said the first time he saw Williams hit, and while the Kid, as they called him, wasn't always much for taking advice, he believed in those words and held them tight for the rest of his life.

Chapter 2: .3995

Williams was manic when he first started playing pro ball. He smiled all the time, laughed all the time. He used to skip after fly balls like he was riding a horse and he would slap his own butt with his glove and shout "Hi-Ho, Silver!" Cedric Durst, his roommate with the minor-league San Diego Padres, remembered Williams once waking up at 6 a.m. and the guy just started jumping up and down on the bed shouting, "Christ, Ced, it's great to be young and full of vinegar!"

You know that expression, "Kid in a candy store?" It's usually said to suggest happiness and there's some of that, but if you've actually seen a kid in a candy store, you know they're out of control. It's all too much. They run around wildly: Wait, let's look at the chocolate, no, the tarts, no, the M&Ms, no . . .

That's how Ted Williams was when he got to the big leagues. He could hardly contain himself. He bragged repeatedly to teammates. When reporters came around—this was before his war with reporters began—he would talk about all the records he was going to set, all the batting titles he was going to win, all the home runs he was going to smash, and they loved it; they wrote it all, and he became a celebrity, something that thrilled him until he realized that with celebrity comes jealousy, and with jealousy comes cynicism, and with cynicism comes, yes, boos.

Hell hath no fury like Ted Williams getting booed.

But that's for later. At the start, he was untamed and joyful and boy, did he hit. First year, right out of the gate, he led the league in RBIs. Second year, he led the league in runs and on-base percentage. Then came the third season, the greatest season. He went into the final game hitting .3995, which, rounded up, is .400. That's how it would have been listed in the stats and on the back of baseball cards: *Ted Williams batted .400.*

And nobody had hit .400 in a decade, going back to Bill Terry in 1930. Nobody had hit .400 in the American League since Harry Heilmann in 1923 and then Ty Cobb before that. Williams wanted the number badly. This was immortality. "He'd get on the same kick every day," his teammate Charlie Wagner told Montville. " 'I'm going to hit .400! I know I can do it! I'm determined to do it!' He was obsessed with the challenge."

Williams was given the option to sit that last day and let his batting average round up to .400. He didn't take that option, something that has been celebrated throughout the years, though I must weigh in to say that part has been overcelebrated and overstated.

Of course he played. Why? He wasn't hitting .400. He was hitting .3995. Sure, it's easy to say that rounds up now but nobody saw it that way then. After he went 1-for-4 the day before, headlines like "Ted Williams Drops Below .400 Level" and "Ted Williams Down to .399" and "Williams Slumps Below Magic Mark" appeared all over the country.

If you want to properly celebrate Williams's insistence, you can celebrate that he stayed in the game even after cracking a single off Dick Fowler in the second inning. That pushed the average up to .4008, or .401 on the back of a baseball card; at that point he could have rested. But he felt great, and he knew that even if he failed to get a hit his next time up, he'd still be hitting .400. At no point for the rest of the game was he ever in danger of dropping below .400.

In fact, the next time up he homered off Fowler to make the average a solid .402, and then he singled again, this time off Porter Vaughan.

And then he singled *again* off Vaughan, 4-for-4, and his average was .405. At that point, he knew that he could go zero for his next five and still be above the .400 line. So he stayed, even played the second game, and ended up 6-for-8 on the day and finished with that familiar .406 average—the last time anyone hit .400.

He famously didn't win the MVP that year, despite hitting .400 and leading the league in homers, runs, slugging, on-base percentage, and walks. That was the season DiMaggio hit in 56 straight games and the writers gave the award to Joltin' Joe. The writers always thought Joe was the better all-around player and leader, but consider this:

DiMaggio *during* the streak: .408/.463/.717, 1.180 OPS.

Williams *all* of 1941: .406/.553/.735, 1.288 OPS.

Chapter 3: Bleeding Hands

Ted Williams fought in two wars. As Bradlee so eloquently writes, he didn't want to fight in either of them. He wanted to play ball. He lamented losing three prime years from 1943 to 1945, when he might have done things that no ballplayer had ever done. He was enraged over being recalled for service in Korea when he was in his 30s.

But he went for his country, and he flew fighter jets. How good a pilot was he? John Glenn chose Williams to be his wingman, so, yeah, that good. "He was excellent," Glenn would say.

You might have heard that Ted Williams almost died on one of his missions over Korea. It's true. As Bradlee writes it, Williams was flying over a village when his plane was hit by small arms fire. His plane was bleeding fuel, and it was flying away from safety, and the protocol was for Williams to eject. But he instantly refused that idea. He knew that if he ejected, he would probably smash his legs—he was 6-foot-4, after all—and would never be able to play baseball again. That was not an option.[*]

---

[*] Bradlee points out that it's a perfect Ted Williams thought that he was more concerned about getting hurt than getting captured. Williams later told a reporter, in his own profane way, that if he had been captured, he would have said, "I'm Ted Williams. I'm a big-deal baseball player. How may I help you?"

Williams's decision to land the plane was perilous, to say the least. His radio was out, his fuel was running dangerously low, he couldn't lower his landing gear. Behind him was a long trail of fire. Then a panel on the bottom of the aircraft just fell off; his plane was essentially a metal skeleton. There is no training for a moment like this. Williams was a lifelong atheist, but in that moment he asked God to, quote, "Save my ass."

He slammed the plane down on the runway and skidded for more than a mile. All around him were sparks and flames. He had no idea when or how the plane was going to stop, but somehow it did, right at the edge of the runway, and he got out of the plane as fast as he could, and he was shaking with fear and outrage (which for him was really one and the same). Then someone came up to him and asked him to sign a piece of paper, which he did.

"What was that?" a friend asked.

"Can you believe it?" Williams said. "That son of a bitch wanted an autograph."

Yes, Ted Williams was John Wayne—the real John Wayne, not the actor who played the role.

He was discharged on July 27, 1953, and two days later he showed up at Fenway Park to talk with Red Sox owner Tom Yawkey. At some point during the talk, Yawkey suggested that Williams go down to the field and take a little batting practice. Williams demurred. He wasn't ready to hit just yet. He'd just gotten back from the war. But Yawkey kept insisting, and Williams finally agreed.

"I'm rusty," he told everyone around the cage before he hit. "It's been more than a year since I've been up to bat."

It had actually been 456 days since he'd gone 2-for-3 against Detroit, homering off Dizzy Trout in his final at-bat. He stepped into the cage anyway and ripped a line drive. Then another. And then he began hitting home runs. The late George Sullivan, a young sportswriter who had become friends with Williams as a Red Sox batboy, was there.

He told Leigh Montville that Williams hit nine home runs in a row.

He told Ben Bradlee Jr. that Williams probably hit 13 home runs in a row.

"He claimed his timing was off," the Boston Globe reported, "but Ted Williams stepped into his old stance and swung as if he had never been away."

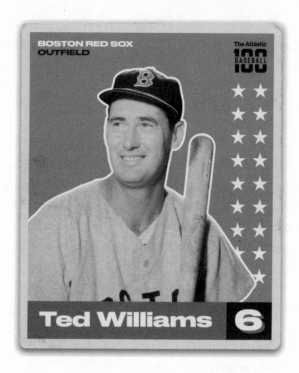

The one thing everyone agreed on was that on his last pitch, Williams rocketed a long home run over the right-field wall. At that point, he stepped out of the cage, flipped the bat to the ground, and walked off while everyone around him watched in awe.

His hands were bleeding.

Chapter 4: Maestros of the Keyboard

Ted Williams hated sportswriters. There's no other word for it. He hated them and hated them and, as his daughter Claudia said, "hated them 'til the day he died."

Williams also read every single thing ever written about him. He used to have the Boston newspapers delivered to him every game day so he could read them before he went on the field. On the road, he would have people back in Boston read him what the writers wrote.

Now, how do you square that? How do you make sense of it?

The safest answer: You don't make sense of Ted Williams. This is part of his legend, the mystery of him and all of his contradictions. On one hand, he was—as a friend said—politically to the right of Attila the Hun. He worked hard all his life to hide his Mexican heritage—his mother was Mexican, as was the uncle who helped teach him the game. Beyond that, he was just about the least politically correct person on earth.

But when he was elected to the Hall of Fame, he put something in his speech about the shameful absence of Negro Leagues stars like Satchel Paige and Josh Gibson. He was asked by the Hall to cut that part out; there was no reason to ruffle feathers on this celebratory day.

Needless to say, he did not cut it out.

"Baseball," he said that day in Cooperstown, "gives every American boy a chance to excel, not just to be as good as someone else but to be better than someone else. This is the nature of man and the name of the game, and I've always been a very lucky guy to have worn a baseball uniform, to have struck out or to have hit a tape-measure home run. And I hope someday the names of Satchel Paige and Josh Gibson in some way can be added as a symbol of the great Negro players that are not here only because they were not given a chance."

It should be noted: Nobody applauded when he said that. It was 1966 and America was on fire. But within a few years, Paige and Gibson were in the Hall of Fame.

He was largely an absentee father whose constant flareups of rage convinced his first daughter, Bobby-Jo, that he was mentally ill. "My dad was sick," she told Bradlee. "And it's a damn shame that, because he was Ted Williams, and because nobody wanted to tell him like it was, including myself, he suffered and progressively became more ill by the years."

He was also a man who raised millions and millions of dollars for children with cancer through the Jimmy Fund and would personally (and very privately) visit hospitals and dedicate the best parts of himself. The announcer Dick Enberg remembered Williams visiting one little boy who grabbed hold of Ted's finger and wouldn't let go. So Williams asked the hospital to bring over a cot, and he lay down until the boy fell asleep. There are a lot of stories like that, too.

Sportswriters saw these acts of generosity, and some of them—probably most of them—wanted to write about it. They wanted to tell about this unseen side of Williams. He threatened them against it. He would say that if anybody wrote about his hospital visits, he would stop coming . . . and who wanted to be the one who pushed Ted Williams to stop visiting hospitals? Nobody. The stories stayed in the notebook. And Williams kept his war against sportswriters intact.

There is another way to square Williams's feelings and that is to say: He needed the sportswriters. He needed the fuel of their criticisms. He needed their insults, their scolding, their cheap shots, their nitpicking in order to summon up the anger necessary to be brilliant. When Williams was young, he used to say that as soon as he made enough money, he was going to quit baseball and go fishing for the rest of his life.

And even if he didn't mean that, he did need something to propel him forward after he had become a star. Fury worked. What did it matter if the vast majority of the words written about Ted Williams were glowing? Those words did nothing for him. It was the bile—most often written by his archnemesis Dave Egan, the Colonel—that spurred him on.

Egan, the Colonel, was a small man physically, but like Williams was a huge personality. He was a Harvard-educated lawyer, a gifted writer, a ferocious fighter for baseball integration, and an alcoholic who was often too drunk to write his own columns. He was also on the take from any organization that could line his pockets.

He didn't like Ted Williams at all. He called Williams "T. Williams Esq." and wrote repeatedly that he was a bad influence on the youth of America. He tried to run Williams out of Boston. He wrote that Williams choked in the clutch. He tore Williams apart for only caring about himself and his own statistics.

"I am on the record stating the Red Sox," he wrote, "will never win the pennant so long as T. Williams Esq. is around to throw sand and monkey wrenches into the gears and machinery."

There were other writers like Egan who tore at Williams (though not quite with the same glee). There were still more who insisted on seeing the worst in the Kid. You already know that Williams lost the MVP award when he hit .400. Well, he also lost it when winning the Triple Crown . . . *twice*. The first time, in 1942, he led the league in average, homers, and RBIs and lost the MVP to Yankees second baseman Joe Gordon. The second Triple Crown, in 1947, he lost it again to his archrival DiMaggio, who by the numbers didn't do *anything* as well as Williams that season.

"I always hit best angry," Williams conceded, and so he powered through it all. Each slight, each insult, led to more hard line drives. Williams led the league in on-base percentage and slugging and OPS+ every full year he played from 1941 to 1951. He won two more batting titles after he came back from Korea; in 1957, at age 38, he hit .388 and posted a 1.257 OPS, the second highest of his career.

He finished five hits shy of hitting exactly .400.

"He said, 'As long as I live, I'll make them eat crow every chance I get,'" Claudia said.

Chapter 5: Bid Kid Adieu

Even a fleet of sportswriters wasn't enough to feed Williams's insatiable need to boil. It's funny, people talked about his incredible eyesight— measured at 20-15 when he was in the service—but it was actually his hearing that was supernatural.

Ted Williams could hear a single boo in a Fenway Park filled with cheers.

Those boos terrorized him all his career. He spit at fans more than once. He supposedly tried to hit a couple with foul balls. When he met awed young fans, he would sometimes say, "You're not one of those boo-ers, are you?"

"He never blamed fans for watching him," Richard Ben Cramer wrote. "His hate was for those who couldn't or wouldn't feel with him, his effort, his exultation, pride, rage or sorrow."

Especially rage. Williams might have been the greatest hitter ever. He also might have been the greatest fisherman ever; he is in two fishing Halls of Fame. But everyone who knew him well will tell you he *definitely* was the greatest swearer ever. Nobody, it seems, could spew blasphemy in the sort of poetic bursts quite like Williams. He was the Ella Fitzgerald of profanity.

In any case, at some point very early in his career, Williams decided that if fans were going to boo him, he would never, ever tip his cap to them. It was an oath that made sense to him, and he kept it his entire career. He hit more than 500 home runs and might have approached 700 had he not gone to war twice. His .482 lifetime on-base percentage is the all-time record. He had a 1.045 OPS as a 20-year-old kid full of vinegar and 1.096 OPS as a 41-year-old with a bad neck and legs that ached all the time. All that time the fans, almost all of them, cheered like mad.

But he still heard the boos, and he never tipped his cap.

Which brings us to the last game. It was September 28, 1960. Williams had turned 42 a month earlier. He'd had one last great season after a dismal and injury-plagued 1959 season—that season was so bad that Yawkey asked him to retire. But Williams refused to go out like that, so he took a $35,000 pay cut and came back and hit .316 with 29 home runs in only 390 plate appearances.

And on that last day, 10,454 dreamers came out to Fenway Park for one last look. It was a dreary day, cold, damp, a brisk wind blew in from right field. John Updike was among those who had come to see if maybe, just maybe, the Kid could hit one more home run. Williams knew what everybody wanted. He tried. He hit two long fly balls, the second of which he believed was as hard as he could hit a ball. Both died on the warning track.

Then came the last at-bat. Baltimore's Jack Fisher was on the mound. His first pitch was a ball. His second pitch was a fastball over the middle of the plate and Williams swung right through it, almost falling to the ground on the follow-through.

Williams knew that Fisher would challenge him with another fastball after that.

Fisher did. He threw one more fastball, and Williams connected, and the ball soared to right field. "From my angle, behind third base," Updike wrote, "the ball seemed less an object in flight than the tip of a tower, motionless construct, like the Eiffel Tower or the Tappan Zee Bridge. It was in the books while it was in the sky."

The ball sailed out, home run No. 521, and Williams ran the bases his usual way, head down, quick as he could—"as if our praise were a storm of rain to get out of," Updike wrote—and he went to the bench. The fans called to him. Teammates pushed him. The umpire asked him to come out. Fisher even paused on the mound to give Williams a chance to take a curtain call. He stayed out of sight.

Then Red Sox manager Pinky Higgins tried to trick Williams into saying good-bye. He sent Williams out to left field for the top of the ninth and then, before the inning actually began, sent Carroll Hardy out there to replace him. His hope was that Williams would hear the cheers—even he would not have been able to hear a boo in that crowd—and just tip his cap on the way back to the dugout.

"Our noise for some seconds passed beyond excitement into a kind of immense open anguish, a wailing, a cry to be saved," Updike wrote. "But immortality is nontransferable."

Ted Williams did not tip his cap. He'd made a promise to himself years before. And he did not break promises to himself. He disappeared into the dugout for good.

"Gods," Updike wrote, "do not answer letters."

Epilogue

In 1999, Ted Williams rode to home plate in a golf cart for the All-Star Game at Fenway Park. He had suffered two strokes and a broken hip in the previous months, but still he stood. The greatest living players—from Henry Aaron to Willie Mays, Bob Feller to Stan Musial, Ken Griffey to Cal Ripken, and all the All-Stars of the day—surrounded him and hugged him. He tipped his cap, and the crowd cheered as loudly as they ever had.

"Hey, McGwire," Williams shouted out to Mark McGwire, the most prodigious slugger in the world then. "You ever smell the wood when you foul one off real hard? You ever notice how it smells like burning wood?"

"I've smelled it," McGwire said. Maybe he had or maybe he was just saying so, but Ted Williams smiled and nodded and said it was the best bleeping smell in the whole world.

No. 5 **Oscar Charleston**

The rest of the group had gone ahead into the museum. We stayed behind. At the entrance of the Negro Leagues Baseball Museum, there's a small and dimly lit room. This is the room where people gather to talk and listen and prepare to experience the Negro Leagues, those baseball leagues where the very best African-American and Latino players in the world could play ball when white supremacy was the law of the land in America.

There isn't much in the little room. There are a few charts showing Negro Leagues migration, a couple of photos, and a statue of Buck O'Neil. The highlight is that it overlooks the Field of Legends, a baseball diamond in the middle of the museum. Beyond the chicken wire, which separates the room and the field, there are 10 bronze statues standing at their baseball positions. The names of the players are familiar to some and, even now, mysterious to others.

1B: Buck Leonard

2B: Pop Lloyd

SS: Judy Johnson

3B: Ray Dandridge

LF: Cool Papa Bell

CF: Oscar Charleston

RF: Leon Day

C: Josh Gibson

P: Satchel Paige

At bat: Martín Dihigo

Let me say something else about the chicken wire, which represents the segregation black fans endured at stadiums across the country. If you unfocus your eyes a bit and look through the chicken wire just so, with your imagination taking the lead, the statues seem to come to life.

Anyway, that's what I thought the day Buck O'Neil and Negro Leagues president Bob Kendrick and I stayed back there with Willie Mays.

"I knew these guys," Mays said as we all looked through the chicken wire and imagined the players as they once were. "Like that guy at third base, Ray Dandridge. I played with him in Minneapolis. He helped me become the ballplayer I became."

Everybody else in our group had gone ahead into the museum. We had stayed behind because of Willie Mays's eyes. Those eyes, which had once been able to differentiate between a fastball and slider simply by the way the baseball's laces moved, had grown terribly sensitive to light. Glaucoma. Even in that dark room, Mays wore sunglasses.

He also wore a thick San Francisco Giants coat, even though it was stuffy. He seemed to be sweating and shivering at once. He was in pain. He seemed exhausted . . . or perhaps more precisely, evaporated. Buck tried to get him to tell some stories, but Mays was not in the mood for stories. He just looked out on the field quietly.

"Willie," Buck said in an effort to break through, "I saw the catch on television the other day."

The catch. Willie Mays made it on September 29, 1954. It was the first game of the World Series, the Polo Grounds, and he went back on a long fly ball hit by Vic Wertz, a fly ball that would have been a home run in almost every other ballpark. Mays turned his back so that anyone who was behind home plate clearly saw the No. 24 on his jersey. He caught the ball over his shoulder and then whirled and threw it back to the infield.

"Willie Mays," announcer Jack Brickhouse shouted, "just brought this crowd to its feet with a catch which must have been an optical illusion to a lot of people."

"You saw that?" Mays said. He smiled a little.

"Only one other guy I ever saw could have made that catch," Buck said.

Seven days after Mays made that catch, the only other man—the statue standing in center field on the Field of Legends—died in a Philadelphia hospital. He was not quite 58 years old and he was almost entirely unknown. His obituary did not appear in the local newspapers.

"Oscar Charleston," Mays said as he looked out on the field.

"He was you before you," O'Neil said.

I want this one ranking to make you angry.

We are now close to the end, and all along I have tried to not mention the rankings. There's is a specific reason for this: The rankings are just a device. Someone once asked Orson Welles if Mr. Thompson, the man who goes in search of Rosebud in *Citizen Kane*, learned anything or grew at all throughout the movie. "He's not a person," Welles raged. "He's a piece of machinery to lead you through."

That's how I view the rankings . . . they are here to give this book shape and to spark a few feelings. Yes, I did use a fairly intricate formula to rank the players—designed with the help of the brilliant Tom Tango—one based on five things in no particular order:

1. Wins Above Replacement

2. Peak Wins Above Replacement

3. How multidimensional they were as players

4. The era when they played

5. Bonus value—This might include postseason performances, leadership, sportsmanship, impact on the game as a whole, if they lost prime years to the war, and numerous other possibilities.

I have no illusions about the formula. It is as flawed as any other system would be. That's why I only used it as a starting point; you may have noticed that many of the players on this list are not ranked as much as they are attached to a number that fits their particular careers. Now, I'll show you why I connected just a few players to certain numbers; some of the reasons are obvious, some less so.

98: Carlos Beltrán (1998 was the first year he appeared in the big leagues)

91: Mariano Rivera (after Psalm 91, the Psalm of Protection)

86: Gary Carter (in honor of his 1986 Mets)

56: Joe DiMaggio (for the hitting streak, obviously)

49: Warren Spahn (1949 was the first of eight times Spahnie led the league in wins)

45: Bob Gibson (his uniform number)

42: Jackie Robinson (his uniform number, the most famous in baseball history)

41: Tom Seaver (his uniform number)

37: Pedro Martínez (his uniform number when he first came up with the Expos)

33: Jimmie Foxx (Double-X wore number 3)

31: Greg Maddux (his uniform number)

27: Mike Trout (his uniform number)

26: Grover Cleveland Alexander (for his famous strikeout in the 1926 World Series)

24: Rickey Henderson (he wore a lot of numbers, but was 24 for the Yankees and others)

20: Tie between Mike Schmidt and Frank Robinson (both were 20)

19: Nobody, the number left blank for the 1919 Black Sox.

I did mess around when matchmaking some other players and numbers, but the point is that I tried to attach a number that fit the player. But that's not to say that I will not defend the individual rankings. I do that all the time. I will happily argue Ted Williams over Ty Cobb, Steve Carlton over Sandy Koufax, Carl Yastrzemski over Ken Griffey. That's a big part of the fun.

I'm just saying I could argue the other side just as easily.

But not on this one. No, this ranking, Oscar Charleston at No. 5, is different.

I want you to *feel* the fury of this ranking, feel it down deep. I want you to think, if you as so inclined, "Look, I'm sure he was terrific, but there's no possible way that Oscar Charleston, who played in a struggling league 100 years ago, could possibly be the fifth greatest player of all time."

Or I want you to think, "Fifth greatest? That's ridiculous. He should be No. 1!"

Or I want you to think, "This is pure political correctness. We have almost no stats on Charleston. We have only a handful of quotes about him. You can't rank someone this high on the list based on a few crusty legends and myths."

Or I want you to think, "It's such an infuriating tragedy that we as an entire nation never got to see the greatest player in the history of baseball."

Or I want you to think, "How is it that I've never even heard of this guy?"

Or I want you to think several of those thoughts at the same time. This ranking, unlike the rest, is a statement and, even more, it's a challenge. Oscar Charleston is the fifth-greatest player in baseball history. I know it. And ranking him here is meant to make you think about what you think.

See, Charleston—Charlie, as he was called—is different. I would say he, more than Satchel Paige, more than Josh Gibson, more than Cool Papa Bell, more than any player in baseball history in my view, represents that time in America when African Americans were invisible to much of the country, when baseball was played exclusively by white men, when being black and playing ball was like howling into the wind.

"I'm truly tempted to research Oscar Charleston," Thomas Boswell wrote angrily in 1999 when Charleston was included on the *Sporting News'* 100 greatest player list. "Was he a 19th-century player? A Negro Leagues star? A legend in Antarctic sandlot ball? Who knows?"

Boswell's column was intended to make a larger point about how modern players regularly get overlooked and under-ranked, a fair criticism about all lists, perhaps including this one.

But he wrongly picked Charleston as his target. Why? Because Charleston is the one who challenges us. It's one thing to honor Paige, who was one of America's most charismatic figures and who actually pitched in the big leagues in his 40s and 50s. It's one thing to honor Gibson, whose home run legends have endured through the years and who died too young.

But Charleston? Even now, if you asked moderate baseball fans across America, how many would even recognize his name?

Yes, I want you to feel rage about this ranking. Because there are only two possibilities. One is that I'm over-ranking Charleston, perhaps out of a raw sentimentality.

The other is that this is about right, that he was one of the greatest—maybe even *the* greatest—baseball player who ever lived and most of America ignored him.

And—here's where the rage part comes in—we'll never know for sure.

There's a famous story written by the legendary sportswriter Grantland Rice called "No Greater Ballplayer." In it, he writes, "It's impossible for anybody to be a better ballplayer than Oscar Charleston."

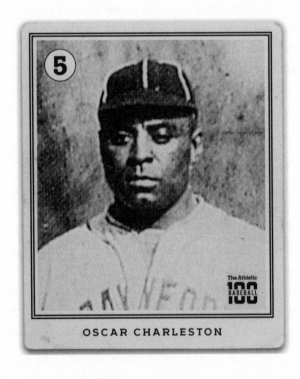

OSCAR CHARLESTON

Rice's story has been quoted repeatedly in all sorts of places. The only problem with it is that the story almost certainly doesn't exist. The only quote that anybody ever uses is the "It's impossible for anybody ..." quote. No one has ever been able to find the story. Even the original source of the quote—the writer John B. Holway—had never actually *read* the story. No, he heard about it from the pioneering sportswriter Ric Roberts.

And, just using common sense, it seems impossible that Rice wrote that story. No white sportswriter wrote about Negro Leagues players in Charleston's day. Yes, Charlie's name would appear in white papers now and again, and he was routinely called "the champion Negro baseball player in the world" or "the colored Babe Ruth" or "the greatest of all Negro players." But that was promotional material. That was to sell tickets to games in town.

They almost never wrote anything real.

There are a few quotes about Charleston from white contemporaries, but it's hard to tell how reliable any of them are. Sportswriter Wendell Smith did quote Honus Wagner in the *Pittsburgh Courier* in 1954:

"Oscar Charleston could have played on any big-league team in history if he had been given the opportunity. He could hit, run and throw. He did everything a great outfielder was supposed to do. I've seen all the great players in the many years I've been around and have yet to see one any greater than Charleston."

There's a line from John McGraw that has come down through the years, though it's not clear that it's real. McGraw supposedly saw Charlie play and said, "I could use that fellow, if I could put a coat of white paint on him."

Dizzy Dean might (or might not) have said: "Charleston could hit that ball a mile. He didn't have a weakness."

Jimmie Foxx, it seems, became friends with Charleston, and he supposedly raved about Charlie in various private settings, though again it's hard to find any actual words.

Ted Williams relayed a story about Charleston he'd heard from Walter Johnson. Seems like the Big Train was facing Charleston in an exhibition game, and Charleston shouted out: "I've done heard all about your fastball, and I'm gonna hit it outta here." After striking out twice, Charleston did indeed crush Johnson's great fastball over the right-field wall for a home run.

It's possible. It is believed that Charleston homered off Johnson in an exhibition game. The trouble with the story is that Walter Johnson himself is quoted telling it about a different Negro Leagues player, Grant "Home Run" Johnson.

The point is, we're unlikely to find more than we have already found.

Racism didn't just block Oscar Charleston. Racism tried to write him out of history. The writer Jeremy Beer just wrote a valuable and superb book called *Oscar Charleston: The Life and Legend of Baseball's Greatest Forgotten Player,* but so much of it is necessarily dedicated to how little we can ever know. Heck, we don't even know how big a man he was. In most places, such as at Baseball-Reference, Charlie is listed at 6-foot-0, 200 pounds. Many of the people quoted about Johnson talk about his size.

But Beer writes that "fully grown, he would be between 5-feet, 8 inches and 5 feet, 9 inches."

So when we ask, "How great a baseball player was Oscar Charleston?" what chance do we have? Heck, we don't even know how tall he was.

Oscar Charleston was born in 1896, a year and a half after Babe Ruth. He began his career at the same time as Ruth. They both threw and hit left-handed. They both began as pitchers. They both left home at a young age. They both started playing pro ball in 1914.

Charlie grew up in Indianapolis. His father, Tom, tried to make ends meet by working in construction. We believe that baseball was an important part of the Charlestons' life, but frankly, we only believe this because Oscar's brother, Roy, was arrested for trying to steal a baseball from a corner store. He was sent to reform school.

Oscar, meanwhile, went to work as a batboy for a good black professional team called the Indianapolis ABCs, this long before the founding of the Negro Leagues. It was written in various stories through the years that he picked up the subtleties of the game from the ABC players.

Charlie left home at age 15 to join the army. It's unclear if he ran away from home to do it, but he probably didn't. In those days, you could join the army at any age if you had a parental consent form. His parents probably sent him. He was shipped off to the Philippines, where in addition to everything else, he ran track and played on the same baseball team as another Hall of Famer, Bullet Rogan.

Even with all the mystery swirling around, there are two things we can say with some certainty about Charleston.

One is that he was a true five-tool talent, and that's a rare thing. The only tool that anyone has ever questioned is his arm—there have been those who called it weak—but he did begin his career as a pitcher and there are various other accounts of him displaying a cannon arm. On his Hall of Fame plaque, his strong arm is specifically mentioned.

The other tools are unquestioned. He could run blazingly fast. He routinely hit .400. He led numerous leagues in home runs. And he played center field like a dream.

Nobody of his day could match that combination. This was why—starting as early as his third year of playing in the Negro Leagues—black sportswriters were already calling him the greatest player of them all. If there is something that stands out as you look through baseball history, it is how few players have truly excelled at every phase of the game.

Then you look at the players of his day. Cobb hit and ran and probably could have hit with power if he wanted, but he couldn't play center field anything like Charlie. Joe Jackson didn't even play center field most of the time, and he certainly didn't hit home runs like Charlie (and he was thrown out of baseball). Ruth hit with unlimited power—Ruth hit with more power than Charlie or anybody else—but he certainly couldn't run or field with Oscar Charleston.

The closest thing in the major leagues to Charlie was probably Tris Speaker, who did hit and hit for average and run the bases and play beautiful defense in center. But here's what Harry Keck, the white sports editor of the *Pittsburgh Sun-Telegraph,* wrote about that: "If you were following the game in the early '20s, you will recall that Tris Speaker frequently was compared with him, not Charleston with Speaker."

Charlie's offensive game was complete. "He could hit you 50 home runs and steal you 100 bases," Buck O'Neil used to say, and this doesn't seem too far from the truth. Just look at 1921. According to the statistics meticulously compiled by Seamheads, Charlie played 82 games that year—almost exactly half of what is now a full season—and he hit .423 with 19 doubles, 14 triples, 17 home runs, 108 runs, 101 RBIs, and 32 stolen bases.

He definitely had blinding speed and has been credited by some as the inventor of the swinging bunt. He ripped the ball; Newt Allen used to say he'd tear the glove right off defenders. There are accounts of him pulling long home runs to right and driving long opposite-field home runs to left. In exhibition games, he homered off Hall of Famers Grover Cleveland Alexander, Jesse Haines, and Lefty Grove.

And yet, his defense was even more celebrated. Charlie played center field so close to second base that people used to wonder if he planned to take the throw from the catcher on stolen base attempts. But nobody could remember anyone ever hitting a ball over his head. "It's like he knew where the ball was going before it was hit," Cool Papa Bell once said. "He would start running back while the pitcher was still winding up."

Negro Leagues owner Cumberland Posey agreed: "Charleston appeared to actually smell where the ball was going to be hit."

"Opposing players," Charleston's teammate Dizzy Dismukes said, "complained that four men played the outfield."

His all-around talent was so overwhelming that writers in the black press often couldn't find a way to sum up his array of gifts. Reading some of those stories is a bit like reading some of the stories written today about Mike Trout (including some of my own). My favorite over-the-top Charleston story was written by William G. Nunn, a longtime sportswriter and, later, a scout for the Pittsburgh Steelers.*

"When nature decides to be generous," Nunn wrote in the *Pittsburgh Courier*, "she can bestow her gifts with the same prodigal abandon shown by the Brewery Irishman cracking old jokes. Occasionally an individual stands colorfully forth from the drab monotony of the nameless herd, seemingly endowed with all those attributes mankind admires and yearns to emulate.

"Such an individual is Oscar Charleston, a meteor now flashing, and for many years, flashing across the baseball firmament with a dazzling luster which is at once a joy to behold and a glorious contrast to the mediocrities of present-day baseball."

He went on to say that Charlie did not only have the speed of Max Carey (who led the National League in stolen bases 10 times) and the arm of the Yankees' Bob Meusel (who twice led the league in assists from right field), and the brains of McGraw and the hitting ability of Rogers

---

* He was also the father of Bill Nunn, who played Radio Raheem in Spike Lee's *Do the Right Thing*.

Hornsby, but he also was a great singer, a gifted writer, and a nearly unbeatable pool hustler.

The second thing we can say with some certainty is that Charlie loved to fight. He had a pretty hot temper, and that would lead to scraps. But he also liked to fight even when he wasn't mad. He used to wrestle with Josh Gibson before games, just for the hell of it.

"There was nothing he liked to do better than play ball," the Negro League star Ted Page told writer Holway, "unless it was fight. With the opposition. Not with his teammates. . . . Josh Gibson never went looking for fights. Charleston would look for them. Charleston wasn't temperamental. He was mean."

There is no shortage of stories about Charleston fighting. He threatened to throw professional wrestler Jim Londos off a train. Cool Papa Bell said he once ripped the hood off a KKK member. Double Duty Radcliffe said he saw Charlie knock out two people in Indianapolis. He got into a fight with at least one soldier—probably several—in Havana after sliding into a hometown player with his spikes up. He once got into a savage fight with a great but hotheaded Negro Leagues player named Oliver Marcelle, and the story goes that it ended with Marcelle hitting Charlie in the head with a bat. Buck O'Neil always said that was ridiculous.

Nobody would *dare* hit Oscar Charleston in the head with a bat.

"Charleston had a stoplight nailed to his chest," Buck said.

Because of all the fighting, Charlie was called by some "the Black Ty Cobb." It was a title he hated, but what could you do? They were always comparing Charlie to some white player—Cobb, Speaker, Ruth, Hornsby. Beer, in his biography, makes the compelling case that Charleston was not mean . . . he was fierce. In those days, fighting was very much a part of baseball, and Charlie put himself in the middle. But he rarely actually started fights. And there are many, many people who said that, deep down, he was a sweetheart.

"What I would say about him," said Mamie "Peanut" Johnson, one of three women to play in the Negro Leagues, "is that he was a beautiful person."

What else do we know? He was devoted to the game. He didn't drink. He didn't smoke. He was a brilliant baseball thinker, someone who had a lot of success after his playing days as a manager. It is said that he was so strong, he could rip the cover off a baseball simply by rubbing it between his hands. It is also said that he was fanatical about punctuality and, as a manager, he would not hesitate to leave behind players who were late to the bus.

Near the end of his life, Charleston worked as a scout and he was instrumental in the Dodgers' signing of Roy Campanella. "I never got the chance to play in the majors because of the color line," he told Wendell Smith, "but I'm going to do all I can now to see that these kids I'm managing get their chance. Everyone who goes up compensates in some way for me."

What are we left with in the end? The stats that have endured show him to likely be a .350 or so hitter with power and speed. The Hall of Fame plaque in Cooperstown states that he was a "Versatile star. Batted well over .300 most years. Speed, strong arm and fielding instincts made him standout center fielder."

O'Neil said that while Mays was the greatest major leaguer he ever saw, Charleston was the greatest baseball player he ever saw.

We are left with the same puzzle we began with. How good was Oscar Charleston? He was as good as you want to believe. In 1940, a reporter named Randy Dixon got together a bunch of experts on black baseball— former players, managers, coaches, umpires, sportswriters, fans—and they all just talked about the Negro Leagues. They made some decisions.

They decided that Cool Papa Bell was the fastest.

Satchel Paige was the goofiest.

Jud "Boojum" Wilson hit the ball the hardest.

Pop Lloyd was the "paragon of deportment."

Martín Dihigo was the most versatile.

Pitcher Willie Foster had the most deceptive delivery.

Biz Mackey was the catcher with the greatest sense of the game.

And, finally, they determined that Oscar Charleston was "the greatest player, all things considered."

That seems about right. If only all things had been considered when Charlie played ball.

No. 4 Henry Aaron

On April 8, 1974, a gray and rainy day in Atlanta, Henry Aaron broke a cherished baseball record.

No, we're not talking about the home run record. That also happened but we'll come back to it.

There were 53,775 people at Atlanta–Fulton County Stadium that day but that was only because the stadium wouldn't hold any more people. It could have been 100,000. It could have been 200,000. It is still the largest home crowd for any home game in Braves history, whether that game was played in Atlanta, Milwaukee, or Boston.

The crowd that day was a moving picture album of Henry Aaron's life. To scan the stadium that day was to scan his years. Herbert Aaron was there, Henry's father. Herbert was the first person to hear Henry's dreams. It was 1948. Henry was 13 or 14. He went to see Jackie Robinson speak at the Davis Avenue Recreation Center. Robinson talked about being relentless, chasing goals, and how a ballplayer's job is not just to get hits, it is to score runs.

"I'm going to be in the major leagues before Jackie retires," Henry told his father that day.

His mother, Estella, was there in the crowd, too. She did not want him to become a ballplayer, not at the beginning. She wanted him to go to college, make something of himself, maybe become a teacher. But she also came to understand that Henry had no room in his imagination for anything other than baseball. He went to the pool hall instead of school. He refused to study anything except the art of hitting a baseball with a bat (or a bottle cap with a broomstick—that was often the only option). He somehow knew that he was going to be a big-league ballplayer when that was an impossible thing for him to know.

Ed Scott was there in Atlanta. He was the man who first signed Henry up to play professional baseball. Aaron was 17 when he joined the Mobile Black Bears, a semipro team made up of grown men—fathers, husbands, factory workers, farmers.

"He was as green as he could be," Scott would say in Aaron's autobiography, *I Had a Hammer*. "He stood up there at the plate upright, no crouch at all, and the other team figured he wasn't ready. The pitcher tried to get a fastball by him, and he hit a line drive that banged against the old tin fence they had around the outfield out there—nearly put the ball through the fence. They walked him the rest of the time."

John Mullen, the nice man who signed Aaron for the Boston Braves and watched out for him, was there. Sadly, Mullen's scout Dewey Griggs was not. He'd died in 1968. Griggs had seen Aaron play for the Indianapolis Clowns and was blown away; he told Mullen to do whatever he had to do to get Aaron signed. But Griggs had an even bigger impact on Aaron's life. Before the game, he walked over and said, casually, "You might want to try hitting with your right hand on top."

Up to that point, Aaron had been hitting cross-handed.

The first time Aaron hit with his right hand on top of the bat, he homered.

Donald Davidson was there in the crowd that day. He had been the Braves' traveling secretary. He had given Aaron his famous uniform number, No. 44. Aaron had not asked for that number specifically, he'd only wanted a repeating number for his uniform. "You're too skinny to have a double number," Davidson had said, but then he made sure that Aaron got the now legendary No. 44.*

---

* Aaron and another 44, Willie McCovey, hold the baseball record for most home runs in a season that also matches their uniform number. Aaron hit 44 homers four times. Davidson would later say his big mistake was not giving Aaron the number 66.

Davidson was also the one who spread the nickname "Hammerin' Hank."

There were celebrities. Pearl Bailey sang the national anthem. Sammy Davis Jr. signed autographs. Georgia governor Jimmy Carter smiled broadly; that smile was about to become world-famous—in less than three years, Carter would be elected president of the United States.

Eddie Mathews was not just there, he was the Atlanta Braves manager. Few teammates have been as connected as Aaron and Mathews. They were the slugging brothers for the Milwaukee Braves for a dozen seasons. They were friends and rivals and balancing influences on each other's lives. Mathews brought Aaron out of his shell. Aaron helped Mathews calm down.

"Henry would hit a home run," their teammate Wes Covington said, "and—where somebody else would say he got lucky—Mathews would say, 'What a shot!' Mathews would hit a home run, and Hank would say, 'Helluva shot!' Their relationship was like fourteen-karat gold."

A band played before the game began. A stockpile of fireworks was set beyond the wall.

And in the second inning of the Braves-Dodgers game, Aaron came up to the plate to face Al Downing. Words cannot revive the sounds of Atlanta–Fulton County Stadium in that moment. The cheering was something more than cheering. Imagine the sound of 53,775 people gathered in one place to see Neil Armstrong land on the moon or to see the Beatles break out on *The Ed Sullivan Show* or to see Mike Eruzione score the goal that beat the Soviets at the 1980 Olympics.

That's how it sounded that day. People had not come to see a baseball game. They had come to be a part of American history, to be in the photograph when something transcendent happened. It isn't often in your life that you go to see something that you know—before it even happens— you will remember forever.

Aaron felt nervous but determined. This would be the day he broke that damned home run record. This would have to be the day; he couldn't take it any longer. He waited for Downing to give him something to hit; the men had faced each other 24 times. They'd each had their victories. Downing had gotten the better of things the first few times they faced off.

"He usually pitched me outside with sliders and screwballs," Aaron would say, and so in 1973, he began to crowd the plate more. That worked:

Aaron cracked a couple of homers off Downing in '73. He crowded the plate again that day, and he somehow blocked out the deafening roars. This was one of his many gifts. "I know it's hard for people to believe," he said. "But I didn't hear anything when I was at the plate."

Downing threw a pitch out of the zone. Another. A third. And a fourth. He walked Aaron on four pitches. The boos from the crowd were murderous.

Then Dusty Baker, Aaron's teammate and friend, smacked a drive and the Dodgers' left fielder Bill Buckner misplayed the ball. And Aaron kept running. People never really appreciated just how good a baserunner Henry Aaron was, but then again, that's the point of all this. There were a lot of things about Aaron people never appreciated. He rounded third and he headed for home. There was no throw to the plate. Aaron scored the first run of the game.

It was the 2,063rd run of his career. That was the record.

It broke the National League record for runs, set by Willie Mays.

This was something meaningful, something profoundly important to Aaron. It went back to the very beginning, when he heard Robinson talk about the importance of scoring runs. To score 2,063 runs you have to average 100 runs for more than 20 years. It is a mind-numbing achievement—think about all those cold April nights, those July steambaths, those meaningless August games and the anxious September games with a pennant in the balance.

Think about the drive, the focus, the sense of purpose needed to score that many runs.

But nobody cared about the runs record, not those in the crowd that day. There were no cheers for that record. Everyone was there for the other thing, and Aaron knew it. There was no time to celebrate. There was no time even to breathe. No, there was nothing at all for Henry Aaron to do except go out the next time and fulfill the destiny he never wanted.

Can a man as beloved and admired and appreciated as Aaron still be underrated? I think so. It comes down to a simple contradiction: His name became synonymous with the home run.

"No matter what it is," Aaron said, "they're gonna always say, 'Hank Aaron and a home run, Hank Aaron and a home run.'"

And Hank Aaron was not a home run hitter.

No, Aaron was a pure hitter. He was an excellent outfielder. He was a superb baserunner. And he was a metronome, pumping out the same brilliant seasons year after year and decade after decade. He led the league in total bases eight times, first as a 22-year-old, last at age 35. Eight times. Nobody—not Ruth, not Williams, not Hornsby, not Musial, not Cobb, not anybody—led the league in total bases as many times.

And the home runs? Well, to turn around the phrase, home runs were a bug, not a feature. Aaron hit the ball very hard and when you hit the ball very hard, some of them go out. He never hit 70 homers in a season like Barry Bonds or 65 homers in a season like Mark McGwire or 60 homers in a season like Babe Ruth or 55 homers in a season like Ken Griffey or 50 homers in a season like Mickey Mantle or even 48 homers in a season like Willie Stargell, Dave Kingman, and Jorge Soler.

Home runs were not the chorus of Henry Aaron's song.

He just hit so many baseballs hard over the years that 755 left the ballpark.

And when a person does something as colossal as hit 755 home runs, it's hard to think of anything else. The magic inventor and writer Jim Steinmeyer talks about a type of stagecraft device called the "dazzler." It is a very bright light that is placed onstage and pointed at the audience's eyes. When that light hits the eyes, everything around the dazzler seems to disappear. "If there's something dark near the dazzler," he says, "you can't see it."

For Henry Aaron, 755 home runs is the dazzler. It blocks the view. People see that, talk about that, argue about that. (When Bonds hit his 756th home run, people argued about it, raged about it; many insisted that Bonds would never be the Home Run King, no matter what the record books said.)

It's a bright light that blinds people to the things that made Henry Aaron so special. People can't see, for instance, how fast Aaron was. He didn't steal bases when he was a young player—almost nobody stole bases in those days, particularly in Milwaukee. In 1957, the Braves stole 35 bases—we're talking about the whole team. In 1958, they stole just 26, dead last in the league.

It wasn't until 1959 that Aaron started feeling the freedom to steal bases. He was 25 years old and had been in the league for five years. He attempted eight stolen bases that year. He was successful all eight times. From 1959 to 1968, Aaron stole 203 bases, seventh in all of baseball, ahead even of Mays. He became just the third player in baseball history to have a 30-30 season.

But here's the big thing: In those 10 seasons, he was successful on more than 80 percent of his attempts. That was the highest stolen-base percentage in the game over that time. How many stolen bases could he have had if he'd tried? There's no telling. For his career, Aaron was successful more than 76 percent of the time, a higher percentage than Robinson, Maury Wills, Lou Brock, Juan Pierre, and, yes, Mays.

"Henry didn't steal bases like Willie," Mathews said, "but goddamn, he could steal bases. He could run like hell, and he didn't even look like he was running. I'll bet you in a footrace, Hank would have beaten Willie."

And what about Aaron as an outfielder? Well, he wasn't a center fielder (he was actually an infielder when he started) and so historically he has been written off by many. But by the Baseball-Reference stats, Aaron was worth 100 runs more than average. By range factor—number of plays made—he often led the league and always finished in the top two or three, and, remember, he played just about his entire career in the same league as another pretty good right fielder named Roberto Clemente. Aaron won three Gold Gloves and might have deserved more.

Again, from Mathews: "He never threw to the wrong base, never missed the cutoff man."

Mostly, though, the dazzler covers up just how complete a hitter Henry Aaron was. If you took away his 755 home runs—just took them away— he would still have had 3,000 hits. Not only does he have the record for most RBIs with 2,297, but he also has the most combined runs and RBIs.

Most Runs plus RBIs

1. Henry Aaron, 4,471

2. Babe Ruth, 4,388

3. Barry Bonds, 4,223

4. Ty Cobb, 4,189

5. Alex Rodriguez, 4,107

And then there's his absurd, almost laughable, breakaway lead in career total bases. If you want to call Henry Aaron the king of something, call him the King of Total Bases. He had 6,856 total bases in his career—700 more than anyone else.

Musial could have hit 350 more doubles and not had as many total bases as Aaron.

Ruth could have hit 250 more home runs and not had as many total bases as Aaron. (Bonds would have needed 220 more homers just to tie Aaron.)

Pete Rose could have cracked another 1,100 singles and not had as many total bases as Aaron.

And let's add something else that people miss: Aaron played in a pitcher's time. He played his prime in a pitcher's ballpark. If you neutralize Aaron's numbers—which is to say you try to put Aaron in what Baseball-Reference calls a "neutral setting"—Aaron's numbers jump from mind-boggling to impossible.

If you neutralize the numbers, Aaron's total bases jump all the way to 7,502—and his lead jumps to almost 1,000 bases. All of his numbers go up including, yes, home runs (all the way up to 824 neutralized homers).

See, when you talk about Aaron and home runs, you put Aaron in the wrong box. He wasn't a slugger and would not stand up to Ruth or Jimmie Foxx or McGwire or a dozen others as a slugger. He never wanted that. Henry Aaron was a ballplayer. He hit for average, hit for power, ran the bases, played good defense, and threw with authority. He did everything well for longer than anyone who ever played this game.

And if he was overshadowed by Mays or Mantle or his blinding consistency or his laconic persona or, yes, that damned home run chase, it didn't matter. He kept going. He kept doing all those brilliant things. Nothing could make him stop.

"You know," Aaron once said, "if I had to pay to go see somebody play for one game, I wouldn't pay to see Hank Aaron. I wasn't flashy. I didn't start fights. I didn't rush out to the mound every time a pitch came near me. I didn't hustle after fly balls that were 20 rows back in the seats.

"But," he added, "if I had to pay to see someone play in a three-game series, I'd rather see me."

I asked Henry Aaron if he had any regrets. A career as perfect as his should be without regrets, at least that's what you would think. But he said that he did have one.

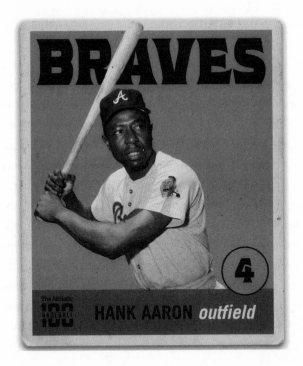

He regretted that he never won a Triple Crown.

"I do think about it," he said. "I missed it three years—not in a row, but three years. And I think if I had really concentrated, really focused on it, I would have won one or two Triple Crowns."

Aaron, for the record, won two batting titles, four home run titles, and four RBI titles. But, alas, he never put the three together in one season.

In 1957, he led the league in homers and RBIs, but his .322 average was fourth behind three of the greatest hitters who ever lived—Musial, Mays, and Frank Robinson.

In 1959, he led the league in hitting at .355 but his 39 homers and 123 RBIs fell short. He finished seven homers behind his Hall of Fame teammate Mathews and finished 20 RBIs shy of Hall of Famer Ernie Banks.

In 1963, he led the league in homers and RBIs, but his .319 average was seven points behind the Dodgers' Tommy Davis. He has always regretted hitting .263 the last two weeks of that season to lose the batting title.

In 1966, he again led the league in homers and RBIs, but he hit just .279 that year—he was getting used to a new ballpark in Atlanta and had shifted his game to take advantage of the home run dimensions.

780 • THE BASEBALL 100

Of course, what could that matter? What could a Triple Crown or two add to a career like Aaron's?

"I just felt . . . I just felt like there was something missing in my career," he said. "I just felt like if I had done what I was supposed to do, I could have won at least one or two Triple Crowns. And that just would have been something. . . ."

He paused here and never finished the thought. I've spent a lot of time thinking about it. I remember years ago, Bob Greene wrote a story about Frank Gifford and how he'd had pretty much the biggest American life imaginable—big man on campus at USC, superstar NFL player, handsome television star, coolest man in the room. But in the end, Greene found that even Gifford looked back wistfully. In his case, Gifford wished he could have been the quarterback rather than the halfback.

This is at the heart of human nature, I guess. I don't believe anyone has had a more perfect career than Aaron—perfect in that he never had a down season and he has several of the most important records. But even Hank Aaron wishes he could have accomplished just one more extraordinary thing.

Let's go back to April 8, 1974. It was the end of the worst time of Aaron's life. He had never wanted to chase Babe Ruth's record. It's just that one day, right around when he turned 32, he began to realize that he had a chance to put up numbers that would match him up with the greatest to ever play the game. And that was too tempting to pass up.

A writer named Lee Allen explained to him that if he stuck around for three or four more seasons, he'd have a real shot at 500 home runs. At that point, only four players ever—Ruth, Foxx, Williams, and Mel Ott—had 500 home runs.

And then if he stuck around for another year or two, he'd get to 3,000 hits. That was a big one; only eight players—eight of the greatest players—had 3,000 hits. Even Ruth and Williams had not done that.

So he kept doing what he always did, and he hit his 500th homer in 1968. He got his 3,000th hit in 1970, but the thing is, that year he began closing in on 600 homers. So he had to do that. He stuck around in 1971 and led the league in slugging and OPS while bashing 47 home runs. What was he going to do? Stop there? No, of course not. So he kept going, and suddenly 700 home runs were in sight, and if 700 homers were in sight, that meant that Ruth's unbreakable record of 714 home runs was in sight.

What was he going to do? Stop?

"If I played out my career in typical fashion . . . the record would show that I had been one of the best ballplayers to come along," Aaron wrote in *I Had a Hammer.* "My credentials would put me in the company of Ruth and Mays and all the others. But I also knew that in the final analysis—in the books and sports columns and barbershops—I wouldn't be in their class. To be in their class, my numbers had to be better than theirs. I didn't agree with it, and I didn't accept it, but it was reality, and I had to deal with it."

And so he dared. He went after Babe Ruth, a black man chasing after a white legend in 1970s America. He hated every minute of it. He hated the racist mail that poured in.

> Dear N—,
> Everybody loved Babe Ruth. You will be the most hated man in the country if you break his career home run record.

> Dear N—,
> You are doing more to hurt baseball than any other that ever played the game. You may break the record and you may replace Babe Ruth in the hearts of the liberal sportswriters, the liberal newspapers, TV and radio . . . but you will never replace the Babe in the hearts of clear-thinking members of our Society.

> Dear Black Boy,
> Listen Black Boy, We don't want no n——Babe Ruth.

> Dear Super Spook,
> First of all, I don't care for the color of s—. You are pretty damn repugnant trying to break the Babe's record.

> Dear Mr. N—,
> I hope you don't break the Babe's record. How do I tell my kids that a n— did it?

> Dear Henry Aaron,
> How about some sickle cell anemia, Hank?

Dear Brother Hank Aaron,

I hope you join Brother Dr. Martin Luther King in that Heaven
he spoke of. Willie Mays was a much better player than you anyway.

On and on and on and on . . . these letters never stopped coming. Polls
showed that most of America was rooting for him. One showed that 87
percent wanted him to get the recognition he deserved by breaking the
record. But what good are polls when the death threats keep coming in?
Thirteen percent of America is still a lot of people. His children needed
security to go to school. He needed an escort every time he appeared in
public. And meanwhile, the reporters kept coming at him, each asking the
same exact questions.

"All I do is lay in bed and stare at the ceiling," he told one reporter who
asked how well he slept.

"Well, isn't it worth it?" the reporter asked.

"I really don't know," he said. "If I go to bed half berzerk, it's not."

No, he didn't sleep. He ate every night in his hotel room alone. He felt
alone. Yet he kept on hitting—and hitting home runs—because somewhere along the way he came to a powerful and painful and undeniable
realization.

The only thing worse than breaking the record would be not breaking
the record.

On April 8, 1974, while a misty rain fell, Henry Aaron came up in the
fourth inning. He was the new all-time National League leader in runs. He
stepped in against Al Downing. The crowd stood and cheered madly. He
shut out the sound like only he could do. The first pitch was a slider and it
was down in the dirt.

Then came the next pitch. Downing said it was a fastball up. Aaron
remembered it as a slider down. They both remember Aaron turning on
it and hitting a long and high fly ball to left field. Neither knew it was gone
off the bat. "But," Downing said, "it kept carrying and carrying."

When it cleared the fence and landed in the glove of relief pitcher Tom
House, fireworks exploded. The crowd exploded. Aaron's heart exploded.
He didn't show it. He rounded the bases the way he always did, unsmiling,
undaunted. He took a moment to shake hands with Dodgers first baseman
Steve Garvey and second baseman Davey Lopes. Even when two college

kids ran on the field and surrounded him—they had run on to congratulate him—he showed no fear or emotion.

He just kept running.

"What a marvelous moment for baseball," Vin Scully said in the booth after letting the crowd tell the story. "What a marvelous moment for Atlanta and the state of Georgia, what a marvelous moment for the country and the world. A black man is getting a standing ovation in the Deep South for breaking the record of an all-time baseball idol."

So many people have asked Henry Aaron what he was thinking in that exact moment. I asked him that, too. He shrugged. How do you explain it? He doesn't have any better answer now than he did that very day when the crowd cheered for 11 straight minutes, and his mother raced on the field and gave him a bear hug that choked the breath out of him, and he was handed a microphone to say what came to mind now that he had passed the Babe.

"Thank God it's over," he said.

A few months after I wrote this chapter, Henry Aaron passed away at age 86. In all, five men in the Baseball 100—Henry Aaron, Bob Gibson, Al Kaline, Phil Niekro, and Tom Seaver—died within months of me writing about them. Each loss hurt, but Aaron was a man apart. And I thought again about him during that home run chase getting all those terrible letters. He read every one, you know. "I had to know what I was up against," he said.

For many years after he broke the record, he did not want to celebrate it. The pain was too fresh. As he grew older, he could never completely forget . . . but he tried to let go of the worst. "I never could understand prejudice, and I still don't," he said. "I just had to get through it."

No. 3 **Barry Bonds**

There are basically two categories of opinion about Barry Bonds and his place in the game. The first opinion is that Bonds was the most absurdly astonishing player who ever played the game and while he certainly made mistakes and alienated people, his sheer awesomeness is what comes through most of all.

These are people who will go every now and again to Bonds's Baseball-Reference page just to gawk at it the way people might stand across the street from the red carpet at the Academy Awards and stare slack-jawed at the beautifully dressed celebrities. In 2004, for example, Bonds got on base more than 60 percent of the time, in large part because—yes, it still looks like a misprint—he was intentionally walked 120 times.

Yes, let's gawk at that.

The second school of opinion is that Bonds's stats and awards and accomplishments must be downgraded—or nullified entirely—because he used steroids to achieve them. This blatant cheating was never punished, not even by an asterisk when he passed the infinitely more admirable Henry Aaron on the all-time home run list. And this is one of baseball's great shames.

In addition, the opinion goes on, he lied about his steroid use constantly, and also he was a thoroughly unlikable guy—many of his team-mates couldn't stand him, many fans say that he turned them off to the game entirely, and away from the field he has been accused of domestic abuse (he was never charged and has denied the allegations)—and it is best for all if he is just wiped out of baseball history entirely except as a reminder that cheaters, in the end, do not win.

You might not share either of these opinions in their entirety or their volume, but I suspect that you lean one way or another. Most people do.

That leads to an intractable problem: There's no way to write about Bonds that suits his two worlds. There is no safe meeting place in between. The people who love Bonds have heard enough about the cheating. Baseball didn't even test then. We have no idea how many other players used steroids. It was a part of the game then. And he was so much better than everyone else. Etc.

And the people who loathe Bonds do not want to hear anything about his steroid-laden numbers—those don't even count—and they don't want to hear weak excuses that it wasn't exactly cheating, and they certainly don't want to hear that he was a Hall of Fame player before he started using because we don't know when he started using. And anyway, he wrecked his own legacy. Nobody did that for him. He could have settled for being one of the best ever and not cheated in the first place. Etc.

So for Barry Bonds, unlike every other player, we have no choice but to write two stories. It works like so: If you like Bonds—or at least respect him enough to read about his greatness without losing your mind—you only need to read the sections headlined "For Bonds Fans."

And if you dislike Bonds—or maybe just don't have any room in your mind for anything but criticism for him—you can stick with the sections headlined "For Bonds Critics."

If you veer into the wrong section, you do so at your own peril.

That's just the deal with Barry Lamar Bonds.

For Bonds Fans

Barry Bonds was born to play baseball. They say that by the time he was three, he could already throw a baseball with near-perfect form. By age five, he could hit overhand pitching. He hit Wiffle balls so hard that he actually broke windows. According to Jeff Pearlman's book, *Love Me, Hate*

GIANTS

BARRY BONDS

Me, the young Barry broke so many windows that his mother, Pat, became a favored customer at the W.J. Bank glass store.

Barry was Mozart on a baseball diamond.

And like Mozart, he grew up knowing that he was not only destined for greatness but for immortality. How could he not be? He was the son of Bobby Bonds, who practically invented the 30-homer, 30-stolen-base season—until Bobby came along, the 30-30 season had only been done four times in baseball history (twice by Willie Mays, once by Aaron, once by Ken Williams). Bobby did it five times by himself.

Barry had Bobby's baseball brilliance, that was clear from the beginning. But he also had his aunt Rosie's athleticism (she reached the 1964 Olympic final in the 80-meter hurdles). He also had his uncle Robert's sheer power (Robert was drafted by the Kansas City Chiefs).

Plus he had this innate understanding of baseball. How did he know so much about this game? One of his first vivid memories was being at Candlestick Park in San Francisco and peppering his godfather Willie Mays with all sorts of baseball questions. And Mays could not believe the intelligence in these questions. This wasn't a 5-year-old; this was a young man asking about how to set up pitchers and how to anticipate balls in the outfield.

Barry Bonds never doubted his destiny, not for one minute. When he played with kids his age (or even a few years older), he was always the best player on the field. And he always wanted more. "He wanted to be great," his high school coach told Pearlman. "A lot of kids just wanted to play. That wasn't enough for him."

Even when he went to major-league ballparks with his dad—at age 6, age 11, age 15—and was allowed to warm up with the big leaguers, he *still* always felt like he was the best player on the field. "I was too young to bat with them," he admitted. "But I could compete with them in the field."

He wasn't exaggerating.

"Bobby had his kid out at the stadium in 1979," Cleveland's longtime PR man Bob DiBiasio said. "Barry was 15. He was better than any of our outfielders at the time."

He was a phenomenon. His hometown Giants took him in the second round out of high school and offered him $70,000 to play ball. Barry went to Arizona State instead, and he set the school home run record and played in two College World Series. He and Oddibe McDowell made up about as great a 1-2 punch imaginable.

And everyone knew that the best was yet to come. The Pirates took him with the sixth pick in the draft and almost immediately began hyping him as the team's next superstar, the next Dave Parker, the next Roberto Clemente, the next Willie Stargell.

"I think one day," his teammate R.J. Reynolds said, "he will put up numbers no one can believe."

For Bonds Critics

Barry Bonds was a pain in the neck from the first time he stepped on a ballfield. Well, to be fair, it couldn't have been easy being the son of Bobby Bonds, baseball's greatest enigma. What a talent Bobby was—he hit and ran and played defense. And he could be utterly charming. He won the Good Guy Award from the Giants' booster club. Twice.

But he was a deeply unhappy man. He was an alcoholic.

"Bobby Bonds," one of his teammates once told me, "was the most miserable person I ever knew inside or outside of baseball."

Bobby was famously distant from his young son. According to one story, maybe true or maybe not, he once slapped a ball out of Barry's throwing hand and grumbled, "No son of mine is going to be left-handed." True or not, he did not offer many encouraging words. He did not show up for Barry's games.

"I resented him when I was a kid," Barry would say. "Not that he was abusive. There's a fine line between abuse and discipline."

Bobby was only 18 years old when Barry was born. Bobby had not even started his pro career yet. In that way, Bobby and Barry sort of grew up in the big leagues together. They each felt the sting every time Bobby got traded. They each endured the shame of Bobby's troubles with alcohol, including his multiple drunk driving arrests. At one game, Barry would always remember hearing the fans chant "502, 502!"—502 being the California police code for driving under the influence.

Perhaps most of all, they each felt the bitterness of expectation; the perpetual cloud hovering over Bobby's head was that he had wasted his otherworldly talent—this even when he set the record with five 30-homer, 30-stolen-base seasons.

"No one gives my dad credit for what he did," Barry would rage as a young ballplayer. "And they put me in the same category. He did 30-30 five times, and they say he never became the ballplayer he should have become. Ain't nobody else done 30-30 five times. Nobody. Zero. So I don't care whether they like me or they don't like me. I don't care."

He didn't care. Or at least that's what he told himself. He was so driven, so single-minded, so arrogant, so difficult. He should have been a first-round pick out of high school; he was as talented as anyone in the draft. But he went to his hometown Giants in the second round. It might have been in part because Bobby had reentered the picture to represent his son, and by then teams had little interest in dealing with the father.

But it also was because Barry couldn't get along with people and played with an attitude that made you wonder if his great talent was even worth it. Legend goes that one scout summed up Bonds with a direct one-word scouting report: *Asshole.*

The Giants didn't come up with enough money and Bonds went to Arizona State, where he was typically breathtaking and typically miserable. Nothing resembling fun ever sparked from Barry Bonds. "I never wanted anything to bother me while I played ball," he said then. "Coach would say to me, 'Barry, bases loaded, one out, how come you're so calm?' I'd say, 'Coach, I don't want to think about it. I just want to swing.' He understood, but not really."

Nobody really understood him. "I never saw a teammate care about him," Arizona State coach, Jim Brock, said. Barry was so disliked by his teammates that Brock at one point held a team meeting and put it up to a vote whether Bonds should be allowed to continue with the team. The majority voted to boot him off. Brock kept Bonds anyway.

"He wanted to be liked, tried so damn hard to have people like him," Brock told *Sports Illustrated*. "Tried too hard. But then he'd say things he didn't mean, wild statements. I tried to tell him that these guys, 20 years from now, would be electricians and plumbers, but he'd be making millions. . . . Still he'd be hurt. People don't realize that he can be hurt—and is, fairly often."

When the Pirates took him in the first round of the draft, Barry's mother told Gene Collier of the *Pittsburgh Press*, "I knew this was one kid who was just going to play baseball and that was it. I guess he's happy. If he's happy, I'm happy."

Does that sound like someone who was happy?

For Bonds Fans

Baseball geniuses do hear their own drumbeat. This certainly didn't start with Barry Bonds. Ty Cobb heard his own. Babe Ruth did. Rogers Hornsby did. Ted Williams did. Reggie Jackson did. Just go down the list. The greatest ones go where that personal drumbeat leads.

Bonds followed a rhythm that only he could hear.

"You can't expect a Thoroughbred to act like a mule," Buck O'Neil used to say about Bonds, a young man he loved.

Understand, Bonds was not an instant sensation in the big leagues. He hit .223 his rookie year. He was moved from center field—the position his godfather Willie Mays made famous—to left field during his second season. He had an impossible amount of pressure heaped on top of him and no matter what good things he did, people could only talk about the things he didn't do.

Bonds scored 95-plus runs his first three full seasons; he posted a 129 OPS+ over that time; he was a fabulous outfielder; he averaged 23 homers and 27 stolen bases a year as a leadoff hitter.

Put it this way: Wins Above Replacement was not invented yet. But in those three seasons, the ones everyone called so disappointing, Bonds had 20 Wins Above Replacement, averaging 6.7 WAR per season. That's pretty close to MVP stuff.

Still, it was the Bonds curse: People only talked about what he could be.

"When it comes to ability, Barry's one of the top five players in the league," his teammate Andy Van Slyke said. "The application has not come yet."

One part of Barry Bonds's life and career that has gone all but unnoticed was how hard he worked to improve. He was relentless about getting better, obsessive about getting better. And it wasn't just one thing. He strove to be a better hitter, a better slugger, a better fielder, a better baserunner. He knew that his arm wasn't the strongest and so he trained himself to charge balls harder than anyone in the game. He understood that he sometimes got home run happy so he worked to develop the best batting eye the game had ever seen since Teddy Ballgame. He was determined to never swing at a bad pitch.

And in 1990, he arrived with the best all-around season for any National League player since Joe Morgan in the mid-'70s. He hit .301/.406/.565, leading the league in slugging percentage. He hit 33 homers, stole 52 bases, scored 104 runs, drove in 114, won a Golden Glove and an MVP award, and led the Pirates to their first postseason appearance in more than a decade.

It wasn't just a breakthrough year. It was an announcement: Baseball's new phenomenon had arrived. In 1991, he led the league in OPS, hit 25 homers, stole 43 bases, drove in 116 RBIs, and won his second Gold Glove.

In 1992, he took it up a whole other notch, leading the league in on-base percentage and slugging, posting his first 1.000 OPS season (spoiler alert: it wouldn't be his last), and leading the Pirates to their third straight postseason appearance. Bonds struggled in all three of those series, which did pin a tag on him as a postseason choker, a tag he wouldn't shed for another decade, when he had a World Series performance for the ages.

In 1993, he left Pittsburgh and went back home to play for the Giants. His first season there was something out of this world. He hit

.336/.458/.677 with a league-leading 46 home runs and 123 RBIs. Teams had no idea what to do with him; they intentionally walked him 43 times. That was his first 10 WAR season. And it was his second straight season with a 1.000 OPS.

Sure, he was enigmatic and problematic; that has always been embedded in his personality. He couldn't connect with teammates. He could barely tolerate the media. And he just couldn't get his arms around the fans' expectations. For Bonds, baseball itself was supposed to be the only thing that mattered. Everything else—*everything* else—annoyed him no end.

"Why can't people just enjoy the show?" he asked. "And then let the entertainer go home and get his rest, so he can put on another show? But in baseball, you get to see us, touch us, trade our cards, buy and sell our jerseys. To me, that dilutes the excitement.

"Autograph seekers! When I go to a movie, after the final credits roll, I get up and leave. It's the end. But I'm supposed to stand out there for three hours and then sign autographs? Fans pay $10 to see 'Batman,' they don't expect to get Jack Nicholson's autograph."

He put on a show like nobody else in the game. In 1995, he had his third 30-30 season even though part of the year was wiped out by baseball's continuing labor squabbles. The next year, he made it a 40-40 season. The year after that, 1997, he hit 40 homers and stole 37 bases.

Then came 1998. Barry Bonds had an incredible year in 1998. I mean, no, it wasn't incredible for *him*, but it was still so remarkable. He hit .303/.438/.609 with 44 doubles, seven triples, 37 homers, 120 runs scored, and 122 RBIs. He won his eighth Gold Glove. He led the league in WAR for the seventh time. It was his seventh straight season with a 1.000 OPS.

And that year, he became the first player in baseball history to hit 400 home runs and steal 400 bases in a career. He was the player of his generation.

It should have been the year of Barry, one celebrated by all. It was, to say the least, not the year of Barry. No, 1998 was the year that people marveled at how far Mark McGwire could hit a baseball. No, 1998 was the year that people pounded their chests along with Sammy Sosa as he rounded the bases an astounding 66 times. No, 1998 was the year that Ken Griffey Jr.—so much more lovable—cracked 56 home runs and drove in 146 and won a Gold Glove (in center field!) and stretched the imagination.

And Bonds? Who? He was just this problematic outfielder who played for an also-ran Giants team and couldn't hit in the playoffs. Yes, all his career, Bonds told people again and again that he didn't care, he didn't care, he didn't care.

But 1998 was the year Barry Bonds discovered he did care very much.

For Bonds Critics

No, Barry Bonds wasn't happy. He was a jerk, that's what he was. There's no way around that. You can't get *that* many people to detest you without being a jerk, without some jackassery, without some obnoxiousness. He didn't exactly hide from the charge. "My job," he explained, "does not say, 'Walk into a locker room and kiss butt.'"

Did people really want Barry Bonds to kiss butt? Or did they just want him to act like a decent human being? You know, to greet teammates, to answer a couple of questions without lashing out, to sign some autographs without an eye roll?

Kiss butt? Be nice? It wasn't clear that Bonds could see the difference.

"Ever since I was a kid," he said, "I have a stamp on my neck: Barry Bonds has a bad attitude and only thinks of himself. Who else am I supposed to think about out there?"

Yes, he stayed at a low boil. He was dismissive of teammates, indifferent to fans, and downright hostile to the media.* Nothing had really changed: He was all about being a great baseball player on the field and absolutely nothing else. And everybody could feel it when watching him play. He had

---

* This personal thing must be said here: Barry Bonds was always nice to me. There was no apparent reason for it. He didn't know me. He hadn't read me. I feel sure he couldn't have come up with my name if he was spotted all the letters except the J. But every time I needed to talk to him, probably a half-dozen times before 1998, a few times after, he was always accommodating, thoughtful—and could this be?—friendly. It was the strangest thing. It was like I reminded him of a childhood friend or something. When I told other writers and people around baseball about this, they shook their heads and promptly told me their own Bonds horror stories. I kept waiting for mine. It hasn't come yet. Maybe it will. But it would not be right or fair for me to discuss Bonds's well-known media hatred without saying that he could be, when he wanted, an engaging, insightful, and pleasant interview. He has a lot of charm. He dispenses it sparingly.

his fans, of course—mostly hometown fans, many who felt as offended by the slights as Bonds himself did—but more turned to Griffey, with his big smile and backward cap and aura of coolness. They turned to Chipper Jones. They turned to Cal Ripken. They turned to Derek Jeter.

They turned to players who made them feel delight. Isn't that the point?

And yes, Barry Bonds was better than they were. He was the best player of his time, one of the best players of all time, even before 1998. But delight? That wasn't his racket.

In 1990, Bonds got the whole city of Pittsburgh to detest him. That year, he went to arbitration and asked for $1.6 million. The Pirates offered about half. Bonds was coming off a season where he hit .248 (even if he did other less obvious things very well), and the Pirates won the case. Barry just about lost his mind.

The next day, his agent, Rod Wright, went to the press. "Barry said, 'If they want me to bat this year, they can find someone else,'" Wright told reporters. "He's fed up. . . . He's so irritated with the organization, he doesn't want to be part of the Pirates. If he could be gone tomorrow, he would be happy."

Yeah, that will get you hated in a town. The newspapers went first.

"Who does Barry Bonds think he is?" Ron Cook asked in the *Pittsburgh Post-Gazette*. "We're not talking about Roberto Clemente or Dave Parker here."

"You heard the cliche, 'He's a good guy to have in the clubhouse,'" Bob Smizik wrote. "It applies to a lot of Pirates. Not to Bonds. He's a bad guy to have in the clubhouse. He is not a leader like Andy Van Slyke, not a terrific guy like Bobby Bonilla, not an unselfish player like R. J. Reynolds. . . . His main interest in the clubhouse is himself."

"Those comments," Bruce Keidan wrote, "made Bonds the Pirates' MDP—Most Despised Player."

Then came the talk radio shows. Barry *had* to be traded. It was practically unanimous. The Pirates looked into dealing him for a frontline starter and another player, but there were no takers, which tells you what everybody around baseball thought about Bonds.

Bonds insisted he didn't care.

"To me, when people say I have an attitude problem, it gives me an edge," Bonds said. "It makes me mad, so I play better." There's undoubtedly something to that: Bonds was hardly the only incredible athlete to be driven by rage. He played Gold Glove defense. He hit home runs. He stole bases. He reached base. And he intimidated like no one else—every year, he drew the most intentional walks.

But what was the cost? In 1990, Bonds hit a long home run in St. Louis and found no one waiting for him at the plate. None of his teammates stood up for him in the dugout. Bonds got their message—"What they were saying is, 'Let us applaud you instead of you applauding you,'" he said—but he wasn't especially moved by the message.

"If I'm supposed to wait for you guys to applaud me," he said, "I could be waiting a lifetime."

For Bonds Fans

Barry Bonds broke the game. That's how good he was after 1998. The theory goes that Bonds saw how people celebrated McGwire and Sosa and others, and he *knew* they were using steroids, and he decided that it was time to go all in.

You can imagine Jack Nicholson's line from *Batman* playing in his head: "Wait till they get a load of me."

There was no testing in baseball then. There was no outcry in baseball then. It was quite the opposite: The game was thriving! The home run was king! Nike reminded everybody that chicks dig the long ball! MLB even put out a comic book of baseball players with enormous muscles. Muscles were in!

So Barry Bonds got muscles. And he tilted baseball.

Let's just look at some of the crazy numbers.

In 2000, at age 35, Barry Bonds hit 49 home runs. It was a career high. He also led the league in walks and OPS+. He finished second in the MVP balloting to his teammate Jeff Kent, though it's unclear why. Bonds did miss 19 games with nagging injuries so maybe that was it.

Anyway, it didn't matter. Bonds would win the next four NL MVP awards.

In 2001, he hit 73 home runs. The record. He slugged .863. The record. He walked 177 times. The record. He homered once every 6.5 at-bats. Impossible. And the record.

In 2002, in some ways, he was even better. .370/.582/.799. That .582

in the middle, yes, that broke Ted Williams's on-base percentage record (.553) set in 1941. Bonds's 1.381 OPS was another record.

He was so good that managers stopped pitching to him with the game on the line (and even when it wasn't). The record for intentional walks in a season before 2002 was 45, set by Willie McCovey in 1969. Managers intentionally walked Bonds 68 times. And get this, they intentionally walked him 13 times in the postseason—that was twice as often as anyone ever before.

In 2003, Bonds missed some time—but managers still intentionally walked him 61 times, and he still hit .341/.529/.749, and he still won his third straight MVP award.

Then came 2004, the most ridiculous season in baseball history. There is simply nothing to compare with Barry Bonds's 2004 season. Everybody had given up on the idea of getting him out, and he was intentionally walked 120 times. There are no words for that and no comparisons in any sport.

Look: Only 60 players in modern baseball history have walked 120 times in a season, period.

In total, he walked 232 times in 2004, another record. He had a .609 on-base percentage, another record. His 1.422 OPS, another record.

Bonds critics—who are not reading this—will tell you that it was the steroids that did it. Come on. You can say that Bonds would not have been capable of anything close to that without steroids, and that is worth discussing. You can say that using steroids is worse than the other kinds of baseball cheating, and that too is worth discussing.

But you can't just erase four years of matchless batting like that. Come on. Bonds wasn't the only one using steroids. He wasn't the only one who pushed boundaries.

He *was* the only one who shot into that stratosphere, to reach an altitude that Cobb and Ruth and Hornsby and Gehrig and Williams and Mays and Aaron and all the rest never reached. Put it this way: When Bonds was intentionally walked 120 times in 2004, do you know who was second? Jim Thome. With 26. Intentional walks were not up around the game. They were only up for him. Bonds was playing at his own level.

It was like he had come from the future.

Yes, he cheated. And it's an affront to those players who didn't succumb to the temptations, to those who played it clean and straight, even when all the incentives pointed toward cheating. But let's be blunt about it: Barry Bonds was never going to be one of those guys. He always pushed the edge. He always played for immortality.

And in this way, he just follows a long line of players whose plaques line the walls of the Baseball Hall of Fame, even while his does not.

For Bonds Critics

Barry Bonds broke the game. That's how good he was after 1998. The breaking of baseball, no, you can't blame that all on him. Others played their roles. But he was the one standing over the busted game at the end, the one holding the sledgehammer. And many people simply will never forgive him for that.

When you look at those late-career Bonds numbers, what do you see? This is the critics' section, so what you see is illegitimacy. When you see 73 home runs and 120 intentional walks and an otherworldly .863 slugging percentage, you also see Ben Johnson's 100-meter world record, whatever that was. You see Marion Jones's three stripped gold medals. You see Lance Armstrong's seven Tour de France victories.

All of it happened but also didn't happen.

But there's something else here, something beyond illegitimacy. In the 1990s, offense exploded in baseball. Dozens of reasons were given, and each of those reasons probably played some part. The strike zone shrank beyond recognition. New ballparks were hitters' paradises. Expansion and injuries diluted available pitching talent more than hitting talent. Players began using harder yet whippier bats. Batters began wearing body armor and so crowded the plate with impunity. The baseballs undoubtedly had more life in them.

And yes, hitters discovered that working out helped a lot. It's astounding it took that long for people to figure it out—it's a bit like the boy in every teen movie failing to realize that the person they really love is the girl next door. But it's true, for a long time baseball people insisted that working out was bad for you, that it made you bulky and less flexible.

Once that myth went away, hitters got much bigger and much stronger. This is true across the board—for players who used steroids and also players who didn't. Ballplayers, just about all of them, practically lived in weight rooms.

Baseball changed. It was fun at first. It was fun in the summer of 1998 when McGwire (who has since admitted using steroids) and Sosa (who has been strongly suspected of using steroids) bashed home runs nightly. Attendance records were smashed. Baseball was front-page news for the first time since the strike.

That was the year, we believe, that Barry Bonds decided to join the party.

His timing could not have been worse, because homer fatigue began setting in almost immediately. In 2000, teams averaged 5.14 runs per game, the highest since 1930, and people started to ask questions. The next year, MLB started testing minor leaguers for steroids.

And the next year is when Bonds became a fully functional Death Star. People couldn't believe how muscular he had become. Comments about how much bigger his head looked filled talk radio and Internet chat rooms (remember those?). And that year, he hit baseballs harder and farther than anyone ever had before. He'd been a power hitter before, sure, but nothing like this. He hit a home run every 6.5 at-bats. There had never been anything like it.

And suddenly this growing scandal had a face. Bonds was the perfect villain. He was generally disliked in and around the game anyway. In 2002, Ken Caminiti talked to *Sports Illustrated*'s Tom Verducci, and he said that at least half the players in baseball were using steroids.

Then José Canseco said that it was actually 85 percent of players, and he wrote two books outing players across the league.

And all this was *exactly* at the time that Bonds was doing those unbelievable things—here, we use "unbelievable" in its most literal sense. Some stared in wonder. But others saw every home run he hit into the bay, every crazy record he set, every intentional walk he was given as a daily reminder that something foul had happened to the national pastime.

Then he took it all a step beyond. He came back to break Aaron's career home run record. He didn't have to do that. He could have walked away when he got hurt at age 40. He had a .300 lifetime batting average. He had 708 career home runs and 506 career steals and he'd won seven MVP awards. His place in the game's stratosphere was secured.

But, no, he would not accept that. By then, most people assumed he'd been a steroid user. By then, most people assumed that much of what he'd done in recent years was fraudulent. He didn't have to come back and break that record that Aaron courageously set under the most crushing pressure imaginable.

But, of course, he did have to come back and break the record because he is Barry Bleeping Bonds and he could still hit like nobody else and relentlessness was always at the heart of his story.

So, sure, he broke the record. He came back at age 41 and again at 42, and in the end, he hit 762 home runs, and he would have kept going, too, if a team had given him a chance. But by then he was indicted for perjury and obstruction of justice in the BALCO scandal—the case would go on for years, and he was convicted of obstruction and then had the conviction overturned. And so teams shut him out.

They've shut him out ever since. So has the Hall of Fame. Baseball fans, too.

For Bonds Fans

Of course he should be in the Hall of Fame. He did everything on a baseball field. He was the greatest player I ever saw. If Rickey Henderson split in two equals two Hall of Famers, as Bill James famously wrote, then you could split Barry Bonds in four and have four Hall of Famers.

He was perhaps the greatest defensive left fielder in baseball history.

He was, with Williams, the most disciplined hitter the game has ever seen (his walks record will probably never be broken).

He hit 700 home runs and stole 500 bases; he was the greatest power-speed threat ever.

He played at a level in the early 2000s that no one, not even Ruth, can match. He was a baseball genius.

Did he cheat? Undoubtedly. Are there cheaters in the Hall of Fame? Undoubtedly. Are there steroid users in the Hall of Fame? Undoubtedly. Are there worse people in the Hall of Fame? Undoubtedly.

The Hall of Fame is for the greatest players who ever lived. He was one of those. Of course he should be in the Hall of Fame.

For Bonds Critics

Of course he shouldn't be in the Hall of Fame. He didn't respect the game. He hurt the sport. He still hasn't ever come clean about what he did so it's hard to believe he feels too much remorse about it. It's an honor granted to the most special players.

Do you really think baseball should honor Barry Bonds?

For that matter, do you really think he should be No. 3 on this list, ahead of Henry Aaron, ahead of Ted Williams, ahead of Stan Musial, ahead of Mickey Mantle? How can you justify that?

When the *Athletic*'s Andrew Baggarly caught up with Barry Bonds, he found a sad and haunted man. "I feel like a ghost," Bonds said. "A ghost in a big empty house, just rattling around."

How you feel about that quote probably says everything about how you feel about him. Are you thrilled that he's getting what he had coming? Do you feel sad that Bonds, who did so many incredible things, cannot find peace?

Or do you feel a little of both?

From his earliest memories, all Barry Bonds ever wanted was to become the greatest baseball player who ever lived. He paid every price. He ignored every doubt. He raged over every hurdle. He cut every corner. He shut himself off from everything else. He brushed aside every other concern. He made more enemies than friends.

And, yes, he became the greatest baseball player who ever lived.

And what was waiting for him at the end? Remember what he said way back at the start of his career: *"If I'm supposed to wait for you guys to applaud me, I could be waiting a lifetime."*

Here's what waited for him at the end: silence.

No. 2 **Babe Ruth**

At a Kansas City Royals fantasy camp not so long ago, one of the campers stood way too deep in right field. No, seriously, he was standing way too deep. He was basically on the warning track. This would have been absurdly deep under any circumstances, but as a reminder, this was at a baseball fantasy camp, where paunchy middle-aged (and former middle-aged) bankers and nurses and small business owners and police officers (and sportswriters) spent their days drinking and reminiscing and pulling muscles, not always in that order.

"Hey," John Mayberry yelled toward the right fielder. "Move in!"

Big John was a slugging first baseman for 15 years in the big leagues. He was good, too. He hit 255 home runs in his career and finished second in the 1975 MVP voting. But at fantasy camp, he was best known for his booming voice and marvelous laugh.

"Move in!" Big John bellowed again, but our intrepid right fielder either didn't hear—a distinct possibility since he was standing in another county—or felt comfortable with his positioning.

"Bring it in!" Big John shouted once more, and when the right fielder still stayed put, he finally lost his patience.

"Hey!" he roared. "BABE RUTH IS DEAD!"

Babe Ruth is not dead. That's the point here. He is not dead and he will never die, and that's what makes him different from anyone across America's sports landscape. Think of it: He was born in the 19th century. He played 100 years ago. There is no other athlete from a century ago who so lingers in our nation's consciousness. Or, to put it more bluntly, nobody would ever argue that any other 1920s athlete is still the greatest ever.

The closest to Ruth is probably the golfer Bobby Jones. He will appear with some regularity on golf top-10 lists—golf fans, like baseball fans, have a particular fondness for the sport's history. But even golf fans would not say Jones was *the* greatest. Yes, Jones got two ticker-tape parades through New York for his golfing glories and he invented the Masters and his swing still looks good on film. But . . . seriously. The guy hit hickory mashies and niblicks on cow pastures. You can't compare him to Tiger Woods, for crying out loud.

Now and again, you might see Bill Tilden or Helen Wills Moody sneak onto a greatest-ever tennis players list. That's nice. Tilden was so dominant in his day that he would, on occasion, purposely lose the first two sets and five games in the third just to make things interesting. Wills Moody won 31 Grand Slam titles. They were fantastic. But, no, nobody seriously considers either of them in the class of Roger Federer, Serena Williams, Rafael Nadal, or Novak Djokovic.

Red Grange was the greatest football player of the day. Howie Morenz was the greatest hockey star of the day. Nat Holman was probably the greatest basketball player of the day—the sport was still too new for any real judgments. . . . Jack Dempsey . . . Man o' War . . . Fritz Pollard . . . Gene Tunney . . . Paul Endacott . . . Walter Hagen . . . George Gipp . . . Gertrude Ederle . . . some of these names might ring a bell, some might not, but they were all the best of that time. None of them fits in a sports talk argument about the greatest ever.

This is just the natural course of sports and time. Every generation brings a new type of athlete: bigger, stronger, faster, better trained, better prepared, better equipped. The world record for the mile in 1927, Babe Ruth's crescendo season, was 4:10. It's about 30 seconds faster now. Johnny Weissmuller set the world record in the 100-meter freestyle in 1922 at an astounding 58.6 seconds—he was the first person to break a minute. It was an extraordinary achievement. That time would not qualify Weissmuller as a boys' or girls' high school All-American now.

So why is Babe Ruth different? He's definitely different. Ruth is not just in the all-time argument for greatest baseball player ever; he *is* the argument.

How? That's the real question, right? How does Ruth stay so vibrant and brilliant and untouchable in our minds when every other athlete's power cracks and fades with the years? How can Ruth, who played in the time of Model Ts and vaudeville, still be the essential baseball player in a world of Teslas and Netflix?

And, in a seemingly unconnected question, why can't they make a decent movie about him?

> "Yes! The Babe! Superman of baseball! The most famous and colorful athlete in the game's history! The incomparable, unpredictable Babe Ruth, American as the hot dog, soda pop and chewing gum, this man was Mr. Baseball himself!"
>
> —the narrator in *The Babe Ruth Story*

Holy cow is *The Babe Ruth Story* bad. A few players ago, I went into pretty grim details about the awfulness of *The Winning Team*, a film about Grover Cleveland Alexander, and that movie is quite terrible. But honestly, upon further review, *The Winning Team* is *The Godfather* when put up against *The Babe Ruth Story*.

I want to give you a sense of just how bad *The Babe Ruth Story* is without actually asking you to see it. There are many ways to do this, but I'll just tell you about one scene. Babe Ruth, played with near-comical awfulness by William Bendix—it's *almost* funny—is taking batting practice when he hits a foul grounder and the baseball hits a dog that had run onto the field. Ruth is mortified and rushes over to the dog and his freckled boy owner.

"I'm sorry, kid," Ruth says. "I didn't mean it. Honest! The pooch just ran out on the field and ..."

"Gee, Babe," the boy says. "Peewee won't die, will he, Babe? He won't die?"

(Please reread this previous line but do it as you would imagine it sounding when spoken in the fastest and most lifeless monotone you have ever heard in your life.)

"No, son, he won't die," Ruth says. "We won't let him die. We're going to take him to the biggest and best hospital in town!"

And this is what they did. They took Peewee to the best hospital in town. Not a veterinary hospital. A people hospital. Ruth, still in full uniform, rushes to the front desk and demands the hospital get the best doctor to operate on the dog. He is furious when the women at the front desk tell him they tend to do most of their work on people. He ducks into an operating room, where he is soon surrounded by doctors.

"Ain't this a hospital?" Ruth rages. "Ain't you guys doctors? Whaddya mean you won't operate just because he's a dog? . . . What's more human than this little pooch?"

I did not make up any of that.

But here's the most remarkable part of *The Babe Ruth Story*—it might not be the worst Babe Ruth movie. No, you have to give full consideration to *The Babe,* made in 1992, starring John Goodman. Film critic Roger Ebert, on the show *Siskel & Ebert,* summed it up this way: "This is a sad movie about a sad man, and although the ads make it look like a comedy, the experience of seeing it is more like living with an alcoholic relative."

That probably sounds harsh if you haven't seen *The Babe*. If you have seen it, you are thinking right now, "Oh, come on, it was way worse than that."

The money scene in *The Babe* is when Ruth visits a sick kid in a hospital.

"Babe's gonna sock you a home run in the game tomorrow," Ruth says. "Will that make you feel better, Johnny?"

And with this, poor Johnny—using all the strength he can muster while enduring whatever terrible disease he has—slowly reaches out his hand and signals (wait for it) that he wants two home runs.

"Two?" Ruth asks in shock. "Two?"

It doesn't seem possible for one life to spur two movies that are that bad. What is it about Babe Ruth's life that seduces filmmakers and at the same time eludes them?

Well, you can see why the story draws them in. The Babe's story seems perfect for the screen. You know all the words to this song already. George Herman Ruth grew up in his father's saloon, where he learned to drink beer, chew tobacco, and commit petty crimes. "I hardly knew my parents," he said. At age seven, his parents sent him for the first time to St. Mary's Industrial School for Orphans, Delinquent, Incorrigible and Wayward Boys.

The courts chose "incorrigible" as young Ruth's ticket into St. Mary's. "I guess I was," Ruth would say.

Once at St. Mary's—he was in and out of the place more or less his entire childhood—he came upon the famous Brother Matthias, a charming 6-foot-6 hulk of a man who became the closest thing Ruth ever had to a father figure. "He taught me to read and write and the difference between right and wrong," Ruth would later say.

It's unclear how much reading or writing the Babe did, and that fuzzy gray area between right and wrong was where he spent most of his time, but Brother Matthias did introduce Ruth to baseball. Ruth always remembered seeing him hit high fly balls with just one hand; he copied that style in his mind. Ruth was a natural. Even as a lefty, he played every position and played them all well. "It was all the same to me," he would say.

Ruth signed with the hometown minor-league club, the Baltimore Orioles, and pitched so well that Orioles owner Jack Dunn almost immediately sold him to the Boston Red Sox for about $10,000. "George Ruth," the *Baltimore Sun* reported, "has jumped from an unknown in an industrial league to one of the brightest stars in baseball in four months."

The next year, at age 20, he won 18 games for Boston as a pitcher and hit four home runs in 92 at-bats. That home run total might not sound like anything special, but this was in the thick of the Deadball Era and those four homers placed him just three behind the league leader, the similarly named Braggo Roth.

For the next five years as a pitcher, Ruth hit at least as many home runs as he allowed.

He really was a terrific pitcher. At 21, he led the league with a 1.75 ERA. At 22, he went 24-13 with a 2.01 ERA. In 1918, at age 23, he pulled off his most famous pitching accomplishment, throwing the last of 29⅔ consecutive scoreless innings in the World Series (a streak that began in 1916). That record would last for 43 years, until it was broken by Whitey Ford.

By 1918, though, it had become clear that while he was a superb pitcher, he was a revolutionary hitter. The game had simply never seen anyone quite like him. Even while playing only 95 games in the field, he led the league in home runs, slugging percentage, and OPS.

In 1919, he became an everyday player and broke the big-league home run record for the first time. He hit 29. It was mind-blowing. Nobody in the 20th century had hit even 25. And Ruth insisted he'd had two home runs stolen from him.

Ruth was sold to the New York Yankees the next year, and he would break his own home run record three more times, hitting 54 in 1920, 59 in 1921 (more than three times the number of homers the Boston Red Sox hit), and 60 homers in 1927. But we can spend all day going over Ruth's records and inconceivable accomplishments and statistics.

Instead, let's just count down from 13.

- 13: Times he led the league in slugging

- 12: Times he led the league in home runs. Also the number of walk-off homers he hit.

- 11: Times he led the league in walks

- 10: Times he led all players—including pitchers—in WAR

- 9: Times he led the league in runs created

- 8: Times he led the league in runs scored

- 7: Times he led the league in extra-base hits

- 6: Times he led the league in total bases

- 5: Times he led the league in RBIs

- 4: Times he hit at least 54 home runs in a season

- 3: World Series wins. Also the times he drove in 160 or more RBIs.

- 2: Times he accumulated more than 400 total bases

- 1: MVP awards and ERA titles and his place on the all-time OPS ranking

What a player. But what tempts the storyteller is the story: Here was a troubled kid who overcame the odds to become the most famous baseball player in the world. He was larger than life in so many ways. He swung around a 52-ounce bat like it was nothing. He hit more home runs himself than every other team in the league. (It's true!) He called his shot in the World Series. (Maybe!)

And as the sportswriters repeatedly wrote: In those days after the 1919

Black Sox threw the World Series, darkening the soul of sports, the Babe gave America hope. "Baseball men," the *New York Times* wrote in Ruth's 1948 obituary, "are almost in accord in the belief that Babe Ruth, more than any individual, and practically single-handed, rescued the game from what threatened to be one of its darkest periods."

And then there was Babe the man. You couldn't help but like him. He was so childlike. So affable. Big heart, you know. He would have picnics on his farm for orphans. He would go to the stadium turnstile and make sure kids got into the ballpark for free. He really would visit sick children in hospitals and, yes, hit home runs for them when he could. A sweetheart. He couldn't remember anybody's name, so he would call everybody "Kid" or "Sport" or "Doc" or he would invent a nickname for them.

And speaking of nicknames, he was a nickname magnet. Nobody had more than the Babe: The Sultan of Swat. The Caliph of Clout. The Colossus of Clout. The Wizard of Whack. The Rajah of Rap. The Bazoo of Bang. The Mammoth of Maul. The Wazir of Wham. The Maharaj of Mash. The Prince of Pounders. The Wali of Wallop. The Potentate of Pow. The Great Bambino, the Big Bam or, least formally, Bam.

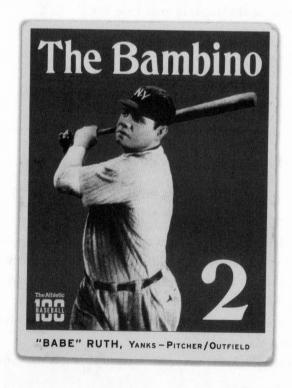

"BABE" RUTH, Yanks – Pitcher/Outfield

What a character. What a guy! He would overload on hot dogs and peanuts and Coca-Cola (and, behind the scenes, less wholesome stuff), and when asked for the secret to his success, he would bellow, "Clean living!" Everybody got a kick out of that.

When teammates in the dugout would ask him what kind of pitch he had hit for a home run, he would shrug and say, "I don't know, but it sure looked good!"

When asked if he had any superstitions, he said: "Yep. When I hit a homer, I make sure to touch all four bases."

When told that his enormous $80,000 salary was bigger than President Herbert Hoover's, he shouted, "I know, but I had a better year."

As the *New York Times* wrote in the lead of its obituary: "Probably nowhere in all the imaginative field of fiction could one find a career more dramatic and bizarre than portrayed in real life by George Herman Ruth."

How could filmmakers resist a story like that? They couldn't.

So why did they fail so miserably? That's tougher.

Do you know why Babe Ruth got sold from the Red Sox? Sure, you've heard the story that Red Sox owner Harry Frazee was stone-cold broke and needed some money so he could produce a Broadway show called *No, No, Nanette*. That story isn't exactly true, though there's truth in it. Frazee did desperately need money. And the $100,000 he got for Ruth—$1.35 million in today's dollars—did keep him solvent and allow him to stay in the theater business and eventually led to him producing his biggest Broadway smash, *No, No, Nanette*.

But there was something else going on, too. Ruth wanted more money. Frazee had gotten used to this dance. Before the 1919 season, Ruth had threatened to hold out and become a boxer if he didn't get $10,000 a year. It wasn't the first time Ruth had held out. But after a prolonged fight, Frazee gave in and offered Ruth a three-year contract at $10,000 a year.

But Ruth had blown up baseball in 1919, setting the home run record and becoming the biggest draw in the game, and he now threatened again to hold out, this time saying he would go into motion pictures.

"Unless they meet my terms," Ruth told reporters, "I am through with major-league baseball. I have several propositions on hand, any one of which would pay me more than $10,000 a year."

The baseball owners could usually count on the newspapers to back them whenever a player sought more money. In this case, however, many writers were so smitten with Ruth that they figured he was worth whatever he asked. "Ruth will be a bigger attraction next year than he was this," the *Buffalo Times* wrote. "If he keeps on his home-run-making way—and there is nothing to indicate he will fail to do so—he alone would be worth at least $100,000 in receipts to any club in 1920."

The story went on for a couple of weeks. Was Ruth bluffing? Would he really quit? Would Frazee pay him $20,000 a year? The simple truth is probably that Frazee could not afford to pay Ruth $20,000 a year—but even if he could, he had lost patience with the Sultan of Swat.

On January 6, 1920, the shocking news hit the papers. Babe Ruth had been sold to the lamentable New York Yankees, who had never won a single pennant in their entire existence. The papers estimated the price was between $125,000 and $150,000, but all anyone knew for sure was that was the highest price ever paid for a ballplayer—double what Cleveland spent when it bought Tris Speaker from the Red Sox less than four years earlier.

When Frazee was asked how he could part with the greatest drawing card in baseball, he did not hold back.

"While Ruth, without question, is the greatest hitter that the game has ever seen," Frazee said, "he is likewise one of the most selfish and inconsiderate men that ever wore a uniform."

Frazee also pointed out that the Red Sox had to suspend Ruth several times for breaking curfew. It was well known by then that Ruth had punched a home plate umpire after not getting a strike call. He broke his toe when kicking a bench after being intentionally walked. He twice went into the crowd to go after a heckling fan. It was less well known that he was an inveterate gambler who spent virtually every night drinking to near unconsciousness, hooking up with prostitutes, and wrecking cars.

So Frazee sold him. He didn't want to sell him. He was, at times, as charmed by Ruth as others. He was entirely blown away by Ruth's talents. Frazee had turned down a $100,000 offer for Ruth before. But with his money situation getting desperate and Ruth's belligerence growing worse, Frazee really didn't see a choice. And he was hardly the only one who felt that way. As Paul Shannon wrote in the *Boston Post,* "Popular as Ruth was, on account of his big-heartedness, [his former teammates] nevertheless realize that his faults overshadow his good qualities."

Or, as Allan Wood, author of *Babe Ruth and the 1918 Red Sox,* wrote, "It would have surprised no one if, for whatever reason, Ruth was out of baseball in a year or two."

In other words, Ruth was almost impossible to pin down. Was he a big-hearted oaf? Yes. Was he a womanizing drunk? Yes. Was he a friendly soul? Yes. Was he a manipulative son of a gun? Yes. Could he be magnanimous? Could he be cruel? Could he be childish? Could he be cynical? Yes is the answer to everything with the Babe.

And maybe that's part of the reason no one has made a good movie about him. How do you make a movie about someone who is everything and nothing at the same time? How do you make a movie about the wind?

" 'The Babe' is a movie that wants to tell the truth behind the legend," Ebert said, "but I don't think it does, and I'm not sure I want to know the truth if it did want to tell it."

Let's talk for a minute about October 1, 1932. That was Game 3 of the World Series, the Cubs versus the Yankees. Babe Ruth and Lou Gehrig each hit two home runs. One of Ruth's home runs has become perhaps baseball's most cherished fable. You've probably heard of it.

They call it "the Called Shot."

Charlie Root was pitching for the Cubs. In the first inning, he got New York's Earle Combs to hit a grounder to short, but Chicago's Billy Jurges threw the ball into the dugout. Root fumed about it and walked Joe Sewell. That brought up Ruth. According to the newspapers, Ruth pointed to the outside corner, as if he wanted Root to throw the ball there. Root obliged, and Ruth hammered it out to give the Yanks a 3–0 lead.

That, actually, was not the called shot.

No, the called shot happened in the fifth inning.

This is how United Press reported it:

With one down in the fifth and the score still tied, Ruth came to bat for the third time. Ruth and the Cubs' players in the dugout had been carrying on a lively repartee throughout the game, and it now reached its height with the Babe waving his hands and yelling at the Chicago players after each pitch.

With the count 2-2, Ruth motioned to the Cubs' dugout that he was going to hit one out of the park, and when a low curve came floating down the alley, he swung with all his powerful body. The ball sailed more than 450 feet to the farthest corner of the center-field bleachers.

So that sort of sounds like he called his shot. "He motioned . . . that he was going to hit one out of the park."

But now look at how the Associated Press reported it:

When he came to the plate in the fifth inning, the Cub bench sitters shouted derisively as he missed the first pitch. The Babe held up one finger and finally two on each hand with the count two and two. Then, wham! He caught Root's next pitch and they never got the ball back. It arched 10 feet over the scoreboard. It was probably the longest home run in Wrigley Field's history. As he trotted around the bags, he held up four fingers, signifying a home run.

So that said he was simply signaling the count. That's how Paul Gallico of the New York *Daily News* had it, too:

The Babe merely held up two fingers to the Cubs' dugout to show that there was still another pitch coming to him. He also did a little plain and fancy leering and then faced Root again with the bat clutched in the ends of his fingers. Windup. Pitch. Flash of ball! Crack! Goodbye!

And of Babe running around the bases, Gallico wrote:

Oh, my New York constituents, how your heart would have warmed had you seen the Babe, thus confounding his enemies, thus making his run.

The *Chicago Tribune* wrote it this way:

Root got him in the hole with two strikes. Guy Bush and Bob Smith, two excellent jockeys, were leaning out of the Cub dugout, doing the best they could to capture the Babe's goat. Bush's line of attack was a lot of choice names he figured would make the Babe a pretty mad fellow. Smith made gestures indicating that he was trying to put the "waamey" (baseball term for jinx) on the Babe.

Babe listened to this and yelled back, apparently unannoyed:

"That's only two strikes, boys. I still have one coming," he cried, meanwhile holding up two fingers. And when the next one came, Ruth sent it to distant parts.

The bulk of evidence suggests Ruth sort of did and sort of didn't call his shot. The way the movies show it—with Ruth pointing to the spot where he planned to hit it—seems to have no basis in reality. If that's what it takes to call a shot, he didn't do it.

But it does seem like he let them know he still had a strike left and that he intended to do something with that strike. And then he unloaded the most mammoth home run anyone at Wrigley Field had ever seen. And this in the World Series!

Isn't that incredible enough?

That's a good question for Ruth. Isn't what he did incredible enough? Why do people have to enhance it? Do you know how they have it in *The Babe Ruth Story*? Ruth doesn't just point once to the spot; he points repeatedly. "Babe Ruth has just made the same gesture again," the announcer shouts. "He's pointing to the flagpole in the center-field bleachers, clearly indicating that's where he means to park that next pitch!"

"Sit down and rest, kid, I'm riding this one out of the park," Ruth says to the catcher.

"Yeah, you and who else?" the catcher says.

"Me and a young pal of mine," Ruth says, speaking of that sick kid in the hospital to whom he had promised a home run.

Why isn't Babe Ruth's story enough for the moviemakers or the myth-makers?

Well, I have a theory.

Babe Ruth, with that swing, with that bat, I got him hitting .140.... I would strike Babe Ruth out every time. I'm not trying to disrespect him, you know; rest in peace, shoutout to Babe Ruth. But it was a different game. The guy ate hot dogs and drank beer and whatever he did. It was just a different game.

—Adam Ottavino

Here's what I believe: At the center of Babe Ruth's brilliance, his wonder, his immorality, is not the story of a tavern keeper's son becoming a hero. It isn't the story of a lovable and incorrigible kid calling his shot or hitting homers for sick children or eating hot dogs until he's ill or of blurry and wild late nights.

No, at the heart of Babe Ruth, I think, is the story of baseball.

Yes, it's corny. I know. But think of it: Baseball is a game that evolved in rural fields around America when the country was young. It was spread, often unwittingly, by soldiers looking for a moment of peace during the Civil War. The game was played for fun by men's clubs, which is why they call baseball locker rooms "clubhouses." Then these clubs began to pay the best players because they wanted to win.

The game's rules shifted and changed until balance was found, until 90 feet seemed just the right distance between the bases, until the mound seemed best situated at 60 feet and 6 inches from home plate, until four balls became a walk and three strikes became an out and three outs became an inning.

Then came fly balls like cans of corn, ground balls that took room-service hops, a song about peanuts and Cracker Jack, crafty left-handed pitchers, umpires who shouted, "Play ball!" and managers who came out to take the ball from one pitcher only to give it to another.

And as all of this began to converge and knit together, baseball surprisingly had something that no other American sport—perhaps no other feature of American life—had: timelessness. This was true on the field, where time was measured by outs instead of clocks.

But it was true off the field, too, where Walter Johnson becomes Bob Feller becomes Nolan Ryan becomes Gerrit Cole; where Ty Cobb leads to Jackie Robinson leads to Pete Rose; Lou Gehrig leads to Cal Ripken Jr.; Willie Mays leads to Mike Trout. The world around baseball progresses so rapidly, too rapidly, and it's all but impossible to keep up.

But baseball, in a large way, stays constant. Still 90 feet. Still 60 feet, 6 inches. Still four balls and three strikes and three outs. They still call locker rooms clubhouses.

Sure, it's not real timelessness. It's a fairy tale we baseball fans tell ourselves. Ottavino is right. It is a different game. Ruth played in a time when black players were shut out. He played in a time before night games, before air travel, before television, before closers, before weight training, before anyone cared about nutrition, before exploding sliders, before 100 mph fastballs, before West Coast games, before a million other things.

But here's the thing: Baseball is the game that lets you pretend time can stand still.

And that, at the heart, is the magic of Babe Ruth. He makes time stand still. Maybe it's pretend. But it feels real. He hits a home run in 1927 and it feels as current and vibrant as if he did it last September. We see his record .690 slugging percentage and we set it side by side with Mike Trout's .581. We see grainy black-and-white film of his big swing and his tiny-step, pigeon-toed running style and we imagine it in full color.

We believe in Babe Ruth because we believe in baseball. The question of "how good would Babe Ruth be now?" might be intriguing, but it entirely misses the point. Babe Ruth is great now, just like he was great in 1975; just like he was great in 1936 when he was elected to the Hall of Fame; just like he was great in 1927 when he hit 60 home runs; just like he was great in 1918 when he was throwing scoreless inning after scoreless inning in the World Series; just as he will be great 100 years from now.

Minutes, hours, months, years—those don't count in baseball. Only outs count. "That's only two strikes, boys. I still have one coming," he shouted at the Cubs before his called shot. And that's where time stands for eternity. Babe Ruth, forever, will still have one strike left.

No. 1 **Willie Mays**

Think for a moment about the first vivid baseball memory you have. Perhaps you have a hollow plastic bat in your hands and a Wiffle ball floats toward you. How old are you? Three? Five? Older? All you want to do is hit the ball. Where does that hunger come from? Who taught you that? Nobody. It is an instinct. You stand rigidly with your legs spread apart and the bat resting on your shoulder—maybe your parents set you up that way like an action figure. The ball dangles in midair like a disco ball. You swing the bat the way you imagine it should be swung, and you connect, perfect contact.

The ball takes off like a leaf caught in the wind, and you begin to run and stumble toward invisible bases that hide in the grass. You run a tight circle around the pitcher—is it your dad? Your mom? Your grandpa? Your best friend?—until you make it all the way around.

And when you get back where you started, you tumble over in the best version of a slide that you can muster. Who taught you how to slide? No one. You just knew.

That memory is Willie Mays.

Or maybe it is this: You and a friend throw a rubber ball (a tennis ball?) against the stairs that climb up to your front door. The sun is so big and warm that it seems to color the cloudless sky yellow. If you throw a ball against those stairs just right—so that the ball hits the upper corner flush—it will take off like a toy rocket. And that's what your friend does. The ball erupts off the stair and goes soaring toward the street, and you turn your back and sprint after it. You can't catch it, but you run just the same because . . . well, just because. And then to your surprise, you find that you start gaining on the ball. You can see it coming down, and you can see that if you reach out, stretch out, thrust out your arm as far as it can possibly go . . .

And maybe you catch it. How did you catch it? You don't know but you feel electricity buzzing throughout your body and you shout out to your friend, "DID YOU SEE THAT?" And your friend jumps up and down excitedly—or, wait, maybe you are the friend—and the two of you spend the rest of the afternoon reliving the catch.

That memory is Willie Mays.

Maybe your memory is of buying a new pack of baseball cards. This might be in the days when baseball cards come with a rectangle of rock-hard chewing gum that tastes like cardboard and rubs your tongue raw like sandpaper . . . or maybe this is years later, when there was no gum, when instead there would be specialty cards inside, maybe an autographed card or one that has a little piece of fabric worn by a major leaguer.

Either way, you pull off the plastic wrapper slowly because you want to savor it all, make the experience last for as long you can. And you slide down the top card just a little so that it reveals only a tiny portion of what card is next. Hmm. Look here. The next player is on your favorite team. Could it be? You don't dare to hope yet. You slide the card down a little more. Yes, it might be. A little more. Yes! The next card is your favorite player, you already know that this next card is now the most valuable thing you own, and you might sleep with it under your pillow or you might put it in one of those baseball card cases for protection. Whatever you do, your life is just a little bit different and better than it was before.

That memory is Willie Mays.

Perhaps you are at a ballpark. Everything looks so green. You'd seen games on television. You've looked at box scores and imagined. But you never believed it could be so green.

The smells overwhelm you—what is that? Beer? Hot dogs? Funnel cakes? Sweat? Yes. All of it. Baseball smells like an amusement park and a backyard barbecue and an afternoon at a movie theater and recess at the playground all at once. Then you hear the sounds, cheers and chatter, boos and a vendor selling peanuts, claps and stomps and groans and hopeful screams that either rise into happy symphonies or trail off into disheartened sighs, all while an organist plays "Hava Nagila" and a Mexican hat dance and a cavalry charge and that nameless song that plays a duet with your rapid heartbeat.

Here we go (YOUR TEAM), here we go (CLAP CLAP).

Maybe you even keep score. You'd have to be a certain age for that to ring true, probably. To keep score, you mark (with your blunt pencil that barely leaves a mark) a 6-3 for a grounder to short or a 9 for a fly ball to right field or you trace that pencil all around the bases and draw a diamond for a home run.

And then a ball is hit deep and the center fielder chases after it, but there is no chance the ball can be caught; the geometry teacher in your head tells you so. Then you see the ball and the man converge, and at the last possible instant the center fielder takes flight and pulls it in, and all at once, all together, people lose their bleeping minds.

"Put a star next to that one," someone tells you, and you do, you put a little star next to the "8."

That memory, most of all, is Willie Mays.

I don't know who the greatest baseball player is. Maybe for our purposes that admission comes 300,000 or so words too late, sure, but I did always believe that admission was present between the words. Can anyone really say if Ichiro Suzuki was better than Tony Gwynn was better than Rod Carew was better than Wade Boggs? If Sadaharu Oh or Buck Leonard could have hit big-league pitching? How do Clayton Kershaw and Sandy Koufax really match up? Can anyone tell you with any real certainty if Cool Papa Bell could have stolen more bases than Eddie Collins or what Joe DiMaggio or Ted Williams or Bob Feller might have done if not for wars?

Can anyone truly know how Mel Ott would have hit for the 1998 Mariners, Carl Yastrzemski for the 1933 Giants, Ken Griffey Jr. for the 1967 Red Sox?

Babe Ruth in modern times? Josh Gibson in the major leagues? Ty Cobb or Cy Young with a live ball? Barry Bonds or Roger Clemens clean?

Willie McCovey with the juicy baseball of 2019? Bob Gibson in this time of many relievers? Mike Trout against the spitball?

Can anyone know?

But wait! Of course we can know. More than that: We do know. We know the answers to all these questions and more because ... well, because we know. See, all along, this journey has not just been about the greatest players in baseball history. It has been about us, too: fans. It's about the things we believe in, the myths we hold dear, the statistics we embrace, the memories we carry.

When a magician performs magic, it doesn't mean anything unless there is someone on the other end feeling wonder.

So, yes, we know who was the greatest ever. We know because baseball goes back more than 150 years to that time when America didn't have a sport or a fully realized identity of its own. Americans boxed and played cricket but who didn't? Football was still rugby. Horses raced. Boats raced. Basketball and hockey had not yet been invented. Golf and tennis had not quite made it over the ocean.

And baseball spread from town to town like gossip. "Baseball is the hurrah game of the republic!" America's poet Walt Whitman said in 1889, and by then he had been writing on and off about the game for 40 years. It didn't look like our baseball at first—it was called "base ball" or "base-ball"—but it got there pretty quickly. And baseball tied communities together. Baseball gave people something to share. Baseball created a new language. And it launched a few million dreams along the way.

And then baseball was always there. It didn't fade away, even when so many other things did. When America grappled with the meaning of "All men are created equal," baseball asked that same question. When America searched for its soul, baseball searched for its soul.

And the greatest players ...

From Cy Young and Christy Mathewson and Honus Wagner

To the Georgia Peach and the Big Train and Oscar Charleston

To the Babe and Lou Gehrig and Satchel

To Joltin' Joe and Ted Williams and Stan the Man

To Hammerin' Hank and Roberto Clemente and the Mick

To Sandy Koufax and Bob Gibson and Yaz

To Reggie and Tom Terrific and Pete Rose

To Mike Schmidt and George Brett and Nolan Ryan

To the Rocket and Barry Bonds and Rickey
To Greg Maddux and Junior and the Big Unit
To Pedro and Ichiro and Mariano
To Albert Pujols and Justin Verlander and Mike Trout
. . . made people feel something more than baseball, something deeper than ground-rule doubles and infield flies and called strikes and an outfielder hitting the cutoff. Who is the greatest player of all time? You know. Maybe your father told you. Maybe you read about him when you were young. Maybe you sat in the stands and saw him play. Maybe you bask in his statistics. The greatest baseball player is the one who lifts you higher and makes you feel exactly like you did when you fell in love with this crazy game in the first place.

The greatest player of all time is Willie Mays.

On August 15, 1951, less than three months after he was called to the big leagues, Willie Mays stood in center field of the Polo Grounds. More than 21,000 people were in the stands that day to see the Giants play the hated Dodgers. You couldn't exactly say there was a pennant race going on yet—

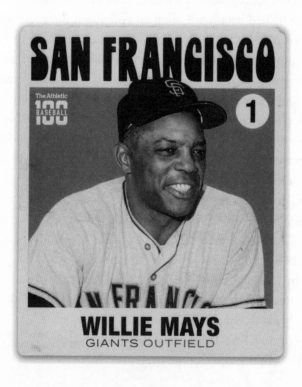

SAN FRANCISCO

1

The Athletic
100
BASEBALL

WILLIE MAYS
GIANTS OUTFIELD

the Dodgers led the Giants by 10½ games—but any Dodgers game was important and, anyway, there was a reason for Giants fans to hope.

The reason was Willie Mays.

He was a new name then; this was before just hearing those three syllables, "Willie Mays," sparked emotion. Mays had started the year playing Triple-A ball in Minneapolis. He was expected to stay there most of the year, perhaps the entire year, but he played so absurdly well from the start that the Giants called for him barely a month into the season.

"I'm not ready," Mays told the Giants manager Leo Durocher over the phone. "I can't hit that big-league curveball."

"What are you hitting now?" Durocher asked.

"Uh, .477," Mays said sheepishly.

"Get your @#$%^ up here!" Durocher shouted.

Mays did, in fact, hit .477 in Minneapolis with 18 doubles, three triples, and eight home runs in 35 games, but that wasn't the crazy part.

No, the crazy part was that his hitting barely mattered. His hitting wasn't what had people in Minneapolis mesmerized and it wasn't why Durocher so badly wanted him. No, the thing that made everybody lose their minds was the way this kid played center field. Nobody had ever seen anything like it. "I can't very well tell a batter not to hit it to him," Gil Hodges would later say. "Wherever they hit it, he's there anyway."

He was everywhere. Mays had patterned his game after his hero, Joe DiMaggio ("I saw him a couple of times in the newsreels," he said), and Mays was even faster than DiMaggio and had a much stronger arm. He could throw out baserunners from anywhere in the outfield. He could run down absolutely anything.

"There were men faster than Willie Mays," Buck O'Neil said. "But I never saw one faster with a fly ball in the air."

But even that doesn't get at why Mays's outfield defense was so life-altering. See, Joe D played the outfield with this quiet grace. It looked effortless. So it was with Tris Speaker and Oscar Charleston. But not Mays. No, Willie Mays going after a fly ball was cotton candy and a carousel and fireworks and a big band playing all at once. His athletic genius was in how every movement expressed sheer delight.

When you watched Mays play center field, you smiled. You laughed happily. You felt your insides warm up like after drinking a perfect mug of hot cocoa.

"I'm not sure what the hell charisma is," Reds slugger Ted Kluszewski once said. "But I get the feeling it's Willie Mays."

The Minneapolis Millers didn't want the Giants to take him away. They tried to keep him a secret, best they could. "Mays, you say?" the team's general manager, Rosy Ryan, would respond to reporters' questions as if it were the first time he had heard the name. He tried to downplay Mays's brilliance. "Yes, that's true," he said after one baseball lifer or another talked about Mays's unrivaled talent for baseball. "But the kid still has some baseball to learn, naturally."

Mays didn't have anything to learn, certainly not in Minneapolis, and Ryan knew it, but you couldn't blame the guy for trying. Anyway, it didn't work. The Giants took him to the big leagues and sent a note of apology to run in the local papers.

Then Mays got off to a rough start in the majors. He started 1-for-26, his only hit being a home run off Warren Spahn. "I'll never forgive myself," Spahn would say. "We might have gotten rid of Willie forever if only I'd struck him out."

Even with the homer, Mays was despondent. He had only just turned 20 years old, and he was not being coy when he told Durocher that he couldn't hit a big-league curveball. He had doubts. After his sluggish start, those doubts turned into fears. Could he make it in the big leagues? Mays was sobbing in the clubhouse when Durocher called him in and told him two things.

One, he said, pull up your pants higher so that umpires stop calling that low strike on you. Mays didn't really listen to that—he always played the game in his own style.

Two, Durocher said he didn't care *what* Mays hit. As long as he played good defense, he would be the Giants' center fielder. Mays did listen to this part. He relaxed. He hit .402 and slugged .696 over the next 24 games. He didn't worry much after that.

All the while, he played defense like no one ever had. In Pittsburgh one day—well, it was July 25, 1951, you can look it up even if it sounds like a folk story—Mays was in center field when the Pirates' Rocky Nelson launched a long fly ball to left-center. Mays took off after it and chased it down but he realized at the very last second that he was too late. He didn't have enough time to get his glove out there to reel it in.

So he simply put out his bare hand and caught the ball.

He couldn't stop smiling after that. He always had a smile in those days anyway, but that catch had turned him inside out with glee. At the end of the inning, he raced into the Giants' dugout in order to get showered with all of the slaps and praise and tributes and good-natured ribbing that such an absurd catch demands. But nobody in the dugout moved. Nobody in the dugout spoke. He was surrounded by complete silence.

"Leo!" he shouted to Durocher. "Did you see that catch I made?"

Durocher looked up stunned as if surprised to see Mays there.

"No, Willie, I didn't see it," Durocher said. "Can you go out there and do it again next inning?"

And with that, all his teammates raced in and crushed Mays with happiness and disbelief. "The finest catch I have ever seen and the finest catch I ever hope to see," Pirates general manager Branch Rickey would say.

Yes, they loved him. Everybody did. "The kid everybody likes," Grantland Rice would call Mays. He played the game with such exuberance, such passion. He would catch fly balls basket-style—with his glove at his waist and turned upside down as if he might be trying to catch pennies from heaven—and while he insisted that this was so he could throw the ball more quickly, the truth was that it was also fun. After games, he would sometimes go play stickball in the streets with kids.

And every sentence, it seemed, he began with a joyful, "Hey!" He loved to talk to people, and as James Hirsch wrote in his book, *Willie Mays: The Life, the Legend:* "His 'Hey' was a high-spirited chirp and because he was terrible with names and was constantly being introduced to strangers, he would follow his greeting with a question: 'Hey, how you doin'?' or "Hey, where you been?'" Reporters started to notice and began to point out how often he would say "hey."

Say hey?

Hey! He was the Say Hey Kid!

Let's go back to that August day in 1951. The score was tied and the Dodgers had runners on first and third with one out. If the Dodgers had scored a run there and won that game, there's a good chance that all the things that people remember about that famous season—the Giants coming back to force a playoff (while using a sign-stealing system), Bobby Thomson hitting the shot heard round the world, Russ Hodges shouting "The Giants win the pennant!" over and over again—would never have happened.

Billy Cox was the runner on third base, and Carl Furillo was at the plate. Furillo hit a fly ball to right-center field. Mays had been shading Furillo to left—Mays's instincts about positioning were normally supernatural—and he had to take off running. People have, through the years, argued about the catch itself. Some have remembered him needing to dive for it. Others said he had to stretch out to the point where a normal human being would have lost balance. Others said he made the catch pretty comfortably.

Nobody argues about what happened next, though. Mays caught the ball and then in one motion whirled and—"like a discus heaver," Jim McCulley wrote in the New York *Daily News*—threw blindly toward the plate. The ball and Cox reached home plate at the same time. An astonished Cox tried to maneuver around and missed the plate. Giants catcher Wes Westrum laid on the tag anyway. Cox was out. The world turned upside down.

"I want to see him do it again," Dodgers manager Charlie Dressen said when asked about the play. "I've been in baseball for 30-odd years and never saw anything like that."

Nobody knows for sure when a baseball cap first flew off the head of Willie Mays. It was probably when he was still a kid in and around Westfield, Alabama. His father, Willie Mays Sr., was called Kitty Cat—or more often just "Cat"—for his quickness on the diamond. He was not, as some have said, a player in the Negro Leagues. He played locally. But that shouldn't give a false impression; Cat Mays was a terrific ballplayer. He used to say that he only made it through the Depression by picking up a few bucks every week playing for various mill teams around town—his services were always in demand.

Cat wanted to raise a ballplayer. The legend goes that when Willie was about six months old, Cat put a baseball on a chair and said, "Go get it." The thing I love most about that story is that, if true, it happened almost exactly at the time when several states away, in Spavinaw, Oklahoma, another dreamer had a son he hoped would become a great ballplayer.

Willie Mays and Mickey Mantle would be connected in many ways throughout their lives.

Cat Mays was not Mutt Mantle, however. He did not force his son into the game. Maybe this was because he did not have to. From the start, Willie wanted to play ball more than anything in the world. He would wait impatiently for his father to come home from the steel mill so that they could play catch.

Willie was a baseball prodigy—well, to be more precise he was, like Mickey, an athletic prodigy. Incredibly, Mays's (and maybe Mantle's, too) best sport was football. He could throw jump passes 60 yards. But there was no place in big-time college or professional sports for a black quarterback then and, anyway, baseball was the driving force in his life. At 16, Cat's friend Piper Davis, manager of the Negro League's Birmingham Black Barons, offered Willie a spot in the outfield. Willie was still so young that he would go to school on weekdays and play games on the weekends.

It was likely around then that his cap first flew off. In those days, Mays was still learning how to be a hitter. He did have some early trouble picking up the curveball. And he could still be overmatched. He remembered the first time he faced Satchel Paige. He rocketed a double off Paige, who had probably wanted to take it easy on the youngster. Then Mays must have smiled a bit too widely at second base because Paige noticed it and walked on over. "That's all for you today, young 'un," Paige said.

"My next three times," Mays would say, "I went whoosh, whoosh, whoosh."

While he needed to learn some things about hitting, he knew all there was to know about playing center field. It's like he was born with it. "I didn't need a book," he would say. He could sense where the ball was going before it was hit. He automatically ran the best route to the ball. And he threw like nobody; he had pitched as a kid and people who saw him swore he could have been Bob Gibson. It didn't interest him.

And around that time, he must have been running and the hat must have gone flying and people watching surely gasped. There's something so sublime about Willie Mays running so hard that he loses his cap. Some said it happened because of the shape of his forehead. Others said it was because of his running style—his head would be up and the bill of his cap would catch the wind. Mays loved the reaction so much that, later, he said that he would start wearing caps that were too big for him, just to give the crowd a thrill.

But in those early days, the cap took off all on its own. And that became his trademark. It led to all sorts of divine moments. On one play, Mays chased after a deep fly ball and just as it arrived, his hat began to fall off. He caught the ball with his glove and the cap with his throwing hand. On another play, Mays was running from first to third when his cap came off and fell into the dirt about where the shortstop normally stands. He stopped instantly—Mays's ability to stop when running at full speed was Barry Sanders–like—scooped up his hat, took off again, and beat the throw by a step.

Giants shortstop Alvin Dark used to chase after him when fly balls were hit out there and pick up Mays's hat for him. "That kid makes so many sensational catches," Dark said, "I feel the least I can do in the way of thanks is to pick up his cap when it comes off."

Then there was Mays's most famous play, the most famous catch in baseball history. It was September 29, 1954, Game 1 of the World Series. Cleveland had won 111 games with what people were calling the greatest rotation the game had ever seen—the Tribe was heavily favored to win the Series.

The score was tied 2-2 in the eighth when Cleveland's Vic Wertz came to the plate with runners on first and second. Wertz was already 3-for-3 on the day. The Giants took out starter Sal Maglie and brought in lefty Don Liddle.

Wertz unloaded on the pitch. The crack of the bat was enough to jolt the sportswriters in the press box. A ball hit that well is almost always a home run. But Wertz had hit the ball to center field, and the game was being played at the Polo Grounds, and that's why something miraculous happened. Most estimates have Wertz's blast going 420 feet or more, which means it would have soared over the center-field wall in Cleveland. But the wall at the Polo Grounds was 483 feet away. Wertz's shot did not even get to the warning track.

Mays had been playing somewhat shallower than normal on the expectation that if Wertz singled, Mays would have to hustle to try to throw out Larry Doby at the plate. Instead, he saw the pitch and—before he even heard the crack of the bat—he turned his back and began running as fast as he could.

That year, 1954, was an incredible one for Mays. He'd missed almost all of the previous two seasons while serving in the army, and he looked rusty for the first three or four weeks of the season. And then, on May 6, things kicked in. Over the next 24 games, he hit .424 with 13 homers. Later in June, he had a seven-game stretch where he went 15-for-26 with seven home runs.

At the All-Star break, he had 31 home runs. He was ahead of Babe Ruth's 60-home run pace. The press kept asking Mays if he thought he had a shot at the record, but at the end of July, he stopped even trying. Durocher had asked him to give up home runs and to, instead, get on base more and spark more rallies.

Here's how good Willie Mays was: He did just that. He hit only five homers the rest of the season. But he also hit .379/.442/.601 with 16 doubles and seven triples. He led the Giants to another pennant. He would win the MVP award and be named the Associated Press's male athlete of the year.

"Willie Mays," Durocher said to the crowd at the Giants' parade, "is the greatest player I ever laid eyes on."

When Wertz hit the shot to center field, Mays knew that he would catch it. Nobody else really did. The fans and sportswriters saw how desperately he was running and thought he would never catch up. Even Dark, who had retrieved Mays's hat after so many great catches, thought there was no way that Mays could catch it, not only because he had so far to run but because he had no angle on it—the ball was hit directly over his head.

But Mays understood the angles of baseball better than anyone in the game's history. He knew even as he ran under the ball that he would catch it. The question he asked himself in real time was not about catching the ball. It was instead: *"How can I prevent Doby from tagging up and scoring all the way from second base?"* Doby could run, and he was aggressive on the bases.

Mays sprinted after the ball and, incredibly, as he got closer to it—with the ball dangling over his head like a lightbulb when a cartoon character has an idea—he began to slow down. He caught the ball over his left shoulder while the No. 24 on his back faced home plate.

And then, he stopped. He just stopped. Even now, as announcer Jack Brickhouse shouted in the moment, it looks like an optical illusion. How can someone just stop like that? It goes against all rules. Then he whirled and threw, "Like some olden statue of a Greek javelin hurler," in the words of the writer Arnold Hano. He threw the ball with such force (and so blindly) that he fell to the ground.

And the cap fell off his head.

Nobody knows for sure where the throw went: The enduring film only shows him making the throw. But we know that it made Larry Doby stop at third. Doby would not score. The Giants would win the game in extra innings and then sweep the Series.

"That was a helluva catch, roomie," Monte Irvin remembered saying. "I didn't think you'd make it."

"I had it all the way," Mays said.

Some years ago, I came up with something called "The Willie Mays Hall of Fame." I came up with the idea because I often hear people complain about certain players getting into the Hall of Fame. They complain by saying, "That's ridiculous. That guy was a good player. But the Hall of Fame is supposed to be for players like Willie Mays!"

Thing is, nobody's like Willie Mays. If he is the Hall of Fame standard, he's the only player in the Hall of Fame.

He's not the only person you could say that about, of course. If the standard for the Hall of Fame was Babe Ruth—meaning that only excellent pitchers who basically invent the home run are eligible—then he would be the only member.

If you want a Young Hall of Fame (only 500-game winners eligible) or a Ryan Hall of Fame (5,700 strikeouts or beat it) or a Cobb Hall of Fame (.366 batting averages and above) or an Aaron Hall of Fame (welcome to all players with 6,800 total bases), yes, those will be one-person museums.

But it's truer for Willie Mays than it is for anybody else. He could, as O'Neil used to say, beat you every way that you can be beaten. There is no one number or single achievement that you can use to sum him up. For Mays, you need to see everything.

Look here:

- 189 different players hit 400 doubles in their careers. Mays hit 523.

- 162 different players hit 100 triples in their careers. Mays hit 140.

- 111 different players hit 330 homers in their careers. Mays doubled that with 660 homers.

- 239 different players stole 250 bases in their careers. Mays stole 338 bases.

Individually, as you can see, these are difficult but not especially rare achievements—Mays cleared each of them by a substantial amount. Now, though, pull them together. How many players have hit 400 doubles, 100 triples, and 330 home runs and stolen 250 bases?

Only one. That's Willie Mays.

"If he could cook," Durocher said, "I'd marry him."

But that's just the hitting and running. Now think of him roaming in center field. In every town, he would make a catch or a throw—or both—that boggled the mind, a catch that would freeze time for every person in the stands.

"Was that your greatest catch?" reporters would ask him.

"I don't compare 'em," he would say. "I just catch 'em."

Now think of his baseball brilliance, the way he could anticipate what was going to happen next, the way he deeply understood every situation and all its possibilities, the way he would take extra bases like they were free mints, the way he would freeze baserunners with a look, the way he would set up pitchers to give him the pitch he wanted.

"There have only been two authentic geniuses in the world," the actress Tallulah Bankhead said. "William Shakespeare and Willie Mays."

"Isn't Willie Mays wonderful?" the first lady of American theater, Ethel Barrymore, asked.

And then, for me, there's the biggest part of all. There was the joy. It is true that as the years went on, Mays grew tired and occasionally cranky. The fans didn't treat him too well when the Giants moved out to San Francisco. Candlestick Park, where he played 889 games, was a cold and windy and desolate place. He, like every black man of his day, endured nastiness and racism. He went through a hard divorce. He had money problems. People tried to take advantage of him.

And he finished his career with the Mets, to the horror of all, by falling down in the outfield.

The only thing Willie Mays could not do on a baseball diamond was stay young forever.

But even to the end, he sparked joy. What do you love most about baseball? Mays did that. To watch him play, to read the stories about how he played, to look at his glorious statistics, to hear what people say about him is to be reminded why we love this odd and ancient game in the first place.

Yes, Willie Mays has always made kids feel like grown-ups and grown-ups feel like kids.

In the end, isn't that the whole point of baseball?

Acknowledgments

Too many years ago, I was a cub reporter at a minor league baseball game when I somehow found myself sitting next to the Hall of Famer Billy Williams. Though Williams did not quite make the Baseball 100, stories about him are scattered throughout this book, and if one was listing the sweetest swings in baseball history, Sweet Swingin' Billy Williams undoubtedly would be among the top five.

In any case, I had a question for him, but it was an embarrassing one. I hesitated and delayed and dithered until finally I decided: What the hell? How often was I going to find myself sitting next to Billy Williams?

"Mr. Williams," I asked, "what's the difference between a curveball and a slider?"

A couple of the more grizzled veteran reporters were within earshot and, predictably, they laughed. I felt my face burn red. It was like asking Mozart the difference between the white and black keys on a piano. But Billy Williams put his hand on my shoulder, and he took my notepad, and he began to diagram the exact difference between the two pitches. For the next 20 or so minutes, he gave me a master class on the curveball and the slider, the challenges of hitting both, the variances between Bob Gibson's slider and Steve Carlton's slider, between Bert Blyleven's curveball and Tom Seaver's curveball.

And at the end of the lesson, he smiled at me and said: "Don't let these other guys fool you. None of them knows the difference between a curveball and slider."

I bring this up here because I realize that there is no way for me to acknowledge or thank all the people who helped me write this book. To do that would essentially mean acknowledging or thanking all those people who helped me fall in love with baseball, which would essentially mean acknowledging and thanking just about every person I've ever known. I'd have to thank Michael Schur and Mike Vaccaro and Michael Orr and Mike Sweeney and Michael Fainer and Mike Schmidt and Mike Trout and Mike Mussina and Al Michaels and an old teacher of mine named Michael who sometimes in class would let us flip baseball cards as a break.

Those are just the Michaels, and that's not nearly all of them.

So, since this chapter cannot list every person in and out of baseball who helped, I am left to simply ask forgiveness from so many people for not mentioning them here. Instead, I will thank the people who had to endure my many moods during the intense writing of this behemoth, beginning with my original editor, *The Athletic*'s Kaci Borowski, who was there with me every day of the original writing and went about as mad as I did. I also want to thank Emma Span and Paul Fichtenbaum and all the good folks at *The Athletic* for their help and support.

And thanks to all those friends who, through texts and calls and support, helped pull me through—Dan and Debby McGinn, Brian Hay, Tommy Tomlinson, Jonathan Abrams, Jim Banks, Jeff Garlin, Ellen Adair, Brandon McCarthy, Nick Offerman, and too many others.

And family—my parents, my in-laws, my two brothers, and mostly my wife, Margo, and my daughters, Elizabeth and Katie, who offered endless love and encouragement and, more often than not, managed to get our dog Westley to stop barking even after the UPS driver dropped off a package. I will also cherish the advice Margo gave me as I came close to the finish line.

"Next time," she said, "how about just the top fifty players?"

Photo Credits

p. 329   No. 52: Adrián Beltré :Photo by Rick Yeatts/Getty Images

p. 337   No. 51: Al Kaline: Photo by Focus on Sport/Getty Images

p. 346   No. 50: Nolan Ryan: Photo by Rich Pilling/MLB Photos via
          Getty Images

p. 353   No. 49: Warren Spahn: Photo by Bettmann

p. 361   No. 48: Ken Griffey Jr.: Photo by Sporting News via Getty
          Images

p. 367   No. 47: Wade Boggs: Photo by Ronald C. Modra/Getty Images

p. 377   No. 46: Eddie Mathews: Photo by Bettmann

p. 386   No. 45: Bob Gibson: Photo by Louis Requena/MLB via Getty
          Images

p. 396   No. 44: Cal Ripken Jr.: Photo by M. David Leeds/Getty Images

p. 406   No. 43: Yogi Berra: Photo by Bettmann

p. 416   No. 42: Jackie Robinson: Photo by Hulton Archive/Getty Images

p. 426   No. 41: Tom Seaver: Photo by Ron Vesely/MLB Photos via
          Getty Images

p. 434   No. 40: Roberto Clemente: Photo by Focus on Sport/Getty
          Images

p. 443   No. 39: Nap Lajoie: Photo by GHI/Universal History Archive
          via Getty Images

p. 454   No. 38: Carl Yastrzemski: Photo by Bettmann

p. 465   No. 37: Pedro Martínez: Photo by Ron Vesely/MLB Photos via
          Getty Images

p. 473   No. 36: Christy Mathewson: Photo by George Rinhart/Corbis
          via Getty Images

p. 483   No. 35: George Brett: Photo by Owen Shaw/Getty Images

p. 492   No. 34: Cy Young: Photo by The Stanley Weston Archive/Getty
          Images

p. 500   No. 33: Jimmie Foxx :Photo by George Rinhart/Corbis via
          Getty Images

p. 508   No. 32: Mel Ott: Photo by New York Times Co./Getty Images

p. 515   No. 31: Greg Maddux: Photo by Timothy A. Clary/AFP via
          Getty Images

p. 525   No. 30: Johnny Bench :Photo by Focus on Sport/Getty Images

p. 532   No. 29: Eddie Collins: Photo by Bettmann

p. 541   No. 28: Randy Johnson: Photo by Matt York/AFP via Getty Images

p. 548   No. 27: Mike Trout: Photo by G Fiume/Getty Images

Index